LAW AND LETTERS
IN AMERICAN CULTURE

LAW AND LETTERS
IN
AMERICAN CULTURE

ROBERT A. FERGUSON

HARVARD UNIVERSITY PRESS
CAMBRIDGE, MASSACHUSETTS
AND LONDON, ENGLAND

Library of Congress Cataloging in Publication Data

Ferguson, Robert A., 1942-
Law and letters in American culture.

Includes bibliographical references and index.
1. American literature—1783-1850—History and
criticism. 2. Law and literature—United States.
3. Law in literature. 4. Lawyers as authors.
5. American literature—Revolutionary period, 1775-
1783—History and criticism. 6. United States—
Intellectual life—1783-1865. I. Title.
PS217.L37F47   1984   810'.9'92344   84-8940
ISBN 0-674-51465-3 (cloth)
ISBN 0-674-51466-1 (paper)

For Eleanor Sanner Ferguson
and in memory of Harry F. Ferguson, Jr.

ACKNOWLEDGMENTS

Alan Heimert and Joel Porte guided this work in its early stages and taught me much about the study of American culture. Lewis P. Simpson read the entire manuscript with care and gave unstintingly of his own expertise, making valuable suggestions and corrections. Jay Fliegelman contributed to my thinking in many areas. I am particularly indebted to my colleagues at the University of Chicago. Robert Streeter offered advice, support, and his own research, and I have benefited enormously from all three. William Veeder improved the manuscript with a close reading that I will continue to value in my future work. James Chandler, Neil Harris, Stanley Katz, James Miller, and Robert von Hallberg all made useful recommendations.

I have relied on some for more than direction. Elizabeth and Howard Helsinger opened their home to me; they listened, urged, questioned, and challenged—always in the right way and at the right time. Priscilla Parkhurst Clark has been my vital intellectual companion; her hand is on every page. John Paul Russo nourished this project from beginning to end. There would have been no book without him. Throughout, he has been the ideal friend of Bacon's description, the one who has made me wiser than myself.

Two grants have facilitated my research, a National Endowment for the Humanities Summer Stipend and a National Endowment for the Humanities Fellowship for Independent Study and Research. I thank the Massachusetts Historical Society for granting permission to quote from the Dana family and Joseph Story papers and the staffs of the Houghton Library at Harvard University, the Regenstein Library at the University of Chicago, the Library of

Congress, the New York Public Library, and the Historical Society of Pennsylvania for helping me with various materials. Earlier versions of chapters 2, 5, 6, and 7 have been published as follows: " 'Mysterious Obligation': Jefferson's *Notes on the State of Virginia*," *American Literature*, 52 (November 1980), 381–406; "Literature and Vocation in the Early Republic: The Example of Charles Brockden Brown," *Modern Philology*, 78 (November 1980), 139–152; "Yellow Fever and Charles Brockden Brown: The Context of the Emerging Novelist," *Early American Literature*, 14 (Winter 1979–80), 293–305; " 'Hunting Down a Nation': Irving's *A History of New York*," *Nineteenth-Century Fiction*, 36 (June 1981), 22–46; and "William Cullen Bryant: The Creative Context of the Poet," *New England Quarterly*, 53 (December 1980), 431–463. I thank the editors and publishers of these journals for their help and cooperation.

CONTENTS

ILLUSTRATIONS

What has been already said rather presupposes than insists upon the importance of a full possession of the general literature of ancient and modern times. It is this classical learning alone, which can impart a solid and lasting polish to the mind, and give to diction that subtile elegance and grace which color the thoughts with almost transparent hues. It should be studied, not merely in its grave disquisitions, but in its glorious fictions, and in those graphical displays of the human heart, in the midst of which we wander as in the presence of familiar but disembodied spirits.

It is by such studies, and such accomplishments, that the means are to be prepared for excellence in the highest order of the profession. The student, whose ambition has measured them, if he can but add to them the power of eloquence, (that gift, which owes so much to nature, and so much to art,) may indeed aspire to be a perfect lawyer.

JOSEPH STORY,
"The Value and Importance of Legal Studies,"
1829

I

THE CONFIGURATION
OF LAW
AND LETTERS

PROLOGUE TO
PART I

I N 1785 John Adams wrote to thank John Trumbull for sending
a copy of *M'Fingal*, the poet's mock-epic on the American Revolution. *M'Fingal* would remain the most popular poem by an American for half a century, but such acclaim meant less to a gentleman
of letters like Trumbull than approval from the social peers for whom
he wrote.[1] Adams was particularly crucial in this regard. He was
Trumbull's former mentor and lifelong political leader, and he had
encouraged the mock-epic in its earliest stages. Along with other
members of the Continental Congress, Adams may even have com-
missioned the first published version of Trumbull's satire in 1775.
"No invoice of goods," the poet later claimed, "was ever more truly
made out and sent to order."[2] The metaphor appropriately links literary
composition to an earlier service—Trumbull's processing of papers
and forms as Adams' law clerk just a year before *M'Fingal*. It is
interesting, then, that Adams used his influence in 1785 to consign
the poet's best effort to an unusable past. Writing from Europe,
Adams' thoughts were firmly on the future: that of his country, his
new ambassadorship to the Court of St. James, and his young son
John Quincy Adams, who was just returning to America to begin
study at Harvard College.

   M'Fingal appeared equal to anything Adams had read in humorous
verse, but he felt "Poetry of superior kinds" should claim Trumbull's
attention now. "I wish you to think of a subject which may employ
you for many years, and afford full scope for the pathetic and
sublime . . . Upon this plan I should hope to see our young America

in Possession of an Heroick Poem, equal to those the most esteemed in any Country." And yet the same plan could never serve for an Adams. With no sense of incongruity, Adams wrote on in alarm over John Quincy Adams' growing passion for poetry. He had just written to assure Harvard's examiners that they could expect an accomplished student of English and French verse. But would these accomplishments now mislead? "If he had it, which is not likely," Adams warned Trumbull concerning John Quincy's talent for poetry, "he will not be so independent of Business as you, and therefore *must not indulge it*, but devote himself wholly to the Law." Trumbull, in short, was to discourage in the son what the father urged upon his former clerk. "I should be glad to hear from you," the letter continued, "as often as your Practice and the Heroick Poem aforesaid will admit."[3]

The incident illustrates a central problem in the interpretation of early American literature—the tendency among critics to forget context in their search for familiar national meanings. At first glance, Adams' letter records the early American writer's plight: Trumbull's entrapment between utilitarian standards (business before poetry) and an artificial literary quest for nationality (the call for an epic poem). These generalizations, the condescensions of a later age, define the formative period through literary weakness. Trumbull's failure to develop into a first-rate satirist, so the argument runs, follows from lack of appreciation, while Adams' rejection of humorous verse represents the narrow-mindedness of a society unreceptive to literature.

Should one, the argument continues, expect real literature from an emerging culture where talent is directed into other channels, where poetic imagination is controlled by civic identification, where even the leisure for literature is lost in definitions of vocational responsibility? The question has dominated literary study of the formative period, and most answers have ignored the vitality and the complexity of republican writings by assuming a "dark ages" before "the long awaited, and long delayed, American Renaissance."[4] In this way developmental theorists of American literature have sacrificed the creative context of early national writings to the success story of a later literature. At stake is the original meaning and strength of the republic's first books. To understand John Adams' language on its own terms is to see a deep commitment to American thought and writing. Adams struggled diligently as a young man to develop an effective literary style. His many essays, treatises, diaries, and the autobiography all attest the high value he placed upon the written word. At least one major achievement in letters followed therefrom. Ezra Pound is not alone in calling Adams' correspondence with Jefferson the central literary accomplishment of the period.[5]

Adams' particular orientation within literature—"I should hope to live to see our young America in Possession of an Heroick Poem" —appears superficial and limited today. But the age, not Adams, tied literature to political ends. Adams wrote to Trumbull during the twilight of the original confederation when nationhood remained the greatest intellectual challenge an American could meet. The struggle for a collective identity imposed aesthetic and intellectual boundaries that we overlook in our mastery of the myths the founding generations had to initiate. Behind everything was Adams' belief that informed expression based on a knowledge of arts and letters was the surest guarantee of a precarious liberty. "Let us tenderly and kindly cherish, therefore, the means of knowledge," he had written his fellow countrymen as early as 1765. "Let us dare to read, think, speak, and write."[6]

This study seeks to recover the lost context out of which Adams and Jefferson, and then Washington Irving, William Cullen Bryant, and other early republicans, dared to read, think, speak, and write. The two Adamses with Trumbull in between, lawyers across three succeeding generations, were part of a now-forgotten configuration of law and letters that dominated American literary aspirations from the Revolution until the fourth decade of the nineteenth century, a span of more than fifty years. Half of the important critics of the day trained for law, and attorneys controlled many of the important journals. *Belles lettres* societies furnished the major basis of cultural concern for post-Revolutionary America; they depended heavily on the legal profession for their memberships. Lawyers also wrote many of the country's first important novels, plays, and poems.[7] No other vocational group, not even the ministry, matched their contribution.

Adams' letter to Trumbull must be understood within this frame of reference. The distinction between law clerk and son becomes less invidious and considerably more complicated when we realize that the subordination of literature to law was a professional guideline born of intellectual proximity. Resolutions favoring law were not in themselves a rejection of the poet's creativity. Georgian England and the America of the early republic rang with the broken promises of members of the bar renouncing polite letters for law. Lawyer-writers invariably preferred "the useful olive to the barren laurel" even as they scribbled volume after literary volume.[8]

Trumbull recognized Adams' rhetorical flourish for what it was, and he concurred without resentment in Adams' assessments of the limits of satire and the crucial importance of a higher poetry on national themes. Adams was an intellectual catalyst. He had encouraged both his son's original literary interests and his law clerk's verse because a knowledge of poetry was part of an eighteenth-century lawyer's training in eloquence. When John Quincy Adams later composed for publication, he did so with everyone's approval, and his poetry maintained the priorities of preceding generations:

> Behold the lettered sage devote
> The labors of his mind,
> His country's welfare to promote
> And benefit mankind.

Trumbull's own reaction kept everything in perspective. John Quincy's verse, he wrote the elder Adams in mixed tones of humor and praise, was "very much superior to the general cast of American and especially *Bostonian* poetry."[9]

To a modern sensibility, the set of epistolary exchanges—and the example could be multiplied a hundredfold—suggests an inadequate or detached view, a looking at literature from the outside. We no longer recognize the peculiar idealism and commitment that Adams and Trumbull brought to seemingly familiar terms like poetry, talent, scope, plan, and young America. The rules controlling literary involvement have changed. The eighteenth-century lawyer possessed literary impulses—"let us dare to read, think, speak, and write"—and to a degree unequaled by others in republican culture. He was, in fact, professionally dependent upon a fusion of law and literature. In the absence of more technical guidelines, the early American lawyer found vocational definition in general knowledge and learned eloquence, in his acceptance of the classical past as a touchstone, in his commitment to public service through the written word.

The first aim of this book is to explore the nexus between law and literature in the early republic and to examine some of the major writers within the configuration. As one might expect, the political writings of such men as Adams, Jefferson, Hamilton, and Madison drew upon legal training, but few have realized quite how great that reliance was in both ideological and structural terms. The central texts of American republicanism acquire new coherence from a legal aesthetic just beneath the surface. Similar lines of force inform early American poetry and fiction. The works of Charles Brockden Brown, Washington Irving, and William Cullen Bryant, among others, were shaped in ways simple and complex by the legal education each writer received. A legal career was an attractive option to ambitious early republicans with literary aspirations, and eighteenth-century legal thought contained many assumptions about the uses and meaning of literature. Once exercised, a vocational preference for law left its own stamp upon a writer's attitudes and motivations.

A second purpose is to examine the rhetoric within republican writings and to reassess its place in American literary culture. The briefest glance at Adams' language reveals the need for a better understanding of ideas rendered too familiar in patriotic forums. As republican idealism moved from intellectual discourse toward re-iteration of myth, the crafted responses in early national writings were soon mistaken for mindless chauvinisms. "From 1790 to 1820 there was not a book, a speech, a conversation, or a thought in the state," Ralph Waldo Emerson believed just thirty years after the fact.[10] The opinion, shared by most modern readers, shows how quickly Americans lost sight of what early republican writers sought to accomplish, how completely Americans tried to disavow a substantial influence.

Donald Davie is only the most recent critic to observe the tendency among Americans to regard their literature as a wholly romantic and post-romantic endeavor to the exclusion of earlier forms and works: "Nobody denies that in the canon of English literature there figure, as of right, the political pamphlets of Jonathan Swift, the political polemics and parliamentary orations of Edmund Burke. But so far as I can see, 'American literature' is very seldom taken to include, as a distinct and ancient literary genre, political speculation and commentary and political oratory." To what extent should the orations of Henry Clay and Daniel Webster, the histories of Francis Parkman, the letters of Adams and Jefferson figure within an American canon? "So far as I know," Davie argues, "not only has the question never been answered, it has perhaps never been asked."[11]

Recent study of Puritan poetry and sermonology may seem to belie Davie's complaint, but the exception only confirms his notion of a truncated canon. Literary critics tend to skip the eighty years from the Great Awakening to the American Renaissance in their haste to associate colonial religious preoccupations with the romantic inwardness of the nineteenth century.[12] The configuration of law and letters fills part of this gap in the American critical tradition. It permits a different approach to pre-romantic texts and encourages unities across the apparent divisions in nineteenth-century literature. Awareness promotes a fresh perspective if just because so many writings of the formative period came from the legal mind. It is perhaps no accident that the neglected literati mentioned by Davie—Adams, Jefferson, Clay, Webster, and Parkman—were all educated to the law.

The study of law in American literature is also long overdue. Despite initiatives by Charles Warren, Richard Beale Davis, Perry Miller, and John McWilliams, the role of legal thought within republican letters remains untold.[13] Miller, in particular, juxtaposed theology and law and outlined the ways in which these competing intellectual frameworks—the evangelical basis and the legal mentality—fought for control of the American mind in the periods between the Revolution and the Civil War. Revivalistic enthusiasm and legal rationality suggested contrasting visions of the republic and a dialectic in post-Revolutionary searches for national identity that pitted millennial utopianism against common law theory. But if scholars have explored the first part of Miller's dialectic—that of the relationship of American literature to early Puritan forms and to religious thought in general—there have been no comparable studies of the connection between literature and law.[14] In the fifteen years since *The Life of the Mind in America* appeared, little has been added to Miller's insistence that lawyers and legal thought were crucial to literary development in the antebellum period. This remains true even though legal historians like James Willard Hurst, Lawrence Friedman, Morton Horwitz, Stanley Katz, William Nelson, Maxwell Bloomfield, and Edward White have recently made their field an excellent barometer for gauging transformations in American thought.[15]

Part I of the pages that follow discusses the meaning, dimensions, and basis of the overall configuration. An opening chapter explores the rapid rise of the legal profession in Revolutionary America and the constitutive influences that placed the lawyer at the center of republican literary activity. The generational continuum already noted in the Adams family and Trumbull remains instructive in this regard and helps to explain how and why the lawyer came to replace the minister as the spokesman of American culture. Chapter 2 focuses on a single text, Thomas Jefferson's *Notes on the State of Virginia*. Generally read as a loose collection of information, *Notes* emerges as a unified work when placed within the framework and theory of eighteenth-century legal thought. Jefferson was the presiding genius of the legal mind in early America, and his reliance upon law for the structural order of his one book has paradigmatic significance. *Notes* illuminates the basic forms of early republican texts and underscores the vitality of legal thought within the literature of the period. Chapter 3 documents the broader context of that vitality in American literature from 1785 to 1840. The lawyer's training dictated patterns of selectivity from the jumble of neoclassical traditions and romantic impulses in eighteenth- and nineteenth-century Anglo-American literature. Properly recognized, these patterns reveal avenues into the hidden structures and public tones of America's first novels and national poems. Chapter 3 also concentrates on the importance of the courtroom as a ceremonial forum in republican culture. Formal legal argument drew large audiences throughout the period, and practicing attorneys had much to do with the rise of a literature of eloquence and oratory. Their emphasis on the spoken word is the key to a strange "rhetoric of spaciousness," a form of early national thought and writing that Americans no longer understand. [16]

Overall, *Law and Letters in American Culture* means to encourage a basic act of recognition and recovery. Recovery, in this sense, implies more than an appreciation of origins. The lawyer-writer at his best was a man of vision who imposed a certain idealism upon the world around him. Notions of a golden age in American law have been properly discounted, but 1765 to 1840 did mark a period when lawyers "spoke and acted with that conscious authority which is characteristic of truly creative founders."[17] The lawyer's deliberate combination of intellectual breadth, artistic insight, and political commitment has been unique in American history—one reason why his definitions of country have been so decisive in shaping the American mind. To study this legacy is to retain the example for a modern culture in which the stark separation of intellect, art, and politics should give every citizen pause.

Americans have kept faith in law as an instrument of social order, but legal thought no longer supplies the ideological coherence it once did.[18] The loss is a serious one in a nation that has defined itself so self-consciously through law. Long ago Tocqueville examined "the most perfect" Constitution and warned that "the government of the Union depends almost entirely upon legal fictions; the Union is an ideal nation, which exists, so to speak, only in the mind, and whose limitations and extent can only be discerned by the understanding."[19] This conception of America insists upon the vital, continuing presence of intellect as both the primary source and the necessary tool of national definition. The Founding Fathers were civic humanists steeped in law as the *ordo ordinans*, the ordering order that arranges values in meaningful patterns. Their decision "to form a more perfect Union" was an act of the imagination that must be shared if it is to be renewed.

CHAPTER 1

IN AMERICA
THE LAW IS KING

"The Road to Honour"

The centrality of law in the birth of the republic is a matter of national lore. "In America the law is king," Thomas Paine the prophet of revolution proclaimed in 1776, and so it has remained ever since in the political rhetoric and governmental councils of the nation. Revolutionary orators and pamphleteers like John Dickinson, James Otis, John and Samuel Adams, Patrick Henry, Thomas Jefferson, James Wilson, and Arthur Lee were members of the profession. Their writings were heavily scored with the citations and doctrines of legal study and contributed decisively to what historians have called the conceptualization of American life.[1] Twenty-five of the fifty-six signers of the Declaration of Independence, thirty-one of the fifty-five members of the Constitutional Convention, and thirteen of the first sixteen presidents were lawyers.[2] All of our formative documents—the Declaration of Independence, the Constitution, the Federalist Papers, and the seminal decisions of the Supreme Court under John Marshall—were drafted by attorneys steeped in Sir William Blackstone's *Commentaries on the Laws of England* (1765–1769). So much was this the case that the *Commentaries* rank second only to the Bible as a literary and intellectual influence on the history of American institutions.[3]

Sociologists have identified the larger patterns involved. Members of the legal profession tend to form the center of an intellectual elite during the developmental phase of a modern state. Conditions were particularly favorable in Revolutionary America for the emergence

of a rational-legal system of authority as opposed to the two alternatives, charismatic and traditional, within Max Weber's theory of
power.[4] But even within the Weberian framework the rapidity of
the American lawyer's climb to power remains astonishing. Entrenched distrust of trained attorneys prevented the development
of an effective legal profession in any of the colonies before the
middle of the eighteenth century, and lawyers only began to assume
real leadership in political affairs after 1760.[5]

Ascendancy came in a rush with the Revolutionary lawyer's reach
for cultural legitimacy. John Adams' first inclination had been to
preach. That was the conventional ambition of colonial intellectuals,
and Adams had to struggle to establish vocational self-respect for a
second choice in law. His journal entries for the 1750s are laced
with self-conscious defenses of the profession and references to "dirty
Dablers in the Law." Not until 1761 could he claim victory: "I have
for my own Part, and I thank God for it, no bad Opinion of the
Law, either as a science, or a Profession."[6] Subsequent generations
would have no need for qualms. By 1787, in his last year at Harvard
College, John Quincy Adams debated a loftier proposition: "the
profession of law against physic and divinity as being most beneficial
to man." Unthinkable forty years before, the same debate was a
foregone conclusion by the turn of the century. "Men of talents in
this country . . . have been generally bred to the profession of the
law," wrote William Wirt, a leader of the Virginia bar, in a typical
statement for 1803, "and indeed throughout the United States, I
have met with few persons of exalted intellect, whose powers have
been directed to any other pursuit. The bar in America is the road
to honour." Thirty years before Alexis de Tocqueville's famous
equation of the legal profession to an intellectual aristocracy, American lawyers already arrogated that status to themselves.[7]

Law attracted men of talent because the profession was lucrative
and secure, but the intellectual ascendancy of the lawyer—his virtual monopoly as republican spokesman—came from ideological
factors. It was an immense advantage that the rhetoric of revolution
had been so patently legalistic. The inalienable rights of rebellion
could be and were derived from right reason and natural law, but
American vehemence depended on the particular expression of these
rights in the common law of England, the statutory enactments of
Parliament, and the various royal charters pertaining to colonial

Washington Giving the Laws to America, line engraving
by J. P. Elven, late eighteenth to early nineteenth century.

Neoclassical expression and legal order reinforce each other in the early republic. In this engraving, Washington, the enlightened lawgiver, is both Moses and Caesar. He enjoys the support of Wisdom and Authority, while History, holding her mirror, points to his eternal fame in the future of America, a future that Mercury confirms. Washington rules through the American Constitution, thus controlling the military power that has tamed the British lion and channeling the natural abundance of the New World. With these potentially dangerous forces under law and order in the foreground, the practical and fine arts (seated in the background) can begin to build a new civilization.

government. Participation in the central Revolutionary debates over parliamentary jurisdiction in the colonies required a detailed knowledge of the same historical, legal sources.[8]

To trace the exact meaning and importance of English legalisms in an American context is difficult; cross-cultural transmissions involve oblique refractions rather than the discrete reflection of whole images.[9] But conceptual necessities magnified the frequency and the scope of American borrowings. J. G. A. Pocock has shown the extent to which common law thought controlled seventeenth- and eighteenth-century political paradigms. He also has summarized the variant borrowed by Revolutionary Americans: "the 'Country' vision of English politics" with its insistence upon a careful equilibrium of governmental organs, its innate suspicion of royal authority, and its invective against standing armies and the excesses of theocratic politics. The Whig vision of history behind these stances assumed an ancient constitution, which, through immemorial common law, guaranteed the rights of Englishmen in perpetuity. The virtues of that ancient constitution had been undermined by the incursions and usurpations of William the Conqueror and his kingly heirs, transforming all of English history into one long struggle for the recovery of lost liberties. In this view the Glorious Revolution of 1688 had been "the triumph of the Common law and lawyers over the king."[10] By extension, the Declaration of Independence in 1776 owed much to an earlier declaration, the Bill of Rights of 1689, and Jefferson's language—"the history of his present majesty, is a history of unremitting injuries and usurpations"—brought a Whig lawyer's perspective to bear upon British America's search for comparable liberties.[11]

Seventeenth-century legal thought furnished a context for understanding history and acting upon it. That of the eighteenth century created a comprehensive, secular vision of country for Englishmen and Americans to define themselves within. A modern political framework had been born in the language of those lawyers who maneuvered to "make the Revolution *legal* in 1688."[12] Legal thought represented an alternative form of explanation, the solution to a century of religious persecution and civil war. By the 1760s, William Blackstone's *Commentaries on the Laws of England* had given the terminology of this new order a final legitimacy by appealing to every eighteenth-century English gentleman's understanding of the status quo and sense of place. Hence, the Revolution of 1688 became, through Blackstone, the *end* of a fifth stage in English history recording "the complete restitution of English liberty, for the first time, since its total abolition at the conquest." In itself the *Commentaries* presumed to be "a general map of the law marking out the shape of the country, its connexions and boundaries, its greater divisions and principal cities." Indeed, Blackstone had such confidence in the scope of his methods that he found it unnecessary "to describe minutely the subordinate limits, or to fix the longitude and latitude of every inconsiderable hamlet."[13]

The impact on early American intellectuals was so profound on so many levels as to constitute one of the greatest instances of paradigmatic migration, innovation, and reconstruction in the history of Anglo-American culture. Legal formulation both created and capped the conservative American Revolution: it provided the rationale for rebellion even as it blocked the continuum of revolution with the archetypical patterns of a new order. Tactically, the radical Whig lawyer's rhetoric and the great secular scope of later eighteenth-century legal thought combined to give the American lawyer every option. Legal terminology was extremely appropriate for partisan debate, but it also could be used to rise above mere politics in a larger vision of country. Intellectually, many eighteenth-century Americans needed an alternative to the religious turmoil wracking colonial culture in the decades after the Great Awakening of the 1730s. Since English legal thought had developed as just such an alternative to religious zeal, American lawyer-writers could use it to express a comparable distaste for the waves of revivalism that swept republican culture in the eighteenth and nineteenth centuries. Figuratively, legal method was also made to order for intellectuals trying to rationalize an unknown new world. In America, where every hamlet was still inconsiderable and where subordinate limits were either vague or the source of bitter contention, Blackstone's permission to ignore aspects of the concrete and to rise to the general proved almost as spellbinding as the explanatory scope the *Commentaries* encouraged. Permission, in this sense, meant the right to rest within a knowledge of ordered abstractions, and it depended upon the fundamental tenets of an English neoclassicism that Americans turned to their own use.

The English legal tradition enabled Anglo-American intellectuals to *assume* a visible link between the observance of natural law and the attainment of civic happiness.[14] Since providence had provided Americans with a continent unspoiled by human history, they could confidently order their new country through a correct, theoretical application of man-made or positive law in harmony with the natural order around them. It is no accident that the Declaration of Independence posits a connection between the scientific "laws of Nature and of Nature's God" and the twenty-seven specific grievances of "the people" against George the Third, king of England. Twelve of the Declaration's "long train of abuses and usurpations" deal explicitly with the legal process in language that juxtaposes the virtue and natural order of law, both abstract and particular, against the artifice and corruption of Old World tyranny.

The assumption of a connection between nature, order, and positive law in Revolutionary America appears most dramatically in that embodiment of popular wisdom, the rabble-rousing Tom Paine. For while *Common Sense* is an electrifying call to arms, it is also a demand for a country defined entirely through law. Paine was no attorney, but in *Common Sense* what he fears most is the "truly alarming" absence of a legal plan. "We may be as effectually enslaved by the want of laws in America," he warns, "as by submitting to laws made for us in England." Because the American colonies are paralyzed in 1776 between the duty of accepting the imposed obligations of English regulation and the responsibility of making law for themselves, they come close to dissolving before the reader's eyes in *Common Sense*. Paine's cry for an immediate constitutional convention supposes a country "without law, without government" on the brink of chaos. In this situation "the law is king" because it remains the only principle of order once the constitutional bonds with England have been sundered. Paine, with an audacity that still amazes, then proves his point by rapidly building his own "settled form of government" for the vast and still-unpopulated American continent. Common sense is his key precisely because it finds law in "the simple voice of nature and reason."[15]

John Adams' "Generous Plan of Power"

While Tom Paine's use of law was superficial, his easy reliance on it and the phenomenal popularity of *Common Sense*—half a million copies were published in 1776 alone—confirm a basic familiarity with and acceptance of legalistic conception in the language of Revolutionary culture. The American lawyer's achievement was to use this familiarity and acceptance to gain control over general discourse in the public domain. With remarkable skill, he converted his own conceptual needs into weapons against his intellectual rivals, seizing upon his advantages as Revolutionary spokesman to drive the American clergy and military away from civic podiums and the positions of communal control. The radical Whig lawyer's rhetoric denouncing religious intolerance and standing armies made a perfect foil for confining the other professions to quarters. No figure was more adept in its use than John Adams. Adams' political writings show how openly attorneys enhanced their position at the expense of others, how easily the lawyer secured an intellectual ascendancy in republican debate, how completely he came to dominate American politics until the Civil War.

Adams perhaps lacked genius—a fact he once bewailed—but his intellect was representative of the times, and his mastery of the lawyer's rhetorical tools was extraordinary.[16] In *A Dissertation on the Canon and Feudal Law* (1765) he is a more radical spokesman than Blackstone, who was writing at the same moment in time, but his technical perspective and sense of sweep are quite similar. *A Dissertation* begins with Adams' analysis of what he calls the two greatest systems of tyranny since the promulgation of Christianity. They are the canon law and the feudal law: the former, "framed by the Romish clergy for the aggrandisement of their own order," and the latter, "originally a code of laws for a vast army in a perpetual encampment."[17] Together the two systems formed a "wicked confederacy" of kings, captains, great officers, and bishops that remained intact until the Reformation established inroads in the name of human liberty. Only in America, where the Reformation received its firmest confirmation away from the canon and feudal systems, did liberty actually flourish. The Puritan forefathers were unfortunately afflicted with "that noble infirmity," religious enthusiasm. but they sensibly rejected "the ridiculous fancies of sanctified effluvia from episcopal fingers," and they favored controls upon "the powers of the monarch and the priest, in every government." Above all, America's first settlers conveyed the general knowledge later generations would need to maintain a spirit of liberty and to resist "unworthy dependencies."

The accuracy of Adams' thesis is not at issue here, only its import for Revolutionary intellectuals. In *A Dissertation on the Canon and Feudal Law* the lawyer emerges as the natural custodian of a liberty that will remain vigorous only through the dissemination of knowledge and awareness among an American citizenry. "It has been observed that we are all of us lawyers, divines, politicians, and philosophers," Adams notes in relating liberty to an unprecedented level of education in the populace around him. The claim in itself could mean little, since the democratization of American culture would require another century and since no Adams would ever occupy the vanguard again. Rather, the point is that lawyers come first in Adams' list because their professional knowledge made them exceptionally conscious of impending dangers to American liberties.

A Dissertation inevitably reads the Stamp Act of 1765 as Parliament's attempt to impose the tyrannical canon and feudal systems upon American politics. Adams presents the problem in such a way that lawyers define the issues, explain what should be done, and then do it while their only serious competitors, the clergy, are assigned the lesser role of celebrating necessary ideals. Significantly, the most important ideal Adams can find for celebration is a ministry divorced from all political power. "Let the pulpit resound with the doctrines and sentiments of religious liberty," he orders. By contrast, the American bar is to "proclaim 'the laws, the rights, the generous plan of power' delivered down from remote antiquity." Adams naturally filters antiquity's plan through a Whig lawyer's perception, through the institutional balances and controls of eighteenth-century British constitutionalism. Administratively, only one figure stands properly equipped to handle both the dangers and the complexities involved. In *A Dissertation* it is one short step to a portrayal of the lawyer as natural leader. "Rulers," Adams reveals, "are no more than attorneys, agents, and trustees, for the people."

Innovative in 1765, Adams' views rapidly became an accepted orthodoxy disenfranchising the clergy from previous functions. By 1775 religious freedom meant absolute separation of church and state for most Americans, and the ministry increasingly abandoned every important option in governmental theory and politics to others. As Carl Bridenbaugh has explained, "American republicanism was emerging naturally in the politics of a society where religious republicanism had long prevailed."[18] Lawyers like Adams and Jefferson worked unceasingly to hasten the change. Their private writings were riddled with fears of real and imagined priesthoods, and they did everything within their power to reduce the political leverage of the American clergy. When Connecticut finally abandoned its state-supported church in 1817, Jefferson wrote Adams to applaud one more victory against "Monkish darkness, bigotry, and abhorrence": "I join you therefore in sincere congratulations that this den of the priesthood is at length broken up, and that a protestant popedom is no longer to disgrace the American history and character." Better attuned to the strength of American revivalism, the more pessimistic Adams wrote back of his continuing doubts and of his fears of foreign influence. "Do you know that The General of the Jesuits and consequently all his Host have their Eyes on this Country?"[19]

The exchange contains a mutual antipathy to theological explanation that transcends time and place. In western thought there are inherent differences between a religious and a legal mentality stretching back at least as far as the fifteenth century and Lorenzo Valla's exposure of the Donation of Constantine.[20] Jefferson and Adams built upon the persistent challenge of legal humanism to religious dogma. The incidental timing of history then magnified their success. For just as the fortuitous conjunction of the Reformation and western colonization forever separated the thought of the New World from that of the Old, so in the eighteenth century the creation of the federal republic during the high phase of European legal thought shaped American civilization around a dominant and distinctive sense of law.

As for the more remote prospect of military ascendancy within America, Adams' comments on standing armies contributed to a mounting phobia that kept the problem from materializing. George Washington as Revolutionary commander complained bitterly that Congressional fears of the military made it impossible to maintain an army, much less fight the British.[21] After the war the first leaders of the federal republic worried aloud about the way "Marius, Sylla, Caesar, Cromwell trampled on liberty with Armies." Mostly lawyers, they spread dark rumors about the Society of the Cincinnati, the organization of retired Revolutionary army officers. When Napoleon rose from the ashes of the French Revolution, anxiety gave way to shrill warnings. The specter of an American Caesar would dominate political invective until the Civil War, and the lawyers who did much of the vociferating were wont to evoke their own predecessor Cicero because he had opposed every form of armed tyranny in Rome.[22]

Meanwhile Washington's personal behavior also undercut potential military involvement in politics. No hero has ever been more justly celebrated for things not done and, hence, prevented. Washington's careful resisting of military intrigue within the Revolutionary Army, his prompt retirement to Mount Vernon, and (with Jefferson's encouragement) his deliberate distance from the Society of the Cincinnati placed effective controls on every military man in America.[23] With a restraint that would characterize most war heroes in American politics, Washington also refused the role of republican spokesman. First citizen by example, he relied upon others for his few memorable public utterances, particularly upon lawyers like Madison, Jefferson, and Hamilton. It was, in fact, the lawyer-poet John Trumbull who prevented Washington's first major address from being "absolutely contemptible" and "a mere schoolboy declamation." If the thought behind the "Circular to the States" of 1783 was Washington's, the public voice was a lawyer's—and by no means for the last time. Alexander Hamilton would supply the main draft of the famous Farewell Address of 1796.[24] What he could not conquer, the lawyer managed to co-opt.

Judicial Review and Cultural Ascendancy

The rise of the doctrine of judicial review early in the nineteenth century made the lawyer's hegemony as republican spokesman official and reveals a great deal about the profession's centrality within American culture. Long before the doctrine became national policy in *Marbury v. Madison* (1803), lawyers were assuming its general validity in America. John Adams had wanted the colonial courts to declare parliamentary acts unconstitutional as early as 1765. Alexander Hamilton of New York, Thomas Jefferson of Virginia, Elbridge Gerry of Massachusetts, James Wilson of Pennsylvania, Oliver Ellsworth of Connecticut, and Luther Martin of Maryland were all leaders of their respective bars when they raised the issue of judicial review again in the late 1780s and early 1790s.[25] In a sense, the lawyer's background *made* him call for a new kind of interpretation and confirmation of fundamental law.

Immersed in the legitimacy of the unwritten and immemorial common law (the *jus non scriptum* rooted in custom predating recorded history), the American lawyer of 1787 suddenly found himself crafting a written constitution with only the vaguest theoretical claim upon the remote past. Arguably, there *was* no past to support the common law in America because the legal definition of custom beyond memory required origins preceding the reign of Richard the First. As St. George Tucker pointed out in his Virginia edition of Blackstone's *Commentaries*, North America had been settled four hundred years too late to qualify.[26] The legitimacy of American law obviously required more immediate sources. And yet every lawyer in America quailed at the thought of a definitive constitution born of a single convention. In 1788 even the tough-minded Hamilton regarded the document drafted the previous summer as "a prodigy to the completion of which I look forward with trembling anxiety."[27] At issue was the lawyer's ability to create new mechanisms of control in the absence of a stable past. Lacking the comforts of precedent, the unreliable present and the even more indefinite future had to be shaped to serve.

One response was to qualify the meaning of the Constitutional Convention as decision-making process. Another was to insist on constant reinterpretation even though the politics of ratification required a moment of faith from everyone. Hamilton as "Publius" warned that only time and experience would smooth or "liquidate the meaning of all the parts" of the new government into "a harmonious and consistent whole."[28] More central to the actual writing of the Constitution, Hamilton's collaborator from the Virginia bar went much further. James Madison believed that all of history carried a negative lesson for the new republic: precedents were valuable only as "beacons which give warning of the course to be shunned." Madison also worried about "the novelty of the undertaking" in Philadelphia. The most the drafters at the Constitutional Convention had been able to do was "to avoid the errors suggested by the past . . . and to provide a convenient mode of rectifying their own errors as future experience may unfold them." Madison made it clear that the evaluations to come would have to be intense and could not be satisfied through the cumbersome formalities of an amendment process. In a statement central to English legal thought from Sir Edward Coke to Edmund Burke, he added: "All new laws, though penned with the greatest technical skill, and passed on the fullest and most mature deliberation, are considered as more or less obscure and equivocal, until their meaning be liquidated and ascertained by a series of particular discussions and adjudications."[29] Only the ongoing legal process could define the republic.

Madison's language contains a procedural tenacity in the face of apprehension that shows how legal thought became the great intellectual adventure of the formative period. For it was one thing to scrutinize every innovation against the traditional forms of English society; quite another to insist on the same stance in an American context that was filled with novelty and lacked basic traditions. What could it mean to "adjudicate" the meaning of piecemeal alteration where everything was new and in constant flux? Applied to the republican experiment, the lawyer's scrutiny demanded all or nothing. And since everything *was* new and changing, since the present *was* always "obscure and equivocal," the price of a moment's inattention might mean total failure. To trust the moment was to accept untested law! Only in these terms can we appreciate the lawyer's virtual obsession with things republican.

Judicial review would become the cultural paradigm for the lawyer's scrutiny. In the absence of legitimizing precedent, the new doctrine provided a mechanism for confirming or rejecting tentative law in a manner that allowed Americans to rely on the present for future decisions. The necessity for some kind of certitude here should not be underestimated. Modern preoccupation with the constitutionalism of checks and balances overlooks the fact that judicial review was designed primarily to catch the dangerous mistakes that every lawyer feared and assumed within the accelerated lawmaking of the new republic.

James Wilson, the most articulate early defender of judicial review, emphasized the role of the doctrine as a safeguard within the legal process, and he did so more than a decade before *Marbury v. Madison*. Judicial review was "a noble guard against legislative despotism," but it was more truly "the glory of the constitution" because it prevented mistakes, unintentional or otherwise, from hardening into system. Wilson saw himself "legislating for a nation, and for thousands yet unborn," and he explained that "it leads me to greater decision on all subjects of a constitutional nature, when I reflect, that, if from inattention, want of precision, or any other defect, I should do wrong, there is a power in the government, which can constitutionally prevent the operation of a wrong measure from affecting my constituents."[30] Temperamentally fearful of all present action, the legal mind gained the courage of its initiatives by making judicial review its intellectual safety valve.

The power of determining the constitutionality of law also gave both sides of the bench the confidence and latitude to argue vital policy instead of dead-letter law. In a developing nation obsessed with its own future glory, no audience could be held by the traditional forms and rhetoric of the past. Before everything else the American lawyer wanted to be heard; the strongest sense of legal propriety would bend before that primal need. Even the conservative Hamilton sounded more like Tom Paine than like learned counsel when he announced that "the rules of legal interpretation are rules of *common-sense*, adopted by the courts in the construction of the laws."[31]

John Marshall was the perfect model and logical extension of the need to speak a contemporary language that all Americans could understand and heed. The architect of judicial review in the federal courts, Marshall was also dismissive of case law in general. In fact, his five greatest constitutional opinions as chief justice of the Supreme Court failed to cite a single previous court decision as authority. Each argument was grounded instead upon appeals to the *principia* of American civilization and upon the grand, inclusive style glimpsed in Adams and Blackstone. Obviously, recourse to judicial review as such was infrequent, but the implications of possible use were sufficient to frame every discussion of constitutional principle. Marshall made the most of this situation, and his methods helped to turn important cases into high ceremonial occasions within republican culture. Already the final arbiter of the law in 1803, the Supreme Court was the great oracle of Americanism by the time of Marshall's retirement in 1835.[32]

In republican society generally, the courtroom speech of both attorney and judge quickly became one of what Clifford Geertz has called "the active centers of social order"—a point within a culture where leading ideas come together with leading institutions and where a governing elite uses the set of symbolic forms involved to express the fact that it is in truth governing.[33] With members of the bar already in control of the legislative and executive processes of government, judicial review meant that lawyers alone would create and evaluate practical policy. The courtroom represented a final and exclusive podium for analyzing and testing formulations within the American experiment. Others might comment, but the business of defining the republic remained the particular prerogative of those who joined the legal profession.

"*Ex Officio* Natural Guardians"

The frailty of new institutions turned the lawyer's business of definitions into a mission for every American to ponder. Most eighteenth-century observers feared that a national government based on republican principles would prove impossible when stretched to the unheard-of scale of the American continent. "You might as well attempt to rule Hell by Prayer," wrote a typical anti-federalist in 1787.[34] Madison's countervailing definitions in Federalist No. 14 and all ensuing efforts to shape the republic try to minimize uncertainties that dominated the American psyche throughout the period. In the words of one commentator:

> No sooner did Americans create their Union than they began to speculate fretfully about how long it would last . . . throughout the early part of the nineteenth century it was a common observation that the Union was evanescent. It was characterized by various writers as "metaphysical and theoretical"; as "a sort of *forced state* . . . of life"; as a mere linguistic creation that had been "spoken into existence"; and that "exists, so to speak, only in the mind."[35]

These anxieties were based upon hard realities and a negative course in events that later Americans have ignored in their eagerness to trace the developing nation. Between 1790 and 1860 virtually every state, major faction, and interest group tried, at least once, to weaken the federal government or break up the union. Political unrest, war, rebellion, economic depression, and uncertain geographic identity were the common lot of the former colonies as they struggled to establish themselves in a union never far from collapse.[36] John Adams spoke for many in 1812 when he described the union as "a brittle China Vase" and "a Palace of Glass" easily destroyed. Ten years later, squarely within the supposed Era of Good Feeling, his son John Quincy Adams meant it when he thanked time and chance for sparing the government he then served as secretary of state. "Although our complicated machine of two co-ordinate sovereignties has not yet fallen to pieces by its own weakness," the younger Adams observed, "it exists in perpetual jeopardy."[37]

Amidst pervasive uncertainty, lawyers assigned themselves to what they conceived to be the crucial problems. They became, in Chancellor James Kent's terms, "*ex officio* natural guardians of the laws" and "sentinels over the constitutions and liberties of the country."[38] Since many construed the emergence of the United States as the first important step in a new age of human progress, the role of guardian easily assumed cosmic overtones. "Of the learned professions, nay of all the sciences," remarked the *American Quarterly Review* in a typical encomium for the period, "it [the law] may well put in a claim for even the highest rank. What, indeed, can be more noble than the aim of that science which is to direct the actions of mankind, and whose foundations rest upon the will of the great ruler of the universe."[39] Republican growing pains enhanced the lawyer's belief that he alone possessed the expertise for proper direction. Hugh Swinton Legaré, probably the most erudite member of the southern bar in the Jacksonian era, spoke for every lawyer when he claimed that a knowledge of jurisprudence was "a glorious distinction among men—especially in an intellectual and free country." "In our land," he concluded, "it is the way to everything desirable and must ever be so . . . It is better than talent—but it helps talent—it is fuel for its fires, a lamp for its feet, and a staff of strength in its right hand."[40]

As long as the law remained "a glorious distinction" and "the way to everything desirable" within a culture that thought of itself as precarious, the lawyer's role as guardian allowed him to control thought and expression. One result was a remarkable symbiosis between law and literary aspiration. Indeed, the lawyer as writer dominated the literature of the early republic because the broad cultural responsibilities of the professional man and the writer's imperatives could be made to appear the same. There is, for example, a strong mutuality in the aims of lawyer and poet in Joel Barlow's plan for *The Columbiad* (1807). "The real object" of Barlow's poem was "to inculcate the love of rational liberty, and to discountenance the deleterious passion for violence and war; to show that on the basis of the republican principle all good morals, as well as good government and hopes of permanent peace, must be founded."[41] In the words of another writer educated to the law, Edward T. Channing, Americans were to "cultivate domestic literature as a source of national dignity" and to use that literature to facilitate "the great experiment of republican influences upon the security, the domestic happiness of man, his elevation of character, his love of country."[42] The lawyer as the expounder and guardian of republican virtue assumed the same guidelines and chose the same themes. His voice and pen served both culture and country in a seemingly endless stream of works instructing and strengthening the American people in the meaning of republicanism.

Supporting the lawyer's assertiveness as ideological guardian was a peculiar and overwhelming self-confidence. His comprehensive sense of relevance and purpose encouraged him to dominate republican culture and to create strong affinities between law and literature. It helped that quite literally everything belonged within the early American lawyer's intellectual purview. When the Supreme Court justice Joseph Story came to bolster the faculty of the Harvard Law School in 1829, his inaugural lecture urged every student to "addict himself to the study of philosophy, of rhetoric, of history, and of human nature." All of Story's recommendations presupposed "the importance of a full possession of the general literature of ancient and modern times." In perhaps the finest single statement of the importance of literature to the early American lawyer, he added:

> It is this classical learning alone, which can impart a solid and lasting polish to the mind, and give to diction that subtile elegance and grace, which color the thoughts with almost transparent hues. It should be studied, not merely in its grave disquisitions, but in its glorious fictions, and in those graphical displays of the human heart, in the midst of which we wander as in the presence of familiar but disembodied spirits.[43]

By 1844 more specialized standards of professionalism existed, standards created in no small measure by Story's nine intervening volumes of legal commentaries. But even at this late date a leader of the bar like Rufus Choate could routinely stress the legal profession's centrality to a "mental culture" based on "admiration of the beautiful, the good, the true in art, in poetry, in thought."[44] The scope and reach of such statements are perhaps the hardest elements for a modern understanding to grasp. It was an age of broad defi-

nitions. In Samuel Johnson's *Dictionary*, literature was simply "learning; skill in letters," both the sum of human thought in language
and its practical applications. Lacking the more specific intellectual
guidelines of statutory or case law, the attorney of the formative
period turned easily and naturally to these more generic proficiencies
for standards of professionalism. Of course, his reliance upon literature as a tool for communicating republicanism reinforced a natural affinity.

An incident involving James Kent, later the chancellor of New
York, and Edward Livingston, who would codify Louisiana law
and become secretary of state under Andrew Jackson, illustrates the
power of that affinity. Riding circuit together as young lawyers in
1786, Kent noted in his journal that Livingston "had a pocket Horace
and read some passages to me, and pointed out their beauties, assuming that I well understood Horace. I said nothing, but was stung
with shame and mortification. I purchased immediately Horace and
Virgil . . . and formed my resolution, promptly and decidedly, to
recover the lost languages." Soon Kent was devoting early mornings
to Latin and Greek, late afternoons to French, and evenings to
English literature in a prodigious quest for "solid happiness and
honor."[45] For Kent and others like him, a neoclassical orientation
made literature the first gauge of professional merit.

Although the lawyer's emphasis upon general literature represented what many would call a pre-professional stage of American
law, the words of Story, Choate, and Kent all illustrate that it was
an emphasis reinforced by the same men who were creating the
complex legal system to follow. Their influence within the profession meant that the movement toward more technical definitions of
expertise came slowly even though the growth in American law
demanded change. "You cannot be men of all work, and lawyers
beside; any more than you can be in two places at the same time,"
Timothy Walker, a disciple of Joseph Story, pleaded as early as
1839, pointing to the bulk and complexity of new American law.
Walker's *Introduction to American Law* would train thousands within
a more selective pursuit of legal knowledge, but the impact of this
narrower focus came in the decades after the Civil War.[46] Until
then, the assumed role of republican guardian and westward expansion preserved the conditions that caused the lawyer to rely on
general literature. It is no coincidence that the final dominating

exponent of the generalist tradition came out of the West. Abraham Lincoln's oratory combined equal portions of Blackstone, Shakespeare, and the Bible. In the first half of the nineteenth century the bond between knowledge, general literature, and law remained paramount, and the epistemological implications involved would shape the meanings Americans attached to all three concepts.

"The General Principles of Universal Law"

James Kent gave the configuration of law and letters its most accurate early expression while lecturing at Columbia College in 1794. He urged every American lawyer to master the Greek and Latin classics as well as moral philosophy, history, logic, and mathematics, and his emphasis was on the ability that flowed from general knowledge. Only an attorney "well read in the whole circle of the arts and sciences" could form "an accurate acquaintance with the general principles of Universal Law." Kent's constitutive metaphor was causal linkage; allusions to chains of subordination, interlocking circles, related systems, comprehensive surveys, and intimate connections all built toward a legal knowledge of universal applicability. Every aspect of what Kent called "the attractive chain of classical studies" was relevant to an infinitely expanding sphere of legal control: "The science of law . . . reaches to every tie which is endearing to the affections, and has a concern on every action which takes place in the extensive circles of public and private life."[47]

Thomas Jefferson's more famous lists of readings for law students were a practical demonstration of the science of law reaching toward every tie. Jefferson, like Kent, believed in the universal order law could provide. He divided legal study into units or "resting places" under the four great systematizers of English law (Bracton, Coke, Matthew Bacon, and Blackstone), and he also found "history, politics, ethics, physics, oratory, poetry, criticism, etc. as necessary as law to form an accomplished lawyer." Jefferson's plans of study were virtual bibliographies of the Enlightenment, requiring fourteen hours of reading a day across a five-year period. His students read physical science, ethics, religion, and natural law before eight each morning; law (in at least three languages) from eight to twelve; politics and history in the afternoon; and poetry, criticism, rhetoric, and oratory "from Dark to Bed-time."[48]

The law student's assigned task was nothing less than a practical omniscience in human knowledge. David Hoffman's *Course of Legal Study; Respectfully Addressed to the Students of Law in the United States* (1817) was the standard manual of its kind well into the 1830s; it covered six years of study and opened with the Bible, Cicero's *De Officiis*, Seneca's *Morals*, Xenophon's *Memorabilia*, Aristotle's *Ethics*, and a long list of other readings in general literature and political philosophy. Hoffman expected his law student to seek "that comprehension of expression peculiar to the poet," and he insisted on the usual litany that "every species of knowledge may prove necessary."[49] Samuel Knapp's *Biographical Sketches of Eminent Lawyers, Statesmen, and Men of Letters* in 1821 added a graphic description of this legal aesthetic at work. "The great lawyers of the present day," Knapp claimed, "bring all the lights of science to raise and adorn the profession." An understanding of literature and science within the courtroom lent "an elevation of feeling and a character to knowledge."[50]

To be sure, few possessed the intellectual dedication that Knapp thought he saw and that Hoffman's guide required. For every Jefferson devoting five full years to legal training, scores of "Blackstone lawyers" entered the profession after a few months of study, self-proclaimed masters of one text. William Wirt could draft for others a Jeffersonian list of books "essential in the preparation of an accomplished advocate," but he began practice in Culpeper County, Virginia, with Blackstone's *Commentaries*, two volumes of *Don Quixote*, and a copy of *Tristram Shandy*.[51] The supposed "golden age of American law" in the first half of the nineteenth century was really a period of very weak collective standards, and many of its greatest leaders from beginning to end—Patrick Henry, John Marshall, Daniel Webster, Abraham Lincoln, and Stephen Douglas, to name only a few—joined the bar after minimal preparation.[52]

Nevertheless, if formal requirements were often lax, the controlling aspirations of an intellectual elite remained firm. John Quincy Adams was hardly an average student, but he received a legal education in the Newburyport, Massachusetts, office of Theophilus Parsons that was typical both in its limitations and in the panoramic directions it encouraged at the end of the eighteenth century. Complaining of Parsons' frequent absences and of the unscholarly atmosphere in a crowded office filled with clients, hangers-on, and lazy fellow clerks, the younger Adams consumed an impressive range of works. His broad reading flowed from Parsons' insistence that "any useful branch of science" was relevant. Conversation ranged across "law, physic, history, poetry, religion, and politics, by turns," and readings included Buffon's *Histoire Naturelle*, the histories of Hume and Gibbon, Shakespeare, Butler's *Hudibras*, and Rousseau's *Confessions*, along with legal texts like Blackstone's *Commentaries* (read three times in a year and a half), *Coke on Littleton* ("the great magazine of legal knowledge"), and numerous books on the forms of pleading.[53] When Adams' contemporary Joseph Hopkinson proclaimed the universal grasp of the accomplished lawyer, he might have had either Adams or himself in mind. Successful Philadelphia lawyer, author of *Hail, Columbia*, congressman, judge, and president of the Academy of Fine Arts, Hopkinson in fact was justifying yet another bibliography for law students, comprising his own "models of history, poetry, and eloquence."[54]

The lawyer's fascination with his endless reading lists is an important key to our understanding of the early American legal mind. The ultimate goal was what Rufus Choate would later find in John Quincy Adams: "the hived wisdom of a life of study and a life of action." Uncertainty over the point of balance between study and action fueled constant debate, but the exchange in itself guaranteed that technical knowledge alone could not make a lawyer in republican society. As one journal of the period pointed out in rejecting this possibility, "Extensive learning, not confined to a particular profession, and varied accomplishments . . . must all unite." It is this expectation of unity—John Quincy Adams' hived wisdom, James Kent's whole circle, Jefferson's balanced systems, and so on—that finally separated the early legal mind from what follows. Rufus Choate was less interested in John Quincy Adams' "universal acquisitions" as such than he was in demonstrating "how those vast accumulations of learning are fused, moulded, and projected, by the fiery tide of mind!"[55] Here is the crux. The excitement in the lawyer's seemingly tedious organization of texts grew from his belief that collection became accumulation; that accumulation, in turn, discovered and, hence, *created* a comprehensive design for America and the world.

The great exemplum of the lawyer's structured, intellectual universe was, of course, Blackstone's *Commentaries on the Laws of Eng-*

relates to
law as a
science of
second nature.

land. Not since Justinian's *Institutes* in the sixth century had there been within western civilization such a successful attempt to reduce to short and rational form the complex legal institutions of an entire society.[56] Even the *Institutes* could not match Blackstone for erudition and literary eloquence. A youthful James Kent first encountered the *Commentaries* during the chaos of the American Revolution. Filled with awe, he immediately decided upon a career in law.[57] For the leaders of the early American bar, living as they were in a new and comparatively rustic culture, Blackstone's *Commentaries* transcended mere knowledge to become a work of beauty and a comforting source of definition; it was a model for aesthetic emulation, a handy methodological scheme of values, a practical example of what one man might accomplish if he but dared to try.

Joseph Story's own admiration knew no limits and reveals the extent to which the *Commentaries* was perceived as literary text: "For luminous method, for profound research, for purity of diction, for comprehensive brevity and pregnancy of matter, for richness in classical allusions and for extent and variety of knowledge of foreign jurisprudence, whether introduced for illustration, or ornament, or instruction, it [the *Commentaries*] . . . stands unrivalled in ours and perhaps every other language."[58] Even Jefferson, who greatly feared the conservative political implications of the *Commentaries*, agreed that of all the basic compendia of laws it represented "the most lucid in arrangement which had yet been written, correct in its matter, classical in style, and rightfully taking its place by the side of Justinian's *Institutes*."[59]

These encomiums to Blackstone deserve careful attention because they point to the source of the lawyer's epistemological self-confidence, his peculiar ability to convert general knowledge into design and then into power in places where others found only confusion. Story and Jefferson valued the aggregation of particulars in the *Commentaries*. Their discovery of comprehensive brevity and lucid arrangement assumed an accumulation beyond mere linkage. Story's praise specifically incorporated long passages from Sir William Jones's *Essay on The Law of Bailments* (1781), the most popular eighteenth-century explanation of Blackstone's importance. Jones, the English linguist, jurist, orientalist, and poet, was a perfect model of the lawyer as man of letters, and his essay on bailments remained an indispensable guide in Anglo-American law for half a century.[60]

Here, in language Story quoted, Jones wrote of "our excellent Black-stone, who of all men was best able to throw the clearest light on this [the issue of bailment], as on every other subject."

While pointing to errors, Jones found the *Commentaries* to be "the most correct and beautiful outline, that ever was exhibited of any human science . . . if, indeed, all the titles which he professed only to sketch in elementary discourses, were filled up with exactness and perspicuity, *Englishmen* might hope at length to possess a digest of their laws, which would leave but little room for controversy." *An Essay on The Law of Bailments* was drafted as just such an initial step toward "filling up" Blackstone's comprehensive design; it closed with a peroration that explained the philosophical basis of such an undertaking and that soon became one of the most frequently quoted passages in Anglo-American law:

> The great system of jurisprudence, like that of the Universe, consists of many subordinate systems, all of which are connected by nice links and beautiful dependencies; and each of them, as I have fully per-suaded myself, is reducible to a few plain *elements*, either the wise maxims of national policy and general convenience, or the *positive* rules of our forefathers, which are seldom deficient in wisdom or utility; if LAW *be a science*, and really deserve so sublime a name, it must be founded on principle, and claim an exalted rank in the empire of *reason*.[61]

Blackstone and his popularizer Sir William Jones supplied a meth-odology of control and a precise delineation of laws that minimized controversy and ensured national cohesion. Here was inspiration for the commentators who shaped the laws of the republic; here was direction for the political leaders who struggled to maintain the example of the Founding Fathers; here was the prospect of form and definition within the densest American wilderness. No wonder the American lawyer came to view himself as the creator of a civ-ilization. "Under [the American lawyer's] influence," ran one at-torney's account from 1840, "new governments are established, courts erected, laws passed, obedience inculcated and enforced, and the great principles of English law and liberty administered in the for-ests, as on the banks of the Thames, or in Westminster Hall."[62]

Science, system, and national identity merged in law to form the "nice links and beautiful dependencies" early republicans needed to create intellectual coherence within a cultural vacuum. With a "few plain elements" of republican theory thrown in, one could use legal thought to impose hierarchy and decorum on the roughest frontier settlement. It was a methodology for ordering this world—and perhaps the next. Samuel Knapp, writing about the legal profession in 1821, assumed as much in making Richard Hooker's famous assertion his own: "Of law there can be no less acknowledged, than that her seat is the bosom of God, her voice the harmony of the world."[63]

Such certainty proved especially irresistible to writers describing a new republic of unprecedented size within a continent still shrouded in mystery. Indeed, one reason why Americans tried so compulsively to explain America to other Americans throughout the first seventy years of their national existence was that the country itself kept changing beyond the conception and even the recognition of its people. The greatest difficulty for the writer of the period was to resolve and, failing that, to circumscribe the unknowns within his experience. Yet the unknowns in themselves were so numerous and so elemental as to require careful manipulation for the sake of clarity and perspective. Creativity really meant the ability to impose order upon unruly material. Hence, the vision of control within eighteenth-century legal thought and the lawyer's faith in universally applicable forms provided ready answers to a serious literary problem. Among early republicans, no one saw farther or displayed more ingenuity in this regard than Thomas Jefferson. There is an elaborate craft to the theory of Americanism that he projected with seeming ease upon his country. Jeffersonian optimism was hard-won, and it represents the clearest example we have of a legal aesthetic at work in early American literature.

CHAPTER 2

MYSTERIOUS OBLIGATION: JEFFERSON'S *NOTES ON THE STATE OF VIRGINIA*

"The Measure of a Shadow"

Nothing illustrates the critical neglect of early republican literature more forcefully than the obscurity of Thomas Jefferson's one book, *Notes on the State of Virginia*. For although Jefferson is a major figure and writer of the age and although *Notes* has been accepted as both an American classic and a vital contribution to the political and scientific thought of the eighteenth century, the book has been largely ignored as a literary text. Even Jefferson's greatest admirers, his biographers, have belittled his creative efforts in this regard. They criticize *Notes* overall as an "unlabored" by-product "tossed off in a few summer weeks," a mere random collection below any standard of authorial planning, a glorified guidebook that Jefferson never really meant to write.[1] These dismissive tones originate in Jefferson's own seeming disregard. He once threatened to burn the entire first edition of *Notes*—some two hundred copies privately printed at considerable expense. "Do not view me as an author, and attached to what he has written," he warned James Madison. "I am neither."[2] Calling his book a private communication unfit for distribution, he tried hard to prevent its general publication.[3] In subsequent letters, *Notes* became "a poor crayon," "this trifle," "nothing more than the measure of a shadow," and "a bad book . . . the author of which has no other merit than that of thinking as little of it as any man in the world can."[4]

Unfortunately, modern observers have taken Jefferson's comments at face value instead of placing them in perspective. *Notes* is

Thomas Jefferson, painting by Thomas Sully, 1822.

Lawyer, author, politician, and ideologist, Thomas Jefferson was the presiding genius of law and letters in the early republic. This portrait was enough to turn the skeptical James Fenimore Cooper into a lifelong follower. Cooper summarized his reaction to the painting in a letter to Pierre Jean David: "On y voit le beau ideal de l'homme et, en même tem[p]s l'homme lui même" [One sees there the beautiful ideal of man and, at the same time, the man himself].

peculiarly an unfinished work, as its author was the first to point out, but it is neither a haphazard nor an unstructured effort. Jefferson devoted much time and energy to his book from its inception in November 1780 to its official publication in London in 1787. He took enormous pains to insure the accuracy of its contents, and years after publication he continued to revise his own copy with a new edition in mind.[5] In denigrating his own work and shunning publication, he responded as any man of letters would in America in the eighteenth century. The true gentleman addressed his work—usually considered a negligible product of leisure—to a small group of social peers. He never wrote for money, rarely signed what he wrote, and tried to avoid the vulgarity of publication.[6]

The slow emergence of *Notes* as a public book affords an excellent example of the way in which a gentleman's work reached a larger audience in the eighteenth century. Jefferson's friends vied for the right to see copies of the manuscript drafts he started circulating in 1781. Access was tantamount to membership within an inner circle, and ensuing pressures from inside the group led naturally toward private printing and publication.[7] Jefferson abided by all of the conventions, but his correspondence implies that he may have been several jumps ahead of his enthusiastic supporters even as he appeared to lag dutifully a half step behind.[8] In any event, once the predictable support from Madison, John Adams, and others produced plans for an English edition, Jefferson's behavior resembled that of anxious authors in every age: irritation over delays in publication, anxiety over printing mistakes, and interest in sales.[9]

The writer's private hopes also belie a lack of interest. The decision in 1785 to run off a private edition of two hundred copies included plans for giving a copy to each student of the College of William and Mary. Jefferson, with his customary faith in the rising generation, acted here with "two great objects" in view: encouragement of slave emancipation in Virginia and the settlement of the state constitution on a new basis (both major topics in *Notes*).[10] It is hard to imagine an author with greater expectations for his text. A man obsessed by notions of design, system, measurement, and style, Jefferson also would have been embarrassed by his biographers' apologies for an apparent absence of form. *Notes*, in fact, possesses a coherent structure that we no longer recognize because of a more general failure to approach the literature of the period on its own terms. We apply our own belletristic standards narrowly and find only weakness in consequence. Placed in the intellectual context of the day, Jefferson's priorities in *Notes* form part of an unexplored literary aesthetic. His book, like the Declaration of Independence before it, turns upon English common law and the great, humanistic legal compendia of the Enlightenment.

"A Patient Pursuit of Facts"

Jefferson's book grew out of a questionnaire circulated during the summer of 1780 to members of the Continental Congress by François Marbois, the secretary of the French legation at Philadelphia. *Notes* was written as a direct response, using the French diplomat's twenty-two explicit queries on the resources of the American states as chapter headings.[11] Detailed answers on manufacturing, demographic patterns, the navigability of rivers, and the nature of animal life fill page after page with charts, measurements, and lists—all suggesting an episodic series of replies to another's questions. In what sense, then, is *Notes* more than a dutiful compilation of information? The very question carries assumptions to guard against. Collection of accurate data—and especially the gathering of information concerning the New World—fascinated eighteenth-century intellectuals. Among Americans in particular, as Daniel Boorstin has pointed out, "the vagueness of the land" and "the scarcity of precise knowledge gave such knowledge as there was a peculiar appeal."[12]

   Jefferson's penchant for organized and minute observation coincided with an American quest for certainties; it also met the prevailing intellectual stipulations of European culture. In places *Notes* clearly is meant for an audience of one, Georges Louis Leclerc, comte de Buffon, the leading French scientist of the day. "Sensible people," Buffon had argued, "will always recognize that the only and true science is the knowledge of facts," and he called for "the exact description of everything" with corresponding, though subordinate, attention to issues of style. Reportage and literary aspiration went hand in hand. Jefferson accepted Buffon's premises in *Notes* even as he meticulously contested the French philosophe's specific theories about America with massive collections of data.[13] "A patient pursuit of facts," he wrote explaining his procedures, "and cautious combination and comparison of them, is the drudgery to which man is subjected by his Maker, if he wishes to attain sure knowledge."[14]

Nor should we expect a different methodology from a man whose professed heroes were Bacon, Newton, and Locke and whose empiricism, in consequence, assumed that facts properly collected would inevitably lead through inductive reasoning toward unified theory and larger vision. Jefferson spoke disparagingly of his own efforts because he knew *Notes* could only begin the climb toward vision, but, a son of the Enlightenment, he believed strongly in the movement toward larger coherence that factual knowledge would bring. This movement gave his own work shape and meaning. *Notes* was "a poor crayon" in the sense that Jefferson firmly expected the future writers then emerging from the College of William and Mary to use his sketch to "fill up" a complete painting. His book was "the measure of a shadow" in that measurements had to be continued every hour as the sun advanced in order "to furnish another element for calculating the course and motion of this member [Virginia] of our federal system."[15]

Jefferson's explicit analogy here between the Newtonian machinery of nature and similar laws of causation for human society was, of course, still another standard assumption of the Enlightenment, one that enabled the author of *Notes* to link what he saw in the physical world with what he wanted to see in society. Behind the meteorological charts of rainfall and wind velocity and the elaborate comparisons of European and American animal life, *Notes*, like every other work to come out of the formative period, is obsessed with the sense of a unique country that Americans were groping to define. Ideological placement of the republic is Jefferson's main theme. *Notes* builds slowly through observation of the natural world and social analysis toward a final peroration on the subject of country in a closing section improbably labeled public revenue and expenses. "Young as we are," Jefferson concludes here, "and with such a country before us to fill with people and with happiness, we should point in that direction the whole generative force of nature." What follows is a summation of America's unique opportunity for creating a new kind of nation based on peace, free trade, virtuous citizenship, and careful harmony within the many advantages nature has furnished the New World (pp. 174–176). The controls of a republican government would guarantee appropriate and unparalleled national growth.

The difficulties in achieving this positive vision involved more than revolutionary rhetoric. The greatest blunder we make in approaching the works of the formative period is to assume the sense of country that the Founding Fathers worked so desperately to create. The year 1781, when *Notes* took shape, was a time of confusion and anxiety in America—particularly for a Virginian and most particularly for Virginia's governor, Thomas Jefferson. Six years later James Madison would become the Father of the Constitution, but in 1781 he was a discouraged member of the Continental Congress writing home to Jefferson of his certainty that the Union would dissolve as the war ended.[16] In Virginia, of course, the war had just begun in 1781, first with an exploratory raid in January by British forces under Benedict Arnold and then with a successful invasion by Cornwallis' army in May that sent Jefferson and his state government fleeing from Richmond. Inadequate military preparation, a crop failure throughout the state, runaway inflation, secessionist movements in the Kentucky territory, and insufficient executive power for dealing with any of these emergencies were complications that left Jefferson helpless to act. Nevertheless, he was blamed for the general collapse by an ungrateful legislature, which decided in June to investigate his conduct as governor. Six months would pass before the next General Assembly voted "to obviate and to remove all unmerited Censure." In the meantime, one of Jefferson's daughters died, his property was overrun and partially destroyed by the British army, he was personally immobilized for a time by a serious riding accident, and his wife's health continued to decline. Her early death in September 1782 would leave Jefferson completely traumatized for weeks on end.[17]

Notes on the State of Virginia was written and revised during this bleak period, the darkest in Jefferson's life. In fact, the whole first draft was composed during the second half of 1781 while the prospect of public censure hung over him. Jefferson would later call this threat "a shock on which I had not calculated," and his entire orientation seems to have been shaken as he announced his permanent retirement at thirty-eight to farm, family, and books. *Notes* represented an attempt to reorder experience and to control the chaos around him.[18] Never a man of action and always an intellectual, Jefferson clearly welcomed a structured excuse for reappraisal. As he put it himself, "I am at present busily employed for Monsr. Marbois without his knowing it, and have to acknowledge to him the mysterious obligation for making me much better acquainted with my own country than I ever was before."[19] No one could have been better primed for the task. For years Jefferson had collected information on America, written on what he described as "loose papers, bundled up without order." *Notes* required an organization for these memoranda and soon became, in Jefferson's phrase, "a good occasion to embody their substance."[20]

Everything about Jefferson's personal situation and the ensuing creative process suggests that *Notes* was no casual effort. The book placed him under mysterious obligation, as he tells us, because it led him toward a better sense of country. Moreover, his growth in knowledge happened at least in part because the need to organize earlier and looser writings—"embody their substance"—produced firmer understanding and control. Taken together, Jefferson's statements indicate unexplored levels of clarity and structure in *Notes*, order imposed on chaos. They also suggest the writer's inclination to combine problems of theme and form. The convergence of revolutionary uncertainties with Jefferson's personal difficulties and with the disarray of his "loose papers" pointed toward demands for control on disparate levels. Jefferson's tentative solution was to submerge each problem in a developmental sense of country. The future of America supplied republican identity and individual meaning as well as textual coherence to *Notes*. Though the process was fraught with aesthetic complications and confusions, it allowed Jefferson to escape the chaos of the moment and to search for incremental meanings within time. Time itself, through Jefferson's optimistic hopes for the future, would suggest an answering promise to anxieties regarding the present; time as theme compensated for structural inadequacies within a text that never claimed to attain finality.

The practical difficulty in seeking a view of country in the 1780s was the sheer unruliness of a subject filled with unknowns. When the author of *Notes* described the Ohio River as the most beautiful on earth (p. 10), it is well to remember that he never traveled far enough west to see it. The notable possibilities of volcanoes along the Mississippi (p. 20) and of carnivorous hairy mammoths extant in the Northwest (pp. 43, 50–54) provide extreme examples of the need to find form in a void. Measuring a half-known world presented related problems. Fearful lest his lists and figures in *Notes* be dismissed as parochial aberrations, Jefferson declares Monticello physically central to Virginia, where "the best average" in data can be expected (p. 76). Ignorant of vital information concerning the Appalachian mountains, he insists upon their orderly appearance: "It is worthy notice, that our mountains are not solitary and scattered confusedly over the face of the country; but that they . . . are disposed in ridges one behind another" (p. 18). A similar mechanism projects geometric and artistic unity over the otherwise formless wilderness of western Virginia. Jefferson's rivers bisect his orderly mountains "at right angles" and move gently eastward toward civilization (pp. 18–19).

Jefferson knew as well as any modern reader that these devices were superficial, even ludicrous; they were strategies of control, not serious formulations. Time and again in *Notes* he shows sophisticated awareness of an investigator's real problems, confessing that a topic is "unripe" for meaningful response and conceding that his answers are incomplete because phenomena remain inexplicable (pp. 2, 33, 54, 81). "It is impossible," he would later add, "for doubt to have been more tenderly and hesitatingly expressed than it was in the *Notes on Virginia*."[21] His use of Marbois's list of queries as chapter headings underlines this point. The text *as question* warns against false information—"Ignorance is preferable to error" (p. 33). It constantly reminds one that, in the absence of knowledge, inquiry imposes order. Significantly, each admission of an incomplete answer also contains Jefferson's realization that the bulk of the New World remains too remote to allow the use of natural philosophy as the primary structural principle for *Notes*.

Though crucial, the point will escape readers concentrating selectively on Jefferson's eloquent and famous descriptions of the Natural Bridge or the Blue Ridge Gap. Neither interest in the natural world nor general philosophical acceptance of nature's blueprint for man can compensate the author of *Notes* for his own lack of information. Not surprisingly, Jefferson turned for relief to the mode of intellectual control he knew best, the law. What does surprise one is the rich implementation of this decision within the structure of *Notes*. The civic tones and disjointed forms of early republican literature take on fresh meaning when we realize that the legal philosophy of the Enlightenment gave Jefferson more than an alternative for discursive method; it also provided an ideal solution to his structural problems. Legal formulation assumed a pattern to incremental

knowledge that enabled Jefferson to fuse the organizational needs
of *Notes* to a developmental sense of country.

"The Most Comprehensive Definitions of Things"

Eighteenth-century conceptions of law encouraged both a particu-
laristic methodology for extracting order from chaos and a comprehensive view of subject matter. Jefferson, perhaps the best legal
scholar in America in 1781, was thoroughly familiar with the works
behind these assumptions.[22] The Dutch jurist, statesman, and poet
Hugo Grotius had written in 1625 that human reason, not religious
explanation, formed the basis of man's understanding of natural
law. Grotius' confidence in secular inquiry and his insistence that
law be presented in "an orderly fashion" and in "a compendious
form" provided the inspiration for Samuel von Pufendorf's *Of the
Law of Nature and Nations* (1673), Jean Jacques Burlamaqui's *Principles
of Natural and Politic Law* (1747–1751), Baron de Montesquieu's *Spirit
of Laws* (1748), William Blackstone's *Commentaries on the Laws of
England* (1765–1769), and related works by such figures as Emmerich
de Vattel, Lord Kames, and Cesare Beccaria.[23]

Jefferson learned from Pufendorf, among others, that it was possible through law "to deliver the most comprehensive Definitions
of Things" and to establish in moral science a certainty analogous
to that in mathematics. Clear connections between natural law and
moral science permitted moral entities to be "superadded to natural
Things" through the "imposition" of the reason of "understanding
Beings."[24] Burlamaqui outlined just how man-made or positive law
logically improved upon natural law and guarded the practical sources
of liberty as well as the identity of a culture. Little known today,
Burlamaqui's *Principles of Natural and Politic Law* served as a major
text among American Revolutionary leaders.[25] Montesquieu's *Spirit
of Laws*, in turn, showed how the inexplicable diversity of country
or countries could be ordered and then reduced through conceptions
of positive law, and Blackstone's *Commentaries* represented the great
exemplum of that accomplishment—a country completely defined
through law.[26]

Just about every substantive idea in *Notes on the State of Virginia*
can be traced in one or more of the legal works in question. Of
more immediate concern here, however, is Jefferson's decision to

use the general form of these writings to provide a structure and organization to *Notes*. The legal treatises of Grotius, Pufendorf, Burlamaqui, Montesquieu, and Blackstone, though enormous compendia, were consciously written as works of literature addressed to a general audience. Even a casual modern reader is struck by the range of subject matter, the reliance on short headings to provide narrative structure, and the rapid shifts in rhetorical strategy from declamatory statement and idle speculation to careful argument, objective proof, and factual narration.

Such combinations were designed to allow sweeping flights in subject matter within concrete methodical structures that needed no explanation. Grotius, in his masterpiece *De Jure Belli et Pacis*, offered the model that others followed. "In order to give proofs on questions respecting this Natural Law," he wrote, "I have made use of the testimonies of philosophers, historians, poets, and finally orators . . . as witnesses whose conspiring testimony, proceeding from innumerable different times and places, must be referred to some universal cause." At the same time, he promised to "arrange in due order the matters [he] had to treat of" and to "distinguish clearly things which were really different" through a "concise and didactic mode of treatment" that would enable his reader to grasp the principles involved "at one view."[27] To do so was, in Pufendorf's words, "to rank [the most comprehensive Definitions of Things] agreeably under their proper Classes, subjoining the general Nature and Condition of every Sort of Beings."[28] The prose of the seventeenth- and eighteenth-century legal philosophers constantly aspires toward eloquence of a kind; but to understand its underlying meaning one must concentrate carefully on the incremental structures supplied by a complex series of chapter and section headings.

Jefferson's use of similar headings in *Notes* solves a number of organizational problems with an ingenuity no one has discussed. As one critic says in summarizing the apparent weaknesses of *Notes*:

> [The book] alternates between statistical description and moral exhortation, between sunny affirmation and anxious apprehension. The audience that it addresses is sometimes foreign, one that must be told that Virginia is organized by counties, and sometimes native, one that must be urged to replace its defective constitution and emancipate its slaves. The scope of the book alternately expands to embrace the

entire United States and contracts to its ostensible subject, as if Jefferson were still unsure whether the phrase *my country* should have its old Virginian application or its new national one.[29]

All such difficulties were intrinsic to the literature of the early republic, of course. When a writer of the period tried to define America for Americans, he faced conflicting definitions of loyalty across communal, county, state, and evolving national ties, and he did so knowing that ultimate literary merit would be judged according to the norms of an extrinsic European readership.[30] Jefferson, a skilled rhetorician well aware of his audiences, uses structure and form to channel the inevitable variations of his discourse. He employs headings to minimize confusion much as the legal writers used them to control their expansive subjects, digressions, and juxtapositions in tone and theme.

Marbois's inserted interrogatives were both "Queries proposed to the Author, by a Foreigner of Distinction" (p. 2) and the questions an everyman might ask about the American unknown. Each appears at the beginning of a section of *Notes* as the symbol of a unified audience, and they function as common denominators signifying to each reader—whether Virginia gentleman, French philosophe, or American democrat—the need to adjust and begin again. Nor is it necessarily a sign of poor organization or rigidity, as too many have suggested, that certain headings in *Notes* barely receive answers at all. Many a chapter in Montesquieu's *Spirit of Laws* was one sentence long.[31] Jefferson understood that the order of headings creates form and narrative structure in such works, and his appreciation of this principle supplies the key to understanding his book. For though he relies on Marbois's questions, Jefferson freely rearranges their sequence and bases his reorganization on the reasoning of the legal treatises he knew so well.

Grotius had argued that failure to separate instituted or positive law from an initial treatment of natural law had been the major obstacle in previous attempts to reduce jurisprudence to the form of an art or science. *De Jure Belli et Pacis* and the major works of Pufendorf and Burlamaqui accept the distinction as a central organizational premise.[32] To achieve the same effect in *Notes*, Jefferson reorders and divides Marbois's random questions and recasts their meaning in context. The table opposite presents a view of this organization by contrasting Marbois's original order of questions to

Marbois's Order	Jefferson's Order
(3)	1. An exact description of the limits and boundaries of the state of Virginia?
(6)	2. A notice of its rivers, rivulets, and how far they are navigable?
(13)	3. A notice of the best sea-ports, and how big are the vessels they receive?
(6)	4. A notice of its mountains?
(6)	5. Its Cascades and Caverns?
(20) (6)	6. A notice of the mines and other subterraneous riches; its trees, plants, fruits, etc.
(21)	7. A notice of all what can increase the progress of human knowledge? [On climate.]
(7)	8. The number of its inhabitants?
(18)	9. The number and condition of the Militia and Regular Troops, and their Pay?
(19)	10. The marine?
(22)	11. A description of the Indians established in that state?
(6)	12. A notice of the counties, cities, townships, and villages?
(1) (2)	13. The constitution of the state, and its several charters?
(10)	14. The administration of justice and description of the laws?
(9)	15. The Colleges and Public Establishments, the Roads, Buildings, etc.?
(17)	16. The measures taken with regard of the estates and possessions of the rebels, commonly called Tories?
(8)	17. The different religions received into that state?
(11)	18. The particular customs and manners that may happen to be received in that state? [On slavery.]
(12)	19. The present state of manufactures, commerce, interior and exterior trade?
(14)	20. A notice of the commercial productions particular to the state, and of those objects which the inhabitants are obliged to get from Europe and from other parts of the world?
(15)	21. The weights, measures, and the currency of the hard money? Some details relating to the exchange with Europe?
(16)	22. The public income and expences?
(4)	23. The histories of the state, the memorials published in its name in the time of its being a colony, and the pamphlets relating to its interior or exterior affairs present or ancient?

Jefferson's rearrangement in *Notes*. As the table demonstrates, *Notes* opens with accounts of Virginia's boundaries, geography, natural life, and climate (pp. 1–81) based on queries three, thirteen, twenty, and twenty-one and on numerous divisions of query six from Marbois's list. The French diplomat's first two questions on the charters and present constitution of the state, representing civil matters, have been dropped to the second half of the book in Jefferson's thirteenth section (pp. 110–129). These changes and others like them create an elementary structural separation in *Notes* between natural phenomenon and social event. Behind the simplicity of the division, however, appear the same elaborate impulses toward continuity that led Grotius to build a unified view from a series of ordered distinctions. Just as the multiplicity of human law might give rise to a science of jurisprudence, so the bewildering physicality of America could be made to yield a unified republic.

The mysteries in natural phenomena were not to be eliminated, but they could be assigned their places within the intellectual construct of natural law. Every selection of facts depends on some principle or initiative. For Jefferson the theoretical assumptions of the natural law philosophers—a nature of uniformity, hierarchy, and larger purpose—provided a necessary sense of order. Indeed, it was easier to infer nature's general design from a world untouched by human history. To take only the most obvious example from *Notes*, Jefferson's mammoth must still live in theory because explorers have found its bones and extinction would be against nature's law. As he writes, "Such is the economy of nature, that no instance can be produced of her having permitted any one race of her animals to become extinct; of her having formed any link in her great work so weak as to be broken." Indian stories of huge animals in the Northwest operate in this context as "the light of a taper" to "the meridian sun" of natural law (pp. 53–54).

The more difficult connection between natural and political order or between natural law and positive law involved a significant intellectual leap, but it was one that the legal philosophers had made with increasing self-confidence as the eighteenth century progressed. One can see the point of connection most clearly through a particular problem in *Notes*. Jefferson's seventh section involves a discussion of Virginia's climate based on painstaking tabulations of rainfall, temperature, and wind velocity recorded twice a day across a five-year period (pp. 73–81). And yet the heading for the section comes from Marbois's twenty-first query, which calls far more grandly for "a notice of all what can increase the progress of human knowledge." Narrow meteorological expertise seems an inappropriate response to the question, but it would not have puzzled François Marbois, the French intellectual for whom it was written. In the eighteenth century, climatological factors were extremely relevant to larger discussions of political theory and, hence, to a belief in human progress based on the forces of political change within the period.

Montesquieu in particular, accepting the general notions that good government should be conformable to nature and that positive law should build from natural law, emphasized the importance of geophysical elements in describing national identity. "Mankind are influenced by various causes," he wrote in *The Spirit of Laws*, "by the climate, by the religion, by the laws, by the maxims of government, by precedents, morals, and customs; from whence is formed a general spirit of nations." In consequence, a true idea of nationality could only be maintained through a detailed understanding of the many aspects of the physical and social worlds that shaped it. The whole function of Montesquieu's book was to examine the importance of these relationships in creating a unique sense of country.[33] A descriptive mode based on particulars promised as much, even as Montesquieu's assumption of an *esprit général* guaranteed final unity within the process. As Peter Gay has suggested in calling Montesquieu the most influential writer of the eighteenth century, coherence emerges in *The Spirit of Laws* through "its author's passion for finding law behind the apparent rule of chance."[34]

Jefferson's personal reliance was profound. While studying law he gave more space in his commonplace book of formal notes to *The Spirit of Laws* than to any other work, and he would later recommend it to his own students as the best general book available on the science of government.[35] In effect, the influence was redoubled because another early intellectual hero in law, Lord Kames, the Scottish jurist and author of *Historical Law Tracts* (1758) and *Principles of Equity* (1760), was a known advocate of Montesquieu's methods. Kames's defense of Scottish nationalism through the uniqueness of Scottish legal traditions prefigures the essential strategy of Jefferson's book.

Notes is a far more coherent text when it is examined in the light of these influences. Mere coverage builds into design if one accepts Montesquieu's belief that effective civil law depends upon issues of climate, geography, and natural wealth.[36] The facts of *Notes* become essential ingredients toward a definition of Americanism that must be reflected in political institutions if the republic is to survive. Accordingly, each of the early sections on physical circumstances within an assumed natural order contributes to a general American spirit and to "specific principles" of civil government that Jefferson believes "are more peculiar than those of any other in the universe." Political customs and practices represent a unique source of virtue in America because they have evolved away from corrupted European counterparts and because they are composed of "the freest principles of the English constitution" in conjunction with "natural right and natural reason" in a New World setting (pp. 84–86, 135–137). Excluding section six with its extensive lists of indigenous flora and fauna, Jefferson gives most space in *Notes* to sections thirteen and fourteen—the central rationale of an American polity based upon charters, constitutions, and the laws of the state (pp. 110–149). These sections, like the political chapters of *The Spirit of Laws*, form the heart of the book. They supply precision and a higher sense of country against earlier uncertainties. Here Jefferson also delivers his pivotal explanation of the Revolution through precedents extracted from the legal charters of the colonies (pp. 110–118). America's assertion of natural right, he argues, was a response to British disregard of lawful forms and has culminated in thirteen independent states "confederated together into one great republic."

The rest of *Notes* builds structurally out of this fundamental assertion of republicanism. Jefferson proceeds to analyze the theoretical problems of republican government as he has come to understand these problems in legal philosophy. Burlamaqui and Montesquieu both had written that republicanism alone was no assurance of liberty, that only positive law (established legal limits in a mixed constitution) provided that guarantee, and that corruption, luxury, and licentiousness would be particular difficulties in any popular government.[37] In keeping with his mentors' assumptions that rulers would become venal and the people careless, Jefferson warns, "It can never be too often repeated, that the time for fixing every essential right on a legal basis is while our rulers are honest, and ourselves united" (p. 161). In context the later sections of *Notes*

represent a political anatomy, fixing every essential right and isolating each potential problem. Jefferson's description of the Virginia
constitution in the second half of section thirteen is peppered with
warnings to Virginians and Americans alike to "bind up the several
branches of government by certain laws" (pp. 120–129). Section
fourteen is dominated by the author's concrete proposals for legal
reforms, and each ensuing section offers abbreviated commentary
on one or more of these reforms. Again and again, legal formulation
offers both a framework of definition and a mechanism of control.

The end of section fourteen and the beginning of fifteen detail
the public educational system that Jefferson, Montesquieu, and Burlamaqui all feel is essential to a true republic and that the author of
Notes ties to his legal system of county and ward government (pp.
146–151). This educational system is to insure an essential general
knowledge of law. "It is in a republican government that the whole
power of education is required," Montesquieu had written, tracing
virtue in a citizenry to patriotic feeling and an informed "love of
the laws."[38] Sections sixteen, seventeen, and eighteen present a
series of measures that will eliminate given threats to republican
virtue: recognition of the continuing legal rights of the defeated
Tories (pp. 155–156), the guarantee of religious toleration by law
within the state (pp. 157–161), and plans for the abolition of slavery
(pp. 162–163). Each measure has been raised previously, though
briefly, in the plan for legal reform in section fifteen. Here Jefferson
explains why his solutions are crucial to the integrity of the republic
and orders his discussion along a continuum of ever-increasing difficulty of implementation, concluding in an image that his Virginia
readers could never accept, "the slave rising from the dust . . . with
the consent of the masters."

Sections nineteen through twenty-two are more haphazard or-
ganizationally because they deal with the vagaries of future danger.
Shorter and more episodic, they constitute a loose catalogue of
prospective problems and solutions using the terminology of luxury
and corruption that any reader of Montesquieu or of the Whig
revolutionary writers will recognize (pp. 164–176). Urbanization,
industrialization, short-sighted commercial measures, standing armies, and inflation are presented one after the other as potential
irritants to the harmony and general spirit of the agrarian republic that Jefferson describes in his peroration at the end of section

twenty-two. Section twenty-three, a list of all existing state histories and formal documents (pp. 177–196), gives a last poignant acknowledgment of what *Notes* would never become: the section is a rough index of the material an American Blackstone would require to write a commentary instead of a note on the state of Virginia.[39]

Notes as a Unified Text

The unified text found within this structural design encourages a new perspective. Critics, assuming only a source book for Jeffersonian political thought, have stressed the passages that affirm the American farmer, nature's order, and the rising glory of America; but Jefferson the ideologue is also a careful observer in his book, and too much of what he sees in Virginia falls short of the republican ideal that is his central theme. Significantly, the prevailing mood of *Notes* as text is one of profound anxiety.[40] When Jefferson brags in *Notes* that the Natural Bridge and the Blue Ridge Gap are worth a voyage across the Atlantic to see, he also admits that his own neighbors lack the wherewithal to travel a few miles to either location (pp. 19–20). He is generally appalled by the cultural ignorance and living habits of his fellow countrymen (pp. 152–153), and he designs his scheme of public education to, in his own words, rake a few geniuses from the rubbish (p. 146). Even minimal levels of general development, he complains, will be undermined by European immigrants who threaten to reduce the American citizenry to an "incoherent, distracted mass" (p. 85). Such views seem out of keeping with Jefferson's supposed faith in the people, but they represent only part of a darker side of *Notes*.

Jefferson the social sophisticate dismisses the towns around him as of no consequence—they are ephemeral things that rise and fall in the accidental circumstances of nature (pp. 108–109)—and he condemns Virginia's tobacco economy: "It is a culture productive of infinite wretchedness" (p. 166). Intrinsic political weakness compounds these social ills. In *Notes* the state's very constitution is illegitimate, badly conceived, and sadly lacking in "a proper complication of principles" (pp. 120–125). Moreover, Jefferson as former governor is personally "confounded and dismayed" because current leaders have readily deserted republican principles in the last stages of the war effort. "Our situation is indeed perilous," he writes, warning against demagoguery, "and I hope my countrymen will be sensible of it" (pp. 126–129). Beyond these immediate problems, Jefferson devotes long pages to theoretical fears of corruption within the state and to the specter of slavery in a republic.[41]

In fact, *Notes* worries the slave issue over three widely separate sections and with growing alarm at each new stage of explanation. Religious tones dominate a hesitant conclusion when it finally comes:

> Indeed I tremble for my country when I reflect that God is just: that his justice cannot sleep for ever: that . . . a revolution of the wheel of fortune, an exchange of situation, is among possible events: that it may become probable by supernatural interference! The Almighty has no attribute which can take side with us in such a contest. (p. 163)

Lewis Simpson already has traced this loss of calm and detachment to Jefferson's conviction that slavery would destroy the republic, but the uncharacteristic switch to apocalyptic terminology also indicates something specific about Jefferson's feelings of helplessness.[42] Of the issues raised in the pessimistic remarks of *Notes*, only slavery resists rational management in Jefferson's hands, and it does so precisely because it defies legal terminology and solution within the intellectual framework of an eighteenth-century lawyer.[43] Slavery exists but against natural law; it becomes, in consequence, a structural incongruity in *Notes*, spilling between and among sections.

Jefferson handles his anxieties in every other area by using legal forms to control realities. As he later summarized the vision behind this procedure, "the elementary republics of the wards, the county republics, the State republics, and the republic of the Union would form a gradation of authorities, standing each on the basis of law."[44] The author of *Notes* can impose his institutional grid of wards or hundreds upon shifting towns or even upon empty space. His decision to place every essential right on a legal basis represents fixed intelligence in the midst of flux, and his draft of a fundamental constitution for the Commonwealth of Virginia appears in an appendix to show the path of civic virtue in spite of corruption and every danger (pp. 209–222).

That even Jefferson, the most optimistic of the Founding Fathers, needed to explain away his fears shows why definitions of country obsessed early Americans. His related ability to sustain optimism through legal formulation also suggests how lawyers came to be the ideological spokesmen of the republic. It is the assurance behind Jefferson's imposed solutions that impresses today—an assurance traced in chapter 1 to the influences of English legal thought upon eighteenth-century philosophy and upon the rhetoric of the American Revolution. Jefferson was the complete master of this English legal tradition. Francis Bacon was his greatest hero because the seventeenth-century lord chancellor had shown others the way, identifying lawgivers and commonwealth builders as the intellectual champions of the modern world.[45] Indeed, Bacon, almost as much as Montesquieu, supplies the primal vision of order within *Notes*. Among Englishmen his *Novum Organum* first presents a secular methodology—"a fixed law, in regular order and without interruption"—in the face of chaos. "There is so great a number and army of particulars," warns Bacon here, "and that army so scattered and dispersed as to distract and confound the understanding . . . unless all the particulars which pertain to the subject of inquiry shall, by means of Tables of Discovery, apt, well-arranged, and as it were animate, be drawn up and marshaled."[46] The many charts of *Notes* cope with a similar "army of particulars" within the American unknown. Jefferson's own tables of discovery represent an assertion of coherence, a kind of Baconian "fixed law, in regular order and without interruption." For an intellect like Jefferson's, with its notorious distrust of theological and metaphysical speculation, Bacon's methods were particularly ideal. Law was the perfect empirical tool, both for discovering the unknown and for imposing a secular, ideological order upon it.

Excitement over the possibilities in legal formulation would dominate American thought for decades after the Revolution because the possibilities themselves were so useful. Isaac Newton had demonstrated how facts properly observed would lead to a unified vision of scientific law, but the English common law—what Jefferson called "the glory and protection of that country"—was a more practical model to work with.[47] Even conservative English intellectuals like William Blackstone derived the spirit of English legal rights from a golden age of Saxon freedom preceding Norman usurpation. Therefore, the common law could be conveniently separated from the royalist taint and corruption that Revolutionary Americans associated with eighteenth-century British culture in general. As an accumulation of history, custom, and legal procedure, it also provided a flexible, empirical sense of order. "Proceeding warily and undogmatically from case to case," writes Daniel Boorstin, "the common law was rich in the prudence of individual cases but poor in theoretical principles; it was adept at solving problems but inept at philosophizing about them."[48] Everything about these intellectual boundaries suited anxious republicans who remained ideologically intense but uncertain of their destinations—so uncertain, in fact, that they would deliberately exclude all mention of "federal" and "national" as words too controversial for the Constitution of the United States.[49] A common law way of thinking avoided orthodoxies that would split the country, and it gave an effective but loose ideological frame to a growing republic. It was, in short, the basic intellectual analogue for the accumulating federalism that would regulate American expansion for a century.

No early American understood the usefulness of legal examination better than Thomas Jefferson.[50] The very structure of *Notes*—an order through accumulation, leaving room for later elaboration—parallels that of the common law, and Jefferson's professional interest in his subject was immense. In an age when practitioners like Patrick Henry and John Marshall joined the Virginia bar after a few months of reading, Jefferson devoted five full years to rigorous study, even teaching himself Anglo-Saxon in order to trace the common law to its roots.[51] He read Grotius, Pufendorf, Montesquieu, and Beccaria in their original Latin, French, and Italian texts; he mastered everything he could find in the related fields of history, ethics, and oratory; and he collected an enormous law library so complete in ancient statutes and reports that the Virginia courts came to treat it as a depository of public records.[52]

The mystic identification of law and country as intrinsic to our national rhetoric is probably the most important legacy of this expertise. Jefferson did more than any other American of his generation to insure that a conception of higher law would dominate political discourse. What is less obvious, however, is the extent to which this rhetoric now masks the compulsive fears that originally gave it meaning. Like most early republicans, Jefferson regarded the uncertainties inherent to his political situation as a perpetual emergency, and he studied law scrupulously because he felt it was the surest mechanism of control in a crisis. Thus, when Jefferson's first inaugural address declares American government to be the strongest on earth because it is "the only one where every man, at the call of the laws, would fly to the standard of the law," it must be understood in light of the potential for emergency within this language and in light of the "anxious and awful presentiments" and "despair" with which Jefferson opens his address.[53]

Because a nation defined through law rested on a republic obsessed with its own frailty, the same combination of assertion and anxiety necessarily dominated the literature of the period. The prose of early republicans is not so much problem-oriented as it is a juxtaposition of problem to solution in cycles of gloom and gladness that never seem to end. *Notes on the State of Virginia* is a type for the manic-depressive tendencies within this process.[54] And Jefferson's creativity is clearest in his use of legal formulation to bridge these extremes through structure and thematic control.

Jefferson's treatment of the American Indian in *Notes* illustrates the point perfectly. Chief Logan's famous speech to Lord Dunmore is evidence that neither intelligence nor sensibility has been lacking in Indian culture. It is also an epitaph for a civilization: "Who is there to mourn for Logan?—Not one" (p. 63). Jefferson's subsequent investigation of Indian burial grounds dramatizes "the melancholy sequel of their history." But there is a larger meaning to this story of disintegration, and it is one that Jefferson welds to his major concern in *Notes*. Total collapse—"I know of no such thing existing as an Indian monument"—occurs because the Indians "never submitted themselves to any laws, any coercive power, any shadow of government."[55] Jefferson's three sections on the counties, constitutions, and laws of the republic, with all of their promise of order and all of their fear of current weakness, follow directly upon the warning explicit in this secular jeremiad. As long as republican anxieties could be met in this fashion, legal formulation offered stability, a marriage of solution and problem that would keep the lawyer at the center of American literary aspirations. *Notes on the State of Virginia* is, in this sense, more than an American classic; it is also a gauge for examining a body of literature in which legal thought controls mental adventure.

The Creativity of the Lawyer-Writer

Notes takes on paradigmatic significance because its strategies of control reflect a forgotten standard of creativity that shaped American writing for decades. What Jefferson searched for and found was a representative voice. Convinced that Americans needed to be taught how to think collectively about their situation, he disciplined his mind and writings to *appear* representative. Imagination, subjective emotionalism, and individual aspiration were less crucial to this end than neoclassical beliefs in fixed standards, hierarchical order, and man's place within society. An appreciation of the fact and basis of preference within these priorities is essential to any real understanding of republican literary tastes. As Allen Tate has insisted, "To the question, What should the man of letters be . . . we should have to find the answer in what we need him to do."[56]

Jefferson saw what needed to be done in his own time with a clarity and breadth of perspective that few writers in any age have been able to match. His immense intellectual influence came through the cultivation of affinities within the American Enlightenment of the eighteenth century and through the creation of symbols and images—Monticello comes first to mind—that would reflect a secular, classical humanism in American thought.[57] These emphases involved deliberate choice within a clear awareness of alternatives. At least Jefferson's private views on literature reveal what one least expects to find, given the neoclassical formalism of the political writings. His letters value literature as much for its subjective appeal as for its ability to advance rationalistic principle. They prefer the expressively emotional over the decorously correct, and they stress the play of the individual imagination as the true source of excellence in a writer.[58] The presence of relatively modern attitudes within an eighteenth-century American mind need not distort established distinctions between neoclassic and romantic, but it does suggest a greater sophistication and a more complicated context for cross-cultural influences than many have been willing to grant. The author of *Notes* is not engaged in a narrow imitation of the neoclassical norms he has mastered so much as he is examining and then selecting from the entire spectrum of available contemporary criticism in search of an appropriate American aesthetic.

In keeping with Jefferson's goals, the language of *Notes* does not seek to transcend the times; it tries instead to embody what one might hope to become within them. Didacticism, sententiousness, and pedantic rationalism are all part of a very deliberate lesson in American idealism, a lesson delivered in *Notes* with a considerable sense of urgency. "The diffusion of knowledge among the people" was "by far" Jefferson's most important priority for the 1780s. He believed that "a crusade against ignorance" (the voice of reason properly used) would "fairly put into the hands of their own common sense" a people who still needed to learn the simple rules of their own best interest.[59] In *Notes* this inculcation of knowledge constitutes the only real safeguard against republican disintegration, and it is a safeguard only in prospect. Urgency flows from a fear that even the people are dangerous in the 1780s because their minds remain unimproved (pp. 147–149).

Jefferson's optimism (his belief that education would provide "the principal foundations of future order") against his pessimism (his alarm over existing levels of discord and ignorance) combined to thrust an enormous burden of responsibility upon the writer. The absence of other educational resources magnified his sense of obligation. The duty of every American writer was to foster the higher level of intellectual homogeneity without which the republic would perish. "It is for the happiness of those united in society," *Notes* tells us, "to harmonize as much as possible in matters which they must of necessity transact together" (p. 84). Every word of Jefferson's book is designed to promote this spirit of harmony in contradistinction to the quarrelsome and unpropitious atmosphere the states were falling into under the Articles of Confederation. Hence, the rhetoric of *Notes* is inclusive and participatory rather than restrictive ("Young as we are, and with such a country before us"); the language builds around abstractions that contain by encompassing ("Civil government being the sole object of forming societies, its administration must be conducted by common consent"); and the general tone is hortatory ("While we have land to labour then, let us never wish to see our citizens occupied at a work-bench, or twirling a distaff").[60]

The originality within Jefferson's style becomes a little easier to grasp if one recognizes its basis in a language of conviction. Creativity consisted in the republican writer's ability to convey ideological certainty without losing sight of the practical complexities that required solution. One rummaged through harsh political realities and a negative view of human nature in search of linkages and social relations that would ease nervous fears and lend system to aspiration. For example, when Jefferson warns in *Notes* that "our rights shall revive or expire in a convulsion," his analysis of detailed problems already has conveyed the assurance that all is avoidable through system or by "fixing every essential right on a legal basis" (p. 161). It is in this sense that a practical political language of caution and antithesis builds into an abstract ideological perspective of affirmation, a peculiar juxtaposition of pessimism and optimism that permeates republican writings. In works like *The Federalist* and *Notes*, gloom over present conditions anticipates a future glory of America that will subsume practical difficulties in republican order and harmony. The writer reinforces his claim to be heard by conveying a pragmatic awareness of the problems every citizen must understand if truly republican solutions are to follow.

Law emerged as such a creative source of expression within the shifting moods of republican literature because it guided the writer's search for conviction. Legal formulation supplied the methodology of linkage we have traced in *Notes*. It dealt in a prudence of means that reached toward ideal totalities, and it cemented the issue of individual freedom within a construct of social order. A combination of advocacy, exhortation, methodological caution, and abstract formulation—in short, the language of the eighteenth-century courtrooms in which Jefferson argued hundreds of cases—was ideal for these purposes.[61] Moreover, at a time when political questions were the controlling passion in American culture, lawyers' language justified expression that was geared exclusively to immediate social solutions. Jefferson, for one, was so committed to the solutions that "an intimate connection" between law and politics would bring that he made knowledge in this area a test of personal efficacy. As he warned his nephew, "He who knows nothing of these will always be perplexed and often foiled by adversaries."[62]

If Jefferson seemed so certain in the law, it was because he could rely on the profusion of answers that law supplied and because these answers, in turn, could produce an integral combination of substance and style. His early readings in eighteenth-century property law offer a final case in point. Using Lord Kames's *Historical Law Tracts*, the law student of the 1760s had copied into his commonplace book the crux of the philosophy of social homogeneity that would inform *Notes:*

> The perfection of human society, consists in that just degree of union
> among individuals, which to each reserves freedom and independency,
> as far as is consistent with peace and good order.[63]

Freedom versus order, the individual within a social context, the
hope for a more perfect society, the search for greater cohesiveness:
these are indeed the themes and values that resonate in *Notes*. But
what is most striking in Kames's sentence is the conjunction of
affirmation and qualification within a projection of balances. The
combination would prove supremely useful to the cautious leaders
of the American Revolution and early republic. High idealism ("the
perfection of human society") is tempered by a countervailing prudence in method couched within the numerous restrictions Kames
and Jefferson place on every means of accomplishment ("just degree," "reserves," "as far as is consistent"). To hope for harmony
among so many divergent elements required the most careful understanding and placement of things within a totality. Law provided
thematic perspective, political control, style, and, not least, an absolutely essential machinery of arrangement.

The persona of the lawyer-writer and, thus, the configuration of
the lawyer in literature lay securely within this machinery of arrangement. In writings where the coordination of parts within a
whole counted for much, the man of letters required the strongest
sense of his own place. The legal profession supplied visible station,
and it formed the base for a republican rhetoric of civic responsibility
and participation. Jefferson, with his typical clarity, summarized
the opportunities involved: "The study of law is useful in a variety
of points of view. It qualifies a man to be useful to himself, to his
neighbors, and to the public. It is the most certain stepping stone
to preferment in the political line."[64] Generations of American intellectuals would accept this formula of the lawyer-writer-activist
serving the community, but over time Jefferson's "variety of points
of view" and his concentric series of involvements with their "stepping stones" of passage would come to haunt the American writer.
The movement of nineteenth-century literature would be toward
an increasingly personal stance and away from social affirmations,
toward what Herman Melville would call the capacity to say "NO!
in thunder."[65] Many an American author would follow Jefferson
into the configuration of law and letters only to struggle with the
initial convenience of that choice.

CHAPTER 3

TO FORM A MORE
PERFECT UNION

"Truth Becomes Infinitely Valuable"

Even as Jefferson's book appeared in London, the Founding Fathers were meeting in Philadelphia "to form a more perfect union," and their success came from the same impulses and strategies that informed *Notes on the State of Virginia*. The Constitution of 1787 is a miracle of concision, emerging as it did from four months of florid effusion and often bitter debate in the Federal Convention. It contains just five thousand words of the plainest prose cast within a one-sentence preamble and seven brief articles. Neither verbiage nor allusion nor admonition interrupts its prescriptive clarity; there is very little linguistic novelty, almost no philosophic innovation, and minimal elaboration. But these evasions are counterbalanced by a series of commitments. Brief rather than cryptic, the Constitution confirms a familiar past. Every word belongs to the realm of common understanding in eighteenth-century American experience; many of these words are taken directly from the constitutions of the states and the Articles of Confederation in a reaffirmation of Whig and republican principle. Moreover, the framers of the vital document are aptly named. The many generalities of the Constitution lie within a precise arrangement of philosophy, tone, and structure. All of these characteristics have been observed, and much has been made of the Founding Fathers' wisdom, their flexibility, their genius of restraint in leaving room for interpretation.[1] But what has not been noted is the extent to which these virtues and the framers' vision, their unerring eye for enduring form, were professionally based.

The Constitution has been many things to many people. It was first and foremost a triumph of expression by lawyers who dominated the Federal Convention as conscious and accomplished men of letters.[2] All of the framers felt Jefferson's urgent need to clarify republican experience, but lawyers in particular shared his language of order, his facility of expression, and, hence, his conviction that a more perfect union was possible. Steeped by profession in the same "learning and literary accomplishments," men like James Madison, Gouverneur Morris, James Wilson, and Edmund Randolph believed in writing things down. They were inclined, in Randolph's words, "to use simple and precise language" within an organization of "general propositions" and "essential principles only," and their debates were filled with adroit recourse to both the flexibility and the specificity of language in quelling controversy. Words like "national," "republic," and "federal" were carefully circumvented in the final document, while others—"president," "congress," "union"— survived only after minute scrutiny. Before everything came a confidence in what Gouverneur Morris called "the language of Reason on this subject."[3] James Wilson, using Bacon and Kames in much the way Jefferson had used them, explained the source of this intellectual self-confidence in a lecture many of the framers attended. The true lawyer possessed a "philosophy of the human mind" that allowed him to "become well acquainted with the whole moral world" and to "discover the abstract reason of all laws." A legal education meant "climbing up to the vantage ground . . . of science"; it was the perfect platform for finding and then articulating "the supreme Law of the Land."[4]

Certainly, the lawyer-framers were responsible for the most impressive intellectual characteristic of the Federal Convention: they kept everyone talking and deciding in spite of essential differences. Professionally comfortable with contention as courtroom counsel, they accepted disagreement as the norm of the Convention but worked through procedure and expression to force resolution. They instinctively recognized that the debater's loose language of persuasion—by analogy the argument before bench and jury—must eventually yield to simple and direct answers that everyone could understand and, understanding, obey. And with surprising unanimity the lawyer-framers worked to that end. They sought a final judgment following advocacy, a judicial decree of sorts in neutral but assertive tones. The Constitution rests upon the flat injunctions of Article VI—"the supreme Law of the Land" to which others "shall be bound"—not upon political rationalization. In general, the framers turned to legal construction for ordering their thoughts and writings. They were precise in their formulations and placed them within a comprehensive intellectual structure, but, with the prudence of a court in session, they made only those decisions forced upon them and labored to maintain vital continuities with the past.

The work of the lawyers of the all-important "committee of style and arrangement" illustrates how the formalism, functionalism, and traditionalism of the eighteenth-century legal mind produced the Constitution. Gouverneur Morris, with the concurrence of Madison, William Johnson, Alexander Hamilton, and the one non-lawyer on the committee, Rufus King, reduced twenty-three disjointed articles to the seven that appear in the final document.[5] By suggesting a more perfect union instead of a new one, the committee of style forged an important link to the legitimacy and wisdom of the past, to the Articles of Confederation, which already insisted upon a perpetual Union. The committee's revised version clarified the new structure of the proposed government but emphasized those elements most congenial to Americans familiar with the legislative orientation of the Confederation. It sought, in other words, to place theory within the guise of precedent.[6]

Articles I, II, and III of the Constitution deal in order with the legislative, executive, and judicial branches of government. Form merges with content to support the doctrines of checks and balances and separation of powers, which are taken from British constitutional thought and from legal theorists like Montesquieu.[7] Articles IV through VII cope with interstate and federal-state regulations, the amendment process, and ratification procedures. While all of these elements contribute to the federal arrangement, the seven articles are clearly deployed in descending order of length, concern, and difficulty.[8] Together, the first three articles form the crux of the Constitution. Each moves from description of a branch of government into issues of qualification and selection for office and then to an enumeration of powers and limitations (extensive for Congress, succinct for the presidency, perfunctory for the courts). Since these enumerations end abruptly without fanfare, one is left with the prospect or intuition of logical extension in each article. Indeed, elaboration *from within* the now-sacrosanct Constitution would not disturb its form, and this flexibility is surely deliberate. For the framers' document, in the manner of *Notes on the State of Virginia*, is a crayon sketch waiting to be filled up. It is another measure of a shadow requiring constant recalculation, another unified text allowing for amendment and ever-greater accuracy.[9] And once again, an encompassing idealism explains the writers' prudence in particulars.

Like Jefferson, the framers approached the task of defining their republic with the controlling terms of eighteenth-century legal thought in mind. When the lawyers on the committee of style revised the preamble of the Constitution, more than literary felicity was involved. They were tying their labors to the universal, unchanging law of reason and of nature. The first version of the preamble— "We the People of the State of [each state named] do ordain, declare, and establish the following Constitution for the Government of Ourselves and our Posterity"—became:

> WE, the People of the United States, in order to form a more perfect union, to establish justice, insure domestic tranquillity, provide for the common defence, promote the general welfare, and secure the blessings of liberty to ourselves and our posterity, do ordain and establish this Constitution for the United States of America.[10]

This new statement of purposes—the ongoing search for justice, domestic tranquillity, common security, the general welfare, and the blessings of liberty—set forth the framers' underlying rationale for change even as it reached toward the fundamental law upon which theorists based all government. Here, within the minimal aims of social compact, was the nexus between natural law and the man-made or positive law encouraged by Grotius, Burlamaqui, and others. By the middle of the eighteenth century, the legal commentators of the Enlightenment had moved from thinking of natural law as a collection of moral abstractions to which conduct should conform to the more particular assertion that natural law could be expressed in a body of ideal legal precepts against which all positive law could then be measured. Special significance must be given to the confidence with which men reached for the general through the concrete. To the extent that positive law partook of the general or represented a proposition espoused by everyone, it could be a manifestation of unchanging natural law and universal reason.[11]

The preamble linked the positive law of the body of the Constitution with the ideal precepts upon which positive law depended. It gave no additional powers, but neither theorist nor citizen would contest the high-minded purposes the preamble set forth. Insofar as a *ratified* Constitution insured these prefatory aims through republican government, it was positive law functioning with an aura of unchanging reason and natural law.[12] The seven linked articles became so many building blocks, which virtuous men could use and subjoin but never legitimately shift, replace, or destroy.

The framers could afford to be flexible because of an underlying permanency. That they thought in such terms appears in their choice of language. In the eighteenth century the words "ordain" and "establish" meant to decree, to settle, or to institute on a stable or permanent basis, which made the members of the Federal Convention lawgivers who were instituting a fixed state or foundation of fundamental principles and settled law.[13] The one apposite verb the committee of style removed from the preamble was "declare." Lawyers steeped in Blackstone knew that to declare implied to contest. A declaration marked the first pleading of a case or controversy within a court of law, and the statement of grievances it contained was more in keeping with an initiation of hostilities—whence the Declaration of Independence of 1776.[14] By 1787 the framers were moving instead to terminate more than a decade of struggle and uncertainty through an appeal to universal accord and higher law. To "ordain and establish" was to aim well beyond a process of pleadings and to resolve conflict in judgment.

National debate over the Constitution was, of course, an incitement to further expression. In the outpouring of writings surrounding ratification, no one had a more dramatic or articulate sense of their achievement than the lawyer-framers themselves. Madison favorably compared the Federal Convention to the "reputed lawgivers" of antiquity, Solon, Lycurgus, and Romulus. Hamilton believed that the process of "reflection and choice" within the Constitution made America "an empire in many respects the most interesting in the world." "Where good government prevails," James Wilson added in proclaiming the new federal arrangement, "there is the country of science and virtue. Under a good government, therefore, we must look for the accomplished man."[15] These statements and others like them depended on a cherished assumption of the Enlightenment—

namely, that knowledge led to virtue when expressed in the language of reason. To that assumption Madison, Hamilton, and Wilson brought their own unmistakable braggadocio, the self-assurance of creators flushed with success. Reason had triumphed in 1787. The Constitution magnified even as it embodied Enlightenment thought. It was visible proof and a lasting token of the bond men saw between knowledge, virtue, and the act of writing.

The same impulses that gave birth to the Constitution left the Founding Fathers with a continuing sense of purpose as men of letters. To accept the Constitution as an artifact of truth and to believe that virtue could be taught was to bring a terrible urgency to the communication of thought.[16] Every framer knew that his new plan of government meant little without reciprocal awareness in the minds of the governed. The mission to instill that knowledge was crucial, and it carried the need for careful language from the Constitution into daily life. John Dickinson, yet another lawyer-framer imbued with Enlightenment idealism, explained how these elements came together. "TRUTH becomes infinitely valuable . . . not as a matter of curious speculation, but of beneficial practice," he argued in his own plea for ratification, "a spirit of inquiry is excited, information diffused, judgment strengthened." The Constitution was a manifestation of truth. It "displayed, explained, and strengthened" the standard of laws protecting all republicans. Under these circumstances, the articulate expression of enlightened citizens became "not only their *right*, but their *duty*."[17] And duty loomed large for Dickinson and those who followed him. The doctrine of *vivere civile* attuned all thought and language to the moral guidance of society.[18]

A corresponding faith in the power of education made learning the servant of pedagogy and pedagogy a manifestation of patriotism. In his role as republican spokesman, the lawyer tied the whole of learning to the legitimizing function of citizenship. His consequent writings were dedicated to country, and took on "a grandeur and elevation before which the mere trifling of amateurs in letters would be humbled and abased."[19] For three generations lawyers spoke and wrote with these thoughts in mind. Their language, addressed to the largest possible audience, "abounded with poetical imagery and ambitious ornaments." Even in courtroom debate they encouraged each other in the most general display of knowledge. The best of lawyers rarely hesitated in "dropping the character of an advocate, to perform the paramount duty of a citizen."[20] The ultimate goal, in the words of Joseph Story, was to apply "the universal empire of juridical reason" to realize "the splendid visions of Cicero, dreaming over the majestic fragments of his perfect republic." This required the combination of literature, philosophy, history, and law found in Cicero himself. It also involved "a new and mighty empire, the empire of public opinion." Polite literature ("from the light essay to the most profound disquisition") was the achievement of the age precisely because it harnessed public opinion to Bacon's "power of knowledge, working its way to universality."[21]

No wonder James Wilson, speaking in 1790 with Washington, Adams, and many other members of the new government in attendance, made his "accomplished man" a lawyer who wrote to and educated other Americans. He began by tracing the glory of Greece directly to her writers, who, in transmitting the virtues of their culture, "excelled those of every other country in abilities and elegance." Indeed, the American republic was every bit the equal of its ancient counterpart "in real worth and excellence." Washington, Adams, and waiting America only needed native writers to prove the point. "When some future Xenophon or Thucydides shall rise to do justice to their virtues and their actions," Wilson assured his audience, "the glory of America will rival—it will outshine the glory of Greece." But where were these writers? To whom did this responsibility truly belong? Since American character could only be defined through "love of liberty, and the love of law," Wilson found his answer within the legal profession.[22] The true lawyer ranged "not without rule, but without restraint, in the rich, the variegated, and the spacious fields of science!" Among American intellectuals, he most easily combined the knowledge, range, and practical experience, the sense of proportion and the eloquence necessary to transmit the virtues of a culture. "To his observation and research every thing is open: he is accustomed to examine and to compare the appearances and the realities of things; to contemplate their beauty, to investigate their utility, and to admire the wonderful harmony, with which beauty and utility coincide."[23]

In the early republic beauty and utility coincided in the great work of bringing an American citizenry to virtue through knowledge. Literature was both an inspiration and an essential tool in this process, and the lawyer was particularly adept in its use. Training reinforced inclination. As James Madison once described the literary aspect of law, "*It* alone can bring into use many parts of knowledge you have acquired and will still have a taste for, & pay you for cultivating the Arts of Eloquence. It is a sort of General Lover that wooes all the Muses and Graces."[24] Here grandiloquence and expediency come together. Phrases like "bring into use," "have acquired," and "pay you" suggest vocational exchange. Finally, it was the nature of legal practice that made the lawyer a lover of all the muses.

"In the Company of Men of Letters"

One can hardly exaggerate the importance of general learning in early American law. Because practitioners lacked court records, case reports, codified statutes, and effective commentaries, mastery of a few essential texts gave professional capability.[25] Alexander Hamilton qualified for the New York bar after six months of reading. James Kent owed his original reputation in the 1780s to a thorough knowledge of one book, Blackstone's *Commentaries.* As late as 1804 the law clerk Daniel Webster read only the briefest list of legal texts.[26] In the generations from Hamilton to Webster general erudition overrode technical expertise as the primary source of professional identity. Higher education in itself supplied the standard gauge if just because a majority of lawyers attended college at a time when scarcely one American in five hundred did so. Inevitably the accomplished attorney applied this distinction to separate himself from the common pettifogger, using his college background of languages and literature to distinguish a community of the competent.[27]

The first third of the nineteenth century heard speech after speech on the centrality of literature to a lawyer's knowledge. "A lawyer in a free country . . . should be well read in the whole circle of the arts and sciences," Kent argued. "He must drink in the lessons and the spirit of philosophy," Joseph Story added, insisting as well upon "full possession of the general literature of ancient and modern times."[28] The Founding Fathers were obvious and convenient models for emulation. Kent followed Alexander Hamilton's careful study of French literature almost as closely as his political conservatism. Story's corresponding admiration of "the love for poetry" in John Marshall helped justify his own interest in verse. Poetry was "a commanding influence" upon the chief justice's "warm and vigorous mind." Marshall, in fact, left the clearest possible image of literary enterprise contributing to professional stature. Until the 1830s his work on the bench and his *Life of George Washington* (1805–1807) were routinely hailed in parallel terms: America's leading jurist had written "the greatest national work which the United States have produced."[29]

Each generation of the antebellum bar went on to extol the literary impulses in the one preceding it. William Wirt immortalized the Revolutionary lawyer's eloquence in his *Sketches of the Life and Character of Patrick Henry* (1817) and was himself canonized by John Pendleton Kennedy's *Memoirs of the Life of William Wirt* (1849). Both biographies were best-sellers for decades, keeping alive the example of the lawyer-writer and the presumption that liberal arts were essential to legal practice.[30] Wirt summarized the link between law and letters and what it could mean in forensic debate: "In the company of men of letters, there is no higher accomplishment than that of readily making an apt quotation from the classics; and before such a body as the Supreme Court these quotations are not only appropriate, but constitute a beautiful aid to argument. They mark the scholar,—which is always agreeable to a bench that is composed of scholars."[31] In this idealized courtroom the greatest compliment one lawyer could bestow upon another was to admire "comprehensiveness of view."[32] Every field of inquiry was relevant when men of letters argued before a bench of scholars. One read quite literally with everything in mind and spoke and wrote to encourage the same versatility and scope in others.

The call for general learning virtually guaranteed belletristic display within the profession. Kent and Story thought of their voluminous commentaries as general literature, and each admired the prose artist in the other's work. "I know not how it is," Story confessed to Kent in a passage typical of their correspondence, "but you carry me a voluntary captive in all your labors, whether in law, or in literature. You throw over everything which you touch a fresh and mellow coloring, which elevates while it warms, and convinces us that the picture is truth and the artist a master."[33] Kent's labors *were* impressive. To an active career on the bench and four volumes of commentaries on American law, he added copious notes on readings in English, Greek, Latin, and French literature, including comments on most of Shakespeare's plays, criticism of writers from Cicero and Juvenal to Mrs. Radcliffe and Carlyle, a whole volume of notes on Scott, and a long essay on his personal hero, Alexander Hamilton.[34] Story's efforts were even more prodigious: an early book of poetry, numerous public addresses, articles rife with literary allusion, a textbook on government, and nine commentaries on distinct fields of law. All of the commentaries were written during Story's joint tenure as associate justice of the Supreme Court and Dane Professor at the Harvard Law School. He was, as one colleague maintained, "incapable of fatigue."[35]

Exceptional in their achievements, Kent and Story were nonetheless typical in their self-conscious display of learning. Theophilus Parsons, Sr., the great chief justice of the Massachusetts supreme judicial court at the turn of the century, published on astronomy and mathematics, wrote a Greek grammar, shaped educational policy as the leading member of the Harvard Corporation, and helped found the Boston Athenaeum.[36] Francis and Joseph Hopkinson—father and son both served on the U.S. District Court of Pennsylvania—wrote volumes of plays, poems, and essays, designed the American flag, made significant improvements on the harpsichord, edited the first American Shakespeare, composed music (including *Hail, Columbia*), and established the Philadelphia Academy of Fine Arts.[37] Their colleagues Charles Ingersoll, Nicholas Biddle, Thomas Wharton, Horace Binney, Pierre Du Ponceau, and a score of others added histories, treatises, translations, plays, language studies, and a seemingly endless supply of poetry and criticism for the journals of the period. Together they made "Philadelphia lawyer" a synonym for culture in the nineteenth century.[38]

The same configuration of law and letters appeared in every state of the union and, notably, in Scotland as well—the Scotland of Kames, Mackenzie, Scott, and Jeffrey. As historians have observed, "it was the lawyers who played the principal role both in the mid-eighteenth and early nineteenth-century stages of the Scottish enlightenment."[39] There were obvious differences between the two cultures, but the parallels suggest another source of the lawyer's vitality in literary forums. In eighteenth-century Scotland and the America of the early republic, the relative weakness of aristocratic influence left room for literati of middle-class origins. Cultural status was as much a question of education and professional achievement as of birth. Moreover, law in Scottish and American society represented both the primary means of public advancement and a vital source of national definition for countering the cultural hegemony of England. The socially mobile lawyer who wrote could join self-interest, vocational identity, and patriotic duty. Literary enterprise brought visible station, professional reputation, and a venue for nationalist sentiment in a confluence of tendencies that guaranteed intellectual self-confidence. The true gentleman of the bar was a gentleman of letters defending cultural ideals.[40]

What set the American experience apart was the way in which actual legal practice reinforced the bond between law and letters. Courtroom litigation dominated the profession in America through the first third of the nineteenth century. Most practitioners rode circuit at least part of the time, handling a large volume of petty cases in different locations as courts moved from one county seat to the next. Local government functioned almost entirely through these courts, and a court in session was always a major event. John Pendleton Kennedy, a lawyer-writer of the 1830s, captured the communal excitement of court day in his novel *Swallow Barn*:

> The sitting of this court is an occasion of great stir. The roads leading to the little county capital were enlivened by frequent troops of the neighboring inhabitants, that rode in squadrons, from all directions. Jurors, magistrates, witnesses, attorneys of the circuit, and all the throng of a country side interested in this piepowder justice, were rapidly converging to the centre of business.[41]

The same excitement prevailed in American cities. Lawyers like William Wirt, Daniel Webster, and Rufus Choate argued their cases before packed courtrooms. The Supreme Court in Washington routinely attracted audiences that Joseph Story called "the taste, the beauty, the wit, and the learning, that adorned the city." And these audiences listened by the hour. In 1824 the Supreme Court was "not only one of the most dignified and enlightened tribunals in the world, but one of the most patient. Counsel are heard in silence for hours, without being stopped or interrupted." Beyond the courtroom, newspapers and journals like the *Port Folio* and the *North American Review* gave extensive coverage to trials, lawyers, and legal material.[42] The trial in republican society was a central ceremony and the courtroom speech its most visible ritual.

These conditions made the advocate a personage among people. "The chairmaker or cabinet maker is known in his town; a good physician for 100 miles; a lawyer throughout America," boasted St. George Tucker, soon to become "the Virginia Blackstone."[43] But the very terms of the lawyer's success also carried him well beyond mere professional expertise. Circuit-riding and the courtroom extravaganza rewarded the entertainer, the cultural spokesman, and the politician. Sheer force of personality and general eloquence found clients, held courtrooms, and won cases. Here was the significance of Wirt's call for literary allusion as "a beautiful aid to argument." Until 1830 the centrality of the courtroom speech made eloquence and extensive learning more important than a knowledge of technical law.[44]

Oratory was the real key to success. "I suppose Chancellor Kent could cite offhand fifty cases to [Daniel] Webster's one on any given subject," a prominent lawyer of the 1820s observed, "and yet, before either court or jury, the odds in favor of Webster would be great indeed." Accordingly, William Wirt's and Robert Walsh's detailed evaluations of members of the Virginia and Massachusetts bars stressed the talent of speakers.[45] William Pinkney of Maryland was the automatic leader of the American bar until his death in 1822 because Story, Marshall, and Roger Taney agreed in calling him the most eloquent advocate they ever heard. Forensic eloquence demanded "the comprehension and vigor of a giant" and "the skill of the artist." Pinkney drew "a splendid portrait" in "the most vivid colors"; he excelled because his oratory left "a single figure, composed of the most discordant materials."[46] Such praise contained the highest sense of a bond between law and literature. In Marshall and Story's search for aesthetic unities, legal knowledge became literary expression.

Something far more basic was also involved in the lawyer's penchant for literary expression, something completely overlooked by scholars of the republican period. Attorneys riding circuit from one court session to another at the beginning of the nineteenth century were the only educated Americans who regularly met and spent time together as a matter of course. Between court sessions, traveling and living together in taverns and inns, they constituted a rare intellectual forum. In consequence, they had the most effective context in America for literary enterprise, and, as we have seen, they were keenly aware of a responsibility to communicate their learning to a general citizenry. Informal exchanges among members of the bar led naturally to verse and criticism in the newspapers and, under certain conditions, to the creation of magazines crucial to the intellectual life of the new nation. "As contributors, editors, and patrons of magazine literature, no other profession furnished as much good material as the law . . . the bar furnished a majority of those who were active in the management of the general magazines and reviews."[47] Many prominent editors were educated to the law: Noah Webster of the *American Minerva* (1793–1797), Joseph Dennie of the *Farmer's Weekly Museum* (1796–1799) and *Port Folio* (1801–1811), William Coleman of the *New York Evening Post* (1801–1829), Charles Brockden Brown of the *Literary Magazine and American Register* (1803–1807), Robert Walsh of the *American Review of History and Politics* (1811–1812) and the *American Quarterly Review* (1827–1837), Washington Irving of the *Analectic Magazine* (1812–1815), Edward and Alexander Everett, Willard Phillips, Edward T. Channing, and Richard Henry Dana, Sr., all of the *North American Review* (1815–1819), as well as John Pendleton Kennedy of the *Red Book* (1819–1821), John Skinner of the *American Farmer* (1819–1830), Theophilus Parsons, Jr., of the *United States Literary Gazette* (1824–1826), William Cullen Bryant of the *New-York Review and Atheneum Magazine* (1825–1826), and Hugh Swinton Legaré of the *Southern Review* (1828–1832).

Collective affinities were at work on every level. A circle of lawyers supplied an obvious network of subscribers and occasional contributors. When Theophilus Parsons, Jr., asked Bryant to submit "two or three dozen names in the west of the State" for the new *United States Literary Gazette*, fifteen of the twenty-seven possibilities the poet suggested were lawyers, and Bryant's list must have been typical. So many contributions to the *Gazette* came from lawyers and were legal in nature that Parsons worried in print about "the charge of too great attention to any one profession."[48] More important still was the way in which practicing attorneys influenced the writers in their midst. Unfortunately, the details of intellectual influence have been lost along with the groups themselves, but one catches a rare glimpse of a forgotten phenomenon in Jeremiah Mason's memoir of New England in the 1790s: "A set of young men, mostly of the legal profession, extending from Greenfield, in Massachusetts, to Windsor, in Vermont, a distance of fifty or sixty miles, were much in the habit of familiar intercourse for the sake of amusement and recreation. They occasionally met in a village tavern, but more commonly at the sessions of the courts."[49] Mason's lawyers—"the extraordinary men who then ranged that country"—included Joseph Dennie (in three years America's leading magazine editor), Royall Tyler (already a significant playwright and novelist), William Coleman (soon to become the influential editor of the New York *Evening Post*), and Thomas Green Fessenden (the gifted verse satirist). Their literary exchanges were typical of legal circles in the period, and their collaborations made Dennie's *Farmer's Weekly Museum* a proving ground for later achievement.

Joseph Dennie, in particular, understood the full import of the lawyer's role in literature at the turn of the century. His *Port Folio* in Philadelphia from 1801, like the *Farmer's Weekly Museum* before it, depended heavily on the contributions of lawyers, and this was a matter of deliberate policy. "In pursuing our literary labours," Dennie declared in the *Port Folio*, "we are solicitous of nothing so much as the approbation of The GENTLEMEN OF THE BAR." As "NATURE'S NOBLEMEN," lawyers formed "THE NATURAL ARISTOCRACY of the country" and displayed "more genius . . . with more learning than any other *cast* in Columbian society." Dennie was certain that American literature would "wholly expire" without the profession's leadership.[50] Literally dozens of Philadelphia lawyers responded by rushing into print, although it was a Massachusetts attorney, none other than John Quincy Adams, who led the charge. Adams saw the *Port Folio* as immensely important to American intellectual growth. "The plan of this undertaking has given me more pleasure than I can express," he observed, contributing article after article to help Dennie "take off that foul stain of literary barbarism which has so long exposed our country to the reproach of strangers, and to the derision of her enemies."[51] Adams was wrong in assuming that America would one day honor the founder of the *Port Folio*, but his excitement, shared by other professional men like Joseph Hopkinson, Gouverneur Morris, and Nicholas Biddle, reminds us of what only Nathaniel Hawthorne would later remember: that Joseph Dennie was "once esteemed the finest writer in America."[52]

"A Library of Eloquence and Reason"

If legal practice was a catalyst for literary endeavor, classicism was the intellectual bond holding law to literature. Others have documented the vitality of the classical tradition from the colonial period, into the Revolution, during the Constitutional Convention, and through the first forty years of the new nation. The rise and fall of the ancient city-states naturally fascinated Americans who worried about their own brand of republicanism. Many found a continuing legacy with the United States as the infant heir of the classical republics. Greek and Roman philosophy, political theory, and history—what Joseph Story called "the prescriptive wisdom of antiquity"—contained lessons for American citizens to master and apply.[53] Many did just that. Alexander Hamilton copied long sections from Plutarch and measured America against the Roman republic as "the utmost height of human greatness." Within the new federal government, he called himself "Paulus" to Jefferson's "Scipio" and Adams' "Brutus." These tendencies were characteristic of the times. Pushed in 1789 to justify his own classicism, Adams announced, "I should as soon think of closing all my window shutters, to enable me to see, as of banishing the Classicks." Thirty years later John Quincy Adams avowed a similar dependency: "to live without having a Cicero and a Tacitus at hand seems to me as if it was a privation of one of my limbs."[54] There was considerable posturing in statements of this sort, but scholars have also found a constitutive influence. Classical thought clearly shaped the values of educated Americans in the early republic.[55]

Already inclined toward classical study, lawyers used their training in Greek and Latin to solve specific professional problems. Hugh Henry Brackenridge's Law Miscellanies in 1814 gave the conventional argument that "a universal knowledge of literary subjects" enlarged the mind, but it also outlined a more exact relationship between classicism and courtroom eloquence. Brackenridge demanded "not the command of words merely, but the delicate selection of words, and choice of terms." Latin and Greek were essential to this purpose: "It is necessary to understand the precise meaning of words; this is not to be collected from dictionaries; so well at least, as from the roots of the words, which are found in those languages from which our own is derived." In the absence of statutes and case law, precision in language study became legal expertise. Greek and Latin also encouraged habits of investigation and instilled maxims of good sense and morality. Here again Law Miscellanies made classical study the student's guide to professional rigor. Inevitably, Bracken-

ridge's own Latinate prose offered a case in point for "grace of
expression" and "distinct speaking and writing." His novel of seven
volumes, the endless *Modern Chivalry*, was intended as "a school
book; a kind of classic of the English language."[56]

Classicism defined professional aspiration as well. "Labour to get
distinct Ideas of Law, Right, Wrong, Justice, Equity," the youthful
John Adams urged himself, knowing full well that the vagaries of
early American law forced him to look elsewhere for answers. "Search
for them in your own mind, in Roman, grecian, french, English
Treatises of natural, civil, common, Statute Law."[57] Because classical scholarship formed the basis of legal study, Adams and other
eighteenth-century practitioners looked for inspiration to the republican lawyers of antiquity, most notably to Marcus Tullius Cicero in the first century B.C. Typically, Adams and his club of
lawyers, the Sodalitas, read Cicero aloud, hoping to lead the Massachusetts bar to "a Purity, an Elegance, and a Spirit, surpassing
any Thing that ever appeared in America." It was, as Adams saw,
the combination of lawyer, statesman, and philosopher that gave
Cicero's work and example such authority.[58] Cicero had written
volume after volume in philosophy, law, and letters, but he also
achieved fame in the judicial courts, held high political office, and
fought for liberty against tyranny in the Rome of Caesar and Pom-
pey. A projection of the same balances made the Ciceronian ideal
the strongest possible vocational model for lawyers in federalist and
Jeffersonian America.

Every early republican intellectual knew Cicero's famous declaration, "The whole glory of virtue is in activity." Activity signified
citizenship and responsibility within the world. The same republicans, however, saw that the context of Cicero's assertion was
professional knowledge, where "profession" meant "the search after
truth." To be drawn away from active life by study was contrary
to Cicero's notion of moral duty, but professional concern necessarily included "opportunities for returning to study" in a *legitimate*
interruption of activity.[59] Once again, it was the combination that
lawyer-writers found so compelling. Cicero emphasized vocational
and public service, but he also conveyed an intrinsic love of learning
and literature within professional knowledge. Since Americans before 1830 automatically accepted conditions in which literary pursuits provided neither a visible income nor independent status, these

balances were important. The subordination of literature to other ends made a virtue of the lawyer's vocational necessities without dismissing the significance of the literary ideal. As a law student in 1816, Hugh Swinton Legaré summarized the possibilities: "The learning that I would aim at is that of Cicero—a learning that can be instrumental in promoting the purposes of active life, in elevating the man of business into ye sage, & the mere statement of wholesome truths, into sublime & touching eloquence."[60]

Language study, the cult of eloquence, and emulation of Ciceronian balances immersed the early American lawyer in literature. So did the presence of poetry in every form of classical writing. "For history has a certain affinity to poetry," Quintilian, the Roman lawyer-educator, claimed for the ancients, "and may be considered in some sense as poetry in prose."[61] Plutarch's *Lives* simply assumed an appreciation of Greek tragedy. Setting forth the laws of the ideal republic, Cicero's *De Legibus* began with the immortality of poetry. To read such works was to recognize with Rufus Choate the truest legacy of Greece and Rome—"admiration of the beautiful, the good, the true in art, in poetry, in thought." The classics were " 'a library of eloquence and reason,' to form the sentiments and polish the tastes, and fertilize and enlarge the mind of a young man aspiring to be a lawyer and statesman."[62] Of course, aesthetic appreciation led easily to professional insistence. "Soak your mind with Cicero," Choate ordered the would-be practitioner. In the law offices of the early republic many an apprentice commenced legal study with a Latin grammar, knowing "he must read *Virgil* and *Cicero* before he could understand *Coke* and *Littleton*."[63]

Before this classicism faded, it shaped literary enterprise in the early republic. The lawyer's classical education gave him the intellectual self-confidence to dominate republican literary forums by placing him squarely within the neoclassical tradition of eighteenth-century literature; it put him just as firmly against the romanticism emerging in Europe at the end of the century.[64] Here, in fact, is a partial answer to questions that still puzzle literary scholars of the period. Why did "imitative" republican writers continue to adhere so closely to the neoclassical modes of eighteenth-century England when confronted with the creative alternative of romanticism? Why was the call for an original national literature answered in borrowed neoclassical terms?[65] The lawyer's choices in literature and his excitement over neoclassical impulses reveal a special kind of creativity.

Americans of the formative period were searching for unities, and a combination of classical and neoclassical values served this end well. Common assumptions such as the harmony of nature, the efficacy of reason, the importance of hierarchy and decorum, and the inherent structure of all knowledge were especially useful in an American aesthetics of order and control. By comparison, the subjective imagination, the originality, the fluid emotionalism and spontaneity of romanticism were inappropriate, even dangerous, to the goal of a collective sense of purpose.[66] The lawyer held republican podiums and dominated republican literature because he offered a vital concept of solidarity and a useful faith in universally applicable forms. He prescribed an ordered liberty that was creative *because* of its guiding balances and subordinations. Since he strove for corporate belief, his language was necessarily didactic and public rather than intimate and personal. In this way an imposed neoclassicism translated into something intrinsic within republican culture. Epic verse, light satire, the moral and political essay, the epistle in prose or verse, the oration—all classical forms used in eighteenth-century English literature—represented obvious tools of implementation.

The vitality of neoclassicism drew upon a premise that the lawyer-writer took as his guiding principle in republican culture: namely, that literature and politics belonged together within a higher sense of civic purpose. As always, Cicero served as reference and inspiration. *De Officiis*—John Quincy Adams called it the manual of every republican—declared that "the chief end of all men" was "to make the interest of each individual and of the whole body politic identical," and that the means to this end was "reason and speech," which united men "in a sort of natural fraternity." It followed that public eloquence on political themes was the highest duty of the educated citizen. Here Cicero placed particular onus upon the legal profession because it was so closely connected to "the gift of eloquence."[67] Virtue, politics, and literary expression merged in the classical image of man finding fulfillment in citizenship. Indeed, for a writer like Joseph Dennie the relationship was a foregone conclusion. "It must be apparent to the most heedless observer," he declared in his prospectus for the *Port Folio*, "that it is the object of this undertaking, to combine literature with politics."[68] The excitement of the lawyer-writer flowed from his recognition of a single controlling analogy. For, as one critic has put it, "the rationale of the Constitution on which was founded the Republic of the United States . . . was also the rationale of the unwritten constitution of the Republic of Letters."[69]

Fisher Ames of Massachusetts left the clearest account of a republic of letters within republican politics—clearest because Ames, even more than his peers, thought in classical parallels. Lawyer, writer, and federalist politician, he found Epaminondas in Washington, Demosthenes and Cicero in Hamilton, and, alas, Philip of Macedonia and Caesar in Thomas Jefferson. "Here let Americans read their own history," cried Ames, pointing to Macedonia's destruction of Thebes twenty-two centuries before. And then, in something of a non sequitur, "Is Virginia to be our Rome? And are we to be her Latin or Italian allies?" In article after article between 1800 and 1805, Ames saw the collapse of Greece and Rome afresh in American experience. "Men who have eyes," he wrote, "are forced to confess, that the progress of our affairs is in conformity with the fixed laws of our nature, and the known course of republics."[70] That the same mind would define American literature in terms of classical Greece is to be expected. And yet Ames was one of the first to think about what American literature might mean on its own terms, and his definition, using the classical tradition as a "symbol system," tells us much about the affinities between law and literature in the forative period.[71]

Ames wanted an imaginative literature that would explain a nation to itself and that would thrive on applause in public forums. "But in the province of the imagination," he specified, "the applause of others is of all excitements the strongest. The excitement is the cause; excellence, the effect." His model was the socially integrated poet of the Greek city-state. "It was enough to inspire the poet's enthusiasm," wrote Ames, "to know beforehand that his nation would partake it." Performance was the key. "All Greece, assembled by its deputies, beheld the contests of wit and valor." Performance circumvented the "cold perusal" of reading; the poet "*saw* with delight his work become the instructor of the wise, the companion of the brave and the great."[72] In the bond of performing artist and audience, Ames captured the nature and meaning of early republican literature, but with one difference. In America, lawyers held the forum and their mode was oratory rather than poetry or drama.

They spoke with such frequency because the republic itself was at stake. For in spite of every political difference, Jefferson, Ames, and their followers all agreed that the republic's greatest strength lay in "the energy and correctness of the public opinion." "We must enlighten, animate, and combine the spirit of freemen," Ames declared; "we must fortify and guard the constitutional ramparts about liberty."[73] No one argued. The republic's leaders fought constantly but not over the importance of public expression. To men of letters the message was the same regardless of party. Their place was the podium; their vehicle, the speech.

"Consider How Winged Are Words"

Americans have always described the first half of the nineteenth century as a golden age of oratory, and, remembering Clay, Calhoun, and Webster, "the true Triumvirate of the Republic," they have generally recognized the lawyer as the orator par excellence. But recognition has not led toward a deeper understanding, and the original reactions of nineteenth-century observers help to explain why. To find that the aim of the orator was to "keep the star-spangled flag of sentiment ever flying" or that American oratory meant "the song of triumph . . . on the beautiful mountains of a promised land" discourages analysis. To know that Clay's voice was "like the swell of a bugle" and that "no man could hear him without a tear" only puzzles a modern reader.[74] Oratory loses its appeal more rapidly than any other mode of discourse, and the great political debates of the antebellum period have been resolved for more than a century. The crucial imaginative and emotive impulses behind intention, logic, and argument, have disappeared. As Daniel Webster knew, "true eloquence, indeed, does not consist in speech . . . Words and phrases may be marshalled in every way, but they cannot compass it. It must exist in the man, in the subject, and in the occasion."[75] The configuration of law and letters recreates just this context by explaining the relation of speaker, speech, and audience in the declamatory literature of the period.

Two of the leading theoreticians of this literature were John Quincy Adams and Rufus Choate. The lectures Adams gave between 1806 and 1809 as Harvard's first Boylston Professor of Rhetoric allowed him to think of himself as "the principal founder" of popular oratory in America. Choate, Boston's leading attorney in 1850 and a self-proclaimed "student of professional forensic rhetoric," was perhaps the last lawyer in America to trace his success to the systematic study and application of classical eloquence.[76] Adams' early comments on the interaction of speaker, speech, and audience explain the lawyer's intrinsic self-confidence in republican forums. Choate's later and more explicit defenses of a fading tradition clarify its original purposes. Together, the two men encompass the age of oratory, commenting on its importance and defining the dominant role of the lawyer.

Adams opened his lectures at Harvard by reminding everyone that "eloquence was POWER" in the republics of Greece and Rome. Oratory, by molding "the mind of man to the will of the speaker," could "yield the guidance of a nation to the dominion of the voice." Adams' students were to "gather fragrance from the whole of paradise" and "distill . . . all the honies of persuasion" in the service of their country. His own assignment was to communicate the "irresistible power of words." In teaching the "Sons of Harvard" true eloquence, Adams gave them "a spear for the conflict of judicial war in the public tribunals." His metaphor contained its own instruction. For if pulpit and bar each used eloquence as "the vital principle," Adams made it clear that "the first and most distinguished station in the ranks of oratory must still be assigned to the eloquence of the bar."[77]

Two conditions made oratory particularly crucial in America. First, eloquence was essential to liberty. Only the orator could both "appal the heart of the tyrant" and "control the wayward dispositions of the people," thus maintaining an appropriate republican balance between monarchical and democratic tendencies. Adams and the generations of intellectuals that followed him could believe so passionately in the power of the spoken word because republicanism was thought to thrive on it. "Under governments purely republican," Adams promised his students, "where every citizen has a deep interest in the affairs of the nation . . . the voice of eloquence will not be heard in vain." Second, eloquence was also essential to order. The size and federal nature of the American republic demanded a spirit of unity that would settle a restive people. "Persuasion, or the influence of reason and of feeling, is the great if not the only instrument, whose operation can affect the acts of all our corporate

bodies; of towns, cities, counties, states, and of the whole confederated empire."[78] Here Adams touched upon an aesthetics of cohesion within nineteenth-century oratory. The speaker's aim—one
modern readers consistently miss—was to include and incorporate
listeners, not to challenge their understanding.

Of course, the unities upon which a sense of cohesion depended
were not always apparent amid the uncertainties and divisive tendencies of the early republic. The orator's preliminary task was to
discover meaning and control; his goal was to present the linkage
and order in American culture. As Adams put it, "The orator gath-
ers the parts, and connects them into an organized body."[79] Half a
century later Ralph Waldo Emerson could still insist on the same
responsibility. The distinguishing characteristic of the orator remained "the conviction communicated by every word, that his [the
orator's] mind is contemplating a whole, and inflamed by the contemplation of the whole . . . which he sees and which he means
that you shall see." The effective speaker fascinated through his
powers of integration. "Where he looks, all things fly into their
places." Emerson made his orator "the true potentate" of American
civilization, and, like many another, he pointed to the lawyer's
natural advantage in assuming the role.[80]

But where were the unities the orator was to find and describe?
How did he gather the parts, exercise control over them, and then
"wield a nation with a breath"? Adams turned for answers to the
universal genius of Cicero. His personal hero's example demonstrated that a knowledge of literature, philosophy, law, and history
were all essential to the orator's craft, leading as they did toward a
universal knowledge and an implied unity.[81] In this Adams relied
on the conventional neoclassical belief that universal knowledge came
closest to approximating an intrinsic order in the world. Even so,
the broadest knowledge was of little avail without a personal eloquence to focus and transmit it, and the key to eloquence was literary
appreciation. Adams reminded his students that Ciceronian ascendancy came through "attainment in literature, the inexhaustible
fountain of eloquence," and he urged them to cherish and cultivate
literary as well as scientific tastes "as the most effectual means of
extending your respectability and usefulness in the world."[82]

Literature was the source of a very different kind of unity; it
encouraged invention, and invention was "indispensable to conceive

and combine any complicated system of arrangement." For Adams, order and invention necessarily came together in effective oratory. "Invention without order is chaos before the creation of light. Order without invention is a mere unintelligent operation of mechanical power."[83] His favorite image of invention, significantly enough, was the Shakespearean poet, naming and ordering the world:

> The poet's eye, in a fine frenzy rolling,
> Doth glance from heaven to earth, from earth to heaven;
> And, as imagination bodies forth
> The forms of things unknown, the poet's pen
> Turns them to shape and gives to airy nothing
> A local habitation and a name.

Adams dared to qualify these lines by tying the orator's inspiration to external truth, but, eager to shape a national identity and intrigued by the power of poetic vision, he seized upon the importance of imagination.[84] Without the personal intuition and unifying appeal of the artist, there could be no higher coherence in a speaker's subject or performance.

Other nineteenth-century observers reached the same conclusion. The orator needed "instruments tuned to a prophet's ear, and swept by a poet's hand" to achieve "celestial harmony." A speaker's greatest impact came through "the grand *union* of the whole" and was due to "mystic principles of art and genius which he employs in the combination and complete work." Literature, in other words, represented a means of creating cohesion through the manipulation of emotion. Eloquence was the specific tool, which the orator forged from literature for this purpose. It was, in Hugh Swinton Legaré's terms, "poetry subdued to the business of civic life."[85] Properly used, literary expression unified both speech and audience. The poeticized figment, extended metaphor, encompassing generalization, and stylized utterance—Henry Clay was said to bring "an amazing weight of expression on to the backbone of a single word"— were so many instruments for using sentiment to control emotion and to turn a crowd of listeners into an effective unit. Certainly, that was the aim. "This distinctive influence," wrote one observer, "the specific influence of the entire organism of a crowd, must continue to be frequently brought into play among us."[86] In the early republic the unity of a listening audience was simultaneously a type for and a step toward a unified country.

There was another unity at work in the visible persona of the
orator. As Adams pointed out, Cicero did more than form an idea
of the subject, he also displayed "the idealized image of a speaker"
to the world.[87] That image was meant to encapsulate the whole
meaning of oratory, and Rufus Choate used none other than John
Quincy Adams to prove the point in a modern context. Adams by
1844 was "old man eloquent," Choate's living symbol of "the power
of a state developed by mental culture":

> See there what the most universal acquisitions will do for the most
> powerful talents. How those vast accumulations of learning are fused,
> moulded, and projected, by the fiery tide of mind! How that capacious
> memory, realizing half the marvels of Pascal and of Cicero, yields up
> in a moment the hived wisdom of a life of study and a life of action,—
> the happiest word, the aptest literary illustration, the exact detail, the
> precise rhetorical instrument . . . one immense torrent, rushing as an
> arrow, all the way from the perennial source to the hundred mouths![88]

Here is the aesthetics of cohesion at work, with Choate fusing every
tendency—classicism, universal knowledge, literary eloquence,
practical application, and patriotic duty—within the controlling image
of a speaker and his audience.

Choate at mid-century was even more convinced than Adams had
been in 1806 that oratory alone could consolidate expanding America:

> Consider how winged are words . . . Consider how soon a wise, a
> beautiful thought uttered here,—a sentiment of liberty perhaps, or
> word of succor to the oppressed, of exhortations to duty, to patriotism,
> to glory, the refutation of a sophism, the unfolding of a truth for
> which the nation may be better,—how soon a word fitly or wisely
> spoken here is read on the Upper Mississippi and beneath the orange-
> groves of Florida, all through the unequalled valley; how vast an
> audience it gains.[89]

He was just as certain of the lawyer's special role in addressing this
vast audience. "I have supposed that our way . . . lies directly into
the city and the forum," Choate told the Harvard Law School class
of 1845. Each student had to realize that his chosen profession,
better than any other, enabled him to serve the state. Without that
realization law became a mere calling, an ignoble matter of bread,
fame, and social place. Lawyers were peculiarly equipped by education and profession "to perform certain grand and difficult and
indispensable duties of patriotism—certain grand, difficult and in-

dispensable duties to our endeared and common native land." Two resolutions headed the list: "to keep the true idea of the State alive and germinant in the American mind" and "to keep alive . . . the calm and grand reason of the law over the fitful will of the individual and the crowd." There was a solemn obligation to speak and to speak often.[90]

Again and again Choate insisted on the intrinsic bond holding law, literature, oratory, and public service together. A consummate lawyer with a large practice, he nevertheless gave part of every day to reading poetry, studying the classics, and translating passages from Greek, Latin, and French. The same diary that recorded these exercises also raged against the growing number of "blockheads" who failed to appreciate the connection between classical scholarship and courtroom eloquence.[91] As a Dartmouth senior, Choate discovered that "learned men are the hope and strength of the nation." The rest of his career was an attempt to serve in that exalted capacity, and he collected a working library of eight thousand volumes for the purpose. Learning was so important because the ultimate power of a civilization depended on its "mental culture." When Choate promised his audiences "the true idea of the state," he automatically assumed the relevance of both ancient and modern literature and history. His orations tried to distill this knowledge and make it part of the philosophical and emotional legacy of every American by speaking "directly to the heart and affections and imagination of the whole people."[92]

It is the intensity of actual performance that astonishes today. Choate once spoke with such vehemence that he feared internal injury, and he was always sick and exhausted after a speech. His efforts were "a series of electric shocks." They "*consolidated* together" audiences, reducing them to "a congregation of statues, spell-bound."[93] What Choate and his audiences finally sought was a higher awareness based upon mutual recognition—a recognition that required this spirit of consolidation. "Here it is, my friends," cried Choate, pointing to the relationship of speaker and audience at the end of one performance, "here—right here—in doing something in our day and generation towards 'forming a more perfect Union'—in doing something by literature, by public speech . . . to leave the Union, when we die, stronger than we found it,—here—here is the field of our grandest duties and highest rewards."[94]

To form a more perfect union meant to think collectively about the national experience, and, as long as this was the case, Americans would approach literature for what it could do rather than for what it was. Public forums inspired a particular kind of creativity. They helped a nation to discover itself. In the words of Daniel Webster, early republicans were studying "to be what they behold."[95] The result was a literature oriented almost entirely toward speech and collective identity. Lawyers were its natural authors. For to form a more perfect union also meant to think in terms of law. As Choate put it, law was "like the structure of the State itself," and Americans were to regard it as "the whispered yet authoritative voice of all the past and all the good." The task of the republican intellectual was to raise this voice until "at last the spirit of the law descends into the great heart of the people for healing and for conservation."[96] Few writers could resist this vision, and those who did were still shaped by it.

II

THE MAJOR
WRITERS

PROLOGUE TO
PART II

The lawyer who wrote faced a complicated series of priorities within republican culture. His legal training, with its premium upon eloquence, required the use of literary expression, but writing itself brought no intrinsic sense of definition. Some aspects of the predicament were, of course, universal and unavoidable. Before the 1820s in America every author's efforts were incidental to a career in the ministry, law, medicine, business, or public service. However, when leaders of the American bar made the combination of law and letters a professional virtue, they magnified the problem for lawyer-writers. Commitment to the profession and service to the community became prerequisites justifying the leisure for writing. The lawyer's pen found purpose only within the life of duty.

Trained as a scholar, the lawyer of the formative period had to remain a man of action, one for whom literature could never become an independent interest. Committed to literary expression, he nevertheless was to exercise that commitment with an external gauge in mind. The value of his writings depended on their usefulness to a republican ideal—an ideal that in itself required careful balances between classical values and the perception of American realities. Even the civic podium, the lawyer's natural literary forum, invoked a spirit of restriction. Public office was an assumed right, but a true gentleman of the bar kept aloof from low politics, never allowing the role of republican spokesman to interfere with his lifelong obligation to the profession.

The greater the devotion to literature, the more distressing these balances and restrictions became. Hugh Swinton Legaré of South Carolina spoke for many intellectuals within the profession when in 1816 he described his own "violent & painful conflict of inclinations between ye desire of future eminence [the law] & that of present gratification [literary pursuits]."[1] So oppressive grew Legaré's struggle to balance literature and law that he finally rejected his education altogether. "Nothing is more perilous, in America," he warned the next generation, "than to be too long *learning*, and to get the name of bookish."[2] Like Legaré in the South, Fisher Ames in Massachusetts loved classical literature and preferred the role of civic orator over "bawling to a jury." Even so, clear distaste for legal practice could never shake established professional priorities. On those few occasions when Ames dared to think of the law as an ancillary matter, he felt like "a mere politician."[3]

Subordination of literature to law also left the lawyer-writer sensitive to the controversies that creativity provokes. William Wirt's *Letters of the British Spy* (1803) became the best-seller of its day, but Wirt suffered acute anxiety when his remarks on active members of the profession ruffled feelings within the Virginia bar. "I meddle no more with the living," he wrote in turning next to a safer topic, a life of Patrick Henry. The biography, a "discourse on rhetoric, patriotism, and morals," was more in keeping with the lawyer's obligation to promote republican culture, and it had the virtue of offending no one. For similar reasons Wirt curbed his inclinations to write drama. Even a good play might lead to "injury with the world."[4]

There were other problems as well. For if the legal profession encouraged the writer, it also created excuses for not writing well. In an age when every gentleman of letters belittled personal achievement, the active life allowed the lawyer-writer to dismiss his literary pursuits as minor concerns. Hence, the published works of Legaré, Wirt, and Ames fell short of a much greater capacity, and Ames spoke for all three men in describing himself as a "ready scribbler" but no author.[5] It was all too easy to settle for a lesser literature. Typically, Charles Ingersoll of Philadelphia devoted enormous time and energy to his history of the War of 1812, while excusing its limitations as a product of leisure hours taken from legal practice.[6] In republican culture claims of insufficient leisure were the author's refrain, a constant and accepted response to criticism.

The same emphasis upon the active life induced Ingersoll to extol a "literature of fact" and to accept America's inferiority in "literature of the imagination" with complacency instead of alarm. His *Discourse Concerning the Influence of America on the Mind* (1823) minimized the distinction by equating literature and public service. "From literature," he wrote, "the transition is natural to the arts, which minister to usefulness, comfort and prosperity, individual and national . . . In all the useful arts and in the philosophy of comfort . . . we have no superiors."[7] Jared Sparks reviewed the *Discourse* in the *North American Review* and carried Ingersoll's argument to its logical conclusion. Americans could "court the muses and loiter in the haunts of ornamental literature" at a later point in time. For now, duty required a literature of "useful intelligence" to "build up the structure of society on the basis of just principles."[8] America itself was the lawyer's book; effective participation within its pages, a kind of authorship.

The utilitarian bias, the patriotic overview, and the other constraints upon the lawyer-writer left him with a painful choice: to bend his creativity within the configuration or to break away altogether. Either way, the struggle left its mark. Chapter 4 examines three post-Revolutionary figures who chose to remain within the law—John Trumbull, Royall Tyler, and Hugh Henry Brackenridge. Poet, playwright, and novelist, they illustrate the predicament of the professional man who retained literary ambitions. Their achievements must be understood within the balances they needed to maintain. Together, Trumbull, Tyler, and Brackenridge also point toward one of the forgotten tragedies in early American literature. Of the three, only Trumbull possessed exceptional talent, but their common problems suggest why the greater intellectual and literary virtuosity of other figures—John Quincy Adams and Daniel Webster, for example—never translated to the printed page.

Chapters 5, 6, and 7 turn next to three writers who did break away. The decision to leave the law constituted the crisis of a lifetime for Charles Brockden Brown, the country's first important novelist, for Washington Irving, its first prominent author, and for William Cullen Bryant, its first national poet. In each case, the crisis of decision led directly into the writer's best work. Vocational anxiety is a fundamental source of emotional power in Brown's *Wieland* and *Arthur Mervyn*, in Irving's *History of New York* and *Sketch Book*, and

An Imaginary Gathering: Washington Irving and His Literary Friends at Sunnyside,
painting by Christian Schussele, 1864.

Shown in this painting of the American literary community at mid-century are, left to right, Henry T. Tuckerman, Oliver Wendell Holmes, William Gilmore Simms, Fitz-Greene Halleck, Nathaniel Hawthorne, Henry Wadsworth Longfellow, Nathaniel Parker Willis, William H. Prescott, Washington Irving, James Kirke Paulding, Ralph Waldo Emerson, William Cullen Bryant, John Pendleton Kennedy, James Fenimore Cooper, and George Bancroft. Seven of the fifteen (Holmes, Simms, Longfellow, Prescott, Irving, Bryant, and Kennedy) formally studied law at least for a time, and an eighth, Cooper, made the law a permanent avocation.

in Bryant's "Thanatopsis" and "To A Waterfowl." Moreover, the search for equilibrium that absorbed Trumbull, Tyler, and Brackenridge appears here—often twisted into bizarre manifestations by the force of a larger talent that *is* breaking away.

Unraveling these permutations through the configuration of law and letters, one rediscovers the nature and form of America's early national poems and first important fiction. The point here is not just that writing was a secondary pursuit in early America, a truism at least as old as Philip Freneau's "Advice to Authors" in 1788, but also that early American literature in itself must be understood against the priority of a separate vocation.[9] It is the intrinsic bond between vocational legitimacy and literary craft that makes the configuration of law and letters such an effective tool of analysis.

Vocational anxiety was particularly great for writers like Brown, Irving, and Bryant because of the special anathema the legal profession reserved for heretics. Beyond the eighteenth-century ideal of the gentleman of letters, which already presupposed visible station and communal leadership, the lawyer's standards gave concrete expression to cultural responsibilities. To deviate was to violate an established code. Criticism from former colleagues at the bar was explicit and intense when a law student or lawyer turned away from the profession. The young man who ignored such criticism soon encountered questions concerning his patriotism and personal integrity in ways that compounded the practical problem of making a living.

Anyone who gave undivided attention to literature and ideas was what John Adams called "a learned Idler."[10] Idleness, in turn, suggested a certain irresponsibility and, in the discourse of men of affairs like Adams and Jefferson, it carried at least an undertone of dismissal. For the lawyers of the Revolution there could be no alternative. The uncertainties of the new republic as well as their own remarkable record of accomplishments meant that service and practical achievement measured the man. Significantly, it was the following generation, living *under* the intimidating example of the Founding Fathers, that turned literary preoccupation into a source of invective and derision. "A mere book-worm is a miserable driveller," wrote Jefferson's younger disciple and personal lawyer William Wirt, "and a mere genius a thing of gossamer fit only for the winds to sport with."[11] By 1817 David Hoffman's standard *Course of Legal Study* was warning against the danger of "pleasing literary pursuits." "Hermits, whether in religion or in literature," Hoffman observed, "have generally found their scheme of exclusive and solitary devotion to a single pursuit, to issue in lassitude and in indolence."[12] Joseph Story, who managed to squelch his own early passion for poetry, quoted Hoffman's admonitions at length in the *North American Review;* they were "useful hints on the law, which should be treasured up by every student."[13] All of these comments were designed to keep the intellectually restless in professional line.

Once again, Blackstone was everyone's model. "Sir William Blackstone never did a wiser thing when he abandoned the writing of poetry," claimed the *American Quarterly Review* in 1832. The transition had been from an "inditer of mongrel verses" to meaningful scholarship and "never-dying renown." Ostensibly a journal devoted to literature, the *Review* called for the renunciation of poetry at the proper moment: "Let all half poets who would be lawyers follow, if they can, the illustrious and sensible example of Sir William Blackstone." Earlier, in 1815, Richard Rush had been even more emphatic. The developing lawyer-writer, like Blackstone before him, should cheerfully "submit in the full spirit of obedience" to the demands of the profession.[14]

As a hermit of indolence, the solitary man of letters became the special target of intellectuals remaining within the profession. Gulian Verplanck's numerous literary projects never supplanted a successful legal and political career in New York, and he thanked his stars that no examples to the contrary crept into his address before the Columbia graduating class of 1830. "Not one of them [those whom I have pointed out to your emulation] was a mere scholar, contented with the bare requirement of learning or of learned fame," Verplanck explained. "Their science, their literature, their talent were all consecrated to the duties of society and the general weal."[15] Always the contrast was between what the *United States Literary Gazette* of Theophilus Parsons, Jr., termed "enlarged and exalted principles of action" and the "purely literary exertions" of those "buried under the dust of libraries."[16] When necessary, the distinction contained a stinging rebuke for the uncommitted. To Henry Longfellow's application for a position with the *Gazette*—the young poet wrote as an unhappy law student in his father's office—Parsons responded in language calculated to injure: "There is a stage in the progress of a bright mind, when the boy has thrown away his toys and marbles, but the young man is still so far a child as to value things more by their elegance and power of amusing than by their usefulness. He plays with his books and thinks he is working when he is only playing hard . . . Get through your present delusion as soon as you can; and then you will see how wise it will be for you to devote yourself to the law."[17]

The constant bombardment of Parsons, Wirt, Verplanck, Story, Hoffman, and other leaders of the bar affected every lawyer-writer but particularly the small minority of adventurers who sought an alternative. Joseph Dennie, the most important journalist in America in 1800, was an early renegade and easily the most defiant. In the 1790s he airily dismissed legal study as a "nauseous pill, not to be poured down the throats of even the vulgar without gilding." Eventually he rejected the legal profession altogether as a "sordid business" that forced the literary man to "batter down a mud wall with roses."[18] Unfortunately, there was no context through which defiance might mature into a personal sense of place and purpose. Dennie edited his *Port Folio* and wrote his popular *Lay Preacher* with the approbation of "Gentlemen of the Bar" first in mind. Later, referring to himself in the third person, he questioned the wisdom of a decision that had produced more unhappiness than literature: "He sometimes, with a sigh, almost regrets that a youthful, perhaps imprudent passion for the Muses, should have been preferred to a more legitimate and lucrative connexion. He still considers the Law as a probable resource . . . when Honour or a power still more imperious may urge the exchange. Possibly, the *useful olive* may refresh his sight with a better if not a brighter hue, than the *barren laurel*."[19]

Imprudent and legitimate, barren and useful, brighter and better, power and honor, the need to consider against the compulsion to regret—Dennie's conflicting terms illustrate a problem without a solution. His indecisiveness, his sense of lost legitimacy, his feelings of inferiority, and his fruitless search for a more appreciative audience were characteristic tendencies among those who followed him in breaking the connection between law and letters. Certainly, the decision to leave legal studies and to write fiction meant disgrace and prolonged adolescence for Brown and Irving—even in literary circles. Bryant's comparable move from law into journalism came in mid-career and only after considerable recognition as a poet, but his experience was no less intense.

Among early critics, only Richard Henry Dana, Sr., realized the full import of the situation "when to make literature one's main employment was held little better than being a drone." Dana, of course, wrote from personal experience. Another to leave the law for a career in letters, he turned the profession's sneer into a personal badge of honor by becoming the "Idle Man" of magazine fiction. He understood better than anyone else how a momentary vocational crisis could develop into a prolonged constitutive influence upon the craft of a writer. Dana's description of Charles Brockden Brown's rejection of law some twenty-five years before his own is particularly instructive in this regard:

> Brown's time came, and then he hesitated, and then his friends talked, or by their marked silence pained him yet more. Unsatisfied in his own mind, and those whose good opinion he fain would have had being against him, he became harassed and dejected . . . He still doubted; and when at last he did resolve, he felt not the relief and vigour of a resolved man; for he feared it might be the yielding of weakness, not the resolution of strength.[20]

Duty and creativity wrestled for the soul of the lawyer-writer, and, as with Jacob and his angel, it was a contest in which only a draw could satisfy. A victory like Brown's brought no resolution, no new name of Israel, only a complete loss of social identity. This trauma then molded the writings to follow, and so it would be for others as long as literature remained a by-product in American culture.

Perhaps inevitably, the problems involved and the solutions sought were most acute in the young. One senses this in Dana's first sentence: "Brown's time came." Vocational uncertainty, the pressures of choices to be made, and the impulse to break away from the world are strongest early in a career. Brown, Irving, and Bryant were at their most creative as indecisive young men under the goad of an adult world's certainties. Youthful rebellion is central to the power of the only works a modern reader remembers. In all three writers, the renegade's defiance vies with a penitential need to please, and much that is creative in their work issues from this struggle. That such anger occasionally unmasks the world pressing upon it should not surprise. To remove these early American writers from the solemn pantheon of national history is to see their youthful anger in context and to realize that the tale of the emperor's new clothes applies with special force in post-Revolutionary America. Not for the last time, a youthful temperament was perfect both for writhing under and for exposing the high-minded bombast of republican culture.

CHAPTER 4

THE POST-REVOLUTIONARY WRITERS: TRUMBULL, TYLER, AND BRACKENRIDGE

"Diligent Observation of All That Is Passing"

Most Americans of the post-Revolutionary era believed with Tom Paine that the cause of America was the cause of mankind.[1] Only with this conviction in mind can one appreciate the compulsion that made republican theory a primary source of creativity in literature. Writers concentrated upon republicanism because nothing less than the history of the world depended on the success of the new United States of America. When in the 1790s America moved in exactly those directions that theorists feared most, concern became obsession. The educated observer saw difficulty at every turn. Territorial expansion pitted East against West and threatened national unity. Then, too, the democratizing course of the Revolution challenged the very form of republicanism. Even prosperity contained a time bomb. If the union somehow survived backwoods rebellions, popular unrest, and party factionalism, luxury would still destroy it. John Adams predicted ruin: "Riches Grandeur and Power will have the same effect upon American as it has upon European minds." "In short my dear Friend," he warned Jefferson, "you and I have been indefatigable Labourers through our whole Lives for a Cause which will be thrown away in the next generation, upon the Vanity and Foppery of Persons of whom we do not now know the Names perhaps."[2]

Post-Revolutionary writers dramatized each difficulty and offered solutions. This process, in turn, automatically favored the lawyer-writer. Republican ideology had been legalistic from the beginning, depending as it did on a framework of laws. Methodologically, the law joined the ideal and the practical in a search for answers—a combination that worked well in the problem-oriented literature of the times. Finally, there was the issue of focus. Many intellectuals watched America with intense curiosity during the formative period, but perhaps only the lawyer did so by training as well as inclination. William Wirt once summarized all of these advantages in a letter on legal education:

> Laborious study, and diligent observation of the world, are both indispensable . . . By the former, you must make yourself master of all that is known of science and letters; by the latter, you must know *man*, at large, and particularly the character and genius of your own countrymen. You must cultivate assiduously the habits of *reading*, *thinking*, and *observing* . . . Learn all that is delicate and beautiful, as well as strong, in the language . . . you must take care to unite . . . the diligent observation of all that is passing around you; and *active*, *close* and *useful thinking*.[3]

John Trumbull (1750–1831), Royall Tyler (1757–1826), and Hugh Henry Brackenridge (1748–1816) were lawyers who shaped imaginative literature in the immediate post-Revolutionary era. They combined "diligent observation of the world" with a knowledge of science, letters, and language; and, inevitably, they wrote of the character and genius of their countrymen. What has not been recognized, however, is the overall significance of the combination. As skilled lawyers and supreme court justices in their respective states, Trumbull, Tyler, and Brackenridge stressed precisely those qualities of observation, of active and useful thinking called for by legal method. In imaginative writing they instinctively turned to the world around them, the first realists in American literature.

In the 1770s and 1780s Trumbull's verse commentaries on the Connecticut clergy and on town life in New England set the tone for a sardonic brand of social criticism. In the 1790s Tyler's and Brackenridge's writings carried the same spirit into drama and fiction. If their works stood virtually alone at the end of the eighteenth century, it was because all three writers resisted the prevailing "school of sensibility." Novels like Brackenridge's *Modern Chivalry* and Tyler's *The Algerine Captive* ran counter to the popular story of feeling and susceptibility dominating early American fiction.[4] The lawyer-writer wanted to control passions, not to stimulate them. Moreover, "diligent observation of all that is passing" encouraged descriptive narrative and anecdotal reportage rather than emotional intricacy or stock romance. In tying his craft so closely to social realities, the lawyer-writer often sacrificed aesthetic considerations, but the same priority made him rummage through experience with peculiar intensity. He gave the new nation its first long, hard look. Here as well were the inclinations behind the first American experiments in dialect and local color. Tyler and Brackenridge head a long line of antebellum lawyers who used the novel to portray a slice of American life. *The Algerine Captive* and *Modern Chivalry* foreshadow John Pendleton Kennedy's *Swallow Barn* (1832), A. B. Longstreet's *Georgia Scenes* (1835), and Richard Henry Dana's *Two Years Before the Mast* (1840).

Trumbull, Tyler, and Brackenridge, seen together, clarify patterns of creativity; their many differences accentuate the important similarities. Trumbull represented high federalism and the traditionalism of an established New England family, while Brackenridge was a western democrat of poor Scottish origins. Tyler came somewhere in between, a moderate in politics who left a respectable situation in Boston to reestablish himself in rural Vermont. Yet regional and even political differences paled against the early American lawyer's vision of country. Brackenridge, the most radical, spoke for all three in announcing the source and the nature of their hopes for America. "Where," he asked, "is the best account to be found of the Roman Commonwealth? In Polybius. In what did its excellence consist? In its balances." The law created and then insured the balanced virtues of a mixed republic. Only a madman could then say, "Down with all law, and give us a free government," because legal formulation was the source of free government. A lawyer's special knowledge made him the natural guardian of republican virtue, and the greatest danger he faced, one identified by all three writers, was *"an uninformed spirit of reform."*[5]

Reform, of course, was everywhere in early republican culture. The legal mind instinctively took and defended a conservative position in the midst of change, and its natural expression was a warning against democratic excess. Mob-rule always seemed just around the corner in Trumbull's townsmen, in Tyler's yeomen, in Brackenridge's frontiersmen. Related issues—creeping materialism, civic corruption, and general licentiousness—contributed to a litany of

American ills. The lawyer-writer always knew how to play upon anxieties in the American psyche. "From the conclusion of this war we shall be going down hill," Jefferson had predicted as early as 1781.[6] Lawyers who wrote later in the century spent much of their time documenting that slide.

Fortunately, a saving vein of humor ran through all of this gloom. In observing the ways of their world, Trumbull, Tyler, and Brackenridge developed a jocose feel for clashes between expectation and reality. They realized before other republicans that the safest and best criticism of the new nation came with a smile. As Trumbull explained *M'Fingal* to John Adams, "The Picture of the Town-meeting is drawn from the life" in "a mixture of Irony & Sarcasm" that served much better than "an unvaried harangue in the Author's own person." "Let me get a man to laugh," Brackenridge noted, "and I put him in good humour." Or more bluntly put, *"we interlard pleasantry to make the boys read."*[7] Indeed, humor represented the cardinal achievement of the lawyer in post-Revolutionary literature. The solemnity of the Founding Fathers gave essential legitimacy and security to early republican growth, but it also suffocated new thought and development. Humor furnished an acceptable means of escape; it distinguished the new generation from the old, and it created alternative modes of expression. Post-Revolutionary writers sorely needed these new approaches in coming to grips with the fading relevance of the Founders' perspective. As the premises of republicanism shifted in the light of experience, humor often bespoke a fresher and more comfortable reality.

The comic voice of the lawyer-writer in the federalist and Jeffersonian eras also channeled resentment. Daniel Webster left the best description of every new American's plight: "We can win no laurels in a war for independence. Earlier and worthier hands have gathered them all. Nor are there places for us by the side of Solon, and Alfred, and other founders of states. Our fathers have filled them."[8] Followers had to be lesser heroes in their "duty of defence and preservation," and the first followers found it hard to think of heroism at all. "I will venture to say," Brackenridge observed in the very first chapter of *Modern Chivalry*, "that when the present John Adamses, and Lees, and Jeffersons, and Jays, and Henrys, and other great men, who figure upon the stage at this time, have gone to sleep with their fathers, it is an hundred to one if there is any of

their descendents who can fill their places."⁹ For the immediate
post-Revolutionary generation, the presence and sometime scrutiny
of the Founding Fathers produced special feelings of inferiority and
exasperation. One thinks of Trumbull's uneasiness and Tyler's vexation in dealings with John Adams or of Trumbull's complaint when
Washington failed to acknowledge the poet's assistance on a public
speech.¹⁰ Brackenridge in particular fared badly in his relations with
the great. He took the Father of His Country to court and lost.
Washington's studied indifference on a social occasion and Jefferson's later rejection of overtures of friendship cut deeply. The novelist once vowed to get even with those "men of place" who ignored
him, and the proof lay in subsequent writings—in Brackenridge's
unflattering aside on Washington in *Law Miscellanies* or in his complex renunciation of Jeffersonian tenets in *Modern Chivalry*.¹¹ Similar
motivations spurred Royall Tyler. His play *The Contrast*, a balanced
appraisal of post-Revolutionary America, was a rare double triumph
of and over experience.

Unsuccessful encounters with the heroes of the republic gave spice
to satire. Humor masked what one critic has called "the paradoxical,
complex estrangement of American men of letters from the Revolution and the new nation."¹² These strains remained uncertain
because the age required writers who would explain and support
the meaning of republican virtue. Nevertheless, an irrepressible
humor pointed the way to later masters of comedy in American
literature. For in using humor, the early lawyer-writer placed comedy on an enduring foundation of realism. Here the point is not
just that Diedrich Knickerbocker benefited from Trumbull's mock-
ery of government by proclamation in *The Progress of Dulness* or
Tyler's satire of Yankee characteristics in *The Contrast*. Trumbull,
Tyler, and Brackenridge showed subsequent generations where to
stand when contesting the grandiosity of republican culture; we are
halfway to the more crafted resentment of Charles Brockden Brown
and the polished buffoonery of Washington Irving.

Trumbull and the "Friends of Order, Justice, and Regular Authority"

John Trumbull's talent made him the most celebrated American
poet of the eighteenth century, and his critical expertise brought

vital leadership to the country's first school of poetry, the Connecticut Wits. But these achievements have always seemed minor when placed against a precocity that promised so much more. By the age of four Trumbull had read the Bible through and was writing verse. At seven, in 1757, he gained admission to Yale College, and, by nine, with Milton and Thomson as guides, he had versified half of the Psalms. He was a leading intellectual at Yale as a young tutor in the early 1770s and a recognized poet before he was twenty-five. All of this activity flowed from a strong, particular, and continuing sense of purpose. From the beginning Trumbull sought "to build a name" in literature, and it was no idle boast when he later wrote John Adams of his determination "to be the most learned Man in America."[13] And yet his best poems, *The Progress of Dulness* (1772–1773) and *M'Fingal* (1775–1782), hardly convey such talent, energy, and ambition. Trumbull was the first to acknowledge his own failure. He excluded everything done in later life, almost forty years, from his *Poetical Works*, when they appeared in 1820.

What happened to the brilliant young writer compared by contemporaries to Swift and Butler? Were American audiences simply unreceptive to the uses and meaning of poetry—particularly satiric poetry? Did Trumbull ossify within a rigid neoclassical tradition? Was this son, grandson, and great-grandson of somber Connecticut clergymen unable to appreciate his own genius for humorous verse? These are the questions biographers have asked in exploring a lost talent, but their answers fail to account for the poet's situation.[14] Trumbull had the intellectual support of community leaders, and his best efforts received popular acclaim. Although committed to neoclassical tenets, he championed the formal study of modern literature on its own terms. Certainly no one in the early republic had a clearer notion of the value and meaning of humor. Satire was "a medicine very salutary in its effects," and Trumbull clearly enjoyed "the groans and distortions of the Patient" who received his "potion." He also understood his central role as a pioneer in American humor. "I have the honour," he once observed, "of being the first, who dared by Satire to oppose the party of controversial Scribblers, & set this part of America an example of the use of Ridicule & Humour, to combat the whims of dogmatical Enthusiasts."[15]

Successful, eager, and perceptive, Trumbull nonetheless stood in the way of his own talent, and his legal career helps to explain why. In effect, the lawyer's goals came to contain those of the poet through the affinities of law and letters in early republican culture. These affinities, the presence of a legal mind within the poetry, are clearest in Trumbull's best works. *The Progress of Dulness* dramatizes the eighteenth-century American intellectual's vocational movement away from the ministry and toward law. *M'Fingal* epitomizes the lawyer's peculiar ambivalence regarding Revolutionary politics. Both poems project the tensions and aspirations that undermined Trumbull's creativity. Examined closely, they illuminate the problems that led toward later silence.

Sixteen hundred lines of jingling tetrameter couplets, *The Progress of Dulness* satirizes three different character types: Tom Brainless, a drudge of a divine, who "deals forth the dulness of the day" from a country pulpit; Dick Hairbrain, who moves from yokel to fop on the strength of his father's wealth; and Harriet Simper, who rises and falls as the traditional coquette in "gaudy whims of vain parade."[16] Of the three sections, only part one, "The Rare Adventures of Tom Brainless," has the bite of true satire. Here Trumbull attacks the loose educational standards of Yale College and the errors of a Connecticut clergy enmeshed in doctrinal wrangling and mediocrity. These were bold targets for an American writer in 1772, particularly for a youth of twenty-two whose father then presided as a leading minister of the region and a trustee of Yale. Trumbull, a true son of New England, meant only to "point out . . . those general errors, that hinder the advantages of education and the growth of piety." Even so, he soon found himself branded "an enemy to truth and learning" by certain "Reverend Gentlemen." Ministers were quick to find "an open reviler of the Clergy" whose "apparent design was to ridicule religion, disgrace morality, sneer at the present methods of education, and, in short, write a satire upon Yale-College and the ten commandments."[17]

The strength of such resentment reveals *The Progress of Dulness* for what it is: the first popular work to document the diminished status of the clergy in Revolutionary America. As one historian has put it, "In 1740 America's leading intellectuals were clergymen and thought about theology; in 1790 they were statesmen and thought about politics."[18] Tom Brainless' inept ministry is the fanciful projection of this change; it "does little good, and little harm," in part because it is so irrelevant (II, 33). Trumbull's characterization traces a descent across the generations. The parson who instructs Tom has forgotten the ancient languages that his pupil can never learn (II, 12–13). "From heaven at first your order came," the poet reminds all brothers of the cloth, but smaller minds have long since reduced truth and conviction to a narrow search for orthodoxy (II, 30). The ministers who gather for Tom's ordination sermon know that Brainless is incompetent both in name and in fact. They admit him anyway:

> What though his learning be so slight,
> He scarcely knows to spell or write;
> What though his skull be cudgel-proof!
> He's orthodox, and that's enough.   (II, 29)

Later in *The Progress of Dulness* Trumbull describes the empty social posturing of a modern church service: "To church the female squadron move, / All arm'd with weapons used in love." The explicit contrast is to the sincerity and vigor of New England's first Community of Saints:

> Each man equipp'd on Sunday morn,
> With psalm-book, shot and powder-horn;
> And look'd in form, as all must grant,
> Like th' ancient, true church militant.   (II, 72)

In a telling juxtaposition, the poet's generation of churchmen struggle against themselves in vain theological debate. No shot and powder-horn here! They are scribbling dogmatists who "fight with quills, like porcupines" (II, 72–73).

Not least in Trumbull's portrait of declension is his pervasive humor. That the poet presumes to satirize "where dreaded satire may not dare" gives final proof of the minister's lost hegemony in American culture (II, 25). Nor is Trumbull slow to trace the implications of a dwindling vitality in religious thought. About to enter the law office of John Adams in Boston, he deliberately stings the clergy with the new choice of young men on the rise:

> [When] fools assume your sacred place,
> It threats your order with disgrace;
> Bids genius from your seats withdraw,
> And seek the pert, loquacious law.   (II, 31)

The shift in professional preferences that began in the generation of John Adams was in full swing when the poet wrote these lines. A decade later, Trumbull's contemporary and sometime collaborator, Noah Webster, summarized the result: "Never was such a rage for the study of the law. From one end of the continent to the other, the students of this science are multiplying without number."[19]

Significantly, Tom Brainless "starves on sixty pounds a year" in his country parish (II, 32). Ministers on fixed incomes were swamped by the inflationary spirals of the Revolutionary and post-Revolutionary periods, while lawyers rode the crest upon the only profession that was both lucrative and secure.[20] Did Trumbull's hopes for wealth and place as a lawyer squelch his penchant for satire? It has been argued that "there was no circle in America into which he [Trumbull] could escape for approval and praise after an onslaught upon the dullards. He had to live among his victims—and eventually expect them to be his legal clients and political supporters." No wonder the poet of 1772 worried about making "a new set of Enemies."[21] He consciously diluted his satire in the last two parts of *The Progress of Dulness*, giving special credence to a couplet in the closing section: "So priests drive poets to the lurch / By fulminations of the church" (II, 75). And yet the same poet was quite willing to challenge and cudgel his "malicious attackers," any one of whom might "have sate for the picture of Tom Brainless."[22] Greater issues than careerism and financial security tempered Trumbull's humor—issues concerned with the intrinsic connection of law and politics and with the intellectual ascendancy of the lawyer in Revolutionary America.

A closer look at *The Progress of Dulness* suggests a troubled and troubling vision of America. The collective cognomen "Tom, Dick, and Harriet" reaches for generic significance, and Trumbull uses his caricatures to excoriate two related evils in American society: impiety and a growing materialism. These ills are the ones deplored by most eighteenth-century American intellectuals in their calls for a return to virtue through education, public service, and a right sense of religion. In fact, the second part of *The Progress of Dulness* ends with just such a call. But Trumbull's happy man who applies "the will of heaven" and "studious pain" to achieve "heart-felt peace of mind" and the praise of his community is a strangely disembodied figment with no part to play in the society of Brainless, Hairbrain, and Simper (II, 56–57). There is no clear path to virtue in *The Progress of Dulness*. For while folly is punished in Trumbull's poem, the fates of his characters raise more questions than they answer.

In part one, laziness and ignorance reward the Reverend Tom Brainless with the obscurity that he manifestly deserves. However, Trumbull saves his sharpest barbs for Brainless' opponents, the New Light Divines who try to rejuvenate the clergy and reconstitute religious fervor in the second half of the eighteenth century. *The Progress of Dulness* may praise the true church militant, but it seeks no modern equivalent. Like Adams and Jefferson before him, Trumbull has absorbed the rational-legal temperament of Lord Kames. He wants nothing to do with dogmatism, enthusiasm, and revivalism as mechanisms of social improvement.[23] Conventionally in favor of piety, he distrusts the wellsprings of emotion that supply religious conviction.

The poet hopes instead that "bright philosophy" and "ethics" will combine with common sense to "teach the laws divine."

> Oh! might I live to see that day,
> When sense shall point to youths their way;
> Through every maze of science guide;
> O'er education's laws preside;
> The good retain, with just discerning
> Explode the quackeries of learning.   (II, 22–23)

The secular humanism in this passage encourages a cool head, not a warm heart. Trumbull's sensationalist stress—"When sense shall point to youths their way"—also leaves plenty of room for the materialism of a Dick Hairbrain or a Harriet Simper. Implicitly, the poet places rationalism and worldly prudence on a par with religious conviction, but since virtue still rests upon piety, the overall result is a kind of moral confusion. Trumbull's solutions compound his problems and reflect uncomfortable transitions in New England life.

The punishments of Dick and Harriet in parts two and three of *The Progress of Dulness* are even more problematic. Fop and coxcomb, Dick fails not because of his moral deficiencies but because of poor fiscal management. In a crass world of Hairbrains, wealth keeps Dick's "name / Rank'd in the foremost lists of fame" and excuses every form of bad behavior (II, 54). Only bankruptcy can expose and condemn. As Trumbull admits, "The coxcomb's course were gay and clever, / Would health and money last for ever" (ii, 56). Harriet Simper's difficulties can be summarized in similar terms: given the opportunity, she fails to marry well. Her coquetry attracts "deserving lovers" along with the usual "powder'd swarm" of dandies (ii, 82, 77). Alas, Harriet does not know when to stop or, more important, whom to choose. The absence of true virtue has less to do with missing her goal in life—a good match—than lack of discernment. Harriet's flaw, like Dick's, is a failure to apply common sense and prudence in worldly matters. Although Trumbull would wish it otherwise, his characters are punished not because they play games with life but because they don't play life's game well enough.

America has become a place in which simple "country manners" give way to the "vain parade" of the "pop'lous city." In *The Progress of Dulness* primitive virtues have been lost, but meaningful culture remains a distant prospect. "The half-genteel are least polite," warns the poet (ii, 69). As if to foreshorten this disastrous middle stage in cultural development, Trumbull hustles Dick and Harriet into premature old age, each within a few lines (ii, 55–56, 86). Unfortunately, the immediate future promises nothing better. In a final thrust Trumbull marries off the vulgar Simper to the ignorant Brainless. Little can be expected from this version of an American union.

Such negativism left the poet of 1773 with a problem. *The Progress of Dulness* undercut an intrinsic optimism in early republican literature and contradicted the poet's own resolutions. Trumbull had written his poem "for the universal Benefit of Mankind" and "to promote the interests of learning and morality." There was bombast in the use of these abstractions but also intense inner conviction. The value of poetry lay in public service. If the story of Tom, Dick, and Harriet failed to "conduce to the service of mankind," then Trumbull "had spent much time in the studies of the Muses in vain."[24]

The subordination of creativity to service put a high premium on the social vision of the writer, and this impulse, in turn, prompted the strongest possible presentation of country during the political turmoil of the 1770s. What *The Progress of Dulness* lacked was an articulate plan for the future of America. One consequence was that its design was "by many . . . ignorantly or wilfully misunderstood" (ii, 60). Trumbull would try to rectify his mistake by including just such a vision in his next major effort, *M'Fingal*, but even then he hesitated—not from a fear of failure but over the uncertain impact of success. The stipulation that a literary work serve given social ends placed a heavy responsibility upon the writer who decided to publish. To those who encouraged the plan of *M'Fingal* in 1775, Trumbull at first opposed "grounds of Diffidence." "But suppose such a piece to succeed," he asked, "What would be its Effect?"[25]

Trumbull feared the discrepancy between creative aims and public reactions, and in *M'Fingal* there was cause for worry. The poet's hopes for his mock-epic of the Revolution were complicated—far more complicated than his first readers realized. On one level, he lampooned the loyalist opposition through the rancorous persona of M'Fingal, a Scottish Tory who condemns the Revolution in a New England town meeting and is tarred and feathered for his pains. Here was the patriotic bluster that early republicans reveled in. Beneath the surface, however, Trumbull sought "impartiality" and wrote to "satirize the follies and extravagancies of my countrymen, as well as of their enemies" (II, 231–232). This more balanced view served other purposes than humor and chauvinism. By looking at both sides, the poet wanted to curb the radical impulses in Revolutionary politics and impose a conservative theory of order.

Like most Whig lawyers of the day and particularly like his mentor and lifelong leader John Adams, Trumbull was for the Revolution but against revolution. Mob excess represented at least as grave a danger to liberty as British tyranny. The democratic tendencies in Revolutionary politics had to be resisted because only a balance of aristocratic and popular components could hope to produce a responsible government. In this Trumbull followed the Polybian view of mixed government set forth by the Whig lawyers of England after the Glorious Revolution and followed closely by Adams and other American leaders in their own Revolutionary debates. There was, of course, much disagreement over the proper arrangement of aristocratic and popular components—Trumbull and generations of Federalists after him wanted "a *speaking* aristocracy *in the face of a silent* democracy"—but everyone agreed that only an impartial rule of laws could safeguard a proper mixture of influences and controls.[26] Accordingly, what Trumbull criticized most in the revolutionary zealots of *M'Fingal* was their loss of respect for law. Too much rebellion undermined the legal foundations of constitutional government.

M'Fingal begins with a communal debate between Honorius, leader of the Whigs, and M'Fingal, who speaks for the Tories, at a town meeting. Even though these exchanges fill two of the poem's four cantos, Trumbull's narrative soon reaches the "Uproar and Rage and wild Misrule" that his character M'Fingal has foreseen as the logical outcome of revolution (I, 95). Meaningful debate quickly becomes impossible. By cantos three and four, as open rebellion succeeds, the "vengeance of resentful Whigs" gives way to "the Mob, beflipp'd at taverns" (I, 165, 124). The last Tories must meet alone at night and in secret. In the concluding lines of Trumbull's mock-epic, they flee in terror as their hiding place is invaded by "the rage of mob" (I, 175). Every form of authority and restraint is swept away in *M'Fingal*. The town constable is tarred and feathered. The chairman of the town meeting, Trumbull's clearest symbol of moderation, literally disappears as he tries "the peace to keep." "Like Sol half seen behind a cloud," he brings the meeting to order, but as tempers flare he moves "out of view, / Beneath the desk." Predictably, no one waits for this invisible moderator to gavel the meeting to a close (I, 10–11, 83–84). Even Honorius loses control. The speaker of the moment when an unidentified shout from outside the hall abruptly terminates debate, Honorius is not heard from again. Whig direction passes from the implicitly aristocratic orator to an unnamed brawler. This final leader in *M'Fingal* is "the stoutest wrestler on the green," and he fights with a worker's spade (I, 104).

Trumbull explains exactly what has happened. Because the town is "torn by feuds of faction," it is subject to mercurial shifts that shake the body politic:

> So did this town with ardent zeal
> Weave cobwebs for the public weal,
> Which when completed, or before,
> A second vote in pieces tore.   (I, 8–9)

These unsettled circumstances gradually destroy the natural order in the state, displacing a necessary aristocratic leadership and turning society on its head.

> For in this ferment of the stream
> The dregs have work'd up to the brim,
> And by the rule of topsy-turvies,
> The scum stands foaming on the surface.

> You've caused your pyramid t' ascend
> And set it on the little end.   (I, 92)

Unleashed, the populace "make the bar and bench and steeple / submit t' our Sovereign Lord, The People" (I, 89). The inevitable result is "Anarchy from chaos" (I, 95). Once law becomes a momentary expression of popular opinion instead of an objective base for mutual restraint, mobs "cry justice down, as out of fashion" and "reduce all grievances and ills / To Magna Charta of your wills" (II, 88). In the pivotal scene of *M'Fingal*, just such a mob arbitrarily tries, sentences, and punishes M'Fingal in what Trumbull calls "an imitation of legal forms . . . universally practiced by the mobs in New-England" during the Revolution. The poet-lawyer calls this imitation of legal forms "a curious trait of national character," and his own constant wordplay upon legal terminology in *M'Fingal* draws attention to a larger problem.[27]

For while *M'Fingal* celebrates the victory of patriotism over tyranny, it also points to a crying need for civic balance and respect for law—virtues lost in the Revolution. In this sense, Trumbull's Scottish Tory summarizes common American fears. By rejecting the British constitution ("That constitution form'd by sages, / The wonder of all modern ages"), the new states are turning away from the old, safe balances, risking "wild confusion" in "new-cast legislative engines" (I, 94–95). New balances must have seemed tenuous indeed in 1782, the year in which *M'Fingal* appeared, and there is much to puzzle over in the poet's brief glimpse of the future:

> This Rebel Empire, proud and vaunting,
> From anarchy shall change her crasis,
> And fix her pow'r on firmer basis;
> To glory, wealth and fame ascend,
> Her commerce wake, her realms extend.   (I, 174)

The only certainty in this vision of empire is present chaos. After the calls to virtue in *The Progress of Dulness*, what is one to make of a future order built so entirely upon commercial prosperity? Post-Revolutionary theorists feared that America lacked the aristocratic components for a properly balanced, mixed form of constitutional government, and Trumbull seems to supply that deficiency here by predicting a new aristocracy of wealth and place.[28] But could an Honorius lead such an empire? Would he want to? And if he could and did, what was to prevent an emerging nation of materialistic Hairbrains?

Trumbull and many others turned for answers to a conservative and legalistic republicanism. "The friends of order, justice, and regular authority," they were certain that a proper respect for law would supply leadership and insure virtue (i, xx). Here was the crux of the matter for conservative republican intellectuals and the literature they wrote. They meant to create a controlling rule of law in a nation of laws, a goal that became an obsession when legal authority was challenged in the 1780s. The poet's last important work, *The Anarchiad* in 1786 and 1787, is a tale of woe precisely because the rule of law has been threatened by a general weakness in the Confederation of States and by the particular turmoil of Shays's Rebellion in Massachusetts. In *The Anarchiad* Trumbull and his collaborators, the other Connecticut Wits, still believe that virtuous leaders can "bid laws again exalt the imperial scale, / And public justice o'er her foes prevail," but in 1786 Shays's "mob-compelling name" has overwhelmed "the new-born state," and "Law sinks before [the] uncreating word" of Chaos. Everyone's worst fears have been confirmed: "Lo, THE COURT FALLS; th' affrighted judges run, / Clerks, Lawyers, Sheriffs, every mother's son."[29]

The poet did not write for publication again. Shays, of course, fell quickly and a stronger constitution soon replaced the weak Articles of Confederation, but the events of the next decade, the democratizing course of the Revolution, left Trumbull and his friends fighting the same ideological battles over and over again. The factional splits between Federalist and Republican, the Whiskey Rebellion of 1794, the conflicts over the Alien and Sedition Acts of 1798, and, above all, the Republican victory of 1800 elicited the same cries of dismay previously heard in *The Anarchiad*.[30] At some point in this period, Trumbull concluded that satiric writings no longer "checked and intimidated the leaders of disorganization and infidel philosophy" as they once had done (i, xxi). A growing threat to law and order from radical democracy required action instead of poetry.

Trumbull served first in 1789 as state's attorney for Hartford County and then as town representative to the legislature. Appointed a judge for the superior court of Connecticut in 1801, he killed whatever was left of the poet. "The character of a partizan and political writer," he explained, "was inconsistent with the station of a judge and destructive of the confidence of suitors in the impartiality of judiciary decisions" (1, xxii). Jeffersonian attacks upon a Federalist judiciary in 1801 may have hastened this movement toward a defensive and exclusive professionalism, but the lawyer's decision necessarily grew from the writer's original aims. The poet of *M'Fingal* and the judge of the superior court were anxious defenders of the same precarious republicanism. Behind the transition was the same legal mind of the period, acting the role of ideological guardian.

Tyler and "Minding the Main Chance"

Less talented but more perceptive than Trumbull, Royall Tyler made better use of a common predicament. As post-Revolutionary intellectuals, both writers belonged to what would always be the next generation; they were ordinary men after a race of heroes. The Founding Fathers fought the Revolution, made the republic, and then lived on to preside over their own creation for another thirty years. Tyler, Trumbull, and their contemporaries worked and wrote within this lengthening shadow. Proclaiming the Revolution that others defined and applying the controversial and often impractical lessons of republicanism to common life—these were the thankless tasks of permanent followers. What distinguished Royall Tyler from other second-generation patriots was his ability to turn an unpromising situation into art. Like Trumbull, Tyler understood that humor could puncture the high seriousness of his times, but he also saw that comedy could reveal a newer and firmer reality. His one masterpiece, *The Contrast*, written in 1787, gave eighteenth-century Americans the most accurate portrait they would receive of themselves.[31]

Tyler's wry appreciation of place came through painful experience. In 1782, five years before the writer's comedy of manners on American life, John Adams took Tyler's measure and found him wanting. Judgment rested upon two separate grounds: Tyler had strayed to the other side of an absolute divide between virtue and vice; also, in the later words of a character in *The Contrast*, he occasionally forgot "to be a man of punctuality and mind the main chance."[32] When Royall Tyler sought the hand of Adams' daughter

"Nabby" in 1782, he was twenty-five, a rising lawyer in Adams' hometown of Braintree, and a recognized man of talent from a good Boston family. As Abigail Adams wrote to her husband, then in Europe negotiating peace with England, Nabby's suitor possessed "popular talents," a "delicate and refined taste," "attainments in literature," an "exceedingly amiable" disposition, and a "mamma . . . in possession of a large Estate." In Braintree he showed "great Steadiness and application" and thus seemed certain of "making a distinguished figure in his profession." On the other hand, Mrs. Adams had to admit that Tyler previously had been "rather negligent in persueing his business in the way of his profession; and dissipated two or 3 years of his Life and too much of his fortune for to reflect upon with pleasure."[33]

Lonely and homesick in Paris, Adams leaped upon every negative implication. A lawyer, he confessed, would be his own choice for a son-in-law but not one who spent his evenings courting ladies, as Tyler seemed to be doing. "I am not looking out for a Poet, nor a Professor of belle Letters," he grumped in response to Abigail's praise. Most of all, Adams worried about those "Errors in Youth" and Tyler's seeming "Gaiety." "Frivolity of Mind . . . never gets out of the Man but shews itself in some mean Shape or other through Life," he advised his wife. Leaving nothing to chance, he also frightened her: "I dont like your word 'Dissipation' at all. I dont know what it means—it may mean every Thing." Out came the heaviest guns. "My Child is a Model," he thundered, " . . . and is not to be the Prize, I hope of any, even reformed Rake." Two months after this salvo, Adams spelled out what a Founding Father could expect in a son-in-law: "Prudence, Talents, and Labour," one "devoted entirely to Study and to Business—to honour & Virtue." The seventeen-year-old Nabby, he promised, could "go with my Consent wherever she can find enough of these." Mother and daughter set sail for Europe in 1784, and the attachment to Tyler was soon severed. Years later, in 1800, Tyler would describe his once future father-in-law in images of unattainability. Then president, though still a quarter of a century before his death, Tyler's Adams "stands on the summit of the age of man, plumes his wings, and prepares to mount to glory."[34] For those who came after, the Founding Fathers were more than mortal; they could be followed but never reached.

The romantic incident is striking because part of Tyler agreed with Adams' assessment and rejection. Not old sins but small, continuing mistakes in propriety ultimately cost Tyler his place in the Adams family. It was as if he deliberately failed a period of probation.[35] There *had* been dissipation, and there would be more. Rumor made him the father of his Harvard College cleaning lady's bastard son. Fact revealed an involved disciplinary record at Harvard in the mid-1770s, at least one public incident of drunk and disorderly conduct, and spendthrift ways. The youthful Tyler might have modeled for Dick Hairbrain. Later, in the 1790s, Tyler emerged as one of the more spirited members of Joseph Dennie's literary circle, which met and wrote in the taverns of Vermont and New Hampshire. His remarkable underground classic on the origin of evil—Eve first discovers and then services Adam's tree of knowledge—appeared in these years.[36] But while Tyler clearly enjoyed himself, a New England conscience made him pay a considerable price in self-esteem. There were strange fits of depression and a feeling of avenues permanently closed by errors in conduct. Indeed, Tyler once smothered an interest in the ministry because "a consciousness of having lived too gay a life in my youth made me tremble lest I should bring in some way disgrace upon the sacred cause!"[37]

A strong sense of public duty accompanied Tyler's awareness of inner discrepancies. Part rogue and playboy, he nonetheless knew how to play the patriot, and he believed in the importance of that role. The soldier, orator, lawyer, lay preacher, judge, professor of jurisprudence, and chief justice of the Vermont supreme court always rose to particular occasions. Major Royall Tyler of the Massachusetts state militia personally quelled a band of insurgents in western Massachusetts in 1787. His speeches to the populace and vigorous military leadership helped to end Shays's Rebellion.[38] For years Tyler performed regularly as a favorite Fourth of July orator, and his speech on the death of Washington in 1800 warned of major difficulties for America in the passing of the Revolutionary generation. "He taught us how to live," Tyler began, using Washington's life as "a practical treatise of the cardinal virtues." Only here could the nation's youth find "their polar star, in their passage through the boisterous ocean of human life." Later the chief justice of 1809 appeared a tower of strength in preserving law and order during a local rebellion. "Our present meeting affords irrefragable evidence that we have still a government existing among us," Tyler reminded his grand jury and refractory neighbors, "a government of our own choice—a government founded in principles of rational liberty: a government which . . . affords ample legal and constitutional redress for public grievances."[39]

In all of these public matters Tyler shared his generation's placement of law at the ideological center of the republican experiment, and his entire professional career, including the preparation of two volumes of Vermont law reports, was dedicated to the same proposition. But what Tyler could never do was devote himself, in Adams' words, "entirely to Study and to Business—to honour & Virtue." He knew the foibles of human nature too well to rely on absolutist standards, and this knowledge made him a sympathetic witness as well as the enforcer of law in Vermont courtrooms. Contemporaries described a professional man "who . . . feels for the errors of others, pities their vices, and compassionates their wants."[40] There were unusual levels of empathy and toleration in the lawyer's point of view, qualities that were also the writer's greatest intellectual strength.

For the playwright life is a mixture in which Honorius is necessary but Hairbrain inevitable; either alone will prove unbearable. *The Contrast* seeks to make these points with humor and grace. Its title is peculiarly apt not just because the play sets a patriot against fops and coquettes but because Tyler insists that each type belongs within his world. By definition, a contrast transcends mere strife; it lends inherent usefulness and a kind of permanence to conflict. As Samuel Johnson identified the term for the eighteenth century, contrast involves "dissimilitude of figures, by which one contributes to the visibility or effect of another." An opposite serves in a mutual process "to shew another figure to advantage." In *The Contrast* Tyler's Revolutionary war hero Colonel Manly seems overly punctilious until the Chesterfieldian seducer Billy Dimple dramatizes the need for proper behavior. Tyler's other characters grope toward each other between these extremes in ways that make them wonderfully human and amusing. Nabby Adams may have been the first to ponder the dramatic ambiguities involved. Was the new lawyer in town as upright as he seemed, she wondered back in June of 1782, or was he "practicing upon Chesterfeilds plan" in "the essence and quintessence of artfulness"?[41] Tyler, of course, was always both,

Colonel Manly *and* Billy Dimple, in a way the Adamses could never understand or condone. *The Contrast* works so well because it insists upon the relationship. Not for nothing are Colonel Manly and Charlotte of the same flesh and blood in Tyler's play. Brother and sister, patriot against coquette, the Manlys square off in an endless exchange that delights because it emanates from one enduring American family.

The first native comedy produced professionally in America, *The Contrast* necessarily draws upon European prototypes. The foppish Billy Dimple and his reluctant fiancée, the sentimental Maria Van Rough, along with Maria's true love, the upright Colonel Manly, are all creatures of eighteenth-century British drama and fiction.[42] Tyler frankly acknowledges his indebtedness on the surfaces of his play. Billy Dimple's knavery—he plans to jilt Maria for the wealthier Letitia while secretly wooing the coquettish Charlotte—owes much to Joseph Surface in *The School for Scandal* (1772), and Tyler spells out the influence by having some of his characters watch and comment on Sheridan's play (pp. 72–73). Maria's agonizing between filial obedience and rejection of the marriage that her father has arranged with the wealthy Dimple comes directly from her readings in Richardson's novels. As one of Tyler's characters explains, "Clary Harlow would have scorned such a match" (pp. 26–27). The structure of *The Contrast* is that of every other eighteenth-century comedy of manners. Dimple's inevitable exposure and the happy union of Maria and Manly cover the customary five acts. Farce follows wit in the usual by-play of servants, in this case Jessamy, Jonathan, and Jenny.

Tyler's originality appears in the way he combines conventional elements, in the way his combinations jar against each other with humorous results, and in the complex picture of America that emerges from these techniques. The many contrasts in Tyler's comedy cut across each other, emphasizing diversity over unity. Luxury and materialism versus virtue and patriotism, rank versus the leveling impulse, experience versus innocence, modernity versus tradition, city versus country, humor versus sentiment—these contrasts interlock in Tyler's characterizations to create multidimensional figures out of stereotypes.[43] Charlotte Manly, for example, is a coquette in the mold of Harriet Simper, and as such she receives her comeuppance in act five, but well before this point her vivacity and effectiveness in the many confrontations of *The Contrast* have added a certain subtlety and substance. Charlotte represents humor in a play that places laughter above all things. In the unequal contest between humor and sentiment, she easily and accurately punctures her natural opponents, Manly and Maria, winning a sympathetic understanding in the process.

Charlotte summarizes what would have been the ready perception of Tyler's immediate audience. For if Colonel Manly stands for the traditional virtues, he is also a ridiculous anachronism in post-Revolutionary New York. Charlotte correctly assesses her brother's heart as "an old maiden lady's bandbox . . . too delicate, costly, and antiquated for common use." His conversation is a "rich old-fashioned brocade" made up of "old scraps of tragedy," and his "regimental coat in the late war" is hopelessly out of place in contemporary society (pp. 42–43, 47, 50–51). "Well said heroics" leave Manly permanently within "the temple of gravity," where only the sentimental (Maria) and the simple (Brother Jonathan) will listen (pp. 47, 92). Charlotte's contrasting love of fashion is frivolous, but it also symbolizes her interest in remaining abreast of the times. As the representative of a volatile present, she most clearly understands the future, predicting the eventual union of "that pair of pensorosos," Manly and Maria (p. 44). Significantly, Charlotte is all energy, verve, and individual enterprise in the face of Maria's inclination "to recline and repose on the bosom of friendship." To Maria's tearful plight, Charlotte responds with the practical common sense of a modern mind and the first stirrings of Jacksonian individualism: "My dear friend, your happiness depends on yourself . . . I would not be forced to make myself miserable: no parent in the world should oblige me to marry the man I did not like" (p. 86).

In the appropriate contrast Colonel Manly is neither modern nor humorous, but a comparable complexity grows out of his own dramatic situation. Readers who find only "a most insufferable prig" forget that Tyler's wooden soldier is the key to the play.[44] True, Manly has "humbly imitated our illustrious Washington" to make his own career "an honourable certificate to posterity," and his "lofty way of saying things" invariably stops conversation (p. 47). However, Tyler plays upon these separations from common life to dramatize the central problem of *The Contrast*. In a work obsessed with issues of national identity, only the patriotic Manly has a vision of his country. The consequence of that vision is much foreboding.

Manly worries about republican "embarrassments" and "public tu-mults," and, comparing the collapse of the Greek city-states to current American dangers, he warns that luxury, "the bane of a nation," is destroying virtue by placing the pursuit of private interest over the common good (pp. 47, 50, 79, 80). "Oh! that my country, would, in this her day, learn the things which belong to her peace!" cries Manly in anguish. The fading altruism of the Revolution must find a place in the new order—a place that will allow patriotism to guide and control a selfish materialism. The Colonel's awkward isolation in *The Contrast* gives this political problem dramatic scope. Tyler's precarious solution—and his way of bringing his Revolu-tionary hero into the present—is to marry Manly into the world of Van Rough, where "it is money makes the mare go" and morality means to "mind the main chance" (pp. 35, 38).

Manly can be duped and ridiculed as an anachronism, but he remains the only real source of authority. America desperately needs that authority in 1787. Like Tyler himself, writing *The Contrast* just after fighting in the militia against Shays's Rebellion, Manly has buckled on his sword to deal with the insurgents (p. 50). The Colonel also curbs the raw energy and pugnacity of that American archetype, Brother Jonathan. The latter would have joined Shays but for the moderating influence of Manly. As "a true born Yankee American son of liberty," Jonathan is jealous of democratic prerogatives, cer-tain that "no man shall master me," and "chock-full of fight" (pp. 54–56, 73, 109). One issue in *The Contrast* is whether this American yeoman will continue to follow Manly, the traditional rural leader, or succumb to Jessamy, Dimple's servant, who promises pleasure and profit in the city. Manly naturally triumphs in the end. He checks the dangerous strength of Jonathan and preserves Charlotte when her own very different brand of vitality leads her into Dimple's clutches (p. 109). Dimple's subsequent challenge reveals the real source of Manly's superiority. "I have a cane to chastise the insolence of a scoundrel," Manly explains, "and a sword and the good laws of my country to protect me" (p. 112). This last, "the good laws of my country," is the lawyer's surest defense and the playwright's increasing concern. Tyler's last plays, *The Island of Barrataria* (after 1813) and *The Judgment of Solomon* (1824–25), are courtroom dramas, which test concepts of law and justice within the structure of gov-ernment.[45]

Examined against each other, the characters of *The Contrast* move from a comedy of manners into a comedy of ideas about the new American nation. Charlotte, Colonel Manly, Billy Dimple, Brother Jonathan, and the Van Roughs project different aspects of the ambiguous image Americans have of themselves at the end of the eighteenth century. When these aspects interact in the world of the play, they dramatize early republican fears. Thus Tyler lampoons the "levelling principle" in Jonathan's comic debate with Jessamy over titles—servant or waiter, "a true Yankee distinction . . . without a difference" (pp. 54–55). Colonel Manly voices another apprehension when he argues that "the noble principle of patriotism" thrives best upon simplicity and parochialism (p. 92). Could chaste republican virtue survive worldliness, or even a growing sophistication? To be sure, Manly raises the issue to justify remaining close at home in contrast to the well-traveled Dimple, but Tyler complicates matters by reminding everyone that Jonathan has joined the Colonel "to see the world" (p. 54). Neither leader nor follower will be quite the same after this first trip to the big city. Brother Jonathan in New York is a comic but disturbing presence.

Throughout *The Contrast* Tyler's characters play off of an obsessive insecurity of the period: the problem of correct behavior. Jonathan's boorish mistakes burlesque the fear of not knowing how to act. "How should you dispose of your time?" Maria asks Charlotte, and the question carries enormous weight for every other figure involved (p. 84). Billy and Jessamy's imitation of Chesterfield, Charlotte's compulsive search for the newest bonnet, Manly's emulation of Washington, Maria's melodramatics, and Van Rough's materialism form the extremes within which acceptable behavior should take place. By making each position a grotesque exaggeration, Tyler safely caricatures a serious issue. Definitions of good behavior always present difficulty, but the bottom line for early republicans must be whether or not a correct code of conduct will pay off in a changing society. Tyler uses this anxiety in *The Contrast* for one of his deftest strokes. When "the path of rectitude" looks bleakest for Maria and Manly, the Colonel adds an amusing consolation to go with "duty" and "honour." "Of this we may be assured," he intones, turning away from true love forever, "that if we are not happy, we shall, at least, deserve to be so. Adieu!" (p. 99).

Royall Tyler made Americans laugh at themselves through their fears and foibles—the first writer in the new nation to do so. It was no mean task bringing "light Censure" (p. 21) to bear upon the self-conscious republican experiment, and no one would prove so adept again before Washington Irving a quarter of a century later. Tyler's careful balances between contrasts created the detachment and supplied the vinegar of true satire. Aware of its sting, Abigail Adams felt certain that *The Contrast* aimed at her new son-in-law, Nabby's choice after Tyler.[46] But surely the playwright reached higher—toward Abigail's husband and the generation of heroes. Tyler must have taken pleasure in the inversion that made Colonel Manly, the Revolution personified, swear loyalty to the materialistic Van Rough (p. 113). One also senses irony behind Manly's naiveté when the hero expresses astonishment over his prospective father-in-law's rejection. "In our country," Manly complains, "the affections are not sacrificed to riches or family aggrandizement" (p. 98). Finally, there is just a touch of derision when Van Rough silences America's wooden soldier: "Come, come, no fine speeches; mind the main chance, young man, and you and I shall always agree" (p. 113). Dramatically, each nuance contributes to the larger uncertainty of whether Manly's honor will survive Van Rough's grasp of the world. Early republicans would ponder this struggle for another thirty years, but of one thing they and *The Contrast* were already convinced. The Founding Fathers had won the girl, and they were going to keep her forever.

Brackenridge and the "Natural Alliance Between Liberty and Letters"

No intellectual could miss the point of Hugh Henry Brackenridge's allegory in the *United States Magazine* of 1779. Unable to win his first love, Miss Muse, the protagonist of Brackenridge's tale moves to Miss Theology, who is "too much pressed upon us," and then to Miss Law, "a grave and comely young lady, a little pitted with the small pox." Miss Law has great promise and possesses prudence and industry, but she is also guarded by "a dry queer genius," a querulous "old fellow of the name of Coke." Understandably, an admirer's eyes easily wander and seize upon the nearest pretty face.[47] Charles Brockden Brown, rejecting law for letters twenty years later, would construct an entire novel upon these tensions in *The Memoirs of Stephen Calvert*. Brackenridge in 1779 necessarily followed a more conservative course. A former chaplain in the Revolutionary army, he joined the Philadelphia bar in 1780 and immediately resettled in the frontier town of Pittsburgh, hoping to make a quick mark in his new profession. Like Trumbull and Tyler, he became a leading lawyer of his region and eventually a judge in the supreme court of his state. A strong sense of vocational responsibility sustained these accomplishments. "The profession of the law is the road to honour and preferment in this country," Brackenridge warned his son, reciting the usual litany. Miss Muse always remained an unworthy alternative. Literature was "a seducing syren from the more profitable pursuits of life."[48]

Yet Brackenridge always wrote and frequently placed the highest value on literary achievement. His energy as Pittsburgh's leading writer rivaled Franklin's in Philadelphia half a century earlier. Brackenridge arranged for the first newspaper in Pittsburgh and became its major contributor. He planned the town's first bookstore and lending library and sponsored the academy that grew into the University of Pittsburgh. Brackenridge's articles on the Federal Constitution in 1788 were courageous responses to regional prejudice against the new government. His *Incidents of the Insurrection in the Western Parts of Pennsylvania in the Year 1794* supplied a vital history of a confusing period. "The Trial of Mamachtaga," an account of a Delaware Indian's bewilderment and natural dignity in a frontier courtroom, drew perhaps the first realistic portrait of an Indian in American literature.[49] Above all, there was *Modern Chivalry*, Brackenridge's eight-hundred-page novel written in seven installments across three decades from 1792 to 1815. A loose collection of anecdotes, incidents, facts, descriptions, observations, speeches, sermons, and poetry on the times, *Modern Chivalry* became popular in the South and West, where it made Brackenridge's name a household word for half a century.[50] In 1815 the author boasted that he could find a copy in every parlor window in Pennsylvania and congratulated himself on "an opus magnum" just one grade below the works of Shakespeare, Homer, and Plutarch. Comprehensive utility was its great strength. "Were all the books in the world lost," he claimed facetiously, "this alone would preserve a germ of every art." Such pretension included an arresting comparison: *Modern Chivalry* more than equaled Thomas Jefferson's entire library at Monticello. "How many are there in an age," Brackenridge wondered, "that could write such a book as this?"[51]

To place Brackenridge's grandiosity against his reservations about literary enterprise is to explore more of the common ground between law and letters in the early republic. In *Modern Chivalry* lawyer and author accept the mutual task of defining American experience, and their joint success lies in the assumed public utility of their work. By 1815 Brackenridge can argue that his novel will "be of service in a republic" because he believes that its earlier portions already have contributed to "a considerable reform of the public way of thinking" as the United States leaves the troubled first decade of the nineteenth century and enters the Era of Good Feeling (pp. 803–806). No lawyer could have expected more of himself. Even the exaggerated humor of *Modern Chivalry* plays upon forms intrinsic to the legal mind of the period. In its self-congratulation, Brackenridge's assumed comprehensiveness, classical stress, utilitarian bias, and bibliographical one-upmanship are the familiar patterns of a lawyer-writer. His allusion to the library at Monticello is also a reminder that Brackenridge has absorbed at Princeton what Jefferson learned earlier at William and Mary, namely, the country rhetoric developed by Whig lawyers in seventeenth-century England.[52]

These influences go a long way toward explaining what Brackenridge means by "such a book as this." Like most members of the legal profession in the 1790s, the author of *Modern Chivalry* feels comfortable only with a system of liberty "gradually moulded to permanence, and durability" (p. 641). He supports practical reform over visionary change (p. 543), careful regulation by positive law (p. 297), absolute respect for legal authority (p. 270), and the goals of balanced government (p. 507). In consequence, he writes against "republicanism run mad" as he sees it in the first decade of the nineteenth century (p. 358). This side of Brackenridge turns *Modern Chivalry* into an elaborate defense of the law.[53]

Of course, the reference to Jefferson, one of many in *Modern Chivalry*, carries another meaning as well. Brackenridge was a lawyer with a particular intellectual heritage to expound and defend. He was a Jeffersonian in politics, fully committed to the democratic trends at work in the new republic. *Modern Chivalry*, patterned on *Don Quixote*, presents Captain John Farrago in the role of "knight-errant" and Teague O'Regan, an uneducated Irish immigrant, as his squire (p. 91). But Farrago and Teague are more than literary pastiches. They come alive as caricatures of the Jeffersonian agrarian ideal and the raw spirit of democracy—a gentleman farmer "of good natural sense, and considerable reading" (p. 6), roaming the country with his energetic but illiterate and often heedless follower.[54] Drama and humor flow from Farrago's attempts to teach the unteachable Teague the refinements of republican virtue. In short, Royall Tyler's veiled conflict between Colonel Manly and Brother Jonathan has moved to center stage in Brackenridge's novel, and the shift signals an exciting new impulse in American literature. Henry Adams first saw the implications. *Modern Chivalry* comes out of the rebellious frontier region of western Pennsylvania and is "more thoroughly American" than any other book of its time, a "satire on democracy . . . written by a democrat and published in the most democratic community of America."[55]

The theme of politics in a democracy gives purpose and momentum to a loose picaresque. Successive installments of *Modern Chivalry* reflect the step-by-step development of democratic thought in America between 1792 and 1815 and form a running commentary on the country's movement from mixed republicanism toward democracy (p. 530). The four volumes of part one progress from conventional satire on the clergy and the military, which every Whig could laugh at in 1792 (pp. 30–41, 69–75), to commentary on the English orientation dividing Federalist from non-Federalist (pp. 88–89), to frankly partisan criticisms of President Washington's levees and financial policies in 1793 (pp. 202–203, 215–219), and finally in 1797 to the full-fledged democrat's call for change despite the terrors of the French Revolution (pp. 312–316). The three volumes of part two, published from 1804 through 1815, then offer a far more elaborate defense of party division (pp. 358, 383). Here Brackenridge equates democracy with virtue (pp. 404, 497, 530), argues for popular suffrage (p. 533), and predicts a progressive society (p. 734).

The link between legal thought and democratic faith in *Modern Chivalry* is the Jeffersonian ideal—an ideal legal in form but democratic in content. As Jefferson in *Notes on the State of Virginia* presents a political-legal theory for unifying a continental republic on democratic terms, so Brackenridge in *Modern Chivalry* applies that theory to test the meaning of the democratic experiment over time and space. Both writers seek a rational democracy between aristocracy and radical democracy, and Brackenridge agrees with Jefferson's plan for achieving this moderate alternative. A government "founded on free principles" must "bind up the several branches of government by certain laws" and can survive only as long as power is "so divided and balanced among several bodies of magistracy, as that no one [can] transcend their legal limits." On the other hand, even the best of governments will degenerate unless power is "shared among all the people." Only the people are beyond corruption and only the people consistently "elect the real good and wise" as leaders, thereby insuring a natural aristocracy based upon virtue and talent. Such a government can be called a rational democracy because it functions as an emblem of the rational, educated mind, making enlightened decisions for an entire organism.[56]

To the writer in a rational democracy falls the crucial task of educating the people in the use of their natural reason and virtue. Brackenridge's acceptance of this role has much to do with his inflated claims for *Modern Chivalry*. "There is a natural alliance between liberty and letters," writes the novelist. "Men of letters . . . naturally ally themselves with the *democratic interest* in a commonwealth." Noting as well that a knowledge of political rights can only come from education and study, Brackenridge reminds his fellow citizens that the lawyer as man of letters had been "the first to give the alarm and assert the rights of the people" during the Revolution (p. 401). Lest the point be missed, *Modern Chivalry* often has the lawyer or judge in the educational role of the man of letters.[57] A writer's general goal is to improve the morals and manners of the people through education (pp. 360, 449, 615); his specific aim, to replace "bandying the term liberty" and "the stirrings of men's minds" with "deliberate reason, and prudent temperament" (p. 348). Goal and aim are possible because "democracy has its strength in strict integrity; in perfect delicacy; in elevation and dignity of mind." In *Modern Chivalry* "the democrat is the true chevalier, who, though he wears not crosses, or the emblazoned arms of heraldry, yet is ready to do right, and justice to every one" (p. 404).

Such an exalted vision of thought and conduct could hardly sustain itself on the rough-and-tumble frontier of western Pennsylvania. One of the few educated men in early Pittsburgh, Brackenridge once likened his situation to that of "a traveller in the Island of Borneo, or other parts of the East Indies, with a thousand monkeys leaping and chattering amongst the trees, and incommoding the Caravan by the fall of excrement." Inevitably *Modern Chivalry* turns into a record of personal disappointment in democratic living and an exposé of the weaknesses in Jeffersonian theory.[58] Captain Farrago, the Jeffersonian farmer, possesses "greater knowledge of books than of the world." Like Don Quixote, he is "unacquainted with the world" until he begins to move within it (pp. 6, 53, 228). His efforts to impose a Jeffersonian perspective upon unfamiliar country supply much of the humor in *Modern Chivalry*.

Amazed at the tenacious corruption and ignorance he finds everywhere, Farrago gradually learns that the human mind is "a strange compound of the rational and irrational, and it is only by turns that the rational predominates" (p. 719). Men do not seek knowledge or follow reason; nor do they choose the best leaders. The Captain's attempt to reason directly with the people leads only to mob violence (pp. 302–308). Every representative assembly and organization in *Modern Chivalry* is made up of fools (pp. 100–103, 674), and "the swinish multitude" persecutes learned men when it finds them (pp. 367–375, 419–420, 430–431). The symbol of this recalcitrant ignorance is the Captain's servant, Teague O'Regan, "a mixture of simplicity with low cunning" (p. 628). Unqualified for any position, Teague finds himself a candidate for Congress, a prospective minister, a likely member of Franklin's Philosophical Society, and a sudden addition to Philadelphia society as Major O'Regan. "The great moral of this book," Brackenridge explains, "is the evil of men seeking office for which they are not qualified" (p. 611). Teague actually becomes an excise officer of the federal government, a judge, and secretary of state in a new western government. Only force and subterfuge can control him. Farrago's many unsuccessful efforts to prepare his servant for public service ridicule the notion of human progress.[59] Brackenridge scores these points by placing Teague in increasing opposition to his master (pp. 735, 748, 781) and by recording the Captain's growing pessimism over the use of reason and the prospect of reform (pp. 658, 782–783).

By the final volume of *Modern Chivalry*, Thomas Jefferson is literally a mammoth ox "out of his district" on the frontier (p. 649). Here, as the personification implies, the leveling principle has advanced to the point where animals are equal to humans. A monkey appears as clerk of courts, and dogs become lawyers (pp. 700–704). In the meantime Captain Farrago has passed westward through settlements named Lack-learning and Mad-cap (pp. 523–526), and he has seen enough to temper the most ardent idealism. As governor

of the newest settlement in the wilderness, Farrago eventually imposes solutions when the people act out of ignorance. "Do you take
me for *Jefferson?*" he asks the assembled populace. "You are mistaken
if you think I have so good an opinion of you" (p. 783). The writer
then steps from "out of sight and behind the curtain" to announce
"having a fling at president Jefferson," but he also acknowledges
having *"erred with him,"* and the admission is an instructive reminder
of the Brackenridge who once wrote a paean to Jefferson as the
statesman and sage who restored Virgin Justice to American soil.[60]

The later Brackenridge remains a Jeffersonian at heart, but his
rhetoric emphasizes forms preserving democracy more than ideology. *Law Miscellanies*, a five-hundred-page compilation of law reports
written in the last decade of Brackenridge's life, explains those legal
forms and symbolizes the author's growing reliance on law and
order.[61] *Modern Chivalry*, in its last installments, becomes a fascinating expression of this shift in perspective. By dipping his pen
"in the inkstand of human nature" and through "the lowest possible
capacity of what is found amongst men," the novelist gropes toward
a different kind of Jeffersonian balance between democracy and law
(pp. 756, 674). The result is perhaps the most perceptive analysis
of changing conditions in early republican culture.

Like every good Jeffersonian, Brackenridge places paramount importance upon education as the guarantee of republican virtue and
worries about the scarcity of sources of learning in an unformed
country. "I take the pulpit, the courts of judicature, and the press,
to be the three great means of sustaining and enlightening a republic," he summarizes at one point (p. 351). But even as he writes,
Brackenridge is documenting the failure of American newspapers
to rise above partisan slander and exposing the incompetence of the
clergy (pp. 331–351, 41, 99–104). Religious enthusiasm and revivalism—"symptoms of a diseased understanding"—also stand in the
way of meaningful education (pp. 255–260, 628–629). Only the
courts of justice remain as "a school of justice, and honor," and
Brackenridge is quick to trace "a strange coincidence between liberty, and an established jurisprudence" (pp. 351, 395).

Reliance on the judicial process as pedagogical tool makes the
courtroom a constitutive metaphor in *Modern Chivalry*. Again and
again Brackenridge used courtroom settings and procedures to in-
struct "Tom, Dick, and Harry, in the woods" in the meaning of

republicanism (p. 471). There are half a dozen trial scenes and as many more commentaries on the law.[62] Humor dominates these episodes, but the underlying lessons are always the same: "Mutual toleration and forbearance, in our sentiments, with regard to the legality, or expedience of measures, is the soul of democracy" (p. 531), and "It is a principle of good citizenship, especially in a republican government, to pay respect to the laws" (p. 270). Knowledge of the law has such general relevance because "the nature of law is liberal; and gives understanding; and wherever there is sound sense, there will be honesty" (p. 699). With the understanding that law gives, one can hope "to see the democracy move in the groove of our noble constitution" (p. 545). For as Brackenridge already has explained, "Legal knowledge, and political learning, are the stamina of the constitution" (p. 433).

Here, in the presumed power of law to instill virtue, is the inspiration of the lawyer-writer in American literature. The intensity of Brackenridge's belief in the integration of positive or man-made law with the principles of universal justice and moral honesty turns writing—"having certain ideas to inculcate"—into duty (pp. 351, 224). The law properly conveyed becomes a patriotic mission. Of course, the legal system itself falls well short of this goal. In *Modern Chivalry* the avarice of Counsellor Grab and the ignorance of Justice Underchin plunge the law into a bottomless pit (pp. 142–147, 286–290). Some areas of the legal system still require basic clarification. "A very material difference," the Captain notes as he watches a court wrestle with distinctions in pleading that will determine whether a convicted defendant will be fined or hung (pp. 152–153). Even a correct sense of the law can misfire through judicial error. Tarred and feathered, Teague O'Regan is remanded to the custody of animal keepers under the laws of *ferae naturae* when the chief justice of the state directs his jury to find Teague a wild beast on the evidence presented (pp. 322–324).

Fools and knaves misuse the law, and men of virtue occasionally blunder. But mistakes in the courtroom strengthen the lawyer-writer's responsibility. Correction lies in "tracing the rules of justice" more carefully for all to see (p. 699). The principles of universal justice rest upon fixed reason, and, as Brackenridge adds, "the application of these principles to particular cases, forms a great part of the common law" (p. 372). By extension, "the common law is general reason adapted to particular cases" (p. 338). It has been worked out across time in a million forgotten courtrooms and constitutes perhaps the clearest product of the rational mind in history. As such, the law of Anglo-Saxon culture requires only proper explanation and occasional amendment to form a perfect safeguard of the new rational democracy in America. *Modern Chivalry* and *Law Miscellanies* are part of the explanatory and amendatory process; they explain the role and application of the law, and in so doing, they preserve the rational democracy that the law allows and, in part, defines.

Brackenridge worries more about an obstacle beyond error and even villainy—the ingrained hostility of the American people themselves to all forms of legal authority. "Down with the lawyers," he observes, "has been the language of the human heart ever since the first institution of society." Now, in post-Revolutionary America, reformist zeal has sharpened a natural antipathy to the law and its agents, and nowhere is this resentment greater than among Brackenridge's own neighbors, the farmers and tradesmen of western Pennsylvania (pp. 486–487, 446–447, 540). Particular measures like the Federalist excise tax on whiskey, along with a general lack of education, have compounded the problem for western communities. "A breath in favor of the law, was sufficient to ruin any man," Brackenridge writes in description of his region in 1795. "It was considered as a badge of toryism . . . To talk against the law, was the way to office and emolument . . . It was the *shibboleth* of safety, and the ladder of ambition."[63] In this precarious situation Brackenridge and America receive a dangerous blow from an unlikely source. Thomas Jefferson's condemnation of the judiciary in 1801— Brackenridge calls it the first and greatest error of Jefferson's presidency (p. 786)—encourages extremists to attack the law itself.[64] The anti-law mobs of the western regions obsess Brackenridge. "It is easier to destroy than to substitute," Brackenridge reminds his readers, and he warns them that demagogues invariably attack the law first (pp. 573, 525). Significantly, Captain Farrago's last address as governor is an abdication speech. He predicts a French Revolution in the West with the guillotine suspended over American necks (p. 784).

Such pessimism gives *Modern Chivalry* a final, mordant twist. Acknowledging the similarity to Don Quixote in the speech that challenges Jeffersonian idealism, Captain Farrago comforts himself by contending that he cannot "be considered as resembling that Spaniard in taking a wind-mill for a giant" (p. 783). Of course not, but the Captain is the chevalier of democracy, and in this role he follows a comparable delusion.[65] Farrago's belief in a rational democracy based upon an educated populace has proven impractical. His attempts "to do right, and justice to every one" have produced neither enlightenment nor reciprocity but rather contempt and rejection. Meanwhile, the plan to prepare Teague for meaningful public service has failed miserably (pp. 142, 735, 783). Farrago represents the intellectual, gentlemanly, republican past; Teague, the ill-mannered, democratic future.[66] Brackenridge projects an inheritance every bit as futile for the nineteenth century as Faulkner, in *Absalom, Absalom!*, means transmission of Sutpen's Hundred to the idiot Jim Bond to be in the twentieth.

Painfully aware of the parallels between Farrago's hopes and his own literary aspirations, Hugh Henry Brackenridge also saw and accepted a more personal failure. In darker moments *Modern Chivalry* appeared "a wide waste, producing nothing profitable" (p. 619). The neglect of his book by republican leaders was a particular source of chagrin to a writer intent on saving his country. "I wish I could get this work to make a little more noise," Brackenridge protested in 1793 after publishing three volumes of *Modern Chivalry*. "Will no body speak? What? Ho! are ye all asleep in the hold there down at Philadelphia?" (p. 250). Behind the complaint was the realization that America's true knights in shining armor had created the republic as Founding Fathers (p. 229). James Madison, a classmate, friend, and sometime collaborator in the Whig Literary Club at Princeton, emerged as one of those knights, while Brackenridge, "lying at the back of a mountain here; the cool west wind blowing on me" (p. 202), remained insignificant on the periphery. Caught between the raw democratic spirit of the West and the more tempered leadership of the East, Brackenridge won the trust of neither. His awareness of the problem turned the lawyer and judge increasingly toward a private world of books and writing. He came to regret the move west, and his confession late in life gave a last eerie echo to Royall Tyler's *The Contrast*.[67] "I have committed a great error," Brackenridge told his son, "in not attending sufficiently to the main chance."

CHAPTER 5

THE CASE OF
CHARLES BROCKDEN BROWN

"A Mere Holder of the Pen"

Nowhere is the bond between vocation and literature more important, or more consistently ignored, than in the writings of America's
first major novelist.[1] Charles Brockden Brown wrote five significant
novels between 1798 and 1800—*Wieland, Ormond, Arthur Mervyn,
Edgar Huntly*, and *Memoirs of Stephen Calvert*—and he used his fiction
as a fantasy world for projecting occupational difficulties. The puz-
zling rebellions of major protagonists, the long descriptions of yellow
fever epidemics, the contradictory nature of Brown's villains, the
matriarchal focus of his stories, and, in general, the emotive basis
of his language all take on new meaning in this biographical context.
Moreover, Brown's preoccupation with vocational problems included a sophisticated general awareness of the early American writer's dilemma. His extensive magazine writings on the subject of
authorship provide the best documentation we have of the tenuous,
uncertain place of the novelist in republican culture.[2]

For Brown the moment of vocational choice always remained
distinct and ominous. "It behooves us," he told the members of his
early literary society, "to make preparations for that awful crisis in
choosing our future parts." Later he added that "the first step . . . is
frequently the point on which our fate hangs suspended, and may
elevate us to an eminent height of happiness, or sink us into the
profoundest abyss of misery."[3] These fears grew out of a particular
crisis in 1793 when Brown rejected the law as his profession after
six years in the Philadelphia law office of Alexander Wilcocks. The

decision led to permanent disapproval from family and friends, and
it plunged Brown into a five-year period of aimless unhappiness, a
personal abyss of misery central to the dark patterns of the later
novels.

The nature of Brown's predicament in 1793 emerges in an eyewitness account by a family friend:

> They [Brown's family] pressed him continually to the practice of
> law . . . he gave expectations of compliance but without sufficiently
> explaining his objections, he secretly fostered a determination adverse
> to their wishes & was fully resolved never to appear at the bar. In
> this very embarrassing situation he became unhappy & often to shake
> off importunities with which he thought he could not comply & yet
> wanted fortitude openly to resist, he wandered from home & gave
> himself up to gloomy reflections.[4]

These observations suggest the stresses on concealment, on secret
guilt, and on perpetual familial conflict in *Wieland, Edgar Huntly,*
and *Arthur Mervyn.* More immediately, the account indicates the
considerable pressure that Brown's family brought to bear upon an
untenable situation. The rejection of law had been a negative decision, without alternatives in an age when literary effort was always
incidental to public service and a career. Even Brown wrote of
vocational application as a firm duty, and, like his family, he regarded his position as an impossible one. "I utterly despise myself . . . Nothing but a wide vacuity presents itself," he wrote in
January 1793 concerning his inability to study law. "Was I born for
nothing?"[5]

The situation plunged Brown into an extended period of despair
so deep as to preclude sustained creative effort for years. More
tangible consequences included social disgrace and financial dependence until the age of thirty; he was the idle fifth son in a
hardworking family of Philadelphia merchants. Indeed, Brown's
entire career in fiction must be understood against the necessary
indulgence and growing impatience of this family of businessmen.
All of the major novels were written while a father and four working
brothers waited for Brown to assume his place in the family concern.
Accordingly, vocational failings were never far from literary craft,
and the novels themselves represented a defense against familial
pressure. The writer even argued, until facts proved him wrong,
that his literature could furnish an independent income.[6] When

Brown in 1801 finally accepted a position in the Philadelphia firm of James Brown and Company, the vocational hiatus of eight years was over. So was the novelist's career.

Brown coped with the pressures of 1793 to 1801 through a series of evasions. As he himself wrote, "I seize any thing however weak and dubious, by which I can hope to raise myself from that profound abyss of ignominy and debasement, into which I am sunk by my own reflections."[7] Physical flight was one recourse. During this period, Brown left Philadelphia for New York whenever possible, and he wrote most of the novels there rather than at home. Philadelphia in 1800 was the primary cultural and literary center of the republic, but for Brown his own city represented only familial obligation and unfulfilled duties.[8] Literature, of course, provided the main defense mechanism for escaping conventional pressures. In a close friend's words, Brown "formed a world of his own in which he delighted to dwell."[9] *Clara Howard or The Enthusiasm of Love* (1801) affords a thinly veiled account of the novelist's personal stance: "He was smitten with the charms of literature, and, greatly to his sister's disappointment and vexation, refused to engage in any of those professions which lead to riches and honour. He adopted certain antiquated and unfashionable notions about the 'grandeur of retreat,' 'honourable poverty,' a studious life, and the dignity of imparting knowledge to others. The desk, bar, and pulpit had no attractions for him" (VI, 318–319). Most of Brown's early protagonists rely heavily upon fantasy and self-absorption as deliberate escapes from reality. When in society, the Rhapsodist waits "impatiently" for solitude because he believes only in the enjoyment of self. His life, as Brown describes it, is "literally a dream." Alcuin, in the early essay of that name, prefers to populate his social sphere with imaginary extensions of his fancy rather than with real people. "The Man At Home" seeks similar self-absorption within what he calls a world of conjecture without limits.[10]

A fantasy world of musings was necessary because there were no kindred minds in 1793 to support either Brown's repudiation of the law or his escape into literary solitude. Fiction lacked respectability as a literary genre in Federalist America, while law represented a major topic of general interest within the realm of letters. When William Wirt and countless others announced that "the bar in America is the road to honour," they meant that law provided the best intellectual challenge as well as the most convenient avenue to wealth and preferment.[11] Hence, William Dunlap, a companion and Brown's first biographer, could legitimately summarize the novelist's choice of literature over law as one between "the error of indulging this romancing vein" and accepting "the duties of real life." Forty years after the event, American intellectuals were still dismissing Brown's "fickleness of purpose" and "poor sophistry" regarding the legal profession. Brown knew what others thought, and he described himself as "one who is conscious that none of his duties are discharged."[12]

The writer's isolation and admission of failure nourished a permanent ambivalence toward his rejected profession. In "A Series of Original Letters" dated 1794, Brown compared the prospect of law, "the road to honour," to the reality he found, "a jumble of iniquities and crudities." He admired the intellectual nature of the law but thought the profession itself contemptible when measured against the goal of an ideal society.[13] The same preoccupation and ambiguity spilled into the later novels. In *Ormond or The Secret Witness* (1799) Brown as narrator dismissed the law because of "its lying assertions and hateful artifices," but he still felt that the professions provided the best means for fulfilling necessary social responsibilities. "The pursuits of law and medicine," he wrote in the same year, "enhance our power over the liberty, property, and health of mankind . . . enabling us to obviate, by intellectual exertions, many of the evils that infest the world." A sketch from 1805 juxtaposed the "tormenting subtleties of Blackstone and Coke" with the knowledge that "law leads more directly and effectually to honour, power, and profit in America." In this period, Brown's *Literary Magazine and American Register* contained heavy-handed burlesques of materialistic law students, descriptions of ideal communities ruined by grasping lawyers, and a reference to the entire field as "my unfortunate profession." Yet the same pages praised the law as "a very prosperous and gainful profession in the United States," traced the security and happiness of many citizens to the abilities of the honorable lawyer, and dismissed those who criticized the profession as knaves and fools.[14]

These uncertainties with their emphasis on honor must be set off against the writer's realization of lost honor. When he left the law in 1793, Brown deserted the separate vocation essential to respectable authorship in early America, but he never relinquished the gentlemanly ideal on which that conception was based. His acceptance of that larger ideal was clearly stated:

> While the *poor author*, that is to say, the author by trade, is regarded with indifference or contempt, the *author*, that is, the man who devotes to composition the leisure secured to him by hereditary affluence, or by a lucrative profession or office, obtains from mankind an higher, and more lasting, and more genuine reverence, than any other class of mortals. As there is nothing I should more fervently deprecate than to be enrolled in the former class, so there is nothing to which I more ardently aspire, than to be numbered among the latter.[15]

Brown was not the recipient of "hereditary affluence," nor did he marry money, as so many of his fictional protagonists would manage to do. The major writer of 1798 to 1801 would always remain the poor author, the "author by trade" whom Brown affected to despise.

His writings, in consequence, are filled with expressions of disregard. In 1794 the future novelist is "unalterably determine[d] never to be an author." Later "The Scribbler" is a "poor beggarly wight" and "a mere holder of the pen" who has "often resolved to cast it away, tired and ashamed of its incorrigible depravity." The protagonist of *Memoirs of Stephen Calvert* actually dismisses all writers of fiction as "preachers of duplicity"; he traces his downfall to a youthful propensity to read their works.[16] Obviously there is a touch of the literary poseur in such disclaimers, for Brown's works also reveal commitment to imaginative writing, respect for the novel as an art form, and pride in authorship. The most famous affirmation came in a letter to Thomas Jefferson along with a gift copy of *Wieland*. "No man," he wrote Jefferson, "holds a performance which he has deliberately offered to the world in contempt."[17] And yet, Brown—a bundle of contradictions—could repudiate all of his own efforts in fiction with expressions of something very close to contempt. It was in 1803, well after the completion of all eight novels, that he delivered his public apologia: "I have written much, but take much blame to myself for something which I have written and take no praise for any thing. I should enjoy a larger share of my own respect, at the present moment, if nothing had ever flowed from my pen, the production of which could be traced to me."[18] These fluctuations between creative satisfaction and self-abasement suggest a writer who trusted his own talent but not its use.

The author of thirty volumes of novels, stories, imaginative narratives, political pamphlets, and magazines, Brown could never decide how to regard this impressive collection, and he was particularly hesitant about the works of fiction. Could the novel constitute an appropriate forum for a man of letters in Federalist and Jeffersonian America? The very act of writing compounded and intensified feelings of inadequacy by drawing attention to the inferior status of the author by trade, and each novel contained the self-scrutiny of one who knew that his craft was intellectually unacceptable to the world around him. These tensions run throughout the fiction, but never more so than in Brown's often ignored *Memoirs of Stephen Calvert*. Here we see how completely specific vocational anxieties could dominate the art of an early American writer.

Memoirs of Stephen Calvert: "The Torments of Idleness"

Although *Stephen Calvert* was not published in book form like the other novels, it was written during Brown's major period and serialized in the *Monthly Magazine and American Review*. William Dunlap reprinted the unfinished work in 1815 in his two-volume biography.[19] A brief summary illustrates the close parallels to Brown's own vocational problems in law. Stephen Calvert is an identical twin, but his brother, Felix, has been lost since birth. They are the sons of an unsuccessful lawyer whose profession is "obnoxious to all his indolent and literary habits" and who is hated by his own father (p. 296). Stephen has been given his lost brother's name, and this circumstance alone raises obvious identity problems when the missing twin reappears. Stephen as protagonist is torn between his feelings for two wealthy women in the novel—a plain cousin, Louisa Calvert, to whom he is formally obligated, and the mysterious, exotic Clelia Neville, whom he loves. His main opponent is a self-appointed mentor and lawyer named Sidney Carlton. Sidney frustrates the hero's every wish, exposes each shortcoming, and delivers periodic judgments on his behavior. Calvert, caught between duty and desire, tries unsuccessfully to keep his relationships with Louisa and Clelia distinct. When Sidney discovers the secret attachment to Clelia Neville, he reveals Stephen's "innate, dastardly, sordid wickedness" for all to see (p. 439). Calvert can face neither his family nor his own feelings of guilt and flees into the wilderness, where he tells his story from a final hiding place.

The hero of *Stephen Calvert* moves within a prism of shame and remorse; he cannot reconcile the external requirements of social obligation with the private dictates of a creative imagination. These lines of force develop in the conflict between artist and lawyer. Sidney Carlton's hold over Stephen is entirely vocational, and the S.C. letter correlation turns the two fictional characters into alter egos for the author. They are the same age, but Sidney easily blocks the inexperienced Stephen from marrying a woman both men seek (p. 337). Sidney, "newly initiated into the legal profession," is formidable and superior in every way, and he is the source of the first uneasiness Stephen Calvert has ever known (p. 311). Nor is the lawyer slow to press his advantage. "You have hitherto dreamed away your life in solitude," charges Sidney. "You have no practical acquaintance with yourself, or with the nature of the beings who surround you. You have nothing but distorted and crude conceptions, and passions lawless and undisciplined" (p. 341). Vocational responsibility entitles Sidney to treat Stephen, the literary recluse, as an erring child whose expressed emotions and plans cannot be taken seriously. The latter's ambitions are "visionary schemes of happiness" based on "incurable frailty" and "tottering structure" (p. 439). Although the lawyer is frequently mistaken in his accusations, Stephen concedes defeat at every turn and blames only himself for allowing "the torments of idleness" to determine his fate (p. 433).

Brown's preoccupation with this unequal contest comes from being on the receiving end of just such a dialogue between 1790 and 1793. In correspondence from these years between Brown and a fellow law student named William Wood Wilkins, the latter plays the assertive, critical role found later in Sidney Carlton.[20] When the uncertain Brown complains of his unhappiness and "unseasonable languors," Wilkins, confident in his own decision to practice law, traces Brown's problem to literary self-indulgence: "Renounce then, I entreat you, your allegiance to fancy! . . . Despise the distressing power of her wand, but bow in manly submission to the sceptre of reason." Brown's unwillingness to follow such advice leads to censure of his moral code, masculinity, and patriotism. He is accused of placing his own amusement before the wishes of his friends and the service of his country. "When will the moment arrive," wonders Wilkins, "when Charles will lay aside that indolence and despondency which is unworthy of him." Though writing to a peer, Brown defers constantly to Wilkins' superiority as tutor and teacher much in the way Stephen Calvert acknowledges Sidney Carlton. "If I condemn myself," Brown notes in self-disgust, "why should I expect not to be condemned by you?"

The two female protagonists in *Stephen Calvert* are projections of Brown's vocational plight, Louisa Calvert representing the virtuous but unattractive option of law and social responsibility and Clelia Neville symbolizing the illicit alternative of the creative artist. As with the law student's initial professional commitment, so Stephen agrees to marry Louisa before he knows her. His active imagination and "the vague encomiums" of relatives have led him to expect an attractive opportunity. Instead, his cousin proves to be tedious, ugly, and boring (p. 314). As a companion for the artist, the good Louisa is particularly hopeless: "Her voice was coarse and monotonous, and wholly unadapted to music; but she was, nevertheless, fond of the art, and when alone, was accustomed to sing" (p. 320). Calvert is ready to marry anyway to improve his financial situation and to avoid the rebukes of family and friends. Nevertheless, his formal proposal is "tinctured with dejection" and "without rapture" (p. 321).

Clelia Neville, on the other hand, appears so beautiful that Calvert's senses are temporarily overpowered. "Clothed with nymph-like and fascinating graces," she is an accomplished painter, musician, and conversationalist, and her voice offers a flexibility of range and tone beyond any Calvert has known (pp. 355–361). Stephen's relationship with Louisa is based on social ties, a sense of duty, and the expectations of the external world; the original bond with Clelia comes instead through an impulsive act of personal generosity. Calvert has saved Clelia from death by fire in a scene where courage, spontaneity, and inspiration necessarily replace studied application and reasoned obligation (p. 322).

The hero is bound to both ladies but by mutually exclusive considerations. Real happiness with either is impossible because of the other, and, analogous to Brown's vocational anxieties, the protagonist can find no avenue toward acceptable fulfillment. Every choice excludes part of Calvert's nature as the incompatibilities of his situation drive him deeper and deeper into intolerable falsehood (p. 393). Meanwhile a powerful and hostile parental sphere watches over these events. Throughout *Stephen Calvert*, the adult world either intrudes with conscious malice or acts out of a narrow self-interest and a conventional rigidity that block the natural feelings of the younger generation.[21] Only the young lawyer, Sidney Carlton, moves easily within this older world, its natural agent.

Stephen Calvert eventually loses everything, including his own identity. Both women have refused him when he finally flees into the wilderness, and though he is unjustly accused, Stephen always remains a guilty suppliant asking forgiveness from a world that sees only an "inconsiderate and headstrong youth" (p. 463). The real Felix Calvert meanwhile has appeared from Europe to reclaim his rightful name and identity. Not surprisingly, this European version of the artist displays an immediate ascendancy over his more parochial American twin. Clelia Neville, the artist's muse, carries a locket in her bosom, and the face upon the locket is that of the real Felix. Stephen's face bears the scars of a New World accident, his hair is dark, and he views things through anxious hazel eyes. Blond and unmarked, Felix exudes "benign complacency"; he has eyes that Clelia calls "an heavenly blue" (pp. 468, 410–411). For Stephen alone the fraternal encounter on the final page of the novel is a cataclysmic "passage into a new state of being" (p. 472). Sidney Carlton has arranged this meeting between Stephen and the long-lost Felix, and it reads like a trade-in for a better model.

Looking back over his story from limbo, the defeated Stephen still regards his moments with the beautiful Clelia as his time of greatest exultation. "I now look back upon them as the tissue of some golden dream," he notes (p. 374). But the ubiquitous lawyer already has condemned Clelia out of hand. After placing spies upon her every action, Sidney's verdict is simple and overriding: "I am convinced of her depravity" (p. 424). Since Stephen cannot long endure the disapproval of family and friends, capitulation is assured. The price of forgiveness will be renunciation of the artistic ideal and acceptance of responsibility within the world. And so, after years of resistance, it must have been for Charles Brockden Brown as well. Late in 1800, shortly after completing what we have of *Stephen Calvert*, Brown quit the literary circle of friends he had made in New York to take his assigned place in the family firm in Philadelphia. Stephen Calvert's acquiescence and loss of identity had unfortunate parallels for American literature. As Donald Ringe has suggested, "with the abandonment of *Stephen Calvert* and with the completion of *Arthur Mervyn* in 1800, the major phase of Brown's career as a novelist was over, and many changes in both his life and his writing were soon to occur."[22]

Wieland: "Judges, Advocates, and Auditors Were Panic-Struck"

The opposing worlds of Stephen Calvert and Sidney Carlton recur throughout Brown's fiction but with shifting consequences. Stephen's imaginative realm of "ideal forms" and "visionary ardours" breaks against social reality because he is "absurd in practice" (pp. 309, 325). He recognizes only the strengths in his adversary, the lawyer, "author of all my subsequent calamities" (p. 311). Brown's other major novels simply reverse the nature of this calamity. In *Wieland, Edgar Huntly, Ormond,* and *Arthur Mervyn*, it is the ordinary vocational world that shatters when it comes into conflict with the realms of the imagination. In each work, central characters are forced to cope with a new level of reality after the rules and laws of society no longer apply.[23]

Brown's need to trivialize the law is an important ingredient in these "transformations." Again and again in the novels, he defensively insists on the law's inapplicability to real problems or its shallowness as a solution to those problems. Indeed, this emphasis helps to explain Brown's noted fascination with William Godwin. *Caleb Williams* was the American writer's favorite novel, in part because law emerges as the real villain in that story. Brown's characters, like Godwin's, receive no comfort, protection, or meaning from the law. Only fools or villains use the law against others, and heroes refuse to use legal remedies even in a just cause.[24]

Wieland, Brown's first published novel, stands for the proposition that rational justice is beyond human capacity.[25] We quickly learn that "the law is a system of expense, delay, and uncertainty" (1, 58). When Wieland slaughters his wife and children after strange voices have drawn him into a fit of religious frenzy, the act has psychological ramifications that prevent any legal system from dealing intelligibly with the tragic results. In Brown's ensuing courtroom scene, the law's officials share a general helplessness: "Judges, advocates, and auditors were panic-struck and breathless with attention" (1, 182). The jury "reluctantly" reaches a guilty verdict, but

Theodore Wieland protests in language that every major character in *Wieland* accepts at some point. "I know not what is crime; what actions are evil in their ultimate and comprehensive tendency, or what are good" (I, 195). Locked within psychological vortices, Wieland easily eludes the law's petty restraints; he repeatedly escapes confinement to wreak havoc among the remaining characters. Laws fail to protect even the most secure from the actions of a madman, and each major character in *Wieland* comes close to madness.[26] Real villains either escape the courts altogether, like Maxwell the seducer, or turn out to be strangely innocent of imputed crimes, as in the case of Carwin the biloquist or ventriloquist.

Brown's repeated theme is the inability of law to control or even to define behavior. In *Arthur Mervyn* the main character wanders through a shadowy world of murder, theft, adultery, forgery, and commercial fraud where legal remedies offer no recourse. As naive as he is, young Mervyn quickly learns that truth and innocence count for little against the inflexible and narrow-minded ministers of the law (II, 112–113). When he finally gains the upper hand, he refuses to use the courts for any purpose. "That is a force which I shall never apply," says Arthur, joining Constantia Dudley of *Ormond* as one whose inherent virtue obviates a recourse to legal sanction (III, 169; VI, 89–90). Edgar Huntly's own attempt to act as a legal agent proves futile and dangerous for all concerned. In the role of a detective or policeman, he investigates the murder of a friend, but his efforts only lead toward darker psychological realities. "Shall we," asks Edgar in growing confusion, "impute guilt where there is no design?" (IV, 87). In the opening pages of *Edgar Huntly*, Brown already has shown that legal imputations of guilt and innocence mean little. Edgar's stubborn efforts to act as an instrument of social justice eventually drive him to the brink of insanity and threaten to destroy everyone around him.[27]

While the novelist used law to illustrate misgivings about the world, he continued to accept the social standards that made his own position such an uncomfortable one. Vocation, or the lack of one, is an important gauge of character in Brown's fiction, and all of the novels inveigh against the dangers of indolence.[28] His villains are invariably men of idleness; they appear as mysterious strangers whose lack of apparent occupation provides the first clue of moral corruption. Welbeck in *Arthur Mervyn* begins as a strange nabob or rich gentleman, one who "does nothing but walk about" (II, 60). His strongest single objection is to work itself: "To be subjected to the necessity of honest labour was the heaviest of all evils, and one from which he was willing to escape by the commission of suicide" (II, 200). These views, of course, form a direct antithesis to Arthur Mervyn's discovery of direction and meaning through his commitment to the medical profession (III, 178). The wealthy Ormond and Carwin, the ventriloquist of *Wieland,* complete an unbroken pattern of dubious figures whose trademark is neglect of vocation. Like Welbeck, Carwin explicitly hates labor of every sort. Since he is also ambitious but dislikes the liberal professions, his situation is one of hopeless dissatisfaction. "I was destitute of all stedfast views. Without profession or habits of industry, or sources of permanent revenue, the world appeared to me an ocean on which my bark was set afloat without compass or sail."[29] Within *Wieland* Carwin functions as just such a vessel, set afloat without purpose or direction. His impulsive use of ventriloquism has no larger aim than amusement, but it starts Wieland, who hears the projected voice as divine revelation, down a grim path of insanity and murder.

Carwin's very aimlessness is significant. More than any other figure in Brown's fiction, he stands for the artist and the artist's unique power. As such, Carwin brings us to the other side of the problem Brown faced in the 1790s—the presumed idleness of the mere artist in republican culture. Just as the novelist needed to portray the law's unimportance to justify professional failure, so he labored to cover his vulnerability as a writer of fiction. *Wieland* opens with a long genealogy that seems extraneous until one realizes that the difficulties of earlier generations neatly bracket Brown's own problems as a working artist.[30] The first two chapters of *Ormond* represent a similar digression. These pages describe the committed artist's inability to cope with the world in mundane vocational terms. Stephen Dudley, trained in Italy to become a professional painter of "comprehensive genius and indefatigable industry," proves completely incompetent when summoned home to run the family's apothecary shop: "The indulgence of his father had contributed to instil into him prejudices, in consequence of which a certain species of disgrace was annexed to every employment of which the only purpose was gain. His present situation not only precluded all those pursuits which exalt and harmonize the feelings, but was detested by him as something humiliating and ignominious" (VI, 7).

The relevance of such opinions to Brown's situation must have been clear enough to the family of merchants in Philadelphia. Brown argues that the artist's aspirations and the businessman's goals form mutually exclusive ambitions. This suggestion, in turn, rests upon an important unstated premise—namely, upon the presumed independent integrity of the artist's role. For if the frameworks of Stephen Calvert and Sidney Carlton exclude each other by definition, then the major issue is inevitable conflict rather than adolescent rebellion; we see alternatives, not a continuum from personal indulgence to social responsibility. The premise remains implicit because Brown could never quite insist upon the artist's separate function. The measure of his vacillation may be taken between the impotence of Stephen Calvert and the extraordinary prowess of Carwin. As the figure for the artist in *Wieland*, the latter uses his talent with breathtaking effect to destroy his enemies.

Brown deliberately endows Carwin with unlimited creativity but no context. Because he must use his gifts in a vacuum, Carwin does so unwisely and in ways that are inevitably misunderstood. As he tells us, "I have handled a tool of wonderful efficacy without malignant intentions, but without caution" (1, 217). The artist's predicament must be seen against the strange power he wields within a world full of misapprehension and disdain. Carwin's normal voice is enough to reduce the proudly rational Clara Wieland to tears when she overhears him asking for a drink of water. Clara, herself a musician and singer, immediately recognizes a superior and awesome talent:

> My brother's voice and Pleyel's were musical and energetic. I had fondly imagined that, in this respect, they were surpassed by none. Now my mistake was detected. I cannot pretend to communicate the impression that was made upon me by these accents, or to depict the degree in which force and sweetness were blended in them . . . my heart overflowed with sympathy and my eyes with unbidden tears.
> (1, 71–72)

But Clara's wonder is matched by fear and distaste because Carwin, "ungainly and disproportioned," does not fit within her own "airy speculations" on art and knowledge. Of course, there *is* no legitimate vehicle for Carwin's talent; he represents the entrapped figure that Brown felt himself to be.

Nevertheless, Carwin as natural artist compulsively uses those forums that are available to express himself. The result is confusion

for others and then conflict. Set against the formal music concerts
and the pedantic disagreements in classical translation that occupy
the Wielands, Carwin's spontaneous creativity provides the first
clear image of the romantic artist in American literature. His power
of assuming any other voice, and hence any other identity, suggests
the imagination transcending its own situation. On the other side,
the Wielands represent the eighteenth-century values and neoclassical intellectual assumptions that dominated the literary circles of
Brown's day—literary circles that repudiated mere stories of the
imagination as unworthy of the true artist. What Carwin actually
destroys is the Horatian ideal of literary retreat, which early Americans only dared to dream of after a life of application and public
service. Theodore Wieland's personal veneration is reserved for Cicero, every early American lawyer's favorite symbol of oratorical
excellence and professional virtue.[31] The juxtaposition to Carwin's
own gift is surely deliberate. Wieland's mastery of classical speech
does not help him against the hidden, magical voice of the modern
artist. The beauty and strength of that voice shatter Wieland's tepid
universe and drive him toward a world of extremes and insanity.

Carwin's own character emphasizes "a passion for mystery" and
a reliance on emotion. He consciously seeks to test and disrupt the
rationalism, tranquillity, and decorum—hallmarks of neoclassicism—that he questions in the Wielands (1, 220, 229). In these
passages Charles Brockden Brown dreams of destroying the world
that threatened his own artistic impulse. When the Wielands' framework of commonplace values collapses, Carwin's exultation is clear.
"I cannot convey to you," he confesses in the face of Clara's hatred,
"an adequate idea of the kind of gratification which I derived from
these exploits" (1, 220).

Arthur Mervyn and *Ormond:*
The "Nameless Charm" of Yellow Fever

The need to disrupt is a potent force in all of Brown's novels, and
each manifestation contains a veiled criticism of vocational life in
the early republic. When yellow fever episodes demolish the conventional worlds of *Arthur Mervyn* and *Ormond* in much the same
way that Carwin shatters society in *Wieland*, the novelist records
each collapse with Carwin's spirit of triumph. This bizarre affinity

with yellow fever moves beyond the dictates of gothic terror in a perfect illustration of the artist's stance *against* his culture.[32] Brown witnessed the horrors of various epidemics in Philadelphia and New York between 1793 and 1798, and he actually contracted yellow fever in New York in September 1798, barely surviving while his roommate and closest supporter, Dr. Elihu Hubbard Smith, died in the same encounter.[33] And yet despite these experiences, Brown's fictional heroes invariably benefit from plague conditions, and each is careful to say so. Arthur Mervyn is "sustained by a preternatural energy" while all around him succumb to disease (II, 214). Amidst grisly descriptions of sickness in *Ormond*, the narrator intrudes to warn that "none can tell whether this descriptive pestilence was, on the whole, productive of most pain or most pleasure" (VI, 71). Wallace, in "The Man At Home," even traces all his happiness to changes enforced by plague conditions. "Yellow fever was, to me," he explains, "the most fortunate event that could have happened."[34]

Significantly, Brown's many descriptions of epidemics all tend to focus on the social and economic inactivity that plague conditions compel.[35] His personal experience had been part of a larger catastrophe, a suspension of normal life. No respecter of social norms, yellow fever paralyzed New York in 1798, bringing an entire city into the vocational hiatus that was Brown's customary lot. Similarly, while the plague in itself produced a lull in general social requirements, the death of Brown's closest friend and his own narrow escape insured a more particular respite from conventional pressures. The writer traded upon his situation to ward off requests from Philadelphia for an immediate return home. "This calamity," Brown wrote from New York shortly after the death of Elihu Hubbard Smith, "has endeared the survivors of the sacred fellowship, W.D. [William Dunlap], W.J. [William Johnson], and myself to each other in a very high degree; and I confess my wounded spirit and shattered frame, will be most likely healed and benefitted by their society."[36] The result was a prolonged period of sympathy among the family of Philadelphia merchants, a spirit of indulgence renewed from similar patterns in Brown's sickly childhood. By the spring of 1800, he had to respond once again to familial criticism, but by then the important novels were written.[37] All four of Brown's major novels were created in the months surrounding his bout with yellow fever, precisely when pressures from home were weakest. "I could muse and write cheerfully in spite of the groans of the dying and the rumbling of hearses, and in spite of a thousand tokens of indisposition in my own frame."[38]

Yellow fever was such a personal catalyst because it also formed the ideal constitutive metaphor for Brown's negative views of American society. Before 1798, the writer had been censured for trying to justify idleness in a world too corrupt for virtuous action. The experience of plague easily and safely symbolized these sentiments at a time when more direct criticisms of country were unacceptable in republican literary circles.[39] In *Ormond* Brown can justify non-involvement and express a certain scorn for conventional endeavor by transposing the corruption of yellow fever to society in general. Here the happiness of mankind is "out of the reach of a member of a corrupt society to control. A mortal poison pervaded the whole system, by means of which every thing received was converted into bane and purulence" (vi, 110). Yellow fever exposes the utter superficiality of conventional standards of conduct and vocation, forcing a return to more basic definitions of behavior. In both *Ormond* and *Arthur Mervyn* plague conditions offer an effective moral gauge for measuring character within a corrupt society. The removal of false social pressures upon Brown's struggling protagonists invariably enables the virtuous to discover a new sense of direction.

Brown's descriptions of yellow fever differ markedly from other contemporary accounts like Mathew Carey's *Short Account of the Malignant Fever Lately Prevalent in Philadelphia* (1793). Carey more typically reads the plague as a divine visitation punishing Philadelphia for superficial extravagance and dissipation. Although he dutifully records the deplorable behavior of many during "the extraordinary public panic," Carey is determined that his reader not draw the real character of the city from this "period of horror and affright." He contrasts "the law of charity victorious" with "the law of self-preservation" and condemns exaggerations of the calamity involved.[40] Brown, on the other hand, ignores divine judgment, insisting that yellow fever reveals ugly social truths about Philadelphia and its people—truths that are disguised by routine in ordinary times. No mere interlude, the plague becomes instead a symptom of larger social problems.

In *Ormond* the pestilence means sudden breakdown on every social level. The collapse is so rapid and complete that one is forced to conclude that all social ties are superficial. The heroine Constantia Dudley fears "this total inactivity," but "the devastation and confusion of the city" immediately redound to her advantage. Yellow fever terminates her tedious vocation as a seamstress and soon eliminates the demands of an avaricious landlord. She returns from the latter's funeral with lightened footsteps to design new measures in home economy and a program in language study (VI, 41–55). Although Constantia suffers a bout of fever and witnesses the destruction of her neighborhood, Brown lists undeniable positive returns: "The yellow fever, by affording her a respite from toil, supplying leisure for the acquisition of a useful branch of knowledge, and leading her to the discovery of a cheaper, more simple, and more wholesome method of subsistence, had been friendly, instead of adverse, to her happiness" (VI, 71). Constantia's inherent virtue insures her survival during the epidemic. By helping others, she in turn is nursed through "a disease where personal attentions are *all in all*." Both *Ormond* and *Arthur Mervyn* are strewn with lesser figures who die horrible deaths either because they selfishly refuse to provide assistance or because they foolishly seek safety in flight.[41]

Arthur Mervyn builds an entire framework out of his own confrontation with yellow fever. In the opening pages of that novel, Arthur is either "without precise object" or the anxious, unknowing pawn of the villain Welbeck's designs (II, 9). "To act under the guidance of another," he complains, "and to wander in the dark, ignorant whither my path tended . . . was a new and irksome situation" (II, 64). The epidemic that stuns Philadelphia galvanizes Mervyn and turns him into a relatively uncomplicated moral agent with a clear course "prescribed by duty" (II, 140). Unsure of his tentative actions in Welbeck's shadowy commercial world, he develops absolute confidence within the more literal corruption of pestilence. Yellow fever has "some nameless charm" for Arthur even before he encounters it (II, 131). When stricken, he turns the fever into an immediate personal asset. The knowledge of infection, he reveals, "instead of appalling me, tended rather to invigorate my courage." It lifts him completely outside ordinary life and places him beyond daily fears (II, 145). In consequence, Arthur's activities become more effective. He experiences a kind of epiphany under plague conditions: "I felt as if the opportunity of combating such

evils was an enviable privilege" (II, 214). Thought to be lazy, ineffectual, perverse, and without prospects, Arthur becomes a prodigy of energy and true righteousness. In fact, yellow fever shapes
his entire future by leading to a worthy career in medicine.

Through their triumphs Brown's fictional characters act out the
novelist's social hostilities in the setting of yellow fever. Constantia
Dudley and Arthur Mervyn operate as figures outside society. Un-
fairly threatened by conventional pressures, they take understandable satisfaction in the collapse of social networks and the fall of the
great to disease. Arthur Mervyn is particularly scornful of "delusive
maxims of decorum" that prevent meaningful moral action (III, 101).
He relies on inward composure to extract himself from one social
complication and embarrassment after another. This composure enables an acknowledged physical weakling and impractical dreamer
to thwart figures of authority and power. Inward resolution also
allows both Arthur and Constantia to conquer the plague.[42] "The
external frame will seldom languish," Arthur concludes, "while ac-
tuated by an unconquerable soul" (II, 169). Implicit in this view is
the assumption in *Ormond* and *Arthur Mervyn* that society falls because it lacks the moral fiber to stand. In a world that has lost its
way in hypocrisy and false standards, Arthur and Constantia are
superior to the disintegration around them because they act "upon
the altar of sincerity" (II, 214).

Inevitably, return to normalcy constitutes the greater danger in
Brown's infested cities. Since the fantasy of Constantia and Arthur's
proven superiority grows out of the novelist's daily frustrations and
failures, it is the resumption of routine that brings unanswerable
problems. The end of yellow fever for Constantia Dudley, "instead
of relieving her from suffering, was the signal for the approach of
new cares" (VI, 71). Calm within the scourge of plague, Arthur
Mervyn fears only the "light and regular" duties of Brown's ironic
happy ending. In these final scenes he suddenly feels an "ominous
misgiving" and "unworthy terrors" (III, 229–230). Together, Constantia's new cares and Arthur's fresh terrors contain a harsh comment on republican culture. For Brown seems to be saying that
Constantia's moral excellence and Arthur's energy have no moral
or aesthetic context in normal society; that virtue and creativity go
unrecognized in a country geared to power and wealth; that only
an extraordinary disruption can restore America to itself. Yellow

fever wrecks more than cities. It challenges the civic vision of the legal guardians whom Brown refused to join.

"The Cold Bounds of Propriety"

At odds with republican culture, Brown made his heroes and heroines outsiders on the brink of rebellion. But if the novelist could resist momentarily through his fiction, the American citizen could never make a comparable public stand, and the distinction separates Brown from the romantic writers who follow him. At the end of the eighteenth century, mere opposition gave no source of identity; society was still the paramount fact in individual life—hence the impulse toward accommodation that always counters rebellion in Brown's novels.[43] Torn by many ambivalences, Brown desperately wanted some kind of agreement with his times. His archness of tone and expression, his use of sentiment, and his celebration of mannered discourse were symptoms of his need to conform to regular eighteenth-century American tastes. In fact, the creativity that modern critics like to stress should be reexamined in this light. The "novelist of ideas" who created confrontations around a series of ideological themes was basically trying to make his fiction more respectable within an intellectual climate that stressed philosophical and civic discourse.[44]

Accommodation—the desire to appear useful in an age of utility— required some kind of integration of the artist within society, and Brown clearly saw the problem in his fiction. Nevertheless, and despite many attempts, a life of frustration kept him from finding a meaningful imaginative solution. Here is the source of those strange bouts of insanity and rebellion that Brown's outsiders undergo as they agree to enter regular social worlds of decorum, balance, leisure, and conventional belief.[45] In *Arthur Mervyn*, to take the most striking example, the protagonist suddenly loses control when he discovers that his unorthodox nature may not fit within Brown's concluding daydream of commonplace success (III, 220–227). The cultured milieu of Achsa Fielding, Mervyn's fiancée, is roughly comparable to the neoclassical society that Carwin destroys. Arthur's prospective marriage raises the same problem of finding independent scope within a setting of measured activities and moderate sensibility. Earlier, he has told us that his pen channels important

emotions and gives meaningful direction (III, 197). Now this instrument of the artist is useless, even inconvenient. "But why am
I indulging this pen-prattle?" asks Mervyn as he accepts his bride.
And he adds, "Take thyself away, quill. Lie there, snug in thy
leathern case, till I call thee, and that will not be very soon . . . Yes;
I *will* abjure thee" (III, 230). Conventional success involves intellectual and creative castration. Arthur's "nameless sort of terror" in
these final pages builds upon his realization of a direct conflict between the artist's needs and the world's demands.

Occasional descriptions of mundane felicity actually reinforce the
novelist's perception of incompatibility. Arthur Mervyn's marriage
to his "lost mamma" in Achsa Fielding affords just one instance of
a compulsive matriarchal focus in Brown's fiction, a focus that points
directly back to the writer's vocational anxieties. Brown's successful
heroes invariably marry older, stronger women who bring legitimizing wealth and the approval of an adult world. This fantasy
world of rich, devoted women reduces vocation to a theoretical
annoyance and relieves related tensions by eliminating all thoughts
of fathers and brothers. The oedipal patterns in these stories protect
the artist from the anger of a vocational world that is patriarchal.[46]
Brown gives his most elaborate account of a matriarchal dream
solution in the same article that summarizes his vocational plight as
the "poor author" or "author by trade."

> There is my friend H——. Can a man be situated more happily? His
> aunt not only secures him and his charming Eleanor from the pos-
> sibility of want, she secures them not only the pleasures and honors
> of extraordinary affluence, but even from the common cares of a
> master of a family. She is his steward . . . The young and happy
> couple have nothing to do but to give themselves up to the delights
> of mutual tenderness, and to fill up the interval between these joys
> with bathing and walking, or with music, conversation, reading and
> writing. He has no other labour on his hands than to decide whether
> the coming hours shall be employed at the clarionet, the pencil, the
> book or the pen.[47]

If this description seems jejune, the destructive tendencies of Carwin, Ormond, Edgar Huntly, and Arthur Mervyn convey the novelist's own misgivings.

Trapped by conflicting concerns, Brown ultimately refused a
synthesis between the artist and republican culture because he had

calculated the depth and nature of his own isolation. "I am aware of the extent to which I expose myself," he wrote in a signed magazine article on the creative process. Here he identified the writer's immediate opponents as "the selfish worldling, the interested parent, the struggles in the path of ordinary ambition, the stupid, the sterile-hearted, the sensual." Behind these particulars came "the censorious eye of the world," which withered poetic sensibilities: "He whose feelings are not acute, sometimes even to disease," Brown warned, "can never touch the true chords of the lyre. To be in constant terror of exceeding the cold bounds of propriety, to be perpetually on the watch against any transient extravagance of mind, is not to be a poet . . . That chilly philosophy which demands the reconcilement of qualities nearly incompatible has always appeared to me far from true wisdom."[48]

These words protest, but they also acknowledge failure. When they first appeared, Brown was already a reluctant associate in the family mercantile business, and, in accordance with the wishes of his eldest brother, James, he no longer wrote novels filled with "gloominess and out-of-nature incidents."[49] The key to his acquiescence, and indeed to the entire career of America's first major novelist, can be seen in a favorite quotation from Shakespeare that Brown placed on the pen of Arthur Mervyn. Asked to share Welbeck's commercial schemes, Arthur slowly writes, "My poverty, but not my will, consents" (II, 51).

CHAPTER 6

WASHINGTON IRVING
HUNTS DOWN THE NATION

"The Scrub-Race for Honor and Renown"

Washington Irving studied and practiced law for ten years at the beginning of the nineteenth century, and, although there is reason to question the depth of his professional commitment, this first career had a decisive influence upon early writings. Irving, with every other law student of the period, expected to tread "the path to honour and preferment—to every thing that is distinguished in public life." He admired Cicero, dreamed of success as a heroic citizen before the bar, and made the customary resolution "to sacrifice *all* to the law."[1] Like Charles Brockden Brown before him and William Cullen Bryant after, Irving was a younger son in a rising middle-class family, one that could afford to tolerate and even encourage a law student's dalliance in literature. The lawyer as writer bespoke the upward social mobility and gentlemanly status that the Irving family sought for its younger members, and there were four older brothers to cope with immediate financial needs through the New York hardware firm of P. and E. Irving. In a hundred ways Irving's brothers paved the way for his literary interests, but their guidance always assumed separate professional ambition within the world. Perhaps in reaction, Irving at nineteen was already yearning for a retirement to literature as Jonathan Oldstyle. Not until his middle thirties in 1819 did the independent man of letters take a stand against fraternal interference and "new plans for subsistence."[2]

Virtually no documentation survives from Irving's career in the law, but personal observations and notebooks allow a rudimentary outline of the involvement. Between 1799 and 1809 Irving studied in the New York law offices of Henry Masterton, Brockholst Livingston, and Josiah Ogden Hoffman. He worked as a law clerk, kept the necessary commonplace book of general readings, passed the examination for the New York bar, and practiced briefly on Wall Street with John Treat Irving, an older brother who later served as First Judge of the Court of Common Pleas.[3] Apparently Irving tolerated these activities instead of making them fully his own—at least his letters complain generally about "this wrangling driving unmerciful profession" and dismiss those "ponderous fathers of the law" who were his intellectual guides. A mediocre student, he usually left his law books to molder on their shelves in "awful majesty of *Folio* grandeur."[4] And yet Irving was never indifferent to the underlying rationale for a legal career. There were two periods of intense professional application, and these periods are of particular interest because they coincide with Irving's first major writings, *Salmagundi; or the Whimwhams and Opinions of Launcelot Langstaff Esq. and Others* (1807–1808) and *Diedrich Knickerbocker's A History of New York* (1809).

In the year before *Salmagundi*, Irving vacillated between a "melancholy slough" and feverish preparation for his approaching bar examination. "I am so completely engrossed with law at present, that I have no time to go about," he wrote in July 1806, six months before his first contribution to the collective *Salmagundi* essays by William Irving, James K. Paulding, and himself.[5] Admission to the bar in November came "more through courtesy than desert," Irving believed, and his feelings of inferiority triggered a long relapse into uncertainty, aimlessness, and professional idleness. "I felt my own deficiency," he later wrote, "and despaired of ever succeeding at the Bar."[6]

A corresponding fear of failure lies behind Irving's sharpest contribution to *Salmagundi*, "On Greatness," and its satire of the alternative he could never realize. Timothy Dabble has all the assurance of a young man in a hurry, the "little great man" who pushes immediately into "the highways and market-places" in search of political advancement, throwing himself into "the scrub-race for honor and renown." Here Irving trivializes the conventional ambitions and virtues that every young lawyer was supposed to possess on the road to honor and preferment. "On Greatness" lumps great

Bryant, Webster, and Irving at the Memorial Services for James Fenimore Cooper, February 24, 1852, photoprint of a sketch by Dan Huntington.

William Cullen Bryant, painting by Samuel F. B. Morse, 1825.

Washington Irving,
painting by John Wesley Jarvis, 1809.

Bryant and Irving, flanking Daniel Webster, appear as they are generally remembered, as older, complacent, and rather conventional public figures. But the important poems and stories were written much earlier—by the vaguely resentful and vocationally uncertain younger men portrayed by Morse and Jarvis. Morse caught Bryant at the age of thirty, just as the major phase of the poet drew to a close; Jarvis painted Irving at twenty-six, as he was writing *A History of New York.*

men together with pimps, bailiffs, and lottery brokers and turns to the dung beetle and jackass for its only images of energy, resolution, and application. "To rise in this country a man must first descend," warns Irving, charting Timothy Dabble's "slimy progress from worm to butterfly." Dabble's personal eloquence, assertiveness, self-interested industry, captivating public manner, and, most of all, his success make him the antithesis of his diffident, dilatory, and ineffectual creator.[7]

A History of New York contains a similar but more intense spirit of negation. By 1809 personal problems had compounded professional aimlessness. Sometime in 1808 the unhappy young lawyer— "I became low spirited & disheartened and did not know what was to become of me"—confessed his love for Josiah Ogden Hoffman's youngest daughter, Matilda. Hoffman, Irving's employer and one of the leading lawyers in New York, offered a full partnership and his daughter's hand, but he also insisted upon a demonstration of professional capacity before the fact. Irving's later account captures the situation and his own anxieties within it:

> I could study any thing else rather than Law, and had a fatal propensity to Belles Lettres. I had gone on blindly, like a boy in Love, but now I began to open my eyes and be miserable . . . I considered myself bound in honour not to make further advances with the daughter until I should feel satisfied with my proficiency in the Law—It was all in vain. I had an insuperable repugnance to the study—my mind would not take hold if it . . . I was in a wretched state of doubt and self distrust.

Desperately, Irving directed his remaining energies away from— indeed, against—the Law. In early 1809 he was secretly hard at work on *A History of New York;* it was a private alternative, an escape from his impossible predicament and a wild stab for the independent reputation that he knew the law would never supply. Then, quite suddenly, the immediate source of tension was gone. Matilda Hoffman's death of a rapid consumption in April 1809 obviated any need to prove professional capacity and commitment. Twenty-six years of age and in "a horrid state of mind," Irving abruptly "abandoned all thoughts of the Law" and turned for solace to his writing.[8] As Diedrich Knickerbocker, Dutch historian and comic old bachelor, he would place himself before the public just eight months after Matilda's death.

Part anodyne, part an expression of sorrow, bitterness, and relief, *A History of New York* is at once a light burlesque comedy set in the colonial past and an atrabilious satire on republican society. Irving's double escape from the law and from the marriage associated with it figures prominently on each level. The lawyer's private alternative to professional ambition becomes the writer's formal act of rebellion. In fact, Irving's emotional rejection of law—fictionally portrayed through the collapse of New Amsterdam—supplies a dramatic unity and thematic coherence that set *A History of New York* apart from his other imaginative works. Vocational resentments form the center of a larger hostility or imagery of estrangement and spur a creativity that has little to do with the muted and sentimental tones of later works or with the "easily pleased Washington Irving" who dilutes Diedrich Knickerbocker's comments in later editions.[9]

The original version of *A History of New York* is nothing less than a "thundering amorphous jeremiad," literally "an attempt to annihilate the history of America."[10] Its driving force is anger, an anger that supplies point of view and an original voice. As many have noted, Irving borrowed heavily from Sterne, Goldsmith, Swift, Addison, Butler, Fielding, Cervantes, and Rabelais, and his book is "the most allusive of all American literary compositions written before 1825." Even so, *A History of New York* is a distinctly American creation and a unified work of the imagination in a sense that Irving's subsequent, more polished books of fiction are not. Crazy old Diedrich Knickerbocker—himself a composite figure drawn from *A Tale of A Tub*, *The Spectator*, and *Tristram Shandy*—brings all external sources under the capacious umbrella of his own anger and frustration.[11] If the Dutch historian constantly wanders, his larger objective, "hunting down a nation," never varies, and his sights remain firmly fixed on "the self-satisfied citizens of this most enlightened republick."[12]

Knickerbocker's embattled America is "garrisoned by a doughty host of orators, chairmen, committee-men, Burgomasters, Schepens, and old women" (p. 432). No rising republic, it is rather "a mighty fungus springing from a mass of rotten wood," one that collapses under its own corrupt weight (p. 133). Throughout the declension of New Amsterdam, Irving's narrator rants compulsively against the "galling scourge of the law" and "the herds of pettifogging lawyers" who reduce the harmony of Dutch civilization to factionalism and then chaos through "the bitterness of litigation" (pp. 123, 216, 130, 181). Small wonder that Knickerbocker's ultimate symbol of destruction is the Yankee circuit-rider: "lean sided hungry pettifoggers, mounted on Narraganset pacers, with saddle bags under their bottoms, and green satchels under their arms, as if they were about to beat the hoof from one county court to another—in search of a law suit" (p. 267).

Washington Irving's comic narrator of a golden age among the first settlers of New Amsterdam depends upon his celebration of a masculine idleness that is divorced from both the need for law and the intrusive industry of women. His placid Dutch burghers do little but eat, sleep, and pull on their pipes in ever-obscuring clouds of smoke. "Making but few laws, without ever enforcing any," they enjoy life because they are satisfied with obscurity and lack all interest in vocational activity, public honor, and civic service (pp. 103, 113, 117, 126, 135–136). The happiest product of this culture in good times and bad is Antony Van Corlear, "a jolly fat dutch trumpeter" and figure for the artist. Antony's creativity and boisterous good humor are rooted in the acceptance of his music by political authority, his imperviousness to legal wrangling, his easy conquests of every available heart, and his good fortune in "having never been married" (pp. 195, 397).

Wouter Van Twiller as the amiable original governor of New Amsterdam secures a golden age in the New World by fining the first court official to bring a lawsuit and deciding that case *against* the merits of the dispute (pp. 119–120). In consequence, "there were neither public commotions, nor private quarrels; neither parties, nor sects, nor schisms; neither prosecutions, nor trials, nor punishments; nor were there counsellors, attornies, catch-poles or hangmen" (p. 130). The only law on record among the first generation of New Amsterdam is a dedication to "the great and good St. Nicholas" as patron saint (p. 107). It is Wouter's successor as governor, Wilhelmus Kieft or William the Testy, who ruins everything by instituting a countervailing reign of laws. Made "testy" by a shrewish wife and too much legal learning, the henpecked William becomes "the Patron of Lawyers and Bum-Bailiffs" and forever destroys the peace and prosperity of his province by making "a multitude of good-for-nothing laws" (pp. 181–185, 211). Peter Stuyvesant, the military adventurer who succeeds William, then completes the fall of Dutch civilization by negotiating legalistic, hence ineffectual, treaties with his neighbors. For the confirmed bachelor Diedrich Knickerbocker, Peter's final alliances are too much like a marriage ceremony—a signal for hostilities to begin (p. 260).

The symbol of Irving's America and focal point of his displeasure in *A History of New York* is Thomas Jefferson's administration of 1801 to 1809.[13] Early republicans had little trouble in recognizing their third president in the figure of William the Testy. Here, as in the earlier *Salmagundi*, Irving satirizes Jefferson's character (his clothes, intellectuality, scientific enthusiasms, and passion for fine horses) and his ideas (the stresses upon education, patriotism, democracy, and republican virtue), as well as his specific programs as president (naval, economic, and foreign policies in general and the inaugural addresses, the Non-Importation Act of 1806, the Embargo Act of 1807, and the Non-Intercourse Act of 1809 in particular). But more than politics informs Irving's hostility.[14] Jefferson and Irving occupied extremes on the American spectrum. Virginia's imposing aristocrat, patriarch, and agrarian theorist easily intimidated the unprepossessing youngest child in an urban, middle-class family of northeastern merchants. It was intellectual versus dilettante and cynic, the man of affairs and practical energy against an adolescent daydreamer, the leading legal mind in America through the eyes of an uncertain law student. As imaginative projection, *A History of New York* seeks to reverse this context of defeat. William the Testy falls through his blind devotion to legal theory, while Diedrich Knickerbocker, as historian, emerges as the only true source of heroism and wisdom. Writers, after all, "are the sovereign censors who decide upon the renown or infamy of our fellow mortals" (pp. 369, 11, 229, 333–334). Knickerbocker celebrates this role of censure, and Irving uses its powers to ridicule his nemesis.

Thomas Jefferson first appears by name in *A History of New York* in the company of a long line of visionaries who use law to create ideal societies. Plato, Aristotle, Grotius, Pufendorf, Algernon Sidney, and Tom Paine are also listed, and they, like Jefferson, make a "ruinous mistake" by ignoring reality in the name of principle (p. 153). William the Testy is "smothered in a slough" of their learning. "Full of scraps and remnants of ancient republics . . . and the laws of Solon and Lycurgus and Charondas, and the imaginary commonwealth of Plato, and the Pandects of Justinian," which is to say, full of the eighteenth-century law student's most basic readings, William is "highly classic, profoundly erudite, and nothing at all to the purpose" (pp. 180–183).

Diedrich Knickerbocker's raillery soars above and about his subject, but there is no mistaking the *point de repère*. Through the satire of Jefferson, Irving calls into question the whole legal vision of America upon which Jeffersonianism is based. He argues that legal administration favors the rich and contentious over the ignorant poor and that it quickly becomes an instrument of oppression (p. 213). America itself has been built upon the unwarranted seizure of Indian land in a history of murder, theft, and fraud legitimized by legal rubrics (pp. 52–61). Similar patterns of injustice run throughout American history. The witchcraft trials of New England are merely conspicuous examples of the way in which courts routinely cloak self-interest and prejudice in the robes of legal authority (pp. 281–284). Moreover, the law as deliberate sham covers an even starker reality: the law as dangerous illusion. Diedrich Knickerbocker will have none of the design for order that law pretends to supply. "Theories are at best but brittle productions" in Knickerbocker's view; they only obfuscate, "gravely accounting for unaccountable things" (p. 48).

Every effort to provide a theory of civilization for New Amsterdam founders upon chaotic reality. By linking the imposition of legal control to the decline and fall of Nieuw Nederlandts, Irving undermines all faith in the saving virtues of law and order. Decisions based upon a theory of law and order, particularly Jeffersonian decisions, only exacerbate existing problems. Accordingly, *A History of New York* is the first American book to question directly the civic vision of the Founding Fathers, and Diedrich Knickerbocker is the natural enemy of Publius, Novanglus, the Pennsylvania Farmer, and other rational, legal spokesmen in early American literature. Irving's comic historian easily ridicules the high seriousness of these republican myth-makers, but the real success of his challenge depends upon his manipulation of basic intellectual affinities. Knickerbocker, like the targets of his satire, is the product of a legal mind, and he knows how to dismantle the sense of country that they built from the legal humanism of the Enlightenment. *A History of New York* is the photographic negative of Jefferson's *Notes on the State of Virginia*.

Diedrich Knickerbocker's "Crazy Vessel"

Certainly, *A History of New York* plays with legal method. One finds the lawyer-writer's customary parody of legal terminology (pp. 37, 62), legal fictions (p. 241), and justification by legal precedent (pp. 52–61). Though short, *A History of New York* faithfully reproduces the elaborate organizational format of a standard legal compendium. Irving divides his little book into volumes, books, brief chapters, and lengthy headings, and he supplies a plethora of footnotes and references—all in mock replication of the machinery in eighteenth-century legal analysis.[15] His intellectual sources are those that buttress the serious writings of Jefferson, Adams, Madison, or Hamilton. References to "the great Buffon," "the learned Grotius," Pufendorf, Vattel, Blackstone, Sir William Jones, and Lord Kames recur here as well as there—except that Knickerbocker uses citations as weapons of disorder and not as touchstones for outline and structure.[16]

Book I opens with a blunt protest against system in general and contests the presumption of scholars to comprehensive knowledge and universal relevance. While "very learned" because it mimics all introductions, Diedrich Knickerbocker's first chapter promises only "divers profound theories and philosophic speculations, which the idle reader may totally overlook" (p. 15). The succeeding narrative, explaining the creation of the world and the discovery of America, openly spoofs the kind of artificial groundwork employed in both legal compendia and general histories of the period.[17] At the outset Irving rejects the Enlightenment's assumption of a discernible relation between natural order and social harmony—an assumption that encourages an epistemology based on the connection of natural law with positive or man-made law and that supports the theory of social contract from Locke to Rousseau. Diedrich Knickerbocker finds too much mystery in nature to justify such exercises in scholasticism. "It is a mortifying circumstance," he warns, "which greatly perplexes many a pains taking philosopher, that nature often refuses to second his most profound and elaborate efforts; so that often after having invented one of the most ingenious and natural theories imaginable, she will have the perverseness to act directly in the teeth of his system, and flatly contradict his most favourite positions" (p. 21). Anyone who ignores this warning is "a blind man describing the glories of light," discoursing "wisely about matters forever hidden" (p. 48).

Irving deliberately apes the strategies employed by Grotius, Pufendorf, and other legal philosophers to achieve intellectual order. Grotius' *De Jure Belli et Pacis* (1625) set the norm in legal method for two centuries by demonstrating how an effort toward comprehensiveness could lead to a unified view. An arrangement of all theories across disciplines relevant to an issue enabled one to construct a "conspiring testimony," which "proceeding from innumerable different times and places must be referred to some universal cause." For Grotius and his many followers in the eighteenth century, similarities in evidence from different sources suggested universal significance, hence, the nature of truth on any given subject.[18] Diedrich Knickerbocker is an avid literalist in this matter. He seizes upon the standard Enlightenment technique with hilarious energy in a *reductio ad absurdum*.

Knickerbocker's "multitude of excellent Theories" on the creation of the world and the discovery of America brings a vast array of sources to a narrative that leads nowhere (pp. 23–41). Ancient cosmogonies combine with modern philosophical accounts from the Congo, the American wilderness, Algeria, France, and England to prove that creating a world is not so difficult a task as everyone imagines. Convinced that discovery of the New World was delayed by Noah's failure to have a fourth son to inherit America, the Dutch historian traces his biblical version through Chaldean, Egyptian, Indian, Greek, Roman, and Chinese sources to affirm "the unquestionable fact" (p. 36). In each case, Knickerbocker easily circles to his original premise but with the added self-satisfaction of universal proof. "When a man once doffs the straight waistcoat of common sense," Irving observes, "it is astonishing how rapidly he gets forward" (p. 32).

All of Knickerbocker's nonsense has a serious goal in mind. Books I and II of *A History of New York* demolish the intellectual foundations for a progressive interpretation of American culture.[19] Conventional beliefs in natural law, the virgin land, manifest destiny, and republican order and virtue all become impossible aboard the Dutch historian's "crazy vessel" (p. 13). Free to present a different understanding of his subject, Irving then turns to the darker view of history and republicanism found within the classical texts of the eighteenth-century law student. Much of the bite in Books IV through VII comes through a consistent and orthodox presentation of this view in the downfall of Dutch New York. Steeped in Homer, Herodotus, Thucydides, Plato, Cicero, Plutarch, Boethius, and their many eighteenth-century heirs, Knickerbocker finds history to be cyclical rather than progressive (pp. 212, 222, 230, 243, 352, 444). He and his contemporaries actually live in degenerate times. Diedrich harks back to a golden age of simplicity and virtue in much the way that Blackstone or a Whig historian regards Anglo-Saxon England with its pure legacy of immemorial common law.[20] His narrative of decline from the reign of Wouter Van Twiller to the end of New Amsterdam under Peter Stuyvesant is told in exactly those terms that every good Whig lawyer from John Adams to Daniel Webster used to express fear of republican collapse.

Irving begins by unmasking republican pretensions to order and control of the kind one finds in *Common Sense*, *The Federalist*, and *Notes on the State of Virginia*. In *A History of New York* every plan and method for ensuring a virtuous society founders upon the organic spontaneity of New World growth. New Amsterdam increases "so rapidly in strength and magnitude, that before the honest burgomasters had determined upon a plan, it was too late to put it in execution" (pp. 102–104). Inevitably, factions develop over the correct form and blueprint for civilization, but while they argue, Knickerbocker's cattle, "in a laudable fit of patriotism," create the streets of New York and set the pattern of Dutch settlement (p. 133). Delusion follows for those who rashly impose their views upon reality. Emerging from swamps and stinkweed, the "immense metropolis" of New Amsterdam parallels Washington, D.C., early in the nineteenth century; they are glorious cities only on paper (pp. 127–128). Experience is the sole teacher in this recalcitrant, empirical world, but her lessons are difficult and hard to apply. "Surely a man has but to travel through the world, with open ears; and by the time he is grey, he will have all the wisdom of Solomon," Knickerbocker explains helpfully, "and then he has nothing to do but to grow young again, and turn it to the best advantage" (p. 343).

Just as the organicism of an emerging culture favors the Dutch in spite of themselves, so this same volatile energy becomes a destructive force once degeneration or corruption sets in. Peter Stuyvesant is the best of Knickerbocker's Dutch leaders, but he is no

match for "the incessant cares and vexations" that turn Nieuw Nederlandts into "a very forlorn, distressed, and woe begone little province" (pp. 242, 246, 376, 387). William the Testy's disastrous reign
of laws has transformed the slumbering inhabitants of New Amsterdam into a meddlesome and contentious people (p. 218). Factionalism, the related presumptions of "the swinish multitude," the
spread of luxury, incompetent leadership, and demagoguery undermine the virtue and strength of Dutch civilization (pp. 378, 381,
412–414). Irving deals here in the patterns of collapse associated
with republics by political theorists from Plato to Montesquieu.
Peter Stuyvesant is not just a lion trapped in the hunter's net and
a bear surrounded by curs, but "a second Cato" facing the same
insurmountable odds as the republicans of antiquity (pp. 404, 436,
392). And once again, destruction proves inevitable: "Neither virtue,
nor talents, eloquence, nor economy, can avert the inavertable stroke
of fate" (p. 444).

As a portrayal of prevalent fears, *A History of New York* raises the
same problems that preoccupy Thomas Jefferson in the second half
of *Notes on the State of Virginia*. The difference is that Jefferson places
issues like factionalism, luxury, and demagoguery in a context that
admits solution, while Irving dismisses Jeffersonian response as part
of the problem. In the reign of William the Testy, a Jeffersonian
emphasis on popular education leads not to an enlightened people
but rather to "juntos of political croakers, who . . . groan over public affairs, and make themselves miserable" (pp. 219–220). Civic
identification and republican virtue also have negative repercussions.
For if patriotism provides a sense of place, chauvinism blinds New
Amsterdam to the reality of its situation in the world and promotes
a dangerous belligerence and jingoism. By the reign of Peter Stuyvesant, the once-placid burgomasters are proclaiming themselves
"the bravest and most powerful people under the sun" and debating
whether or not to exterminate Great Britain (pp. 408–410). One
has only to think of Henry Clay and his war hawks plunging America toward the disastrous War of 1812 to see the relevance of Irving's
humor.[21]

"Words of Battle" was Irving's expression for "talking of patriotism & principle," and he clearly feared the bellicosity such language could induce.[22] Chauvinism always confuses in *A History of
New York*, and at every level. Knickerbocker's "old 'seventy-six' of

a governor," Peter Stuyvesant, is also an "imp of fame and prowess" whose search for glory unwittingly compounds the "valour of tongue" and "gallant vapouring" that replace common sense and probity in New Amsterdam (pp. 246, 399, 410). The military adventurism of Peter the Headstrong brings about the final ruin of Dutch New York; it leads directly to British invasion and the fall of New Amsterdam in a narrative that approximates the collapse of ancient Athens in the Peloponnesian War.[23] Meanwhile, the Dutch historian's overt veneration for Stuyvesant as national hero gives a final twist to the problem of patriotism. Preoccupied with his favorite's resemblance to Ajax, Hercules, Coriolanus, Achilles, Charlemagne, Peter the Great, and other heroes, Knickerbocker details Stuyvesant's flaws without realizing their significance. Patriotic blinders have left him "a very numscull at drawing conclusions" when it comes to a full understanding of his own subject (pp. 243–246, 263–264, 344–345, 392). His many descriptions of "hyperbolic bursts of patriotism" and of "choleric" reactions thereto are, of course, comic (p. 408). Nevertheless, the Irving behind this mask is describing an angry, aggressive culture, a nation "insatiable of territory" (p. 391). Beyond humor, *A History of New York* finds America well on its way to Herman Melville's bleak description of 1855: "Intrepid, unprincipled, reckless, predatory, with boundless ambition, civilized in externals but a savage at heart, America is, or may be, the Paul Jones of nations."[24]

Subversive Voices

Such deliberate negation carried Irving dangerously beyond the sphere of commentary allowed by republican orthodoxy at the beginning of the nineteenth century. In celebrating new national convictions, the Founding Fathers created a rhetoric in which opponents were either fools, knaves, or outright traitors. The ensuing acrimony between Federalists and Jeffersonians—unmatched in American politics for virulence—demonstrates how slowly a consensus allowing loyal opposition developed.[25] There was, in short, little public ground for Washington Irving to stand on in his implicit rejection of democratic republicanism, and Irving clearly understood the dangers in store for open heretics. "The Little Man in Black" of *Salmagundi* dramatizes the proposition that "an individual who is once so unfortunate as to incur the odium of a village is in a great measure outlawed and proscribed; and becomes a mark for injury and insult." A direct precursor of Diedrich Knickerbocker, the little man in black is persecuted to death for harmless deviations from the communal norm.[26] Irving's Dutch historian is a far more serious renegade, yet he thrives while the merely eccentric intellectual of *Salmagundi* perishes. The difference—what Diedrich Knickerbocker adds to the little man in black—is a saving mask of comic humor.

Of course, Irving's reliance upon humor is immediate and obvious in *A History of New York*, but his methods and the underlying safeguards they permit deserve closer attention. Knickerbocker is the first in a long line of literary personae who trade upon a subversive vein of humor in American literature—a humor that plays upon chaos and affirms common individual traits (cunning, endurance, physical prowess) over and against civic identities and the ideological building blocks of republican culture. Subversive humor exposes apparent virtue and conventional aspiration through reference to a lower but firmer reality. Laughter follows from a realization of the gap between what is and what ought to be or from "recognition of the insuperable defects of actuality."[27] These juxtapositions were everywhere in the jumble of airy hopes and primitive realities of early republican culture, and, as the examples of John Trumbull, Royall Tyler, and Hugh Henry Brackenridge have made clear, lawyer-writers were especially adept at finding comic incongruities. Deflating comparisons came easily to men whose professional needs required a mastery of both patriotic rhetoric and the rough-and-tumble tactics of the early American courtroom. They had only to examine their own experience.

What distinguishes Irving from earlier comic lawyer-writers is the courage of one who has stepped completely outside the welter of incongruities that he describes. Irving holds nothing back in *A History of New York*. At the same time, his stance as a thoroughly alienated outside observer allows the artistic detachment upon which all good satire depends.[28] For while the gap between appearance and reality in Irving's satiric vision grows from such conventional devices as mock-encomium, mock-epic, and the fantastic tale, it is the separate integrity of Diedrich Knickerbocker's ironic voice that ensures integral dramatic effect. To accept that voice on its own terms—and the reader has no choice in this matter—is to be doubly disarmed from protesting the views it secures. Knickerbocker may be a whimsical crank, but he is the only source of coherence in *A History of New York*, and he carefully attaches the reader to his own elaborate and dramatic search for "the chaste and simple garb of truth" (pp. 93, 99, 167). At the beginning of Book IV, he even announces the moment in time when the independent observer must fall completely under the historian's spell, held "by the button" and "fairly in my clutches."[29]

Since irony must work through indirection, there is no one moment for seizing upon and denying the image of America that accompanies Knickerbocker's gradual embrace of his audience. When, for example, he reveals his fat, sleepy burghers placing a "scrupulously honest" hand or foot upon the scales in fur trade with the Indians, we laugh at reality through the appearance (p. 87). The necessarily heroic adventurers who discover Manhattan, "four indubitably great men," are also ruthless desperadoes and riffraff who come from the lowest of the low (literally excrement) and fight among themselves as the "tough breeches" of this world (pp. 89–96). Both levels of description are ridiculous in this narrative, and, hence, they come together with dramatic force in the consistently comic tones of the Dutch historian. The irascible Diedrich is characteristically frank about this process. Were Jason and his Argonauts "heroes and demigods" or "a mere gang of sheep stealers on a marauding expedition"? (p. 71). They were both, and Knickerbocker's insistence upon this simultaneity in Dutch New York inevitably discloses a nation of swindlers and belligerents beneath America's pious myths of the Founding Fathers. The indirections of irony allow Irving to make this point while evading the responsibility of a stance for or against. Alvin Kernan has summarized the advantages admirably in his study of satire: "Irony is the perfect rhetorical device for catching the pretense which reveals itself as sham, since its two terms [appearance and reality] permit the poet to create both the pretense and the truth at once. He no longer need tell us, as the sermonist or reformer does, that men are not what they seem to be; he dramatizes the gap men drive between what they seem to be and what they are; he creates, like other poets, the very thing he exposes."[30] One cannot, in other words, divorce an accepting laughter at Knickerbocker's New York from Irving's critical presentation of America.

The particular kind of laughter Knickerbocker provokes is another safeguard against the potential intolerance of a republican ortho-doxy. For neither satire nor comedy but rather an adroit mixture of the two informs *A History of New York*, and it is the combination that protects the writer from censure. Like every satirist, Irving uses a manifest fiction (Knickerbocker's fanciful narrative of Dutch New York) to attack discernible historic particulars in his own world (a nation of lawyers and "the self-satisfied citizens of this most enlightened republick"). And yet Irving's attack lacks the icy mind, the calculating strategy, the persistently rational approach to life, and the intensity of true satire.[31]

As a blend of satire and comedy, *A History of New York* under-mines more than it attacks. More precisely, it uses a "comedy of confusion" to ridicule order and system within the world.[32] Knick-erbocker's elaborate difficulty in shaping an accurate picture of his subject trivializes comparable efforts to create a meaningful sense of country in post-Revolutionary America (p. 98). Here, in fact, is one explanation for the enormous popularity of *A History of New York* in the early decades of the nineteenth century. Knick-erbocker's deliberate confusion is an amusing antidote for early Americans steeped in civic pomposity and high-minded searches for national order. Because comedy works through a special relaxation of concern by annihilating the concern itself, it tempo-rarily frees the mind from the desires and emotions that require action.[33] Irving's absurd parallels allow his tense fellow republi-cans to laugh away their anger and anxieties. His explicit analogies between the problems of Dutch New York and the new United States comically inflate or deflate serious issues away from a level of meaningful concern.

For Diedrich Knickerbocker, problems of country are at once petty and cosmic. America's "voluminous budgets of complaints" prove only that "your enlightened people love to be miserable," but each grievance must still be cited because even the smallest is "suf-ficient reason, according to the maxims of national dignity and hon-our, for throwing the whole universe into hostility and confusion" (p.231). Impulsive and emotional, the voice behind this irony con-stantly challenges the rational republican rhetoric it seeks to expose through laughter. As such it is both comic and subversive. "I could make every mother's son of ye grandfatherless," warns Diedrich, sick of constant debate over his republican heritage and the Founding Fathers (p.230). His main targets are "statesmen, orators, civilians, and divines; who by dint of big words, inflated periods, and windy doctrines, are kept afloat on the surface of society, as ignorant swimmers are buoyed up by blown bladders."[34]

The success of Irving's freewheeling humor is clear from the darkness it conveys without offending. Convinced that learned men "weave whole systems out of nothing," Diedrich Knickerbocker is intent upon reversing that process, "winnowing away all the chaff of hypothesis, and discarding the tares of fable" until literally nothing remains (pp. 48–50, 10). Inexorably, *A History of New York* marches down "the wide-spread, insatiable maw of oblivion" until everything "has returned to its primeval nothingness" (pp. 13, 443). Nevertheless, this spirit of negation remains comic because of Knickerbocker's own boundless, affirmative energy and elaborate play upon republican optimism and order.

At his angriest, Irving is unsuited for the more bitter art of Swift or Pope, but craft as well as temperament is responsible for the lighter humor and more cautious piquancy of *A History of New York*. Irving instinctively knows that direct attack will not meet with a receptive audience—an assumption in keeping with the intellectual movement of the eighteenth century away from satire and toward a more joyful and kindly theory of laughter.[35] His criticizing voice has to be comic because the more negative art of satire cannot reach the needs of an American culture still straining for affirmations. Accordingly, Knickerbocker's whimsical humor, excitement over the world, and enthusiasm for his own history round off the sharper edges of *A History of New York*. As old Diedrich summarizes this final perspective, "I look up to [the world] with the most perfect good nature, and my only sorrow is, that it does not prove itself worthy of the unbounded love I bear it" (p. 455). Good nature covers but does not hide a resentment that seizes the pen as "trusty weapon" (p. 334).

"In Harmony with the Feelings and Humors of My Townsmen"

The republican contesting American virtue, the historian rejecting a progressive view of country, the lawyer spurning a nation of laws—these are not the images that Americans retain of their first successful man of letters. Irving quickly retreated to safer ground and became what critics generally find, a placid portent of new beginnings in American literature.[36] He soon grew uneasy about his angry early works, *Salmagundi* and *A History of New York*, and by 1829 he was dedicating his craft to the civic vision that Diedrich Knickerbocker destroys.[37] Eventually, Irving even convinced himself that *A History of New York* represented "a temporary jeu d'esprit." "The Author's Apology" of 1848 worries about Knickerbocker's presumptuous trespasses, unwarrantable liberties, and rashness, stressing instead the older Irving's need to be "in harmony with the feelings and humors of my townsmen."[38]

As often happens, anger disappeared with success. The first edition of *A History of New York* earned between two and three thousand dollars—an astonishing sum for the times—and it made Irving the talk of the town.[39] Burdened by vocational failure, the young author easily found himself "quite flushed with this early taste of public favour." "I was noticed caressed & for a time elated by the popularity I gained . . . Wherever I went I was overwhelmed with attentions."[40] In 1809 Irving also lacked a controlling sense of self as a writer; there was, in consequence, no intellectual coherence to his alienation, no sense of purpose to sustain opposition. Not until *The Sketch Book of Geoffrey Crayon, Gent.*, in 1819, did Irving achieve real understanding of his craft, and by then his motivations were quite different. Diedrich Knickerbocker and Geoffrey Crayon were both the products of crisis. The bankruptcy of the Irving family business in 1818 was a comparable intellectual catalyst to the vocational problems and personal tragedy of 1809, but Irving's artistic needs had shifted drastically in the interim.

A History of New York flows from the bewilderment of one who has just realized the unfair pain that life inflicts upon the living. *The Sketch Book*, in contrast, represents a calculated move by Irving the bankrupt to regain lost caste or, as he also puts it, "to reinstate myself in the worlds thoughts."[41] The first book counters; the second seeks to reconcile and rejoin. Diedrich Knickerbocker gleefully juxtaposes starving poets to "a fat round bellied alderman" of a world (p. 351), while the gentlemanly Crayon avoids every incongruity in search of a dignified, harmonious stance for the writer as observer. The former's ingenuous search for "the chaste and simple garb of truth" has little to do with Crayon's "escape from the commonplace realities of the present."[42] A rambling language of exposure turns into the crafted sentimental tale.

Between the two voices of Knickerbocker and Crayon came a decade of virtual silence. It is a mark of Irving's general immaturity at twenty-seven that the success of *A History of New York* led not to new assurance and direction but to intellectual collapse. The celebrated author sank into "dismal dejection" and drifted "without aim or object." Uninterested in law and unable to write, Irving took a desultory role in the family business, calling himself "a mere animal; working among hardware and cutlery." Editorship of the *Analectic Magazine* (1813–14) did little to alleviate his apathy. "I became weary of every thing and of myself," Irving concluded in retrospect. A self-proclaimed idleness—"idle habits and idle associates & fashionable dissipation"—really meant a retreat to the indolence of youth but without the saving prospect of growth.[43]

These facts reveal *A History of New York* for what it is—an acting-out of childhood experience and arrested adolescent frustrations. Irving is certainly correct in calling it "a raw juvenile production."[44] The golden age of Wouter Van Twiller allows a nostalgic rendition of infancy and early boyhood. The first Nieuw Nederlandts is an "infant settlement," "a sturdy brat," and "a chubby overgrown urchin, clinging to its mother's breast." Eating, sleeping, and other domestic cares are its only activities.[45] Chronologically, the reigns of William the Testy and Peter the Headstrong move on to depict adolescence and early manhood with explicit references to Irving's vocational daydreams, first in the law and then in the military. William's legal wranglings project Irving's hostilities as a legal apprentice as do Diedrich Knickerbocker's complaints about writing. "Up early and to bed late," grumbles the Dutch historian, "poring over worm-eaten, obsolete, good-for-nothing books, and cultivating the acquaintance of a thousand learned authors, both ancient and modern, who, to tell the honest truth, are the stupidest companions in the world" (p. 42). These words apply with equal force to the life of a law student in 1809. In a similar way, Irving's personal dreams of military adventure between 1807 and 1815 find comic parallels in Peter Stuyvesant's chivalry. During the genesis of the Knickerbocker history, the young writer drew elaborate sketches of soldiers in his commonplace book. Then, as a rather incongruous

Colonel Irving of the Iron Greys, he was momentarily "roused and stimulated" by the War of 1812.[46] Of course, neither the law nor the military led Irving anywhere, and his doubts and later disappointments were rooted in the legal and military ruins of *A History of New York*.

The great irony of Washington Irving's career is that the dead ends of *A History of New York* produce far more energy and originality than the fresh start of *The Sketch Book* and everything that follows. Geoffrey Crayon's muted tones are harder won and based on a deeper understanding, but Knickerbocker's insistent voice is more clearly original, creative, and authentic.[47] Trapped in grief and aimlessness, the younger writer swings wildly but with telling effect. Geoffrey Crayon, on the other hand, is trying to make his way in the world. He first promises to alter his manners as an American in Europe and soon censures the behavior of others, complaining of "a querulous and peevish temper among our writers."[48] As early as 1823, Irving summarized the new patterns that would dominate all of his later writings: "I prefer summon[ing] up the bright pictures of life that I have witnessed and dwelling as much as possible on the agreeable." Creativity meant "an activity in my imagination . . . apt to soften and tint up the harshest realities."[49] The satirist has withdrawn.

Harsh realities do appear in *The Sketch Book*, but, as Irving suggests, they have been softened and tinted. Typically, his ordeal of bankruptcy surfaces in "Roscoe," "The Wife," and "Rip Van Winkle," but the bitterness and humiliation Irving personally felt have been filtered from these fictional accounts.[50] Roscoe, as a successful writer, is a superior being, "independent of the world around him" and, hence, untouched by financial ruin. When Roscoe's estate is auctioned off, the people are thronging wreckers. Retainers of the law then loiter like lizards and toads around a dry fountain, but even these "ill favoured beings" cannot reach the writer who is safely locked within "the superior society of his own thoughts." In "The Wife," a bankrupt fears the effects of financial ruin upon his delicate wife only to find that she is delighted with the humble cottage and simple life they must now lead. Rip Van Winkle's patrimonial estate has dwindled to a patch of Indian corn and potatoes, but he is temperamentally equipped to "take the world easy," perfectly content with his poverty.[51] Here are the defense mechanisms Irving used in his own situation rather than descriptions of the reality he found.

Throughout *The Sketch Book* death, sickness, and squalor are limned in delicate colors and framing discourse. The dead are cared for by the living, the sick by the hale, the poor by the rich, allowing Irving to draw the sting from life's terrors. "Half venturing, half shrinking," Crayon narrates as a man of care and sorrow. He travels the world as an idler one step above genteel poverty in a way that faintly recalls Diedrich Knickerbocker's more amusing shabbiness and comic fear over the landlady's bill.[52] Significantly, it is the posthumous writings of the Dutch historian within Crayon's *Sketch Book* that everyone remembers. "Rip Van Winkle" and "The Legend of Sleepy Hollow" captivate because they consciously reach back toward the more jaundiced eye and sharper tongue of the earlier persona.

"Rip Van Winkle" opens with a comic defense of Knickerbocker's stance *against* his culture. The idle Rip, as many have shown, is a natural renegade. His "insuperable aversion to all kinds of profitable labor" and his final success combine to make him a subversive force within republican culture.[53] "The Legend of Sleepy Hollow" comes even closer to the residual source of Knickerbocker's sardonic strength. Ichabod Crane, the outsider frightened away by the headless horseman of neighborhood lore, first appears as "the genius of famine descending upon the earth" in Irving's magic valley of prosperous farmers. Sleepy Hollow represents a retreat from the world and its distractions, the one peaceful exception within a restless country of incessant change. Ichabod is its mortal enemy because he is from the outside and holds such worldly and vocational ambitions. His unlimited appetites ("the dilating powers of an Anaconda") and interest in land speculation portend destruction. The most Brom Bones ("hero of the country round") can do is to divert Ichabod away from Sleepy Hollow. Like his regional counterparts invading Peter Stuyvesant's Nieuw Nederlandts, the avaricious Yankee schoolteacher is an intrinsic consequence of American growth and character and therefore unstoppable.[54]

Ichabod Crane's eventual and inevitable climb in the world represents both an unpleasant memory and a final barb from the author. For Ichabod ultimately becomes a New York lawyer who takes the traditional path to public office and succeeds as a justice of the city courts. Like Timothy Dabble before him, he is another "little great man" in republican culture. Irving's concluding postscript reaches back to former tirades against the legal profession and is an echo of problems not forgotten. Here Knickerbocker uses "pepper and salt" and "a triumphant leer" to point out that those who "have reason and the law on their side" will never understand Ichabod's story. Here too is the satirist's parting shot.[55] Irving's literary career extends across another forty years, but it remains almost entirely within the narrower emotional range of a sentimental readership. Unfortunately, the headless horseman of Sleepy Hollow is the Doppelgänger for a writer who would henceforth ignore the intellectual wit and sharp humor that made him famous.

CHAPTER 7

WILLIAM CULLEN BRYANT:
THE CREATIVE CONTEXT
OF THE POET

"The Poet of Our Woods"

America's first national poet was a young and rather angry lawyer in western Massachusetts just after the War of 1812. William Cullen Bryant wrote verse for another fifty years, but most of his important poems were finished before he decided, in 1825, to try journalism in New York City. These facts mark the creative context of a poet who has been victimized by more false impressions than any counterpart in American literature. Inflated by literary nationalists in his own day and dismissed as a mere precursor by later generations, Bryant survives, if at all, as one of the bearded schoolroom bards— "the dear old poet" once toasted jocularly by Hawthorne, Melville, and Oliver Wendell Holmes on a picnic in the Berkshires.[1] More recent observers, looking beyond the stereotype, have been drawn to the complications in the later career. For Bryant also served for forty-three years as editor-in-chief of the New York *Evening Post*, leaving critics with an absorbing problem: how to reconcile the idle dreamer who shuns worldly strife in poems like "Green River" and "A Winter Piece" with the self-made millionaire, the political commentator, the eager campaigner advising Abraham Lincoln on cabinet appointments.[2]

Whittier and Emerson were certain that the newspaper-man's "daily twaddle" and penchant for the "thistles and teazles of politics" undermined both his virtue and his creativity. Friends countered by isolating the high-mindedness of the poet in a separation of functions. "Not even the shadow of his business must fall upon the consecrated haunts of his muse," claimed John Bigelow in a typical defense of his business partner.[3] This debate created the "chaste and tidy envelop of the Man of Letters" that scholars have recently corrected by documenting Bryant's many involvements. But the very premises of modern reactions have kept attention upon the public figure of mid-century.[4] We need to concentrate upon the true poet of thirty years before—the more elusive Bryant who wrote "Thanatopsis" and "To A Waterfowl" when James Monroe was president. Missing is a firm sense of the creative framework available to Bryant between 1814 and 1825. What kind of poet was it possible to be in Federalist New England during the Era of Good Feeling? We know that Bryant was influenced by Archibald Alison's *Essays on the Nature and Principles of Taste* and by Wordsworth's critical essays and *Lyrical Ballads*.[5] But how did Alison's associationist views and aesthetic principles translate within early republican circles? What did it mean to read Wordsworth and write nature poetry in a frontier wilderness?

Answers to these questions may suggest an intrinsic context for the poet, but they are not easy to formulate. Scholarly generalizations placing Bryant between the neoclassical and romantic impulses of Europe say little about his actual situation in America, and we are only beginning to understand the responsiveness of Bryant and other early American intellectuals to Scottish moralists like Alison.[6] Bryant also faced a different natural setting than the English romantics did. In fact, he committed himself to both the difference and the importance of locality and context. "Let me counsel you," he advised his brother John, "to draw your images, in describing Nature, from what you observe around you . . . The skylark is an English bird, and an American who has never visited Europe has no right to be in raptures about it."[7]

Bryant was a close observer; more than the skylark was missing from the unbroken forests around him in western Massachusetts. As his friend the painter Thomas Cole noted, the American landscape was "destitute of many of those circumstances that give value to the European." The distinctive characteristic of native scenery was "wildness"—a trait that often produced "a mysterious fear" in men.[8] When Bryant hinted of a landscape without expression in his "Lectures on Poetry," he glimpsed the same "blank desertion, no familiar shapes / Of hourly objects" that Wordsworth more openly feared in *The Prelude*. The grasp of the English poet was always superior, but Wordsworth and the other writers of the romantic movement had the advantage of a more visible "mooring place" or haven—the safer nature of the English rural parish—to return to and recover within.[9] More artificial means were needed in America to deal with the blank face of Nature. Bryant's waterfowl flies through "desert and illimitable air," along a "pathless coast," and within a "cold, thin atmosphere" that turns into a swallowing abyss (III, 26–27). Up against limitless space and an absence of form, the poet learned to frame his own gaze in ways we no longer recognize or accept.

This search for order emphasized self-control. "We cannot eradicate the imagination, but we may cultivate and regulate it," Bryant said in language closer to his Calvinist heritage than to romanticism (V,15). Order also required a nature becalmed. The tranquillity of "Inscription For The Entrance To A Wood" (III, 23–24), the sweet and quiet eye of Bryant's fringed gentian (III, 221), and the soft breath of "The West Wind" (III, 41–42) were all part of a general plan to "see the lovely and the wild / Mingled in harmony on Nature's face" (III, 102). Ultimately, one controlled nature by placing it within the social context of man. Despite the popular image of "The Poet of Our Woods," Bryant's nature poems invariably lead to civilization and away from the settings they purport to celebrate.[10]

"Forced to Drudge for the Dregs of Men"

Bryant's insistence on calm control ultimately undermined his talent. Critics have noted the growing serenity of tone and mood that robbed the later poetry of urgency and strength by removing all possibility of conflict.[11] But no one has appreciated the crucial connection between this loss in tension and the poet's shift in vocations. Bryant's creative decline was gradual; nevertheless, its origins can be traced clearly to the year in which he left the law for a more satisfying career in journalism. "Thanatopsis," "The Yellow Violet," "Inscription For The Entrance To A Wood," "To A Waterfowl," "Green River," "A Winter Piece," "The West Wind," "The Rivulet," "I Broke The Spell That Held Me Long," "Autumn Woods," "Mutation," and "November" were written before the move to New York in 1825. There is no later series of comparable power, and few of Bryant's better poems came after 1830.

Bryant the lawyer was a better poet than Bryant the journalist because of the vocational tensions in the younger man's life—tensions carrying into his verse and cutting across habitual calm. Quick success in New York removed the major source of disruption and anxiety. "I have got to be quite famous as the editor of a newspaper . . . This is better than poetry and magazines," he wrote in 1826, after jumping from a small literary journal to the influential *Evening Post*.[12] By 1829 Bryant was controlling the *Evening Post* and calling journalism an indispensable and noble vocation. He found it infinitely more useful than law.[13] As was the custom among early American editors, Bryant of the *Evening Post* rarely ventured into the outside world either in search of news or to record noteworthy events. Typically he saw a small number of subordinates and visitors in the quiet ambiance of his office where, in the words of a business partner, "his command of his irritabilities and passions was so complete that he breathed an air perpetually serene and bright."[14] This satisfaction in the newspaperman proved dangerous for a poet already inclined toward assurance and reserve.

Quite the reverse had been true of the lawyer-poet in western Massachusetts who often lost his temper in courtroom debate (I, 204). Vocational uncertainties in the young lawyer lie at the center of Bryant's early creativity. "Thanatopsis" and "To A Waterfowl," both pleading for a higher sense of meaning and direction beyond individual experience, date from his hesitation and self-doubt just before Bryant opened his legal practice in Plainfield, Massachusetts.[15] Many of his nature poems from 1815 to 1825 play upon the juxtaposition of ideal nature against the real world of man, but Bryant's clear unhappiness as a law student and lawyer adds a new dimension to the conventional device.

In "Inscription For The Entrance To A Wood," Nature's "abodes of gladness" have meaning mostly because "the world is full of guilt and misery," causing the speaker to loathe his life within it (III, 23). Bland descriptions of scenery in "The West Wind" receive fresh intensity through a closing simile linking nature to man's dissatisfaction (III, 42). The poet of "Green River" delights all the more in his wanderings because they come in moments snatched from study and care (III, 31). A similar happiness in "A Winter Piece" follows from relief in "hours I stole / From cares I loved not, but of which the world / Deems highest" (III, 34–35). The contrast in a poem like "Green River" is not simply between an idle dreamer and the man of the world, but between the escaping poet and the lawyer who is:

> forced to drudge for the dregs of men,
> And scrawl strange words with the barbarous pen,
> And mingle among the jostling crowd
> Where the sons of strife are subtle and loud. (III, 33)

Significantly, Bryant's greatest poetic productivity came in 1824 when his legal practice became most distasteful and when he agonized over a growing desire to quit the profession. With power and immediacy he poured his anxieties into the poetry of this period. Two poems in particular, "Autumn Woods" and "Mutation," written together in 1824 and published in the *United States Literary Gazette* within a month of each other, appear almost as a type for inner struggle (III, 111–114). Like anyone vacillating over an important decision, Bryant was ambivalent about change and the necessity for it. "Autumn Woods" longs for a season that will never end and glorifies the static, escapist desire to remain dreaming in nature's colored shades, away from "the tug for wealth and power." "Mutation," on the other hand, quickly renounces "short-lived pleasure," rejoices in rapid fluctuations in time and feelings, and finishes with a couplet exalting the freshness of change: "Weep not that the world changes—did it keep / A stable, changeless state, 'twere cause indeed to weep." Both poems rely dramatically upon the presence of "passions and the cares that wither life." The poet endures "fiercest agonies," "dreams of horror," "strong secret pangs of shame," as well as sudden moments of joyful release—all emotions in keeping with Bryant's state of mind when deciding to leave the law against the advice of colleagues and friends.[16]

The strength and persistence of Bryant's dissatisfaction help to explain why the poet's unhappiness remained such a goad during the creative years of 1811 to 1825. As early as 1812, the beginning law student was threatening to desert his studies. "Would not blacksmithing," he complained, "be as good a trade as any for the display of one's abilities?" Letters over the next four years confessed a continuing aversion, and he shrank from the prospect of actual practice. "The day when I shall set up my ginger-bread board is to me a day of fearful expectation," he wrote in 1815. "The nearer I approach to it the more I dread it."[17] Bryant overcame these fears, but the lawyer's letters show him moving from initial distaste toward an active hatred for what he called "this beggarly profession," "a shabby business," and "the disagreeable disgusting drudgery of the law."[18]

Disenchantment did not spring from failure. Starting in 1811, Bryant studied law for four years under two of the leading attorneys in Massachusetts, Samuel Howe of Worthington and William Baylies of Bridgewater. Both men remained advisers well beyond the point in 1815 when their protégé was admitted to the Massachusetts bar at the precocious age of twenty. Bryant subsequently maintained a superior practice for the times in Great Barrington, one of the larger towns in Berkshire County. He argued before the Massachusetts supreme court at least four times, became a justice of the peace, performed his duties as the elected town clerk of Great Barrington, and served as one of the town's tithing men. It was the record of an accomplished lawyer and leading citizen covering fourteen years.[19]

Why should a successful lawyer come to resent his profession so intensely? Biographers have responded too narrowly, looking to Bryant's outrage over a particular judicial decision and assuming general moral repudiation of the entire legal system. Neither the details of the court case in question nor the pragmatic politics of the later newspaperman support this image of high-minded absolution. After *Bloss v. Tobey* in 1824, Bryant did indeed claim that the state supreme court's decision to arrest judgment for his client Bloss was "a piece of pure chicane" cheating Bloss of his just award. But Chief Justice Isaac Parker's opinion in the case supplies a less idealistic context for Bryant's disgust. The court made its decision to arrest judgment with extreme reluctance and only because of a very basic error in pleading on the part of counselor William Cullen Bryant. Moreover, Bryant's client was left with an alternative remedy.[20]

Bryant's disillusionment as a lawyer grew from a much more complicated sense of failure, one that explains why vocational anxieties transferred so readily into the early poetry. In the 1820s the poet discovered that he could not succeed on his own terms as a writer while practicing law. His realization was based upon the peculiar twist and urgency that New Englanders of the period brought to early American conceptions of authorship. Of course, no American before the 1820s made a living from writing, but Bryant and his contemporaries, as gentlemen of letters, turned the burden of a separate profession into an important source of literary identity. Literature in isolation meant a life of sterility and irresponsibility; intellectual respectability required involvement within the world. These tenets were especially central to cultural identity in New England at a time when economic woes and the demise of the Federalist party left many intellectuals warning of regional collapse and calling for a reassertion of civic vitality.

For Bryant's generation the central statement of the writer's cultural responsibilities came in Joseph Stevens Buckminster's *Phi Beta Kappa* address at Harvard College in 1809, "On the Dangers and Duties of Men of Letters." Forty years after the event, George Ticknor, the leader of Boston literary circles, could marvel over Buckminster's impact: "The very tones of his voice stir us still as with the sound of a trumpet. They sank deep into many hearts; and more than one young spirit, we have reason to think, was on that day and in that hour . . . consecrated to letters."[21] Buckminster insisted that utility was the object of study, that the effective jurist, statesman, theologian, and historian was worth "a whole cabinet of *dilettanti*." Contrasting active and inactive learning, he expressed his contempt for those who avoid "the common contests and occupations of active life . . . relinquishing its real duties in the luxurious leisure of study."

Buckminster inserted a Calvinist energy and rectitude that tied the man of letters' sense of station to the Congregationalist's belief in corporate responsibility. He also added that spirit of gloomy anxiety and cosmic uncertainty unavoidable in a New England divine. The duty of the man of letters was even heavier in America because "every where there are dangers and evils" within "the awful history of our times," because American educational backwardness represented a threat to progress, because the age of revolution had left "the minds of men in an unsettled state," and because intellectuals in the New World were "so insulated" within a "vast territory." Republican culture was too thin and precarious to allow anything but the most serious communal obligation in the American writer. Nor was this all. The theme of Buckminster's exhortation was the necessity of a *balanced* involvement in civic affairs that managed somehow to avoid mere politics and daily dissension. Political ambition, concern for popularity, even too much curiosity over the minutiae of politics would plunge the literary man within "the service of vulgar and usurping faction," thus destroying all possibility of virtuous learning. Like his Puritan ancestors, the New England man of letters was expected to live in the world but not to be of it.[22]

The young Bryant would have known of Buckminster's oration—it was the most important comment on literary vocation in New England before Emerson's "American Scholar"—but he heard similar precepts every day of his life from a mother who proudly traced her ancestry to the *Mayflower* pilgrims and a father who strove to be the man of letters Buckminster described. "Never be idle," Sarah Snell Bryant constantly admonished her children (I, 58). In his late seventies, her dutiful son would still feel uneasy when unemployed (II, 336), and he was always critical of the unsettling idleness he found as a traveler in Europe. Implicit in every stage and moment of Bryant's career was the seventeenth-century warning of John Cotton: "Yet if thou hast no calling, tending to publique good, thou art an uncleane beaste."[23]

The poet's father was both the concrete example behind the call to duty and the "preceptor" responsible for Bryant's literary precocity.[24] Dr. Peter Bryant maintained an extensive medical practice around the Hampshire town of Cummington, served as a representative and senator in the Massachusetts general court, made himself an accomplished musician, collected one of the best libraries in the region, and wrote poems of his own under the sobriquet "student in physic." He admired Timothy Dwight and John Trumbull as much for their public stances as for their verse, and his closest friends were professional men "uniting dignity and grace of deportment to fine intellectual endowments, wide reading, liberality of thought and act, and public spirit" (I, 64–65).

Dr. Bryant evaluated his son's creative efforts, rewarded the best poems with gifts of money, submitted pieces to knowledgeable critics, and even arranged for publication. Always, however, warm encouragement assumed a corresponding involvement in the world and a balance *between* literary enterprise and vocation. There is, in fact, an unnoticed lesson in the doctor's unilateral submission of "Thanatopsis" to the *North American Review*, an event so electrifying it sent editors rushing into the street to glimpse a true Poet.[25] Peter

Bryant sought publication only after his son refused to do so. He acted to reassert the need for equilibrium against the poet's resolution to sacrifice literature entirely to law. When Dr. Bryant died in 1820, his son dutifully praised the father's balanced "years of toil and studious search," promising to copy the example through life (III, 51). This promise and the values behind it explain why the creative writer remained editor of the *Evening Post*, a man of letters in public service, long after wealth freed him of every necessity.[26] Earlier, the poet had searched in vain for a similar fulfillment in law, pouring his frustrations into the only poems we remember.

Bryant entered the legal profession assuming high patriotic usefulness, gentlemanly status, and disinterested study within "the amiable and admirable secrets of the law."[27] Actual practice as one of only three lawyers in isolated Great Barrington proved far less inspiring. Bryant found himself professionally at the center of every town quarrel with "an extremely exciteable, and not very enlightened population."[28] His docket books from the period do not convey the high usefulness he imagined; they are filled with cases like *Sarah Bacon v. Sylvester Halbert:* "plf's [plaintiff's] action for selling cheese on promise that it was good—it turned out rotten and good for nothing." A lawyer's business in western Massachusetts involved the settlement of petty contract disputes, the resolution of boundary line grievances, the eviction of tenants on behalf of absentee landlords, and the collection of money from unwilling and frequently indigent debtors who were also neighbors.[29] In a word, legal practice plunged Bryant directly into the factionalism and petty dissension that Buckminster had warned the man of letters to avoid at all costs. No wonder the new journalist of 1825 wrote so happily from New York of escape from "innumerable local quarrels and factions." "[I] am aloof," he announced, "from those miserable feuds and wranglings that make Great Barrington an unpleasant residence, even to him who tries every method in his power to avoid them."[30]

By comparison, leadership of the *Evening Post* provided the best possible platform for a man of letters who wished to serve his country while remaining outside of politics. The newspaper editor always inveighed against mere faction, and usually managed to separate himself from the worldly conflicts he wrote about.[31] The effect of this separation on the poet was profound. As early as 1826, Bryant had believed that "poetry lifts us to a sphere where self-interest cannot exist, and where the prejudices that perplex our every-day life can hardly enter" (v, 18–19). Now that sphere could be protected from intrusive tensions. "It is remarkable, indeed," wrote his son-in-law Parke Godwin in 1883, "how few traces of the agitations and sharp collisions of his life are left on his poems" (I, 399). Richard Henry Dana, Sr., praising what later readers would condemn, congratulated the poet in 1864 for "the freedom from all appearances of effort" in his new collection, *Thirty Poems*. The volume itself was a "semi-angelic creature" allowing only "beautiful and harmless earthly things" to approach its pages. "I thank you," wrote Dana, "for the pleasing consciousness of subsidence into a perfect calm which it brought upon me" (II, 207–208). Emerson and Whittier had been exactly wrong in their criticisms. It was not politics and worldly affairs that ruined the poet but a deliberate emotional detachment from these affairs consistent with lifelong goals as a man of letters.

"The Lesson Nature Taught"

The separation of life and art kept Bryant from thinking like the American Wordsworth that many have called him. From the English romantics, he accepted emotions as a guide, plain language as his base, and nature as the source of all inspiration.[32] None of these premises, however, could mean the same thing for an American weaned upon Calvinism and Federalist politics. The poet actually distrusted expression of feeling, and he was notorious among American literati for his personal lack of warmth. In poetry he preferred "calm power and mighty sweep" to "empty gust of passion" because, like many another New Englander, he knew that the human heart was "a garden covered with weeds" and that "the government of passion" was the paramount issue in human development.[33] Nature was indeed an inspiration, but Bryant's background made him look beyond nature toward republican idealism for definition and purpose. "It is the dominion of poetry over the feelings and passions of men," he wrote in 1826, "that gives it its most important bearing upon the virtue and welfare of society . . . It [poetry] cherishes patriotism, the incitement to vigorous toils endured for the welfare of communities" (v, 16–17). These are the claims of an early republican searching for controls and of a citizen accepting collective obligation; they have little to do with a romantic poet's assertion of individual feeling and imagination.

Regulation, utility, and communal growth are the themes of a social vision. Wordsworth, of course, made numerous statements on passions conquered, on the poet's role within the world, and on the moral usefulness of poetry in society, but always with the underlying assumption of an individual speaking with feeling to other individuals: "The poet writes under one restriction only, namely, the necessity of giving immediate pleasure to a human being . . . not as a lawyer, a physician, a mariner, an astronomer, or a natural philosopher, but as a Man."[34] By contrast, Bryant described a poet addressing many Americans at once and on matters of social identity. His insistence upon a direct link between poetry and civic welfare also meant that more was at stake than Wordsworth's desire to give immediate pleasure. The private poet was a public teacher responsible for the nation's good—and, inevitably, answerable to it. Thus, Bryant in 1826 could unite eloquence and poetry and compare the public orator to the poet: "Eloquence is the poetry of prose; poetry is the eloquence of verse . . . Let the same man [the orator] go to his closet and clothe in numbers conceptions full of the same fire and spirit, and they will be poetry" (v, 13).

The interchange of concepts does more than explain the way Bryant, New York's first citizen, moved so easily between his writing desk, the editor's office, and the public speaker's platform; it also indicates how directly doctrines of republican virtue influenced the voice of the early poet. Bryant in 1818 dated the beginning of American poetry from the War for Independence and Francis Hopkinson's "Battle Of The Kegs" (v, 48). He considered "The Ages"—his survey in verse of the evolution of human liberty through the climax of the American Revolution—to be a credo, placing it first in every collection of poetry.[35] And he envied those American intellectuals born just a little earlier amidst "the public actions of the men who achieved our Revolution, noble examples of steady rectitude, magnanimous self-denial, and cheerful self-sacrifice for the sake of their country" (v, 333–334). Bryant's summary of Friedrich von Schiller's goals as a writer applied much more forcefully to his own and revealed how intrinsic a political vision was to the practicing poet: "The office of him who labored in the field of letters, he thought, was to make mankind better and happier by illustrating and enforcing the relations and duties of justice, beneficence, and brotherhood, by which men are bound to each other; and he never forgot this in anything which he wrote" (vi, 219–220).

Modern readers, interested only in the more timeless nature poet, tend to set aside such aspirations as well as Bryant's poems on civic subjects. Making use of scholarly divisions between "The Poems of Nature" and "The Poems of Progress," they forget that Bryant's sense of mission as an early American never allowed the distinction.[36] The chauvinistic remarks that critics would like to dismiss as products of a superficial literary nationalism actually came from an encompassing and urgent idealism. Bryant and his contemporaries believed political changes were transforming the world. The frailty of republicanism in New England, still recovering from the Hartford Convention, only underlined the importance of ideological involvement.[37] A correct sense of country, as distinguished from mere patriotism, was the major intellectual concern of the age—so much so that it shaped most other theoretical considerations.

Just as the poet of the woods always needed more than the rustic ideal, so nature in isolation failed to provide sufficient scope for the early republican's needs. It is true that the initial nature poems are remembered for celebrating retreat from the world, but retreat itself lacks permanent legitimacy in Bryant's view. By way of comparison, there is little of the "wise passiveness" in meditation defended so vehemently by Wordsworth in "Expostulation and Reply" (1798) or of the separate, viable place in nature of Coleridge's "Reflections on Having Left a Place of Retirement" (1795). The reveries of Bryant's "Inscription For The Entrance To A Wood," "Green River," and "A Winter Piece" take place during stolen hours, and each assumes return to the active world and its cares (III, 23, 31–38). The "certain flight" of the bird in "To A Waterfowl" teaches a "lesson," but the poet's corresponding steps will lie within the world of men where that lesson in direction can be applied (III, 26–27). Even the modest flower in "The Yellow Violet" is less an image in nature than it is a type for social behavior:

> But midst the gorgeous blooms of May,
> I passed thee on thy humble stalk.
>
> So they, who climb to wealth, forget
> The friends in darker fortunes tried.　(III, 22)

Later nature poems continue to stress the familiar observer who enjoys communion with nature but yields this pleasure for responsibilities in the world. There are holy men who hide themselves in the wilderness of "A Forest Hymn," but Bryant is not one of them, identifying himself instead with another group—"holy men / Who deemed it were not well to pass life thus" (III, 133). One senses something furtive about the hiding holy men of "A Forest Hymn," and in later poems their position stands revealed as clear evasion of duty. Bryant's "William Tell" (1827) assumes a man of nature. Nevertheless, "the lesson Nature taught" is a socially integrated vision of a liberated Switzerland, which prepares Tell for the great work of setting his country free (III, 198). Again, in "The Antiquity of Freedom" (1842), Freedom is an armed warrior who rests in nature's peaceful shades but dares not remain or sleep there for fear of Tyranny's ambush (III, 305–307).

Bryant's longest poem, "Sella," written in the dark year of 1862, is an explicit statement of the artist's obligation to leave nature behind in exchange for service to country. This trite excursion into fairyland has been uniformly misread as a piece of pure escapism from wartime pressures, but the poem itself suggests a more interesting conclusion.[38] Sella, a consort of water nymphs in nature, grieves when family members block all return to the natural world of pure enjoyment. Then, incredibly, she becomes a hydraulic engineer, using her knowledge of nature's waterways to build canals, mills, reservoirs, and an industrial age. A hundred new cities mourn her death in old age as the moving force and matriarch of society. Blocked from a narrow, personal indulgence in nature's kingdom, the artist learns to think of larger service and turns her talent to the more important work of constructing a successful civilization (IV, 101–120). For Bryant, the responsible intellectual could always return to the higher realm of nature but only as a visitor who is "sent back to the world with . . . moral perceptions cleared and invigorated" (V, 19–20).

Characteristically, nature prefigures the poet's best hope for society and is used for this purpose (III, 109). Many of Bryant's poems depend on a positive frame of natural imagery to provide either a perspective for viewing social activity or a suggestion of future historical events. Hence, the image of a pleasant wilderness in "The Conjunction of Jupiter and Venus" leads quickly to a political discussion of American ascendancy and the unhappiness of modern Greece (III, 180–183). "The Prairies" begins as a description of that setting but becomes an imaginary political history of the region (III,

228–232). The mountain scenery of "To The Apennines" provides a platform for viewing the "armed nations" that have swept through European history (III, 244–246). Bryant's accent in each poem falls upon human history, not nature's beauty.[39] Thus, in "The Twenty-Second Of December," a celebration of the first American settlement, human event surpasses natural setting when pilgrim fame appears "greener still" than the wonders of the New World (III, 220).

Bryant's main problem in such correspondences was that he observed carefully enough to know that nature cut across every one of them. The nature of blessed repose turns demonic to kill an innocent child in "A Presentiment" (III, 273–274) and brings nameless horror in "The Hurricane" (III, 195–197). Breezes first carry birds, then "seize and dash them dead" in "The Winds" (III, 288–291). The poet limits the implications of such savage imagery by comparing the wild winds to European tyrants soon to be conquered—political theory rather than nature's mercy restores order—but even nature's predictable return to "hymnings sweet" fails to answer the poet's leading question, "Why rage ye thus?"

There is a chaos and potential for evil in nature that offends Bryant's search for order. He shrinks in fear from her power in "Midsummer" (III, 172), from her hostility to man in "The New and The Old" (IV, 77–78), and from her indifference in "The Rivulet" (III, 82–85). The poet who remains in the woods finds inscrutable mystery instead of larger meaning. Even more terrifying, he encounters complete absence of form. "The Unknown Way" (1845) illustrates Bryant's appreciation of this peril (IV, 12–14). Here the poet describes the two paths of life: one a hard, dusty, open road within civilization and the other a path in nature through a flowering woodland where the shade is cool, the *Horatian secretum iter*. More than civic responsibility keeps the poet on his harder route. At the last, nature's way is unknown and, therefore, dangerous; the inviting path may end, in Bryant's words, "like human life, on a trackless beach."

Scottish Influences: "The Mighty Spell of Mind"

Bryant's anxieties suggest a different poet from the placid sentimentalist that scholars have found.[40] His apparent calm masked apprehensions and underlying tensions. Certainly, he was aware of the discrepancies in his thought between natural harmony and chaos, between feeling and distrust of emotion, between bucolic retreat and civic vision, between artistic reverie and social obligation. And his recognition of these problems can be seen in the series of intellectual resolutions he developed from readings in the Scottish moralists. Early republicans, in search of controls, seized upon the philosophical constraints offered by the Scottish common-sense school, and Bryant was no exception. As early as 1812, he read and accepted Archibald Alison's *Essays on the Nature and Principles of Taste* (1790), Thomas Reid's *Inquiry into the Human Mind on the Principles of Common Sense* (1764), and Dugald Stewart's *Elements of the Philosophy of the Human Mind* (1792).[41] Indeed, William Hudson, Robert Streeter, and William Free already have shown how the aesthetic thought of Archibald Alison, based on associationist psychology, shaped Bryant's "Lectures on Poetry" and encouraged his literary nationalism.[42] The same influences carried into the poetry where Bryant used Reid, Stewart, and particularly Alison to regulate his anxieties.

Numerous affinities attracted the republican poet to the Scottish moralists—not least were fear of "an ill-regulated imagination" and of "immoderate passions," acceptance of nature's guiding laws, belief in an innate moral sense for interpreting those laws, and insistence upon man's essential definition within society.[43] But these particulars were less important than the support the American received for crucial strategies as a poet. Alison's *Essays* contained a moral justification for the role of the civic poet, a psychological basis for linking man's various levels of experience, and an aesthetic premise for separating the complexities of nature from the natural harmonies Bryant wanted to celebrate. Alison, in other words, provided the rationales that Bryant needed to control his poetry.

Like many of the Scottish moralists, Alison combined social conservatism and belief in an innate moral sense with associationism and a sensationalist conception of knowledge. He offered a tempered idealism that acknowledged the world while emphasizing the individual's ability to control perception within it and an associative theory of the imagination that stressed comprehensiveness and synthesis rather than subjectivism or skepticism.[44] These assumptions were extremely welcome ones to American intellectuals torn between ideological certainties and republican unrest. Alison's principal inquiry in his *Essays* was to analyze the "Law of Mind" behind the complex emotions of beauty and sublimity. He believed that "the artist is able to awaken this important exercise of imagination, and to exalt objects of simple and common pleasure, into objects of Beauty or Sublimity." Few ideas could have created more excitement among American writers bent upon instilling love of country in a republican citizenry. Alison's insistence that "National associations" increased the emotions of sublimity and beauty only magnified his importance.[45]

By separating sensation and perception from ensuing emotional responses, Alison placed aesthetic experience—emotions of taste—completely within the human mind:

> Thus when we feel either the beauty or sublimity of natural scenery . . . we are conscious of a variety of images in our minds, very different from those which the objects themselves can present to the eye. Trains of pleasing or of solemn thought arise spontaneously within our minds; our hearts swell with emotions, of which the objects before us seem to afford no adequate cause.

Here, Alison's use of the association of ideas became both an explanation of discrepancy and the essence of complex emotion. He argued that an initial strong feeling—arising from perception of a worthy object—triggered in the imagination a train of corresponding images from previous experience. "The object itself," he believed, "appears only to serve as a hint, to awaken the imagination, and to lead it through every analogous idea that has place in the memory." By definition, this process moved beyond an immediate context toward a larger synthesis, but the divisions were such as to interrupt the experience at any point. One could perceive without feeling initial emotion, and one could feel emotion without exciting the imagination into the train of images that became complex emotions of sublimity or beauty.[46]

The Scottish moralist's premises led him toward troubling but exciting conclusions. Even if observers saw the same things, they were not going to emerge with the same emotional experiences; they would fail to remain even close without a series of mental correspondences to work with.[47] New Englanders like Bryant, Edward T. Channing, Jared Sparks, and George Bancroft read Alison and debated a particular problem in this regard. Were Americans handicapped by the absence of what Bryant called "the associations of tradition"? Was a republican citizenry in danger of merely perceiving the new country without experiencing its sublime grandeur?[48] If so, Alison placed special responsibility on poets as fertile sources of sublime association, and he told them how to proceed. Mental processes, he insisted, not only allowed combinations of different levels of associations but virtually required them. The train of ideas that might become associated with a poem, scene, or painting easily combined moral, natural, social, and political experiences from the memory.[49] Alisonian aesthetics gave intellectual permission to artists to present moral and civic issues in nature poetry—an opportunity that went hand in glove with the early American writer's obligation to create a virtuous sense of country out of proper associations.[50] This is part of what Bryant meant when he spoke of the dominion of poetry over the feelings as a crucial influence upon the virtue and welfare of society (v, 16).

Belief in the centrality of mental activity also allowed the artist a breathtaking ascendency over the physical world. Since desirable aesthetic response came largely from an internal principle of connection, one was free to ignore or even to change what Alison called "that confusion of expression which so frequently takes place even in the most beautiful scenes of real Nature." *Essays* becomes one long celebration of the artist's control as Alison establishes a continuum of the sublime based upon the artist's corrective powers. The art of gardening rises above the confusion of nature, and landscape painting is superior to both because of the artist's greater aesthetic control in that medium. Over all stands the poet who, "with the mighty spell of mind at his command," is most capable of giving to expression a unity of character not necessarily found in nature. Of course, the true poet uses expression not to supplant nature but to discover its designs; discovery is the highest experience of the sublime. "Nothing is more delightful," concluded Alison, "than in any subject where we at first perceived only confusion, to find regularity gradually emerging, and to discover, amid the apparent chaos, some uniform principle which reconciles the whole."[51]

Here were solutions to Bryant's contradictions and fears. He clearly depended on Alison's search for design, his belief in analogies drawn between the natural and moral spheres, his emphasis upon the power of national associations, and his confidence that the complexity of nature could be circumscribed through intellectual control. Time and again, the poet reaches for the aesthetic unity that associationism allowed an observer to impose upon nature. In "The Path"—something of an answer to "The Unknown Way"—human direction overcomes a dreary wilderness when a pathway built by the poet suggests highways linking cities and nations (IV, 138–141). "The Old Man's Counsel" shows how a selective use of images and types from nature will bring, in the face of darkness, a recognition of divinity in the elements (III, 293–296).

These were the strategies that an early republican could use to control the world, and they were certainly the ones a New England heritage encouraged. Alison, after all, was another Protestant divine who accepted the material world as a scene of moral discipline. When Bryant in 1826 described the poet's power in drawing analogies and correspondences "between the things of the moral and of the natural world," he could have spoken with either Archibald Alison or Jonathan Edwards in mind.[52] In fact, the detailed parallels between individual poems of Bryant's and passages from *Essays on the Nature and Principles of Taste* reveal a profound reliance. Alison found Nature to be man's one unreproaching friend amid the agitations of society; he warned that professional life and activity in the world could dull one's sensibilities; and he urged true intellectuals to seek dignified self-command and a predominance of mind over temporary emotion. The same themes were virtual compulsions in Bryant's early poetry.[53]

The Still Voice of "Thanatopsis"

The poet's masterpiece, "Thanatopsis," depends upon the context we have traced, and the influence is crucial because Bryant wrote a poem qute different from the one modern readers have found. Despite prevailing interpretations, "Thanatopsis" is not a dialogue between the persona of the poet and a voice in nature. Even the earliest proponent of a shift in speakers within the poem, Carl Van Doren in 1915, was bothered by seeming inconsistency in nature's point of view, and every hypothesis since then has presented its own problems. Are there many voices in "Thanatopsis" or only two? Has the poet returned in a concluding section or does dialogue lapse into monologue? Is exchange finally unequal because man cannot hope to reach nature's philosophical level or because of Bryant's own uncertain craftsmanship?[54] Scholarly debate will prove endless because discussion is based upon a faulty premise and upon too much attention given to the supposed poet of nature. There is only one speaking voice in "Thanatopsis"—that of the poet guiding his reader through a train of related mental associations toward sublime emotion and a sense of unified calm.

The extraordinary tonal uniformity of "Thanatopsis"—always a problem for those seeking an exchange—offers intuitive support for a single voice. So does the tripartite division in Puritan sermonology that informs the poem.[55] For in sharing the structure, the rhetorical tone, and the directive, didactic thrust of a sermon, "Thanatopsis" must function within genre as a discourse of formal instruction and not as dialogue. Everything about Bryant's background substantiates this conclusion. Like most early republicans, he preferred oratory as a literary form, and his poems rely heavily on the sustained eloquence of pulpit and platform.[56]

If the initial section of "Thanatopsis" corresponds to the doctrine of a sermon, Bryant's text is clearly Alison's *Essays on the Nature and Principles of Taste.*

> To him who in the love of Nature holds
> Communion with her visible forms, she speaks
> A various language; for his gayer hours
> She has a voice of gladness, and a smile
> And eloquence of beauty, and she glides
> Into his darker musings, with a mild
> And healing sympathy, that steals away
> Their sharpness, ere he is aware. When thoughts
> Of the last bitter hour come like a blight
> Over thy spirit, and sad images
> Of the stern agony, and shroud, and pall,
> And breathless darkness, and the narrow house,
> Make thee to shudder, and grow sick at heart;—
> Go forth, under the open sky, and list
> To Nature's teachings, while from all around—
> Earth and her waters, and the depths of air—
> Comes a still voice.[57]

William Hudson has shown how Bryant used Alison's belief in a healing principle of nature and how the poet may have been influenced in this passage by Alison's description of autumnal decay and melancholy. In addition, Alison wrote frequently of the "expression" of nature's general form, and he gave Bryant his central premise: "The gaiety of Nature alone, is beautiful to the cheerful man; its melancholy, to the man of sadness."[58]

Alisonian aesthetics furnished Bryant with a procedure for "Thanatopsis," a methodological approach that makes dialogue between man and the external world extremely unlikely. In *Essays on the Nature and Principles of Taste* nature either reflects man's moods or awakens him to an internal process of moral emotion, but it is incapable of intellectual exchange. "Matter in itself is unfitted to produce any kind of emotion," explained Alison the sensationalist. Mind, on the other hand, held a sway that is hard to reconcile with Nature's apparent dominance within "Thanatopsis" in all theories of a dialogue. "Our minds," wrote Alison, "instead of being governed by the character of external objects, are enabled to bestow upon them a character which does not belong to them." Nature is a catalyst at the beginning of mental process; it is "fitted to awaken us to moral emotion; to lead us, when once the key of our imagination is struck, to trains of fascinating and of endless imagery."[59]

A train of inward images and emotions is exactly what we find in "Thanatopsis." In an earlier introduction dating from 1815, Bryant had placed his poem within the "better genius" of a poet who "would thus commune" through a series of mental images.[60] The subsequent personification of nature in Bryant's final version eliminates this device, but a careful reading shows that point of view always remains in the mind of a single observer. Nature in "Thanatopsis" speaks only to one who first "holds / Communion with her visible forms" in an approximation of Alisonian sensation and perception. The language of nature appears "various" because it mirrors changes in human emotion and works within the thought of man ("she glides into his darker musings"). In consequence, the still voice of the poem requires an ear already listening to nature's teachings; it comes "from all around—Earth and her waters, and the depths of air" or through a conscious appreciation of nature's comprehensive design. Even the noun "Communion"—foregrounded in line two in a striking variation upon the verb form of 1818—confirms Bryant's focus upon an individual mind facing mystery. In Calvinist New England the very concept of the Sacrament bespoke mental preparation and introspective analysis of emotion. Bryant was fully aware of the literary tradition in sacramental meditations that turned private religious devotion into poetic experience.[61]

Unity of mind and voice are significant because they point toward the actual strategy of Bryant's masterpiece. "Thanatopsis" is not an exchange between a poet of the woods and his source of inspiration but rather a deliberate movement *away from nature* by a nineteenth-century American in search of other controls. We already have examined Bryant's apprehensions regarding the natural world; here nature actually becomes the source of terror that Edmund Burke called the ruling principle of the sublime.[62] Read in isolation, the short second section of the poem is a dark vision of Nature's role in the destruction of man.

> Yet a few days, and thee
> The all-beholding sun shall see no more
> In all his course; nor yet in the cold ground,
> Where thy pale form was laid, with many tears,
> Nor in the embrace of ocean, shall exist
> Thy image. Earth, that nourished thee, shall claim
> Thy growth, to be resolved to earth again,
> And, lost each human trace, surrendering up
> Thine individual being, shalt thou go
> To mix for ever with the elements,
> To be a brother to the insensible rock
> And to the sluggish clod, which the rude swain
> Turns with his share, and treads upon. The oak
> Shall send his roots abroad, and pierce thy mould.

In associationist terms, Bryant is creating the simple, unified emotion (in this case fear) that the ensuing train of mental association and sublime emotion will depend upon.[63] Structurally, we have moved from philosophical assertion to the emotional center of "Thanatopsis"; from the thought of fear ("when thoughts of the last bitter hour come") to horrifying violation ("pierce thy mould"). Bryant's blank verse is usually filled with monosyllabic vocabulary. But in these last three lines only three words are minimally longer in a relentless march of masculine rhythms that helps to snuff out all personality. From such devastation there can be no recovery in nature.

Instead, the solutions in the last two sections of Bryant's poem come from the human world. Organic decay and individual mortality in nature are replaced by a reassuring commonality in human life. Death becomes a social experience: "All that breathe / Will share thy destiny." In a typical reach for dimension, Bryant also uses cosmic size both to create sublime effect and to insure an anthropocentric universe.[64] Nature's forms "are but the solemn decorations all / Of the great tomb of man," while sun and stars shine down as mourners upon the "one mighty sepulchre" that is earth. Enveloping nature is soon saturated in metaphoric language from the human condition. The dying recline and sleep on couches in nature's resting-place of chambers and silent halls. Patriarchs, kings, tribes, and caravans fill the forests in a society of the unseen dead. The poet allows his reader an Alisonian control over this external world. "Pierced" by roots in section two, we are now encouraged to "pierce the Barcan wilderness." The result is indeed the hoped-for calm emphasized by the Scottish moralist:

> sustained and soothed
> By an unfaltering trust, approach thy grave,
> Like one who wraps the drapery of his couch
> About him, and lies down to pleasant dreams.[65]

Lost on modern readers, these comforts are peculiarly interesting in light of the anxieties and social concerns of the early republican. Bryant solves many problems at once in "Thanatopsis." The vast reaches of the western wilderness are suddenly populated with a living dead that bring form and even decorum to nature. The Oregon River—"in the continuous woods / Where rolls the Oregon"—was a favorite symbol of uncharted frontier for Americans in the first third of the nineteenth century.[66] When Bryant announces "yet the dead are there," he implies a previous human reach and dominion that will inevitably come again. The poet's use of dimension to discover uniform design and to achieve sublime effect also carries a reassuring political statement. There is a striking democracy in Bryant's society of the dead that owes much to republican instincts. The dead kings and patriarchs of the New World are the anachronisms of forgotten and lesser civilizations. But lying now in equality alongside matrons, maids, and speechless babes, they strangely prefigure and now corroborate the republican values of a more progressive era within "the long train of ages."

The very stillness of social vision in "Thanatopsis" is a final, implicit source of comfort to a poet who feared a turbulent American society and faced an unwelcome vocational decision within it. Writing "Thanatopsis" in the fall of 1815 just before beginning actual legal practice, Bryant was confronting the same "employments" that seem trivial and cause loss of perspective in his poem ("each one as before will chase / His favorite phantom"). He frequently formed his descriptions of vocational difficulties from slave imagery, and the last lines of "Thanatopsis" should be understood as an attempt to rise above such narrow, worldly cares.[67]

> So live, that . . .
> Thou go not like the quarry-slave at night,
> Scourged to his dungeon, but, sustained and soothed
> By an unfaltering trust, approach thy grave.

The problem Bryant wrestled with all of his life was how to serve his community while retaining the saving perspective of the true poet in touch with both nature and society.

Believing in civic involvement, the man of letters still expected the poet to function above the world. "Thanatopsis" not only revolves around this conviction, it is the ultimate portrayal of the balance Bryant tried to achieve.[68] In this sense, movement from a preoccupation with "the narrow house" or coffin of section one to celebration of earth's mighty sepulchre in section three represents a decision to accept the world. As social forms circumscribe nature in "Thanatopsis," they lend philosophical support to the speaker's decision. Bryant's final injunction, "So live," is the declaration of this acceptance, and it encompasses citizen and lawyer as well as poet. Nevertheless, the "unfaltering trust" on which emotional resolution depends is the higher achievement of the poet alone. In "Thanatopsis" trust wins over fear through aesthetic experience and artistic control. Eventual calm builds legitimately out of craft and vision. Here, in the demonstrated prowess of the poet, is Bryant's highest moment. No American poet, with the possible exception of Edgar Allan Poe, would reach any higher for a generation to come.

III

BREAKDOWN AND RESOLUTION

PROLOGUE TO
PART III

S TILL CENTRAL to republican experience in 1825, the configuration of law and letters disappeared with the Civil War. The
prominence of men like James Kent, Joseph Story, John Quincy
Adams, Daniel Webster, Henry Clay, and John C. Calhoun sustained intellectual vitality through the second quarter of the nineteenth century, but the example that these figures set died with
them. One by one the conditions supporting the configuration became less relevant in republican life. Changing definitions of law
and literature emerged in the Jacksonian era. At issue was a modern
American culture imposing new meaning on established forms.

The priorities that held the early American lawyer to literature
were brittle, and this was a period of extraordinary social, economic,
and intellectual flux. Serious erosion began in the second decade of
the century. Between 1789 and 1815 American law developed through
basic constitutional issues and through a delineation of general problems in property, contracts, debt, and ejectment. "I saw where
justice lay," wrote Chancellor Kent, "and the moral sense decided
the court half the time . . . I might once in a while be embarrassed
by a technical rule, but I most always found principles suited to
my views of the case."[1] The War of 1812 undermined this broad
philosophical approach by creating many of the more complex
branches of modern law. The British blockade disrupted coastal
shipping, ruined intercontinental trade, and forced new efforts in
domestic manufacturing, internal transportation, and mechanical
invention. Overnight the law required experts in admiralty and

insurance law to handle the tangled aftermath of confiscations and losses. Similar needs quickly developed in corporation and patent law.[2]

Technical competence triumphed over general learning and philosophical discourse as case law accumulated. Where only three appeals in corporation law came before the Supreme Court prior to 1815, the case load in this new area required a textbook by 1832. In fact, there were suddenly too many textbooks on American law rather than too few. "The multiplication of books is becoming, or rather has become, an evil that is intolerable," wrote Kent in 1830, referring to the growing mass of case reports and legal digests. "Those who have the best practice, are tasked almost beyond endurance," added David Dudley Field in 1844. "The multiplication of law-books, and, above all, the multiplication of courts, have quadrupled their labors." Mastering the law "from the foundation to the summit" quickly became a full-time occupation for Field's "true lawyer."[3] By mid-century it was an extraordinary figure indeed who could encompass law and literature and remain active in both.

Philosophically, the shift from general principles to textbook law created a very different sense of subject. It dictated a relative stress on positive or man-made law over natural law. The early lawyer searched for a declaration derived from common usage and consistent with nature. His successor, the reader of case reports, thought in terms of the specific commands that society had placed upon itself.[4] Each had a particular approach to the printed page. The first looked for connections and resemblance; the second, for distinction and precision. The first, for eloquence and ethical foundation; the second, for material support. Their respective needs made general literature useful to the former and increasingly irrelevant to the latter. And the second kind of lawyer inevitably swallowed the first. The American penchants for written constitutions and for a national law distinct from European antecedents only hastened the victory of legal positivism.

Another blow to the affinity between law and literature came in the collapse of the classical tradition. The administration of John Quincy Adams, 1825 to 1829, closed the era in which classicism determined intellectual thought in American culture. Within the legal profession the process took longer; nevertheless, a knowledge of classical literature became increasingly peripheral to legal practice as educational standards deteriorated within the bar. Legal historians have noted that "the tide of early nineteenth-century democracy carried before it all previously existing standards of admission to the profession." By 1840 educational requirements for admission to state bar associations had been lowered everywhere, and a broad knowledge of general literature had been dropped as a prerequisite to argue before the higher courts.[5] Again, David Dudley Field bore witness: "The bar is now crowded with bustling and restless men . . . The quiet, decorous manners, the gravity, and the solid learning, so often conjoined in a former generation, are now rarely seen together. A new race has sprung up and supplanted the old."[6] Classical literature did not interest this new race of lawyers, and the profession soon lost the common ground it once enjoyed for literary appreciation and expression.

The lawyer's more frequent choice of technical expertise over general learning was also a reaction to Jacksonian influences. While anti-lawyer sentiment stretched back as far as the Revolution, the egalitarian tendencies of the 1830s exacerbated hostility by segregating a professional elite. Jacksonian democrats spoke of subjecting the bar to popular controls. To protect themselves, lawyers moved toward a narrower, but safer, basis of identification. Abdicating the sweeping assertiveness of their predecessors, the new practitioners of the 1840s claimed legitimacy through specific utilitarian skills that lawyers alone could perform. Political service, literary enterprise, and public speaking belonged in a different (and increasingly suspect) category.[7] By 1850 the expansive post-Revolutionary lawyer, the courtroom orator who relied on general jurisprudence, belles-lettres, and the classics, was an anachronism. Few tried to follow the generations of Adams, Webster, and Choate, and those who did were doomed to failure. Indeed, one of the poignant stories of mid-century was the attempt of men like John Pendleton Kennedy and Richard Henry Dana, Jr., to realize the ideal of the gentleman lawyer-writer even as that ideal fell to pieces.

The law itself began to serve radically different national needs.[8] In the decades following the Revolution, Americans depended on formally structured legal institutions because they lacked functional equivalents for ordering their society. The law supplied a vital image of cohesion, a useful paradigm for order in the world. It expressed corporate harmony, a crucial ingredient of every early republican's moral sense of self. Fixed standards, firm precedents, and immutable law were part and parcel of an ideology of union, an aesthetics of cohesion. But by 1830 the same premises were blocking a radically different sense of national development. Precedent and fixed law were clumsy tools for coping with a burgeoning economy of land speculators, textile mills, turnpike companies, and railroad corporations. Moreover, Americans no longer needed expressions of communal solidarity in quite the same way. Jacksonian individualism accepted national identity as a given, stressing instead personal freedom from artificial social institutions and arguing for unrestrained self-interest as the surest guarantee of communal growth and virtue.[9]

Always a function of communal expression, the law adjusted to Jacksonian impulses. By 1850, "law, once conceived of as protective, regulative, paternalistic and, above all, a paramount expression of the moral sense of the community, had come to be thought of as facilitative of individual desires and as simply reflective of the existing organization of economic and political power."[10] This shift transformed the lawyer's role in American society. As long as law reflected the order and virtue of the republic, lawyers could speak for the entire community. But once law became a deliberate instrument of social policy for particular kinds of individuals, the attorney who operated in this process became a narrower agent of competing concerns. As the increasingly technical representative of vested interests, he found less and less reason to function as the ideological guardian of his culture.

Significantly, the role of ideological guardian was a growing problem even for the established generation of lawyer-orators. In the decades before the Civil War, republican principle began to founder on a basic incompatibility in the American experiment. Sectional strife over slavery in a free republic made national identity a dangerous subject. Leaders like Webster, Clay, and Choate spoke less of principle and more of compromise between conflicting ideals. Their appeal to necessity turned the union into an intrinsic virtue rather than an experiment for fostering virtue in men. The Missouri Compromise in 1820, the Congressional gag rule of 1836, the Compromise of 1850, and the Kansas-Nebraska Act of 1854 were successive and inadequate attempts to preserve; they were not ventures in understanding or ideological clarification. Daniel Webster's "Seventh of March" speech in 1850, one of the set-pieces of nineteenth-century oratory, capped this trend; it was less an enumeration of principles than a plea to sacrifice principle for the sake of union, more a recognition of practical limitations than a vision of moral action.

> There are men who, in reference to disputes of that sort, are of the opinion that human duties may be ascertained with the exactness of mathematics. They deal with morals as with mathematics; and they think what is right may be distinguished from what is wrong with the precision of an algebraic equation . . . They are apt, too, to think that nothing is good but what is perfect, and that there are no compromises or modifications to be made . . . But we must view things as they are.

This is a far cry from the Webster of 1825 who spoke of "great objects" and "settled conviction," and expected Americans to "extend our ideas over the whole of the vast field in which we are called to act."[11]

The lawyer's centrality to compromise glorified his position as the American peacemaker. "The lawyer has entrusted to him the social life of man," ran a typical account from the 1840s. "This is his function, to preserve the social life in security and soundness."[12] However, the price of the peacemaker's inflated role was bankruptcy in the face of war. Because the failure of compromise was peculiarly the lawyer's own, it paved the way for a broader rejection of his influence. The anathema heaped upon Webster over the Compromise of 1850 and the even greater outrage in 1857, following the Supreme Court's effort to settle the slavery issue in *Dred Scott v. Sanford*, bespoke a general loss of faith in the lawyer and his republic of laws. "Webster never goes behind government," sneered Thoreau in "Civil Disobedience," "and so cannot speak with authority about it . . . The lawyer's truth is not Truth, but consistency or a consistent expediency." Emerson in 1854 pointed directly to the futility of successive compromise efforts. "These things show that no forms, neither constitutions, nor laws, nor covenants, nor churches, nor bibles, are of any use in themselves," he concluded. "The Devil nestles comfortably into them."[13]

The writers of the American Renaissance proposed new affirmations to replace the lawyer's corporate identity and institutional solutions. "I give you myself before preaching or law," Walt Whitman announced in "Song of the Open Road." "Be not disheart, d," he added later in "Drum-taps," "affection shall solve the problems of freedom yet." Here Whitman also delivered the new generation's clearest repudiation of the old:

> (Were you looking to be held together by lawyers?
> Or by an agreement on a paper? or by arms?
> Nay, nor the world, nor any living thing, will so cohere.)[14] •

New affirmation *required* rejection of the old; the romantic artist's assertion of individual feeling and personal revelation necessarily questioned a public eloquence based on civic identity. And yet these obvious polarities explain less than many have imagined. For in reacting against, the writers of the American Renaissance also sought to improve upon. Crucial continuities remained between old and new. Certainly, the American Renaissance assimilated early republican thought and language even as it qualified traditional usage. When Emerson "set the private man first," arguing that "he only who is able to stand alone is qualified to be a citizen," he nonetheless retained the concept of citizenship. His dismissal of the public oration as "an escapade, a non-commital, an apology, a gag" did not prevent oratory from being the proximate source of Emersonian language. When Emerson criticizes "the mind of this country" in "The American Scholar," when Thoreau finds "the only true America" in *Walden*, when Whitman chants "A Nation announcing itself" in "By Blue Ontario's Shore," they engage in the same compulsive search for a better sense of country, the same urgent certainty that Americans will benefit collectively from the writer's vision of the whole.[15] These expressions and countless others like them show that civic tones and feelings of communal obligation remained an intrinsic part of American literature through the creative outburst of the 1850s.

Such continuity in literary expressions owed something to the lawyer's continuing ideological presence through every change in national life. Despite Whitman's disclaimer, Americans most assuredly *did* expect to be held together by lawyers. Nor was it happenstance that a lawyer did more than anyone else to preserve the union in the ensuing rupture. Abraham Lincoln redefined American republicanism, replacing the right of revolution with a mystic concept of loyalty. "Let every American, every lover of liberty, every well wisher to his posterity, swear by the blood of the Revolution, never to violate in the least particular, the laws of the country," Lincoln declared. The Civil War, a new bloodletting of monstrous proportions, transformed a republic of laws into a nation under law.[16] The lawyer was never lost in this shift, but after 1865 he was first civil servant within the state rather than the guardian of republican virtue in America and the world.

As Jefferson exemplifies the original form and direction of the legal mind in America, so Daniel Webster illustrates the changing nature of that mind in the first half of the nineteenth century. Chapter 8 concentrates upon the career and writings of Webster to explain the breakdown in the configuration of law and letters and to clarify the meaning of oratory in American literature. In the 1820s Webster was his country's foremost courtroom advocate, over-shadowing others in his mastery of constitutional law and in the importance of cases argued. But the rapidly growing complexity of the law soon robbed him of the ability to hold his own in many cases and led to an embarrassing dependency on friends for knowl-edge of the law. In the 1830s and 1840s colleagues like Horace Binney and Charles Sumner, fresh out of Harvard Law School, were catching the great orator in simple ignorance of the law during courtroom disputes. Over the same thirty-year period, Webster remained America's leading public spokesman, "the central heart of a national sentiment." His goal, in the words of a contemporary, was "to place the great names of the several states on the bead-roll of the one indivisible Republic," and his success in the courtroom led him to assume that the right speech before the proper jury would unify a nation.[17] That goal and that assumption ruled the literature of the period.

Using the Richard Henry Danas, father and son, as guides, chap-ter 9 analyzes the transition from neoclassic to romantic in American literature. Mirror images of each other, the Danas encompass the first half of the nineteenth century. Richard Henry Dana, Sr., aban-doned the legal profession to become the country's first important romantic critic and the "Idle Man" of periodical fiction during the Era of Good Feeling. His son, who wrote *Two Years Before the Mast* (1840) as a law student preparing for the bar, soon rejected literature for law and eventually became United States attorney for the Dis-trict of Massachusetts in the 1860s. Together their writings suggest important continuities in nineteenth-century fiction and reveal the changing role of the legal mind in American culture. Tendencies here have much to do with the American Renaissance that followed.

The tenth and final chapter explores the way in which the democratic continuum in American life shook the lawyer's confidence in his forms and ideas. One after the other, the leading intellectuals of the early bar gave way to the gloomiest predictions. Progressive historians have tended to dismiss this pessimism as narrow-mindedness, but it was the presence of vision, not its absence, that brought despair to the likes of Fisher Ames, Gouverneur Morris, William Wirt, John Quincy Adams, and Daniel Webster. Well versed in classical models of government, the early American lawyer rarely forgot that his favorite heroes from antiquity, the lawyer-orators Demosthenes and Cicero, died resisting the successful efforts of despots to subvert republican rule. His readings in Thucydides, Plutarch, Tacitus, Machiavelli, and Montesquieu left him brooding over, in Joseph Story's words, "the melancholy lessons of the past history of republics down to our own."[18]

The greater one's theoretical understanding and the closer one looked at reality, the harder it became to rest within the initial abstractions defining American culture. It was hardly a coincidence that new American writers turned toward romanticism at just that moment when neoclassicism began to force a negative vision of country. Chapter 10 interprets these changes as well as the lawyer's own recourse to a more sharply defined, modern professionalism. The new expert solved the old generalist's problems by sacrificing the role of ideological spokesman. There was, however, a strange and notable exception. In the South the old-style generalist and the overall configuration of law and letters continued to thrive throughout the nineteenth century. Chapter 10 concludes with an explanation of this forgotten phenomenon and with a last look at the configuration through the disillusioned eyes of James Fenimore Cooper. A brief epilogue on Abraham Lincoln then shows how the deepest pessimism could turn to affirmation in the mind and thought of the Emancipator. To understand this process is to see the power and appeal of Lincoln's accomplishment in a new light.

CHAPTER 8

DANIEL WEBSTER:
COUNSEL FOR THE DEFENSE

"If I Am Any Thing, It Is the Law . . . That Has Made Me What I Am"

Daniel Webster dominated American courtrooms and shaped national politics from the War of 1812 to the Compromise of 1850. His countrymen thought him a unique national treasure, much in the way they thought of Plymouth Rock or Bunker Hill. No comparison was too grand. Webster's brow was finer than Shakespeare's, his head more beautiful than Goethe's. His very manner induced a mystical confidence. "Fidgety men were quieted in his presence," wrote one observer, "women were spellbound by it, and the busy, anxious public contemplated his majestic calm with a feeling of relief." When Webster died in 1852, the *New York Times* mourned the passing of the greatest man in the world, one who "rarely had his equal since the morning of time."[1] Even Webster's harshest critics assumed preeminence. "Since Charlemagne, I think there has not been such a grand figure in all Christendom," wrote Theodore Parker in his public condemnation. Ralph Waldo Emerson also censured Webster, but he noted qualities "such as one cannot hope to see again in a century," qualities that distinguished Webster "above all other men." "Webster," Emerson concluded, "is a man by himself of the great mould." He was "the completest man" that the world knew.[2]

The subject of these encomiums had a conforming mind and a flawed personality. Moreover, the public performances that enthralled contemporaries seem neither visionary nor profound today.

The interesting thing about Webster's immense personal magnetism is that it did not impose the extraordinary so much as it served the conventional. He embodied intellectual aspirations more than he guided them, and his speeches sought to convince men of what they already knew. And yet Webster was "the completest man." He was the most important lawyer-writer of the age. Thomas Jefferson, John Adams, John Quincy Adams, and then Joseph Story and James Kent were the theoreticians and scholars of the configuration of law and letters. Daniel Webster became its great personal exponent, its mouthpiece, its defender. He was a Whig lawyer using public forums to update the Whig theory of history in a democratic republic. It was in this sense that he could be called *the* American mind of the period.[3]

Webster took the written Constitution of 1787 and placed it safely in time out of memory by tying its significance to the abstract will of the people—that will in itself representing an expression of timeless fundamental law. What had been a "mechanical contrivance of wise men" thus became "an organic fact, springing from the intelligence, hearts, and wills of the people."[4] Every time the Defender of the Constitution spoke, the country formed a courtroom, the ideal citizen arose as his client, and the American people became a jury with whom decisions finally rested. The case in question was always the same: "that other sentiment, dear to every true American heart,—Liberty *and* Union, now and for ever, one and inseparable!"[5]

The orator understood the source of his own power. "If I am any thing," Webster announced late in life, "it is the law . . . that has made me what I am . . . The law has been my chief stimulus, my controlling and abiding hope, nay, I might say, my presiding genius and guardian angel" (IV, 88). The law could be so many things because it pervaded every aspect of the mind and career. In the first decade of the nineteenth century, just as Webster began legal practice in New Hampshire, John Quincy Adams summarized both the centrality of oratory in American culture and the unique advantage of the lawyer. The law alone gave training in each of the three branches of oratory delineated by the ancient Greeks: judicial or forensic oratory, which dealt with decisions of natural justice, equity, or positive law in a courtroom situation; demonstrative or epideictic oratory, which celebrated or condemned some person or event in the marketplace: and deliberative oratory, which tried to influence a decision on public policy within an assembly.[6] Daniel Webster became the one nineteenth-century American to master all three classical divisions of the orator's craft. Starting with judicial oratory, which Adams had designated as the most difficult, he eventually dominated every podium except the pulpit in an age when speech controlled thought and action.[7]

The law also prepared Webster ideologically for the forums that it opened to him. The young regionalist who entered national politics defending states' rights soon found out that his most important clients in the courtroom wanted protection from local regulation and from state interference.[8] Webster learned the doctrine of national supremacy in cases like *McCulloch v. Maryland* (1819) and *Gibbons v. Ogden* (1824). In the first, with the Bank of the United States as his client, he established that a state may not tax an instrumentality of the federal government. In the second, representing a steamboat company, he undercut state regulation of shipping by insisting upon the broadest possible federal jurisdiction over internal commerce.

These courtroom arguments, and others like them in the 1820s, formed a lingua franca for the political debates that followed. Webster's forensic power in the nullification crisis of the 1830s came from his precise manipulation of legal terms in support of a strong central government. In the Senate, Webster constantly pushed Calhoun and other nullifiers back upon the technical meaning of words like *"adopt, ratify, ordain, establish,"* back upon "the plainly written fundamental law" (VI, 186–188). The Constitution was neither a compact acceded to by the states nor a contract but rather "the result of a contract." Before ratification, the framers' document had been "a deed drawn but not executed" or "the mere draught of an instrument." Once accepted by the people in representative conventions, it "received the sanction of the popular will" and thus became *"a fundamental law."* As such, the Constitution, like any other law, was "not the agreement, but something created by the agreement; and something which, when created, has a new character, and acts by its own authority." That *something* reached beyond the language of the law—"the agreement itself is merged in its own accomplishment"—toward the higher realms of a mystical union (VI, 198–201).

Beyond issues of substance, the law taught Webster how to speak once he knew what to say. The trademarks of his oratory—clarity, simplicity, and logical pattern—came from professional experience. The strength of the influence can be seen in Webster's preference for lucid prose over the florid style of his time. Virtually every contemporary critic noticed the difference. A few simple words from Webster were "like a cup of cold water to a man thirsting among hogsheads of lavender," wrote Emerson after a long day next to the speaker's platform. While others reached for "splendor of diction, and magnificence of metaphor," Webster openly rejected "the pomp of declamation" and derided "costly ornaments and studied contrivances of speech."[9]

In fact, Webster entered the law with just such an ornate style and had it beaten out of him in the courtroom. "I have some of your pounding in my bones yet," Webster wrote Jeremiah Mason twenty years after the fact (xvii, 489). Both antagonist and mentor, Mason was the acknowledged leader of the bar in Portsmouth, and Webster left a clear record of what he learned when he moved there in 1807:

> Before I went to Portsmouth my style was florid, and I was apt to make longer sentences and to use longer words than were needful. I soon began, however, to notice that Mr. Mason was a cause-getting man. He had a habit of standing quite near to the jury . . . and then he talked to them in a plain conversational way, in short sentences, and using no word that was not level to the comprehension of the least educated man on the panel. This led me to examine my own style, and I set about reforming it altogether.[10]

His mature style in the courtroom grew out of a single premise: "The power of clear statement is the great power at the bar."[11] And the famous orator brought the same lesson to the speaker's platform. "Clearness, force, and earnestness," he announced in his discourse on Adams and Jefferson, "are the qualities which produce conviction" (I, 307).

Webster could put such a professional emphasis on clarity and the plain style because of the nature of legal practice in the first third of the nineteenth century. Early American lawyers spent much of their time reducing technicalities to tenets that juries, lay judges, and their audiences could follow easily. No one excelled Webster in this capacity, though many brought a similar conviction to the process.[12] The decision to simplify for a common understanding assumed that the machinery of the law rested upon general principles that everyone understood; this was true because the laws of nature made it true. The young Webster, like Jefferson before him, accepted a universal natural law that preceded and supported positive or man-made law.[13] Belief in a connection enabled Webster to use generalities from natural law as citations in *Dartmouth College* and *Ogden v. Saunders;* it also encouraged him to find larger meaning when an audience understood a properly delivered argument. Here is the symbiotic tie between Webster and his listeners and, generally, between speaker and audience in antebellum America. The oration was so much more than itself because it communicated fundamental truths that all would acknowledge.[14]

For a lawyer with Webster's record of success in the courtroom, forging an understanding with his listeners came naturally. There was an irresistible analogy to be drawn between the spellbound jury making its decision and a national audience trying to comprehend its political situation. The right address to either—properly timed, properly given, and properly understood—necessarily led on to resolution. Webster assumed that when he spoke in front of a jury "the minds of commonly sensible men may be conducted to high results of argument." Since the law was "an instrument and means of instruction to the mass of the people," since trial by jury was "the popular teacher of our system," and since juries decided correctly in "a vast majority of cases," he also assumed "there can be no better tribunal than the people brought together in the jury-box" (IV, 91–92).

The ultimate parallel to the jury's verdict was a national election, and Webster drew the analogy, always hoping that his orations would lead to the presidency. His political career was one long attempt to bring America into a single ideological forum for the speech that would make decisions possible. In this sense, the peroration in the Reply to Calhoun involved more than idle sentiment when it was delivered in 1833: "I rely on the true American feeling, the genuine patriotism of the people, and the imperative decision of the public voice" (VI, 237). The politician expected such a decision through the lawyer's experience, and the two roles appeared so interchangeable because the political oration, like the jury charge before it, was designed to make the law "the keystone of the arch" of American civilization (VI, 67–68). After the seminal speeches of the 1830s, few distinguished between the great courtroom advocate and the Defender of the Constitution—Daniel Webster least of all.

Certainly, the politician depended on the lawyer. Always and on every level, Webster's answer lay in the law. The law established liberty even as it maintained order, acting now on one side, now on the other (IV, 91). It reached to the highest as well as the lowest; it regulated necessary passions and eliminated dangerous excess (I, 276). "The fire of liberty burns brightly and steadily in your hearts," Webster reminded one audience, in describing the posture it was to assume, "while DUTY and the LAW restrain it from bursting forth in wild and destructive conflagration" (IV, 316). The politician could trade in patriotic fervor because the lawyer defined the negative boundaries. Indeed, Webster made the latter's task an intrinsic responsibility. "The profession of the law," he believed, "is the support of public liberty" (IV, 91). Americans differed from other peoples in their acceptance of the law and its agents: "They have learned this one great lesson, that there is no security without law" (IV, 299). The "prescribed forms of the law" literally defined America. "When we depart from that," Webster explained, "we shall wander as widely from the American track as the pole from the track of the sun" (XI, 224). The United States formed "a great, popular constitutional government, guarded by the law and by judicature, and defended by the affections of the whole people" (x, 97). As every member of that popular government knew, "the law is the supreme rule for the government of all" (IV, 300). Conformity to truth demanded obedience. Webster agreed with Blackstone that the law included "something permanent, uniform, and universal" (x, 219).

The theme is everywhere in the thirty-year span of speeches, but with a notable change. Over time Webster came to use the law in a different way. Believing in a "fixed and settled character by law" in 1850, he meant something both more and less than he did in 1820 in calling upon "the authority of human laws" (x, 85; I, 222). And here, as in so many areas, Webster represented the spirit of his times. A corresponding general shift in attitudes regarding the law separates modern American civilization from the early republic. Webster, who fascinated so many in courtrooms, speaking halls, and the Senate, had much to do with that shift.

"The Most Consummate Orator of Modern Times"

The power of the speaker still overshadows the power of the speech. Webster at the podium reminded witnesses of heavy cannonading. He overwhelmed his audiences, and his command over them was legendary. With a single bellow for silence, he quelled a huge and unruly crowd at Bunker Hill in 1825, ending "an appalling moment" of general panic. *"Be silent yourselves,"* he thundered to those in authority, *"and the people WILL obey!"* They did, instantly. Another Olympian shout stilled the mob that gathered for his discourse on Adams and Jefferson.[15] Special emphasis on the word "onward" once caused an entire audience to lean forward as if pushed. "So Moses might have appeared to the awe-struck Israelites as he emerged from the dark clouds and thick smoke of Sinai," ran one account of Webster speaking in the Senate.[16] However overblown, the image fairly captures Webster in his own time. He was the lawgiver delivering the word to a waiting people, and his first readers inevitably held that image when they made his published works an absolute standard. The collected orations gave the best available summary of American purpose. They were "an outline framework of the American Character and the American History" and constituted the highest expression of a culture. "Webster's speeches," Emerson wrote in 1834, "seem to be the utmost that the unpoetic West has accomplished or can."[17]

What survives the speaker who heightened immediate effect by wearing blue and buff, the colors of the Revolution? What remains of the literature that inspired another age? Webster left perhaps eight speeches that still stand as monuments of their kind: *Dartmouth College v. Woodward* (1818) and *Gibbons v. Ogden* (1824), both argued before the Supreme Court, the Plymouth Oration (1820), the First Bunker Hill Address (1825), the Commemorative Discourse on Adams and Jefferson (1826), and three speeches in the Senate of the United States, the Second Reply to Hayne (1830), the Reply to Calhoun (1833), and the Constitution and the Union Speech (1850).[18] No one else in American culture, not even Abraham Lincoln, who owes a greater debt to Webster's speeches than has been imagined, can match the overall range and power of these performances.

Three speeches from the canon—the *Dartmouth College* argument, the Plymouth Oration, and the Second Reply to Hayne—will be closely examined here. Each affords a first great example within a distinct branch of oratory (judicial, demonstrative, and deliberative), and each sheds light on the younger Webster who, as the chronological pattern of his masterpieces attests, was the greater orator. The *Dartmouth College* argument established Webster's reputation before the Supreme Court, and it marked the first time Webster enthralled a national audience. The Plymouth Oration moved the aged John Adams to proclaim Webster "a great mind" and "the most consummate Orator of modern times." Many agreed when Adams called this speech the most perfect expression of "the genuine spirit of New England."[19] Finally, the Second Reply to Hayne ranks even today as the most important political address delivered in antebellum America. Its impact made Webster "a whole species in himself."[20]

Of all his flights in eloquence, Webster preferred the courtroom arguments—in part, one suspects, because there he saw the most tangible results. He once cited *Dartmouth College v. Woodward* and *Gibbons v. Ogden* as his greatest intellectual triumphs. In the first case, Webster's opening speech left John Marshall in tears, and the lawyer had the supreme satisfaction of receiving a final decision from the chief justice that went "the whole length" of his own position. Six years later in *Gibbons v. Ogden*, Marshall once again followed Webster idea for idea, supporting the latter's claim that Marshall had taken the argument "as a baby takes in its mother's milk."[21]

Joseph Story, then sitting on the Supreme Court, most accurately described the overall impact of Webster's performance in *Dartmouth College*: "The whole audience had been wrought up to the highest excitement; many were dissolved in tears; . . . many were sinking under exhausting efforts to conceal their own emotions."[22] Webster's manner had much to do with the effect: "It is, sir, as I have said, a small college, And yet *there are those who love it*" (xv, 11). But in this first major performance the lawyer spoke before a relatively small and sophisticated professional audience of lawyers and their clients. More than histrionics was involved, and Justice Story's own behavior provides an important key. An indefatigable note-taker on the bench, Story took nothing down on this occasion. "Everything was so clear, and so easy to remember," he is supposed to have explained, "that not a note seemed necessary" (xv, 11).

Clarity of presentation sustains a perfect sense of placement at every stage of the *Dartmouth College* argument, and that placement in itself builds to a dramatic climax around essentials. Holding every listener, even those who stray easily, Webster intersperses summaries at periodic intervals. The first thirty pages of the argument reduce to a single paragraph at a crucial organizational moment (x, 224). Webster is a model of concision when he needs to be. His gift for placement also includes a wonderful instinct for narrative—a trait that appears most dramatically in criminal cases like "The Defence of the Kennistons" and "The Murder of Captain Joseph White," where the lawyer becomes a powerful storyteller recapitulating crimes and punishments (x, 173–193; xi, 41–105). In *Dartmouth College* the same sense of drama and pace smooths away complexities and underlines important points.

Two questions arise in *Dartmouth College* (x, 230, 231). Is Dartmouth College a private corporation with certain privileges and immunities for its trustees or a public corporation subject to the modifications of state legislation? And who is to settle that question, the state legislature or the federal court? Webster dramatizes both issues, translating abstractions into flesh and blood and individual points of view. In the first instance, Eleazar Wheelock, the founder of the Dartmouth Corporation, rises from his grave to gaze in dismay at the wreckage of his private and personal project. "Little did he suppose that this charter secured to him and his successors no legal rights" (x, 210). In the second, Webster animates both the college and the Supreme Court in a direct appeal. The Court alone can prevent Dartmouth from being "prostrated for ever" (x, 233). "Sir, you may destroy this little institution," Webster tells John Marshall; "it is weak; it is in your hands!" (xv, 11). Personification would always remain a favorite tactic for holding and channeling attention. When historical figures like Lafayette, Washington, Adams, Jefferson, and Madison appear in the political orations, they almost always adumbrate complex political points of view.

The most impressive aspect of the *Dartmouth College* performance is the way in which it foreshadows all of the politician's subsequent thematic concerns. The argument contains, at least in embryo, everything the Defender of the Constitution would want to say to the American people. No fact better illustrates the central role of the legal career in the formulation of Webster's general language and thought.[23] The perennial question of who should decide the law—

federal court or state legislature—carries directly from *Dartmouth College* in 1818 through the Reply to Calhoun in 1833, and Webster's response remains the same; the federal court should decide (VI, 212–216). Welding the present to the past is another favorite strategy as early as *Dartmouth College*. The common law principle of *stare decisis*, which binds a court to the rules laid down in previous decisions, informs virtually every page of Webster's argument. Judicial precedents abound, ones that will soon translate within the political arena into reverence for the Constitution and the intention of the founders as past gauges of present merit.

Already in *Dartmouth College* the Revolutionary Founders appear as "the wise men of that day" who change little and then only with reluctance (x, 231). By 1826, Webster is arranging these Founders, separate stars, into fixed and eternal constellations that guide Americans "with the united blaze of a thousand lights" (I, 324; II, 71). His public speeches, like the Bunker Hill Monument itself, function as "a memorial of the past, and a monitor to the present" (I, 262). *Dartmouth College* supplies the beginnings of a vocabulary for these later speeches. Phrases like "laws of the land, within the meaning of the constitution" (x, 219), "the people have thought otherwise" (x, 232), and "regard to law" (x, 233) percolate through Webster's argument. Unmistakably the political orator finds his voice in the courtroom.

Dartmouth College also conveys the developing *method* of Webster's eloquence. One sees the youthful orator of 1818 learning how to use immediate circumstance to reach toward a general and participatory inclusiveness. As Webster knew, "true eloquence, indeed, does not consist in speech . . . It must exist in the man, in the subject, and in the occasion" (I, 307). *Dartmouth College* accepts this idea; the lawyer imposes himself upon his situation by first dwelling within it. The argument opens with what one listener aptly termed an easy, conversational tone (xv, 10). Webster states the question before the court, then "the substance of the facts," then the specific points he will prove and their relation to the nature of the Court's jurisdiction (x, 195–200). Gradually these narrow particulars form a broad frame of reference through Webster's understanding of the general rights of contract and of property at stake in the case (x, 211, 216, 221, 229). Everyone is made to feel the violation Webster's client has suffered and the potential for injustice elsewhere if that situation remains uncorrected. By the middle of Webster's peroration, "all the literary institutions of the country" appear in "certain and immediate" danger, and the entire state of New Hampshire stands accused of blatant disregard of the law of the land (x, 232–233). A campus squabble between academic factions has become a national issue affecting every citizen's safety. "It is more!" Webster concludes, with a cry calculated to alarm those in power. "It is, in some sense, the case of every man among us who has property of which he may be stripped" (xv, 11). There is, in short, a culminating inclusiveness in the *Dartmouth College* argument, and the strategy is deftly linked to courtroom procedures and formulations. Accepting those procedures and formulations initially means little more than believing in the power of the Supreme Court, but, somewhere within the presentation, believing in the Court becomes a matter of accepting Webster's argument.

The lawyer of *Dartmouth College* understands the importance of arguing or building from context, and this knowledge always remains the true source of his rhetorical power. Context for Webster includes many things: a sense of place and timing, acceptance of restraint, and adherence to form. A courtroom requires all of these elements. What Webster understands better than any other orator of his day is that the same rules of persuasion apply in other forums. The commemorative addresses and political speeches invariably commence with a recognition of audience that states and then uses the basis of the occasion, though never more brilliantly than in the Second Reply to Hayne, where Webster's simple rereading of the formal resolution before the Senate sweeps aside the abstract bombast of his opponent (vi, 3–4). Timing is everything in his oratory. The speaker who responds to Robert Hayne of South Carolina can shine so immediately because he uses notes that have been "tucked away in a pigeon hole" and kept there for the moment of greatest impact.[24] Webster rarely manufactures the situations of his speeches. He has patience. He rises only to the momentous occasion, and he speaks in reaction to others. As in the courtroom, it is the case that makes the context; the speaker keeps his seat until his time and turn. From professional experience, Webster knows how much procedures can heighten expectation. Time after time, his political audiences wait for the announced speech that finally comes only when Senate formalities yield the most opportune moment.

The true orator speaks carefully, infrequently, and only in the most appropriate situations. In contrast, Henry Clay seems a "tall orator" because he speaks so often and on trivial occasions.[25] From the beginning, Webster emphasizes a few outstanding speeches, rushing them into print while they still hold the popular imagination. Again, timing is the issue, as the aftermath of *Dartmouth College* demonstrates. *"You must therefore write out your argument,"* Webster warns his fellow counsel, Joseph Hopkinson, a month after the Supreme Court's decision. "I will examine, compare, correct, & edit it . . . This is a work which you must do for *reputation*. Our College cause will be known to our children's children." The statement is as farsighted as it is self-serving. Webster's reputation can be so great in part because he takes such good care of it.[26]

As *Dartmouth College* manifests the methods of the speaker, so the Plymouth Oration reveals the substance of his appeal. The oration, a bicentennial celebration of the Pilgrims' landing in 1620, tries to reassure a nineteenth-century audience that feels increasingly cut off from a vanishing past and an uncertain future. Webster uses place and an imaginative projection of time to allay this very real anxiety in his countrymen.[27] Like the Greek battlefield of Marathon before it, Plymouth Rock transmits "consequences through ages," creating "a solid and permanent interest" as a symbol of "all the succeeding glories of the republic." Imagination "kindles at the retrospect," enabling Americans "looking before and after, to hold communion at once with our ancestors and our posterity." Thus, when past, present, and future come into proper relation with each other, lonely separation gives way to meaningful apposition. Webster's goal is to transform "mere isolated beings, without relation to the past or the future" into citizens "closely compacted on all sides with others" as "links in the great chain of being" (1, 181–186).

The rest of the Plymouth Oration fortifies the emotional lesson that Marathon and Plymouth Rock have taught through "genius of place." Immediately after these opening examples, Webster divides his speech into a tripartite elucidation of America's past, present, and future (1, 187). Since "we live in the past by a knowledge of its history," the first section gives an account of the first New England settlement, its founding and its relation to later periods. The Pilgrims emerge as "republicans in principle," and their every action points toward later independence and greatness. They are causes in an "operation tending to prepare things for this great result"

(I, 181, 188, 200). The second section of the speech then deals with the present in a short notice of the progress of New England (I, 187). Here Webster takes considerable pains to link the material prosperity of his own day with the moral virtue of the Founders. The developments that enabled even eighteenth-century Americans to "look back with joy, and even admiration" have increased until "the imagination hardly keeps pace with the progress of population, improvement, and civilization" (I, 206–207). This history of "astonishing increase" leads naturally into Webster's third section, on America's mission to come. The future is the hope and anticipation of the present. It is the faith Americans have in the republican institutions that will welcome new generations to "the immeasurable blessings of rational existence" (I, 181, 210, 226).

As Webster's narrative gradually makes clear, the ultimate power holding past, present, and future together comes from the hand of the law. The Pilgrims' intimate knowledge of government and law makes them "*at home* in their country" on their first day there. "Every thing was civilized but the physical world" (I, 190, 198). The same knowledge protects the present: "That which is elsewhere left to chance or to charity, we secure by law" (I, 217). As in *Dartmouth College*, Webster's thesis boils down to "the fundamental laws respecting property." Five pages of the Plymouth Oration are given over to a detailed analysis of "the laws which regulate the descent and transmission of property" in America, England, and France (I, 211–215). The conveyance of land represents the most vital connection between past, present, and future; this is where the past helps or hinders the future most. Webster argues that the early American practice of distributing freehold estates generally and easily without primogeniture or other entailments created a culture in which equality of property fostered republican institutions. He finds the same practice still at work in 1820 and calls it the single greatest guarantee of the future of the republic. "The people possess the property, more emphatically than it could ever be said of the people of any other country, and they can have no interest to overturn a government which protects that property by equal laws."

How, it might be asked, did this lecture on property law so move the reserved Boston Brahmin George Ticknor that he nearly collapsed from the stimulation? "I was never so excited by public speaking in my life," wrote Ticknor, hours after hearing the Plymouth Oration. "Three or four times I thought my temples would burst with the gush of blood."[28] The answer lies in Webster's understanding of the role of his audience. Animated obedience is the participatory mode of nineteenth-century listeners *demonstrating* their understanding. For just as the orator brings "his hearers up to his theme" by "the fit expression of his thought," to quote a nineteenth-century critic, so the listening audience tries "to receive and repay mutual sympathy" in "forgetfulness of all but the orator's presence and words."[29] Depending upon these elements, Webster incorporates his Plymouth audience into the process of conveyance that forms his constitutive metaphor. Speaker, speech, and audience become a public exercise in self-esteem through which the property of all Americans is transmitted from one generation to the next.

Webster begins the act of incorporation by informing his listeners that they have gathered at Plymouth Rock to leave "some proof that we have endeavored to transmit the great inheritance unimpaired." This exercise is necessary not just because republican principles must be conveyed anew but also because those in attendance, the second generation after the Revolutionary Founders, need to feel that "we are not altogether unworthy of our origin" (I, 183). The Declaration of Independence is the title-deed of American liberties (I, 303). Webster's speech amounts to a search of that title at the moment of transmission, but transmission in itself is something beyond speech, something accomplished in the interstice between the speaker and his audience. "We are in the line of conveyance," Webster announces, after showing that republican institutions, like property, must be "transmitted, as well as enjoyed" (I, 220). "We would leave for the consideration of those who shall then occupy our places, some proof," he concludes, and the reiterated phrase "some proof" then forms a peroration (I, 225). In the end, proof of conveyance lies in the audience's unified reaction to the total experience. Everything comes together in a common moment of feeling to be shared by those who rise in "long succession, to fill the places which we now fill" (I, 225). The nature of this moment is like the one Walt Whitman creates, reaching toward futurity, in his greatest poem, "Crossing Brooklyn Ferry": "What thought you have of me now, I had as much of you."[30] Or, in Webster's comparable words, "We would anticipate their concurrence with us in our sentiments of deep regard for our common ancestors" (I, 225).

Both feeling and phrase flow from the aesthetics of cohesion in nineteenth-century oratory. The underlying premise, one every orator of the period shares, is that sympathetic emotion recasts an audience from "A simple addition of the individuals that compose it" into "a certain social organism."[31] More than most, Webster draws upon that organic sympathy for substantiation. An audience "proves the feeling which the occasion has excited," he confesses in one instance (I, 235). The need for cohesion (proving *the* feeling) is especially relevant for a political leader lecturing on law, order, and "a true spirit of union and harmony" (I, 254). Webster's audience *must* unify for him to find in them "one cause, one country, one heart" (I, 244). Also and well beyond ideology, the man of action needs to believe that speech will lead to decision. The implied assent of a collective body of listeners enables Webster to "hold fast the great truth, that communities are responsible, as well as individuals" (I, 282).

"No Lawyer Could Give Any Other Answer"

Sympathetic emotion, cohesiveness, and communal assent reach their heights for Webster in 1830 with the Second Reply to Hayne. In what has been called "the finest statement of the true basis of our nationalism," a whole generation comes together under an acknowledged leader to conquer a moment of serious regional division within the body politic.[32] The speech itself is a cornerstone of modern American culture. More widely read than any other Congressional address of the age, it resonates with a common nationality at a time when most republicans still saw their country as a compact between the states. Webster's words formalize a shift in the American mind toward the idea of a single, democratic union. The very language of the speech—"the people's Constitution, the people's government, made for the people, made by the people, and answerable to the people" (VI, 54)—carries over and into those ultimate announcements of national identity made by Abraham Lincoln during the Civil War.[33]

The Second Reply to Hayne also represents the crest of the lawyer's involvement in general American literature and thought. For although Webster's ideas are political in implication, they draw heavily upon nineteenth-century traditions in the law, and they owe much of their force to a conscious mastery of literary expression. This speech, as Chancellor James Kent knew at the time, rescues constitutional law "from the archives of our tribunals and the libraries of lawyers" so that it can be "placed under the eye, and submitted to the judgment, of the American people." Webster takes the thought and even the language of courtroom decisions like *Dartmouth College, Gibbons v. Ogden*, and *McCulloch v. Maryland* and adapts them for legislative chambers and a lay audience.[34] His eloquence is great because so practiced. All of the earlier strategies of the courtroom speaker culminate here: the insistence on procedural place and decorum (VI, 3–8), the construction from narrow context toward the most general inclusiveness (VI, 4, 75), the use of "studied plainness, and as much precision as possible" (VI, 50), the acceptance of the "greater harmony" and meaning of past principle (VI, 49–50), the reliance upon Blackstone for constitutional theory and practice (VI, 53, 71), the play upon "the great question" of constitutional prerogatives (VI, 53), and, over all, Webster's rendition of the legal mind as "that mighty grasp of principle" in American culture (VI, 62).

Literary skill also supports the lasting eloquence of the Second Reply to Hayne. The original speech was delivered from twelve loose sheets, but these scattered notes served only the speaker and his immediate audience.[35] Webster knew better than to rely on the performer's tricks where publication was concerned. With posterity in mind even before the fact, he arranged for a personal amanuensis to record every word of his performance. The orator then turned writer, carefully revising the stenographer's transcript and delaying publication by almost a month while he clarified, strengthened, eliminated, and reorganized. Webster's revisions for publication were always elaborate and sometimes laborious. As the best analyst of the stylist has revealed, "He tormented reporters, proof-readers, and the printers who had the misfortune to be engaged in putting one of his performances into type." That Webster took particular care with the Second Reply to Hayne is clear; his original notes, first full transcript, and published oration all differ radically from each other.[36]

The craft behind the final product appears everywhere in Webster's euphonious language but also in his controlling sense of imagery and organization. Two constitutive metaphors shape the

Webster Replying to Hayne, painting by G. P. A. Healy, 1851.

Healy's portrait of Webster replying to Hayne in 1830 captures the configuration of law and letters at its height. To convey the intensity of the moment, Healy crowded the great and near-great into his listening gallery, including, among others, John Quincy Adams, George Ticknor, Joseph Story, Henry Longfellow, and even Alexis de Tocqueville, who did not come to America until 1831. Tocqueville later summarized the real meaning of performances like Webster's when he wrote, "The government of the Union depends almost entirely upon legal fictions; the Union is an ideal nation, which exists, so to speak, in the mind."

speaker's ideological concerns. Images of water support a ship of state, while more abstract images of conflict and warfare allow Webster to play the man of peace.[37] The Second Reply to Hayne opens with a famous example of the former: "Mr. President,—When the mariner has been tossed for many days in thick weather, and on an unknown sea, he naturally avails himself of the first pause in the storm, the earliest glance of the sun, to take his latitude" (VI, 3). Surely by design, Webster's subsequent justification of a strong central government begins with a description of the additional lighthouses, improved harbors, and safer waterways that the federal commerce power can bring to navigation (VI, 24). The speech ends predictably when "the tempest" that prepares to strike the nullifiers' "floating banner" yields before the sun shining upon "the gorgeous ensign of the republic." Old Glory's "ample folds" then "float over the sea and over the land," while "every wind under the whole heavens" cooperates in "Liberty *and* Union, now and for ever, one and inseparable!" Angry waves have given way to "a copious fountain of national, social, and personal happiness" (VI, 71, 75). The same peaceful conclusion resolves an extended contrast in which Robert Hayne's "anger," "challenge," "loathed calumnies," "blows," "accusations," "attacks," and "warfare" come up against Daniel Webster's "integrity of heart and magnanimity of feeling" (VI, 7, 8, 14, 41, 46, 15). Hayne's methods mean "States dissevered, discordant, belligerent, on a land rent with civil feuds, or drenched, it may be, in fraternal blood!" Webster's attitude leads instead to "the prosperity and honor of the whole country." Fortunately, the people will know how to choose between them, and Webster, as always, asks for their decision (VI, 73–75).

The craftsman reaches a higher level of skill in the formal unity of his effort. For although Webster's arguments seem episodic and even haphazard, they actually conform to a plan that Americans in 1830 knew and appreciated. The Second Reply to Hayne adheres to the six stages of development set forth in classical oratory: exordium, proposition, explication, argument, pathetic rendition, and peroration. The classical formula may have been instinctive for a speaker who memorized long passages of Cicero's oration, but Hugh Blair's *Lectures on Rhetoric and Belles Lettres* (1783) turned the formula into a convention for nineteenth-century listeners.[38] Never is Webster more impressive as a writer than here, when he holds the

political debater to the hermetic, organizational integrity of the formal oration. The step-by-step progression of the Second Reply to
Hayne from exordium to peroration shows again the professional
man's natural regard for form and procedure. "His exordium is
known by heart, everywhere," wrote one contemporary of Webster's opening, with its storm-tossed mariner.[39] The proposition, or
enunciation of the subject, comes immediately after in the rereading
of the Senate resolution, and this second section may be said to
include as well Webster's digressive objection to Hayne's method
of discourse on the floor of the Senate (VI, 3–20). The explication,
or illustration of the cause, then occupies six pages in the published
oration, starting with Webster's pronouncement, "I come to the
point of the alleged contradiction" (VI, 20–26). Webster contrasts
New England's view of the common good with South Carolina's
narrow assertion of states' rights. As with any other speech, the
next section on reasoning, or argument, fills the bulk of Webster's
effort (VI, 26–70). The orator begins his formal argument by stating
"I will answer the inquiry, not by retort, but by facts," and he
adopts the customary practice of delivering weaker points first, defending himself and New England before turning to the higher cause
of the Union.

The ensuing pathetic part of the Second Reply to Hayne represents one of Webster's master strokes. The task of the orator at
this stage is to put his listeners into the situation of debate. Webster
accomplishes that and more by placing both Hayne and the audience
in the scene at the moment when an act of nullification would require
resistance to federal law and would be, thus, an act of treason (VI,
70–73). Since Robert Hayne commanded the state militia of South
Carolina in 1830 as its major-general, Webster plausibly makes him
lead the nullifiers in person and in a way that requires the use of
the sword. "Direct collision, therefore, between force and force, is
the unavoidable result of that remedy for the revision of unconstitutional laws which the gentleman contends for." The famous peroration follows swiftly, returning as it should to the Union, the
ultimate strength of the orator's cause (VI, 74–75). There is, in sum,
considerable method in the way Webster made men *shed tears like
girls* with the Second Reply to Hayne.[40]

As before, the substance behind the method comes from Webster's view of the law. "One of two things is true," he observes in

reply to Hayne; "either the laws of the Union are beyond the discretion and beyond the control of the States; or else we have no constitution of general government" (VI, 64). Therefore, doctrines of nullification, with their claims of "the right of constitutional resistance," are unlawful weeds in the garden of American constitutionalism (VI, 53, 50). Blackstone's *Commentaries* recognizes a right of revolution against an oppressive and intolerable government, but that right of revolution does not confer another right to interrupt a law for lesser offense. "I cannot conceive that there can be a middle course," Webster argues, "between submission to the laws, when regularly pronounced constitutional, on the one hand, and open resistance, which is revolution or rebellion, on the other." To dramatize the distinction the debater then separates the irresponsibility of mere "feelings" from a proper sense of "legal control," and, thus armed, he turns upon Hayne, a lawyer who also has read Blackstone (VI, 52–55).

In the created scene of the penultimate section of Webster's speech, General Hayne must answer the question of his soldiers when they ask "to be informed a little upon the point of law" before implementing nullification:

> They know he has read Blackstone and the Constitution . . . They would inquire, whether it was not somewhat dangerous to resist a law of the United States. What would be the nature of their offence, they would wish to learn, if they, by military force and array, resisted the execution in Carolina of a law of the United States, and it should turn out, after all, that the law *was constitutional*. He would answer, of course, Treason. No lawyer could give any other answer.   (VI, 71)

Since a lawyer *must* lead, the lawyer who leads truly already has appeared in Webster's speech. Samuel Dexter of New England, "with a mind of true greatness and comprehension," has solved just such a crisis more than two decades before. Dexter represents all of New England in the Embargo Crisis of 1808, and he finds everyone's answer through the courts. "In the old-fashioned way of settling disputes," Webster proudly notes of both lawyer and client, "they went to law" (VI, 62).

To say that the greatest speech of the antebellum period comes from a lawyer and describes lawyers and the law is to recognize the dominant role of the lawyer-writer at work in early American culture. But 1830, the year of the Second Reply to Hayne, marks a turning point, and the speech itself contains troubling weaknesses. In the exigency of the moment against Hayne, Webster pushes toward extremes. One is struck, for example, by the rigid constraint in alternatives to *either* law *or* revolution at a time when the democratic revolution in republican ways is a continuous and vital part of national development. In the midst of division, Webster calls "for the Constitution as it is, and for the Union as it is" because "it was the very object of the Constitution to create unity of interests" (VI, 14, 24). But what if that saving document in acknowledging slavery became a source of division instead of the symbol of unity? What if the lawyer in his interpretation of "the plain words of the instrument" no longer reached the real issue of debate? (VI, 73). What if the eloquence of even the best orator failed to extract a viable solution in the crises to come? Webster spoke for his time, but time itself was changing from under the speaker in his moment of triumph.

"He Poisoned the Moral Wells of Society with His Lower Law"

Webster remained at the center of American politics for twenty-two years after the Second Reply to Hayne, and what happened to him in this period happened to the configuration of law and letters in general. In these years Webster struggled to maintain combinations that worked spontaneously in the first third of the century. His first problem was to follow the success of 1830, and he complicated the issue by assuming that success precluded mere repetition. By 1831 the debater believed that his contest with Hayne had ended with a "harmony of sentiment" in his favor. "The doctrines of nullification have received a severe and stern rebuke from public opinion," he told a New York audience gathered in honor of his victory. A decisive expression of "the controlling authority of the people themselves" had settled the nature of the Union once and for all (II, 61–62, 57). When the controversy persisted despite this claim, Webster blamed a perverse minority. A sense of déjà vu crept into his responses to later challenges. It was as if the lawyer of *Dartmouth College* had been asked to deliver his case over and over again.

John C. Calhoun, a more formidable opponent than Hayne, brought the doctrine of nullification back for Senate debate in 1833, and

Webster's reply was, if anything, a more concise and effective definition of the Union. But part of Webster spoke in frustration this
time. Referring back to 1830 as the real moment of crisis for the
country, he reminded the Senate that he had risen then against
Hayne on the same question and that circumstances had changed
for the better in 1833 because of it. "Since that day, Sir," Webster
explained, "the public opinion has become awakened to this great
question . . . it has reasoned upon it, as becomes an intelligent and
patriotic community, and has settled it, or now seems in the progress
of settling it, by an authority which none can disobey, the authority
of the people themselves" (VI, 183).

Calhoun was trying to appeal an unappealable judgment, failing
to see that the people's decision in 1830 made him an isolated and
slightly ridiculous figure in 1833. Webster only needed to point out
that his opponent received "no succor from public sympathy." Not
stopping there, however, he drew a telling corollary: the people's
decision and Calhoun's corresponding weakness made Webster's
own response less significant (VI, 182–183). Nevertheless, he agreed
to review once more the historical changes that turned a weak confederation into a powerful union. "If men will open their eyes fairly
to the lights of history," he remarked in some exasperation, "it is
impossible to be deceived on this point" (VI, 206). The orator's acute
sense of timing was clearly offended by the redundancy of his position, but he saw no alternative and closed with yet another call
upon the people—a call that cleverly turned the burden of repetition
into high drama. His own appropriate part, Webster told his audience, required a never-ending appeal. The Defender of the Constitution would invoke "the PEOPLE" continuously, "earnest as ever,"
even after time and reiteration made voice and speaker feeble (vi,
238).

The Reply to Calhoun reached a national audience, but could one
hope for that much again and again? In 1833 Webster still believed
that words, "things of mighty influence," controlled both human
passions and political discussions, but he also knew that rhetoric
was vain when words lost their power (VI, 186; I, 307). Repetition
made sense only as long as it could be justified as part of the national
learning process (I, 324). To maintain the same subject after Americans had mastered the meaning of the Constitution would turn its
Defender into "a feeble imitator of other men's language and sen-

timents" (IV, 271). Inevitably, the 1830s and 1840s meant preaching to the converted. In areas of general consensus, national definition involved the increasingly pointless task of making "all admit, what none deny" (XI, 222). Forever linked with the idea of the Union, Webster tried to avoid overexposure. "I must not allow myself to pursue this topic," he announced on one occasion in 1843. "It is a sentiment so commonly repeated by me upon all public occasions, and upon all private occasions, and everywhere, that I forbear to dwell upon it now" (III, 209).

A very different problem developed in those areas of deepening national controversy. The Founders supplied crucial evidence for clarifying the Constitution, but that basic source of understanding could not resolve the growing number of issues that lay "beyond all contemplation or expectation of the original framers of the Constitution" (x, 38). Webster was also learning that even the best explanation of the Constitution failed to convince those who really disagreed. "The Constitution was intended as an instrument of great political good," its Defender noted ruefully in 1842, "but we sometimes so dispute its meaning, that we cannot use it at all" (III, 136). As sectional strife grew, eloquence itself appeared a source of disruption. Webster began to realize that political speech divided Americans where it once had united them. "The curse of this country is eloquent men," he observed in 1845.[41] These admissions and others like them implied a truth Webster hated to face directly. Oratory no longer governed; it no longer led toward consensus. The analogy between the courtroom decision of a judge or jury and a political decision made in public forums had never been more than that, and it was rapidly becoming much less.

By 1850 the man who once called words mighty influences for rationality saw his countrymen routinely mistaking violent talk for eloquence and reason (x, 90). A consummate irony during debate over the Compromise of 1850 involved Clay, Calhoun, and Webster together; each of the Senate's three great orators rose in turn to condemn public speaking as a source of the nation's problem. Clay claimed that inflammatory speech had transformed Congress into a raging furnace where calm had reigned just two months before. Calhoun warned that no number of eulogies could save the Union. Webster complained that the whole language of the country had been depraved and corrupted by Congressional debate. A second irony followed. When speech failed, Stephen Douglas manipulated behind the scenes to create the Compromise of 1850.[42] His success meant that the days of the orator in American culture were numbered.

Oratory came to play a smaller part in the courtroom as well. Webster's great talent for summarizing basic principles effectively and eloquently became less and less relevant within the increasingly technical jurisprudence of the 1830s and 1840s. As early as 1822 the lawyer worried about his lack of expertise (XVI, 70). By 1835 he felt severely handicapped (XVIII, 10). Webster had never been what the profession called "a deep read lawyer."[43] "Many other students read more than I did and knew more than I did," he confessed late in life. "But so much as I read, I made my own" (XVII, 51). This firm knowledge of basic texts more than sufficed in the earlier decades of the century, when a personal hero like Samuel Dexter could dismiss an opponent's "basket full of law books" by saying, "One plain dictate of common sense, one clear maxim of the Common Law is worth a cartload of such rubbish."[44] But Webster faced a new situation in the 1830s, one in which common sense and clear maxims could not compete with a detailed knowledge of statutory and case law.

The old-style generalist in law was retreating before a more formally trained expert. Between 1837 and 1845 Webster allowed his practice to decline. He disliked what the transformation in the profession meant and held to early priorities when he did appear in court, searching for ways to apply basic American principles.[45] When *Luther v. Borden* in 1848 afforded a rare chance to invoke national definitions, he jumped at the opportunity to spurn current legal practice in the name of a more general ideal. The case came to the Supreme Court against the dramatic backdrop of the Dorr Rebellion in Rhode Island. Webster, with a vivid presentation of the facts, tried to "relieve the drudgery of perusing briefs, demurrers, and pleas, in bar, bills in equity and answers." Just like the orator of *Dartmouth College* of thirty years before, he wanted to "introduce topics which give sprightliness, freshness, and something of an uncommon public interest to proceedings in courts of law" (XI, 219, 241). Again the nation listened, but the only audience that mattered, the justices on the bench, listened now with a more specialized sense of legal practice in mind. The Court ruled that *Luther v. Borden* involved purely political matters on which it could not pass judgment.[46] It rejected Webster's strategy.

Embattled politically and increasingly cut off from the professional source of a functional oratory, Webster depended more and more upon emotional language beyond the immediate scope of rational discourse.[47] Melodramatic invocation began to overshadow ideological explanation. The first Bunker Hill address, in 1825, ended with a call for enlarged conceptions and the extension of ideas; the second, in 1843, with the exclamation "Thank God, I—I also—AM AN AMERICAN!" (I, 254, 283). Within this more sentimental mode, Webster pushed earlier positions toward new extremes. The spokesman for the Whig theory of history in nineteenth-century American culture originally termed the Revolution a natural and necessary result in the development of the country, but the debater's grouping of nullification and secession with revolution soon made the very idea of rebellion unacceptable. Rejection of constituted authority belonged to an earlier ideological stage that should not be repeated (I, 202; VI, 189–194). By 1843 the Revolution seemed more miracle than logical sequence, and only a fool or a madman would want to try it again (III, 207–208). There was less flexibility in these later stances. In Webster's thought the Constitution always had been the standard for planning future development, but that instrument of rational guidance gradually became a totemic constraint. "In itself it is already complete and perfect," the orator told an audience in 1847. Duty now came before thought. A presumptuous man might think of improvement; a patriotic one would resist every change (IV, 99–100).

These rigid and often sentimental later speeches contained two uncomfortable truths about the beginning of modern American political thought. First, the Webster of the 1840s was articulating a more emotional basis for national identification, and that basis has dominated political expression in the United States ever since. He pinpointed the change from a republic, which assumed an intellectual right of revolution, to a nation-state, which depended upon notions of loyalty and collective mission.[48] The Civil War and martyrdom helped Abraham Lincoln complete the change in the 1860s, but Webster, fifteen years before, supplied the major element when he linked patriotism to a mystical regard for established law. History has been vague on this contribution, and the oversight hides a second and more painful truth. When Daniel Webster perfected the central image of the law-abiding citizen, he did so to answer moral protests against slavery. His "undeviating devotion to legalities" in enforcing the Fugitive Slave Law of 1850 made him a target of abolitionist sentiment at the time and "the forgotten man of American conservatism" ever after.[49] Ideological vindication—the celebration of lawful obedience in the nation-state—came only later and indirectly with Appomattox, when Lincoln received credit for the ideas of victory. Nevertheless, it was Webster who made "law and order" a national virtue. That this political slogan was used initially to resist the extension of suffrage and to protect the institution of slavery should give every American pause.[50]

Thomas Jefferson's *Notes on the State of Virginia* first formalized intellectual debate over the relations of slavery, law, and morality in the republic. Jefferson found the situation impossible not because the law failed to handle slavery—there was a considerable body of slave law in the southern states even in 1787—but because laws on slavery could never rest upon the higher morality of natural law. Since subsequent theorists also justified their jurisprudence as an extension of higher law, they could never reconcile republican principles with the institution of slavery. This was the contradiction that gradually infected the entire culture. When sectional strife and abolitionist sentiment over slavery reached a breaking point in 1850, Webster cut to the heart of the contradiction with a response that offended many. He made the Constitution itself the practical manifestation of higher law, thus justifying slavery as the unavoidable price of holy Union. His critics accused him of substituting law for morality. Actually, he was edging toward a modern, positivist definition of the law in which man-made law became the source of *all* entitlements.[51]

Webster summarized his position while acting as legal counsel for the party of "law and order" in *Luther v. Borden*. Far from offering a right of revolution, the Constitution was an instrument for exercising existing authority. Under its aegis, the legal process could be seen as "one uniform current of law, of precedent, and of practice" in "the stream of public authority" (XI, 227–230). The metaphor was particularly useful for one easily alarmed by "the spray of the waves of violent popular commotion" (XI, 243). When real commotion came in 1850, Webster knew how to handle it. He opened the famous Seventh of March speech on Constitution and Union with another image of stormy seas and then called for calm through a series of legal remedies that would restore "that quiet and that harmony which make the blessings of this Union so rich" (x, 57–58). His historical review of the law of slavery and the language of the Constitution authenticated the legality of slavery within the Union in and after 1787 (x, 61–66). The complex issue of slavery in the new territories also had "a fixed and settled character, now fixed and settled by law which cannot be repealed" (x, 85). Finally, the compromise measures before the Senate called for "the enactment of proper laws" for the return of fugitive slaves escaping from the South (x, 86–87). In this way, real grievances could be redressed as "matters of law"; all else was agitation, opinion, sentiment, and mutual crimination and recrimination (x, 92).

Webster's speech placed a heavy onus on the law as the final source of national unity. Only one other statement of the period, the *Dred Scott* decision of the Supreme Court in 1857, would try to impose such a legal solution upon sectional strife. When the Compromise of 1850 itself became the law of the land, northern outrage concentrated upon the Fugitive Slave Law and upon Daniel Webster, who, as Millard Fillmore's new secretary of state, was the federal officer responsible for its enforcement.[52] Webster, in turn, made support of the Fugitive Slave Law a test of loyalty and disobedience a question of treason (IV, 256–262, 275). He taunted his adversaries. They argued from "the din and roll and rub-a-dub of Abolitionist writers" or from "the ideas of the higher law that exists somewhere between us and the third heaven," and they foolishly forgot that the Constitution itself guaranteed the restitution of runaway slaves (x, 165; IV, 275).

The acrimony reflected a major ideological realignment. For while the Defender of the Constitution maintained a certain consistency on the slave issue, the intellectual spokesman for a culture was changing, and the crux of that change involved a lost dimension in the meaning of the law.[53] Ultimately, the lawyer's special moral stature in public forums rested on the assumption that higher law supported the civic design of the American experiment. Questioning that higher law meant calling the previous understanding of most Americans into question. At Plymouth Rock in 1820, Webster encouraged the legal profession to eliminate the African slave trade as a practice "contrary to the principles of justice and humanity within the reach of our laws." To destroy "this work of hell" was a solemn duty that would bring the laws of man into line with the justice of Heaven (I, 221–222). Thirty years later, a different Webster dismissed all higher law as the false code of abolitionism. Where exactly was the higher law, he jested, and how high was it? (XIII, 435). The orator who tried to make the republic consistent with its principles in 1820 now argued to preserve a Union of absolute and inherent meaning. In a description of country that ignored three million American slaves, he praised a beneficent government that trampled upon no man's liberty (X, 97–98). Morality and law, principle and practice, ideology and oratory no longer cohered in a single speaker. Webster no longer functioned as the moral spokesman of his generation, and it was no accident that his most eloquent detractors, men like William Ellery Channing, Theodore Parker, and Ralph Waldo Emerson, grounded their own morality in theological traditions.

Webster was the focal point of larger forces at work. The debate over slavery reached an old imbalance in the literary consciousness of the nation. When post-Revolutionary lawyer-writers wanted to exclude clergymen from the high office of defining the republic, they invoked separation of church and state and substituted a secular theory of moral value based upon Enlightenment thought. Sectional strife hardly touched the doctrine of church and state, but it gradually destroyed the moral vantage point of the legal mind in American culture. The bitter debates between North and South taught lawyer-politicians like Webster, Clay, and Stephen Douglas that idealism complicated the task of political resolution. They learned that compromise required a language of accommodation rather than talk of higher law, and they adjusted accordingly.[54] But even as the legal mind was accepting the practical limits of its situation, its counterpart in religion was refusing every implication and seizing abandoned moral ground.

By labeling the law a servant of slavery, religious voices put lawyers on the defensive and regained a prominent role in the discussion of civic matters and public policy. As early as 1839 William Ellery Channing pointed a clerical finger at the law as the shield protecting slavery. The great apostle of Unitarianism believed in "a higher law than the Constitution," and that law abhorred human bondage. In 1842 Channing's pamphlet "The Duty of the Free States" recast Webster's stand on slavery at Plymouth Rock two decades before. Channing wrote, as Webster had spoken, "to bring into harmony the law of the land and the law of God," but the minister's mechanism was the lawyer's turned upside down. "In this country," Channing declared, "no law, no constitution can prevail against the moral convictions of the people."[55] Later, after the Compromise of 1850, Theodore Parker made the name Webster synonymous with the fallen nature of all human law. Webster, the great lawyer and defender of national principles, had failed to grasp the real meaning of universal law, and the result for America had been devastating. "No living man," lamented Parker, "has done so much to debauch the conscience of the nation; to debauch the press, the pulpit, the forum, and the bar . . . He poisoned the moral wells of society with his lower law."[56] Emerson wrapped Webster, Clay, and Calhoun together, calling them "attorneys of great & gross interests" who ignored "the cause of right." Even as he blamed the legal profession for turning Webster into a moral skeptic, Emerson wondered how other lawyers could have been so blind as to allow the law to be discredited. Webster's "legal crime" demoralized the entire community. His Fugitive Slave Law brought a free and Christian state down to the cannibal level.[57] All of these denunciations involved an ironic reversal. In the crisis over slavery, ministerial figures now wielded the higher law, and they used it as lawyers once did, to define national virtue and to lead Americans back to the primal business of definitions.

Clerical resurgence also came at a crucial moment in the literary life of the country. The ministry never reestablished the intellectual ascendancy it held in colonial times, but radical divines influenced a new and powerful force in American thought. The moral outrage of the antislavery movement and the creative impulses of the American Renaissance ran together at mid-century, mixing a language of prophetic warning with radically private modes of expression. Out of this combination came a fresh perspective on moral issues, a perspective that regarded the legal mind as a natural enemy. The rising novelists, poets, and essayists of the 1850s wrote of their distaste for lawyer's law, and they often inserted Daniel Webster to prove their point.

"I Cannot Now Read Webster's Speeches"

There was an inevitable antagonism: Webster stood for the old modes of expression and against the innovative ideas of the American Renaissance. He was the natural enemy of the new literary order, or at least its most visible opponent. By presiding over a declamatory literature, he shaped the literary tastes of those who called oratory and public debate "the characteristic germs of a national litera- ture."[58] Webster's speeches were filled with literary allusions, and he spoke often on the duties and place of the man of letters in republican culture. In his view, Adams and Jefferson used early acquisitions in literature to become great, but they demonstrated their greatness by putting public service before contemplative pur- suits. "Literature sometimes disgusts," Webster explained, when it is not linked to utility and public action (I, 300, 319). At its most important, literature helped to secure free institutions. It was "a happy restraint" and "the graceful ornament of civil liberty" (I, 224).

This subordination of literary expression to republican principles involved nothing new, but people listened when they heard Webster on the subject. Webster, for his part, spoke with such confidence because he personified the conventional gentlemanly ideal of learn- ing dedicated to service. Poetry was "the handmaid of true philos- ophy and morality" in that it brought the past and the future into line with the present (I, 183). Since the true orator tried to do the same and since the law also secured the present and future through the past, there could be no contradiction between poet, orator, and lawyer as long as each exercised the highest of functions. All three succeeded in the same way by relying upon clarity, fullness, and force to educate an audience.[59] All three also accepted the same intellectual frame of reference. For Webster, every responsible thinker necessarily concentrated on one problem, "the contemplation of what has been done on the great question of politics and govern- ment." This was "the master topic of the age" (I, 248). Alexander Pope rose above other poets precisely because he celebrated "con- nections, mutual dependencies, and relations," which governed pol- itics as well as literature. As Webster summarized the point, "What the poet says of the great chain that holds all together in the moral, intellectual, and physical world, is applicable to the bond which unites the States" (IV, 289–290).

Every assumption ran counter to the new romantic impulses of the 1830s. From its foundation and pillars to its entablatures and august dome, the temple of justice was a neoclassical structure that glorified the frame of human society (III, 300). Webster used it to link past and present, to symbolize order, and to circumscribe experience with abstractions. Since knowledge was cumulative, he spoke to reach "a more elevated tribunal than ever before existed on the earth . . . the tribunal of the enlightened public opinion of the world" (I, 250; III, 120). Romanticism, on the other hand, discarded Pope and the great chain of being. It put the inspired moment before historical placement, the concrete over the abstract, imagination above social order, and individual readers ahead of public audiences. Nothing could resolve these contradictions. At issue was the very definition of the writer in American culture.

Politics sharpened contradiction. Webster always tried to reconcile differences by placing them within a comprehensive view of things.[60] Virtually every major speech aimed for harmony by insisting upon the Union and the Constitution as the common denominators of all Americans. To this strategy, which owed much to a neoclassical theory of linkage, local feeling and the voice apart were prime dangers. Webster saw sectional strife as "feeling less than wholly American," and he blamed local resentments, local jealousies, and local interests for undermining the common cause (I, 265). The Constitution harmonized everything into one great whole (IV, 289). Gradually, however, separate voices and private interpretations were turning it into a polyglot that contained as many tongues as the Tower of Babel (VI, 196). Coherence required the single and elevated voice of one in touch with universals and a sense of the whole. Neoclassicism encouraged such a voice in a way that romanticism did not. Webster lacked these actual terms of distinction, but it was an easy matter for him to equate his own "old-fashioned way of stating things" with the rationality of "the old school," and it was just as easy to assign the new way of thinking, "a dreamy and undisturbed state, flowing or not flowing, according to its own impulse," to the emotionalism of sectional opposition (XI, 222; IV, 181). His denunciation of those who placed personal feeling above civic duty had far-reaching implications (VI, 55). Although the debater's point effectively isolated southerners like Robert Hayne and John C. Calhoun as irresponsible visionaries, the same tactic separated Webster from younger northern intellectuals who were beginning to stress the individual's private relation with the universe.

The balances, tradition, and orthodoxy of neoclassicism urged consensus, compromise, and preservation of the Union. The individualism, sympathetic feeling, and reformist zeal of romanticism encouraged more particular stances—regional identification on the one side, the problem of slavery on the other. These tendencies and affinities did not always control, but political and literary issues often coincided in the language of debate. Thus, Webster described a nationwide struggle between sound principle and disorganizing sentiment, while Henry David Thoreau dubbed the same conflict a choice between narrow expediency and wise speculation.[61] Each man's terminology applied to his understanding of literary polarities beyond the political. Webster gloried in the conflict as the distinctions became clear. To the lawyer and man of affairs, the feelings and intuitions of transcendentalism were "so refined and invisible as to hang on the very verge of nonsense or nonentity" (xviii, 129). When the higher law became a weapon in transcendentalists' hands, Webster dismissed the two together. He assumed that only a "transcendental and ecstatic" conscience could enter the imaginary realm of higher law, and he quickly turned "a little professional" to contrast the firm reality of lawyer's law (xiii, 435). The transcendentalists naturally responded in kind. It was in rejecting mere law that Thoreau condemned Webster in 1849: "The lawyer's truth is not Truth, but consistency or a consistent expediency."

The writers of the American Renaissance cut their teeth on Daniel Webster. They toyed with his image lovingly as they tried to destroy it, and the marks they left were a sign of their own development. Emerson, the leader of the movement, wrote often of Webster's greatness. The subject was simply too rich for him to ignore, even after regard turned to scorn.[62] In 1830 "Mr. Webster's noble speech in answer to Hayne" contained "beauty and dignity of *principles*." By 1839 the same "recorded eloquence" lacked nerve and dagger, and Emerson soon confessed "I cannot now read Webster's speeches." In the intervening decade, the essayist had forged his own philosophy of individualism in seminal works like "Nature," "The American Scholar," and "The Divinity School Address." "We lose our invention, & descend into imitation," he wrote again in 1852, and by this point he could tell Americans in a single sentence the problem that he saw: "Mr. [Edward] Everett [makes] your literary opinions, and Mr. Webster your politics from the same sources."[63] Since the sources Emerson referred to were European and not American, the explicit challenge to literary orthodoxy was twofold. Emerson rejected the general notion that Webster's speeches gave "the best characteristics of a generous nationality," and he dismissed the larger assertion that American literature represented "the *left arm of national glory*."[64] Patriotic oratory no longer reached the essence of American experience because the assumption on which it was based, the subordination of literary to political expression, was false.

Emerson's followers dramatized his discoveries in the literature of the 1850s and after. Henry Thoreau jeered at "the hip-hip-hurrah and mutual-admiration-society style" of the political speech. Celebrations of national identity could not give a sincere account of a person, much less of a nation. Social virtue, which oratory instilled, meant nothing more than "the virtue of pigs in a litter, which lie close together to keep each other warm."[65] The most private voice of the age made the same point with lighter humor. "I'm Nobody! Who are you?" asked Emily Dickinson:

> How dreary—to be—Somebody!
> How public—like a Frog—
> To tell your name—the livelong June—
> To an admiring Bog![66]

Implicit in these statements was a belief in private meanings that automatically diminished public figures. Walt Whitman celebrated many selves in his poetry, but he saw an unappetizing "duplicate of every one" in public situations. That self was "smartly attired" with "countenance smiling, form upright," and it kept with the customs, "speaking of any thing else but never of itself."[67]

Webster was an obvious target. In the tension between public and private that permeates the literature of the American Renaissance, he appears the hypocrite or worse. "Song for Certain Congressmen" and "Blood-Money," two early poems by Whitman, turn Webster into an unprincipled manipulator and a modern Judas.[68] Hawthorne's *House of the Seven Gables* in 1851 is a political romance full of ironic references to slavery, the prejudice of Jim Crow, and class rivalry. Judge Jaffrey Pyncheon, who causes his poor cousin to gnash her teeth against human law, is Nathaniel Hawthorne's blackest villain. He goes his way as a man of the law, using "festive eloquence" in the wake of "Webster's mighty organ-tones." Lest anyone miss the point, Hawthorne observes "the voice that speaks, and the pen that writes for the public eye and for distant time . . . inevitably lose much of their truth and freedom by the fatal consciousness of so doing." Only "a hidden stream of private talk" ever touches the real meaning of Jaffrey Pyncheon. In *The House of the Seven Gables*, eloquence no longer means what it says, and Webster stands for false success.[69]

Melville's *Mardi* in 1849 casts the Defender of the Constitution in the role of a snaky parasite sucking on a shark. "Leech-like," he sticks to his subject in the fashion of "a false brother in prosperity" or "a beggar to the benevolent." The travelers of *Mardi* visit the central temple of Vivenza (the Capitol in Washington), where they admire the mighty brow of Saturnina, an image for Webster. But here again, Webster represents mere outward show. The wise Babbalanja reminds everyone to "measure brains, not heads."[70] Two years later *Moby-Dick* also looks to the inner man for meaning. A far more subtle allegory of the Union, Melville's masterpiece tells the story of thirty *Isolatoes* "federated along one keel." When the white whale's predestinating head sinks the *Pequod*, only Ishmael, who repudiates the debased politics of his day, survives. He is carried from the sunken ship of state by Queequeg's "coffin life-buoy" in an ironic repudiation of Daniel Webster's own version of political collapse.[71] "I am looking out for no fragment upon which to float away from the wreck," cried Webster in the exordium of March 7, 1850, which Americans knew by heart (x, 57). Queequeg, "George Washington cannibalistically developed," provides just such a fragment, and the Ishmael whom it saves tells a very different story about America.

CHAPTER 9

THE RICHARD HENRY DANAS:
FATHER AND SON

"When He Fell, We All Fell with Him"

Some individuals personify the wholeness of an age; others reflect the incompleteness of its parts. Daniel Webster, in the first category, spoke confidently for the nineteenth century and symbolized its conventions. The Richard Henry Danas, father and son, were more shadowy figures caught up in changes that they only partially understood. As traditional as Webster in politics and social matters, they accepted many of the new impulses sweeping through nineteenth-century intellectual thought, and those impulses were complex. It was not just that Webster admired Pope over all other poets while the Danas preferred Wordsworth.[1] The whole manner in which Americans approached politics, society, and literature was changing. Webster belonged to old ways of thinking. The Danas fell somewhere between the old and the new and faced uncomfortable choices in consequence. Those choices, rather than specific achievements, are what make the Danas interesting. Their failures underscore the contradictions between neoclassical and romantic in republican culture, and their successes illustrate the slow and painful growth of a peculiarly American romanticism. For if Webster embodied the configuration of law and letters, the Danas represented its collapse, and they were the first to realize as much.

Richard Henry Dana, Jr., admired Daniel Webster for what his own career lacked. Webster, "the only *statesman* in the land," was a giant amidst "push-pin politicians." He was "the great man of the age, with a voice, action & presence almost god-like, answering fully to the call." That voice commanded where later ones merely charmed or excited admiration. When Webster died in 1852, Dana wrote, "No man represented so completely, in our day, at least, the mighty, innate, inaccessible superiority of dialectic intellect." It was altogether fitting that no death since Washington's had so moved the nation.[2] The contrast of social vision to the puerile manipulation of push-pins, the association of voice with action and control, the assertion of solution within the context of speech, and the glorification of a dialectic or argumentative intellect—these were the strengths of the lawyer-writer who dominated public forums through the correct application of republican ideology. Dana saw Webster as the last intellectual link to the Founding Fathers, and he knew that his own generation was losing control of the Founders' creation. Somehow the connection between social vision and professional training had been broken.

Dana could even identify the moment of final rupture: 1850, when Webster stopped being Webster. "We have all mourned over him," Dana said of Webster in 1851, "because we felt that when he fell, we all fell with him."[3] Famous author, rising lawyer, charter member of the Free-Soil Party, Dana was just thirty-six at the time—young enough to oppose the new Fugitive Slave Law, old enough to see that his personal affinities still lay with Webster. Webster's fall implicated every lawyer-writer because of Dana's overwhelming sense of decline. Every achievement in Dana's own life yielded before that dark assumption. *Two Years Before the Mast*, published in 1840, made a major contribution to the thriving genre of American sea fiction, and it guaranteed membership in the most exclusive literary circles. Dana's courtroom defenses of fugitive slaves in the 1850s, his expertise in maritime law, and his crucial argument for Lincoln's wartime policies in the *Prize Cases* of 1863 brought him renown within the legal profession and an honorable place within the moral, commercial, and political development of the country. Meanwhile, financial success restored the fallen fortunes and the prestige of an ancient family line. But Dana extracted small satisfaction from his accomplishments. "My life has been a failure, compared with what I might and ought to have done," he wrote his son in 1873. "My great success—my book—was a boy's work, done before I came to the Bar." More reflection brought greater desperation. "I feel that my life will have been a failure (under all my circumstances) unless I do something more," he wrote again in 1879, just three years before his death.[4]

If one event convinced Dana of his own futility, it was the Massachusetts constitutional convention of 1853. The young Webster had dominated the previous convention of 1820, shaping the state constitution on conservative principles and quickly establishing himself as a statesman of the first order. Dana's father, Richard Henry Dana, Sr., had witnessed Webster's greatest performance then and encouraged the obvious parallels. That first convention had been a turning point in a young lawyer's political career—why not the second, too? But careful study of the 1820 debates and his own major role in the convention of 1853 brought Dana defeat rather than victory, ridicule instead of reputation. He proved utterly ineffective in the public fight for ratification, and he saw the voters of Massachusetts reject the new constitution; they objected at least in part to provisions that Dana had written.[5] The would-be statesman wanted to recover the past for an electorate in search of its future. When the call came in 1853, it was for answers that he was unprepared to give. The inherently conservative configuration of law and letters no longer held American audiences. As Dana summarized his situation a year later, "My duties as lawyer, scholar, and publicist are all out of the way."[6]

Forebears made Dana especially conscious of failure. His grandfather and father, Francis Dana (1743–1811) and Richard Henry Dana, Sr. (1787–1879), entered the legal profession with the same larger aspirations. In fact, the three Danas span the entire period of the configuration of law and letters, and their respective decisions reveal a great deal about the changing nature of nineteenth-century intellectual life. Francis Dana typified the early American lawyer's grasp of his culture. Admitted to the Massachusetts bar in 1767, he played a minor but distinct role in the Revolution. He was a member of the Continental Congress, chairman of the committee on the army that brought vital political support to Washington at Valley Forge, secretary to John Adams during the original peace negotiations in France and Holland, and then ambassador to Russia. Only poor health kept him from serving as one of the framers in Philadelphia in 1787, and a year later he was instrumental in the Massachusetts convention that ratified the Constitution of the United States. Eventually, Francis Dana became chief justice of the supreme judicial court of Massachusetts, a position he held for fifteen years from Washington's presidency into the second administration of Jefferson. As chief justice he sustained "an elegance but little known in those days," riding circuit in the finest of carriages, and his grand jury charges epitomized New England Federalism in its days of glory. An admiring Richard Henry Dana, Jr., captured the total effect: "His whole style was that of a great magistrate, & he sustained the dignity of the office with no little of the aristocratic bearing."[7]

Unfortunately, Francis Dana's success also magnified failure in the next generation. Richard Henry Dana, Sr., never recovered from the disastrous speculations of an older brother who dissipated family fortunes in the first decade of the nineteenth century. Indeed, much of Dana Sr.'s writing dealt with the shock of this lost status. Of his father the chief justice he noted, "I can never think of his exalted character without a sense of my own littleness." The merest memory, he added, "makes the present tasteless, & takes away the vigour of my hope in what is to come." Written in 1819, these words came not from a pining adolescent but from a man of thirty-two, and they expressed a final determination to reject the law for a private life as "The Idle Man" in literature.[8]

This decision was a public admission of defeat in 1819. Contemporaries like George Ticknor, Edward T. Channing, William Hickling Prescott, and Alexander Everett also abandoned the law for various literary pursuits, and Henry Longfellow, James Russell Lowell, and Francis Parkman followed suit a generation later, but these men relied upon independent wealth or another vocation for status, and most had both.[9] Dana Sr. could name only an honorary assistantship at the *North American Review*, and even this tenuous association—"all gentlemen and no pay"—was taken away in 1819 when failure to succeed in the logical sequence of editors prompted his resignation.[10] By 1822 he had just the smallest of patrimonies, an occasional lecture series, and his own writings to fall back upon. "I am a miserable cripple," he had announced earlier, revealing the hypochondria that would support another half-century of idleness.[11] The boy of twelve who remembered Washington's death would live to see Rutherford B. Hayes elected president, and every year brought fresh complaints and new failures. "I was shabbily enough treated in my honest endeavours for an humble place," he told his son later. Alas, "the *life* of the mind, through long disappoinment, had become permanently languid."[12] In 1848 Lowell's *A Fable for Critics* sounded a final note of satire over all of this pathos: "That he once was the Idle Man none will deplore,/ But I fear that he will never be anything more."[13]

The lesson in contrast of the two older generations was not lost on the third. Richard Henry Dana, Jr., noted both the positive model and the negative example, and nothing pleased him more than the resemblance so many saw between himself and his grandfather.[14] His own mission in life was clear from the beginning: he would restore the family name. Even the mechanics of success were obvious. Dana "always considered it a settled thing" that he would be a lawyer, and his earliest memory of childhood, "looking through a small side window to watch my father as he went off to Court at Concord," established permanent expectations.[15] For his part, Dana Sr. did everything possible to enforce the difference between father and son. A "feeble, sickly creature," too weak to ride or walk or even write at times, he nevertheless required "steady labour," even "strenuous effort & industry," from his child. "Do all you can to make yourself a good and useful man," he wrote to the boy of nine. Later, he enumerated qualities that made his son "peculiarly fit" for the legal profession.[16]

Precedent, familial pressure, pride, and ambition all pushed Richard Henry Dana, Jr., toward the law, but conditions in 1840, the year he entered practice, no longer favored the old balances between law and letters or the related notion of the gentleman in public service. Dana, of course, believed in those traditional goals, as his account of Harvard Law School between 1837 and 1840 makes clear: "Free from all the details, chicanery & responsibilities of practice, we were placed in a library, under learned, honourable & gentlemanly instructors, & invited to pursue the study of jurisprudence, as a system of philosophy . . . All exercises were voluntary, there were no rewards or punishments, no rank, & no police or supervision." By 1839 the law student was so impressed that he carried the same system back into Harvard College as a part-time instructor in elocution. "I accepted the plan of the law professors," he later wrote, "& the first day that I met my classes told them that I had nothing to do with their parietal government; that we met merely as gentlemen who were pursuing the same studies & exercises, & that I had no eyes, ears or tongue for anything else."[17] These passages take much for granted. The messy world and its problems are kept at bay, handled by someone else and removed from the intellectual process. Significantly, Dana also experienced his best years as a writer, 1837 to 1840, in this arrangement. The gentleman of letters as law student wrote *Two Years Before the Mast* in 1838, and the conditions that made his achievement possible—"free from all the details, chicanery & responsibilities of practice"—disappeared the moment academic preparation became professional reality.

The world of the law student and teacher could be defined in a single word: gentlemanly. The more complicated world of the lawyer could not be so reduced, and Dana's attempts made even the young man an anachronism in his own time. The problem was twofold. On the one hand, Dana's idea of the gentleman forced him beyond private and academic life. The true gentleman, after all, sought the discipline and responsibility of active public service. On the other hand, Dana's rigid criteria for gentlemanly status (breeding, refinement, cultivation, delicate perception, decorum, restraint, and elevation) eliminated all but a few of those who sought an active life in business.[18] Only the rare exception qualified for Dana's exacting designation, and this was particularly the case in the legal profession. Even Joseph Story could be condemned for arguing at table "like a lawyer" and prosing "like a book worm"; he "forgot that he was a gentleman dining out." On another occasion Dana found only one gentleman—"he seemed a pearl among swine"— after ransacking the entire practicing bar of Providence, Rhode Island. The search for a proper gentleman became an obsession in the journal, one with a foreseeable conclusion. "In 30 years there will not be a *gentleman* left in the country," Dana predicted in 1843, approving the words of his uncle, Washington Allston.[19] Of course, it was the gentleman as eighteenth-century replica, as the reincarnation of Chief Justice Francis Dana, that seemed so nearly extinct.

Dana's own modernity compounded the problem of repeating the past. He thought of the grandfather but *like* the father. That father, Richard Henry Dana, Sr., had been the first modern American critic, the first to value the romantic impulses in nineteenth-century literature, and he had used those impulses to justify his retreat from public life. Since romanticism stressed a creative imagination yearning for natural simplicity, the editor of *The Idle Man* easily separated a private life of the mind from the corrupting and vulgar world of work and society. Indeed, the distinction governed the elder Dana's writings and entered into the psychological legacy of the son.[20] Richard Henry Dana, Jr., would also regard vocational matters with a deep and permanent distaste. "How I loathe the business & petty things of the world," wrote the lawyer, praying for an independence from professional duties. He faced these duties but with "a dread . . . received from my father," and he complained that they robbed him of insight into "all that is simple & pure in nature!"[21]

Never happy, Dana struggled with a growing sense of discrepancy. His life soon became a cycle of extremes—total immersion in the law giving way to sudden collapses and escapes in travel. Sea voyages and hiking treks restored the exhausted lawyer as if by magic. Within hours of leaving his Boston office, Dana would move from physical breakdown to prodigious displays of energy that astonished the sailors and mountain men with whom he liked to consort.[22] These trips were obvious mechanisms of release; they were also psychic imitations of Dana Sr.'s permanent retreat from vocation, and, as such, they required the father's way of thinking. Dana called his excursions "an abandonment to nature & nature's unsophisticated men," and he used them to reach for a more crucial identity away from public life. "I was intended by nature for a general roamer and traveller by sea and land," he explained in one of many dismissals of the lawyer's priorities.[23] Both word and gesture bespoke a romantic's view of the world. Abandonment to nature signified a return to vital resources and an awareness of something lost that might also be forbidden.

The first romantic gesture was the escape to California as a common sailor in 1834, a decision made in violation of every social norm and leading directly to *Two Years Before the Mast*. But only one other trip, a voyage to Cuba when Dana was forty-five, led to a published work.[24] After 1840 writing became part of the lawyer's public identity: literature, one more thing to avoid during those travels when Dana was most himself. "I make it a rule," he observed, "never to read or study when I am away on these excursions . . . I will rather lie down & bask in the sun, or throw stones in the air & catch them than put my mind to any labor, or allow one thought of business, or law or literature to enter it."[25] In effect, the writer left the neoclassical ideal of balanced involvements far behind. Unable to renew the old continuities between public writing, civic duty, and personal identity, Dana thought more and more in terms of exclusions and bifurcations. And yet he always remained the gentleman of letters fulfilling public duties and holding "any poor-author fancier" in contempt.[26] Out of date and over-refined, the stance further isolated and constrained the writer. Dana lived and wrote *between* traditional and modern understandings. New ways of thinking had pushed him to separate public and private where the creative process was concerned, but he never accepted the essence of modern literature. He never saw the overriding importance of giving public expression to private thought, and, in consequence, he left the best of his mature writings hidden away in his journal.

These faults are easier to describe than to explain. No nineteenth-century writer received a more thorough grounding in his craft than Dana. Father and uncle—Richard Henry Dana, Sr., and Washington Allston—specified the importance of literature and the more particular meaning of its modern expression. Ralph Waldo Emerson was an early teacher. Another uncle was Edward Tyrrel Channing, the Boylston Professor of Rhetoric at Harvard College, who, in the words of Thomas Wentworth Higginson, "probably trained as many conspicuous authors as all other American instructors put together."[27] Dana lived in almost daily contact with his uncles, and, as the subsequent editor of both men's writings, he formalized an intimate knowledge of their thought. It was Channing who suggested the topic of Dana's Harvard commencement address in 1837, "Heaven Lies about us in our Infancy," a line from Wordsworth's "Ode on the Intimations of Immortality." The address itself, wrote one auditor, "was of that Swedenborgian, Coleridgian, and dreamy cast which it requires a peculiar structure of mind to understand, much more to relish."[28] Clearly Dana understood the tenets of romanticism.

For the working artist, however, there is always an enormous gap between theoretical understanding and creative application. The Danas, both father and son, mastered the meaning of romanticism but never its working implications and never its voice. They failed because the emerging modes of expression at work in nineteenth-century American culture required new ways of regarding the self—ways that unsettled everything the Danas stood for in republican society. Neoclassicism assumed an identity that reached through civic action toward the presumed identity of other men and women.

Romanticism, concerned more with ego and self-expression, compelled a prior discovery and assertion of personal identity. As the first suggested relation, so the second implied opposition, and the difference underlined absolute philosophical divisions. Were truths self-evident or were truths evident to the self?[29] The Danas could never decide, and their uncertainty meant that the configuration of law and letters no longer answered such questions.

Richard Henry Dana, Sr.: "Turning the Mind Long Inward"

Richard Henry Dana, Sr., could legitimately call his own works "a part of our literary history."[30] Between 1817 and 1827 he wrote America's first sustained critique of romanticism, penned the country's most perceptive reviews, praised Charles Brockden Brown's genius before other critics found even merit, and helped create the genre of American gothic fiction. Too, Dana Sr. lived long enough to see his most unpopular evaluations turn into conventional doctrine. He knew the satisfaction of having been right all along: "Much that was once held to be presumptuous novelty" in the Era of Good Feeling became, in his words, "little better than commonplace" by 1850 (I, IV). The precursor, however, took no satisfaction in what followed. "Emerson & the other Spiritualists, or Supernaturalists, or whatever they are called, or may be pleased to call themselves" were a bad influence; "madness is in their *hearts*," wrote Dana Sr.[31] There was, in short, a basic failure in sympathy that illustrates how thoroughly republican culture tangled the notions of neoclassic and romantic. Dana Sr., the purveyor of a European romanticism, saw not a counterpart in American transcendentalism but rather an extreme manifestation that exceeded essential controls. Neoclassical in form, those controls were part of a political orthodoxy that no early republican could ignore—part of the long contest between order and originality in American literature. Dana Sr. earned a special place in that contest by laboring to combine the incompatible.

Every major tenet of romanticism receives attention in Dana Sr.'s early *North American Review* articles.[32] An essay from 1817, "Old Times," chooses feeling and imagination over affected refinement and cold rationality, nature over society, ancient custom over modern practice. The writer wants a mind as organic and creative as the earth itself, and he looks for the "wild and adventurous starting up in the midst of the common objects of life" (II, 3–11). A review of Washington Allston's poetry from the same year makes poetry the highest ideal of a culture, rejects didacticism in literature, and applauds balladic simplicity. Again the contrast is between the freedom, energy, and spontaneity of man in nature against the confinement, artificiality, and "hot stir of pent society" (II, 103–105, 125–128). Two more reviews from 1818 and 1819 turn abstract premise into explicit accusation. Here Dana Sr. censures critics who condemn Wordsworth and Coleridge in the name of Pope; they substitute profession for sincerity, wit for feeling, ornament for simple reflection, and reason for natural impulse (II, 133–134, 149, 178–200, 261–267). The true critic hopes instead for awakened associations, "living forms struggling to break forth," and "a holier calm" from "the riot of the imagination" (II, 179, 196, 263).

The same ideas carry into the poems and stories of the 1820s. "The Changes of Home," "Factitious Life," "The Early Spring Book," "The Moss Supplicateth for the Poet," and "Daybreak" all extol in verse the simple, organic, natural world in which "the whole man *lived* his feelings" (I, 35–84, 114–118, 121–124, 139–144, 63). Like many another romantic poet, Dana Sr. employs pastoral settings, aeolian harps, and mystic hieroglyphs to convey one central message: "How simply nature teaches truth!" (I, 35–36, 79, 99, 116). His fictional protagonists also turn to nature as a special source of meaning. Looking to the "blessed and silent communion" of the elements, Tom Thornton, in the story of that name, wants to "mingle with the air, and be all a sensation too deep for sound,—a traveller among the stars, and filled with light" (I, 186). Edward Shirley of "Edward and Mary" combines a distaste for the world at large with delight in the purifying influences of nature. In this account of threatened love, nature invariably sympathizes with the hero's shifts in mood (I, 223–224, 262, 269). In "Paul Felton," Paul walks the hills, looking for sympathy in nature. Nature is "power, and intellect, and love, made visible," and it allows Paul moments of truth: "He was as a part of the great universe, and all he looked upon, or thought on, was in some way connected with his own mind and heart" (I, 274, 277). In each story spontaneous impulses cut across careful reason, and external landscapes merge with stages of mind to emphasize the organic link between man and nature (I, 203–204, 218, 232–239, 294, 328).

Yet these writings perplex because they promise so much more than they give. Original in intent, they are imitative in effect. They fail through a basic paradox: the poems and stories of Richard Henry Dana, Sr., are romantic in theory but neoclassic in practice, and the combination robs each point of view of its intrinsic worth. The same paradox, of course, applies to other writers in the first decades of the nineteenth century, but Dana Sr.'s stature as a romantic theorist poses the problem in its purest form.[33] How could such a critic fail to see the gap between assertion and execution in his own work? Why do neoclassical premises remain so firmly entrenched in poems and stories that strive so hard for something else? The negatives traditionally used to explain literary weakness in the early national period do not apply in this case. Neither parochial nor utilitarian, the publications of Dana Sr. show that he possessed the time, the opportunity, the literary sophistication, and the desire to achieve much in poetry and fiction.

Conflicting aims hurt Dana Sr. far more than inadequate means. He writes for a world that requires him to be too many things at once. A romantic critic, he is also a gentleman of letters with the responsibility of defining man's place in society. As republican citizen, he believes in social subordination as a basis of ordered liberty, and his dutiful expression of that belief is profoundly neoclassical in scope and tone, adding decorum, propriety, duty, hierarchy, and control to the cardinal virtues of imagination and natural impulse.[34] These unlikely combinations breed contradiction and crop up everywhere in Dana Sr.'s stories, poems, and reviews.

The published works are a battleground of conflicting values. One celebration of "the wild and adventurous" insists upon the necessity of order and constraint in master-servant relations (II, 7–11). The reviewer who wants passions to be "living, sentient, speaking, acting beings" also confesses to "fears of being unduly sprightly . . . sacrificing our dignity and decorum" (II, 354, 289). Feelings are vital, but the most natural impulse must bow to social convention. Thus, a call for honest feeling does not excuse Washington Irving for allowing a husband to show public affection in "The Wife." Still other parts of The Sketch Book lack proper refinement because Irving stoops to describe passion outside of love (II, 308–309). Dana Sr. admires Charles Brockden Brown for accomplishing what he himself cannot: "Instead of living as only one of the multitude of keen and clever men at the bar, and then dying and being forgotten, [Brown] is going down . . . as the earliest author of genius in our literature" (II, 341). But no amount of originality can justify the bad taste of Brown's free-thinking tracts or the vulgarity of that moment in *Ormond* when the beautiful Constantia Dudley washes foul linen (II, 333–336).

Greater writers would soon turn the ambiguities between personal feeling and social conformity into high art. Less gifted, Richard Henry Dana, Sr., nonetheless glimpses the possibility; he is the first to understand that the American story involves an unending adjustment of twin obsessions, impulse and order. Predictably, his heroes are divided men. They cling to decorum and nicety during the sharpest of inward crises, and cling they must since insanity lies close to the surface in Dana Sr.'s fiction. Characters who lose sight of the prescribed forms of conduct go mad.[35] Protagonists like Tom Thornton, Edward Shirley, and Paul Felton have romantic temperaments, but their safety depends upon a neoclassical equilibrium that guards against the dangers of introspection. Romanticism has taught Dana Sr. that imagination can be a perilous thing:

> The imagination grows forgetive, and the mind idles, in its melancholy, among fantastic shapes; all it hears or sees is turned to its own uses, taking new forms and new relations, and multiplying without end; and it wanders off amongst its own creations, which crowd thicker round it the farther it goes, till it loses sight of the world, and becomes bewildered in the many and uneven paths that itself had trodden out. (I, 223)

More simply, "turning the mind long inward upon itself" means "making ourselves miserable" most of the time. Social interaction alone can correct the resulting imbalance. "To know ourselves," Dana Sr. explains, "we must be content, sometimes, to go out of ourselves" (II, 434). Happiness requires recognition of one's "double character"; one's "outer and inner machinery" must balance (II, 423).

"Paul Felton" (1822), a minor masterpiece in the American gothic between Brown and Poe, tells what happens when man's inner machinery takes over.[36] Accepting the romantic postulate that imagination guides perception, Dana Sr. writes a nightmare of the imagination run wild. Paul Felton has been raised in melancholy isolation by his widowed father, a background that inhibits meaningful intercourse with the world. Incapable of balancing outer and inner priorities, he retreats inward where everything is "pent-up and secret action." Soon all is "at war and in opposition in his character," and his mind welcomes extremes, "not knowing how to measure its joys when they came" (I, 270–272, 295). This mind is "in a peculiar degree single," which means that the passion of the moment utterly controls what Paul comprehends. Gradually, obsessions rob Paul of all sense of reality and turn him into a homicidal maniac (I, 287, 295–296, 313, 333, 338, 341). He murders his wife, Esther, who, as the symbol of social interaction, has tried to save him (I, 287, 347, 353–354). It is Esther who delivers the author's overall indictment of Paul: "You have brooded all alone over your melancholy thoughts, till they have bewildered you" (I, 280, 282, 284).

Inner bewilderment is such a source of terror in "Paul Felton" because it happens so easily and because Paul differs only in degree from the more social beings around him. As the story makes clear, everyone experiences unwilled mental aberrations, which suddenly appear "like visitants from hell" (I, 317–318). This is the organic mind receiving and projecting associations. Left alone, however, the mind uses these sensations too freely and quickly becomes an engine of delusion. Paul separates himself from "what is homely and substantial in this world we live in" and, hence, fails to protect himself from intrinsic impulses (I, 313). "I would not be what I am," he mourns, rightly fearing his own inner psyche (I, 342, 353). The rest is an ugly, inevitable sequence. In accepting an organic theory of the mind, Dana Sr. understands that the imagination welcomes delusion and thrives on madness. Paul easily manufactures a private hell as real as the external world, and that hell expands in his narcissistic enjoyment of the act of creation (I, 338).

"Paul Felton" recounts the mind's helpless pleasure in its own madness when all avenues of escape have been sealed off. Even Paul's classical education and his love of nature hurt more than they help. The former supplies a certain clarity and simplicity, but it also alienates Paul from modern society (I, 271, 276–277). Nature presents even graver problems; she is indifferent, leaving Paul "a withered thing amid her fresh and living beauty" (I, 274). Worse, she sometimes stimulates the darker recesses of his mind. A desolate wasteland directly behind the house of Paul and Esther accentuates each feeling of isolation and delusion (I, 293–294, 304–305, 338, 363). Moreover, "a spider" in the madman's eye feeds on a correspondence in nature. When Paul plans the murder of Esther, he is deep in the wilderness, literally supported by "some giant spider" of a pine tree (I, 329, 337–341). Man and nature have come together, but in horror and catastrophe instead of transcendence and a higher reality.

The reversal of romantic aspirations is surely deliberate. Dana Sr. accepts a vital link between the imagination and the natural realm, but he fears the way "quickly associating processes of the mind" magnify emotion, and he sees too much of a blank wilderness, "the place of death," to rest easily in nature (II, 50; I, 88–89, 305). New ideas compete with old solutions. Dana Sr. wants an objective truth to secure the subjective reality that he has come to believe in. Caught between combination and contradiction, he is the first American writer to face the epistemological problems of nineteenth-century thought.[37] Where is absolute order in a contingent universe? When do feelings represent fact? What is truth? "Paul Felton" ushers these questions into American fiction, where they lead to either a quest for ultimate meaning or a search for particular order. The isolated hero quests for meaning, social man searches for his place, and the two vie for position in every major work of the American Renaissance. Paul Felton, alas, is an early uncertain mixture of both. The man who would challenge the universe shrinks from the impropriety of a ride in his fiancée's carriage (I, 281, 284). He is the *isolato* as public figure, a stance that begins in confusion and ends in madness because it has "too much to do with the senses" (I, 315). Something beyond mere perception must clarify Paul's world, something that will fix meaning and establish order.

That something is the early American's regard for the law—the only answer Dana Sr. gives to the writer's problems. "Law as Suited to Man" in 1835, almost two decades after the lawyer rejects his profession, tries to resolve the incongruity between subjective thought and objective order by inserting the legal philosophy of Edmund Burke (II, 55–57). In itself the attempt is a firm indication of the citizen still at work in the romantic theorist. Torn between unacceptable alternatives, Dana Sr. wants to prove "there is nothing without us which fails of reaching that which lies within." He answers the great questions of romanticism with one of his own: "And must not Law, then, give form and pressure to every part of man?" Properly understood, the law joins mind and matter, allowing "no jarring nor discordant influences within or without." Reciprocity is the key to harmony here, a reciprocity that effectively externalizes the romantic's psychological theories of correspondence. Burke . has traced not only "the reachings of law into man's finer nature" but also "the delicate, electric *aura* which this individual nature gives back, and diffuses through every fiber of the great, general frame." Accordingly, the law is an infinite abstraction "producing congruity, and giving continuity" between "outer political rule" and "the finest feelings in man's individual being." It meets man everywhere and on every level, its divine purpose being "to bring man into the likeness of the pattern" (II, 62, 69, 58–59). As for so many other early American intellectuals, the law gives Dana Sr. a principle of unity in an uncertain world; it secures "the resemblances and relations of things to each other" and ties "the upper and lower, the inward and outward world to one great end" (II, 57). The language sounds familiar because it is what lawyers since Thomas Jefferson had been using to order American culture.

Even so, "Law as Suited to Man" belongs to 1835. The essay consciously imposes traditional solutions upon new problems, and as such it illustrates the special dilemma of the legal mind of the 1830s better than any other document of the period. Indeed, the contradictions here suggest an impossibility beyond mere difficulty. The republic, literature, and law—all of the controlling constants— change suddenly into variables in the Jacksonian era. When Dana Sr. deplores "the very absence of checks and balances, and settled orders," he also unwittingly announces a formal break in the bonds that once held law to literature (II, 95). Each theoretical affirmation in "Law as Suited to Man," and there are many, is qualified by a list of perceived ills. Practice so violates theory in this description of America that one senses a permanent disjunction. Put another way, the republican man of letters no longer encompasses reality in 1835. His patterns of discourse do not reach the new levels of psychological process that now appear as part of every understanding. A new self-consciousness has brought another dimension to the conflation of moral and legal perspectives and with devastating implications.[38] In "Law as Suited to Man" Dana Sr. tries to build a house with paint and brush. He desperately needs the citizen's more elementary context, but the aspirations of romanticism, which question or ignore a writer's institutional affiliations, prevent a simple return to old ways of thinking. Despite every explanation to the contrary, the legal philosopher and the romantic critic remain absolute opposites in Dana Sr.'s essay, split between social assertion and psychological insight.

"There is nothing more serious than poetry," says the literary critic in "Law as Suited to Man," a statement in support of individual creativity that no other American of his generation dared to make. This side of Dana Sr. writes to keep the mind alive, the imagination in motion, the fancy in play, and all principles of association in action (II, 72–74). And yet the same essayist deserts "man, in his short-lived, individual character" in favor of "the person abstracted from these, and representative of permanent Law" (II, 60). He hopes instead to help each well-defined class find its place—"all brought about by and carried through the harmonizing Orders of a great general Law" (II, 72–73). The civic humanist of an earlier day could join these differences by making self-fulfillment a question of citizenship.[39] Not so the intellectual of the 1830s, who began to see an increasing gulf between self and society. In 1835, the year "Law as Suited to Man" appeared, Ralph Waldo Emerson was thirty-one and ready to write that "things are not huddled and lumped, but sundered and individual."[40] For Richard Henry Dana, Sr., the same notion meant a terrifying "principle of severance" and the certainty of communal paralysis (II, 58).

Taken together, Emerson and Dana Sr. capture a crucial moment in American intellectual thought. Paradigms of social and psychological process often merge or even clash without crisis, but here they are reconstituting in a way that requires a direct reversal in modes of thought. In celebrating "the new importance given to the single person," Emerson claims that man explains society instead of the other way around. "The world is nothing, the man is all," he announces, thus becoming the first American really to accept the romantic *within* romantic theory. Much is at stake in this acceptance, and not least is Emerson's immediate deduction that the law be seen as an internal matter: "In yourself is the law of all nature."[41]

The very basis of law has become a subject of dispute in Jacksonian America. By 1835 the question is no longer *if* law is suited to human life but *how*. Courtrooms are treating the law less and less as an eternal set of principles derived from natural law and more and more as an independent instrument of social policy that lawmakers have created.[42] This change is Dana Sr.'s greatest fear. Assuming a definitive link between natural law and man-made or positive law, "Law as Suited to Man" returns again and again to the contradiction between eighteenth-century legal philosophy and nineteenth-century judicial positivism (II, 58–59). Either the law "presses upon every part of the ductile spirit of man," or it is just a machine, "supplying conveniences and furnishing levers and springs to help on the more general purposes of man" (II, 57, 55). Either it has "a necessitated beginning and continuance in our very nature," or it is "a mere arbitrary institution set up by man himself, out of convenience and choice" (II, 59). Either "it bodies itself forth in orders of men," or it is "a caterer to the self-conceit of man" (II, 62–63). These distinctions mark the difference between order and chaos in "Law as Suited to Man." For if legal positivism turns the law into a more flexible social instrument, it also traps law within the civic milieu, rendering it useless as a philosophical bridge between levels of existence. Gone is the "kindly adaptation" between outward forms and inward needs (II, 62). Lost are fitness in gradation and a relationship in orders (II, 63).

Painfully, the writer knows that his solutions no longer solve. The predictions of "Law as Suited to Man" counter its preferences. In this, the last original essay the elder Dana published, America suffers from a "mad restlessness which sets at naught all Law," and at fault is "the want of an agreement between the ordinary courses of Providence and our outward public Form of Law" (II, 74, 95). These truths, once admitted, render the prescriptive tones and remedies of the traditional man of letters obsolete. For the writer who would connect law and literature, expression has lost all context except in a glorification of the past. Hence, the past for Dana Sr. becomes richly variegated marble; the present, "an uncouth, dead mass of pudding stone" (II, 39). As for the future, it contains "some fearful rebuke," and the prophet faces it only to prepare his children for "a world to which we would not trust ourselves" (I, 431). A final image of Dana Sr. as writer appears in his son's journal, where he takes pen to paper only to stop paralyzed "in the anxious, uncertain state . . . which interrupts all his labors now; a sense that it is his duty to work, & a morbid sensitiveness which makes every day & every hour an unfit time to work at." His subject? Musing upon the experiences of life from the twilight shadows of an empty room.[43]

Richard Henry Dana, Jr.: "The Life of a Common Sailor"

Two Years Before the Mast gives the son's answer to the father's predicament. Richard Henry Dana, Jr., goes to sea in 1834 to escape his father's house. To be sure, "love of adventure & the attraction of the novelty" enter into this decision, but Dana emphasizes another motive, "anxiety to escape from the depressing situation of inactivity and dependence at home." A severe attack of measles weakens Dana's eyes in 1833, and he finds himself sharing both the experience and the meaning of Dana Sr.'s domestic idleness. The parallel is safely obscured in financial terms but still terrifying: "I was obliged to leave college, & lingered about at home, a useless, pitied & dissatisfied creature. My father was at this time embarrassed in his pecuniary condition, & I felt that I was a burden upon him." Deploring a situation that describes both father and son—"loss of all employment & any prospect of advancement in life"—the boy of eighteen sails before the mast as a common sailor.[44] He seeks an entire change of life, barely looks toward shore upon departure, and, despite the inevitable seasickness of the novice, experiences a strange pleasure in the very act of separation.[45] For separation is the other side of bondage; it is here a form of liberty.

In California the young seaman enjoys the occasional Boston newspaper more than letters from home (p. 250). And no wonder! Dana Sr.'s letters complain constantly of a father's pain in separation. "I would not for worlds suffer again what I suffered then," he writes, urging an early return, "it wrung me as if it would wrench soul & body asunder . . . I had thought my heart to be like an over-winter apple, that had hung ungathered, juiceless & shrunken up." When Dana answers with glowing descriptions of happy days and good health ("I have not had a sick day or even a head-ache since I left you"), the father does not hide his ambivalence. "Y'r letter, tho' it told me you were safe & well, instead of making me happy, by a mysterious working of the soul, made me 'as sad as night' for several days."[46] A corresponding sense of depression strikes the son when he reenters Boston harbor after an absence of two years: "I found that I was in a state of indifference, for which I could by no means account . . . a state of very nearly entire apathy." Dropping anchor means a simultaneous loss of purpose and occupation, and it returns Dana to the Boston of his previous problems (pp. 354–355). The rough, sunburned sailor who steps ashore is astonished by "the pallid & emaciated appearance of the gentlemen." As for the women, they appear "mere shades," and the whole city seems shrouded in sickness. Here, of course, is the familial malaise writ large, and Dana quickly learns to insert the seaman's intervening experience to avoid contagion.[47]

None of these underlying tensions disturb the flow of affection between child and parent, but *Two Years Before the Mast* never mentions the father, and it explicitly rejects the once-shared "quiet, sedentary, life at home" (p. 316). Dutiful, loving, even protective, Dana must displace the psychic example of his father to survive in the world. Appropriately, his favorite tale from childhood, his father's semi-autobiographical story "The Son," makes a boy play the role of a man. In this account of a dying woman who resembles Dana's own mother in character and plight, there is one crucial circumstance to separate fiction from fact: no father appears to interrupt a son's embracing grief. The reversals here are revealing ones. Dana Sr. regresses in "The Son," placing his own grief over the death of a wife in an adolescent perspective to minimize the ignominy of his own paralysis. Meanwhile the younger Dana, as reader, usurps his father's role, reliving the memory of the mother, "the sanctum sanctorum with us all," as chief mourner and "Daydreamer."[48] Similar patterns of retreat and assertion dominate each writer's understanding of the world around him.

Two Years Before the Mast begins with an adolescent's flight to California and chronicles the passage to manhood—a passage that requires the initiate's acceptance and mastery of a corporate identity. The boy learns to live within the world of men through the responsibilities that he meets there. Too many readers neglect this theme; they emphasize the adventurism in Dana's narrative and trivialize its practical sense of accomplishment as "honest boyish enthusiasm for the right name of every rope."[49] In fact, one must separate voyage from book. The boy-sailor escapes Boston by going to sea. The author, five years older, is a law student about to begin practice in the same city, and he means *Two Years Before the Mast* to "be of some use to me in Boston in securing to me a share of maritime business."[50] Everything depends upon this older writer's precision. His technical expertise is at once a personal demonstration of manhood, an assertion of professional availability, and an epistemological reordering of the world that his father left in chaos. Law and letters meet in these several purposes but in strange new ways and on radically different terms.

Dana reaches for definition in exactly those areas where Dana Sr.

is most vague. Vocation and context remain abstract in the father's stories: they are always concrete and never in doubt in the sailor's narrative. *Two Years Before the Mast* gives the place and function of every man aboard the ship *Pilgrim* from the captain to the cook. The daily location of that ship, the weather it faces, the general routine, the purpose behind every procedure, the work of the moment, the cost of labor (twelve dollars a month per sailor), and the larger task at hand (collecting forty thousand hides along the coast of California) are matters of minute and frequent record. Dana overwhelms with facts and figures, and this continuous stream of information solves two problems. It bolsters the legitimacy of the "green hand" who tells the story of his voyage to and from California, and, more subtly, it guarantees a world of surface realities. The first is very important to the novel of initiation.[51] The reader learns alongside a "completely bewildered" informer who opens himself "to the full impression of everything" around him (pp. 7–10). This dual process of discovery and revelation dominates the story, creating a natural bond between narrator and audience and instilling a mutual sense of accomplishment in the parallels of performance and understanding. From the landlubber's bout of seasickness and first meal at sea, to acceptance "as a son of Neptune" on crossing the equator, to hearing the strange sound "Land ho!" and not knowing what it means, to steering around Cape Horn, to "smelling hell" on the return trip in winter, to everyone's surprise back in Boston over the " 'rough alley' looking fellow" out of the Harvard boy, *Two Years Before the Mast* chronicles the movement from "beginner" to "regular *salt*" (pp. 12–14, 24, 26, 31, 280, 354, 7–8). The successful completion of each new task gives Dana the right to speak. His careful explanation of those tasks is both proof of performance and the capstone of satisfaction that the reader shares in comprehension of the page. "I got through without any word from the officer," runs a typical closure, "and heard the 'well done' of the mate . . . with as much satisfaction as I ever felt at Cambridge on seeing a *'bene'* at the foot of a Latin exercise" (p. 73).

The sailor's eagerness is part of his compulsive need to belong— a psychological truth that locks all identity and thought within the narrative of fact. Success *as* a crew member prefigures every other consideration. When Dana finds "that I—home-bred, gentleman-bred, college-bred—could stand it as well as the roughest of them," he means "after this, I shall be up to anything."[52] Self-discovery has become a function of performance and participation, not of thought. In this sense, *Two Years Before the Mast* hardly resembles the philosophical confrontation between man and nature that some want to find.[53] Although a boundless sea at dawn arouses "a feeling of loneliness, of dread, and of melancholy foreboding," Dana quickly submerges such "day-dreaming" in the crew's routine (p. 13). He emphasizes the way collective man combats the elements, and his favorite recurring image of life aboard ship is of the men in full chorus singing "Cheerily, men!" or "Heave round hearty!" over a common task (pp. 107, 179, 259–260, 273, 308, 321). The sublimest sights, an iceberg in sunshine and a massive electrical storm, come through the first-person plural, the "we" of the crew's perspective (pp. 297–298, 334–338). The isolated, idle sailor, even in sickness, is a man in disgrace and a figure without an identity (pp. 19, 71, 276, 303–307, 397–398). These priorities keep Dana's promise "to present the life of a common sailor as it really is," but they also constitute a way of coping with the world and man's place in it (p. 6). The search for membership lifts all uncertainty to the surface of circumstance where it can be resolved in action.[54]

Two Years Before the Mast, like the voyage it describes, copes with contradiction by literalizing the task at hand. Certainly contradictions appear. Do what he may, the would-be sailor remains a gentleman's son, and every controversy, real or imagined, serious or trivial, sets the two separate identities against each other (pp. 42, 113, 162, 265–266). It is the gentleman's son who speaks when Dana receives orders to stay in California longer than expected. As no common sailor ever could, he countermands his captain by citing a higher authority in Boston. Dana is quite explicit about what he has done, and so is the crew in response:

> "Oh yes!" said the crew, "the captain has let you off, because you are a gentleman's son, and have got friends, and know the owners . . . !" I knew that this was too true to be answered, but I excused myself from any blame, and told them that I had a right to go home, at all events. (pp. 265–266)

Intractable as experience, this conflict in identity actually disappears on the higher level of the text. *Two Years Before the Mast* is necessarily cyclical in its psychological thrust because book and narrator com-

plete themselves only when flight gives way to return. The boy
who goes to sea must prove himself in the man who arrives back in
port. Exercising "a right to go home" thus becomes Dana's ultimate
task. For that final and definitive act of accomplishment, gentleman
and sailor must join. The reader accepts this coordination of opposites as part of a necessary resolution, and he is helped by the
fact that sailor and gentleman always have been one *in the telling*.
A narrator who compares ship's officer to Latin professor obviously
speaks for more than jack tar. His voice, subsuming the contradictions of class and vocation, allows a unified perceptual aesthetic to
emerge. One finds this aesthetic in the gentleman's heightened
awareness of the sailor's life, the real source of power in *Two Years
Before the Mast*. As Dana explains the phenomenon, "We must come
down from our heights . . . if we would learn truths by strong
contrasts" (p. 252).

But if contrast aids perception, it complicates the issue of identity.
Caught between roles, Dana knows that the uncomfortable alliance
of gentleman and sailor cannot last.[55] He needs a firmer sense of
overall place—something beyond membership—to explain himself
and make ends meet. These matters come to a head in the famous
flogging scene (pp. 100–104). Each crisis in personal relationships
separates gentleman from sailor in *Two Years Before the Mast*, but the
flogging incident completely divides the two in its ugliness and
extremism. When Captain Thomas ties and personally whips two
sailors for supposed insubordination, he fulfills an earlier promise
to turn the *Pilgrim* into "hell afloat" (p. 10). His actions transcend
every conceivable level of acceptable behavior:

> He danced about the deck, calling out as he swung the rope,—"If
> you want to know what I flog you for, I'll tell you. It's because I like
> to do it!—because I like to do it!—It suits me! That's what I do it
> for!"
>
> The man writhed under the pain, until he could endure it no longer,
> when he called out, with an exclamation more common among for-
> eigners than with us—"Oh, Jesus Christ! Oh, Jesus Christ!"
>
> "Don't call on Jesus Christ," shouted the captain; "*he can't help you.
> Call on Captain T*____, he's the man! He can help you! Jesus Christ
> can't help you now!"

Dana leans "sick, and horror-struck" over the side of the ship. Disgusting for everyone, the scene is impossible for him. While the

gentleman recognizes and articulates an intolerable breach of ethical imperatives that should not be borne ("A man—a human being, made in God's likeness—fastened up and flogged like a beast!"), the sailor sees only his own helplessness ("If a sailor resist his commander, he resists the law, and piracy or submission are his only alternatives"). As the former rails against tyranny and blasphemy, so the latter insures the passive acceptance of everything as mere punishment. Here is an intolerable impasse, one that must be broken if personal integrity and self-respect are to survive.

Dana's response informs both his book and his life. In the "dark hole" of the forecastle, listening to the scourged seamen's moans, he swears to help when circumstances permit. However, the promise itself is more an assertion of caste than an oath of allegiance: "I . . . vowed that if God should ever give me the means, I would do something to redress the grievances and relieve the sufferings of that poor class of beings, of whom I then was one" (p. 104). There is no spirit of solidarity here. This pledge comes from the gentleman, and the condition of its fulfillment requires prior separation from the sailor's lot. *Two Years Before the Mast* meets the forecastle vow from above. The very title accentuates a *temporary* affiliation ("having intended only to be gone eighteen months or two years"), and the text, necessarily the product of a gentleman's pen, marks a return to social standing even as it memorializes the mutual experience of shipmates (p. 91). Dana writes about seamen from their perspective in order to dramatize "the hardships of their daily life," but his purpose is to diminish those hardships, and social correction of this sort belongs in the gentleman's sphere. Accordingly, gentleman replaces sailor at the moment of explanation (pp. 6, 357–374). An unconscious parody of the method in later life clarifies its implications. Disguised as a sailor in the streets at night, Dana would open his seaman's coat, revealing "the dress of a gentleman," as he lectured the prostitutes who approached him.[56] An unwitting double exposure, the sailor's masquerade still sets the gentleman's performance. For Dana, problems always have their solution in the proper understanding and adjustment of social hierarchies.

Two Years Before the Mast answers the problem of the scourged sailor with an explanation that is social in focus and corporate in form. When Herman Melville presents a similar scene in *White Jacket* (1850), the accused sailor wants to drag his captain overboard rather than submit to the cosmic insult of a flogging. Flogging contradicts "the Law of Nature," and White Jacket's mind automatically resists with "the instinct diffused through all animated nature." Shipmates intercede just in time to prevent an act of overt mutiny, and in the end White Jacket escapes the whip because he is innocent and because intervention comes from Jack Chase, the archetypal handsome sailor who stands for "the Rights of Man, and the liberties of the world." But all of this—the imagined resistance, the crew's successful intervention, the punishment rescinded—is a fantasy triggered by the contrasting reality of *Two Years Before the Mast*.[57] One of the sailors on the *Pilgrim* is flogged *because* he tries to intercede for the other; natural justice has no meaning in this order of things. For Dana the harsh conditions aboard ship are given constraints. He supports the captain's absolute authority and corporal punishment as institutional necessities, and he blames social relations, not individuals, for the flogging incident (pp. 358, 363–364, 92). It is the captain's severity *up against* the misguided leniency of his first mate that creates trouble. Tensions ease as soon as the same captain's new officer shows himself to be, in Dana's telling description, "not so estimable a man, perhaps, but a far better mate of a vessel" (p. 184).

Context and function define everything here. Context makes the assigned role of a soldier a more humiliating punishment for a sailor than flogging (p. 123). Function keeps "good officer" and "good man" from being synonymous categories and prefers the first when the two contradict each other. Aboard the *Pilgrim* moral abstraction bends to the mechanics of operation. Better practice and more efficient application, not philosophical correction, must solve the flogging issue. Dana wants a more careful administration of existing laws and stricter accountability after a captain's authority has been exercised. His ultimate appeal is to the legal officials in the courts (pp. 359, 368–369). Rather than direct public action—"I fully believe that any public and strong action would do harm"—the situation calls for professional men who will bring the common law to bear in those cases of excessive punishment. In this way, the sailor's general hardships can be "modified by circumstances" and the particular evil of flogging will achieve "the gradual working of its own cure." Judge, jury, and "a fair administration of the laws" perform "the less easy and less exciting task of gradual improvement." Properly used with the tools of general education, they represent "the issue of things working slowly together for good" (pp. 359–364).

These are the answers one should expect of a law student in the late 1830s, and as such they reflect the changing nature of the legal mind in American culture. Social conservatism remains the most obvious feature of that mind, but Dana's sharper stress upon man-made law as an instrument of social policy separates him from Dana Sr. a generation before. The son has moved closer to the fields of legal positivism that his father feared.[58] For although *Two Years Before the Mast* does not embrace positive law and formalism wholeheartedly, it clearly rejects natural law theory in favor of a more self-contained functionalism, and the significance of this shift for the lawyer-writer is vast. In the early republic an incremental ordering of facts and ideas could assume a prior and parallel ordering in nature. Thomas Jefferson could write *Notes on the State of Virginia* with the understanding that natural law could bridge the gap between different levels of reality. A lawyer's public mode of explanation was instinctively connective and encompassing. By 1840 *Two Years Before the Mast* must make its own world entirely out of human expertise. Order has become an hermetically sealed system of functions properly performed. In Dana's narrative the sailor protects himself from larger uncertainties by knowing exactly what he is doing aboard the *Pilgrim*. He does not confront the world around him so much as he accepts a careful role within it.

The strategy is crucial because it also answers the new lawyer's needs in 1840. Specialization and the burgeoning complexity of legal thought have transformed the profession that Dana enters in that year. Expertise within a closed context has replaced ideological synthesis and intellectual comprehensiveness. Closer to his modern equivalent than his early republican predecessor, Dana as lawyer must define himself in his knowledge and application of statute law, and he must look toward specific codifications rather than general statements for a sense of order.[59] These changes naturally lead the mid-century lawyer toward technical vantage points and away from literary expression. The interests of law and literature no longer merge as they once did, and there is no better example of the discrepancy than the subsequent tacks of Melville and Dana, those two most famous sailors in American literature. After *White Jacket*,

Melville writes *Moby-Dick or, The Whale* (1851), the ultimate exploration of myth and cosmic meaning. After *Two Years Before the Mast*, Dana writes *The Seaman's Friend: Containing A Treatise of Practical Seamanship, with Plates; A Dictionary of Sea Terms; Customs and Usages of the Merchant Service; Laws Relating to the Practical Duties of Master and Mariners* (1841); it is, in the author's words, "purely a business book."[60] These works set romance against manual, rumination against codification. Writer and lawyer have moved into separate spheres.

The American Renaissance: "Right Before the Mast"

The narrowing professionalism of the mid-century lawyer is the visible side of a curious reversal in American literature. For even as leaders of the bar reject natural law in the name of a more technical expertise, a new breed of literary intellectual rises to seize that abandoned legacy. Few have noticed how frequently the writers of the American Renaissance resort to higher law as a mode of explanation, and no one has appreciated the continuities involved. Melville, Emerson, Thoreau, and Hawthorne are reacting against the past, against the civic tones and themes of early republican literature; nonetheless, it is Melville, the romantic novelist, who reaches back to natural law to condemn flogging, and not Dana, the student of law. Nor is Melville alone. Emerson and Thoreau both rely upon what Emerson calls "the transcendent simplicity and energy of the Highest Law." In their writings natural law frames a moral landscape in which "virtue is the adherence in action to the nature of things."[61] Less earnest and infinitely more ironic, Hawthorne still allows for a higher law at work in human affairs. The providential deaths of Arthur Dimmesdale in *The Scarlet Letter* and of Jaffrey Pyncheon in *The House of the Seven Gables*, like that of Billy Budd in Melville's last story, deliberately hint at divine justice. Of course, each of these deaths also introduces more problems than it solves— a salutary reminder that higher law serves a very different purpose in the fictions of Hawthorne and Melville than it did in the orations and treatises of the founding generations.[62]

The integument of republican society in the eighteenth century, natural law theory occupies a much less strategic position by 1850. In the polemical writings of the American Renaissance it appears in many guises—as moral antidote and rhetorical tool, as epistemological gauge and mythic answer—but it no longer functions as the controlling ideological norm of a culture. The difference separates Dana and Melville, among others, and at stake is the whole notion of a writer's creative purpose. What bothers the narrator of facts excites the romantic novelist. Dana, a true lawyer-writer, makes order his highest priority in *Two Years Before the Mast*. He uses a linear record of accumulating observation to hold everything in place. Presenting the sailor's life "like any other practical subject," he sticks "closely to fact in every particular" (pp. 5–6, 357–358). This approach leaves little room for natural law. The same search for order that once required an understanding of natural law now ignores that understanding as idle speculation. By way of contrast, Melville shadows forth vague immensities and philosophical ambiguities in his fiction. He invokes natural law to bring in other levels of meaning, to suggest imaginative correspondences, to encourage moral generalization, and to oppose social convention. The protagonist of *White Jacket* speaks of a plurality of worlds. His voice "helps to shape eternity," his desires "stir the orbits of the furthest suns," and his feelings "mold the whole world's hereafters."[63] Natural law is one more means of achieving philosophical scope and intensity.

Melville's flexibility stands out in the comparison with Dana—a flexibility distinctly modern in its implications. While *Two Years Before the Mast* uses a rigid, linear point of view to insure basic definitions and to show that a good man can conquer his world, *White Jacket* superimposes many different points of view to prove that "this old-fashioned world of ours" is "full of all manner of characters—full of strange contradictions."[64] Melville and the other figures of the American Renaissance write to convey a complexity that evades easy understanding. Their major symbols are always ambiguous, and their narratives link the internal and enigmatic landscape of the mind to external reality. The letter "A" signifies many things besides adultery in *The Scarlet Letter*. When Arthur Dimmesdale rips aside his shirt to show the mark on his chest, Hawthorne offers no fewer than four interpretations of *what is seen* there, and all of them "necessarily have been conjectural."[65] Ahab's scar, the anatomy sections of the whale, the white whale itself, the doubloon nailed to the mast of the *Pequod*, and Queequeg's coffin lifebuoy are just a few of the ambiguous symbols in *Moby-Dick*, a work that dedicates itself to "the image of the ungraspable phantom of life" and puts truth "far beyond all utterance." Man's "larger, darker, deeper part remains unhinted" because it is "vain to popularize profundities, and all truth is profound."[66]

Such works are modern in two senses of the term, psychological and historical. They tie reason to emotion in a compound vision of reality with all of the heightened possibilities for sincerity, subjectivity, and irrationality that this brings to literature, and they are written during a vital moment of transition from old to new. Americans in 1850 have begun to assume the concepts of country that earlier generations had to reiterate so constantly, but they are also locked in a controversy over slavery that defies rational resolution. They face as well unprecedented social change. Industrialization, large-scale immigration, social atomization, technological innovation, racial discrimination, and urbanization—the familiar issues of the twentieth century—start to disrupt American life at this point in time, straining traditional values and compelling recognition of strange, new forces and unfamiliar practices in society.[67] There are, in short, more questions than answers in 1850. The stage has been set for a different kind of literature, one that deals in problems instead of solutions. As Hawthorne summarizes the point of view that will dominate subsequent American fiction, "This is such an odd and incomprehensible world . . . a man's bewilderment is the measure of his wisdom."[68]

In addition, democratic politics and romanticism, both anti-authoritarian in tone, prompt the writers of the American Renaissance to put the self before the citizen. Thoreau best captures the shift in emphasis in "Civil Disobedience," where he dismisses government as "a sort of wooden gun to the people themselves," claiming that "we should be men first, and subjects afterward." "It is not desirable," he concludes, "to cultivate a respect for the law, so much as for the right." This position resembles White Jacket's response to his captain. In both instances a higher standard based on the distinction between natural right and social authority justifies opposition. Both works assume the right of revolution that natural law gives to a people whose inalienable rights have been violated, but here, through romantic individualism, social rebellion has become a personal right of resistance. "Let your life be a counter-friction to stop the machine," writes Thoreau.[69] Emerson's persona in "The

Divinity School Address," Hester Prynne of *The Scarlet Letter*, Holgrave of *The House of the Seven Gables*, Ishmael of *Moby-Dick* stand against society in the name of a higher understanding. Here, natural law invariably challenges the social framework that it once supported, and behind the reversal is a new concept of country. Emerson dedicates his journal to the Spirit of America. Thoreau self-consciously begins his experiment at Walden on the Fourth of July. Hawthorne calls "our sacred Union" the best hope of mankind, and Melville sees his countrymen as "the peculiar chosen people—the Israel of our time." They mean, however, something quite different than earlier writers who catalogue republican virtues and institutional safeguards. In the great literary works of mid-century, America is its land and its people.[70] Virtue abides in the democratic whole rather than in civic arrangement.

All of these changes—subjective individualism, anti-authoritarianism, skepticism, philosophical pluralism, and democratic nationalism—catch the Richard Henry Danas in the middle. Inspired by romanticism, father and son initiate the exploration of opposites that will figure so prominently in the work of the next generation. Trained as lawyers, they also retain modes of discourse that recall early republican tones and content. These starts and stops reflect a writer's greatest difficulty: the ability first to hear and then to master a new voice in literature, the capacity to reach beyond acceptance to real use. The Danas articulate more than they themselves can receive as practicing artists, which is why their writings support even as they resist the American Renaissance. One studies this tangled record to discover exactly how intellectual assertion becomes literary practice in the new literature of the 1850s and to understand why that transition is impossible for so many intellectuals of the period.

Dana Sr.'s acceptance of man's "double character" in 1831 parallels Emerson's "propounding . . . of the double consciousness" twenty years later. "There is an outer and an inner machinery, a set of processes of thoughts and feelings for his fellow-men, and another set for himself," writes Dana Sr., describing human psychology in a complex world. "A man must ride alternately on the horses of his private and his public nature," answers Emerson.[71] The same kind of parallelism appears in the next generations. When Melville reads *Two Years Before the Mast*, he confesses "a sort of Siamese link of affectionate sympathy"—an admission of similarity that transcends mere subject matter. Certainly, Dana's promise to describe "the light and the dark together" anticipates Melville's insistence that white and black are sides of the same whole. "Enjoy the bright, keep it turned up perpetually if you can," the latter advises, "but be honest, and don't deny the black." It is because the sailor's perspective so obviously represents a way of looking from the other side that Melville borrows openly and knowingly from Dana. "When I go to sea," Ishmael announces in the opening chapter of *Moby-Dick*, "I go as a simple sailor, right before the mast."[72] One basis of this shared perspective involves the interest in fact and particularity, which Dana imbibes emotionally as a sailor and then intellectually as a student of law and passes along to Melville. The anatomy sections of the whale and the descriptions of the whaling industry in *Moby-Dick* owe much to the example of *Two Years Before the Mast* and perhaps even more to Dana's direct advice. "About the 'whaling voyage'—I am half way in the work, & am very glad that your suggestion so jumps with mine," Melville writes Dana. There is, however, an interesting qualification. Melville inserts another level of inquiry above the factual examination that Dana apparently urged: "Blubber is blubber you know . . . & to cook the thing up, one must needs throw in a little fancy."[73]

Melville asks for an accuracy thoroughly absorbed by imagination, and his letter measures the distance between mere narrative and a new kind of prose romance. The Danas simply lack the sense of ambiguity that distinguishes the writers of the American Renaissance; flexibility seems to be the missing ingredient. But what is this flexibility, genius aside? What does Melville have that the Danas can only talk about? Look for example at one more similarity with a difference. When the elder Dana develops his theme of madness in "Paul Felton," he connects Paul to a wild nature boy named Adam in a relationship that points toward *Moby-Dick* and the far greater bonding process between Captain Ahab and Pip, the small black shipkeeper of the *Pequod*.[74] The pairings, though, serve very different purposes. Dana Sr. uses Paul and Adam to threaten the common sense and decorum of society with the insanity of seclusion. By way of contrast, Melville explores an open-ended spectrum of psychological opposites in a world that is socially more secure. The design of "Paul Felton" makes Adam a contrived duplicate of Paul's delusions; he is another social outcast with the same problems. Ahab and Pip, on the other hand, meet in mutual recognition from conflicting extremes of madness. Ahab's unbounded egotism touches Pip's complete loss of identity—"One daft with strength, the other daft with weakness"—and both characters poignantly understand that sanity exists somewhere along the "man-rope" in between. Real drama lies within. Nothing that Ahab and Pip do or say together disturbs life aboard the *Pequod* in the way that Paul and Adam shake their American village. "Paul Felton" signals a terrifying loss of social control that Dana Sr. must correct at all costs. Able to assume the social fabric that Dana Sr. protects, Melville challenges the universe instead. Ahab injects himself into Pip's life to take the place of "the omniscient gods oblivious of suffering man." What the writers of the American Renaissance draw upon, they also transform. In Melville's hands a clumsy mechanism has become a deft psychological and philosophical probe.

The point is not just that *Moby-Dick* questions from within while "Paul Felton" depends upon externals. Melville has learned to achieve positive vision from a negative stance. This constitutes a new skill, a new organ of perception, in American literature. One realizes its importance by remembering that "the honor of a literature lies in its capacity to develop 'a great quarrel within the national consciousness.' "[75] The writers of the 1850s understand that to make anew means first to disrupt; creativity has a subversive component. Thus it is that Thoreau, like Melville, consciously turns to Dana's central image to warn against the dangers of "tradition and conformity" in American culture. "I did not wish to take a cabin passage," he explains in the concluding chapter of *Walden*, "but rather to go before the mast and on the deck of the world, for there I could best see the moonlight amid the mountains."[76] Dana's temporary flight from proper Boston—one quickly subsumed in the sailor's eagerness to be the best of citizens aboard ship—has become Thoreau's permanent rebuke to all forms of authority. In *Walden* new ways of seeing demand a break with tradition. Those who define themselves through society, the officers who rule from *behind* the mast, cannot appreciate the separate world that moonlight suggests. Moonlight, after all, is the medium of the spirit; it evokes Hawthorne's "neutral territory, somewhere between the real world and fairy-land, where the Actual and the Imaginary may meet."[77]

This new aesthetic of the American Renaissance excludes the legal mind from literary enterprise. Hawthorne can describe the possibilities in a moonlit room, and Melville can tell Hawthorne that "truth is ever incoherent," but in the law reality is always otherwise.[78] Practitioners with clients must deal in facts, certainty, affirmation, and assurance. They accept complexity and nuance only to solve problems. Reason is their tool; institutional continuity, their control. Of the emotional vortices and philosophical doubts that undermine the professional search for answers, they have little to say. Plays upon the ambiguous, the unique, and the bizarre—these possibilities excite the modern writer, and they also run counter to every lawyer's interests and goals. Since 1850 the best American writers have aimed for an original show of consciousness. Lawyers have thought ever more consciously of standards, norms, and rules.

The Richard Henry Danas dramatize this divergence as it begins in the middle third of the nineteenth century. Philosophically, they see both the light and the dark in life, but they see as citizens who serve the light in a nation of laws. Rationalism and civic-mindedness, what the ancients called *civitas*, compel the Danas to choose between alternatives and to present social affirmations. Psychological awareness and a more personal sense of country allow the writers of the American Renaissance to balance alternatives in a more creative tension. The difference is the chasm between early American and modern literature. The Danas are on one side of the divide, Emerson and his followers on the other.

CHAPTER 10

END OF THE
CONFIGURATION

Vision and Despair: "The Law Is Now and Has Long Been Our Only Strength—But It Is Crumbling Under Us"

Virtually every lawyer-writer in America viewed the changing nature of his country with alarm. Most feared and rejected the democratic impulses that recast republican culture between the Revolution and the Civil War. A minority from Thomas Jefferson through Andrew Jackson and beyond welcomed democratization but condemned other trends like the growth of commercialism, the consolidation of political power, the emergence of special interests, and the rise of corporations.[1] Both groups assumed for themselves the role of ideological guardian; both saw symptoms of corruption and decline; both gave way to anger and despair in the face of change. Among the conservatives, every transition provoked an expression of loss. The message was identical when Fisher Ames announced the collapse of the republic in 1804, when James Kent found destruction all around him in 1832, and when Rufus Choate called the Union a "fragile creation, which a breath can unmake" in 1850.[2] For the democrats, the same transitions were marred by an overwhelming sense of danger. Even the greatest celebration of democratic spirit, Andrew Jackson's Farewell Address as president in 1837, concentrated more on evils than affirmations. "Knowing that the path of freedom is continually beset by enemies who often assume the disguise of friends," Jackson told his countrymen, "I have devoted the last hours of my public life to warn you of the dangers."[3]

At its worst the lawyer-writer's pessimism stifled insight and effort. "There is a kind of fatality in the affairs of republics," Fisher Ames concluded in 1805, "that eludes the foresight of the wise as much as it frustrates the toils and sacrifices of the patriot and the hero."[4] Weak as prophecy, this statement accurately described a common state of mind. One after another the wise men, patriots, and heroes of the early American bar lamented their unavoidable decline. The greater their personal success, the sharper their claims of helplessness and doom. "When? Where? and how? is the present Chaos to be arranged into Order?" John Adams asked Thomas Jefferson in 1813. Gouverneur Morris, Revolutionary leader and drafter of the Constitution, put the same questions in more ominous form. "I should be glad," he wrote in 1814, "to meet with some one, who could tell me what has become of the union, in what it consists, and to what useful purpose it endures."[5] The most important man of letters in the next generation, the one-time lawyer and famous lexicographer Noah Webster, deliberately made the nation's failure his own. "I have labored in vain and spent my strength for naught," he explained in 1835, noting that "the true principles of republican government are now abandoned by all parties." Three years before, Jefferson's leading disciple, William Wirt, had dubbed himself " 'a disappointed man' . . . disappointed in my country and the glory that I thought awaited her;—disappointed, most sadly, in the intelligence and virtue which I had attributed to our countrymen;—disappointed in life itself, which is, indeed, all vanity and vexation of spirit."[6] These expressions of woe were endemic rather than occasional. As their correspondence reveals, John Marshall, Joseph Story, James Kent, and Daniel Webster traded similar notions and with great frequency. No major event of the period passed without some leading lawyer predicting imminent and utter ruin.

Two explanations have been offered for the pervasive dolor of the antebellum bar: either the early lawyer's pessimism grew out of his "philosophy of restriction," which required a guarded view of human nature and "definition by negation," or, more generally, his pessimism was a secularized manifestation of the American jeremiad.[7] While suggestive, these theories are inadequate. The first ignores chronological change, and the second misreads the actual form of the early lawyer's complaint. The initial or functionalist argument does not distinguish between lawyers who performed the same negative function with a different attitude. Why should the role of social watchdog have depressed certain generations or figures more than others? Jefferson, Madison, Hamilton, and other first republicans built positive visions out of a philosophy of restrictions. After the Civil War, legal theorists created "the age of faith" in American law.[8] What separated earlier and later optimists from James Kent and Joseph Story, or, for that matter, what about the *philosophical* optimism of such figures as Kent and Story? Only a more precise understanding can answer these questions, and precision in this case precludes the mustering of nay-sayers under the comprehensive banner of the jeremiad. The unhappy voice of the antebellum lawyer delivered its own message. Less strident than a jeremiad, that message was also infinitely darker.

Generically, the American jeremiad began as a political sermon linking social criticism and spiritual renewal in seventeenth-century Puritan culture. It directed God's chosen people toward the fulfillment of their assigned mission on earth, and it predicted the awful consequences of failure. Always a warning, it gradually took the form of any public exhortation that sounded an alarm over the endangered national covenant, and so nineteenth-century orators and twentieth-century critics have understood the term. And yet admonition and lamentation alone do not account for the enormous vitality of the country's first enduring literary genre. America's Jeremiahs spoke with a conviction that the national mission would be fulfilled. Their cry of declension always contained a deeper message of hope. Above all, the jeremiad secured a vision of the future in which Americans completed their ordained errand in history.[9] The lawyer's lament differed in two respects; it took the form of personal communication rather than public exhortation, and it left no room for affirmation. Men like Daniel Webster and Joseph Story— Fisher Ames was the great exception—maintained an official optimism and then gave way to despair in their confidential letters. Webster could expound upon the nation's prosperity and "the true principles of the best, the happiest, the most glorious Constitution of a free government," even as he privately confessed that "almost everything is gone, or seems rapidly going."[10] In the 1840s Story preferred "severe scrutiny" over "serious alarm" in a speech on national problems, but he drew a much bleaker picture for James

Kent. "For myself," he wrote to Kent, "I do not believe in the practicality of maintaining our Republic against such fearful odds. The Law is now and has long been our only strength—but it is crumbling under us."[11]

Webster's and Story's distinction between public assertion and private admission is instructive. When a minister chastised his flock from the pulpit, he performed a professional duty of correction. His announcement of divine displeasure and coming punishment removed all discrepancy between secular and sacred history by showing that God at least still cared. It also encouraged a wayward people to repent and reform. In contrast, the lawyer's negative asides ran against his assumed role as national guardian. At best his despair was a whispered acknowledgment to colleagues of mutual defeat; the nation no longer followed their lead. At worst the whispers themselves implied a loss of intellectual function. Since the Revolution, lawyers had assumed a certain prerogative in interpreting the republican experiment. Rufus Choate summarized the underlying premise: "Because we are lawyers, we are statesmen. We are by profession statesmen."[12]

But what if actual circumstance contradicted the lawyer's confident visions of republicanism? Only two conclusions were possible. Either the lawyer had missed the true course of the experiment that he once formulated or the experiment itself was failing. Both rationales engendered feelings of helplessness and lost preeminence. By 1832 John Marshall was ready to "yield slowly and reluctantly to the conviction that our constitution cannot last." He did so not just because of political differences with Andrew Jackson but because he saw no sign of true republicanism, as he understood that term, in the new leaders of the South. "Our opinions are incompatible with a united government even among ourselves," he informed Joseph Story. "The union has been prolonged thus far by miracles." In New York James Kent gave vent to similar emotions: "I have no hope that this corrupt and fanatical age can be reformed without harsh applications, and I think we are running down fast to the lowest depths of degradation."[13]

Such gloom came out of a sharp debate over the meaning of American civilization. At issue was the role of law in government, and at stake was the nature of the republic itself. John Adams, John Marshall, Joseph Story, James Kent, Daniel Webster, and other

Judge Story, painting by Charles Osgood, 1837.

Their innate conservatism and classical education led most early American
lawyers to view democratic change with alarm. Joseph Story, associate
justice of the Supreme Court from 1811 to 1845, looked at the Jacksonian
era and applied "the melancholy lessons of the past history of republics
down to our own." He came to expect the collapse of the country that he
had served for so long.

conservative members of the early American bar all believed in what they called "an empire of laws, not of men." Their republic enshrined the law of nature, a rule of right and reason, within organs of government that protected the rights of men against the encroachment of minorities *and* majorities. Accordingly, they emphasized the form of government created by a constitution, and they looked for a finely articulated arrangement of institutions to distribute and to check power. In essence their rule of law was a "method of counterpoise" that skillfully mixed and balanced refractory and antagonistic parts.[14] Self-regulating, that rule nonetheless required highly educated managers to maintain and explain its balanced intricacies. This was the ground on which the conservative bar established its own importance. Because each intricacy derived from a general notion of right and reason, a theorist could also hope for its universal expression and enforcement. More than a learned flourish impelled Associate Justice Story to use Cicero when he announced the Supreme Court's decision in *Swift v. Tyson* (1842)—"*apud omnes gentes, omni tempore, una eademque lex*" (for all people and all times, one system of law). It was in this sense that Story and others of his generation could be called legal pantheists.[15]

From the beginning, however, another theory of republicanism influenced post-Revolutionary politics. This second theory looked to the inalienable power of the people as the source of all government and emphasized the right of those outside government to reach and restrict those within.[16] The two theories—what can be termed the institutional view and the participatory view—were implicitly antithetical, but it was the democratic continuum in American politics that turned abstract alternatives into clashing orthodoxies. The move toward universal manhood suffrage, the direct election of government officials, the shift from political caucuses to public nominating conventions, and the growth of the party spoils system forced a constant reiteration of differences between 1800 and 1850. Each change, depending upon the observer's orientation, signaled either a terrible loss of institutional integrity or a vital gain in the people's access to government. The shrill tone of antebellum politics—its hysteria, its paranoia, its plain nastiness—owed much to a deliberate spirit of contradiction as the second view slowly displaced the first in the American mind.[17]

Although most conservative intellectuals found themselves on the losing side of this acrimonious debate, the lawyer-writer expressed the deepest sense of defeat. In his case democratization threatened identity itself because he alone had included political expertise in his definition of professionalism or claim to special knowledge. He *professed* to know more about republicanism than others —precisely the claim that a participatory theory of republicanism could not allow. No, the people alone knew their best interest. Moreover, if true wisdom resided in the people, then the special knowledge of an elite was a dubious contribution to republican virtue. By the 1830s an expert's knowledge was a dangerous thing, and all of the professions were under attack as strongholds of aristocratic privilege.[18] The Jacksonian's faith in spontaneous action and self regulation made the rule of law a contradiction in terms. Joseph Story saw all of this and more from his seat on the Supreme Court between 1811 and 1845. "How can a Republic long continue, when the People . . . refuse to listen to the counsels of Wisdom and Experience?" he asked near the end, admitting failure.[19] The lawyer as man of letters had lost his audience and knew it. No one was listening.

His classicism confirmed the lawyer's despair. From Plato he accepted the value of a mixed republic of laws over a people's democracy. *The Republic* taught that popular rule soon led to despotism and that even the ideal state tended toward disintegration. The writings of Thucydides, Plutarch, Livy, Sallust, and Tacitus—full of the collapse of Greek and Roman culture—then became so many demonstrations of Plato's theory of decay.[20] For every lawyer who resisted parallels between the fall of the ancient republics and the struggle of American democracy, ten drew them. Rare was the alarm that failed to mention Caesar in some New World version of Tacitus' *Annals of Imperial Rome*. Fear of the distant past helped to create what has been called "the tremendous concern of the legal generation of 1820 to 1850 for the imposition of negatives upon the emerging society."[21]

Other Americans read the classics, but lawyers took the analogies between ancient and modern peculiarly to heart. As one leader of the South Carolina bar described his profession in 1843, "We nearly resemble the Roman Republic."[22] Nothing could have been further from the truth, of course, though intellectual leaders of the bar took a strange comfort in the imagined resemblance. If the classical or-

ators, the greatest lawyers of all time, could not reverse the mach-
inations of tyranny, could their American analogues accomplish
more? To recount the failures of Demosthenes and Cicero was to
subsume personal responsibility for the safety of republicanism in
historical cycles of rise and fall. Participating in this most frequent
of professional rituals, Joseph Story reduced the presidency of Andrew Jackson to "a dream"; he had been "called back to the last
days of the Roman republic, when the people shouted for Caesar,
and liberty itself expired with the dark but prophetic words of
Cicero."[23] The highest accolade one nineteenth-century lawyer could
bestow upon another was to recognize Ciceronian qualities that
appeared on the verge of extinction. When Daniel Webster eulogized
John C. Calhoun with the words "We saw before us a Senator of
Rome, while Rome survived," he knew himself to be *ultimus Ro-
manorum*.[24]

Every orientation places unrecognized constraints upon the imagination. Here preoccupation with the classical past contained un-
spoken fears of an American future. Nothing illustrates the lawyer-
writer's failing ascendancy at mid-century more vividly than his
inability to cope with the dynamism of the expanding nation. By
definition, "intellectuals elicit, guide, and form the expressive dispositions within a society."[25] The most expressive disposition in and
after Jacksonian culture was change, and this was the very characteristic that the lawyer-writer could not accept. Put another way,
the lawyer as national guardian was turning away from the earliest
and most enduring aspiration of life in the New World, its vision
of the future, its faith in progress. He had lost his grasp of what
America was *becoming*. The questions are, how did this happen and
why?

The Vanishing Generalist

Two exceptions prove the rule of the lawyer's pessimism: Charles
Grandison Finney (1792–1875) and David Dudley Field (1805–1894).
Finney, practicing in upstate New York, saw the face of Jesus across
his darkened law office one evening in 1821 and immediately abandoned one profession for another. Soon he was the leading revivalist
in America, guiding what is known as the Second Great Awakening
into the 1830s.[26] Field, for his part, developed into the most powerful

corporate lawyer of the age with a clientele in New York City that came to include robber barons like Jay Gould and James Fisk as well as "Boss" Tweed of Tammany Hall. More memorable than any courtroom triumph, however, was Field's lifelong attempt to reform the American legal system. He became famous as the heart and soul of the codification movement in nineteenth-century legal thought.[27] Joining the very different careers of Finney and Field was an essential optimism—an optimism that embraced the early lawyer's belief in comprehensiveness. Significantly, both men fought hardest against the narrow professionalism of immediate colleagues. Mere evil and lawlessness stood in their way less than "false instruction given to the people" and "the theories and prejudices of the profession, hardened by the incrustation of centuries."[28] Charles Grandison Finney and David Dudley Field were embattled generalists in an increasingly specialized age. Each discovered himself by challenging relevant vocational norms.

Finney's frequent recourse to the law, the profession he abandoned almost half a century before, was easily the most remarkable feature of his *Memoirs* in 1868. Writing at the age of seventy-six, the autobiographer had a long and successful career in religion and theology to present: the confrontation with Lyman Beecher and the conservative clergy at the New Lebanon convention of 1827, the major revivals of the 1830s, the controversial printed lectures and sermons, and, not to be forgotten, the crucial roles first as a founder and professor and then as the president of Oberlin College. These were the events that others would remember. For Finney, however, the law deserved special attention because it explained the nature of his achievement. As the *Memoirs* made clear over and over again, law books and "the close and logical reasonings of the judges" taught him to care for the precision and effectiveness of language in a way that no religious training ever could. So great grew Finney's appreciation of this difference between himself and other ministers that in later life he "seldom felt that [he] was one of them."[29] The same care for language in context defined Finney's phenomenal record as a preacher: "I was bred a lawyer. I came right forth from a law office to the pulpit, and talked to the people as I would have talked to a jury." His sermons sounded practical, direct, common, and, above all, persuasive; those of others appeared dignified, abstruse, ornate, and remote—all in all "a speech in language but partially understood." Consciously modeling his performances on the jury address, only Finney knew how to reach an audience. The traditional minister failed not in spite of his preparation but because of it. The burden of orthodoxy made him "David in Saul's armor."[30]

Finney was a strange hybrid and so were his opinions. His criticisms of the regular clergy revealed a deep distrust of all formal preparations and esoteric knowledge. No matter what the issue in the *Memoirs*—religious doctrine, education in general, personal health, the design of a building—the self-educated revivalist always knew more than the trained theologians, professors, doctors, and architects around him. Orthodox ministers were only the most visible failures in a long line of impractical theorists who never understood reality.[31] This side of Finney bespoke the Jacksonian's contempt for special expertise. But another side exempted the law in particular from every aspersion. Finney often referred to the value of his own training—two years in a law office in Adams, New York—and he remained "very fond" of his first profession. Nothing pleased him more in later life than his religious influence upon lawyers. Their conversion figured prominently in most of Finney's revivals, and he concentrated on them whenever he could. "I have always been particularly interested in the salvation of lawyers, and of all men of the legal profession," he confessed. Lawyers were "more certainly controlled by argument, by evidence, and by logical statements, than any other class of men." They were "the most accessible class" in a proper presentation of the Gospel, and their social prominence in the act of conversion helped others to see the Truth.[32]

The obvious contrast between Finney's regard for lawyers and his distrust of ministers suggests a complicated dynamic at work. When the revivalist accepted "a retainer from the Lord Jesus Christ to plead his cause," he became God's lawyer in thought and word.[33] But that spiritual mission also meant leaving major intellectual affinities behind. For despite Finney's claims to the contrary and irrespective of religious affiliation, most leaders of the antebellum bar rejected revivalism. In "the great issue of the nineteenth-century, the never-ending case of Heart versus Head," the revivalist temperament and the legal mind were natural enemies; the emotionalism of the one necessarily clashed with the intellectual discipline of the other.[34] Indeed, Finney instinctively saw the contradiction. His fondness for the law did not blind him to the fact that "all was dark in that direction" and "shut up" the moment he converted.[35] Why, then, the continuing play upon a lost identity? The answer to this question helps to account for Finney's extraordinary hold over nineteenth-century audiences. God's lawyer was a very special kind of revivalist. His unique combination of professional modes responded to communal as well as personal longings.

Certainly, the revivalist as lawyer made the most of both frameworks. With other proponents of the Second Great Awakening in American culture, he rejected the Calvinist notion of God's arbitrary grace for an elected few, assuming instead that every individual possessed the means of salvation. This was the key to mass revivalism in the nineteenth century—its pietistic stress upon the devotional over the intellectual ideal in Christian experience and its commitment to converting whole communities at a time. Finney's new evangelism plunged him directly into the major democratic movements of the period.[36] His conversion allowed a moderate Whig lawyer to find virtue in the people themselves. It opened the way for a communal spokesman to regain the popular audiences that the conservative legal profession had been losing. Conversely, the one time lawyer remained to help control those audiences. Finney curbed the excess emotionalism of his listeners when he could, and his background in the law supplied much of his skill in crowd manipulation.[37] Old training and new fervor combined in the preacher's sense of mastery. His clear message to a willing people made everything possible. "If the church will do all her duty," Finney urged the ministers around him in 1835, "the millennium may come in this country in three years."[38] Here the revivalist in his self-confidence owed something to the lawyer before his jury. If the redeemed nation ever came, both knew it would be because of " 'good sense in addressing the people.' "[39]

David Dudley Field brought the same untiring zeal to a different idea of reaching the people. As he put the central concern of his life, "It is the first duty of a government to bring the laws to the knowledge of the people." Codification, reducing the chaotic mass of nineteenth-century law to order, was the great means to this end. It involved neither more nor less than "writing [the law] in a book of such dimensions and in such language that all can read and comprehend it." The people, of course, could never write such a book; that was the task of "the true lawyer" who understood what was needed and knew best how to supply it.[40] In fact, Field went much further. "A code is or should be an homogeneous work," he wrote. "It should have the impress of one mind, or at most of a few minds." Here was a sense of mission at least as exalted as Finney's. Field, with perhaps a few others, wanted "to look at the law of the land as a whole, to lop off its excrescences, reconcile its contradictions, and make it uniform and harmonious." As a first step he meant to transform the hundreds of volumes of New York case law, the entire common law tradition, and all relevant statutes, commentaries, and court procedures into "four or five pocket-volumes" that every American could understand.[41] Not for nothing did this New York business lawyer compare himself to Justinian, Francis Bacon, and Alfred the Great! The analogies were apt for one so consciously engaged in "the first attempt ever made to codify the common law of England." Field hoped for the highest of stations. He would be the lawgiver of millions for all time to come.[42]

Defeats—and there were many—never punctured the codifier's assurance or resolve. Field began his drive for legal reform in 1839, and within ten years New York had a preliminary Code of Civil Procedure. Largely the work of Field, this preliminary code became law in nine other states before the Civil War. But although it eliminated convoluted forms of common law pleading and simplified many issues of jurisdiction, the Code of 1848 was only the first step in a master plan that failed. Four other codes—a more complete code of civil procedure, and political, penal, and civil codes on substantive law—never gained acceptance in New York. Even the preliminary enactment lost its integrity; relentless modification soon tore it apart, leaving a jumbled mass, seven times the size of the original pocket-volume. Beyond New York just five states out of forty-two embraced the full intent of codification.[43] Field did not hide his exasperation. "Are we to go on forever in a hopeless search for something certain and something stable?" he chided the legal profession in 1884. The question, asked in Field's eightieth year, carried a direct challenge. "Order can be brought out of this confusion," he insisted. "It is only our own profession that has hitherto prevented it." Half a century of struggle supported the assertion. At the gates of reform, preventing entrance, stood "a case-hardened lawyer . . . with a battered shield on his breast and an old javelin in his hand." Inevitably, Field made himself Cicero, "studying how to make the law an open book."[44]

His self-confidence came from the methodological certainties and ideological hopes of the early bar. Field dismissed "the mere practicing lawyer" of his own day. The ideal man of the law was a scholar: "He must have comprehended the greatness of the whole, the harmony of its parts, and the infinite diversity of its particulars." Anyone who strove for less was "an imposture."[45] So far the codifier said no more than "the old lawyers" whom he consciously emulated, but he made their argument his own when he linked comprehensiveness to codification. A code was "a comprehensive statute"; it brought the particular to the level of the general and the comprehensive, and as such it encouraged the lawyer's peculiar power in thought.[46] For those who hesitated to use that power, there was the shining example of the Constitution—itself "a great code in a small compass." It followed that "such a work is the inevitable outcome of American institutions" and that "all the instincts of republicanism are in its favor." Field envisaged

> a CODE AMERICAN, not insular but continental, as simple as so vast a work can be made, free in its spirit, catholic in its principles! And that work will go with our ships, our travelers, and our armies; it will march with the language, it will move with every emigration, and make itself a home in the farthest portion of our own continent, in the vast Australian lands, and in the islands of the southern and western seas.[47]

Against these aspirations, opposition could sound like ignorance. But what if such a code—"as simple as so vast a work can be made"— proved too simple? Field's detractors included most of his colleagues, and they denied his first premise. The legal profession had lost its faith in the power of abstraction. Generalization no longer explained experience.

Finney and Field shared a distrust of complexity. This was part of their appeal, and this was the source of their difficulty with a new breed of intellectuals in American culture. Finney's revivalism supplied a single answer to every problem from alcoholism to slavery to government itself. His message touched an anxious people beset with growing pains. "And what shall we do, to lift up the standard, to move this entire nation and turn all this great people to the Lord? We must DO RIGHT." God would handle the matter from there. "Let us mind our work," Finney concluded, "and let the Lord take care of the rest."[48] Field's codification movement assuaged the same uncertainties. His plan to reduce "the shapeless and incongruous mass" of the legal process into "reasonable compass and an intelligible form" struck a vital chord in a republic of laws. A national code promised to strengthen each citizen's sense of self as it led toward a more perfect civilization.[49] One should not underestimate either of these appeals among nineteenth-century audiences. Another generalist of the age, Abraham Lincoln, would combine Finney's religious tones with Field's mystic homology of law and nation in a final definition of country. But for ordinary times and everyday life, Americans needed an entirely different set of assumptions to cope with the spiraling complexity around them. They lived on the brink of what has been called "a profound change in the conditions of satisfactory explanation."[50]

The New Professionalism: Mid-Century and After

The generalist in thought was disappearing. Intellectuals, recognizing that no one person could encompass modern culture, rejected comprehensiveness as a goal and turned to other methods and standards of inquiry. The most dramatic alternative involved the validation of emotive sensations and perceptions. Intuition, imagination, and self-realization gave the individual observer new modes of investigation and understanding. This was romanticism with its interests in uncharted interiors, organic growth, the unique, and the individual—interests that flourished in the dynamic, adventurist landscape of nineteenth-century American civilization.[51] A second alternative met the growing implausibility of the generalist head on. Modern professionalism simply replaced the individual inquirer with collective, specialized inquiry. As one historian has summarized the change, "In an increasingly interdependent society, truly authoritative opinion could come only from full-time inquirers organized in a highly disciplined community of inquiry, one whose members would police each other's work with ruthless intensity."[52] The professional and the romantic: virtually every intellectual became one or the other as American culture developed into an uneasy mixture of both, a professionally run society with romantic aspirations. Did one secure a place in an assumed order through particular knowledge or did one intuit the whole through a sense of sympathetic correspondence? Answers to this question ranged between talent and genius, expertise and art, pragmatism and idealism, technical reason and imagination, depending upon the context. Of more immediate concern, however, is the fact that every answer split the lawyer-writer down the middle. At mid-century the attorney's skill and the writer's creativity appeared a contradiction in terms.

Old-style lawyers reacted in three ways. Many despaired over a fragmenting world. A few, like Finney and Field, sustained inclusive views through a personal sense of mission. Still others began to accept the overriding complexity of the law as an intellectual norm, and this third group represented the future. The generation that first came to the bar in the 1840s readily adapted to change, though some looked back with nostalgia. When Rufus Choate, one of the last generalists to lead the profession, died in 1859, Richard Henry Dana, Jr., described himself as "the master of a small coasting vessel, that hugs the shore" in contrast to Choate, "a great homeward-bound Indiaman, freighted with silks and precious stones, spices and costly fabrics . . . with the nation's flag at her mast-head, navigated by the mysterious science of the fixed stars."[53] The simile aptly conveyed a specialist's sense of loss. But that which was lost could also seem irrelevant. George Templeton Strong, the consummate New York office lawyer of the 1850s, offered a more condescending view of the past, gently mocking "the Lycurgic D.D. Field" as one of many "elder respectabilities."[54] The new practitioner did not share Choate and Field's old-fashioned need for cosmic unity. It was enough to find the detail and application of the law without worrying about comprehensiveness and theoretical compatibilities. For if the law of nature, the moral law, the law of nations, and the civil law seemed "curiously interwoven," to cite a textbook from 1857, those relations barely touched the civil law "as a distinct branch of knowledge." Nature, morality, and nationality were one thing; the civil law, quite another. Only the latter deserved to be counted in "the profession of the law, the study of the law, the science of the law."[55]

The grand style of the generalist really ended with the Civil War.[56] What the growing professionalism of the 1840s and 1850s questioned, the more inductive jurisprudence of the 1870s and 1880s openly condemned. Christopher Columbus Langdell (1826–1906), the first dean of the Harvard Law School, secured another triumph of the particular over the general in 1870 when he introduced the case-by-case method of teaching that would shape modern legal education. Langdell thought of the law as a separate science: those who entered its exclusive preserve kept to primary sources, to the cases and statutes in the legal process itself.[57] Then in 1881 Oliver Wendell Holmes, Jr. (1841–1935), proclaimed "the failure of all theories which consider the law only from its formal side." The most prominent figure in American jurisprudence for the next half century, Holmes denied the possibility of "logical cohesion of part with part" in the law. Jurists who still believed in natural law or in the connection of law and morality were naive.[58] As for the giants of the past, Holmes kept them there. "Story's simple philosophizing has ceased to satisfy men's minds," he told a Harvard Law School audience in 1886. Modern lawyers needed a different kind of knowledge. They had to forget the traditional "rag-bag full of general principles" in which abstractions emerged "like a swarm of little bodiless cherubs fluttering at the top of one of Corregio's [sic] pictures." The whole legal system had to be restated with a microscopic intensity that would complement panoramic scope and reveal the "precise contours" and "innermost meanings" of each doctrine. This was legal positivism carried to its logical conclusion. And "the new work" required an equally new generation of experts. Holmes, as an erstwhile law student named Henry James saw first, represented the specialist par excellence.[59]

Ironically, the changing meaning of the law received its most eloquent statement in a work of fiction. Sometime between 1886 and 1891 Herman Melville wrote *Billy Budd, Sailor (An Inside Narrative)*, his story about a young sailor's court-martial and execution aboard a British man-of-war on the high seas. The essential action takes place in a paragraph and can be summarized in less.[60] Billy Budd, innocence personified, kills the ship's master-at-arms, John Claggart, with a single impulsive blow when Claggart falsely accuses him of mutiny before their captain, Edward Fairfax Vere. Billy strikes because a stutter prevents him from speaking; he is then charged, tried, sentenced, and hanged by Captain Vere and a drumhead court for the capital offense of hitting a superior. The precision of established law stipulates no less, and the Captain's orchestration of Billy's conviction reflects, in the words of a critic, "a positivist's condensation of a legal system's formal character."[61] Vere's sense of duty here, in friction with his larger awareness as "a veritable touchstone" of humanity, gives Melville's parable of crime and punishment—unintentional crime and, therefore, unjust punishment—its power, its capacity to horrify. The law is the inflexible surface of "an inside narrative." Those who use it adhere "to the frontage, the appearance" and condemn "to summary and shameful death a fellow creature innocent before God."

Forty years separate the punishment scenes in *White Jacket* and *Billy Budd*, the difference between the American Renaissance and the Age of Realism. In 1850 Melville chooses to interrupt martial discipline with a higher moral law. Nothing can stop the inexorable execution of God's angel in 1891.[62] The modernity of *Billy Budd* consists in its portrayal of a legal system that explicitly denies all natural and spiritual connections. Amidst much deliberate ambiguity, Melville labors to sustain a basic separation of realms, and that separation is surely what he alludes to in declaring that *Billy Budd*, unlike Hawthorne's tales, "is no romance."[63] When Billy shouts farewell to the *Rights-of-Man*, the mercantile ship from which he is impressed into military service, he loses all touch with natural law. Later, the death of Claggart appears an act of divine justice in the eyes of Billy's witness, defense counsel, prosecutor, and ultimate judge, Captain Vere, but this recognition has no effect upon the legal proceedings at hand. "Struck dead by an angel of God!" cries Vere over the fallen Claggart. "Yet the angel must hang!" The drumhead court then follows his lead, enforcing the law as written and disregarding natural and religious feelings. Private conscience must yield to "that imperial one formulated in the code under which alone we officially proceed." All else is irrelevant, "a matter for psychologic theologians to discuss."

Melville's presentation of Vere's opinions borrows heavily from the professional orthodoxy that Langdell, Holmes, and others popularized in the second half of the nineteenth century. The writer creates a situation in which tragedy has to happen, the consequence of that orthodoxy. Unmistakably, it is precision of language, an excluding logic, insistence upon context, and an overruling distrust of moral philosophy—traits of the modern professional—that kill Billy Budd. "For my own part," wrote Holmes in the same decade, "I often doubt whether it would not be a gain if every word of moral significance could be banished from the law altogether, and other words adopted which should convey legal ideas uncolored by anything outside the law"—a thought repeated endlessly in American law schools ever since. Purged thus of "confounding morality," the law gained in the clarity of specialization what it lost in "the majesty got from ethical association."[64]

Holmes's proposal was one that no early American lawyer could have understood. To "convey legal ideas uncolored by anything outside the law" raised a wholly different conception of the subject. Holmes spoke of the law as "a business with well understood limits, a body of dogma enclosed within definite lines."[65] These limits and lines, which exclude more than they include, necessarily required another kind of audience. The antebellum lawyer addressed the people and used much the same language at the bar, from the bench, and behind the podium. Holmes thought of other lawyers or what he once welcomed as "the little army of specialists."[66] The subrogation changed everything that the profession wanted to accomplish with thought and language. Modern lawyers would enfold themselves and their subjects in expertise. The price of their intellectual precision would be a deliberate rejection of comprehensive ideas and a corresponding loss in communicative power. Legal knowledge in the twentieth century would reach only the few; it would have less and less to do with America's general search for self-expression.

The Separate South

If little has been said on regional differences within the configuration of law and letters, it is because similarities prevailed in the first third of the nineteenth century. The courtroom orator and his alter ego, the lawyer-writer in literature, shaped intellectual discourse everywhere. That is why Robert Hayne and Daniel Webster could move an entire nation in 1830; their senatorial exchange touched universal sensibilities. Twenty years later that common ground had disappeared. By 1850 the old-style lawyer was an anachronism in New England and the Mid-Atlantic states, and he survived in the West only as long as frontier conditions favored general knowledge over expertise. The generation of Stephen Douglas and Abraham Lincoln would be the last in the law to make eloquence its stock in trade, the last to mix Blackstone, Shakespeare, and the Bible as primary sources in the courtroom—the last, that is, north of the Mason-Dixon line.[67]

The configuration continued to thrive in the South. From Virginia through Georgia the courtroom orator became more important in 1850, not less, and the lawyer-writer solidified instead of losing his control over literary and political forums. Modernization and the new professionalism extended west but not south, and the ensuing contrast in professional standards compounded sectional misunderstanding. In pointing to misunderstandings, the South could justly claim that the North had changed, but it would never appreciate the powerful exception to that charge. Lincoln, after all, came out of the frontier West. An old-fashioned generalist who rode the circuit, he appeared in national politics as one of the last men of the North to share a language and mode of presentation with the South, a fact that made him peculiarly formidable in the great intellectual debates of the Civil War.

Men trained in the law utterly dominated Southern literature between 1830 and 1870. Edgar Allan Poe (1809–1849) alone among the major writers belonged in a separate category, and Poe left the South in 1837. John Pendleton Kennedy (1795–1870) and William Gilmore Simms (1806–1870) were the significant novelists; Henry Timrod (1828–1867) and Sidney Lanier (1842–1881), the most important poets. The influential theorists were John C. Calhoun (1782–1850), William Harper (1790–1847), Thomas Roderick Dew (1802–1846), George Fitzhugh (1806–1881), James Henry Hammond (1807–1864), and Albert Taylor Bledsoe (1809–1877). The leading humorists were A. B. Longstreet (1790–1870), Johnson Jones Hooper (1815–1862), and Joseph Baldwin (1815–1864). All of these writers studied law, and they were only the most prominent figures in a much larger tradition of gentlemen of letters at the bar. In the words of one nineteenth-century observer, "The major portion of such literary work as was done at the South was done by lawyers."[68] Indeed, the apologetic tone in this summary—"such literary work as was done"—contains its own truth. Often mentioned, the lawyer-writer in the South has yet to be examined in context.

Many of the original conditions supporting the configuration persisted in the South. An agrarian economy deterred specialization while sustaining old customs and small-town society. Even in the twentieth century a southern critic could label his culture "a superficial Victorian veneer pasted over what was still an eighteenth-century way of living."[69] Neoclassical values continued to define intellectual achievement. Until at least 1900, oratory held its place, politics remained a controlling theme, and gentlemen of letters outnumbered professional writers. These tendencies encouraged the lawyer-writer, as did the traditional conservatism, rationalism, and secularism of the southern mind.[70] In literature the result was "Confederate prose" or "the nineteenth-century Ciceronian Southern style"; it was "the mode of discourse inevitable in a society which gives itself up to politics and the law."[71]

In mid-nineteenth-century southern culture, the connection between politics, literature, and the law remained in force. And yet to assume a simple preservation of early republican principles—a frequent rhetorical ploy of regional spokesmen—ignores the way in which the present uses the past for its own purposes. Even sacred ideas function as the corollaries of current needs. As long as national and regional identities coincided, a situation that lasted well into the 1840s, the South could rest within the shared civic thought and literature of the formative period. But that security became a threat when sectional strife reached a breaking point in the 1850s. Suddenly the South had to invent a literary nationalism to counter its own Americanism. Overnight the region struggling to be a nation demanded of its writers a wholly reconstituted "Southern Republic of Letters."[72] "Let all your game lie in the constant recognition & assertion of a *Southern Nationality!*" William Gilmore Simms instructed his friends. Thus, and at the very moment that the North was moving toward a more individual and imaginative literature, the South necessarily plunged back into the civic forms of the past in search of a new image of itself and of its meaning in history.[73] That quest made the rhetoric of nationhood—the combination of politics and the law—fresh again, and it insured the continuing ascendancy of the lawyer-writer, who, in defining one nation in 1776, was well equipped to create another in 1861.

Defeat in 1865 set the obsession with politics in stone. In the 1850s southerners had asked themselves, "What have we become?" With Appomattox that question resolved itself into "What have we done?" or, in the loaded language of one postwar lawyer-writer, "Can any good come forth of a generation that believed that their fathers were traitors?"[74] Justification replaced explanation. Before the war, civic involvement had been the supreme manifestation of intellectual achievement in the South, but Reconstruction pushed southern leaders out of public life, forcing them to make the most of the role of ceremonial spokesman. Patriotism, always the first duty of the true southerner, became a literary style, a matter of correct expression where action was impossible.[75]

These changes kept the civic voice at the center of literary aspiration and the public man of letters over the professional writer. And here, once again, the lawyer-writer held a natural advantage over such competitors as the defeated soldier and the failed politician. His task was twofold: he sought to reconcile the Old South and the New in one more attempt at communal definition, and, with the entire region as his client, he appeared as defense counsel on appeal after an adverse judgment.[76] Thomas Nelson Page (1853–1922) captured the essence of this second stance as late as 1892 when, still insisting on "the legal, constitutional right to secede," he described the South as the victim of an unfair trial: "In the supreme moment of her existence [the South] found herself arraigned at the bar of the world without an advocate and without a defence."[77] Southern literature in the last third of the nineteenth century always returned to that supreme moment in the past. It wanted to reopen the case and plead the cause anew. It tried through eloquence to achieve what had been lost forever on the battlefield, reaching back to the literature of the early republic in poignant echoes that chronicled "the South living the long aftermath of its confused and disastrous attempt to establish itself in history as a nation."[78]

Regional peculiarities in the law itself reinforced the Southern lawyer's broad social role. Because commercial law developed very slowly in the South, the generalist ruled legal practice much longer than elsewhere, and his ability to unify communal sympathies remained a vital professional skill. Then, too, the southern lawyer always had to be more than a lawyer. As scholars have shown, the law constituted just one of several competing modes of social order in the antebellum South.[79] The code of honor and slavery both impinged upon formal legal prerogatives. The leaders of the Old South settled matters of slander, libel, assault, battery, and other differences of opinion on the field of honor, bypassing courtroom remedies and overtly breaking state laws that prohibited dueling. At the same time, slavery barred a third of the South's population from the legal rights of citizenship, and it placed the plantation owner above the law by allowing him to wield absolute power over those people who were his personal property. These tendencies were part of "the unwritten constitution of the Old South," and, in restricting the meaning and application of the legal process, they created a paradox. The more restricted the law became, the more expansive the lawyer had to be.

The southern practitioner had no choice but to incorporate the code of honor and slavery into his professional life. To have relied exclusively upon conventional legal expertise, as lawyers in the North and West increasingly did, would have been social and political suicide. In the words of one Tennessee lawyer, born in 1816:

> To carry a personal grievance into a court of law degraded the plaintiff in the estimation of his peers and put the whole case beneath the notice of society. The party defendant in such cases declined to appear before the court . . . If his enemy declined to meet him in personal combat, society reversed the decision of the court, ostracized the successful plaintiff and lionized his enemy.[80]

It was just as impossible to avoid a stand on slavery. Silence on the issue was tantamount to treason; assertion, part of the conventional formula of regional identity. Lawyers were particularly important in this context because the South needed answers to those incongruities between natural law and slavery that gave abolitionists a theoretical advantage and slaveowners since Jefferson so many qualms.[81]

Whatever the penalties of avoidance, the rewards for participation were great. Pro-slavery arguments electrified Southern audiences more effectively than other subjects, guaranteeing rapid political advancement. Throughout the antebellum period, lawyer-writers led the way in justifying the peculiar institution. They redefined natural rights and dissociated natural law from embarrassing contractual theories of obligation.[83] John Lyde Wilson (1784–1849) was both a lawyer and an ex-governor of South Carolina when he published *The Code of Honor; or Rules For The Government of Principals and Seconds in Duelling* in 1838. Wilson declared "a right to appeal to arms" the appropriate response "where the laws of the country give no redress for injuries received," and he was convinced that honor "would quit the country and inhabit the wilderness with the Indians" if the practice were effectively prohibited by law. How far he wandered from the spirit of the courtroom—and how foreign compromise became in the South—can be read in one of the final dicta of his dueling manual: "Words used in retort . . . will not satisfy,—words being no satisfaction for words."[84]

In trying to reconcile slavery, dueling, and the rule of law in a republic, the southern lawyer embodied the contradictions of his culture. His predicament, in fact, led him to look to the intellectual comprehensiveness of the eighteenth-century bar and away from the growing precision of the nineteenth-century expert. Only the former encouraged the loose inclusiveness so suitable for the unwritten code of the South.[85] Of course, mere inclusion could never eliminate contradiction, but the effort created an expansive social persona that reduced conflicting systems of order to personal modes of behavior. The lawyer in the Old South absorbed alternative roles into a single, enveloping grand style. This is the reason why descriptions always make him something more than himself. Thus, the true lawyer in South Carolina in 1806, fictionalized as Mr. Verdict, is both a practitioner and the proprietor of a small plantation, and his integrity and authority are such as to render the legal process obsolete. Mr. Verdict settles his cases through informal arbitration; he willingly serves as "the judge or umpire of both parties," and, in consequence, "now scarcely ever comes to town but on club nights."[86] The planter, a code name for slaveowner, has safely absorbed the lawyer while safeguarding the latter's skills and reputation for the administration of an informal, unwritten code.

Modern sketches of the phenomenon follow the same lead. The ideal antebellum lawyer is always a planter, always the absolute and unquestioned leader of his community, always a literary presence. His use of the law is informal and idiosyncratic rather than precise. Classical works outnumber law books in his library, and he respects authority more than authorities. In his hands the common law is common sense—an instrument instead of a standard.[87] To give a final, succinct description in full:

> The South was an aggregate of farms and plantations, presided over by our composite agrarian hero, Cicero Cincinnatus. I can think of no better image for what the South was before 1860, and for what it largely still was until about 1914, than that of the old gentleman in Kentucky who sat every afternoon in his front yard under an old sugar tree, reading Cicero's Letters to Atticus. When the hands suckering

the tobacco in the adjoining field needed orders, he kept his place in the book with his forefinger, walked out into the field, gave the orders, and then returned to his reading under the shade of the tree. He was also a lawyer, and occasionally he went to his office, which was over the feed-store in the county seat, a village with a population of about 400 people.[88]

Even in caricature this figure is remarkable for the variety of functions he must perform. He is farmer, intellectual, overseer, classicist, lawyer, political leader, and, not least, gentleman of leisure. And all of the foregoing make another: the writer, the composite hero who labors to hold the bitter contrasts in southern life together.

These character traits lead directly to the central aesthetic of southern literature in the nineteenth century. "Cicero Cincinnatus," in presiding over that literature, imposes his need to resolve the differences around him. His books mediate between privilege and tyranny, simplicity and ignorance, honor and anger, comparison and prejudice. A. B. Longstreet's *Georgia Scenes* (1835) encloses the violence and crudity of the backwoods within the sophisticated voice of a lawyer-narrator who is above "the humbler walks of life" but close enough to describe and evaluate them. This "stranger" gets along with "the boys of Upper Hogthief" even though his story plays off the gulf between.[89] The same phenomenon occurs in William Gilmore Simms's minor classic "How Sharp Snaffles Got His Capital And Wife" (1870). An educated outsider known as "The 'Jedge' " receives and re-tells a border hunter's tale, and he links town culture and frontier life in the process.[90] Many of the novels of Simms, and of John Pendleton Kennedy as well, supply a similar kind of neutral territory for bringing aristocrat and yeoman, planter and plain farmer, together.[91]

Ultimately, however, the tradition of southern harmony is a matter of personal style imposed from above. Joseph G. Baldwin's *Flush Times of Alabama and Mississippi* (1853) blends every contrast into the figure of the lawyer as communal spokesman. From the polished jurist to the rural pettifogger, this figure appears in every sketch, and Baldwin's special triumph is his ability to make an alloy that encompasses the whole. Old Caesar Kasm, to take the best example from *Flush Times*, combines high honor and low vituperation in a comic mixture of decorum and chicanery. Slaveowner, lawyer, duelist, old-fashioned Federalist, and a Virginia gentleman who has seen better days, the appropriately named "Sar Kasm" wins a weak case through sheer force of will.[92] His character and his victory personify the predicament and, unfortunately, the hope of the Old South.

Ever more conscious of the contradictions around them and in them, the twentieth-century counterparts of Caesar Kasm tend to be tragic rather than comic figures. Cicero Cincinnatus appears in modern fiction mostly to watch what remains of southern culture destroy itself. He is the solitary holder of a negative wisdom, and, hence, of a terrifying woe. One thinks here of Judge Rumford Bland, the blind, syphilitic "ruined angel" who names Thomas Wolfe's *You Can't Go Home Again* (1934), or of Jeremiah Cobb, the chief magistrate in William Styron's *Confessions of Nat Turner* (1966) as he drunkenly mourns over "my Virginia, blighted domain!"[93] By far the greatest of these figures is Gavin Stevens, William Faulkner's "bucolic Cincinnatus" and "designated paladin of justice and truth and right." Stevens, attorney and then district attorney in Faulkner's Jefferson County, also wonders whether his "heat-miraged land" will outlast an awful corruption, but he has finally learned that the attempt to win Sar Kasm's case brings only despair, and this is the beginning of a better understanding.[94] In one of those startling continuities in American literature, Stevens looks back beyond his own contradictions to the higher ideal of the Founders. The courthouse in Jefferson, built by black hands as well as white, is "the center, the focus, the hub; sitting looming in the center of the county's circumference like a single cloud in its ring of horizon." As such, it appears "protector of the weak, judiciate and curb of passions and lusts, repository and guardian of the aspirations and the hopes." This vision gives Stevens courage to face the old predicament head on and in a new way. As he explains to Temple Drake, symbol and type of a false southern honor, "What we are trying to deal with now is injustice."[95]

James Fenimore Cooper in "A Country of Laws"

Assessing the value of the configuration of law and letters within the larger canon of American literature presents a different and final problem. That the configuration supplies another way of approaching and entering the American mind is clear. That it explains the thought and behavior of certain writers and that it imposes its own aesthetic upon a series of texts have been matters of demonstration. But value, at least in literary terms, implies more than understanding or even importance. What has the configuration really added to American culture? And, since literary enterprise has largely discarded the lawyer-writer's methods in the twentieth century, what of value has been lost? Such questions should be asked, and a final example, the fiction of James Fenimore Cooper, provides a context for answers.

Cooper (1786–1851), like Daniel Webster and the Richard Henry Danas, spanned the major period of concern, and his writings projected both a theory of value and a prescient sense of loss. Although the man behind the writings neither read nor practiced law in the formal sense, he frequently appeared in court against the newspaper editors who "libelled" his work. He was also, in the words of his daughter, "partial to legal reading, and often studied some questions of that nature with deep interest, and without any other object than the pleasure of the investigation itself."[96] Cooper, in other words, assumed the traditional role of the landowning gentleman who studied and maintained the laws of his realm. He used his pen to serve his nation, calling himself an "American who wishes to illustrate and enforce the peculiar principles of his own country, by the agency of polite literature."[97] And these familiar priorities yielded familiar consequences. Across thirty years and thirty-two novels, Cooper took as his central theme the unfolding nature of the republic of laws in American culture.[98] Three novels in particular lend themselves to a summary of Cooper's achievement: *The Pioneers* (1823), *Home As Found* (1838), and *The Ways Of The Hour* (1850).[99] Each exemplifies the writer's talent for depicting his society through symbolic characterization, each effectively dramatizes the central problem of the republic at a particular stage of development, each offers its own insight into the meaning of the law in American culture. Together, they cover Cooper's writing career at regular intervals, revealing the chronological development of his thought and methods and underscoring the permanent or fixed assumptions of his social theory.[100]

Home As Found, the middle novel, summarizes the writer's hope for America (pp. 162–165). Here, using human development as a metaphor, Cooper steps back from his story to describe the three stages in the growth of a new country from childhood through adolescence to adulthood. At the commencement of Cooper's ideal settlement, "Good-will abounds; neighbor comes cheerfully to the aid of neighbor; and life has much of the reckless gayety, careless association, and buoyant merriment of childhood." The inhabitants of a new community, though from different social and educational strata, "meet, as it might be, on a sort of neutral ground, one yielding some of his superiority, and the other laying claims to an outward show of equality" through "mutual wants and mutual efforts." Soon, however, "society begins to marshal itself, and the ordinary passions have sway. Now it is that we see the struggles for place, the heart-burnings and jealousies of contending families, and the influence of mere money." This adolescent stage of invidious comparison and unruly competition is "the least inviting condition of society," but it can give way to the third and last condition, maturity, only when "men and things come within the control of more general and regular laws." A refined legal system establishes the necessary "division into castes that are more or less rigidly maintained, according to circumstances." All three of the novels in question take place in Cooper's middle period or least inviting stage of civilization—*The Pioneers* at the beginning, *Home As Found* in its full sway, and *The Ways Of The Hour* in a sort of arrested or stunted adolescence that is dangerous for all concerned. The problem, as Cooper makes clear, is that the law has been displaced from its *natural* function.

In *The Pioneers*, set in 1793, civil law and natural law come into direct and irreconcilable conflict through the characterizations of Marmaduke Temple, the judge and leading citizen of the rural village of Templeton, and Natty Bumppo, the aged hunter who has lived on the site since it was a wilderness.[101] Bumppo, in breaking Judge Temple's new game laws, runs afoul of local magistrates and ends up in the Judge's courtroom, where he is punished for his offenses. Natty argues against Temple's law with the force of "reason" and the consistency of his own actions in nature as evidence. His point of view contains its own accusation: "I b'lieve there's some who thinks there's no God in a wilderness!" The Judge's only response to this charge is a non sequitur. "Attend to your plea, Bumppo," he instructs the accused (pp. 377–383). Significantly, the only real villains in this encounter are lesser figures who have helped to engineer Bumppo's violation of the law. Temple and Bumppo both have right on their side. The Judge must look to the onward march of civilization, which, as several incidents prove, will destroy the natural world unless strict laws of conservation are administered.[102]

For his part, Natty flees westward to reestablish the simpler harmonies that nature makes possible (pp. 475–476).

Cooper sides with civilization in this conflict but not without
qualms. Civil authority in Templeton appears a paltry thing at best.
The minor officials of the village are corrupt self-seekers who use
the law for their own advantage (pp. 335–347). Of the two lawyers
who appear in Judge Temple's court, both "cunning in the law,"
Lippet is an ambulance-chasing pettifogger and Van der School a
hopeless pedant (pp. 29, 144–147, 287–280, 348–350). Then, too,
Richard Jones as sheriff always seems on the brink of a rash or
unjust act that only Judge Temple can curb (pp. 180, 251–252, 270,
365–368, 448–453). Cooper uses the relationship to dramatize the
importance of bending executive might to judicial control, but he
raises a subtler possibility in making sheriff and judge blood relatives
of the same household. Richard Jones is Marmaduke Temple carried
to excess. In very different degree, the two men share the same
faults: carelessness, a certain disregard of others, cupidity, and an
insistence upon their own way (pp. 11–15, 37–39, 84–85, 177–180,
323–333).

One of Cooper's master strokes is the flawed character of his town
leader. Marmaduke Temple's eagerness for wealth and position have
left a "slight stain" (p. 23). His "infirmities," as Cooper calls them,
have helped him to forget the Indian claims upon his land, and they
encourage his propensity to solve moral issues with money (pp. 238,
8–10, 42, 252, 338, 395). And yet he clearly constitutes the ideal
communal leader in Templeton. Cooper's point is that the best of
men remains a faulty guide in and by himself. As the Judge reminds
his daughter, "The laws alone remove us from the conditions of the
savages" (p. 395). Private conscience without the externalization of
reason and revelation, without the law guided by religion, must
always fail. Cooper, throughout his fiction, places the moral or
divine law at the foundation of all civil law.[103] Marmaduke Temple
symbolizes the hope of harmonizing civil, moral, divine, and natural
law into the social reality of the future. "Mount Vision," the perspective from which Temple first dreams of his city in the wilderness, is meant to incorporate "Hawk-eye," Natty's view, in the end
(pp. 236, 303). In fact, *The Pioneers* actually begins with that act of
incorporation in a cameo picture of Templeton some thirty years
after the events of the novel. A beautiful and thriving village nestled
into the natural environment, Judge Temple's finished creation ex-

hibits "how much can be done, in even a rugged country, and with a severe climate, under the dominion of mild laws" (pp. 1–2).

Home As Found, written fifteen years after *The Pioneers* and set in the 1830s, returns for a closer look at Templeton, and it discovers that "no country has so much altered for the worse in so short a time" (p. 224). When the enlightened gentry of this generation climb Mount Vision, they see only "the envy, rapacity, uncharitableness, and all the other evil passions of man!" (p. 131). Templeton has moved farther away from the desired reconciliation of civil, natural, and divine law, not closer. The stability and sense of hierarchy necessary for such harmony have vanished (pp. 424–426). Natty Bumppo is now a barely remembered "mocking spirit" (p. 204). Religion itself has been subjected to the leveling process through "a loose habit, that is insensibly taking the place of the ancient laws of propriety" (pp. 186–189). To use Cooper's metaphor, America has turned into a runaway carriage crashing downhill (p. 56).

The "Representative American" amid all of this declension is Aristabulus Bragg, lawyer and agent for the Effinghams as they return to their ancestral home, "that model of the composite order" built by Marmaduke Temple (p. 128). Bragg, the willing servant of Effingham interests, has absolutely no intellectual interest in either their model or the order behind it. Proud to be an American, he has no understanding of the principles on which his country is based.[104] And yet nothing can stop this "compound of shrewdness, impudence, common-sense, pretension, humility, cleverness, vulgarity, kind-heartedness, duplicity, selfishness, law-honesty, moral fraud, and mother-wit" (p. 10). As the name implies, Aristabulus Bragg aspires to a higher status than he deserves with even the White House in his purview (pp. 30, 73). Manifestly, the law has stumbled in its fundamental educational purpose. Bragg has become "expert in all the practices of his profession" without accepting the decorum and control that legal study was supposed to inculcate (p. 10). It is just a question of time before he leaves the Effinghams to strike out on his own. Meanwhile the Effinghams use the reluctant Bragg to help prove their title in a land dispute with the public. Succeeding in this attempt, they fail utterly in their larger purpose. "I will teach [the people]," claims Edward Effingham, "what they now do not appear to know—that we live in a country of laws." Alas, the lesson of *Home As Found* runs quite the other way. A "spirit of misrule" is abroad in the land (pp. 207–220).

The Ways Of The Hour carries Cooper's fears to their logical conclusion by subverting the actual legal process. The writer's last novel, it has been called "the most damaging of Cooper's attacks on American society," and it owes much of its forgotten power to the writer's careful dramatization of changes in the legal system.[105] In Biberry, New York—the misplaced *r* turns the town into "Bribery"—an innocent woman named Mary Monson is convicted of first-degree murder on the loosest circumstantial evidence. Jury tampering, wholesale intimidation, and a purchased press figure prominently in this decision, which is reversed only when the supposed murder victim appears in court (p. 462). However, the real antagonists in *The Ways Of The Hour* are Thomas Dunscomb and Squire Timms, Mary Monson's two defense attorneys. "My heart is full of the failing justice of the land," mourns Dunscomb in 1850, the last in a long line of Cooper gentlemen (p. 271). By way of contrast, Timms engages in every sordid practice that the times allow. "Things are changed in Ameriky, Mr. Dunscomb," announces Timms, the logical outgrowth of Aristabulus Bragg. "The people are beginning to govern; and when they can't do it legally, they do it without law" (p. 138). Popular opinion has replaced the law, undermining the true basis of the republican experiment.

Only Timms proves effective in the trial of Mary Monson. Helpless in a world where "talk and prejudice" outweigh "principles and facts," Dunscomb retires from the law a disenchanted man (pp. 218, 177, 496). Timms, on the other hand, is "scamp enough for anything." He heads for the state senate, where he will soon be "whining about 'republican simplicity' " (p. 512). The ruled has become the ruler in this topsy-turvy world. Moreover, Timms succeeds by deliberately turning his back on the original meaning of America:

> I think it will be wisest to let the law, and old principles and the right, and *true* liberty, quite alone . . . A good deal is said about our fathers, and their wisdom, and patriotism, and sacrifices; but nobody dreams of doing as they *did*, or of reasoning as they *reasoned*. Life is made up, in reality, of these little matters in a corner. (p. 228)

This reality defeats Dunscomb and, by extension, his creator, and Cooper shows as much by turning Mary Monson into a far more effective attorney than either of her counsel.

In the curious denouement of *The Ways Of The Hour*, Mary wins her own case through new evidence and a brilliant cross-examination that carries the day (pp. 456–462, 469–479). Such unacceptably masculine behavior on the part of a Cooper heroine is perhaps the writer's clearest indication that the times are out of joint. The lady, always Cooper's symbol of civilization, has been corrupted by her upbringing in a false world. Mary, in fact, is declared insane for her pains, though this designation cannot be legally established (p. 479). Just as interesting is the resentful onlooker. Baffled, ineffective, obsolete, and most of all silent, Dunscomb has lost all sense of purpose in the moment of Mary's triumph. Everything he stands for has been either dismissed or twisted. Dunscomb has become a last figuration for the predicament of the lawyer as republican spokesman in American culture.

The striking thing about Cooper's novels is their clarity of vision, their ability to capture complex political and social problems in imaginative literature. Individual representations fall into stereotypical patterns, but the interaction of these representations breathes nuance and spontaneity into "Cooper's agonized scrutiny of the American character." In the exchanges and the relationships of Judge Temple and Richard Jones, of Aristabulus Bragg and the Effinghams, of Dunscomb and Timms, the novelist tackles the problems of making republican institutions adequate to American life.[106] And he demonstrates those problems with an impressive precision of language and thought. His incorporation of social analysis within a fictional mode can be questioned but not the conviction that motivates it. One does not have to accept Cooper's conservative vision of American society to share his passionate belief in what one critic has called "the social utility of moral understanding."[107]

Cooper always strives to make the meaning of America clear—a goal that writers and other intellectuals seem to have lost sight of in the twentieth century. There is a skill in making intricate issues come alive in prose, and Cooper's sincerity and attention to detail in this attempt often make him a more effective craftsman than even he must have realized. When Dunscomb in *The Ways Of The Hour*, to take a final example, seeks to make God and not the Constitution the "palladium of our liberties," the claim exists on many levels (p. 19). Dunscomb is Cooper the conservative Christian gentleman insisting upon the religious basis of all moral and social order. He is also just a touch of the natural philosopher, Natty Bumppo crying that God be put back in the wilderness. Then again, he represents the traditional lawyer who, in context, is objecting to a secularizing legal positivism, in this case the Code of David Dudley Field that has been passed in New York shortly before Cooper wrote. The Code, "as extravagant and high-flying an invention as ever came from the misguided ingenuity of man," has separated the law from its natural and moral roots (pp. 14, 45, 69). In *The Ways Of The Hour* neither the virtue of the redeemed nation nor the natural rights of the citizen can be quite the same now that human law is its own justification.

These stances of the Christian gentleman, the natural philosopher, and the traditional lawyer were an uneasy mixture of the timely and the anachronistic in 1850. Cooper played upon a prevalent anxiety when he voiced alarm over the growing secularization of American thought, but his solutions imposed the past upon the present. His last novels tried to force a choice *between* religion and the modern world, *between* God and the Constitution. In making God the only legitimate source of political liberty, the lawyer Dunscomb quietly affirms what Cooper had proclaimed three years before in *The Crater*, a novel in which "that dread Being" prepares to destroy the earth itself: "Let those who would substitute the voice of the created for that of the Creator, who shout 'the people, the people,' instead of hymning the praises of their God . . . remember their insignificance and tremble. They are but mites amid millions of other mites, that the goodness of providence has produced for its own wise ends."[108]

If such passages failed to move Cooper's contemporaries, it was because fewer and fewer Americans were willing to define themselves just so as conventionalized Edwardsian sinners in the hands of an angry God. Something more was needed in 1850, something that would recognize the citizen's hold upon the world without weakening a corresponding claim upon the ideal. Cooper wrote just before the creation of a new theology for the secular nation-state. By placing God *within* the Constitution, Abraham Lincoln would eliminate the choice that Cooper had to make.

LINCOLN:
AN EPILOGUE

T HE NATURE of Abraham Lincoln's achievement has been a
fascinating and lively source of debate for more than a century
now—fascinating because the debate involves changing assumptions
about the national character, lively because critics have found so
many different reasons for greatness. The nineteenth-century images of the self-made man and the democratic leader out of the West
celebrate more than explain. More recently, Lincoln has become a
poetic figure imposing himself upon the nation through the magic
of language, a consummate pragmatist who marshals the realities
beyond mere ideology, and the moral touchstone of a troubled society.[1] Still more recently, he has appeared the liberating spokesman
of a post-heroic generation, the founder and first martyr of a new
civil religion, and a dual personality whose ability to resolve inner
conflicts tallies with the needs of a divided nation.[2] Diverse, even
contradictory, these interpretations all share the assumption that
Lincoln somehow made himself into a type of American civilization.
In the words of Roy Basler, the leading scholar of Lincoln materials,
"The essential effort of Lincoln's life was to identify himself, by
words and in relationships to his contemporaries, as a representative,
symbolic hero."[3] Representative of whom and symbolic of what
have been the questions over which so many have agreed to differ.

The configuration of law and letters brings fresh meaning to this
search for a representative figure. Lincoln is the last Blackstone
lawyer to lead the nation. He speaks and writes from within a
recognized tradition, and, to the extent that he consciously crafts a

larger persona "by words and in relationships to his contemporaries," he finds his models among such predecessors as Thomas Jefferson, Henry Clay, and Daniel Webster. For Lincoln, Jefferson is "the most distinguished politician of our history"; Clay, "freedom's champion" and "my beau ideal of a statesman"; Webster, "greatly devoted to the Union" and an inspiration in oratory.[4] No classicist, Lincoln nonetheless functions as part of a continuing Ciceronian ideal—the ideal of the rational man who reaches his highest attainment in an encompassing and eloquent wisdom concerning the civil world around him. The wartime president's language strives for and builds within such a mode of eloquent, forensic wisdom, and yet it is also its own language.[5] Genius turns what it finds into something else. Lincoln transforms the legacy of Jefferson, Clay, and Webster, and that transformation is at least one measure of his conscious achievement.

The legal aesthetic of early nineteenth-century thought persists in Lincoln the public speaker from beginning to end. As with earlier lawyer-writers, the law provides an ordering device and source of definition, and it proves that divine and human law connect in the American experiment. These familiar premises explain Lincoln's call for a political religion in 1838:

> To the support of the Constitution and Laws, let every American pledge his life, his property, and his sacred honor . . . Let reverence for the laws, be breathed by every American mother . . . let it be taught in schools, in seminaries, and in colleges;—let it be written in Primmers, spelling books, and in Almanacs;—let it be preached from the pulpit, proclaimed in legislative halls, and enforced in courts of justice. And, in short, let it become the *political religion* of the nation. (I, 112)

Even bad laws should be "religiously observed" if just for the sake of example. To understand, accept, and obey the laws of the land is to participate in the higher destiny of America and to receive personal meaning in the process. "If ever I feel the soul within me elevate and expand to those dimensions not wholly unworthy of its Almighty Architect," Lincoln explains a year later, "it is when I contemplate the cause of my country" (I, 178). The same theoretical concerns have a central place in the First Inaugural Address more than twenty years later (IV, 262–271). "I hold, that in contemplation of universal law, and of the Constitution, the Union of these States

Abraham Lincoln, by an unknown photographer
at Mathew Brady's gallery, in Washington D.C., about 1862.

Lincoln used the tradition that made him even as he pondered change. In
the process he gave final expression to the Ciceronian ideal of forensic
eloquence in American culture.

is perpetual," argues the new president, supporting the notion of an eternal Union first with "fundamental law" and then with a more tactical "legal contemplation" of national history. Since the Union, formalized in law, guarantees permanent safety and order, "the central idea of secession, is the essence of anarchy." Here, once again, social well-being and individual happiness demand obedience to law, including the odious Fugitive Slave Act. "I do suggest, that it will be much safer for all, both in official and private stations, to conform to, and abide by, all those acts which stand unrepealed, than to violate any of them." Only in this way can all Americans, North and South, find and fulfill "the better angels" of their nature.

The style behind the assertions is also familiar. Lincoln places highest value upon the encompassing abstraction that will hold things in place. "All honor to Jefferson," he writes in 1859, "—to the man who, in the concrete pressure of a struggle for national independence by a single people, had the coolness, forecast, and capacity to introduce into a merely revolutionary document, an abstract truth, applicable to all men and all times, and so to embalm it there, that to-day, and in all coming days, it shall be a rebuke and a stumbling-block to the very harbingers of re-appearing tyrany and oppression" (III, 376). Subsequently as president, he introduces comparable abstractions to define, embalm, and, hence, eliminate a struggle for national *identity* by a *divided* people. Take, for example, the controlling figure of "our national homestead," the constitutive metaphor of the Annual Message to Congress for 1862 (v, 527–537). Proving first that American lands form one "great body" and are "well adapted to be the home of one national family," Lincoln reduces the Civil War to "the passing generations of men," noting that the earth itself "abideth forever." Everything comes down to the question whether *this* generation ("we waste much strength in struggles among ourselves") "shall nobly save, or meanly lose, the last best, hope of earth."

Lincoln speaks with the voice of a circuit-riding lawyer. He argues from ideas presented as fundamentals, from principles rather than precedents.[6] Clarity, structure, balance, and plainness are the building blocks of this language, what Lincoln himself calls "the solid quarry of sober reason" (I, 115). His essential medium is the speech. "Extemporaneous speaking should be practised and cultivated," he warns the would-be practitioner. "It is the lawyer's avenue to the public. However able and faithful he may be in other respects, people are slow to bring him business if he cannot make a speech" (II, 81). Making a speech requires a practical knowledge of rhetoric, an instinct for arranging particulars, and the ability to entertain an audience through the mastery of language, which in Lincoln's case means a complicated mixture of popular dialect, biblical phraseology, and literary cadence. On the Illinois court circuits of the 1840s, eloquence still counted for much. How one spoke was at least as important as what one knew, and it was hardly a coincidence that Lincoln's law partners, Ward Hill Lamon and William Herndon, shared his fondness for Shakespearean declamation.[7]

The remarkable thing about Lincoln is that he employs the tools and ideology of his profession without being bound by them. Moderation and caution remain but not the worship of the past that so characterizes the legal mind of the period. Unlike so many of his predecessors, Lincoln recognizes the need for innovation. Where Daniel Webster fixes the Founding Fathers in permanent constellations of inspiration, Lincoln finds "a *once* hardy, brave, and patriotic, but *now* lamented and departed race of ancestors" (I, 108). And with unerring instinct, he looks to Thomas Jefferson, the one major lawyer-writer among the Founders who welcomed change. The point cannot be overstated. Virtually an anachronism as an old-style lawyer in 1861, Lincoln redefines his country by seeing past the failures in the system that produced him. As he tells his countrymen in 1862, "the dogmas of the quiet past, are inadequate to the stormy present . . . as our case is new, so we must think anew, and act anew" (V, 537).

The inadequacies of the past become manifest in the debased oratory and rising acrimony of the 1840s and 1850s. Lincoln reaches political maturity on the losing side of the debate over the Mexican War and amid growing agitation over slavery. From the former he learns the danger and distortion of patriotic language turned to baser aims. Fought for territorial gain, the Mexican War is "unnecessarily and unconstitutionally commenced" and then maintained "by fixing the public gaze upon the exceeding brightness of military glory" (I, 446, 439). A false language of principle disguises naked self-interest. Slavery, however, is worse, much worse. The hidden cancer in the Constitution, slavery literally eats away principle in the name of self-interest. The potential spread of slavery, through the doctrine of popular sovereignty in the territories, "deprives our republican example of its just influence in the world," and it creates "an open war with the very fundamental principles of civil liberty— criticising the Declaration of Independence, and insisting that there is no right principle of action but *self-interest*" (II, 274, 255–260). Language itself has lost its power to convince by the time of the Kansas-Nebraska Act of 1854.[8] "Who after this will ever trust in a national compromise?" asks Lincoln in repudiation (II, 272).

His practical answer to the problem of slavery in 1854 does not differ markedly from Daniel Webster's; Lincoln proposes that slavery be limited to "its existing legal rights" under the Constitution, no more and no less. But the rhetoric surrounding this answer suggests a radically new perspective. "Our republican robe is soiled, and trailed in the dust. Let us repurify it. Let us turn and wash it white, in the spirit, if not the blood, of the Revolution" (II, 276). Lincoln realizes that an essential ingredient has been lost in the compromises between 1820 and 1854. He remembers what Tocqueville had claimed twenty years before: "The Union is an ideal nation, which exists, so to speak, only in the mind."[9]

From this viewpoint, Stephen Douglas' tactics in the 1850s represent a desertion of principle and an attack on the eternal ideal of the republic. Not for nothing does Lincoln contrast Douglas' "round, jolly, fruitful face," a symbol of political patronage, against his own "poor, lean, lank, face" of principle (II, 506). Technically, the Lincoln-Douglas debates of 1858 are fought out upon the question of whether or not a majority can define and, hence, limit the nature and scope of fundamental liberties, whether or not a people who want slavery may establish it in their midst simply by voting for it. As a matter of positive law, Douglas finds such a power, basing his argument on the latest compromise resolutions of Congress and the *Dred Scott* decision of the Supreme Court. "All you have a right to ask is that the people shall do as they please," Douglas tells his audiences; "if they want slavery let them have it; if they do not want it, allow them to refuse to encourage it" (III, 325). As a matter of basic principle, Lincoln denies that the fundamental liberties of a minority can be legislated away in this manner. To be able to do so reduces the "once glorious" Declaration of Independence to "a mere wreck" and "mangled ruin" (II, 406). At issue is not a political decision of the moment but "the eternal struggle between these two principles—right and wrong—throughout the world" (III, 315). By encouraging the possibility of slavery among any majority that wants it, Douglas is "blowing out the moral lights around us." He is "penetrating the human soul and eradicating the light of reason and the love of liberty in this American people" (III, 29).

Defeat in the election of 1858 inevitably increases these apprehensions. Influence has defeated the sacred principles of republicanism (III, 27; II, 547). "But soberly," writes Lincoln a year later, "it is now no child's play to save the principles of Jefferson from total overthrow in this nation" (III, 375). His Cooper Institute Address in New York early in 1860, the speech that wins an eastern following overnight and the Republican presidental nomination three months later, is one more attempt to dramatize and fix "our moral, social, and political responsibilities."[10] Again, Lincoln condemns Douglas' "sophistical contrivances"; they are "reversing the divine rule" by "groping for some middle ground between the right and the wrong." Moreover, the uncertainties that such contrivances have engendered make a new assertion of faith imperative. "LET US HAVE FAITH THAT RIGHT MAKES MIGHT," Lincoln concludes, "AND IN THAT FAITH, LET US, TO THE END, DARE TO DO OUR DUTY AS WE UNDERSTAND IT" (III, 550).

That Lincoln's positions on slavery and civil rights are more in keeping with a modern view than those of Douglas should not disguise the fact that his legal thought is more traditional. Douglas, the legal positivist, supports existing legislative and judicial remedies as the only acceptable standards of control. Lincoln, on the other hand, believes that "he who moulds public sentiment, goes deeper than he who enacts statutes or pronounces decisions" (III, 27). He places the debate (and the Union itself) on the level of universal values or natural rights, *beyond* the convenient artifice of men, and his extraordinary rise to prominence between 1858 and 1860 suggests that many Americans agreed with him. The moral crisis over slavery turns back the clock in legal thought for a moment in time; it allows a classic generalist to circumvent modern legal positivism just long enough to make a last contribution to the axioms of American republicanism. By insisting that positive or man-made law remains subject to a higher norm, Lincoln bolsters a dwindling, old-fashioned faith in constitutionalism while accommodating a new rise in reformist zeal and religious revivalism in the 1850s. Indeed,

the balanced complexity of the appeal defines the presidency that
follows.

Lincoln enters the White House in 1861 with an almost mystical
faith in the law, great powers of eloquence, a presumption of change,
and the determination to protect the national ideal through a proper
and necessary re-articulation of principle. He looks to the Declaration of Independence for guidance; it is "the sheet anchor of American republicanism" because it contains "the principle of 'Liberty
to all' " or "*the* word, *'fitly spoken'* "; it is the "apple of gold," with
the Union and the Constitution as "the *picture* of *silver*, subsequently
framed around it." Lincoln's priorities are clear: "The *picture* was
made *for* the apple—*not* the apple for the picture." His mission,
and that of every other American, must be to "act, that neither
picture, or *apple* shall ever be blurred, or bruised or broken" (II, 266;
IV, 169). His problem as president is that the picture *has* been blurred
and the apple perhaps bruised. As he assesses the difficulty in 1864:
"The world has never had a good definition of the word liberty,
and the American people, just now, are much in want of one. We
all declare for liberty; but in using the same *word* we do not all mean
the same *thing*" (VII, 301). The greatest utterances of the Lincoln
presidency seek a solution to this problem, namely, the precise
relation between liberty and law or how men will articulate the
meaning and scope of liberty. The overall issue is the same as in
1858. But Lincoln now speaks from a better platform and against
the dramatic backdrop of the Civil War, and he has discovered from
the Lincoln-Douglas debates that his real goal must be to place the
whole matter *above* debate.

In a first step, Lincoln reaffirms his previous assertions. Americans must accept the statement that all men are created equal as
"the great fundamental principle upon which our free institutions
rest," and they must recognize the Declaration of Independence—
"*that immortal emblem of Humanity*" and "majestic interpretation of
the economy of the Universe"—as the temporal embodiment of an
eternal ideal (III, 327; II, 546–547). The president-elect reinforces
these earlier statements on his way to Washington in February of
1861. At Philadelphia, in Independence Hall, the Declaration becomes not only the fountain of all meaningful political thought but
also the source of "hope to the world for all future time." And,
significantly, Lincoln couches his comments in the form of an oath

before "Almighty God," an oath that mentions and then repeats the prospect of his own personal sacrifice in the name of principle (IV, 240–241). Others have pondered this sudden "note of fathomless emotion" and recourse to divine sanction, but more can be said about the method involved.[11] The new president's heightened language instinctively combines legal abstraction and religious feeling in different and powerful ways.

Lincoln has learned that belief and not reason must support his hope for a universally accepted definition of liberty. Unfortunately, disputants will not agree over vital issues that are left to logic. "The plainest print cannot be read through a gold eagle," he observes in recognition of the economics that cut across principle in discussions of slavery (II, 409). Then, too, his debates with Douglas have convinced him that knowledge alone will not bring better understanding. "One would start with great confidence that he could convince any sane child that the simpler propositions of Euclid are true," Lincoln writes soon after, in 1859; "but, nevertheless, he would fail, utterly, with one who should deny the definitions and axioms." The election of 1858 has turned upon just such a denial and evasion of "the definitions and axioms of free society" (III, 375). The people must transcend themselves to accept a communal imperative against self-interest, and the Civil War, with its heightened imperatives, accentuates the requirement. Liberty may indeed guarantee individual development and national prosperity—frequent assumptions in Lincolnian rhetoric—but these assumptions neither justify nor explain ultimate sacrifice, the appalling human losses of the war itself. Lincoln, who speaks often of the soldier and his family, responds by bringing his policies "in consonance with [God's] will" and by conflating a "precious birthright of civil and religious liberty" (VI, 39–40). So compelling is this fusion of faith and politics for the wartime president that he actually contemplates an amendment that would insert God into the Constitution.[12]

In effect, Lincoln reshapes the doctrine of separation of church and state for his own times and purposes. Jefferson, Adams, and the other lawyer-writers of the early republic used the doctrine to disenfranchise their natural enemy, the clergy, in discussions of public policy. But the factors that enabled this act of displacement— natural law theory, the voice of reason, the secular aspirations of the Enlightenment, and the fear of an established church—no longer

dominate intellectual thought in 1861. In the interim, rational discourse has failed to resolve sectional strife. Evangelistic Protestant-
ism and revivalism in general have become ever more powerful
catalysts in the progressive democratization of American culture,
and the ministry's leadership of the antislavery movement has enabled it to regain a prominent role in political debate.[13] Lincoln rides
the crest of a clerical abolitionism, and his appeal must be understood
in terms of a deliberate amalgamation of rational, legal statement
and moral, religious fervor. He surpasses all other American spokesmen because he alone manages to unite the two separate strands of
American oratory, law and religion, in a truly encompassing eloquence.

Several things are crucial here. By combining legal and religious
impulses, Lincoln brings the lawyer-writer back to the primary
source of all thought; he revitalizes the constitutive orientation of
the intellectual toward the sacred.[14] Strength flows from his virtually
unique ability to wrap political explanation in divine mystery:

> God wills this contest, and wills that it shall not end yet. By his mere
> quiet power, on the minds of the now contestants, He could have
> either *saved* or *destroyed* the Union without a human contest. Yet the
> contest began. And having begun He could give the final victory to
> either side any day. Yet the contest proceeds.   (v, 404)

Lincoln himself partakes of this mystery—"So true is it that man
proposes, and God disposes"—by making himself "an humble instrument in the hands of the Almighty" (VII, 301; IV, 236, 190). He
preempts the ministry where earlier lawyer-writers from Jefferson
to Stephen Douglas simply rejected it. Accordingly, when the radical clergy try to seize the initiative on emancipation, Lincoln dis-
arms them with a humor that depends upon his own preconceived
language of mission:

> I hope that it will not be irreverent for me to say that if it is probable
> that God would reveal his will to others, on a point so connected with
> my duty, it might be supposed he would reveal it directly to me; . . . it
> is my earnest desire to know the will of Providence in this matter.
> (v, 420)

God's chosen instrument should not be superseded even by the
church and will not brook interference. As the first Annual Message
to Congress warns everyone, a single mind *must* control the ship of
state (v, 51).

Ultimately, however, the use of religious language has less to do
with political vantage points than it does with the compulsions to
believe and to convince others. Lincoln cannot bear the possibility
of a meaningless war. The president-elect's great unpublished fragment on the Constitution and the Union begins with the controlling
assumption that "all this is not the result of accident. It has a philosophical cause" (IV, 168). Later, anguishing over the double horrors
of slaughter and failure, he concludes, "We cannot but believe, that
he who made the world still governs it" (V, 478). "I have been driven
many times upon my knees," he tells the newspaperman Noah
Brooks, "by the overwhelming conviction that I had nowhere else
to go."[15] Out of this conviction, a message to be communicated at
all cost, comes the vital connection between God's inscrutable purposes and the known plan of the Union. "Let us diligently apply
the means," runs a typical passage from 1863, "never doubting that
a just God, in his own good time, will give us the rightful result"
(VI, 411). Such language invites consent rather than response. Since
the necessary thrust of an appeal to belief is toward orthodoxy, the
premises that a listener accepts on faith ("never doubting") must not
be questioned. Lincoln's two greatest public efforts assume this
form. The Gettysburg Address and the Second Inaugural Address
are not just religious statements. They are formal benedictions that
foreclose all possibility of reply, speeches that end all speech within
the oratorical tradition of American literature.[16]

In an age when the speech lasts two hours, neither of Lincoln's
two masterpieces fills five minutes (VII, 22–23; VIII, 332–333). Both
deprecate the spoken word ("The world will little note, nor long
remember what we say here," "Little that is new here could be
presented"), and each minimizes the speaker.[17] The first-person singular pronoun appears just once, in the first paragraph of the Second
Inaugural Address, and then only as a parenthetical expression.
Lincoln virtually ignores his audiences of the moment, and he has
little interest in an "immediately popular" effect (VIII, 356; VII, 24).
His language appears abstract, biblical, muted. It reaches for scope
("this continent," "the world," "the earth," "all nations") and toward
a permanence that is revealed in the order of things ("The Almighty
has His own purposes"). And yet this deliberate tapping of eternal
truths works because Lincoln maintains the firmest sense of relevance and context. His stated purpose always is to be practical while
remaining just and constitutional (VI, 370). He avoids the "merely

pernicious abstraction" and needless controversy by refusing the question that "has not been, nor yet is, a practically material one" (VIII, 402–403).

In other words, the spiritual leader continues to accept the pragmatic focus of the courtroom advocate. If the former argues that "men should utter nothing for which they would not willingly be responsible through time and in eternity," the lawyer in Lincoln knows that this will never happen and that one must always argue the case at hand (V, 535). The latter recognizes that every crisis takes place in a murky present that resists the permanent and the eternal. Of leaders in every event "we shall have as weak, and as strong; as silly and as wise; as bad and good," and, therefore, the man of vision still studies every particular for itself as part of an accumulating record "to learn wisdom from" (VIII, 101). There could hardly be a better definition of how the legal system is supposed to work. An appreciation of process balances vision, and never more so than in Lincoln's understanding of the central concept of liberty. On one level, liberty is a fixed ideal in the overall plan of the universe. On another, it must be treated as a practical tool within the realm of expedience. In declaring all men equal—"equal in 'certain inalienable rights, among which are life, liberty, and the pursuit of happiness' "—the Founders did not "confer" these elements as matters of fact. "They meant simply to declare the *right*, so that the *enforcement* of it might follow as fast as circumstances should permit" (II, 406). Lincoln the ideologue never forgets the power of circumstance, and his language, at its best, blends the ideal with the possible. This curious mixture of intellectual largesse and restraint supplies much of the precise emotive power in the two speeches that everyone remembers.

The Gettysburg Address welds the two notions of fundamental liberty and human equality together in a definition of country. "Four score and seven years ago our fathers brought forth on this continent, a new nation, conceived in Liberty, and dedicated to the proposition that all men are created equal"—conceived *then*, in 1776, in Liberty but dedicated *now*, forward in time, in the demonstration or proof of the proposition that all men are created equal.[18] This bond of principles, which holds past, present, and future together, allows the speaker to pose "a new birth of freedom" through the continuing dedication of the living, who must complete "the unfinished work" that the soldiers at Gettysburg "have thus far so nobly advanced." Characteristically fusing religious and political themes, Lincoln allows the notions of sacrifice and redemption ("those who here gave their lives that that nation might live") to stand simultaneously for the spiritual rebirth of the individual and the preservation of democracy in the larger life of the nation.[19] In both senses, "those dead shall not have died in vain." It is "under God" that Americans will experience their new birth of freedom and that, in an echo from Daniel Webster, "that government of the people, by the people, for the people, shall not perish from the earth."[20]

The Second Inaugural Address then makes the Civil War the direct consequence of an *insufficient* dedication to the principle of equality. Slavery is "the *cause* of the conflict." Lincoln, without condemning the South ("Let us judge not that we be not judged") calls the defense of slavery both an aberration against republican principle and a cosmic "offence" worthy of divine punishment. "It may seem strange that any men should dare to ask a just God's assistance in wringing their bread from the sweat of other men's faces." The war comes "as the woe due to those by whom the offence came," and it has continuing meaning for all as an act of purification:

> If God wills that [this mighty scourge of war] continue . . . until every drop of blood drawn with the lash, shall be paid by another drawn with the sword . . . so still it must be said "the judgments of the Lord, are true and righteous altogether."

On such a stage, mutual compassion and renewed belief in the proper principles of the moral and social order are the only plausible human reactions. And so the moving peroration:

> With malice toward none; with charity for all; with firmness in the right, as God gives us to see the right, let us strive on to finish the work we are in; to bind up the nation's wounds . . . to do all which may achieve and cherish a just, and a lasting peace, among ourselves, and with all nations.

The many voices of a national leadership speak as one here. All the sources of American thought recombine. Lincoln is the spiritual leader correcting and then blessing his congregation in benediction, the Ciceronian orator defining his country, and, not least, the lawyer-politician acting out his highest social role, that of peacemaker.[21] One of these voices, and thereby all, reaches every American.

NOTES

Prologue to Part I

1. *M'Fingal* was the favorite American poem until Longfellow's *Evangeline* appeared in 1847. Adams wrote to thank Trumbull for the final, expanded version of 1782. See Victor E. Gimmestad, *John Trumbull* (New York: Twayne, 1974), p. 105, and Alexander Cowie, *John Trumbull, Connecticut Wit* (Chapel Hill: University of North Carolina Press, 1936), pp. 181–182.

2. For a brief account of Adams' role in *M'Fingal* and for Trumbull's comment on composition, see Gimmestad, *John Trumbull*, pp. 84–88. For evidence from 1774, the year of Trumbull's clerkship, that Trumbull was an intimate in political discussions in the Adams circle, that his talent as a poet was much admired at the time, and that Adams was interested in encouraging literary satires on the political events of the day, see L. H. Butterfield, ed., *Diary and Autobiography of John Adams*, 4 vols. (1961; rpt. New York: Atheneum Press, 1964), II, 85–86; L. H. Butterfield, ed., *Adams Family Correspondence* (Cambridge, Mass.: Harvard University Press, 1963–   ), I, 98; and Charles Francis Adams, ed., *The Life and Works of John Adams*, 10 vols. (Boston: Little, Brown, 1850–1856), IX, 334. See also the exchange of letters between Adams and Trumbull from November 1775 in Robert J. Taylor, ed., *Papers of John Adams* (Cambridge, Mass.: Harvard University Press, 1979), III, 278–279, 298–301.

3. John Adams to John Trumbull, April 28, 1785, contained in full in *Historical Magazine*, 4 (July 1860), 195. (Emphasis added.) See also John Adams to Benjamin Waterhouse, April 24, 1785, in Adrienne Koch and William Peden, eds., *Selected Writings of John and John Quincy Adams* (New York: Alfred A. Knopf, 1946), p. 72.

4. Robert E. Spiller, Willard Thorpe, Thomas H. Johnson, Henry Seidel Canby, and Richard M. Ludwig, *Literary History of the United States,*

3rd edition, rev. (New York: Macmillan, 1963), pp. 130, 121. For a good recent discussion of these problems, see William Hedges, "The Myth of the Republic and the Theory of American Literature," *Prospects: An Annual of American Cultural Studies*, 4 (1979), 101–120.

5. Ezra Pound, *Guide to Kulchur* (1938; rpt. New York: New Directions, 1952), pp. 184, 254, 264.

6. For good examples of Adams' early literary resolutions and comments on writing, see *Diary and Autobiography of John Adams*, I, 84, 168, 255. The quotation is from "A Dissertation on the Canon and Feudal Law," *The Life and Works of John Adams*, III, 448–449, 462.

7. "Out of forty of the more important critics of the day, twenty had been trained for the law." William Charvat, *The Origins of American Critical Thought, 1810-1835* (Philadelphia: University of Pennsylvania Press, 1936), pp. 5–6. For a quick summary of the lawyer's dominance of early journals, see Frank Luther Mott, *A History of American Magazines, 1741–1850* (New York: Appleton, 1930), pp. 154–156.

8. Typical of the period, the quotation is from Sir William Jones (1746–1794) as it appeared in Lord Teignmouth [Sir John Shore], *Memoirs of the Life, Writings, and Correspondence of Sir William Jones* (Philadelphia: W. M. Poyntell, 1805), pp. 130, 125–127. Similar comments appeared in the prefaces of Jones's books. Jones, the English jurist, poet, and linguist, was an important influence on Americans of the Revolutionary generation, and Teignmouth's later biography made him a model for decades. See Robert A. Ferguson, "The Emulation of Sir William Jones in the Early Republic," *New England Quarterly*, 52 (March 1979), 3–26.

9. For Trumbull's personal rejection of literature, see Cowie, *John Trumbull*, pp. 130–131, 207. For his acknowledgment to Adams of the limits of satiric verse and his comment on John Quincy Adams' poetry, see John Trumbull to John Adams, April 27, 1793, quoted in Gimmestad, *John Trumbull*, pp. 120, 142. See also John Quincy Adams, "Justice: An Ode," *Poems of Religion and Society* (New York: William H. Graham, 1850), p. 98.

10. Edward Waldo Emerson and Waldo Emerson Forbes, eds., *Journals of Ralph Waldo Emerson*, 10 vols. (Boston: Houghton Mifflin, 1909–1914), VIII, 339.

11. Donald Davie, "American Literature: The Canon," *Trying to Explain* (Ann Arbor: University of Michigan Press, 1979), pp. 187–198.

12. Hedges, "The Myth of the Republic and the Theory of American Literature," *Prospects*, 110.

13. Charles Warren, *A History of the American Bar* (1911; rpt. New York: Howard Fertig, 1966); Richard Beale Davis, "The Early American Lawyer and the Profession of Letters," *Huntington Library Quarterly*, 12

(February 1949), 191–205; Perry Miller, ed., *The Legal Mind in America from Independence to the Civil War* (Garden City, N.Y.: Doubleday, 1962); Perry Miller, *The Life of the Mind in America from the Revolution to the Civil War* (New York: Harcourt, Brace, and World, 1965); Richard Beale Davis, *Intellectual Life in Jefferson's Virginia, 1790–1830* (Knoxville: University of Tennessee Press, 1972); and John P. McWilliams, Jr., *Political Justice in a Republic: James Fenimore Cooper's America* (Berkeley: University of California Press, 1972).

14. Miller, *The Life of the Mind in America*, pp. 93–95, 100, 121–124, 133–138. For only the most recent works exploring relationships between literature and religion, see Sacvan Bercovitch, *The American Jeremiad* (Madison: University of Wisconsin Press, 1978); Ann Douglas, *The Feminization of American Culture* (New York: Alfred A. Knopf, 1977); Michael T. Gilmore, *The Middle Way: Puritanism and Ideology in American Romantic Fiction* (New Brunswick, N.J.: Rutgers University Press, 1977); and Giles Gunn, *The Interpretation of Otherness: Literature, Religion, and the American Imagination* (New York: Oxford University Press, 1979).

15. James Willard Hurst's exposure of the weaknesses in traditional hermetic studies of constitutional law and his call in 1960 for more useful definitions of law in terms of social functions has produced a harvest of important interdisciplinary studies in legal history in the 1970s. The books of Lawrence Friedman, Morton Horwitz, and William Nelson, among others, all seek, in Friedman's words, to treat American law "as a mirror of society" because "legal history is a way of studying the general history of the country's character and development." The rejection of singular dramatic cases as the basis of study in favor of examination of the regular instances in which law, economy, and society interact has yielded a degree of "transformation" in law and a level of integration in cultural values previously unrecognized. James Willard Hurst, "The Law in United States History," *Proceedings of the American Philosophical Society*, 104 (1960), 518–526; Lawrence M. Friedman, *A History of American Law* (New York: Simon and Schuster, 1973), pp. 10, 23; Morton J. Horwitz, *The Transformation of American Law, 1780–1860* (Cambridge, Mass.: Harvard University Press, 1977); William E. Nelson, *Americanization of the Common Law: The Impact of Legal Change on Massachusetts Society, 1760–1830* (Cambridge, Mass.: Harvard University Press, 1975); Stanley N. Katz, "Introduction," *A Brief Narrative of the Case and Trial of John Peter Zenger* (Cambridge, Mass.: Harvard University Press, 1972), pp. 1–35; Maxwell Bloomfield, *American Lawyers in a Changing Society, 1776–1876* (Cambridge, Mass.: Harvard University Press, 1976); and G. Edward White, *The American Judicial Tradition: Profiles of Leading American Judges* (New York: Oxford University Press, 1976).

16. Richard M. Weaver, "The Spaciousness of Old Rhetoric," *The Ethics of Rhetoric* (Chicago: Henry Regnery, 1953), pp. 164–185.

17. Anton-Hermann Chroust, *The Rise of the Legal Profession in America*, 2 vols. (Norman: University of Oklahoma Press, 1965), II, 285.

18. For the importance of law as the transcendent idea supplying unity in Enlightenment thought, see Ernest Cassirer, "Law, State, and Society," *The Philosophy of the Enlightenment*, trans. Fritz C. A. Koelln and James P. Pettegrove (Princeton, N.J.: Princeton University Press, 1951), pp. 238–242. As a product of the Enlightenment, American legal thought has always been concerned with "the formulation and application of integrating ideas to bring values into some ordered pattern." James Willard Hurst, *Law and Social Order in the United States* (Ithaca, N.Y.: Cornell University Press, 1977), pp. 47–48.

19. Alexis de Tocqueville, *Democracy in America*, 2 vols. (1835; rpt. New York: Alfred A. Knopf, 1945), II, 166–167.

1. In America the Law Is King

1. Thomas Paine, *Common Sense*, in Philip S. Foner, ed., *The Complete Writings of Thomas Paine*, 2 vols. (New York: Citadel Press, 1945), I, 29. Bernard Bailyn, "General Introduction: The Transforming Radicalism of the American Revolution," *Pamphlets of the American Revolution* (Cambridge, Mass.: Harvard University Press, 1965), I, 26–27, 18, 409–417.

2. Daniel J. Boorstin, *The Americans: The Colonial Experience* (New York: Random House, 1958), p. 205.

3. Daniel J. Boorstin, "Preface to the Beacon Press Edition," *The Mysterious Science of the Law: An Essay on Blackstone's Commentaries Showing How Blackstone . . . Made of the Law at Once a Conservative and a Mysterious Science* (Boston: Beacon Press, 1958).

4. Edward Shils, "Intellectuals in the Political Development of New States," *The Intellectuals and the Powers and Other Essays* (Chicago: University of Chicago Press, 1972), pp. 392–393, and Seymour Martin Lipset, "Establishing National Identity," in *The First New Nation: The United States in Historical and Comparative Perspective* (1963; rpt. Garden City, N.Y.: Doubleday, 1967), pp. 17–26.

5. Boorstin, *The Americans: The Colonial Experience*, pp. 196–197. See Charles Robert McKurdy, "Lawyers in Crisis: The Massachusetts Legal Profession, 1760–1790," Ph.D. diss., Northwestern University, 1969, pp. 7–8, 23–35; and Thomas R. Meehan, "Courts, Cases, and Counselors in Revolutionary and Post-Revolutionary Pennsylvania," *Pennsylvania Magazine of History and Biography*, 91 (January 1967), 3–34. For a summary of early American prejudice against the legal profession and the lawyer's rapid

rise in the eighteenth century, see Lawrence M. Friedman, *A History of American Law* (New York: Simon and Schuster, 1973), pp. 10, 23.

6. L. H. Butterfield, ed., *Diary and Autobiography of John Adams*, 4 vols. (1961; rpt. New York: Atheneum Press, 1964), I, 43, 138, 184, 196. See also L. Kinvin Wroth and Hiller B. Zobel, eds., *Legal Papers of John Adams*, 3 vols. (Cambridge, Mass.: Harvard University Press, 1965), I, lii–lvii.

7. Robert A. East, *John Quincy Adams: The Critical Years, 1785–1794* (New York: Bookman Associates, 1962), pp. 64–65; William Wirt, "Letter VIII," *The Letters of the British Spy* (1803; rpt. New York: Harper and Brothers, 1844), p. 206; Alexis de Tocqueville, *Democracy in America*, 2 vols. (1835; rpt. New York: Alfred A. Knopf, 1945), I, 272–273.

8. My thought and language here owe much to Bernard Bailyn, *The Ideological Origins of the American Revolution* (Cambridge, Mass.: Harvard University Press, 1967), pp. 20, 3–31, 76–79.

9. Harry Levin, "Preface," *Refractions: Essays in Comparative Literature* (New York: Oxford University Press, 1966), ix–x.

10. J. G. A. Pocock, *The Ancient Constitution and the Feudal Law: A Study of English Historical Thought in the Seventeenth Century* (1957; rpt. New York: W. W. Norton, 1967), pp. 30–55, 232–233, 241; Pocock, *Politics, Language and Time: Essays on Political Thought and History* (New York: Atheneum Press, 1973), pp. 124–126; and Pocock, *The Machiavellian Moment: Florentine Political Thought and the Atlantic Republican Tradition* (Princeton, N.J.: Princeton University Press, 1975), pp. 506–552. The quotation on the Glorious Revolution is from G. M. Trevelyan, *The English Revolution, 1688–1689* (1938; rpt. New York: Oxford University Press, 1967), p. 71. For a complete account of the lawyer's crucial role in the Revolutionary Settlement of 1688, see Michael Landon, *The Triumph of the Lawyers: Their Role in English Politics, 1678–1689* (University, Ala.: University of Alabama Press, 1970).

11. Thomas Jefferson, " 'Original Rough Draught' of the Declaration of Independence," and "A Summary View of the Rights of British America, 1774," in Julian P. Boyd, ed., *The Papers of Thomas Jefferson*, 19 vols. (Princeton, N.J.: Princeton University Press, 1950–), I, 424, 121–137. For an excellent general placement of the "Whig science of politics" within the context of the American republic, see Gordon S. Wood, *The Creation of the American Republic, 1776–1787* (1969; rpt. New York: W. W. Norton, 1972), pp. 3–45.

12. Landon, *The Triumph of the Lawyers*, p. 246.

13. William Blackstone, *Commentaries on the Laws of England*, 4 vols. (1765–1769; rpt. Chicago: University of Chicago Press, 1979), I, 4, 35, and IV, 400–436.

14. Blackstone, "Of the Nature of Laws in General," *Commentaries*, I,

41. Blackstone, of course, relies upon the explicit assumptions of the linkage between natural law and civic order as seen by John Locke and other social contract theorists.

15. Thomas Paine, *Common Sense*, in Foner, ed., *The Complete Writings of Thomas Paine*, I, 43, 25, 37, 29, 31, 6.

16. "Why have I not Genius to start some new Thought. Some thing that will surprize the World," Adams wondered in 1759—*Diary and Autobiography of John Adams*, I, 95. For an excellent study of Adams' intellectual strengths and weaknesses and his representative qualities overall, see Edmund S. Morgan, *The Meaning of Independence: John Adams, George Washington, Thomas Jefferson* (New York: W. W. Norton, 1976), pp. 3–25.

17. The quotations in the following two paragraphs are all from *A Dissertation on the Canon and Feudal Law*, in Charles Francis Adams, ed., *The Life and Works of John Adams*, 10 vols. (Boston: Little, Brown, 1850–1856), III, 445–464.

18. Carl Bridenbaugh, *Mitre and Sceptre: Transatlantic Faiths, Ideas, Personalities, and Politics* (New York: Oxford University Press, 1962), p. 307. For a more recent and detailed account of the development of a secular or civil millennialism in the early republic and an explanation of the ways in which the clergy adjusted to its diminished role, see Nathan O. Hatch, *The Sacred Cause of Liberty: Republican Thought and the Millennium in Revolutionary New England* (New Haven: Yale University Press, 1977).

19. Thomas Jefferson to John Adams, May 5, 1817, and John Adams to Thomas Jefferson, May 18, 1817, in *The Adams-Jefferson Letters: The Complete Correspondence Between Thomas Jefferson and Abigail and John Adams*, ed. Lester J. Cappon, 2 vols. (Chapel Hill: University of North Carolina Press, 1959), II, 512–515.

20. See, for example, Quentin Skinner, *The Foundations of Modern Political Thought*, 2 vols. (New York: Cambridge University Press, 1978), I, 201–208; II, 123–134.

21. John C. Fitzpatrick, ed., *The Writings of George Washington from the Original Manuscript Sources, 1745–1799*, 39 vols. (Washington, D.C.: U.S. Government Printing Office, 1931–1944), VI, 112, 137, 155, 422; XIX, 131.

22. "Minutes of Debate in the First United States Senate," *Diary and Autobiography of John Adams*, III, 219. For the classic and single most effective criticism of the Society of the Cincinnati, see Thomas Jefferson's letter to an uncertain George Washington. TJ to George Washington, April 16, 1784, in Boyd, ed., *The Papers of Thomas Jefferson*, VII, 105–110, and TJ to James Madison, December 28, 1794, in Andrew A. Lipscomb and Albert E. Bergh, eds., *The Writings of Thomas Jefferson*, 20 vols. (Washington, D.C.: Thomas Jefferson Memorial Association, 1905), IX, 294–295. More generally, see Edwin A. Miles, "The Whig Party and the Menace of Caesar,"

Tennessee Historical Quarterly, 27 (Winter 1968), 361–379; Stephen Botein, "Cicero as Role Model for Early American Lawyers: A Case Study in Classical 'Influence,' " *Classical Journal*, 73 (Spring 1978), 313–321; and Howard Mumford Jones, "Roman Virtue," *O Strange New World: American Culture, the Formative Years* (New York: Viking Press, 1964), pp. 227–272.

23. James Thomas Flexner, *George Washington*, 4 vols. (Boston: Little, Brown, 1965), II, 491–508, 522–528, III, 63–68, 235, and *Writings of George Washington*, XXIX, 70–72, 113–116, 151–153, 170–172, 186–188.

24. For John Trumbull's remarks on Washington's "Circular to the States" and a claim for his own important role, see his letter to John Adams, July 8, 1805, quoted in Victor E. Gimmestad, *John Trumbull* (New York: Twayne, 1974), p. 109. For Hamilton's extensive advice and redrafting of Washington's farewell address, see *Writings of George Washington*, XXIX, 48–61, 178, 190–192, 214–238.

25. For the history of judicial review in America before John Marshall's decision established the doctrine in the federal courts in *Marbury v. Madison*, 1 *Cranch* 137, 2 *United States Supreme Court Reports, Lawyers' Edition*, 60 (1803), see Julius Goebel, Jr., *Antecedents and Beginnings to 1801, in* Paul A. Freund, ed., *History of the Supreme Court of the United States*, 9 vols. (New York: Macmillan, 1971), I, 50–95, 125–142, 209, 227, 301–302, 338, 589–592, 704–707, 778–784. See also William E. Nelson, "Changing Conceptions of Judicial Review: The Evolution of Constitutional Theory in the States, 1790–1860," *University of Pennsylvania Law Review*, 120 (June 1972), 1166–85. For John Adams' early views on judicial review at the time of the Stamp Act crisis, see *Diary and Autobiography of John Adams*, I, 263–270.

26. St. George Tucker, *Blackstone's Commentaries: with notes of Reference, to The Constitution and Laws, of the Federal Government of the United States; and of the Commonwelath of Virginia*, 5 vols. (Philadelphia: William Y. Birch and Abraham Small, 1803), I, 76.

27. Hamilton, "Federalist No. 85," in Alexander Hamilton, John Jay, and James Madison, *The Federalist: A Commentary on the Constitution of the United States, Being a Collection of Essays written in Support of the Constitution agreed upon September 17, 1787, by the Federal Convention* (1787–1788; rpt. New York: Random House, 1937), pp. 570–574. Later references to *The Federalist* will be to this edition.

28. Hamilton, "Federalist No. 85," "Federalist No. 82," *The Federalist*, pp. 574, 534.

29. James Madison, "Federalist No. 37," *The Federalist*, pp. 226, 229.

30. James Wilson, *Lectures on Law Delivered in the College of Philadelphia in the Years one thousand seven hundred and ninety, and one thousand seven hundred and ninety one*, in Robert Green McCloskey, ed., *The Works of James Wilson*,

2 vols. (Cambridge, Mass.: Harvard University Press, 1967), 1, 330–331.

31. Hamilton, "Federalist No. 83," *The Federalist*, p. 539.

32. A description of Marshall's attitude on case citation is contained in Leonard Baker, *John Marshall: A Life in Law* (New York: Macmillan, 1974), pp. 552–555. The best single description of Marshall's style and of the basis of his court decisions is in G. Edward White, "John Marshall and the Genesis of the Tradition," *The American Judicial Tradition: Profiles of Leading American Judges* (New York: Oxford University Press, 1976), pp. 9–12. For the classic analysis of the absence of citation in Marshall's major decisions, see Charles Warren, *A History of the American Bar* (Boston: Little, Brown, 1911), p. 403. The five cases Warren alludes to are *Marbury v. Madison*, *Cohens v. Virginia*, *McCulloch v. Maryland*, *The Dartmouth College Case*, and *Sturgis v. Crowninshield*. The connection between Marshall's concept of judicial review, his broad sense of republicanism, and his assumption that the Supreme Court was the guardian of the republic has been traced by Robert Kenneth Faulkner, *The Jurisprudence of John Marshall* (Princeton, N.J.: Princeton University Press, 1968), pp. 200–223.

33. Clifford Geertz, "Centers, Kings, and Charisma: Reflections on the Symbolics of Power," in Joseph Ben-David and Terry Nichols Clark, eds., *Culture and Its Creators: Essays in Honor of Edward Shils* (Chicago: University of Chicago Press, 1977), 150–171.

34. Thomas B. Wait to George Thatcher, November 27, 1787, in "The Thatcher Papers," *Historical Magazine*, 2nd series, 6 (November 1869), 258. See also Jackson Turner Main, *The Antifederalists: Critics of the Constitution, 1781–1788* (Chapel Hill: University of North Carolina Press, 1961), pp. 129 ff. For other relevant comments from various anti-federalists, see Cecelia M. Kenyon, ed., *The Antifederalists* (New York: Bobbs-Merrill, 1966), pp. 10–11, 209–214.

35. George Forgie, *Patricide in the House Divided: A Psychological Interpretation of Lincoln and His Age* (New York: W. W. Norton, 1979), p. 13. Forgie's references, in order, are to Edward Everett in 1826, Rufus Choate in 1850, the *Southern Quarterly Review* in 1842, and Alexis de Tocqueville in 1835.

36. Lipset, *The First New Nation*, p. 38. For other recent examinations of the precarious situation and uncertainties of early republicans, see John R. Howe, "Republican Thought and the Political Violence of the 1790's," *American Quarterly*, 19 (Summer 1967), 147–165, and more generally, James Sterling Young, *The Washington Community 1800–1828* (New York: Columbia University Press, 1966); Linda K. Kerber, *Federalists in Dissent: Imagery and Ideology in Jeffersonian America* (Ithaca, N.Y.: Cornell University Press, 1970); and Fred Somkin, *Unquiet Eagle: Memory and Desire in the Idea of American Freedom, 1815–1860* (Ithaca, N.Y.: Cornell University Press, 1967).

37. JA to TJ, June 28, 1812, *The Adams-Jefferson Letters*, II, 311; John

Quincy Adams to James Lloyd, October 1, 1822, in Worthington C. Ford, ed., *Writings of John Quincy Adams*, 7 vols. (New York: Macmillan, 1913–1917), VII, 311–313.

38. James Kent, "Address Delivered Before the Law Association of New York City, October 21, 1836," in William Kent, ed., *Memoirs and Letters of Chancellor James Kent* (Boston: Little, Brown, 1898), pp. 235–236.

39. "Eminent British Lawyers: A Review," *American Quarterly Review*, 12 (1832), 267.

40. Originally appeared in Hugh Swinton Legaré, "Codification," *Southern Review*, 7 (May to August, 1831), 411–412. See also Mary S. Legaré, ed., *Writings of Hugh Swinton Legaré*, 2 vols. (Charleston, S.C.: Burges and James, 1845), II, 501.

41. Joel Barlow, "Preface," *The Columbiad*, in William K. Bottorff and Arthur L. Ford, eds., *The Works of Joel Barlow*, 2 vols. (1825; rpt. Gainesville, Fla.: Scholars' Facsimiles and Reprints, 1970), II, 382.

42. Edward T. Channing, "Independence in Literary Pursuits, Phi Beta Kappa Address at Harvard College, August 27, 1818," reprinted in *Key Reporter*, 26 (Spring 1961), 4. More generally on this theme, see Russel Blaine Nye, "The Quest for a National Literature," *The Cultural Life of the New Nation, 1776–1830* (New York: Harper and Row, 1960), pp. 235–237.

43. Joseph Story, "Value and Importance of Legal Studies: A Discourse Pronounced at the Inauguration of the Author as Dane Professor of Law in Harvard University, August 25, 1829," in William W. Story, ed., *The Miscellaneous Writings of Joseph Story* (Boston: Little, Brown, 1852), pp. 527–529. See also Arthur E. Sutherland, "Joseph Story: 1829–1845," *The Law at Harvard: A History of Ideas and Men, 1817–1967* (Cambridge, Mass.: Harvard University Press, 1967), pp. 92–139.

44. Rufus Choate, "The Power of a State Developed by Mental Culture: A Lecture Delivered Before the Mercantile Library Association, November 18, 1844," and "The Position and Functions of the American Bar, as an Element of Conservatism in the State: An Address Delivered Before the Law School in Cambridge, July 3, 1845," in Samuel G. Brown, ed., *The Works of Rufus Choate with a Memoir of His Life*, 2 vols. (Boston: Little, Brown, 1862), I, 411, 414–438.

45. Kent, *Memoirs and Letters of James Kent*, pp. 24–27.

46. Timothy Walker, "Ways and Means of Professional Success, being the Substance of a Valedictory Address to the Graduates of the Law Class, in the Cincinnati College . . . delivered, March 2, 1839," *Western Law Journal*, 1 (September 1844), 545. Walker's impact upon law students from 1837 to 1905 is outlined briefly in Perry Miller, ed., *The Legal Mind in America from Independence to the Civil War* (Garden City, N.Y.: Doubleday, 1962), pp. 239–240.

47. James Kent, "An Introductory Lecture to a Course of Law Lec-

tures: Delivered November 17, 1794," reprinted in *Columbia Law Review*, 3 (May 1903), 330–343.

48. TJ to Dabney Terrell, February 26, 1821, in Lipscomb and Bergh, eds., *The Writings of Thomas Jefferson*, xv, 318–323; TJ to John Minor, August 30, 1814, in Paul Leicester Ford, ed., *The Works of Thomas Jefferson*, 12 vols. (New York: G. P. Putnam's Sons, 1905), xi, 420–426. See also Morris L. Cohen, "Thomas Jefferson Recommends a Course of Law Study," *University of Pennsylvania Law Review*, 119 (April 1971), 823–844.

49. David Hoffman, *A Course of Legal Study; Respectfully Addressed to the Students of Law in the United States* (Baltimore: Coale and Maxwell, 1817), pp. 1–40, 304, xii. For an indication of the importance of Hoffman's guide in the 1820s and 1830s, see Warren, *A History of the American Bar*, p. 540.

50. Samuel Knapp, *Biographical Sketches of Eminent Lawyers, Statesmen, and Men of Letters* (Boston: Richardson and Lord, 1821), pp. 22–23.

51. Howell J. Heaney, "Advice to a Law Student: A Letter of William Wirt," *American Journal of Legal History*, 2 (July 1958), 256–258.

52. Standards for becoming a lawyer varied enormously from one state to another between 1789 and 1820, but gradually, as James Willard Hurst has pointed out, "the tide of early-nineteenth-century democracy carried before it almost all previously existing standards of admission to the profession." For the complexities involved, see Hurst, *The Growth of American Law: The Law Makers* (Boston: Little, Brown, 1950), pp. 250, 249–375; Anton-Hermann Chroust, "Bar Organizations and Their Decline," *The Rise of the Legal Profession in America*, 2 vols. (Norman: University of Oklahoma Press, 1965), ii, 129–172; Maxwell Bloomfield, "Upgrading the Professional Image," *American Lawyers in a Changing Society, 1776–1876* (Cambridge, Mass.: Harvard University Press, 1976), pp. 136–190, Lawrence M. Friedman, *A History of American Law* (New York: Simon and Schuster, 1973), pp. 275–278. See also Charles M. Haar, ed., *The Golden Age of American Law* (New York: George Braziller, 1965).

53. John Quincy Adams, *Life in a New England Town: 1787–1788. Diary of John Quincy Adams, While a Student in the Office of Theophilus Parsons at Newburyport*, ed. Charles Francis Adams, Jr. (Boston: Little, Brown, 1903), pp. 42, 36, 111, 60–67, 133, 121, 158, 72.

54. Hopkinson is quoted in "Law and Lawyers," *Southern Review*, 3 (May 1829), 435.

55. For Rufus Choate's comments on John Quincy Adams in this paragraph, see "The Power of a State Developed by Mental Culture," in Brown, ed., *Life and Works of Rufus Choate*, i, 409. See also "Eminent British Lawyers: A Review," *American Quarterly Review*, 12 (1832), 268.

56. Boorstin, *The Mysterious Science of the Law*, pp. 3–4.

57. Kent, *Memoirs and Letters of Chancellor Kent*, p. 18.

58. Joseph Story, "Review of Hoffman's Course of Legal Study," *North American Review*, 6 (November 1817), 52.

59. TJ to Dr. Thomas Cooper, January 16, 1814, Lipscomb and Bergh, eds., *The Writings of Thomas Jefferson*, XIV, 54–63. The same letter deplored the appearance of what Jefferson called "Blackstone lawyers," practitioners who relied exclusively upon this one source.

60. See Robert A. Ferguson, "The Emulation of Sir William Jones in the Early Republic," *New England Quarterly*, 52 (March 1979), 1–26.

61. Sir William Jones, *An Essay on The Law of Bailments* in Lord Teignmouth [Sir John Shore], ed., *The Works of Sir William Jones*, 13 vols. (London: John Stockdale, 1807), VIII, 327–328, 455. See also Joseph Story, "Review of Hoffman's Course of Legal Study," *North American Review*, 6 (November 1817), 53.

62. [W. W. Fosdick], "The Profession of the Law," *Western Law Journal*, 7 (December 1849), 101.

63. Knapp, *Biographical Sketches of Eminent Lawyers, Statesmen, and Men of Letters*, p. 9, and Richard Hooker, *Of the Laws of Ecclesiastical Polity*, in W. Speed Hill, ed., *The Folger Library Edition of the Works of Richard Hooker*, 4 vols. (1593–1662; rpt. Cambridge, Mass.: Harvard University Press, 1977), I, 142.

2. Mysterious Obligation: Jefferson's *Notes on the State of Virginia*

1. Dumas Malone, *Jefferson the Virginian*, in *Jefferson and His Times*, 5 vols. (Boston: Little, Brown, 1948–1974), I, 376–379; Gilbert Chinard, *Thomas Jefferson: The Apostle of Americanism*, 2nd edition, rev. (Boston: Little, Brown, 1946), pp. 119–120, and Merrill D. Peterson, *Thomas Jefferson and the New Nation: A Biography* (New York: Oxford University Press, 1970), p. 249. Of course, all three writers appreciate the importance of *Notes* as a political, scientific, and historic document and as a crucial sourcebook for examining Jefferson's ideas.

2. TJ to James Madison, May 11, 1785, in Julian P. Boyd, ed., *The Papers of Thomas Jefferson*, 19 vols. (Princeton, N.J.: Princeton University Press, 1950–1974), VIII, 147–148. Cited hereafter as *Papers*. The Princeton edition, projected at sixty volumes, is now complete through 1791. For correspondence and works after this date, I use Andrew A. Lipscomb and Albert E. Bergh, eds., *The Writings of Thomas Jefferson*, 20 vols. (Washington, D.C.: Thomas Jefferson Memorial Association, 1905). Cited hereafter as *Writings*. I have modernized Jefferson's spellings.

3. Jefferson admonished each of his friends receiving a private copy of *Notes* to avoid all possibility of publication, and he placed inscriptions

to this effect in each copy. See *Papers*, VIII, 246. See also TJ to John Page, May 4, 1786, *Papers*, IX, 444.

4. For these disparaging comments, see in order, TJ to Rev. James Madison, August 13, 1787, *Papers*, XII, 31; TJ to James Madison, February 8, 1786, *Papers*, IX, 264–265; TJ to John Melish, December 10, 1814, *Writings*, XIV, 220; and TJ to Alexander Donald, September 17, 1787, *Papers*, XII, 133.

5. Jefferson began work on *Notes* in November 1780 but was interrupted by official duties as the wartime governor of Virginia. The bulk of the first draft was apparently written in August 1781, though Jefferson made further addenda in the autumn to complete it. In the winter of 1781–82 and again in the winter of 1783–84, he made revisions that trebled the size of the original draft. He used his extensive correspondence to collect additional data from friends. Further changes were completed in Paris before publication—a process Jefferson monitored carefully to insure accuracy. In later years, he kept a personal copy of the London edition of 1787 in which he made numerous marginalia. As late as 1810, he wrote of his plans to revise and enlarge *Notes* in a new edition. These facts can best be drawn from the collection of correspondence regarding *Notes* in E. Millicent Sowerby, *Catalogue of the Library of Thomas Jefferson*, 5 vols. (Washington, D.C.: U.S. Government Printing Office, 1952–1959), IV, 301–330. See also William Peden, "Introduction," *Notes on the State of Virginia* (1954; rpt. New York: Norton, 1972), xi–xxv.

6. William Charvat, *The Profession of Authorship in America, 1800–1870*, ed. Matthew J. Bruccoli (Columbus: Ohio State University Press, 1968), pp. 6–10.

7. For the pressures from Jefferson's circle of private readers, see Francis Hopkinson to TJ, November 18, 1784, *Papers*, VII, 535; Charles Thomson to TJ, March 6, 1785, *Papers*, VIII, 16; and George Wythe to TJ, January 10, 1786, *Papers*, IX, 165.

8. Jefferson knew that his own generous distribution of private copies in France was forcing the issue of publication regardless of the advice he sought from friends. See TJ to James Madison, September 1, 1785, *Papers*, VIII, 462.

9. For the encouragement of Adams and the ever-reliable Madison, see John Adams to TJ, May 22, 1785, *Papers*, VIII, 160, and James Madison to TJ, November 15, 1785, *Papers*, IX, 38. For Jefferson's impatience over delays and his concern over printing accuracy and his discreet interest in sales, see TJ to Abbé Morellet, July 2, 1787, *Papers*, XI, 529–530, and Jefferson's various letters to his publisher John Stockdale in *Papers*, XI, 107, 183, and XII, 488.

10. TJ to the Marquis de Chastellux, June 7, 1785, *Papers*, VIII, 184.

11. Marbois's list of twenty-two queries is contained in *Papers*, IV, 166–167.

12. Daniel J. Boorstin, "The Vagueness of the Land," *The Americans: The National Experience* (New York: Random House, 1965), pp. 221–274, particularly pp. 236–237.

13. Jean Piveteau, ed., "Buffon et la Méthode," *Oeuvres Philosophiques de Buffon* (Paris: Presses Universitaires de France, 1954), pp. 15, 22. See also Peter Gay, *The Enlightenment: An Interpretation*, 2 vols. (1969; rpt. New York: Norton, 1977), II, 152–156. For accounts of Jefferson's controversies with Buffon in *Notes*, see Marie Kimball, *Jefferson: War and Peace, 1776 to 1784* (New York: Coward-McCann, 1947), pp. 279–288, Ruth Henline, "A Study of *Notes on the State of Virginia* as an Evidence of Jefferson's Reaction Against the Theories of the French Naturalists," *Virginia Magazine of History and Biography*, 55 (July 1947), 233–246, and Lawrence Lane, "An Enlightened Controversy—Jefferson and Buffon," *Enlightenment Essays*, 3 (Spring 1972), 37–40.

14. Thomas Jefferson, *Notes on the State of Virginia*, ed. William Peden (1954; rpt. New York: Norton, 1972), p. 277. All future references in the text are to this edition.

15. *Papers*, XII, 31, and *Writings*, XIV, 220–221. For more specific evidence of Jefferson's belief that the minute observations of *Notes* would lead to general theories of solid foundation, see TJ to John W. Campbell, September 3, 1809, *Writings*, XII, 307, and TJ to Lewis Caleb Beck, July 16, 1824, *Writings*, XVI, 71–72.

16. James Madison to TJ, November 18, 1781, in William T. Hutchinson, William M. E. Rachal, and Robert A. Rutland, eds., *The Papers of James Madison*, 12 vols. (Chicago: University of Chicago Press, and Charlottesville: University Press of Virginia, 1962–   ), III, 307–308.

17. The historical facts in this paragraph and Jefferson's place within them are from Dumas Malone, *Jefferson the Virginian*, pp. 327–369. The "Resolution of the House of Delegates, June 12, 1781," seeking an investigation of Jefferson's conduct as governor and the belated "Resolution of Thanks to Jefferson by the Virginia General Assembly, December 12, 1781," are in *Papers*, VI, 88, 135–136.

18. For an interesting recent essay detailing Jefferson's feelings, see William J. Scheick, "Chaos and Imaginative Order in Thomas Jefferson's *Notes on the State of Virginia*," in J. A. Leo Lemay, ed., *Essays in Early Virginia Literature Honoring Richard Beale Davis* (New York: Burt Franklin, 1977), pp. 221–234. Jefferson's bitter comments concerning his situation at the time are in: TJ to James Monroe, May 20, 1782, *Papers*, VI, 184–185; TJ to George Washington, May 28, 1781, *Papers*, VI, 32–33; TJ to General Lafayette, August 4, 1781, *Papers*, VI, 111–

112; and TJ to Edmund Randolph, September 16, 1781, *Papers*, VI, 117–118.

19. TJ to the Chevalier D'Anmours, November 30, 1780, *Papers*, IV, 168.

20. "Autobiography," *Writings*, I, 90–91.

21. Quoted in Merrill D. Peterson, *Thomas Jefferson and the New Nation*, p. 263.

22. The best analysis of Jefferson's expertise in law is Edward Dumbauld, *Thomas Jefferson and the Law* (Norman: University of Oklahoma Press, 1978), pp. 10, 28, 33, 75, 88–120, 132–135.

23. Hugo Grotius, "Prolegomena: 1, 8, 9, 11," *De Jure Belli et Pacis*, trans. William Whewell, 3 vols. (Cambridge, Eng.: Cambridge University Press, 1853), I, 37, 44–46. See also Ernst Cassirer, *The Philosophy of the Enlightenment*, trans. Fritz C.A. Koelln and James P. Pettegrove (1951; rpt. Boston: Beacon Press, 1955), pp. 234–241.

24. Samuel von Pufendorf, *Of the Law of Nature and Nations*, trans. Basil Kennett, 4th edition (London: J. Walthoe, 1729), pp. 1–3 (Bk. 1, Ch. 1). See also Leonard Krieger, *The Politics of Discretion: Pufendorf and the Acceptance of Natural Law* (Chicago: University of Chicago Press, 1965), pp. 52–54.

25. Jean Jacques Burlamaqui, *The Principles of Natural and Politic Law*, trans. Thomas Nugent, 5th edition, 2 vols. (Cambridge, Mass.: Hilliard, 1807), I, 134–140 (Pt. 2, Ch. 6), II, 16–24 (Pt. 1, Ch. 3), II, 38–49 (Pt. 1, Ch. 7). For the impact of Burlamaqui's thought on Jefferson's writings, see Morton White, *The Philosophy of the American Revolution* (New York: Oxford University Press, 1978), pp. 39, 161–163, 188. See, more generally, Ray Forrest Harvey, *Jean Jacques Burlamaqui: A Liberal Tradition in American Constitutionalism* (Chapel Hill: University of North Carolina Press, 1957).

26. Baron de Montesquieu, *The Spirit of Laws*, trans. Thomas Nugent, 2 vols. (Cincinnati: Clarke, 1873), I, 5–8 (Bk. 1, Ch. 3); William Blackstone, "Introduction," *Commentaries on the Laws of England*, facsimile of the 1st edition of 1765–1769, 4 vols. (Chicago: University of Chicago Press, 1979), I, 35.

27. "Prolegomena: 40, 56, 59," *De Jure Belli et Pacis*, I, 66, 77–78.

28. *Of the Law of Nature and Nations*, p. 1.

29. Thomas Philbrick, "Thomas Jefferson," in Everett Emerson, ed., *American Literature 1764–1789: The Revolutionary Years* (Madison: University of Wisconsin Press, 1977), p. 162.

30. For the uncertainties involved in the literature of the early republic, see particularly William L. Hedges. "The Myth of the Republic and the Theory of American Literature," *Prospects: An Annual of American Cultural Studies*, 4 (1979), 101–120, and Lewis P. Simpson, "The Symbolism of Literary Alienation in the Revolutionary Age," in William C. Havard and

Joseph L. Bernd, eds., *200 Years of the Republic* (Charlottesville: University Press of Virginia, 1976), pp. 79–100.

31. Compare, for example, queries three and ten in *Notes on the State of Virginia* with Montesquieu's one-sentence chapters in *The Spirit of Laws*, I, 32 (Bk. 3, Ch. 11), II, 127 (Bk. 24, Ch. 12), and II, 140 (Bk. 25, Ch. 1).

32. "Prolegomena: 30, 41," *De Jure Belli et Pacis*, I, 60, 66–67.

33. *The Spirit of Laws*, I, 339 (Bk. 19, Ch. 4), and I, 5–8 (Bk. 1, Ch. 3).

34. Gay, *The Enlightenment: An Interpretation*, II, 324–325.

35. Gilbert Chinard, "Introduction," *The Commonplace Book of Thomas Jefferson: A Repertory of His Ideas on Government* (Baltimore: Johns Hopkins University Press, 1926), pp. 31–38, 257–296. Jefferson's praise of Montesquieu was qualified by the flaws he found in *The Spirit of Laws*, but his general admiration for the French legal theorist's ideas is clear from TJ to Thomas Mann Randolph, Jr., May 30, 1790, *Papers*, XVI, 449.

36. *The Spirit of Laws*, I, 7 (Bk. 1, Ch. 3).

37. *The Principles of Natural and Politic Law*, II, 58–61 (Pt. 2, Ch. 1), II, 68–71 (Pt. 2, Ch. 2), II, 145 (Pt. 3, Ch. 5) and *The Spirit of Laws*, I, 126–144 (Bk. 8), I, 172–186 (Bk. 11, Chs. 4–6), I, 210 (Bk. 12, Ch. 1). Jefferson follows the suggestion in these passages that only a proper disposition of laws in relation to a constitution guarantees liberty.

38. *The Spirit of Laws*, I, 38–39 (Bk. 4, Ch. 5), and *The Principles of Natural and Politic Law*, II, 120–122 (Pt. 3, Ch. 2).

39. Although a commentary could be a book of notes, its formal meaning as used by Blackstone and as presented in Jefferson's own Latin-English dictionary implied more formal and elaborate control. *Notatio* means a marking or observing or a taking notice of. The process leaves a *Nota*, evidence. *Commentatio*, on the other hand, implies more extensive organization and could specifically mean "a description, as of a country, and giving an account of it in writing"—Adam Littleton, *Littleton's Latin Dictionary in Four Parts*, 6th edition (London: J. Walthoe, 1735), and Sowerby, *The Library of Thomas Jefferson*, v, 87. Jefferson, a keen Latin scholar, understood the distinction involved. He resisted pressures from within his own circle to give *Notes* "a more dignified title." See, for example, Charles Thomson to TJ, March 6, 1785, *Papers*, VIII, 16.

40. Thomas Philbrick and William J. Scheick have identified some of the anxious tones in *Notes;* see Philbrick, "Thomas Jefferson," p. 166, and Scheick, "Chaos and Imaginative Order in Jefferson's *Notes*," p. 224.

41. For Jefferson's frequent comments on corruption and disintegration in the state, see *Notes on the State of Virginia*, pp. 85, 120–121, 148–149, 161. He deals with slavery first in section eight on population (p. 87), then in section fourteen on laws (pp. 138–143), and finally in his discussion of manners and customs in section eighteen (pp. 162–163).

42. Lewis P. Simpson, *The Dispossessed Garden: Pastoral and History in*

Southern Literature (Athens, Ga.: University of Georgia Press, 1975), pp. 27–30.

43. John Locke placed slavery completely outside the social compact, and Montesquieu, while analyzing slavery in detail, declared the practice contrary to natural law and to the fundamental principles of *all* societies. Montesquieu found slavery particularly dangerous for a country with moderate laws. It is worth adding that Jefferson wrote *Notes* during the crest of abolitionist movements in both England and France. See John Locke, *Two Treatises of Government*, in *The Works of John Locke*, 12th edition, 9 vols. (London: C. and J. Rivington, 1824), IV, 212 (Bk. 1, Ch. 1), and IV, 351–352 (Bk. 2, Ch. 4); Montesquieu, *The Spirit of Laws*, I, 270–283 (Bk. 15, Chs. 1–15). See also Peter Gay, "Abolitionism: A Preliminary Probing," *The Enlightenment: An Interpretation*, II, 407–423.

44. TJ to Joseph C. Cabell, February 2, 1816, *Writings*, XIV, 422.

45. Francis Bacon, "Of Honour and Reputation," *Essays of Counsels Civil and Moral*, in James Spedding, Robert L. Ellis, and Douglas D. Heath, eds., *The Works of Francis Bacon* 14 vols. (London: Longman, 1857–1874), VI, 505–506. Jefferson's admiration for Bacon was so unstinting that he carried Bacon's picture with him when he traveled, and he organized his own vast library of six thousand volumes around Bacon's intellectual distinctions. Bacon was the first in Jefferson's "trinity of the three greatest men the world had ever produced." See Douglas Adair, *Fame and the Founding Fathers*, ed. Trevor Colbourn (New York: Norton, 1974), pp. 13–15, and TJ to Dr. Benjamin Rush, January 16, 1811, *Writings*, XIII, 4.

46. "Aphorisms 100, 102," *Novum Organum; or True Directions Concerning the Interpretation of Nature*, in *The Works of Francis Bacon*, VIII, 136.

47. Jefferson, "A Summary View of the Rights of British America, 1774," *Papers*, I, 122.

48. Boorstin, *The Americans: The National Experience*, p. 41.

49. James Madison, "June 19–20, 1787," in Adrienne Koch, ed., *Notes of Debates in the Federal Convention of 1787* (New York: Norton, 1969), pp. 140–156.

50. For Jefferson's specific acceptance of both the order *and* the flexibility in what Boorstin calls "the common-law way of thinking," see *Notes on the State of Virginia*, p. 137. Here Jefferson bases his entire revision of Virginia's laws upon English common law, but he carefully resists the "dangerous" inclination to reduce the common law to a single text.

51. Julian Boyd also raises the discrepancy between Jefferson's preparation and the more superficial legal studies of his contemporaries in "Jefferson's Expression of the American Mind," *Virginia Quarterly Review*, 59 (Autumn 1974), 541–542. That Jefferson turned to Anglo-Saxon "for explanation of a multitude of law-terms" is clear from TJ to Herbert Croft, October 30, 1798, *Writings*, XVIII, 363.

52. Dumbauld, *Thomas Jefferson and the Law*, pp. 3–17, 121–124. For Jefferson's actual use of Latin, French, and Italian in his legal studies, see Chinard, ed., *The Commonplace Book of Thomas Jefferson*, pp. 47, 257–316, 369.

53. "Inauguration Address, March 4, 1801," *Writings*, III, 317–321.

54. William Hedges comments forcefully upon the "pronounced manic-depressive tendencies" in early American literature in "Charles Brockden Brown and the Culture of Contradictions," *Early American Literature*, 9 (Fall 1974), 137.

55. *Notes on the State of Virginia*, pp. 92–97. Critics looking for the revolutionary Jefferson have tended to stress his suggestion in these pages that no law among the American Indians is preferable to too much law among civilized Europeans. What they overlook is that the full context of Jefferson's remarks shows his support for what he presents as a separate generalization: "Great societies cannot exist without government."

56. Allen Tate, *The Man of Letters in the Modern World* (Cleveland, Ohio: World Publishing, 1955), p. 11.

57. Lewis P. Simpson, *The Dispossessed Garden*, pp. 24–25. More generally, see Henry F. May, *The Enlightenment in America* (New York: Oxford University Press, 1976).

58. For both the terminology and the ideas in these two sentences, I am indebted to Stephen D. Cox, "The Literary Aesthetic of Thomas Jefferson," in J. A. Leo Lemay, ed., *Essays in Early Virginia Literature*, pp. 235–243. For relevant letters containing the views mentioned, see TJ to Robert Skipwith, August 3, 1771, *Papers*, I, 76–81; TJ to Charles McPherson, February 25, 1773, *Papers*, I, 96–97; TJ to John Adams, April 20, 1812, and October 12, 1813 in *The Adams-Jefferson Letters: The Complete Correspondence Between Thomas Jefferson and Abigail and John Adams*, ed. Lester J. Cappon, 2 vols. (Chapel Hill: University of North Carolina Press, 1959), II, 298, 385.

59. TJ to George Wythe, August 13, 1786, *Papers*, X, 244–245.

60. *Notes on the State of Virginia*, pp. 174, 84, 165.

61. Jefferson's case books indicate a total of 939 cases from February 1767 to November 1774. For more detailed information and actual examples of Jefferson's style in courtroom debate, see Dumbauld, *Thomas Jefferson and the Law*, pp. 88–120.

62. TJ to Thomas Mann Randolph, Jr., July 6, 1787, *Papers*, XI, 557–558.

63. Chinard, ed. *The Commonplace Book of Thomas Jefferson*, pp. 19–20, 107.

64. TJ to Thomas Mann Randolph, Jr., May 30, 1790, *Papers*, XVI, 449.

65. Herman Melville to Nathaniel Hawthorne, April 16, 1851, quoted

in Jay Leyda, ed., *The Portable Melville* (New York: Viking Press, 1952), p. 428.

3. To Form a More Perfect Union

1. For a standard analysis of the Constitution, see Clinton Rossiter, *1787, The Grand Convention* (New York: Macmillan, 1966), pp. 257–273.

2. Thirty-one of the fifty-five framers were lawyers, but sheer numbers only begin to convey lawyers' domination of the Convention. Clinton Rossiter divides the framers by importance into principal participants, influentials, very usefuls, on down to ciphers, disappointments, and dropouts. Three of the four principals were lawyers, and the exception, George Washington, was peculiarly silent as the president of the Convention. Seven of the eleven influentials, five out of seven of the very usefuls, five of the six most frequent speakers, and four of the five members of the "committee of style and arrangement" who drafted the final document were educated in law. Rossiter, *1787, The Grand Convention*, pp. 224, 247–252. See also Winton U. Solberg, ed., *The Federal Convention and the Formation of the Union of the American States* (New York: Bobbs-Merrill, 1958), pp. 388–406.

3. For an analysis of the general requirements of "learning and literary accomplishments" (a college education and proof of expertise in classical languages and literatures, and in ancient and modern history and philosophy) within the eighteenth-century American bar, see Charles Warren, *A History of the American Bar* (1911; rpt. New York: Howard Fertig, 1966), pp. 157–187, 195, 198, 307. The comments of Edmund Randolph and Gouverneur Morris appear in Max Farrand, ed., *The Records of the Federal Convention of 1787*, rev. ed., 4 vols. (New Haven: Yale University Press, 1937), II, 137, 237. See as well Ernst Cassirer, *The Philosophy of the Enlightenment*, trans. Fritz C. A. Koelln and James P. Pettegrove (Princeton, N.J.: Princeton University Press, 1951), pp. 238–241.

4. Wilson's remarks are from his introduction to "Lectures on Law Delivered in the College of Philadelphia in the Years 1790 and 1791," in Robert Green McCloskey, ed., *The Works of James Wilson*, 2 vols. (Cambridge, Mass.: Harvard University Press, 1967,) I, 90–91. Reference to "the supreme Law of the Land" is from Article VI of the Constitution. Morton Horwitz has admirably summarized the way in which the eighteenth-century legal mind believed in the discovery and application of preexisting legal rules based on natural law and a sense of the unchanging and inherent rightness or justice of the law. Morton J. Horwitz, "The Emergence of an Instrumental Conception of American Law, 1780–1820," in Donald Fleming and Bernard Bailyn, eds., *Law in American History* (Boston: Little, Brown, 1971), pp. 291–298.

5. Compare the original working copy of the Constitution as reported by the committee of detail on August 6, 1787, with the version of the committee of style, which was dated September 12, 1787. Farrand, *Reports of the Federal Convention*, II, 565–603.

6. ". . . the Union shall be perpetual . . ." Article XIII, Articles of Confederation—1777, in *The Federal and State Constitutions, Colonial Charters, and Other Organic Laws of the United States*, ed. Benjamin Perley Poore, 2 vols. (Washington, D.C.: Government Printing Office, 1878), I, 11. Significantly, it is the organization of the revised version of the Constitution, with its strong initial stress upon the legislative branch, that allows Madison to argue that "if the new Constitution be examined with accuracy and candor, it will be found that the change which it proposes consists much less in the addition of NEW POWERS to the Union, than in the invigoration of its ORIGINAL POWERS." "Federalist No. 45," in Alexander Hamilton, John Jay, and James Madison, *The Federalist: A Commentary on The Constitution of the United States, Being a Collection of Essays written in Support of the Constitution agreed upon September 17, 1797, by the Federal Convention* (1787–1788; rpt. New York: Random House, 1937), p. 303. All further references to *The Federalist* are to this edition.

7. "The celebrated Montesquieu," in particular, was a frequent authority cited by speakers within the Federal Convention and by *The Federalist*. Farrand, *The Records of the Federal Convention*, I, 71, 308, 391, 485, 497, 580; II, 34, 530; III, 109, 197; and *The Federalist*, pp. 49, 50, 53, 282, 285, 313, 315, 504. Significantly, all but one of these references came from a lawyer-framer.

8. The framers opened with a complete account of their proposed bicameral legislature and gave it their most detailed attention because they believed their fellow Americans were particularly anxious on this point, because their own greatest fears were of legislative tyranny, because they counted on the representative principle to distinguish modern republicanism from the failures of the ancient world, and because every social theorist since John Locke believed "the constitution of the legislative is the first and fundamental act of society." See Farrand, *The Records of the Federal Convention*, I, 185–186, 249–254, 372; "Federalist No. 10, 39, 48," *The Federalist*, pp. 53–62, 243, 322; and John Locke, "An Essay Concerning the True Original, Extent, and End of Civil Government," in "Two Treatises on Government," *The Works of John Locke in Nine Volumes*, 12th ed. (London: C. Baldwin, 1824), IV, 464 (Ch. 19, no. 212).

9. Following "the design of a great Confederacy," Madison believed that it was "incumbent on . . . successors to improve and perpetuate." He and the other framers knew that "a faultless plan was not to be expected" from the Federal Convention, and they predicted that "useful alterations will be suggested by experience." As noted in chapter 1, Madison and

Hamilton were particularly aware of the need for ongoing interpretations and possible amendment of the Constitution as "new law." See "Federalist No. 14, 37, 43," *The Federalist*, pp. 85, 226–229, 286.

10. Both Madison and Morris would later claim that Morris was the author of these changes in the preamble, but the larger consultation process of the committee of style remains shrouded in mystery. The Convention accepted the committee's final draft of the preamble with the single deletion of the word "to" before "establish justice." See Farrand, *The Records of the Federal Convention*, II, 565, 590, 605; III, 499. See also Rossiter, *1787, The Grand Convention*, p. 225.

11. The thought and language of this paragraph owe much to Roscoe Pound, *The Formative Era of American Law* (Boston: Little, Brown, 1938), pp. 14–26. Pound notes here as well that natural-law thinking dominated legal thought in America for the three generations after independence and that consensual natural law (the political idea that what everyone agrees to is declaratory of natural law) was particularly dominant in the thinking of early republicans. See as well Hugo Grotius, *De Jure Belli et Pacis*. trans. William Whewell, 3 vols. (Cambridge, Eng.: Cambridge University Press, 1853), I, xlix, 9, 16–17 (Prolegomena 15, 16, and Bk. 1, ch. 1, no. 9–12); Jean Jacques Burlamaqui, *The Principles of Natural and Politic Law*, trans. Thomas Nugent, 5th ed., 2 vols. (Cambridge, Mass.: Hilliard, 1807), I, 1, 36–37, 130–131, 184–185, and II, 111–113 (Pt. I, ch. 1, no. 1; Pt. I, ch. 5, no. 10; Pt. II, ch. 5, no. 7–8; Pt. II, ch. 12, no. 1–2; and Pt. III, ch. 1, no. 6–9); and Emmerich von Vattel, *Le Droit des Gens, ou Principes de la Loi Naturelle, appliqués à la Conduite et aux Affaires des Nations et des Souverains*, trans. Charles G. Fenwick (Washington, D.C.: Carnegie Institution, 1916), pp. 13–14 (Vol. I, Bk. 1, ch. 2, no. 13–19).

12. Just as the preamble set forth an appeal to fundamental and natural law, so the ratification process in the final article, Article VII, encouraged the application, after the fact, of a consensual theory of natural law. These emphases led many Americans to "a notion of the Constitution as declaratory of natural law." Roscoe Pound, *The Formative Era of American Law*, p. 26.

13. In Samuel Johnson's *Dictionary of the English Language*, to *ordain* meant to appoint, to decree, to settle, to institute, to set in office, to invest with ministerial function; to *establish* was to settle firmly or fix unalterably. *Establishment*, in turn, referred to a fixed state, model of a government, settled regulation, or to foundation, fundamental principle, settled law.

14. William Blackstone, "Of Pleading," *Commentaries on the Laws of England*, 4 vols. (1765–1769; rpt. Chicago: University of Chicago Press, 1979), III, 293–301 (Bk. 3, ch. 20).

15. "Federalist No. 38," *The Federalist*, pp. 233–234; "Federalist No.

1," *The Federalist*, p. 3; "Oration Delivered on the Fourth of July 1788, at the Procession formed at Philadelphia to Celebrate the Adoption of the Constitution of the United States," *The Works of James Wilson*, II, 776.

16. For the relationship of knowledge, education, and virtue in Enlightenment thought, see Quentin Skinner, *The Foundations of Modern Political Thought*, 2 vols. (Cambridge, Eng.: Cambridge University Press, 1978), I, 88–94; Peter Gay, *The Enlightenment: An Interpretation*, 2 vols. (1969; rpt. New York: W. W. Norton, 1977), II, 52, 497–517; and J. A. Passmore, "The Malleability of Man in Eighteenth-Century Thought," in Earl R. Wasserman, ed., *Aspects of the Eighteenth Century* (Baltimore: Johns Hopkins University Press, 1965), pp. 21–46.

17. John Dickinson, *The Letters of Fabius, in 1788, on the Federal Convention*, in *The Political Writings of John Dickinson, Esquire, Late President of the State of Delaware, and of the Commonwealth of Pennsylvania*, 2 vols. (Wilmington: Bonsal and Niles, 1801), II, 72–73, 115–116.

18. For the role of the doctrine of *vivere civile* (the ideal of active citizenship in a republic) in western thought and in early American culture, see J. G. A. Pocock, *The Machiavellian Moment: Florentine Political Thought and the Atlantic Republican Tradition* (Princeton, N.J.: Princeton University Press, 1975), pp. 4, 56, 349–350, 466, 506–552. For the influence of civic concerns upon American writing in the early republic, see Lewis P. Simpson, *The Man of Letters in New England and the South: Essays on the History of the Literary Vocation in America* (Baton Rouge: Louisiana State University Press, 1973), p. 21.

19. E. P. Whipple, "Daniel Webster as an Author," *North American Review*, 59 (July 1844), 45.

20. The context of these quotations is Joseph Story's approving descriptions of such early giants at the bar as Samuel Dexter and William Pinkney in *The Miscellaneous Writings of Joseph Story*, ed. William Wetmore Story (Boston: Little, Brown, 1852), pp. 786–791, 795–799.

21. Joseph Story, "Progress of Jurisprudence, An Address delivered before the Members of the Suffolk Bar, at their anniversary, September 4, 1821, at Boston," and "Characteristics of the Age: A Discourse pronounced at Cambridge before the Phi Beta Kappa Society of Harvard University, August 31, 1826," *The Miscellaneous Writings of Joseph Story*, pp. 215, 341, 357.

22. "Lectures on Law," *The Works of James Wilson*, I, 69–70.

23. "Lectures on Law," *The Works of James Wilson*, II, 565.

24. James Madison to William Bradford, September 25, 1773, in William T. Hutchinson, William M. E. Rachal, and Robert A. Rutland, eds., *The Papers of James Madison*, 12 vols. (Chicago: University of Chicago Press, and Charlottesville: University Press of Virginia, 1962–   ), I, 96.

25. For facts and figures on the early American bar this section relies on Lawrence M. Friedman, *A History of American Law* (New York: Simon and Schuster, 1973), pp. 91–293; Maxwell Bloomfield, *American Lawyers in a Changing Society, 1776–1876* (Cambridge, Mass.: Harvard University Press, 1976); and Anton-Hermann Chroust, *The Rise of the Legal Profession in America*, 2 vols. (Norman: University of Oklahoma Press, 1965), II, 3–91, 129–223.

26. Perry Miller, *The Life of the Mind in America from the Revolution to the Civil War* (New York: Harcourt, Brace, and World, 1965), p. 110; Julius Goebel, Jr., ed., *The Law Practice of Alexander Hamilton: Documents and Commentary*, 2 vols. (New York: Columbia University Press, 1964), I, 47–48; and Charles Warren, *A History of the American Bar*, pp. 186–187. Webster's comment is quoted in Warren.

27. For relevant figures on education in America see Evarts Boutell Greene, *The Revolutionary Generation 1763–1790* (New York: Macmillan, 1943), pp. 122–128; Jackson Turner Main, *The Social Structure of Revolutionary America* (Princeton, N.J.: Princeton University Press, 1965), pp. 246–250; Russel Blaine Nye, "The Idea of an American University," *The Cultural Life of the New Nation, 1776–1830* (1960; rpt. New York: Harper and Row, 1963), pp. 171–194; and Friedman, *A History of American Law*, p. 267. As Friedman notes, of the 2,618 trained lawyers who practiced in Massachusetts and Maine between 1760 and 1840, 71.4 percent, or 1,859, were college-trained. For the term "community of the competent" and an argument that professionalization must be understood not as a measure of quality but of community, see Thomas L. Haskell, *The Emergence of Professional Social Science: The American Social Science Association and the Nineteenth-Century Crisis of Authority* (Urbana: University of Illinois Press, 1977), pp. 18–19, 27, 66–80.

28. James Kent, "An Introductory Lecture to a Course of Law Lectures, Delivered November 17, 1794 . . . in Columbia College," *Columbia Law Review*, 3 (May 1903), 338. Joseph Story, "A Discourse Pronounced at the Inauguration of the Author as Dane Professor of Law in Harvard University, August 25, 1829," *The Miscellaneous Writings of Joseph Story*, pp. 528–529.

29. William Kent, *Memoirs and Letters of James Kent, LL.D., Late Chancellor of the State of New York* (Boston: Little, Brown, 1898), pp. 36–37; Joseph Story, "Public Life and Services of Marshall," *North American Review*, 26 (January 1828), 5. For the original version of this oft-repeated praise of Marshall's biography of Washington, see John Bristed, *America and Her Resources, or A View of the Agricultural, Commercial, Manufacturing, Financial, Political, Literary, Moral, and Religious Capacity, and Character of the American People* (London: Henry Colburn, 1818), p. 357. See also Charles

Jared Ingersoll, *A Discourse Concerning The Influence of America on the Mind: Being An Annual Oration Delivered Before the American Philosophical Society, at the University in Philadelphia on 18th October 1823* (Philadelphia: Abraham Small, 1823), pp. 13–15.

30. For a good account of the influence of Wirt's biography of Henry, of Kennedy's biography of Wirt, and of Wirt's general importance as a model for emulation, see Maxwell Bloomfield, *American Lawyers in a Changing Society*, pp. 173–190.

31. Quoted in John P. Kennedy, *Memoirs of The Life of William Wirt, Attorney General of the United States*, 2 vols. (Philadelphia: Lea and Blanchard, 1849), II, 441.

32. See, for example, *The Miscellaneous Writings of Joseph Story*, pp. 23, 790–791, 795, 799.

33. Kent prefaced his commentaries with assurances of their "general application"; they were "useful and ornamental to gentlemen in every pursuit" and were meant for "the general reader." James Kent, *Commentaries on American Law*, ed. Oliver Wendell Holmes, Jr., 4 vols. (Boston: Little, Brown, 1884), II, ix–x, and IV, 2–3. See also Joseph Story to James Kent, October 25, 1831, quoted in *Memoirs and Letters of James Kent*, p. 229.

34. *Memoirs and Letters of James Kent*, pp. 240–243, 254, 281–331. See also John Theodore Horton, *James Kent: A Study in Conservatism* (New York: DaCapo Press, 1969), pp. 45–47, 76–77, 114–115.

35. For Story's own "love of poetry" and his comments on the publication of his poems, see his "Autobiography," in *The Miscellaneous Writings of Joseph Story*, pp. 37–38. For a list of his commentaries written while at the Harvard Law School, see Arthur E. Sutherland, *The Law at Harvard: A History of Ideas and Men, 1817–1967* (Cambridge, Mass.: Harvard University Press, 1967), pp. 98, 107–108.

36. Theophilus Parsons, Jr., *Memoir of Theophilus Parsons, Chief Justice of the Supreme Judicial Court of Massachusetts; with Notices of Some of His Contemporaries* (Boston: Ticknor and Fields, 1859), pp. 152, 235, 260–307, 404–445; and Frank Gaylord Cook, "Theophilus Parsons," *Great American Lawyers*, ed. William Draper Lewis, 8 vols. (Philadelphia: John C. Winston Co., 1907–1909), II, 81–97.

37. Francis Hopkinson, *The Miscellaneous Essays and Occasional Writings of Francis Hopkins*, 3 vols. (Philadelphia: T. Dobson, 1792), and Burton A. Konkle, *Joseph Hopkinson 1770–1842: Jurist, Scholar, Inspirer of the Arts* (Philadelphia: University of Pennsylvania Press, 1931), pp. 1–11, 45–51, 74–84, 147–154.

38. Gary Nash, "The Philadelphia Bench and Bar, 1800–1861," *Comparative Studies in Society and History: An International Quarterly*, 7 (January 1965), 203–220. More generally, see Albert H. Smyth, *The Philadelphia*

Magazines and Their Contributors, 1741–1850 (Philadelphia: Robert N. Lindsay, 1892), pp. 110–130, and Harold M. Ellis, *Joseph Dennie and His Circle: A Study in American Literature from 1792 to 1812* (1915; rpt. New York: AMS Press, 1971).

39. John Clive and Bernard Bailyn, "England's Cultural Provinces: Scotland and America," *William and Mary Quarterly*, 3rd series, 11 (April 1954), 200–213. See also Ian Simpson Ross, "The Law and Edinburgh," *Lord Kames and the Scotland of His Day* (Oxford: Oxford University Press, 1972), pp. 8–43.

40. See generally Edwin Harrison Cady, *The Gentleman in America: A Literary Study in American Culture* (Syracuse, N.Y.: Syracuse University Press, 1949), pp. 1–126. Cady demonstrates that the seventeenth-century concept of the gentleman already contained emphases on education and a knowledge of law. He then traces the ways in which education and professional knowledge became a matter of central importance in America, where gentlemanliness was more of a cultural ideal than a class distinction.

41. John Pendleton Kennedy, *Swallow Barn Or A Sojourn In The Old Dominion* [1832] (New York: Hafner, 1962), p. 167. For a thorough description and analysis of the phenomenon of circuit-riding, see Daniel H. Calhoun, *Professional Lives in America: Structure and Aspiration 1750–1850* (Cambridge, Mass.: Harvard University Press, 1965), pp. 59–87. See also Friedman, *A History of American Law*, pp. 270–275, and Thomas R. Meehan, "Courts, Cases, and Counselors in Revolutionary and Post-Revolutionary Pennsylvania," *Pennsylvania Magazine of History and Biography*, 91 (January 1967), 3–34.

42. *The Miscellaneous Writings of Joseph Story*, p. 786, and newspaper description of the Supreme Court of 1824 quoted in Charles Warren, *The Supreme Court in United States History*, 3 vols. (Boston: Little, Brown, 1923), 1, 467, 473. For specific examples of journal coverage of legal matters, see *Port Folio*, 1 (September 12, 1801), 292–293, 1 (October 3, 1801), 316–317, and 1 (October 10, 1801), 526–527; and "Trial of Robert Goodwin On An Indictment of Manslaughter," *North American Review*, 11 (1820), 114–124. The *Port Folio* carried a regular section called "Law Intelligence." My own research shows that customarily one tenth and sometimes as high as one fifth of each issue of the *North American Review* from 1815 to 1830 dealt with legal material.

43. St. George Tucker to Theodorick and John Randolph, June 12, 1787, quoted in Main, *The Social Structure of Revolutionary America*, p. 200.

44. "Eminent British Lawyers: A Review," *American Quarterly Review*, 12 (1832), 268. As the anonymous reviewer put it, "Mere knowledge of the technicalities of the law does not constitute the lawyer in America— eloquence goes far to make the advocate here—but even that is not all-

sufficient; extensive learning, not confined to a particular profession and varied accomplishments (which may in one sense, indeed, be considered some of the constituents of eloquence) must all unite."

45. George Washington Strong to John Nelson Lloyd, December 31, 1827, quoted in Allan Nevins, "Introduction," *The Diary of George Templeton Strong*, 4 vols. (New York: Macmillan, 1952), I, xv. For examples, see William Wirt, *The Letters of The British Spy* [1803] (New York: Harper, 1844), pp. 213–214, and Robert Walsh, "The British Spy in Boston: Letter III," *Port Folio*, 4 (November 17, 1804), 361.

46. For all of the comments of Pinkney by Marshall, Story, Taney, and others, see Warren, *A History of the American Bar*, pp. 260, 280–281, 367.

47. Frank Luther Mott, *A History of American Magazines, 1741–1850* (New York: D. Appleton, 1930), pp. 154–155.

48. William Cullen Bryant to Theophilus Parsons, Jr., January 19, 1824, in *The Letters of William Cullen Bryant*, ed. William Cullen Bryant II and Thomas G. Voss, 2 vols. (New York: Fordham University Press, 1975), I, 149–151. Theophilus Parsons, Jr., "Law Books," *United States Literary Gazette*, I (1824–25), 250.

49. Jeremiah Mason, *Memoirs and Correspondence of Jeremiah Mason*, ed. George Stillman Hillard (Cambridge, Mass.: Riverside Press, 1873), pp. 28–32.

50. Joseph Dennie, "Miscellany," *Port Folio*, new series, 3 (April 25, 1807), 259, and "Legal Character," *Port Folio*, 5 (April 20, 1805), 112–113. See also "Prospectus of A New Weekly Paper Submitted to Men of Affluence, Men of Liberality, and Men of Letters," attached before *Port Folio*, 1 (January 3, 1801), 1. Dennie welcomed all of the professions in this prospectus, but he couched it in terms of a lawyer's contract and emphasized that "lawyers are splendidly distinguished for *polite*, as well as professional studies."

51. John Quincy Adams to Thomas Boylston Adams, March 21, 1801, in *The Writings of John Quincy Adams*, ed. Worthington C. Ford, 7 vols. (New York: Macmillan, 1913–1917), II, 521. For Adams' prominent participation in the *Port Folio* and for information on the many other lawyers who wrote for its pages, see Harold Milton Ellis, *Joseph Dennie and His Circle: A Study in American Literature from 1792* (1915; rpt. New York: AMS Press, 1971), Guy R. Woodall, "The Relationship of Robert Walsh, Jr., to the *Port Folio* and the Dennie Circle: 1803–1812," *Pennsylvania Magazine of History and Biography*, 92 (April 1968), 195–219, and Randolph C. Randall, "Authors of the *Port Folio* Revealed by the Hall Files," *American Literature*, 11 (January 1940), 379–416.

52. Nathaniel Hawthorne, "Thomas Green Fessenden," *American*

Monthly Magazine, 5 (January 1838), 31. For a collection of Dennie's journalistic writings, see Joseph Dennie, *The Lay Preacher* [1796], ed. Harold M. Ellis (New York: Scholars' Facsimiles and Reprints, 1943).

53. *The Miscellaneous Writings of Joseph Story*, p. 376. For relevant readings on the classical tradition in America, see Gilbert Chinard, "Polybius and the American Constitution," *Journal of the History of Ideas*, 1 (January 1940), 38–58; Howard Mumford Jones, "Roman Virtue," *O Strange New World: American Culture, The Formative Years* [1952] (New York: Viking Press, 1964), pp. 227–272; Richard M. Gummere, *The American Colonial Mind and the Classical Tradition* (Cambridge, Mass.: Harvard University Press, 1963); Gordon S. Wood, "The Appeal of Antiquity," *The Creation of the American Republic, 1776–1787* [1969] (New York: Norton, 1972), pp. 48–53; Linda K. Kerber, "Salvaging the Classical Tradition," *Federalists in Dissent: Imagery and Ideology in Jeffersonian America* (Ithaca, N.Y.: Cornell University Press, 1970), pp. 95–134; Edwin A. Miles, "The Young American Nation and the Classical World," *Journal of the History of Ideas*, 35 (April–June 1974), 259–274; and Meyer Reinhold, ed., *The Classick Pages: Classical Reading of Eighteenth-Century Americans* (University Park, Pa.: American Philological Association, 1975).

54. Alexander Hamilton's Pay Book and Alexander Hamilton to Gouverneur Morris, June 22, 1792, in *The Papers of Alexander Hamilton*, ed. Harold C. Syrett, 24 vols. (New York: Columbia University Press, 1961–1976), I, 391–407, and XI, 545. Also Alexander Hamilton, "Federalist No. 34," *The Federalist*, p. 204; John Adams to Benjamin Rush, June 19, 1789, in *Letters of Benjamin Rush*, ed. L. H. Butterfield, 2 vols. (Princeton, N.J.: Princeton University Press, 1951), I, 518; and John Quincy Adams, "May 10, 1819," *The Diary of John Quincy Adams: American Diplomacy, and Political, Social, and Intellectual Life from Washington to Polk*, ed. Allen Nevins (New York: Frederick Ungar, 1969), p. 216.

55. "Such classicism was not only a scholarly ornament of educated Americans; it helped to shape their values and their ideals of behavior." Wood, *The Creation of the American Republic*, p. 49.

56. Hugh Henry Brackenridge, *Law Miscellanies Containing an Introduction to the Study of The Law; Notes on Blackstone's Commentaries, Shewing the Variations of The Law of Pennsylvania from The Law of England . . . And a Variety of Other Matters Chiefly Original* (Philadelphia: P. Byrne, 1814), xii, xiv; Hugh Henry Brackenridge, *Modern Chivalry* [1796–1815], ed. Claude M. Newlin (New York: Hafner, 1968), p. 77. See also Leo M. Kaiser, "An Aspect of Hugh Henry Brackenridge's Classicism," *Early American Literature*, 15 (Winter 1980–81), 260–270. Kaiser documents Brackenridge's commitment to classical expression and the many uses of Latin phrases in *Modern Chivalry*.

57. *Diary and Autobiography of John Adams*, ed. L. H. Butterfield, 4 vols. (1961; rpt. New York: Atheneum, 1964), I, 73.

58. *Diary and Autobiography of John Adams*, I, 63, 251–255. "As all the ages of the world have not produced a greater statesman and philosopher united than Cicero," Adams wrote in 1787, "his authority should have great weight"—"Preface," *A Defence of the Constitutions of Government of the United States*, in *The Life and Works of John Adams*, ed. Charles Francis Adams, 10 vols. (Boston: Little, Brown, 1850–1856), IV, 295. See, more generally, Stephen Botein, "Cicero as Role Model for Early American Lawyers: A Case Study in Classical 'Influence'," *Classical Journal*, 73 (Spring 1978), 313–321, and Reinhold, ed., "Cicero," *The Classick Pages*, pp. 49–63.

59. Cicero, *De Officiis*, trans. Walter Miller (Cambridge, Mass.: Harvard University Press, 1961), p. 21 (I, vi, 19). "All these professions [astronomy, mathematics, dialectics, and civil law] are occupied with the search after truth; but to be drawn by study away from active life is contrary to moral duty. For the whole glory of virtue is in activity; activity, however, may often be interrupted, and many opportunities for returning to study are opened." For the general importance of this passage to American literati, see Simpson, *The Man of Letters in New England and the South*, p. 21.

60. Hugh Swinton Legaré to Francis Walker Gilmer, October 1, 1816, quoted in Richard Beale Davis, "The Early American Lawyer and the Profession of Letters," *Huntington Library Quarterly*, 12 (February 1949), 202.

61. H. E. Butler, trans., *The Institutio Oratoria of Quintilian*, 4 vols. (Cambridge, Mass.: Harvard University Press, 1961), IV, 21 (x, i, 31).

62. "The Power of a State Developed by Mental Culture: A Lecture Delivered before the Mercantile Library Association, November 18, 1844," and Rufus Choate to Richard S. Storrs, Jr., January 2, 1841, in Samuel Gilman Brown, *The Works of Rufus Choate with a Memoir of His Life*, 2 vols. (Boston: Little, Brown, 1862), I, 411, 47.

63. Quoted in Claude M. Fuess, *Rufus Choate: The Wizard of the Law* (New York: Minton, Balch, 1928), p. 222. See as well accounts and requirements within the early American bar in Warren, *A History of the American Bar*, pp. 184, 197–200, 307.

64. Miller, *The Life of the Mind in America*, pp. 118, 147.

65. For the best presentation of the problems and questions concerning the neoclassical tradition in America, see Leon Howard, "The Late Eighteenth Century: An Age of Contradictions," M. F. Heiser, "The Decline of Neoclassicism 1801–1848," and G. Harrison Orians, "The Rise of Romanticism 1805–1855," in Harry Hayden Clark, ed., *Transitions in American Literary History* (New York: Octagon Books, 1975), pp. 51–244.

66. For a good summary of the distinctions between neoclassicism and

romanticism, see Walter Jackson Bate, *From Classic to Romantic: Premises of Taste in Eighteenth-Century England* (1946; rpt. New York: Harper and Row, 1961).

67. Cicero, *De Officiis*, pp. 293 (III, vi, 26), 53–55 (I, xvi, 50), and 239–241 (II, xix, 65–66). Also John Quincy Adams, *Lectures on Rhetoric and Oratory, Delivered to the Classes of Senior and Junior Sophisters in Harvard University*, 2 vols. (Cambridge, Mass.: Hilliard and Metcalf, 1810), I, 136.

68. Joseph Dennie, "Prospectus of A New Weekly Paper Submitted to Men of Affluence, Men of Liberality, and Men of Letters," *Port Folio*, 1 (January 3, 1801), 2.

69. See Lewis P. Simpson, "Federalism and the Crisis of Literary Order," *American Literature*, 32 (November 1960), 264.

70. Fisher Ames, "Eulogy on Washington," "A Sketch of the Character of Alexander Hamilton," "The Dangers of American Liberty," and "The Republican No. 1," in *Works of Fisher Ames with a Selection from His Speeches and Correspondence*, ed. Seth Ames, 2 vols. (Boston: Little, Brown, 1854), II, 87, 261, 373, 352–353, 252–253.

71. More attention should be paid to the work exploring the connections between ideology and thought. Clifford Geertz uses the term "symbol system" to mean an extrinsic source of information "in terms of which human life can be patterned—extrapersonal mechanisms for the perception, understanding, judgment, and manipulation of the world." Geertz, "Ideology as a Cultural System," in David E. Apter, ed., *Ideology and Discontent* (New York: Free Press, 1964), pp. 62–63.

72. "American Literature," *Works of Fisher Ames*, II, 428–442 (emphasis added).

73. "Laocoon. No. II," and "Character of Brutus," *Works of Fisher Ames*, II, 126, 273.

74. There are numerous contemporary accounts of nineteenth-century oratory, but the quotations here are from the two most thorough studies of the subject. See Edward G. Parker, *The Golden Age of American Oratory* (Boston: Whittemore, Niles, and Hall, 1857), pp. 120, 4–6, 15, and Francis Walker Gilmer, "Sketches of American Orators," *Sketches, Essays and Translations* (Baltimore: Fielding Lucas, Jr., 1828), p. 43. For three modern studies on which this section relies, see Richard M. Weaver, *The Ethics of Rhetoric* (Chicago: Henry Regnery, 1953), Daniel Boorstin, "A Declamatory Literature," *The Americans: The National Experience* (New York: Random House, 1965), pp. 307–324, and Barnet Baskerville, *The People's Voice: The Orator in American Society* (Lexington: University Press of Kentucky, 1979).

75. Daniel Webster, "A Discourse in Commemoration of the Lives and Services of John Adams and Thomas Jefferson, delivered in Faneuil Hall, on August 2, 1826," *The Writings and Speeches of Daniel Webster*, 18 vols. (Boston: Little, Brown, 1903), I, 307.

76. "July 31, 1826," *The Diary of John Quincy Adams*, p. 363, and Fuess, *Rufus Choate*, pp. 125–130.

77. John Quincy Adams, *Lectures on Rhetoric and Oratory*, I, 19, 29–31, 66, 62, 50, 319.

78. John Quincy Adams, *Lectures on Rhetoric and Oratory*, I, 16–17, 30–31, 71–72, also I, 45, 68–69. See as well Linda K. Kerber's interesting discussion of Adams' lectures in *Federalists in Dissent*, pp. 126–131.

79. John Quincy Adams, *Lectures on Rhetoric and Oratory*, I, 108.

80. Ralph Waldo Emerson, "Eloquence," *The Complete Works of Ralph Waldo Emerson*, 12 vols. (Cambridge, Mass.: Riverside Press, 1883–1893), VII, 92, 89, 65. This essay first appeared in the *Atlantic Monthly*, 2 (September 1858), 385–397.

81. John Quincy Adams, *Lectures on Rhetoric and Oratory*, I, 104, 99, 126–127, 102.

82. John Quincy Adams, *Lectures on Rhetoric and Oratory*, I, 49–50, 126, II, 395.

83. John Quincy Adams, *Lectures on Rhetoric and Oratory*, I, 394.

84. John Quincy Adams, *Lectures on Rhetoric and Oratory*, I, 165–167, 383. Adams quoted here from *A Midsummer Night's Dream*, v, i, 12–17, with an interesting inaccuracy. Shakespeare's "shapes" becomes "shape," increasing the poet's unifying power within the world.

85. Gilmer, *Sketches, Essays and Translations*, p. 51, Parker, *The Golden Age of American Oratory*, p. 152, and Hugh Swinton Legaré, quoted in Baskerville, *The People's Voice*, p. 77.

86. Parker, *The Golden Age of American Oratory*, pp. 43, 12. For an extended analysis of the way in which a nineteenth-century orator was supposed to unify and then play upon his audience, see "Eloquence," *The Complete Works of Ralph Waldo Emerson*, VII, 63–98.

87. John Quincy Adams, *Lectures on Rhetoric and Oratory*, I, 108–110.

88. Rufus Choate, "The Power of a State Developed by Mental Culture: A Lecture Delivered before the Mercantile Library Association, November 18, 1844," in *The Works of Rufus Choate*, I, 409. For a recent analysis of Choate's larger importance to the period, see Jean V. Matthews, *Rufus Choate: The Law and Civic Virtue* (Philadelphia: Temple University Press, 1980).

89. "Power of a State Developed by Mental Culture," *Works of Rufus Choate*, I, 410.

90. "The Position and Functions of the American Bar, as An Element of Conservatism in the State: An Address Delivered before the Law School in Cambridge, July 3, 1845," *Works of Rufus Choate*, I, 414–417.

91. "Fragmentary Journal," *Works of Rufus Choate*, I, 85–91, 93–98, 136–137.

92. Fuess, *Rufus Choate*, pp. 34, 235, 241. See also "The Power of a

State Developed by Mental Culture," and "The Importance of Illustrating New-England History by a Series of Romances like the Waverley Novels, Delivered at Salem, 1833," *Works of Rufus Choate*, I, 394–413, 320.

93. Edward G. Parker, *Reminiscences of Rufus Choate, The Great American Advocate* (New York: Mason Brothers, 1860), pp. 57, 490–491; Fuess, *Rufus Choate*, p. 78; "Memoir of Rufus Choate," *Works of Rufus Choate*, I, 73.

94. "Speech Delivered at the Constitutional Meeting in Faneuil Hall, November 26, 1850," *Works of Rufus Choate*, II, 326.

95. "The Character of Washington, A Speech delivered . . . on the 22nd of February, 1832," *The Writings and Speeches of Daniel Webster*, II, 71.

96. "The Position and Functions of the American Bar," *Works of Rufus Choate*, I, 436.

Prologue to Part II

1. Hugh Swinton Legaré to Francis Walker Gilmer, August 24, 1816, in Richard Beale Davis, "The Early American Lawyer and the Profession of Letters," *Huntington Library Quarterly*, 12 (February 1949), 200.

2. Hugh Swinton Legaré to T. C. Reynolds, February 6, 1841, in Mary Swinton Legaré, ed., *Writings of Hugh Swinton Legaré, Prefaced by a Memoir of His Life*, 2 vols. (Charleston, S.C.: Burges and James, 1846), I, 236.

3. Winfred E. A. Bernhard, *Fisher Ames: Federalist and Statesman, 1758–1808* (Chapel Hill: University of North Carolina Press, 1965), pp. 121, 290, 313, 355.

4. William Wirt to Dabney Carr, June 8, 1804, and March 3, 1813, in John Pendleton Kennedy, *Memoirs of the Life of William Wirt, Attorney General of the United States*, 2 vols. (Philadelphia: J. B. Lippincott, 1860), I, 116, 307. See also William R. Taylor, *Cavalier and Yankee: The Old South and American National Character* (New York: Doubleday, 1963), pp. 54–55.

5. Bernhard, *Fisher Ames*, pp. 121, 290, 313, 355.

6. William M. Meigs, *The Life of Charles Jared Ingersoll* (Philadelphia: J. B. Lippincott, 1897), p. 327.

7. Charles J. Ingersoll, *A Discourse Concerning the Influence of America on the Mind* (Philadelphia: Abraham Small, 1823), pp. 13–14, 23–24.

8. Jared Sparks, "Review of Ingersoll's *Discourse Concerning the Influence of America on the Mind*," *North American Review*, 18 (1824), 161–162.

9. Philip Freneau, "Advice to Authors," *The Miscellaneous Works of Philip Freneau, Containing His Essays and Additional Poems* (Philadelphia: F. Bailey, 1788), pp. 42–48.

10. John Adams to Thomas Jefferson, August 14, 1813, in *The Adams-Jefferson Letters: The Complete Correspondence Between Thomas Jefferson and Ab-*

igail and John Adams, ed. Lester J. Cappon, 2 vols. (Chapel Hill: University of North Carolina Press, 1959), II, 366.

11. William Wirt, "Public Letter Written December 30, 1832," *Southern Literary Messenger*, 1 (October 1834), 34.

12. David Hoffman, *A Course of Legal Study; Respectfully Addressed to the Students of Law in the United States* (Baltimore: Coale and Maxwell, 1817), p. 27.

13. Joseph Story, "Review of Hoffman's Course of Legal Study," *North American Review*, 6 (November 1817), 66.

14. "Eminent British Lawyers: A Review," *American Quarterly Review*, 12 (1832), 289. Richard Rush, *American Jurisprudence*, quoted in Perry Miller, ed., *The Legal Mind in America from Independence to the Civil War* (New York: Doubleday, 1962), pp. 47–49.

15. Gulian Verplanck, *An Address Delivered Before the Philolexian and Peithologian Societies, August 2, 1830 on the Evening Preceding the Annual Commencement of Columbia College* (New York, 1830), pp. 33–34.

16. "Review," *United States Literary Gazette*, 3 (October 1825–April 1826), 260.

17. Theophilus Parsons, Jr., to Henry Longfellow, August 16, 1825, in Lawrance Thompson, *Young Longfellow 1807–1843* (New York: Macmillan, 1938), p. 76.

18. Quoted in Harold M. Ellis, *Joseph Dennie and His Circle: A Study in American Literature from 1792 to 1812* (1915; rpt. New York: AMS Press, 1971), pp. 47, 62.

19. Joseph Dennie, "Editor's Notes," *Port Folio*, 5 (April 1805), 112–113.

20. Richard Henry Dana, Sr., "The Novels of Charles Brockden Brown," *Poems and Prose Writings*, 2 vols. (New York: Baker and Scribner, 1850), II, 327, 340–341. [Originally from the *United States Review and Literary Gazette* for 1827.]

4. The Post-Revolutionary Writers: Trumbull, Tyler, and Brackenridge

1. Thomas Paine, *Common Sense*, in Philip S. Foner, ed., *The Complete Writings of Thomas Paine*, 2 vols. (New York: Citadel Press, 1945), I, 3, 45. Paine saw American independence as the greatest opportunity for human improvement since Noah. Cooler minds were less extreme, but Alexander Hamilton and John Jay raised the same notion of mission in Federalist No. 1 and No. 2, and one finds the idea everywhere in the literature of the period.

2. John Adams to Thomas Jefferson, October 9, 1787, *The Adams-*

Jefferson Letters: The Complete Correspondence Between Thomas Jefferson and Abigail and John Adams, ed. Lester J. Cappon, 2 vols. (Chapel Hill: University of North Carolina Press, 1959), 1, 203.

3. William Wirt to a Law Student, December 20, 1833, in *The Southern Literary Messenger*, 1 (October 1834), 35.

4. See Tremaine McDowell, "Sensibility in the Eighteenth-Century American Novel," *Studies in Philology*, 24 (July 1927), 383–401, and Russel B. Nye, *The Cultural Life of the New Nation* (1960; rpt. Harper and Row, 1963), p. 254. More recently, see Wendy Martin, "The Rogue and The Rational Man: Hugh Henry Brackenridge's Study of a Con Man in *Modern Chivalry*," *Early American Literature*, 8 (Fall 1973), 189, and Donald T. Siebert, "Royall Tyler's 'Bold Example': *The Contrast* and the English Comedy of Manners," *Early American Literature*, 13 (Spring 1978), 3–11.

5. See Hugh Henry Brackenridge, *Modern Chivalry*, ed. Claude M. Newlin (1937; rpt. New York: Hafner, 1968), pp. 414–416, 386, 544.

6. Thomas Jefferson, *Notes on the State of Virginia*, ed. William Peden (1954; rpt. New York: W. W. Norton, 1972), p. 161.

7. John Trumbull to John Adams, November 14, 1775, quoted in Victor E. Gimmestad, *John Trumbull* (New York: Twayne, 1974), p. 88; Hugh Henry Brackenridge, *Modern Chivalry*, pp. 479, 443.

8. Daniel Webster, "An Address delivered at the Laying of the Cornerstone of the Bunker Hill Monument at Charlestown, Massachusetts, on the 17th of June, 1825," *The Writings and Speeches of Daniel Webster*, 18 vols. (Boston: Little, Brown, 1903), 1, 253–254.

9. Brackenridge, *Modern Chivalry*, p. 7.

10. John Trumbull to John Adams, July 27, 1805, quoted in Gimmestad, *John Trumbull*, pp. 108–109. "Why was I totally neglected at the first organization of the general Government?" Trumbull asked Adams, recounting his assistance to Washington as a speech writer. See also G. Thomas Tanselle, *Royall Tyler* (Cambridge, Mass.: Harvard University Press, 1967), pp. 10–19.

11. For descriptions of Brackenridge's encounters with Washington and Jefferson, see Claude Milton Newlin, *The Life and Writings of Hugh Henry Brackenridge* (Princeton, N.J.: Princeton University Press, 1932), pp. 62–68, 229–234. See also Hugh Henry Brackenridge, *Law Miscellanies: Containing An Introduction to The Study of the Law . . . With Some Law Cases, and A Variety of Other Matters Chiefly Original* (1814; rpt. New York: Arno Press, 1972), pp. 257–258. For Brackenridge's jocular promise to punish indifference through his pen, see *Modern Chivalry*, pp. 156–157.

12. Lewis P. Simpson, "The Symbolism of Literary Alienation in the Revolutionary Age," *The Brazen Face of History: Studies in the Literary Consciousness in America* (Baton Rouge: Louisiana State University Press, 1980), p. 24.

13. For the most complete record of Trumbull's achievements as a child prodigy, see *Extracts from the Itineraries and Other Miscellanies of Ezra Stiles, D.D., LL.D., 1755–1794, With a Selection from His Correspondence*, ed. Franklin Bowditch Dexter (New Haven: Yale University Press, 1916), p. 400. For Trumbull's comments, see "While You, my Friend, to Flow'ry meads resort" and John Trumbull to John Adams, February 6, 1790, both quoted from Victor E. Gimmestad, *John Trumbull* (New York: Twayne, 1974), pp. 13, 127.

14. See Leon Howard, *The Connecticut Wits* (Chicago: University of Chicago Press, 1943), pp. 66, 77; Alexander Cowie, *John Trumbull: Connecticut Wit* (Chapel Hill: University of North Carolina Press, 1936), pp. 4, 62–63, 144; and Gimmestad, *John Trumbull*, pp. 81–82, 152.

15. John Trumbull, "Preface," *The Progress of Dulness, Part Second* (New Haven: Thomas and Samuel Green, 1773), vi. For Trumbull's comment on his role as a humorist, see Gimmestad, *John Trumbull*, p. 43.

16. John Trumbull, *The Progress of Dulness*, in *The Poetical Works*, 2 vols. (Hartford: Samuel G. Goodrich, 1820), II, 33, 65. Unless otherwise indicated, all later references to Trumbull's poetry are from this edition and are listed in the text. Trumbull's introduction, paginated with a series of separate arabic numerals in *The Poetical Works*, is referred to by roman numerals in the text to avoid confusion.

17. *The Poetical Works*, II, 10. See also "Preface," *The Progress of Dulness, Part Second*, vii–x. (One must turn to the first edition of the poem in 1773 for these comments. Trumbull excluded his angry response to the clergy's criticisms from his collected works.)

18. Edmund S. Morgan, "The American Revolution Considered as an Intellectual Movement," in Arthur M. Schlesinger, Jr., and Morton White, eds., *Paths of American Thought* (Boston: Houghton Mifflin, 1963), p. 11. For the ministry's own recognition of its diminished status in post-Revolutionary America see Emory Elliott, *Revolutionary Writers: Literature and Authority in the New Republic* (New York: Oxford University Press, 1982), pp. 38–45.

19. Quoted in Charles Warren, *A History of the American Bar* (1911; rpt. New York: Howard Fertig, 1966), p. 322.

20. See Jackson Turner Main, *The Social Structure of Revolutionary America* (Princeton, N.J.: Princeton University Press, 1965), pp. 96–102, 203–207.

21. Howard, *The Connecticut Wits*, p. 78. See also John Trumbull to Silas Deane, January 8, 1772, quoted in Cowie, *John Trumbull*, p. 101.

22. John Trumbull, "Preface," *The Progress of Dulness, Part Second*, v–vi.

23. For the best treatment of Kames's influence on Trumbull and of Trumbull's satire of the New Light Divines, see Howard, *The Connecticut*

Wits, pp. 65 ff. See also *The Progress of Dulness*, in *The Poetical Works*, II, 22–23.

24. *The Progress of Dulness, Part Second* is "published for the universal Benefit of Mankind." The other quotations in this paragraph are all from Trumbull's "Preface to the Third Part," *The Poetical Works, f145ii*, 60.

25. John Trumbull to Silas Deane, May 27, 1775, quoted in Gimmestad, *John Trumbull*, p. 81.

26. The words in quotation are those of Samuel Stone, a Hartford minister of the previous century, but they have been used as a slogan to summarize all "Federalists of the Old School." See David Hackett Fischer, *The Revolution of American Conservatism: The Federalist Party in the Era of Jeffersonian Democracy* (1965; rpt. New York: Harper and Row, 1969), pp. 4, 17. For the centrality of Polybius' view of mixed government to Revolutionary and post-Revolutionary thought, see Richard M. Gummere, *The American Colonial Mind and the Classical Tradition: Essays in Comparative Culture* (Cambridge, Mass.: Harvard University Press, 1963), pp. 177–182, and Meyer Reinhold, ed., *The Classick Pages: Classical Reading of Eighteenth-Century Americans* (University Park, Pa.: American Philological Association, 1975), pp. 121–127.

27. *M'Fingal*, in *The Poetical Works*, I, 112–113. For Trumbull the law student and lawyer's use of legal terminology in his poem, see I, 17, 18, 20, 32, 36, 37, 38, 42, 71, 88, 89, 165, 172.

28. For a brief discussion of these early republican fears over the components of mixed constitutional government, see J. G. A. Pocock, *The Machiavellian Moment: Florentine Political Thought and the Atlantic Republican Tradition* (Princeton, N.J.: Princeton University Press, 1975), pp. 513–517.

29. David Humphreys, Joel Barlow, John Trumbull, and Dr. Lemuel Hopkins, *The Anarchiad: A New England Poem*, ed. Luther G. Riggs (New Haven: Thomas H. Pease, 1861), pp. 23–24, 6–7. Throughout *The Anarchiad* the collapse of legal standards remains a central theme. See, for example, pp. 9, 16–17, 30, 36–37, 51, 57, 61.

30. See Linda K. Kerber, *Federalists in Dissent: Imagery and Ideology in Jeffersonian America* (Ithaca, N.Y.: Cornell University Press, 1970), and Richard E. Ellis, *The Jeffersonian Crisis: Courts and Politics in the Young Republic* (New York: Oxford University Press, 1971).

31. "No other writer of the eighteenth century gave Americans so perfect a glass of their existence." Kenneth Silverman, *A Cultural History of the American Revolution* (New York: Thomas Y. Crowell, 1976), p. 560.

32. Royall Tyler, *The Contrast, A Comedy; in Five Acts*, ed. James Benjamin Wilbur (Boston: Houghton Mifflin, 1920), p. 113. All later references to *The Contrast* are to the Wilbur edition.

33. John and Abigail Adams' correspondence over their daughter Ab-

igail's attachment to Royall Tyler extends from December 1782 to the summer of 1784 and will soon appear in full in the fifth volume of *Adams Family Correspondence*, edited by L. H. Butterfield and published by Harvard University Press. For the quotations that appear in this paragraph and the next, see L. H. Butterfield, "Introduction," *The Earliest Diary of John Adams* (Cambridge, Mass.: Harvard University Press, 1966), pp. 18–27, and G. Thomas Tanselle, *Royall Tyler* (Cambridge, Mass.: Harvard University Press, 1967), pp. 10–18.

34. Royall Tyler, "An Oration on the Death of George Washington," in Marius B. Péladeau, ed., *The Prose of Royall Tyler* (Rutland, Vt.: Charles E. Tuttle, 1972), p. 279.

35. When Nabby left for Europe, she and Tyler had a tentative understanding, with her parents' permission. Inexplicably, Tyler failed to write regularly and became foolishly temperamental around family relatives, who reported every slip to Nabby's parents in Europe. See Tanselle, *Royall Tyler*, pp. 16–17.

36. For Tyler's early misconduct, see Tanselle, *Royall Tyler*, pp. 6–8, and Butterfield, "Introduction," *The Earliest Diary of John Adams*, p. 23. See also Harold Milton Ellis, *Joseph Dennie and His Circle: A Study in American Literature from 1792 to 1812* (1915; rpt. New York: AMS Press, 1971), pp. 65–66, 95. Tyler's bawdy poem, "The Origin of Evil, an Elegy," was published anonymously in pamphlet form in 1793. It appears in full in Marius B. Péladeau, ed., *The Verse of Royall Tyler* (Charlottesville: University Press of Virginia, 1968), pp. 10–15.

37. Quoted from Tanselle, *Royall Tyler*, p. 35.

38. Tanselle, *Royall Tyler*, pp. 20–22.

39. "Oration on the Death of George Washington," and "Charge to the Grand Jury of Chittenden County, August 1808 in *The State of Vermont v. Cyrus B. Dean*," in *The Prose of Royall Tyler*, pp. 269, 273–274, 278, 362–365, 408.

40. Quoted from Tanselle, *Royall Tyler*, p. 38.

41. Abigail Adams 2nd to Elizabeth Cranch, June [1782], *Adams Family Correspondence*, ed. L. H. Butterfield and Marc Friedlander (Cambridge, Mass.: Harvard University Press, 1973), IV, 335.

42. Tanselle, *Royall Tyler*, pp. 53–54. For more detail on works that may have influenced Tyler in *The Contrast*, see Herbert R. Brown, "Sensibility in Eighteenth-Century Drama," *American Literature*, 4 (March 1932), 47–60, and Arthur H. Nethercot, "The Dramatic Background of Royall Tyler's *The Contrast*," *American Literature*, 12 (January 1941), 435–446.

43. Two recent analyses explore some of these diversities and complexities in *The Contrast*. See Roger B. Stein, "Royall Tyler and the Question of Our Speech," *The New England Quarterly*, 38 (December 1965), 454–

474, and Donald T. Siebert, Jr., "Royall Tyler's 'Bold Example': *The Contrast* and the English Comedy of Manners," *Early American Literature*, 13 (Spring 1978), 3–11.

44. See George O. Seilhamer, *History of the American Theatre from 1774 to 1797*, 3 vols. (1889; rpt. New York: Francis P. Harper, 1896), II, 226, and Siebert, "Royall Tyler's 'Bold Example'," *Early American Literature*, p. 9.

45. For comment on the lawyer's interest in the question of justice in Tyler's last plays, see Walter J. Meserve, *An Emerging Entertainment: The Drama of the American People to 1828* (Bloomington: Indiana University Press, 1977), p. 102.

46. Abigail Adams to Mary Smith Cranch, July 16, 1787, noted in Butterfield, "Introduction," *The Earliest Diary of John Adams*, p. 29.

47. Hugh Henry Brackenridge, "The Cave of Vanhest," in Daniel Marder, ed., *A Hugh Henry Brackenridge Reader 1770–1815* (Pittsburgh: University of Pittsburgh Press, 1970), pp. 91–92.

48. H[enry] M[arie] Brackenridge, *Recollections of Persons and Places in The West* (Philadelphia: James Kay, Jun., 1834), p. 139, and "Conclusion," *Gazette Publications*, in Marder, ed., *A Brackenridge Reader*, p. 377. [Originally printed in 1806.]

49. For effective summaries of Brackenridge's achievements in the early republic, see Daniel Marder, *Hugh Henry Brackenridge* (New York: Twayne, 1967), pp. 18–19; Marder, ed., *A Brackenridge Reader*, pp. 10–15, 41, 131, 266; and Joseph J. Ellis, "Hugh Henry Brackenridge: The Novelist as Reluctant Democrat," *After the Revolution: Profiles of Early American Culture* (New York: W. W. Norton, 1979), pp. 73–110.

50. Arthur Hobson Quinn, *American Fiction* (New York: D. Appleton-Century, 1936), p. 11.

51. Hugh Henry Brackenridge, *Modern Chivalry*, ed. Claude M. Newlin (1937; rpt. New York: Hafner, 1968), pp. 727, 807, 803. All later references to *Modern Chivalry* in the text are from the Newlin edition.

52. For an excellent analysis of the importance of English Whig rhetoric in the language and conception of *Modern Chivalry*, see Michael T. Gilmore, "Eighteenth-Century Oppositional Ideology and Hugh Henry Brackenridge's *Modern Chivalry*," *Early American Literature*, 13 (Fall 1978), 181–192.

53. Claude Milton Newlin, " 'Modern Chivalry, Part II': A Defense Of The Law," *The Life and Writings of Hugh Henry Brackenridge* (Princeton, N.J.: Princeton University Press, 1932), pp. 251–266.

54. See Lewis Leary, *Soundings: Some Early American Writers* (Athens, Ga.: University of Georgia Press, 1975), p. 170. For the complex interaction of Farrago and Teague in *Modern Chivalry*, see Emory Elliott, *Revolutionary Writers*, pp. 182–217.

55. Henry Adams, *History of The United States of America*, 9 vols. (1889–1891; rpt. New York: C. Scribner's Sons, 1921), I, 124–125. The third volume of *Modern Chivalry* in 1793 was the first literary work written, printed, and issued west of the Allegheny mountains.

56. Thomas Jefferson, *Notes on the State of Virginia*, ed. William Peden (1954; rpt. W. W. Norton, 1972), pp. 120, 129, 148–149, and Thomas Jefferson to John Adams, October 28, 1813, in *The Adams-Jefferson Letters*, ed. Lester J. Cappon, 2 vols. (Chapel Hill: University of North Carolina Press, 1959), II, 388–389. For direct parallels in Brackenridge's writings, see *Modern Chivalry*, pp. 21, 270, 399, 404, 414, 423, 426–427, 433, 497, 507, 529–530, 543–544. See also Newlin, *The Life and Writings of Hugh Henry Brackenridge*, pp. 250, 259, and Lewis P. Simpson, "The Symbolism of Literary Alienation in the Revolutionary Age," *The Brazen Face of History: Studies in the Literary Consciousness in America* (Baton Rouge: Louisiana State University Press, 1980), pp. 23, 35.

57. Among commentators on Brackenridge, only Lewis P. Simpson has seen the intrinsic connection between law and writing in *Modern Chivalry*. See Simpson, *The Brazen Face of History*, pp. 35–37.

58. Quoted in Newlin, *The Life and Writings of Hugh Henry Brackenridge*, p. 220. This comment first appeared in the Pittsburgh newspaper, *The Tree of Liberty*, on September 13, 1800. Brackenridge's disappointments in politics and the persecution he suffered at the time of the Whiskey Rebellion are fictionalized in *Modern Chivalry*, pp. 13–17, 282–284, 302–326. See also Marder, *Hugh Henry Brackenridge*, pp. 43–54, 90.

59. For two examinations of Brackenridge's interest in the irrational in human nature and the role of his characterization of Teague, see Amberys R. Whittle, "*Modern Chivalry*: The Frontier as Crucible," *Early American Literature*, 6 (Winter 1971–72), 263–270, and Wendy Martin, "The Rogue and the Rational Man: Hugh Henry Brackenridge's Study of a Con Man in *Modern Chivalry*," *Early American Literature*, 8 (Fall 1973), 179–192.

60. *Modern Chivalry*, pp. 173, 786. Brackenridge wrote "Jefferson, In Imitation of Virgil's Pollio" early in 1801 when he was leader of the Jeffersonian democrats in western Pennsylvania. He also tried to draw Jefferson into regular correspondence, promising for his part to send the party leader "hints, or indicia of the public mind on occasional subjects." Jefferson responded only briefly but also gave Brackenridge a personal copy of *Notes on the State of Virginia*. The poem and relevant correspondence are quoted at length in Newlin, *The Life and Writings of Hugh Henry Brackenridge*, pp. 230–235.

61. Hugh Henry Brackenridge, *Law Miscellanies: Containing An Introduction to the Study of the Law, Notes on Blackstone's Commentaries . . . and A Variety of Other Matters, Chiefly Original* (1814; rpt. New York: Arno Press, 1972). For a perceptive placement of *Law Miscellanies* in Brackenridge's

changing viewpoint, see Marder, *Hugh Henry Brackenridge*, pp. 117–119.

62. For the formal courtroom scenes in Brackenridge's novel, see *Modern Chivalry*, pp. 152–153, 285–290, 323–324, 430–432, 546–547, 701–702. Lessons in law appear on pp. 35–36, 137–139, 143–147, 220–224, 338–339, 453–454, 542–545.

63. Hugh Henry Brackenridge, *Incidents of the Insurrection in the Western Parts of Pennsylvania in the Year 1794*, 3 vols. (Philadelphia: John M'Colloch, 1795), III, 22.

64. For the best work on this subject, see Richard E. Ellis, *The Jeffersonian Crisis: Courts and Politics in the Young Republic* (New York: Oxford University Press, 1971). For the depth of anti-law attitudes in the period, see Maxwell Bloomfield, "Antilawyer Sentiment in the Early Republic," *American Lawyers in a Changing Society, 1776–1876* (Cambridge, Mass.: Harvard University Press, 1976), pp. 32–58.

65. For an analysis of Farrago's delusions as Don Quixote, see Joseph H. Harkey, "The *Don Quixote* of the Frontier: Brackenridge's *Modern Chivalry*," *Early American Literature*, 8 (Fall 1973), 193–203.

66. Teague as inheritor is described by Ellis, *After the Revolution*, p. 100, and Leary, *Soundings*, p. 173.

67. Marder, *Hugh Henry Brackenridge*, pp. 58–62; Henry Marie Brackenridge, *Recollections*, pp. 131, 140.

5. The Case of Charles Brockden Brown

1. The many recent studies of Charles Brockden Brown have affirmed his significance, but they have also ignored the historical context of his craft. As William Hedges correctly notes, "Recent studies on the whole give us no very clear sense of Brown as a person who lived in a particular time and place." Hedges, "Charles Brockden Brown and the Culture of Contradictions," *Early American Literature*, 9 (Fall 1974), 110.

2. Brown's *Literary Magazine and American Register* contained a wide range of articles debating the proper place and function of fiction within society. See "On Novel Writing," 2 (December 1804), 693–694; "Novels," 3 (January 1805), 16–17; "The Sorrows of Werter," 6 (December 1806), 451; and "On The Cause of the Popularity of Novels," 7 (June 1807), 410–412. See also "The Difference Between History and Romance," *Monthly Magazine and American Review*, 2 (April 1800), 251–253.

Brown's novels are collected in *Charles Brockden Brown's Novels*, ed. David McKay, 6 vols. (Philadelphia: David McKay, 1887). Except for *Memoirs of Stephen Calvert*, references to Brown's novels in the text are to this edition.

3. For Brown's statements on his vocational anxieties see William Dun-

lap, *The Life of Charles Brockden Brown: Together with Selections From The Rarest of His Printed Works, From His Original Letters and From His Manuscripts Before Unpublished*, 2 vols. (Philadelphia: James P. Parke, 1815), I, 25, and II, 117. Hereafter cited as Dunlap. See also "The Reflector, No. II," *Literary Magazine and American Register*, 4 (August 1805), 104–105.

4. "The Diary of Thomas Pym Cope," December 15, 1809. Transcript by Harry R. Warfel of a diary in the possession of Mrs. George W. Emlin of Philadelphia. I am indebted to Warner B. Berthoff for my copy of this transcript. That Brown felt these tensions but studied law seriously between 1788 and 1793 is clear from surviving notes and commonplace books in his own hand. See *Charles Brockden Brown Manuscripts, 1715–1824*, 14 vols., in the possession of the Historical Society of Pennsylvania, V, IX, X.

5. For the negative context of Brown's decision against law and for the rejection of his position by family and friends, see Dunlap, I, 40–47. Brown wrote most extensively of man's positive duty to work and to be of service within the world in "Walstein's School of History" in *The Rhapsodist and Other Uncollected Writings by Charles Brockden Brown*, ed. Harry R. Warfel (New York: Scholars' Facsimiles and Reprints, 1943), p. 153, and in "Sketch of The Life and Character of John Blair Linn" in John Blair Linn, *Valerian, A Narrative Poem* (Philadelphia: Thomas and George Palmer, 1805). Brown's self-critical remarks in the text are from a letter written on January 22, 1793, cited in David Lee Clark, "Unpublished Letters of Charles Brockden Brown and W. W. Wilkins," *University of Texas Studies in English*, 27 (June 1948), 103.

6. Dunlap, II, 11, 99–100.

7. Dunlap, I, 53.

8. Brown once compared the "pure airs and brilliant prospects" of New York to the "uniform, monotonous and dull" appearance of Philadelphia. Of the latter, he added "more irksome, more deadening to my fancy is this city, on its *own* account, than ever" (Dunlap, II, 101). For convincing evidence that Philadelphia in 1800 was the leading cultural center in the Republic, see Van Wyck Brooks, "Philadelphia in 1800," *The World of Washington Irving* (New York: E. P. Dutton, 1944), pp. 1–26.

9. Dunlap, I, 40.

10. See "The Rhapsodist" and "The Man At Home," in *The Rhapsodist*, pp. 6–7, 46, and Brown, *Alcuin: A Dialogue* (New York: T. and J. Swords, 1798).

11. Lack of respect for the novel in early American literary circles is summarized by William Charvat, *The Origins of American Critical Thought 1810–1835* (Philadelphia: University of Pennsylvania Press, 1936), pp. 136–140. Wirt claimed that he knew "few persons of exalted intellect" in America outside his profession. William Wirt, "Letter VIII," *The Letters of The*

British Spy (1803; rpt. New York: Harper, 1844), p. 206. Brown's magazine gave *The British Spy* a very mixed review. See *Literary Magazine and American Register*, 1 (January 1804), 261.

12. For these negative appraisals of Brown's vocational situation see, in order, Dunlap, I, 17, 41–43; Edward Tyrrel Channing, "The Life of Charles Brockden Brown: Review of William Dunlap's Biography of Brown," *North American Review*, 9 (May 1819), 61, 58–77; and William H. Prescott, "Charles Brockden Brown, The American Novelist," *Biographical and Critical Miscellanies* (1834; rpt. London: Richard Bentley, 1845), pp. 7–8. Brown's own comment is from Clark, "Unpublished Letters of Brown and Wilkins," p. 103.

13. "A Series of Original Letters," in Warfel, ed., *The Rhapsodist*, pp. 103, 108–109, 114–124. These letters appeared in print in 1798, but Warfel traces their composition largely to 1795.

14. *Ormond*, VII, 18–19. For the rest of Brown's comments on law in this paragraph, see, in order, "Walstein's School of History," in Warfel, ed., *The Rhapsodist*, p. 153; "A Sketch of the Life and Character of the Author," in Linn, *Valerian, A Narrative Poem*, p. vii; *Literary Magazine and American Register*, 5 (May 1806), 330–332; 4 (October 1805), 270; 6 (November 1806), 359–360; and *American Register or General Repository of History, Politics, and Science*, 1 (1806–1807), 175.

15. "Extracts From a Student's Diary: Authorship," *Literary Magazine and American Register*, 1 (October, 1803), 8–9. The emphasis is Brown's. Ernest Marchand first traces this comment to a "hankering for the gentlemanly tradition of authorship." Marchand, "Introduction to the Hafner Library Edition," *Ormond or The Secret Witness* (New York: Hafner, 1962), p. xlii.

16. For Brown's negative comments on writing, see Dunlap, II, 92, 264–265, 330.

17. Letter from Charles Brockden Brown to Thomas Jefferson, December 15, 1798, in David Lee Clark, *Charles Brockden Brown: Pioneer Voice of America* (Durham, N.C.: Duke University Press, 1952), p. 163. See also "A Student's Diary," *Literary Magazine and American Register*, 1 (March 1804), 405.

18. "The Editor's Address To The Public," *Literary Magazine and American Register*, 1 (October 1803), 4. Also quoted in Dunlap, II, 60.

19. *Memoirs of Stephen Calvert*, in Dunlap, II, 274–472. Subsequent page references to *Stephen Calvert* in the text are from Dunlap, II.

20. All of the quotations in this paragraph are from Clark, "Unpublished Letters of Brown and Wilkins," pp. 75–107.

21. The forces of adult repression are intense in *Stephen Calvert*. Stephen's grandfather plans the murder of his own son, Stephen's father (pp.

294–296). Louisa Calvert and Clelia Neville are both brutalized by "parental tyranny" when young (pp. 301–302, 399–401). Stephen fears the "vigilant eye" of his mother and will do anything to avoid her disapproval (pp. 321, 451).

22. Donald A. Ringe, *Charles Brockden Brown* (New York: Twayne, 1966), p. 112.

23. Criminal insanity shatters the peaceful worlds of *Wieland* and *Edgar Huntly*. Clara Wieland and Edgar Huntly are then forced to confront parallel impulses within themselves. The yellow fever epidemics and ensuing panics lead to similar situations in *Ormond* and *Arthur Mervyn*.

24. Brown always insisted upon "the transcendent merits of *Caleb Williams*" as a model for his own work. Dunlap, II, 107. George Sherburn writes about the law as the essential villain in Godwin's novel in Sherburn, "Introduction to the Rinehart edition," *The Adventures of Caleb Williams or Things As They Are* (New York: Rinehart, 1960). That Brown was attracted by Godwin's distaste for legal regulation is clear from several magazine articles that touch on the subject. See *Literary Magazine and American Register*, 2 (August 1804), 361–369, and 3 (March 1805), 194–195.

25. Warner B. Berthoff, "The Literary Career of Charles Brockden Brown," Ph. D. diss., Harvard, 1954, p. 135. For an analysis of Brown's objection to law in another novel, see Carl Nelson, "A Just Reading of Charles Brockden Brown's *Ormond*," *Early American Literature*, 8 (Fall 1973), 170–174.

26. Brown liked to demonstrate that "the wisest and soberest of human beings is, in some respects, a madman." Dunlap, II, 377. Both Wielands, Edgar Huntly, Arthur Mervyn, Philip Stanley, and Stephen Calvert all prove this proposition within the novels. Brown's premise of sudden, unexplained madness has been traced, in part, to his interest in Lockean psychology. See Arthur Kimball, *Rational Fictions: A Study of Charles Brockden Brown* (McMinnville, Ore.: Linfield Research Institute, 1968), pp. 55–59.

27. For explicit indications that legal distinctions and social remedies become irrelevant in *Edgar Huntly* when placed against larger psychological truths, see IV, 67–69, 254–263.

28. In *Jane Talbot*, for example, the hero must first recover from "indolent habits" and a "rooted incapacity" before he is allowed to marry the heroine (V, 177, 199). Achsa Fielding, the source of wisdom in *Arthur Mervyn*, warns that "the worst foes of man . . . are solitude and idleness" (III, 208). Both Theodore Wieland and his father succumb to madness while idle men (I, 30, 41). Even Stephen Calvert notes "the salutary effects of occupation." Dunlap, II, 433.

29. "Memoirs of Carwin, The Biloquist," in Dunlap, II, 212, 215, 222.

30. Generations of Wielands summarize Brown's conflict between lit-

erature and the family mercantile business. Grandfather Wieland is a dis-inherited gentleman who must convert his love of music and literature from "sources of amusement" into "means of gain." His literary efforts provide a "scanty subsistence" and he dies young. By contrast, the next Wieland is brought up entirely within the narrow framework of "mercantile servitude." His success and contentment depend upon this very narrowness (I, 26–27).

31. For the nature of the Horatian ideal in America see Howard Mumford Jones, "Roman Virtue," *O Strange New World: American Culture, The Formative Years* (1952; rpt. New York: Viking, 1964), pp. 245–250. For the importance of Cicero to Republican lawyers, see Stephen Botein, "Cicero as Role Model for Early American Lawyers: A Case Study in Classical Influence," *The Classical Journal,* 73 (1977–78), 313–321. Conflict between romantic impulse and neoclassical restraint is general in Brown's fiction. See Michael D. Bell, " 'The Double-Tongued Deceiver': Sincerity and Duplicity in the Novels of Charles Brockden Brown," *Early American Literature,* 9 (Fall 1974), 150–151, and Paul Witherington, "Brockden Brown's Other Novels: *Clara Howard* and *Jane Talbot,*" *Nineteenth-Century Fiction,* 29 (December 1974), 263.

32. An enthusiastic reader of *The Castle of Otranto, The Mysteries of Udolpho, Caleb Williams,* and other gothic novels of terror, Brown clearly understood the literary potential of the horror in yellow fever. For Brown's detailed familiarity and interest in gothic fiction, see Lulu Rumsey Wiley, *The Sources and Influence of the Novels of Charles Brockden Brown* (New York: Vantage, 1950), pp. 72–95.

33. Dunlap, I, 3–12. Here, in a letter, Brown described Dr. Smith's altruistic service and his final suffering in some detail: "The disease, in no case, was ever more dreadfully and infernally malignant."

34. "The Man At Home," in Warfel, ed., *The Rhapsodist,* p. 85. The passage originally appeared in *Weekly Magazine,* 1 (1798), 322–323.

35. David Lee Clark argues that Brown may have decided to write about yellow fever as early as 1793 and certainly by 1796: *Charles Brockden Brown: Pioneer Voice of America,* pp. 156–157. For the best examples of Brown's interest in how "employments of life would be suspended" under plague conditions, leaving everyone "suddenly bereft of all activity," see *Literary Magazine and American Register,* 1 (1803–1804), 6, as well as *Arthur Mervyn,* II, 129–130, 140, and *Ormond,* VI, 53–54.

36. Dunlap, II, 10.

37. Biographical details are scant, but Brown apparently was always a family favorite indulged because of a frail constitution (see Dunlap, I, 41, 49). For evidence of increasing familial pressure by April 1800, see Brown's defensive letter on "book-making" in Dunlap, II, 100.

38. Counting the lost *Sky-Walk* and *Memoirs of Stephen Calvert*, Brown wrote eight novels. He apparently was at work on all four major novels between September and November 1798, or during and immediately following his exposure to yellow fever. *Wieland*, published in September 1798, was completed and printed during the epidemic; *Ormond* was published in February 1799; *Arthur Mervyn*, in two parts in May 1799 and July 1800; and *Edgar Huntly or Memoirs of a Sleep-Walker*, in August 1799. Brown's observation on the facility with which he wrote during the epidemic of 1798 is contained in Dunlap, II, 96. For Warner Berthoff's passing comment on the timing of Brown's creativity, see Berthoff, "The Literary Career of Charles Brockden Brown," p. 32. For a good account of Brown's methods of composition in this crucial period, see Sydney J. Krause, "*Ormond*: How Rapidly and How Well 'Composed, Arranged and Delivered'," *Early American Literature*, 13 (1978–79), 238–249.

39. William Hedges already has shown how Brown's use of yellow fever is a general criticism of eighteenth-century tenets of rationalism and pietism. Hedges, "Benjamin Rush, Charles Brockden Brown, and the American Plague Year," *Early American Literature*, 7 (1972–73), 295–309. Hedges contrasts Rush's Enlightenment views with Brown's intellectual skepticism. Arthur Kimball more generally finds in Brown's plague scenes "an ambiguous warning to Americans." *Rational Fictions: A Study of Charles Brockden Brown*, pp. 193, 195–199. Warner Berthoff best describes how Brown uses accepted scientific theory "to express his moral image of society: the conception of a materially tainted atmosphere." "The Literary Career of Charles Brockden Brown," p. 145. For a good example of Brown's early renunciation of the world's corruption and the negative reactions of his peers, see Dunlap, I, 41–43.

40. Mathew Carey, *A Short Account of the Malignant Fever, Lately Prevalent in Philadelphia . . . From August 1, to the middle of December 1793*, 4th ed. (Philadelphia: Mathew Carey, 1794), pp. 6, 10, 21, 23, 45, 58 (the first edition appeared in November 1793). For an analysis of the central importance of Carey's account at the time, see J. H. Powell, *Bring Out Your Dead: The Great Plague of Yellow Fever in Philadelphia in 1793* (1949; rpt. New York: Time, 1965). Brown clearly read the Carey account, and the two writers agreed in many aspects of their coverage.

41. The comment on the importance of nursing and attention is from a letter Brown wrote during the plague of 1798 (Dunlap, II, 5). Both *Ormond* and *Arthur Mervyn* depend heavily upon this assumption, which was shared by Carey in *A Short Account of the Malignant Fever*, p. 72. For examples of selfish behavior leading to a chain reaction of multiple deaths note the cases of Whiston in *Ormond*, VI, 46–47, and of Thetford and his family in *Arthur Mervyn*, II, 158–160.

42. Of Arthur Mervyn, we learn that "nothing was more remarkable than his impenetrability to ridicule and censure" (III, 20). In a false society, this demeanor is a virtue. Sheer composure enables Arthur to handle the angry bully Philip Hadwin (III, 88–92) and to correct his own father in public (III, 127–128). Mervyn's composure, however, is most important against yellow fever. Brown apparently believed that terror or unusual emotion increased or ripened infection (VI, 68–69). This premise was shared by many contemporaries. "The effect of fear in predisposing the body for yellow fever and other disorders, and increasing their malignance, when taken, is well known," wrote Carey, *A Short Account of the Malignant Fever*, p. 77. Brown seizes upon the idea to link virtue with survival and lack of virtue with fatal contagion.

43. For two different but parallel descriptions of the intellectual shift in nineteenth-century thinking from identification *within* a social context toward individual identity formed *against* social norms, see Quentin Anderson, *The Imperial Self: An Essay in American Literary and Cultural History* (New York: Alfred A. Knopf, 1971), pp. 55–58, and Morse Peckham, *Beyond the Tragic Vision: The Quest for Identity in the Nineteenth Century* (New York: George Braziller, 1962), pp. 87–100, 160.

44. The nature of Brown's special creativity in fiction is summarized by Donald A. Ringe, "Charles Brockden Brown," in Everett Emerson, ed., *Major Writers of Early American Literature* (Madison: University of Wisconsin Press, 1972), pp. 273–294. See also Warner B. Berthoff, " 'A Lesson on Concealment': Brockden Brown's Method in Fiction," *Philological Quarterly*, 37 (January 1958), 45–57, and William Hedges, "Charles Brockden Brown and the Culture of Contradictions," *Early American Literature*, 107–142.

45. Philip Stanley in *Clara Howard*, Edgar Huntly, Arthur Mervyn, and even Clara Wieland each experience destructive and irrational impulses just as entrance or return to the conventional world becomes possible.

46. Arthur Mervyn, Philip Stanley, Henry Colden, and Edgar Huntly are just a few of the heroes in Brown's fiction who plan to marry protective women of wealth and wisdom. The pattern becomes an obsession in Brown's last two novels, *Jane Talbot* and *Clara Howard*. By contrast, the fathers of Constantia Dudley, Stephen Calvert, Jane Talbot, Arthur Mervyn, Carwin, and Louisa Calvert are weaklings or worse. Brothers are forces of evil or incompetence in *Jane Talbot*, *Edgar Huntly*, *Wieland*, *Ormond*, and *Arthur Mervyn*. Older sisters are invariably virtuous, supportive, and protective. Brown's merchant father and four brothers set a conventional example that must have given the "idle" Charles many uncomfortable minutes.

47. "Authorship," *Literary Magazine and American Register*, 1 (October 1803), 9.

48. "Desultory Observations On The Sensibilities and Eccentricities of Men of Genius: With Remarks on Poets," *Literary Magazine and American Register*, 7 (April 1807), 294.

49. Dunlap, II, 100.

6. Washington Irving Hunts Down the Nation

1. Biographical fragment in a draft of a letter to Mrs. Amelia Foster, April–May 1823, in *Washington Irving, Letters*, ed. Ralph M. Aderman, Herbert L. Kleinfield, and Jenifer S. Banks, 2 vols. (Boston: Twayne, 1978), I, 738, and WI to Amos Eaton, December 15, 1802, *Letters*, I, 6. (The emphasis in the quotation is Irving's.) See also Stanley L. Williams, *The Life of Washington Irving*, 2 vols. (1935; rpt. New York: Octagon Books, 1971), I, 15, 24–25.

2. Washington Irving, *Letters of Jonathan Oldstyle* (1824; rpt. New York: Columbia University Press, 1941), pp. 2, 35, 60. (The Oldstyle letters originally appeared in Peter Irving's newspaper, the *Morning Chronicle*, in 1802 and 1803.) For Irving's declaration of his own literary intentions and personal independence, see WI to Ebenezer Irving, March 3, 1819, *Letters*, I, 540–541.

3. All facts on Irving's legal career are from Williams, *Life of Irving*. For Irving's commonplace book containing references to readings in Herodotus, Homer, Aristotle, Pliny, Plutarch, and other classical authors, see "Notes Taken While Preparing Knickerbocker, 1807–8," in the possession of the Houghton Library, Harvard University.

4. WI to Amos Eaton, December 15, 1802, and WI to Gouverneur Kemble, May 24, 1806, in *Letters*, I, 6, 217.

5. WI to Gouverneur Kemble, May 26, 1806, and WI to Henry Ogden, July 1806, *Letters*, I, 219, 222.

6. Biographical fragment, *Letters*, I, 739.

7. Washington Irving, "On Greatness, By Launcelot Langstaff, Esq.," in William Irving, James Kirke Paulding, and Washington Irving, *Salmagundi; or the Whimwhams and Opinions of Launcelot Langstaff Esq. and Others* (Philadelphia: Lippincott and Co., 1873), pp. 349–359. ("On Greatness" first appeared in "Salmagundi No. 15," dated October 1, 1807.)

8. Biographical fragment, *Letters*, I, 739–741.

9. All analyses of Irving as an angry young man must begin with William Hedges, *Washington Irving: An American Study, 1802–1832* (Baltimore: Johns Hopkins University Press, 1965), pp. 8–10. The concept of an "imagery of estrangement" in Irving's writings is Hedges'. For comments on Irving's later reputation as the genial man of letters, see Williams, *Life of Irving*, I, 22, II, 147–148, 374n.

10. Williams, *Life of Irving*, I, 116, and Martin Roth, *Comedy and America: The Lost World of Washington Irving* (Port Washington, N.Y.: Kennikat Press, 1976), p. 115.

11. Williams, *Life of Irving*, I, 114, and Roth, *Comedy and America*, p. 114, 196n. Roth demonstrates how *A History of New York* subsumes Irving's many external sources, and he also documents the growing number of scholars who see *A History of New York* as Irving's most creative work. For a precise delineation of Diedrich Knickerbocker's origins in Fielding, Sterne, and Swift, see James E. Evans, "The English Lineage of Diedrich Knickerbocker," *Early American Literature*, 10 (Spring 1975), 3–13.

12. Washington Irving, *Diedrich Knickerbocker's A History of New York*, ed. Stanley Williams and Tremaine McDowell (New York: Harcourt, Brace, 1927), pp. 132, 65. All later references in the text are to this edition, which follows the original version of December 1809. Irving altered his book in later editions, softening the satire and removing its bitterest sections.

13. *A History of New York*, pp. 179–187, 202–209; *Salmagundi*, pp. 18, 30, 52–53, 101, 150–151, 292–293. For the explicitness of Irving's satire of Jefferson, see Edwin A. Greenlaw, "Washington Irving's Comedy of Politics," *Texas Review*, 1 (April 1916), 291–306, and Stanley Williams and Tremaine McDowell, "Introduction," *Diedrich Knickerbocker's A History of New York*, lxi–lxxiii. That Irving's satire extends into New York state politics as well is clear from Mary Weatherspoon Bowden, "Knickerbocker's *History* and the 'Enlightened' Men of New York City," *American Literature*, 47 (May 1975), 159–172.

14. For Irving's general detachment from politics, see Donna Hagensick, "Irving—A Litterateur in Politics," in Ralph M. Aderman, ed., *Washington Irving Reconsidered: A Symposium* (Hartford: Transcendental Books, 1969), pp. 53–60, and Allen Guttmann, "Washington Irving and the Conservative Imagination," *American Literature*, 36 (May 1964), 165–173.

15. In later editions, Diedrich Knickerbocker openly admits this technique of comic inflation: "I have pursued the latest rules of my art . . . and wrought a very large history out of a small subject." Edwin T. Bowden, ed., *A History of New York* (New Haven: College and University Press, 1964), pp. 82–83. [Bowden uses the 1812 edition of Irving's work.]

16. *A History of New York*, pp. 17, 28, 45, 47, 62, 83, 153.

17. For the standard delineation of Irving's parody upon a variety of history texts, see Williams and McDowell, "Introduction," *Diedrich Knickerbocker's A History of New York*, xliv–li. For the nature of legal compendia of the period, see chapter 2.

18. Hugo Grotius, "Prolegomena: 40, 56, 59," *De Jure Belli et Pacis*, trans. William Whewell, 3 vols. (Cambridge, Eng.: Cambridge University Press, 1853), I, 66, 77–78.

19. For the destructive tendencies of Knickerbocker's treatment of history, see Roth, *Comedy and America*, pp. 114–115, and Hedges, *Washington Irving: An American Study*, pp. 85, 107. Knickerbocker "asserts through irony and humor the virtual meaninglessness of history." Hedges, "Knickerbocker, Bolingbroke, and the Fiction of History," *Journal of the History of Ideas*, 20 (June–September 1959), 317–328.

20. *A History of New York*, p. 106. See also Sir William Blackstone, Book IV, Chapter 33, *Commentaries on the Laws of England* (1765–1769; rpt. Chicago: University of Chicago Press, 1979), IV 400–436, and J. G. A. Pocock, *The Ancient Constitution and the Feudal Law: A Study of English Historical Thought in the Seventeenth Century* (1957; rpt. New York: W. W. Norton, 1967).

21. See, for example, John C. Miller, ed., "The Coming of the War of 1812: Three Speeches before Congress," *The Young Republic, 1789–1815* (New York: Free Press, 1970), pp. 159–174.

22. WI to William P. Van Ness, February 20, 1811, and WI to Gouverneur Kemble, January 10, 1838, *Letters*, I, 307, II, 918–920.

23. From the beginning, Diedrich Knickerbocker promises to use the "profound political speculations" of Thucydides. *A History of New York*, p. 9. Just as her military prowess and growing strength leads Athens' enemies to band against her, so Peter Stuyvesant's victories at Fort Casimer and Fort Christiana draw the attention of the British. Peter's disastrous venture into New England then functions as a comic parallel to the ill-advised Sicilian expedition of Athens, described in Books VI through VIII of Thucydides' history. Both Thucydides and Irving also inveigh against the tendencies toward incompetent leadership and belligerence in republics. See *A History of New York*, pp. 376–377, 390–396, 408–410, 445–446, and Thucydides, *History of the Peloponnesian War*, trans. Rex Warner, rev. ed. (Middlesex, Engl: Penguin, 1972), pp. 87, 103–108, 409–599. From his general readings in the classics and from Machiavelli, Irving noted in his legal commonplace book that "there is no surer way to ruin a democracy, than to set it on bold undertakings, which it is sure to misconduct." "Notes Taken While Preparing Knickerbocker, 1807–8."

24. Herman Melville, "Chapter 19: They Fight the Serapis," *Israel Potter: His Fifty Years of Exile* (1855; rpt. New York: Sagamore Press, 1957), p. 170.

25. *Common Sense*, for example, identifies all opponents of the Revolution as "interested men, who are not to be trusted, weak men who *cannot* see, prejudiced men who will not see, and a certain set of moderate men who think better of the European world than it deserves." *The Complete Writings of Thomas Paine*, ed. Philip S. Foner, 2 vols. (New York: Citadel Press, 1945). I, 21. In *The Federalist* all opposition is based entirely upon "views, passions, and prejudices little favorable to the discovery of truth."

Alexander Hamilton, "Federalist No. One." Failure to acknowledge any integrity in opposition naturally led to extreme reactions in political debate. See Linda K. Kerber, *Federalists in Dissent: Imagery and Ideology in Jeffersonian America* (Ithaca, N.Y.: Cornell University Press, 1970), and John R. Howe, Jr., "Republican Thought and the Political Violence of the 1790s," *American Quarterly*, 19 (Summer 1967), 147–165.

26. *Salmagundi*, pp. 404–411. See also William Hedges, *Washington Irving: An American Study*, pp. 8–9.

27. The distinction between subversive and reputable humor is made and then traced by Walter Blair and Hamlin Hill, *America's Humor from Poor Richard to Doonesbury* (New York: Oxford University Press, 1978), pp. 162–171. See also James Feibleman, *In Praise of Comedy: A Study in Its Theory and Practice* (New York: Macmillan, 1939), pp. 189–191.

28. The importance of detachment in the point of view of satire is noted in Walter Blair, *Native American Humor (1800–1900)* (New York: American Book Company, 1937), p. 6; Alvin B. Kernan, *The Plot of Satire* (New Haven: Yale University Press, 1965), p. 12; and Wayne C. Booth, *The Rhetoric of Fiction* (Chicago: University of Chicago Press, 1961), p. 331.

29. *A History of New York*, pp. 175–177. For Irving's specific techniques as an intrusive narrator in *A History of New York*, see Evans, "The English Lineage of Diedrich Knickerbocker," *Early American Literature*, 3–13.

30. Kernan, *The Plot of Satire*, p. 84.

31. For my terms in defining satire and then for distinguishing comedy from satire, see Edward W. Rosenheim, Jr., *Swift and the Satirist's Art* (Chicago: University of Chicago Press, 1963), pp. 25–31, and Kernan, *The Plot of Satire*, pp. 200–220.

32. Hedges, *Washington Irving: An American Study*, pp. 262 ff., and Roth, *Comedy and America*, pp. 116–122.

33. Elder Olson, *The Theory of Comedy* (Bloomington: Indiana University Press, 1968), pp. 23–35, 46–47.

34. *A History of New York*, p. 205. Irving's interest in exposing political bombast is discussed in David Durant, "Aeolism in *Knickerbocker's A History of New York*," *American Literature*, 41 (January 1970), 493–506.

35. For the movement from wit toward humor and toward "a more joyful and kindly theory of laughter," see Stuart M. Tave, *The Amiable Humorist: A Study in the Comic Theory and Criticism of the Eighteenth and Early Nineteenth Centuries* (Chicago: University of Chicago Press, 1960), pp. 74 ff.

36. See, for example, Lewis Leary, "Washington Irving: An End and a New Beginning," *Soundings: Some Early American Writers* (Athens, Ga.: University of Georgia Press, 1975), pp. 292–329.

37. For Irving's expressions of embarrassment concerning his first works, see *Letters*, I, 541, 550, 741, and Williams, *Life of Irving*, II, 269–276. By

1829 Irving was already talking of his biography of Washington as "my great and crowning labor" and as a "universally popular" work and a "valuable and lasting property" for Americans. WI to Peter Irving, December 18, 1829, *Letters*, II, 494. Terence Martin has shown how Irving's later historical protagonists ("images of exactly what made America what it wanted to be") contradict the earlier fictional heroes in "Rip, Ichabod, and the American Imagination," *American Literature*, 31 (May 1959), 137–149.

38. "The Author's Apology" from the revised edition of *A History of New York* in 1848, quoted in full in Bowden, ed., *A History of New York*, pp. 350–352.

39. For the financial success and great popularity of *A History of New York*, see Williams, *Life of Irving*, I, 118, 411.

40. Biographical fragment, *Letters*, I, 741.

41. Biographical fragment, *Letters*, I, 743.

42. *A History of New York*, p. 93. Also Washington Irving, "The Author's Account of Himself," *The Sketch Book of Geoffrey Crayon, Gent.*, ed. Haskell Springer (Boston: Twayne, 1978), p. 9.

43. Biographical fragment, *Letters*, I, 741–742, and WI to Henry Brevoort, May 15, 1811, *Letters*, I, 316. See also WI to Henry Brevoort, June 8, 1811, *Letters*, I, 322–323. For Irving's career with the *Analectic Magazine*, see Hedges, *Washington Irving: An American Study*, pp. 107–115.

44. WI to John G. Lockhart, August 20, 1819, *Letters*, I, 558.

45. *A History of New York*, pp. 104, 111, 136. See also Roth, *Comedy and America*, p. 135. Arguably, all of Irving's best fiction plays upon his fascination with arrested adolescence. His greatest heroes are "childish, primitive images of what America could not assimilate into the national self-image." Martin, "Rip, Ichabod, and the American Imagination," p. 148. Rip Van Winkle, in particular, passes "from childhood to second childhood with next to nothing in between." He is "the ego arrested at the infantile level in an Oedipal situation." Philip Young, "Fallen from Time: The Mythic Rip Van Winkle," *Kenyon Review*, 22 (Autumn 1960), 547–573.

46. "Notes Taken While Preparing Knickerbocker, 1807–8," and "Biographical fragment," *Letters*, I, 741. For Irving's short military career in the New York State Militia, see Williams, *Life of Irving*, I, 142–143.

47. Recent studies have tended to agree upon the greater creativity of the younger Irving. See Hedges, *Washington Irving: An American Study*, pp. viii, 30, 237–238, 265; Roth, *Comedy and America*, pp. 84, 143, 155; and Lewis Leary, "The Two Voices of Washington Irving," in Motley Deakin and Peter Lisca, eds., *From Irving to Steinbeck: Studies in American Literature in Honor of Harry R. Warfel* (Gainesville: University of Florida Press, 1972), pp. 13–26.

48. *The Sketch Book*, pp. 8, 48.

49. Biographical fragment, *Letters*, I, 743–744.

50. Biographical fragment, *Letters*, I, 742. "I underwent ruin in all its bitterness & humiliation—in a strange land—among strangers. I went through the horrible ordeal of Bankruptcy."

51. "Roscoe," "The Wife," "Rip Van Winkle," in *The Sketch Book*, pp. 16–19, 22–27, 30–31. Here and in the following paragraph I paraphrase from Irving's language in my descriptions.

52. Geoffrey Crayon is a vague figure in *The Sketch Book*, but these characteristics can be gleaned from various remarks. See, in particular, "The Author's Account of Himself," "The Voyage," "The Art of Book Making," "The Stage Coach," "L'Envoy," *The Sketch Book*, pp. 9, 15, 61, 156, 299. See also *A History of New York*, pp. 1–6, 444.

53. "Rip Van Winkle," *The Sketch Book*, pp. 28, 30, 40–41. See also Blair and Hill, *America's Humor from Poor Richard to Doonesbury*, pp. 165–171.

54. "The Legend of Sleepy Hollow," *The Sketch Book*, pp. 272–297. See, in particular, pp. 272–275 and 280–281. For an analysis of Ichabod Crane's role as despoiler in the world of Sleepy Hollow, see Herbert F. Smith, "The Spell of Nature in Irving's Famous Stories," *Washington Irving Reconsidered: A Symposium*, pp. 18–22. The role of the Yankee in Irving's fiction has been traced by Donald A. Ringe, "New York and New England: Irving's Criticism of American Society," *American Literature*, 38 (January 1967), 455–467.

55. "The Legend of Sleepy Hollow," *The Sketch Book*, pp. 295–297. Terence Martin argues that Rip and Ichabod together represent the defeat of the imagination and the end of the creative side of Irving's career in "Rip, Ichabod, and the American Imagination," pp. 137–149. See also Martin Roth, "The Final Chapter of Knickerbocker's New York," *Modern Philology*, 66 (February 1969), 248–255, and Robert A. Bone, "Irving's Headless Hessian: Prosperity and the Inner Life," *American Quarterly*, 15 (Summer 1963), 167–175.

7. William Cullen Bryant: The Creative Context of the Poet

1. James T. Fields, *Yesterday With Authors* (1871; rpt. Boston: Houghton Mifflin, 1901), pp. 52–53.

2. For biographical details, see Charles H. Brown, *William Cullen Bryant* (New York: Scribner's Sons, 1971), pp. 151–152, 174, 184, 211, 418, 481. See also Herman E. Spivey, "Bryant Cautions and Counsels Lincoln," *Tennessee Studies in Literature*, 43 (Second Quarter 1966), 99–103.

3. See, in order, "To A Poetical Trio in the City of Gotham," *The Complete Poetical Works of John Greenleaf Whittier* (Boston: Houghton Mifflin,

1895), pp. 510–511; Letter from Ralph Waldo Emerson to Margaret Fuller, May 4, 1838, *The Letters of Ralph Waldo Emerson*, ed. Ralph L. Rusk, 6 vols. (New York: Columbia University Press, 1939), II, 129–130; and John Bigelow, *William Cullen Bryant* (1890; rpt. Boston: Houghton Mifflin, 1896), p. 109.

4. Albert F. McLean, Jr., *William Cullen Bryant* (Boston: Twayne, 1964), p. 17; Brown, *Bryant*, pp. 1, 208–522; and Judith Turner Phair, "Introduction," *A Bibliography of William Cullen Bryant and His Critics, 1808–1972* (Troy, N.Y.: Whitston, 1975), pp. 1–29. McLean identifies the image of the man of letters and the need for correcting it. Both Brown and Phair emphasize the later journalist and political figure.

5. See William P. Hudson, "Archibald Alison and William Cullen Bryant," *American Literature*, 12 (March 1940), 59–68; Alan B. Donovan, "William Cullen Bryant: 'Father of American Song'," *New England Quarterly*, 41 (December 1968), 505–520; and Gay Wilson Allen, *American Prosody* (New York: American Book Company, 1935), pp. 30–31.

6. For a recent argument calling for more extensive application of the Scottish moralists within early American history and literature, see Garry Wills, *Inventing America: Jefferson's Declaration of Independence* (New York: Doubleday, 1978).

7. William Cullen Bryant II and Thomas G. Voss, ed., *The Letters of William Cullen Bryant*, 3 vols. (New York: Fordham University Press, 1975–   ), I, 319–320. Cited hereafter as *Letters*.

8. Thomas Cole, "Essay on American Scenery," *American Monthly Magazine*, 1 (January 1836), 4–5, and James Thomas Flexner, *That Wilder Image: The Painting of America's Native School from Thomas Cole to Winslow Homer* (Boston: Little, Brown, 1962), p. 40.

9. "Lectures on Poetry," in *The Life and Works of William Cullen Bryant*, ed. Parke Godwin, 6 vols. (New York: Appleton, 1883), V, 24. All subsequent references in the text to Bryant's works are from this edition. William Wordsworth, *The Prelude, or Growth of A Poet's Mind*, ed. Ernest de Selincourt, 1st edition (London: Oxford University Press, 1926), p. 24. De Selincourt places authorship of the passage in the latter half of 1799.

10. "The Poet of Our Woods" was an encomium for Bryant in the nineteenth century. See Eugene Benson, "The Poet of Our Woods," *Appleton's Journal of Literature, Science, and Art*, 2 (December 18, 1869), 568–569, and Walt Whitman, "My Tribute to Four Poets," *Specimen Days and Collect*, ed. Floyd Stovall (1882; rpt. New York: New York University Press, 1963), p. 267. For more complete accounts claiming that Bryant was only at home in nature, see Caroline H. Kirkland, *Little Journeys to The Homes of American Authors*, ed. Elbert Hubbard (New York: Putnam's Sons, 1896), pp. 57–59, and more recently Roderick Nash, *Wilderness and the*

American Mind, rev. ed. (New Haven: Yale University Press, 1973), pp. 74–75.

11. McLean, *Bryant,* pp. 37–38.

12. *Letters,* 1, 209.

13. *Life and Works,* 1, 253, 339.

14. Bigelow, *Bryant,* pp. 114–115.

15. Bryant once claimed to have written a draft of "Thanatopsis" in 1811 or 1812, "probably the latter," which would place composition just after the keen disappointment of leaving Williams College and during his initial exposure to legal studies. But William Cullen Bryant II marshals considerable evidence for composition in the autumn of 1815. He also argues that the law student's fears of public speaking in courtroom debate lie behind the emotional force of both "Thanatopsis" and "To A Waterfowl." William Cullen Bryant II, "The Genesis of 'Thanatopsis'," *New England Quarterly,* 21 (June 1948), 163–184, and "The Waterfowl in Retrospect," *New England Quarterly,* 31 (June 1957), 181–189.

16. Lawyers objecting to Bryant's decision included close supporters like Willard Phillips and Charles Sedgwick. *Life and Works,* 1, 200–201.

17. *Letters,* 1, 23–24, 56, and 34, 41, 44–45, 58, 76.

18. *Letters,* 1, 71, 105, 166, 177, 193.

19. For Bryant's legal career, see Brown, *Bryant,* pp. 64–75, 88, 94; Bigelow, *Bryant,* pp. 33–38; and *Life and Works,* 1, 143–145, 159.

20. For assertions that *Bloss v. Tobey,* 2nd Pickering Massachusetts Reports 320–30 (1824), turned the high-minded poet in other directions, see *Life and Works,* 1, 201–202; Brown, *Bryant,* p. 121; and *Letters,* 1, 16, 147.

21. Joseph Stevens Buckminster, "On the Dangers and Duties of Men of Letters," *Monthly Anthology and Boston Review,* 7 (September 1809), 146–158. For Ticknor's comment and for an excellent treatment of Buckminster's influence, see Lewis P. Simpson, "Joseph Stevens Buckminster," *The Man of Letters in New England and the South: Essays on the History of the Literary Vocation in America* (Baton Rouge: Louisiana State University Press, 1973), pp. 22, 3–31.

22. Perry Miller and Thomas H. Johnson, "This World and the Next," *The Puritans,* rev. ed., 2 vols. (1938; rpt. New York: Harper and Row, 1963), 1, 281–290. For an exciting study demonstrating how this Puritan doctrine generally influenced nineteenth-century American literature, see Michael T. Gilmore, *The Middle Way: Puritanism and Ideology in American Romantic Fiction* (New Brunswick, N.J.: Rutgers University Press, 1977).

23. John Cotton, *The Way of Life. Or God's Way and Course, in bringing the soule into; keeping it in, and carrying it on, in the wayes of life and peace* (London: L. Fawne and S. Gellibrand, 1641), p. 449. For Bryant's criticisms of European idlers, see *Letters,* 1, 417, 428–432, 460.

24. Donald M. Murray, "Dr. Peter Bryant: Preceptor in Poetry to William Cullen Bryant," *New England Quarterly*, 33 (December 1960), 513–522. For the poet's own acknowledgments of his father's literary guidance, see *Life and Works*, I, 22–36; III, 51; IV, 196.

25. *Life and Works*, I, 148–154; *Letters*, I, 28, 71, 76; and Brown, *Bryant*, pp. 78–81.

26. Bryant was generally prosperous after 1840 and became a wealthy man before 1860. Although he frequently complained that newspaper work drained his creativity, he remained an active journalist until the year of his death in 1878. For relevant financial figures, see Bigelow, *Bryant*, pp. 91–92, and Brown, *Bryant*, pp. 427, 481. See also *Letters*, II, 27, 35, 64, 97.

27. *Letters*, I, 25–26.

28. *Letters*, I, 184.

29. Docket Book for Court of Common Pleas, October 1823–February 1825, *William Cullen Bryant's Personal Miscellaneous Papers*, New York Public Library. For a general description of legal practice in the region at this time, see Anton-Hermann Chroust, *The Rise of the Legal Profession in America*, 2 vols. (Norman: University of Oklahoma Press, 1965), II, 15.

30. *Letters*, I, 184, 193.

31. Bigelow, *Bryant*, pp. 112–115; Brown, *Bryant*, p. 431; Phair, *A Bibliography of Bryant*, pp. 13–15. The diarist Philip Hone noted at least one lapse in the editor's aloof demeanor, describing a fight between Bryant and a rival editor in the streets of New York on April 20, 1831. *The Diary of Philip Hone, 1828–1851*, ed. Allan Nevins, 2 vols. (New York: Dodd, Mead, 1927), I, 40–41.

32. Throughout the nineteenth century, Bryant was known as the American Wordsworth. His "Lectures on Poetry," delivered before the New York Athenaeum in 1826, relied upon Wordsworth's critical writings. Compare Wordsworth's "Preface to the Second Edition of . . . the *Lyrical Ballads*," *The Poetical Works of William Wordsworth*, ed. Ernest de Selincourt, 2d edition, 5 vols. (Oxford: Clarendon, 1952), II, 386–387, and "Lectures on Poetry," *Life and Works*, V, 8–10, 19.

33. See Nathaniel Hawthorne, *The Heart of Hawthorne's Journal*, ed. Newton Arvin (Boston: Houghton Mifflin, 1929), pp. 285, 299; Emerson, *The Letters of Ralph Waldo Emerson*, III, 29; James Russell Lowell, "A Fable for Critics," *The Writings of James Russell Lowell*, 10 vols. (Boston: Houghton Mifflin, 1890), IX, 51. See also "The Poet," *Life and Works*, IV, 136, and *Letters*, I, 24.

34. Wordsworth, "Preface to the Second Edition . . . *Lyrical Ballads*," II, 395.

35. Brown, *Bryant*, p. 101.

36. See McLean, *Bryant*, pp. 39–65, 85–108; Bigelow, *Bryant*, pp. 108–109, 140–141; and Tremaine McDowell, "Introduction," *William Cul-*

len Bryant: Representative Selections, With Introduction, Bibliography, and Notes (New York: American Book Company, 1935), pp. 16–23, j31–39.

37. Gordon S. Wood analyzes the "moral dimension" and "utopian depth" of an early American republicanism that produced "extraordinarily idealistic hopes for the social and political transformation of America," in Wood, *The Creation of the American Republic, 1776–1787* (1969; rpt. New York: Norton, 1972), pp. 47–48. For Bryant's espousal of this brand of republicanism, see "The Ages" and "The Lapse of Time," *Life and Works*, III, 53–68, 124–126, and *Letters*, II, 521. Bryant's intense interest in the uncertain events surrounding the Hartford Convention of 1814 is clear from *Letters*, I, 42–50.

38. Parke Godwin's analysis of "Sella" in *Life and Works*, II, 188–189, is followed by Brown, *Bryant*, pp. 446–447.

39. For similar uses of natural imagery as a frame for political scenes, see "Earth," "The Fountain," "The Winds," *Life and Works*, III, 238–241, 282–291.

40. Bryant has been dismissed for "lack of complexity" and "bareness of thought" and has been criticized for being oblivious to difficulties and aspiring to no more than the "homely simpleness of a one-room cabin." George Arms, *The Fields Were Green: A New View of Bryant, Whittier, Holmes, Lowell, and Longfellow, with a Selection of Their Poems* (Stanford: Stanford University Press, 1953), pp. 9–11. More recently, Bernard Duffey finds Bryant "existing apart from the complications of creed and doctrine," relying upon the "comforts of self-approval" and a "unity of early nineteenth-century man" for his "poetry of coherence." Duffey, *Poetry in America: Expression and Its Values in the Times of Bryant, Whitman, and Pound* (Durham, N.C.: Duke University Press, 1978), pp. 6–8, 32, 42.

41. In general, see William Charvat, "Sources in Scottish Philosophy, Aesthetics and Culture," *The Origins of American Critical Thought, 1810–1835* (Philadelphia: University of Pennsylvania Press, 1936), pp. 27–58. Terence Martin has demonstrated how important the American search for constraints and controls was in acceptance of Scottish thinking in Martin, *The Instructed Vision: Scottish Common Sense and the Origins of American Fiction* (Bloomington: Indiana University Press, 1961). For Bryant's readings, see Tremaine McDowell, "Cullen Bryant Prepares for College," *South Atlantic Quarterly*, 30 (April 1931), 132.

42. Hudson, "Alison and Bryant," pp. 59–68; Robert E. Streeter, "Association Psychology and Literary Nationalism in *The North American Review*," *American Literature*, 17 (November 1945), 243–254; and William J. Free, "William Cullen Bryant on Nationalism, Imitation, and Originality in Poetry," *Studies in Philology*, 66 (July 1969), 672–687.

43. See, in order, Dugald Stewart, "Section v: Inconveniences resulting from an Ill-regulated Imagination," *Elements of the Philosophy of the*

Human Mind (London: Strahan and Cadell, 1792), pp. 508–509; Henry Home [Lord Kames], "Chapter Sixteen: Sentiments," *Elements of Criticism* (1762; rpt. New York: A. S. Barnes, 1874), pp. 247–248; Thomas Reid, "Section 24: Of the Analogy Between Perception and the Credit We Give Human Testimony," *An Inquiry into the Human Mind on the Principles of Common Sense*, and "Part Three, Chapter Four," *Essays on the Active Powers of Man*, in *Philosophical Works*, ed. Sir William Hamilton, 2 vols. (Hildesheim, Germany: Georg Olms Verlagbuchhandlung, 1967), I, 195–198, and II, 586. See also Charvat, *The Origins of American Critical Thought*, p. 58.

44. For the philosophical distinctions in this paragraph, I am indebted in part to Walter Jackson Bate, "The Growth of Individualism: The Premise of the Associaton of Ideas," *From Classic to Romantic: Premises of Taste in Eighteenth-Century England* (1946; rpt. New York: Harper and Row, 1961), pp. 93–118, and to Walter John Hipple, Jr., *The Beautiful, the Sublime, and the Picturesque in Eighteenth-Century British Aesthetic Theory* (Carbondale: Southern Illinois University Press, 1957).

45. Archibald Alison, *Essays on the Nature and Principles of Taste* (1790; rpt. Edinburgh: Bell and Bradfute, 1811), I, xxiv–xxv, 34.

46. See, in order, Alison, *Essays*, I, 176–177, 5–6, 17–18, 161, 58, 8–10.

47. Alison, *Essays*, I, 18–21, 63–66.

48. *Life and Works*, V, 24. See also Streeter, "Association Psychology and Literary Nationalism," 243–254. At least one observer, Tocqueville, was convinced Americans were "insensible to the wonders of inanimate nature." Alexis de Tocqueville, *Democracy in America*, ed. Phillips Bradley, 2 vols. (New York: Alfred A. Knopf, 1945), II, 74.

49. Alison, *Essays*, I, 65, 118, 34, and II, 422, 437, 444.

50. For my thinking on the relations of aesthetics and morals in Alison and the impact of this doctrine on Americans, I am indebted to Robert E. Streeter's unpublished manuscript, "Moralistic Criticism and Association Psychology in *The North American Review*, 1815–1835."

51. Alison, *Essays*, I, 120, 134, and II, 67, and, more generally, *Essays*, I, 120–148, and II, 55–67.

52. Compare "Lectures on Poetry," *Life and Works*, V, 19, with Alison, *Essays*, II, 440–447, 58, 420, and Jonathan Edwards, *Images or Shadows of Divine Things*, ed. Perry Miller (New Haven: Yale University Press, 1948), pp. 44, 52, 61, 130. For an argument drawing the Edwardsian parallel, see Donovan, "Bryant: 'Father of American Song'," 506–508.

53. Compare Alison, *Essays*, II, 446, I, 20–21, 89–95, and II, 387–394, with Bryant's "Green River," "A Winter Piece," "I Broke The Spell That Held Me Long," "I Cannot Forget With What Fervid Devotion," and "To The Fringed Gentian," in *Life and Works*, 31–38, 99, 165, 221.

54. See Carl Van Doren, "The Growth of 'Thanatopsis'," *Nation*, 101

(October 7, 1915), 432–433, and Tremaine McDowell, "Bryant's Practice in Composition and Revision," *PMLA*, 52 (June 1937), 474–502. The most forceful and thorough advocate of a dialogue in "Thanatopsis" is Albert McLean in McLean, *Bryant*, pp. 65–80. For an argument moving from two voices to many, see E. Miller Budick, " 'Visible' Images and the 'Still Voice': Transcendental Vision in Bryant's 'Thanatopsis'," *ESQ: Emerson Society Quarterly*, 22, No. 2 (1976), 71–77. George Arms, in a view contested by McLean, suggests a return to the poet as speaker in the final lines of the poem; Arms, *The Fields Were Green*, pp. 14–15.

55. Albert F. McLean, Jr., brilliantly traces how "Thanatopsis" parallels the formulaic divisions of doctrine, reasons, and uses in Puritan sermonology in "Bryant's 'Thanatopsis': A Sermon in Stone," *American Literature*, 31 (January 1960), 474–479. Bryant's interest in the tones and forms of religious expression was always intense. He apparently wrote precocious sermons of his own in childhood. "Autobiographical Fragment," *Life and Works*, I, 5, 9, 15, 21, 26, and Brown, *Bryant*, p. 13.

56. For an indication of how many of the intonations in Bryant's poetry come from oratory, see Marvin T. Herrick, "Rhetoric and Poetry in Bryant," *American Literature*, 7 (May 1935), 188–194. Bryant may even have had a particular speech in mind for "Thanatopsis" in Pericles' funeral oration. See Gerald J. Smith, "Bryant's 'Thanatopsis': A Possible Source," *American Notes and Queries*, 13 (June 1975), 149–151.

57. I accept the Godwin text of "Thanatopsis" based upon the 1821 version but including Bryant's minor changes in 1836 and 1871. *Life and Works*, III, 17–22. For a detailed account of the changes with relevant dates, see McDowell, *Bryant: Representative Selections*, pp. 389–392.

58. Hudson, "Alison and Bryant," 61–63, Alison, *Essays*, I, 11–15, 17, 92.

59. Alison, *Essays*, I, 176, and II, 428, 437.

60. For earlier versions of "Thanatopsis," I rely on Tremaine McDowell's presentation of Manuscript B in "Bryant's Practice in Composition and Revision," 482. Manuscript B actually has been traced to 1815 by William Cullen Bryant II in "The Genesis of 'Thanatopsis'," 180–181. My analysis here should be understood against the general view that a comparison of Manuscript B and the 1821 version proves a shift in perspective from a persona of the poet to a voice in nature.

61. Internal preparation and intense meditation were essential duties required of all Calvinists approaching the Lord's Table. For a recent discussion of how these elements apply within English and American poetry, see Robert Daly, *God's Altar: The World and the Flesh in Puritan Poetry* (Berkeley: University of California Press, 1978), pp. 71–81.

62. "Indeed terror is in all cases whatsoever, either more openly or

latently the ruling principle of the sublime." Edmund Burke, "Terror," *A Philosophical Enquiry into the Origin of our Ideas of the Sublime and Beautiful* in *The Works of the Right Honourable Edmund Burke*, 3 vols. (London: J. Dodsley, 1792), I, 120. Bryant read Burke in his father's library while still a boy, and the Englishman's influence on Bryant's "Essays on Poetry" has been recognized. See Brown, *Bryant*, p. 144. Alison's own debt to Burke and the many examples of terror in his discussions of the sublime would have reinforced Burke's teachings for Bryant. See Alison, *Essays*, I, 75, 83, 162, 193–196, 221.

63. Alison, *Essays*, I, 156–157.

64. For a discussion of Bryant's frequent stress upon the enormous dimensions of the world around him, see Donald Ringe, *The Pictorial Mode: Space and Time in the Art of Bryant, Irving, and Cooper* (Lexington: University Press of Kentucky, 1971), pp. 213–214. Both Burke and Alison discuss at length the issue of scope as a fundamental source of the sublime. Burke, "Why Visual Objects of Great Dimensions are Sublime," *A Philosophical Enquiry*, in *Works*, I, 206, and Alison, *Essays*, I, 324–325, and II, 23, 66–67.

65. See Alison, *Essays*, II, 386–402.

66. The basis of Bryant's use of the Oregon River in "Thanatopsis" is discussed by Vernon F. Snow, "Where Rolls the Oregon," *Western Humanities Review*, 10 (Summer 1956), 289–292.

67. In various letters, Bryant described his life as both a lawyer and a journalist in terms of slave imagery. See *Letters*, II, 26–27, 35, 91.

68. Bryant's struggle for balance was constant in these early years. "Alas, Sir," he wrote to his law tutor in 1817, "the Muse was my first love and the *remains* of that passion which not *rooted out* yet chilled into extinction will always I fear cause me to look coldly on the severe beauties of Themis [Law]. Yet I tame myself to its labours as well as I can." *Letters*, I, 71. There is every reason to believe that the anxieties implicit in this comment were uppermost in the poet's mind while he was "lounging away three months at my father's," writing "Thanatopsis," and nerving himself to open legal practice in a nearby town. *Letters*, I, 64.

Prologue to Part III

1. William Kent, *Memoirs and Letters of James Kent, LL.D.* (Boston: Little, Brown, 1898), p. 159.

2. For these developments, see Charles Warren, *A History of the American Bar* (1911; rpt. New York: Horward Fertig, 1966), pp. 276–291, 496–497.

3. Kent is quoted from Warren, *History*, p. 522. David Dudley Field,

"The Study and Practice of the Law," *United States Magazine and Democratic Review*, 14 (April 1844), 345, 351.

4. For distinctions between natural and positive law in American culture, see Redmond J. Barnett, "Professionalism and the Chains of Slavery," *Michigan Law Review*, 77 (January–March 1979), 669–677, and Robert M. Cover, *Justice Accused: Antislavery and the Judicial Process* (New Haven: Yale University Press, 1975), pp. 1–30.

5. Howard Mumford Jones, *O Strange New World: American Culture, the Formative Years* (New York: Viking, 1968), p. 265. Jones pinpoints the collapse of the classical tradition. For the collapse in educational standards within the nineteenth-century bar, see James Willard Hurst, *The Growth of American Law: The Law Makers* (Boston: Little, Brown, 1950), p. 250, and, more generally, pp. 249–375. See also Anton-Hermann Chroust, *The Rise of the Legal Profession*, 2 vols. (Norman: University of Oklahoma Press, 1965), II, 49, 129–172.

6. David Dudley Field, "The Study and Practice of the Law," p. 345.

7. For the best analyses of the changes presented in this paragraph, see Maxwell Bloomfield, "Law vs. Politics: The Self-Image of the American Bar (1830–1860)," *American Journal of Legal History*, 12 (October 1968), 306–323, "Lawyers and Public Criticism: Challenge and Response in Nineteenth-Century America," *American Journal of Legal History*, 15 (October 1971), 269–277, and "Antilawyer Sentiment in the Early Republic," *American Lawyers in a Changing Society, 1776–1876* (Cambridge, Mass.: Harvard University Press, 1976), pp. 32–58.

8. My language and thought in this paragraph and the next owe much to Morton J. Horwitz, *The Transformation of American Law, 1780–1860* (Cambridge, Mass.: Harvard University Press, 1977), pp. 3, 26–30, 253. See also Lawrence M. Friedman and Harry N. Scheiber, "Preface," *American Law and the Constitutional Order: Historical Perspectives* (Cambridge, Mass.: Harvard University Press, 1978), vii–viii, and William E. Nelson, *Americanization of the Common Law: The Impact of Legal Change on Massachusetts Society, 1760–1830* (Cambridge, Mass.: Harvard University Press, 1975), pp. 87, 143, 172–174.

9. See, for example, John William Ward, "Jacksonian Democratic Thought: 'A Natural Charter of Privilege'," in *The Development of an American Culture*, ed. Stanley Cohen and Lorman Ratner (Englewood Cliffs, N.J.: Prentice-Hall, 1970), pp. 44–64.

10. Horwitz, *The Transformation of American Law*, p. 253.

11. Daniel Webster, "Constitution and Union, A Speech Delivered in the Senate of the United States of America, March 7, 1850," and "An Address delivered at the Laying of the Corner-stone of the Bunker Hill Monument at Charlestown, Massachusetts, on June 17, 1825," *The Writings*

and Speeches of Daniel Webster, 18 vols. (Boston: Little, Brown, 1903), X, 58, 64–65, and I, 254.

12. Henry N. Day, *The Professions* [1849], quoted by Perry Miller, *The Life of the Mind in America from the Revolution to the Civil War* (New York: Harcourt, Brace and World, 1965), p. 207.

13. Henry David Thoreau, "Civil Disobedience," *The Writings of Henry David Thoreau*, 20 vols. (Boston: Houghton Mifflin, 1906), IV, 384. Ralph Waldo Emerson, "The Fugitive Slave Law: Lecture Read in the Tabernacle, New York City, March 7, 1854," *The Works of Ralph Waldo Emerson*, 12 vols. (Boston: Houghton Mifflin, 1909), XI, 220–221. For accounts of American reactions to Webster after the Compromise of 1850 and to the Supreme Court after *Dred Scott v. Sanford*, see Richard Currant, *Daniel Webster and the Rise of National Conservatism* (Boston: Little, Brown, 1955), p. 169, Robert G. McCloskey, *The American Supreme Court* (Chicago: University of Chicago Press, 1960), pp. 94–96, and Don E. Fehrenbacher, *The Dred Scott Case: Its Significance in American Law and Politics* (New York: Oxford University Press, 1978), pp. 417–595.

14. Walt Whitman, "Song of the Open Road" [1856], and "Over the Carnage Rose Prophetic a Voice" [1860–1865], *Leaves of Grass*, ed. Harold Blodgett and Sculley Bradley (New York: New York University Press, 1965), pp. 159, 315–316.

15. Emerson, "Speech at the Kansas Relief Meeting in Cambridge, Wednesday Evening, September 10, 1856," "Spiritual Laws," "The American Scholar, An Oration delivered before the Phi Beta Kappa Society, at Cambridge, August 31, 1837," *The Works of Ralph Waldo Emerson*, XI, 244, II, 145, I, 113; Thoreau, *Walden*, in *The Writings of Henry David Thoreau*, II, 228; Whitman, "By Blue Ontario's Shore," *Leaves of Grass*, p. 340.

16. Abraham Lincoln, "Address Before the Young Men's Lyceum of Springfield, Illinois, January 27, 1838," *Collected Works of Abraham Lincoln*, ed. Roy P. Basler, 8 vols. (New Brunswick, N.J.: Rutgers University Press, 1953), I, 112. See also George M. Frederickson, "The Doctrine of Loyalty," *The Inner Civil War: Northern Intellectuals and the Crisis of Union* (1965; rpt. New York: Harper and Row, 1968), pp. 130–150, and, more generally, George B. Forgie, *Patricide in the House Divided: A Psychological Interpretation of Lincoln and His Age* (New York: W. W. Norton, 1979).

17. See R. Kent Newmyer, "Daniel Webster as Tocqueville's Lawyer: The *Dartmouth College* Case Again," *American Journal of Legal History*, 11 (April 1967), 127–147, and Edward G. Parker, *The Golden Age of American Oratory* (Boston: Whittemore, Niles, and Hall, 1857), pp. 87–88.

18. Story is quoted from Miller, "Definition by Negation," *The Life of the Mind in America*, p. 215.

8. Daniel Webster: Counsel for the Defense

1. Edward G. Parker, *The Golden Age of American Oratory* (Boston: Whittemore, Niles, and Hall, 1857), p. 49; James Parton, *Famous Americans of Recent Times* (1867; rpt. Boston: Houghton Mifflin, 1895), p. 57; *New-York Daily Times*, Monday, October 25, 1852.

2. Theodore Parker, "Discourse Occasioned By The Death of Daniel Webster," *Additional Speeches, Addresses, and Occasional Sermons*, 2 vols. (Boston: Rufus Leighton, Jr., 1859), I, 249; Edward Waldo Emerson and Waldo Emerson Forbes, eds., *Journals of Ralph Waldo Emerson*, 10 vols. (Boston: Houghton Mifflin, 1909–1914), VI, 430, 342; VII, 218; VIII, 335. See, more generally, Irving H. Bartlett, *Daniel Webster* (New York: W. W. Norton, 1978), for the puzzle of Webster's greatness.

3. Parker, *Golden Age*, p. 84. See also Daniel Walker Howe, *The Political Culture of the American Whigs* (Chicago: University of Chicago Press, 1979), pp. 8, 69–95.

4. Edwin P. Whipple, "Daniel Webster as a Master of English Style," *The Great Speeches and Orations of Daniel Webster* (Boston: Little, Brown, 1889), lx.

5. "Second Speech on Foot's Resolution delivered in the Senate of the United States on January 26, 1830," James W. McIntyre, ed., *The Writings and Speeches of Daniel Webster*, 18 vols. (Boston: Little, Brown, 1903), VI, 75. All subsequent references to Webster's writings and speeches in the text are from this edition.

6. John Quincy Adams, *Lectures on Rhetoric and Oratory, Delivered to the Classes of Senior and Junior Sophisters in Harvard University*, 2 vols. (Cambridge, Mass.: Hilliard and Metcalf, 1810), I, 45–46, 50, 111, 250–319.

7. Daniel Boorstin, *The Americans: The National Experience* (New York: Random House, 1965), pp. 307–311.

8. The connection between Webster's emerging nationalism and the legal cases he argued as a young lawyer has been noted in Robert F. Dalzell, Jr., *Daniel Webster and the Trial of American Nationalism 1843–1852* (Boston: Houghton Mifflin, 1973), pp. 25–26.

9. See Whipple, "Daniel Webster as a Master of English Style," *Great Speeches*, xx; George Ticknor Curtis, *Life of Daniel Webster*, 2 vols. (New York: D. Appleton, 1870), I, 252–253; and Maurice G. Baxter, *Daniel Webster and the Supreme Court* (Amherst: University of Massachusetts Press, 1966), pp. 10–11. Emerson's comment is from April 1835 in Ralph L. Rusk, ed., *The Letters of Ralph Waldo Emerson*, 6 vols. (New York: Columbia University Press, 1939), I, 444. For the conventional orator's conscious magniloquence, see Francis Walker Gilmer, "Sketches of American Orators," *Sketches, Essays, and Translations* (Baltimore: Fielding Lucas, Jr.,

1828), p. 30. Webster's comment is in McIntyre, ed., *Writings and Speeches,* I, 307.

10. Quoted from Walker Lewis, ed., *Speak for Yourself, Daniel: A Life of Webster in His Own Words* (Boston: Houghton Mifflin, 1969), p. 42. See also, for the original source, Curtis, *Life,* I, 90. For corroborating evidence of this move toward simplicity, see Alfred S. Konefsky and Andrew J. King, eds., *The Papers of Daniel Webster: Legal Papers,* Volume 1, *The New Hampshire Practice* (Hanover, N.H.: University Press of New England, 1982), pp. 165–169.

11. From a letter to Richard Milford Blatchford in 1849, quoted in Peter Harvey, *Reminiscences and Anecdotes of Daniel Webster* (Boston: Little, Brown, 1877), p. 118.

12. Bartlett, *Daniel Webster,* p. 75.

13. For the importance of concepts of natural law to Webster the lawyer, see Baxter, *Webster and the Supreme Court,* pp. 37–38, and McIntyre, ed., *Writings and Speeches,* IV, 90.

14. For an analysis of how the "perceived consensus of the period" on fundamental truths shaped nineteenth-century American oratory, see Richard M. Weaver, "The Spaciousness of Old Rhetoric," *The Ethics of Rhetoric* (Chicago: Henry Regnery, 1953), pp. 166–170.

15. Josiah Quincy, *Figures of the Past* (Boston: Little, Brown, 1926), pp. 115–116; Claude Moore Fuess, *Daniel Webster,* 2 vols. (Boston: Little, Brown, 1930), I, 297–298, 302.

16. Parker, *Golden Age,* pp. 93–94; Charles W. March, *Reminiscences of Congress* (New York: Baker and Scribner, 1850), pp. 146–147.

17. Parker, *Golden Age,* pp. 84–85; Emerson and Forbes, eds., *Emerson's Journals,* III, 308.

18. Listed below are the formal titles and locations of the speeches in question in McIntyre, ed., *Writings and Speeches:* "The Dartmouth College Case: Argument before the Supreme Court of the United States, at Washington, on the 10th of March, 1818" (X, 194–233), with "Peroration to the Dartmouth College Argument" (XV, 9–13); "The Case of Gibbons and Ogden: Argument made in the Case of Gibbons and Ogden, in the Supreme Court of the United States, February Term, 1824" (XI, 3–23); "First Settlement of New England: A Discourse delivered at Plymouth, on the 22d of December, 1820" (I, 181–226); "The Bunker Hill Monument: An Address delivered at the Laying of the Corner-stone of the Bunker Hill Monument at Charlestown, Massachusetts, on the 17th of June, 1825" (I, 235–254); "Adams and Jefferson: A Discourse in Commemoration of the Lives and Services of John Adams and Thomas Jefferson, delivered in Faneuil Hall, Boston, on the 2d of August, 1826" (I, 289–324); "Second Speech on Foot's Resolution: Delivered in the Senate of the United States on the

26th of January, 1830" (VI, 3–75); "The Constitution not a Compact between Sovereign States: A Speech delivered on the 16th of February, 1833, in reply to Mr. Calhoun's Speech, on the Bill 'further to provide for the Collection of Duties on Imports' " (VI, 181–238); "The Constitution and the Union: A Speech delivered in the Senate of the United States, on the 7th of March, 1850" (X, 56–98).

19. John Adams to Daniel Webster, December 23, 1821, in Charles M. Wiltse and Harold D. Moser, eds., *The Papers of Daniel Webster: Correspondence*, Volume 1, *1798–1824* (Hanover, N.H.: University Press of New England, 1974), pp. 297–298.

20. Parton, *Famous Americans*, p. 98. Emerson argued that "The Second Reply to Hayne" made Webster president in everything but name from 1830. Emerson and Forbes, eds., *Emerson's Journals*, VI, 381.

21. Harvey, *Reminiscences*, pp. 140–142; McIntyre, ed., *Writings and Speeches*, XV, 12; Wiltse and Moser, eds., *Papers*, I, 241.

22. *Daniel Webster Papers 1800–1895*, 13 vols. (Washington: Library of Congress), XII, 18013 [on microfilm, reel 6].

23. The importance of this relationship is also raised in Baxter, *Webster and the Supreme Court*, p. 241.

24. Harvey, *Reminiscences*, p. 152.

25. Daniel Webster to Edward Everett, February 23, 1825, in Wiltse and Moser, eds., *Papers*, II, 33. See also Webster's anonymous editorial comment on Henry Clay in Charles M. Wiltse, ed., *Microfilm Edition of the Papers of Daniel Webster*, 41 reels (Ann Arbor: University Microfilms, 1971), reel 7, 008041–008058.

26. Daniel Webster to Joseph Hopkinson, March 22, 1819, in Wiltse and Moser, eds., *Papers*, I, 251. For Webster's careful attention to the timing and publication of his speeches, see Wiltse and Moser, eds., *Papers*, I, 285, and Bartlett, *Daniel Webster*, pp. 101, 109, 158–159.

27. For American feelings of isolation and general anxiety at this time, see Fred Somkin, *Unquiet Eagle: Memory and Desire in the Idea of American Freedom, 1815–1860* (Ithaca, N.Y.: Cornell University Press, 1967), pp. 5, 7, 17, 33, 38, 45, 169–175.

28. Quoted from a letter written on December 21, 1820, in George S. Hillard, Anna Eliot Ticknor, and Anna Eliot Ticknor, eds., *Life, Letters and Journals of George Ticknor*, 2 vols. (Boston: James R. Osgood, 1876), I, 330.

29. March, *Reminiscences*, pp. 147–148.

30. Walt Whitman, "Crossing Brooklyn Ferry," *Leaves of Grass: Comprehensive Readers Edition*, ed. Harold W. Blodgett and Sculley Bradley (New York: New York University Press, 1965), p. 163.

31. Ralph Waldo Emerson, "Eloquence," *The Complete Works of Ralph*

Waldo Emerson, 12 vols. (Cambridge, Mass.: Riverside Press, 1883–1893), VII, 64–65.

32. Fuess, *Daniel Webster*, I, 398; Dalzell, *Trial of American Nationalism*, pp. 26–27.

33. Fuess, *Daniel Webster*, I, 383–384; Richard N. Current, *Daniel Webster and the Rise of National Conservatism* (Boston: Little, Brown, 1955), pp. 60–63; Lewis, ed., *Speak for Yourself*, p. 217; and Bartlett, *Daniel Webster*, pp. 117–121. See as well "Address Delivered at the Dedication of the Cemetery at Gettysburg, November 19, 1863," in Roy P. Basler, ed., *The Collected Works of Abraham Lincoln*, 8 vols. (New Brunswick, N.J.: Rutgers University Press, 1953), VII, 23, and Holman Hamilton, *Prologue to Conflict: The Crisis and Compromise of 1850* (Lexington: University of Kentucky Press, 1964), pp. 14–15.

34. McIntyre, ed., *Writings and Speeches*, II, 43–44. See also Baxter, *Webster and the Supreme Court*, p. 241, and Fuess, *Daniel Webster*, I, 373, 379, 381.

35. Webster's original "Notes on the Reply to Hayne" appear in McIntyre, ed., *Writings and Speeches*, VI, 287–292.

36. Whipple, "Daniel Webster as a Master of English Style," *Great Speeches*, xxiii; Fuess, *Daniel Webster*, I, 375, 383; and McIntyre, ed., *Writings and Speeches*, VI, 293–296. Of the eighty-five pages that Webster finally gave to the printer, more than sixty are in his own hand. For another instance of Webster's great care with the language of his published orations, see Curtis, *Life*, I, 252–253.

37. For an interesting treatment of the theme of violence in Webster's speech, see Wayne Fields, " 'The Reply to Hayne': Daniel Webster and the Rhetoric of Stewardship," *Political Theory*, 11 (February 1983), 15–16.

38. For Webster's claim of close familiarity with the works of Cicero, see Wiltse and Moser, eds., *Papers*, I, 13. For appropriate examples of the organization of the formal oration in Cicero's writings, see *De Oratorio*, Book II, 77–84, and *De Inventione*, Book I, 20–109. For the modern understanding of the parts of a formal oration, I rely upon the terminology and explanations of Hugh Blair, *Lectures on Rhetoric and Belles Lettres*, ed. Harold F. Harding, 2 vols. (Carbondale: Southern Illinois University Press, 1965), II, 157, 169, 174, 179, 182, 189–192, 200. Harding, in an introduction, explains Blair's immense impact on nineteenth-century orators and their audiences. For the connection between nineteenth-century legal training and Blair's *Lectures*, see Richard Beale Davis, "Law and Oratory," *Intellectual Life in Jefferson's Virginia 1770–1830* (Knoxville: University of Tennessee Press, 1972), pp. 367–370.

39. March, *Reminiscences*, p. 135.

40. March, *Reminiscences*, p. 142.

41. William H. Gilman et al., eds., *The Journals and Miscellaneous Notebooks of Ralph Waldo Emerson*, 16 vols. (Cambridge, Mass.: Harvard University Press, 1960–1982), IX, 166.

42. Henry Clay, "Speech of Mr. Clay on the Foregoing Resolutions, Delivered February 5th and 6th, 1850," in Calvin Colton, ed., *The Works of Henry Clay*, 6 vols. (New York: A. S. Barnes and Burr, 1857), III, 304; John C. Calhoun, "Speech on the Slavery Question, delivered in the Senate, March 4th, 1850," in Richard K. Crallé, ed., *The Works of John C. Calhoun*, 6 vols. (New York: D. Appleton, 1854), IV, 559; Webster, "The Constitution and the Union: A Speech delivered in the Senate of the United States, on the 7th of March 1850," in McIntyre, ed., *Writings and Speeches*, X, 90. See also Hamilton, *Prologue*, pp. 81, 147–149.

43. See William Plumer, "Reminiscences of Daniel Webster," in McIntyre, ed., *Writings and Speeches*, XVII, 546.

44. Quoted in Charles Warren, *A History of the American Bar* (1911; rpt. New York: Howard Fertig, 1966), p. 310.

45. See R. Kent Newmyer, "Daniel Webster as Tocqueville's Lawyer: The *Dartmouth College* Case Again," *American Journal of Legal History*, 11 (April 1967), 127–147, and Baxter, "Preface," *Webster and the Supreme Court*, vi–viii. Under financial pressure, Webster reluctantly returned to more active practice at the end of his life, but, as Baxter points out, he was most active and most successful in the courtroom between 1819 and 1827. Webster did, however, adapt to a greater specialization. See Konefsky, "Introduction," *Legal Papers*, I, xxxviii.

46. See Charles Warren, *The Supreme Court in United States History*, 3 vols. (Boston: Little, Brown, 1923), II, 462–469.

47. On the issue of the orator's growing emotionalism, see Dalzell, *Daniel Webster and the Trial of American Nationalism*, pp. 189, 199–203. Webster in 1847 specifically calls for an attachment to the Union not from "philosophical reasoning" but through "heartfelt *sentiment*." McIntrye, ed., *Writings and Speeches*, IV, 102.

48. See, for example, George M. Fredrickson, *The Inner Civil War: Northern Intellectuals and the Crisis of the Union* (New York: Harper and Row, 1965), pp. 184–189. Fredrickson argues here that the Civil War created a "new respect for nationalism and the positive state," increased respect for "the maintenance of order," and made "the very concept of 'revolution' or 'rebellion' anathema to many Northerners." Webster's speeches ten years before began this process.

49. Current, "Posterity, Its Judgment," *Daniel Webster and the Rise of National Conservatism*, pp. 197, 184–202.

50. The term "law and order" appears at least as early as 1796 in American culture, but it was the Dorr Rebellion in Rhode Island in 1842

that turned the phrase into a political slogan. Here, the two factions were "Dorr and Free Suffrage" and "Law and Order." Webster, of course, was the attorney for the side of law and order in *Luther v. Borden* (1848), and he applied the same language to the larger arena of sectional strife, which may have encouraged the emergence of the "Law and order party," the designation taken by the pro-slavery faction in Kansas in 1854. See *A Dictionary of American English on Historical Principles*, ed. Sir William Craigie et al., 4 vols. (Chicago: University of Chicago Press, 1936), III, 1404.

51. For my terminology and an interesting discussion of modern positivist definitions of the law, see Roberto Mangabeira Unger, *Law in Modern Society: Toward a Criticism of Social Theory* (New York: Free Press, 1976), pp. 83–86.

52. The secretary of state administered the federal courts when Webster held that cabinet office. See Bartlett, *Daniel Webster*, pp. 263–268.

53. On constitutional grounds, Webster could always find a consistency in his successive rhetorical positions on slavery. Eliminating the slave trade did not specifically violate the Constitution. Failing to return slaves or trying to abolish slavery in the existing states did. See the Constitution of the United States, Article I, section ii, 3; Article I, section ix, 1; and Article IV, section ii, 3.

54. For those actually engaged in the mechanics of compromise like Daniel Webster, the higher law appeared "some useless abstraction" because it was "not a safe law to be acted on, in matters of the highest practical moment." The need for agreement between North and South made the Union itself "a great practical subject" and "not a mere topic for ingenious disquisition or theoretical or fanatical criticism." The survival of the Union no longer allowed a rigid idealism. "I get along with the Nullifiers," Webster wrote his son in 1847, "without making any sharp points." See McIntyre, ed., *Writings and Speeches*, XIII, 434–435, and XVIII, 245.

55. My argument owes much to an excellent discussion of Channing's attitude on the law in Andrew Delbanco, *William Ellery Channing: An Essay on the Liberal Spirit in America* (Cambridge, Mass.: Harvard University Press, 1981), pp. 132–135. For Channing's direct views, see William Ellery Channing, "Remarks on the Slavery Question, in a Letter to Jonathan Phillips, Esq.—1839," and "The Duty of The Free States: Part II.,— 1842," *The Works of William E. Channing, D.D.*, 1st Complete American Edition, 6 vols. (Boston: James Munroe, 1841–1843), V, 17–19, and VI, 283–291, 318.

56. Parker, "Discourse Occasioned by the Death of Daniel Webster," *Additional Speeches*, I, 239, 256, 278. See also Henry Steele Commager, "Slavery and the Higher Law," *Theodore Parker* (1936; rpt. Boston: Beacon Press, 1967), pp. 197–213.

57. Emerson and Forbes, eds., *Emerson's Journals*, VIII, 344, 184–194. Emerson left the ministry in 1832, but his language and thought always relied heavily upon theological traditions. See as well Aileen S. Kraditor, "Religion and the Good Society," *Means and Ends in American Abolitionism: Garrison and His Critics on Strategy and Tactics, 1834–1850* (New York: Random House, 1967), pp. 78–117, and Dalzell, "Preface," *Webster and the Trial of American Nationalism*, xi–xii.

58. Parker, *Golden Age*, p. 83.

59. Harvey, *Reminiscences*, p. 118.

60. Webster actually used the phrase "comprehensive views of things" as the highest accolade he could bestow upon his ideal in the law, Jeremiah Mason. McIntyre, ed., *Writings and Speeches*, IV, 186. Most commentators of the period identified this aspiration as a favorite strategy in Webster's oratory. See Parton, *Famous Americans*, pp. 110–111; Parker, *Golden Age*, pp. 59–61; and March, *Reminiscences*, pp. 146–147.

61. McIntyre, ed., *Wrtings and Speeches*, III, 300; Henry Thoreau, "Civil Disobedience," *The Writings of Henry David Thoreau*, 20 vols. (Boston: Houghton Mifflin, 1906), IV, 384. The quotation from Thoreau's works at the end of this paragraph is from the same source.

62. By 1843, when Webster visited Concord to handle cases in the courts, Emerson already felt that ambition had ruined the politician, but he still saw Webster as "a schoolmaster among his boys," and he admitted that Webster completely filled his own thoughts: "I doubt if I shall get settled down to writing until he is well gone from the county." Emerson and Forbes, eds., *Emerson's Journals*, VI, 429, 433. Hawthorne and Thoreau also wrote of their fascination over Webster's greatness, and they did so both early and late in their careers.

63. Emerson and Forbes, eds., *Emerson's Journals*, II, 296; V, 205, 420. Gilman et al., eds., *Journals*, XIII, 109.

64. For these conventional assertions of the day, often repeated by the traditional man of letters, see George Ticknor, *"Speeches and Forensic Arguments* by Daniel Webster," *American Quarterly Review*, 9 (June 1831), 420, 456, and James A. Hillhouse, "A Discourse, Pronounced on the 7th of April, 1836, before the Brooklyn Lyceum, On the Relations of Literature to a Republican Government," in *Dramas, Discourses, and Other Pieces*, 2 vols. (1839; rpt. New York: Benjamin Blom, 1967), II, 132.

65. *The Writings of Henry David Thoreau*, VIII, 170; X, 397.

66. Thomas H. Johnson, ed., *The Poems of Emily Dickinson*, 3 vols. (Cambridge, Mass.: Harvard University Press, 1963), I, 206–207. This is No. 288 in Johnson's numbering of the poems.

67. Walt Whitman, "Song of the Open Road," *Leaves of Grass*, p. 158.

68. Walt Whitman, *The Early Poems and the Fiction*, ed. Thomas L.

Brasher (New York: New York University Press, 1963), pp. 44–48. See Brasher's explanatory notes to these poems as well.

69. Richard Clark Sterne, "Hawthorne's Politics in *The House of the Seven Gables*," *Canadian Review of American Studies*, 6 (Spring 1975), 74–83, and Nathaniel Hawthorne, *The House of the Seven Gables*, in William Charvat, Roy Harvey Pearce, Claude M. Simpson, eds., *The Centenary Edition of the Works of Nathaniel Hawthorne*, 13 vols. (Columbus: Ohio State University Press, 1962–   ), II, 24, 50–51, 85, 187–210, 273, 122, 310. Just a year before, in 1850, Hawthorne wrote a more extended parody of Webster as "old Stony Phiz" in a short story, "The Great Stone Face." *The Complete Works of Nathaniel Hawthorne*, 13 vols. (Boston: Houghton Mifflin, 1883), III, 428–431. See also Julian Hawthorne, *Nathaniel Hawthorne and His Wife*, 2 vols. (Boston: James R. Osgood, 1885), I, 476–478.

70. Herman Melville, *Mardi and A Voyage Thither*, in Harrison Hayford, Hershel Parker, G. Thomas Tanselle, eds., *The Writings of Herman Melville* (Evanston: Northwestern University Press, and Chicago: The Newberry Library, 1970), III, 54, 515–516.

71. My interpretation of *Moby-Dick* relies heavily upon Alan Heimert, "*Moby-Dick* and American Political Symbolism," *American Quarterly*, 15 (Winter 1963), 498–534. For the relevant quotations in this paragraph, see Herman Melville, *Moby-Dick or, the Whale*, ed., Charles Feidelson, Jr. (New York: Bobbs-Merrill, 1964), pp. 166, 720–724, 82. For a recent analysis suggesting that Melville may have been preoccupied with Daniel Webster in his fiction, see Allan Moore Emery, "The Political Significance of Melville's Chimney," *New England Quarterly*, 55 (June 1982), 201–228.

9. The Richard Henry Danas: Father and Son

1. Richard Henry Dana, *Poems and Prose Writings*, 2 vols. (New York: Baker and Scribner, 1850), II, 178–200. Cited hereafter as Dana Sr., *Writings*. Robert F. Lucid, ed., *The Journal of Richard Henry Dana, Jr.*, 3 vols. (Cambridge, Mass.: Harvard University Press, 1968), II, 527. To eliminate confusion, Richard Henry Dana, Sr., will be referred to by the somewhat unorthodox designation of Dana Sr. in the text, and Richard Henry Dana, Jr., will be referred to as Dana.

2. Lucid, ed., *Journal*, I, 96, 167, and II, 689, 513–515.

3. Quoted in Samuel Shapiro, *Richard Henry Dana, Jr.: 1815–1882* (East Lansing: Michigan State University Press, 1961), p. 65.

4. Quoted in Charles Francis Adams, *Richard Henry Dana, A Biography*, 2 vols. (Boston: Houghton Mifflin, 1895), II, 380, and in Shapiro, *Richard Henry Dana, Jr.*, p. 183.

5. For Webster's growth in reputation through his participation in the

constitutional convention of 1820, for Dana and his father's acceptance of the parallel in 1853, for Dana's own preparations for the constitutional convention of 1853, for his subsequent success as a delegate, and for the final failure of the constitution of 1853, see Lucid, ed., *Journal*, I, 164, and II, 542–565, and Shapiro, Chapter VI, "The Constitutional Convention of 1853," *Richard Henry Dana, Jr.*, pp. 68–83.

6. Richard Henry Dana, Jr., to Sarah Watson Dana, September, 3, 1854, quoted in Adams, *Richard Henry Dana*, I, 332.

7. For the two quotations in this paragraph, see Lucid, ed., *Journal*, I, 346, and II, 605. For relevant information on Francis Dana's life, see Richard Henry Dana III, "Francis Dana," *Cambridge Historical Society: Publications*, 3 (April 1908), 56–78, and Richard Henry Dana, Jr., "Francis Dana," *Pennsylvania Magazine of History and Biography*, 1 (1877), 86–95.

8. Richard Henry Dana, Sr., to William Ellery, September 20, 1819, *Dana Papers: Massachusetts Historical Society*. Hereafter referred to as *MHS Papers*. Dana Sr. studied law in Boston, Providence, and Baltimore between 1809 and 1812, gained admission to the Massachusetts bar in 1811, served as Cambridge property tax assessor in 1816 and 1817, and even sat in the state legislature, but by 1819 all thought of a public life in law had passed. The unhappy emotional record of these years appears in predictable correspondence with William Ellery, the maternal grandfather. Ellery, who combined law and politics in his own right to become a signer of the Declaration of Independence and a leading citizen of Rhode Island, insisted upon professional application and described the wondrous system of Lord Coke's works, the honors of the world, the call to public duty, and a plan for putting away "childish things." Dana Sr., the struggling grandson, wrote back first of idleness, unhappiness, stagnation, and "this mighty chaos of learning" that was Lord Coke, and later of "sufferings, & disappointments," "defects," shame, and failure. See William Ellery to Richard Henry Dana, Sr., November 9, 1809, January 22, 1809, February 28, 1811, January 4, 1812, April 22, 1813, March 7, 1817, and Richard Henry Dana, Sr., to William Ellery, October, 1809, January 1, 1817, March 1, 1817, November, 1818, all in *MHS Papers*.

9. Ticknor, Channing, Longfellow, and Lowell all became professors at Harvard College. Alexander Everett entered the diplomatic service. Prescott and Parkman, prohibited from more active lives by severe health problems, justified themselves through volume after volume of scholarly history. Ticknor, Longfellow, Lowell, Prescott, and Parkman inherited or married wealth. See David B. Tyack, *George Ticknor and the Boston Brahmins* (Cambridge, Mass.: Harvard University Press, 1967), pp. 32–36; C. Harvey Gardiner, *William Hickling Prescott, A Biography* (Austin: University of Texas Press, 1969), pp. 23–68; Martin Duberman, *James Russell Lowell* (Boston: Beacon Press, 1966), pp. 36–141; and Richard Beale Davis, "The

NOTES TO PAGES 244–247

Early American Lawyer and the Profession of Letters," *Huntington Library Quarterly*, 12 (February 1949), 191–205.

10. Van Wyck Brooks, *The Flowering of New England, 1815–1865* (New York: E. P. Dutton, 1936), pp. 111–117. For the chronological facts of the life of Richard Henry Dana, Sr., see Richard Henry Dana III, "Unpublished Memoir of Richard Henry Dana, Sr.," in M. A. De Wolfe Howe, *Later Years of the Saturday Club, 1870–1920* (Boston: Houghton Mifflin, 1927), pp. 37–42.

11. Richard Henry Dana, Sr., to William Ellery, February 4, 1818, *MHS Papers*.

12. Richard Henry Dana, Sr., to Richard Henry Dana, Jr., August 9, 1841, *MHS Papers*.

13. James Russell Lowell, "A Fable for Critics," *The Complete Writings of James Russell Lowell*, 16 vols. (Cambridge, Mass.: Riverside Press, 1904), XII, 54.

14. Lucid, ed., *Journal*, I, 129, 164, 172–177, 346; II, 489, 605, 608, 661, 667.

15. Richard Henry Dana, Jr., "An Autobiographical Sketch," in Lucid, ed., *Journal*, I, 37, 4.

16. Richard Henry Dana, Sr., to Richard Henry Dana, Jr., August 17, 1831, August 19, 1831, October 14, 1831, August 11, 1831, April 7, 1824, and October 20, 1838, in *MHS Papers*.

17. Richard Henry Dana, Jr., "An Autobiographical Sketch," in Lucid, ed., *Journal*, I, 37–39.

18. For Dana's definitions of the concept of the gentleman as he understood it, see Lucid, ed., *Journal*, I, 103, 234, 326. Robert Lucid's introduction to the journals gives an excellent analysis of the implications for Dana's own career. See "Introduction," xvi–xxiii.

19. See Lucid, ed., *Journal*, I, 53, 109, 149. Also, I, 56–57, 139, 234; II, 518, 822.

20. For examples of distinctions made by Richard Henry Dana, Sr., between a private world of virtue and a vocational world of corruption and danger, see "The Changes of Home," "The Factitious Life," and "Edward and Mary," in Dana Sr., *Writings*, I, 35–84, 222–269. Dana's letters to his son also contain direct warnings on the dangers involved. See Richard Henry Dana, Sr., to Richard Henry Dana, Jr., September 26, 1837, December 11, 1840, December 24, 1840, in *MHS Papers*.

21. Lucid, ed., *Journal*, I, 213–214, 37, 199; II, 664.

22. Lucid, ed., *Journal*, I, 71, 268–269, 360–383; II, 836; III, 927. See also Lucid, "Introduction," xxxiii–xxxiv.

23. Lucid, ed., *Journal*, II, 457, and Adams, *Richard Henry Dana*, I, 332.

24. As Dana described his decision to sail before the mast, it was "to

relieve myself from ennui" and "the attractiveness of the romance and adventure of the thing." Lucid, ed., *Journal*, I, 26–27. For an analysis of the romantic implications, see Lucid, "Introduction," xxxi, and Bliss Perry, "Dana's Magical Chance," *The Praise of Folly and Other Papers* (Boston: Houghton Mifflin, 1923), pp. 53–62. For Dana's one other publication from his travels, see *To Cuba and Back: A Vacation Voyage* (Boston: Houghton Mifflin, 1859).

25. Lucid, ed., *Journal*, II, 456–457.

26. Lucid, ed., *Journal*, II, 435, and I, 56–59, 102–103.

27. Lucid, ed., *Journal*, I, 13. Thomas Wentworth Higginson, *Old Cambridge* (New York: Macmillan, 1899), p. 14, and Brooks, *The Flowering of New England*, pp. 43–44. Some of Channing's students were Dana, Emerson, Thoreau, Oliver Wendell Holmes, Wendell Phillips, Charles Sumner, James Russell Lowell, and Edward Everett Hale. At least one of the above, Thoreau, acknowledged that he learned to write as Channing's pupil.

28. Lucid, ed., *Journal*, I, 36. The eyewitness account of Dana's performance, a Dr. John Pierce's, is quoted in Adams, *Richard Henry Dana*, I, 22.

29. For these distinctions between neoclassic and romantic, see J. G. A. Pocock, "On the Non-Revolutionary Character of Paradigms: A Self-Criticism and Afterpiece," *Politics, Language, and Time: Essays on Political Thought and History* (New York: Atheneum, 1973), p. 275, and M. F. Heiser, "The Decline of Neoclassicism," in Harry Hayden Clark, ed., *Transitions in American Literature* (New York: Octagon Books, 1967), pp. 154–155.

30. Dana Sr., "Preface," *Writings*, I, iv. All subsequent references to these writings in this section will appear in parentheses in the text.

31. Richard Henry Dana, Sr., to William Cullen Bryant, May 21, 1840, *MHS Papers*.

32. For a summary of the dominant characteristics of romanticism, all of which appear in Dana Sr.'s writings, see G. Harrison Orians, "The Rise of Romanticism, 1805–1855," in Clark, ed., *Transitions*, pp. 166–167.

33. For descriptions of the general conflict between neoclassic and romantic values in American literature and for my own use of these descriptions, see Leon Howard, "The Late Eighteenth Century: An Age of Contradictions," and Heiser, "The Decline of Neoclassicism," in Clark, ed., *Transitions*, pp. 52–53, 139–143.

34. See Heiser, "The Decline of Neoclassicism," in Clark, ed., *Transitions*, pp. 94–98.

35. Tom Thornton's life is a prolonged fight between personal passion and social duty. When passion conquers all sense of social responsibility, Tom goes crazy. Edward Shirley moves in one page from mental chaos to

a defense of superficial etiquette as a control—"We all stand in need of these rules." The shift and a timely inheritance from "an old-fashioned, thorough-bred gentleman" keep melancholy from slipping toward madness and death. Utterly shattered by his mother's death, Arthur in "The Son" carefully pays "the debt to society required of him" by leading her funeral procession with perfect "spiritual composure." His resolution enables "thoughtful tranquillity" and "gentle cheerfulness" to conquer torpor, indistinctness, melancholy, and unconnected thought. Dana Sr., *Writings*, I, 192–199, 210–213, 236–240, 262–265, 383–386.

36. For a recent analysis of the place of "Paul Felton" in the American gothic and for a description of the role of imagination in the story, see Donald A. Ringe, *American Gothic: Imagination and Reason in Nineteenth-Century Fiction* (Lexington: University Press of Kentucky, 1982), pp. 123–127. See, as well, Ringe, "Early American Gothic: Brown, Dana, and Allston," in Kenneth Walter Cameron, ed., *Romanticism and the American Renaissance: Essays on Ethos and Perception in the Age of Emerson, Thoreau, Hawthorne, Melville, Whitman, and Poe* (Hartford: Transcendental Books, 1977), Part II, 3–8.

37. For a perceptive article on the plight and situation of Dana Sr., see Doreen Hunter, "America's First Romantics: Richard Henry Dana, Sr. and Washington Allston," *New England Quarterly*, 45 (March 1982), 3–30.

38. See, for example, Harold Bloom, "The Internalization of Quest-Romance," in Bloom, ed., *Romanticism and Consciousness: Essays in Criticism* (New York: W. W. Norton, 1970), p. 6. Bloom refers to the "high cost of Romantic internalization" when it shows itself "in the arena of self-consciousness."

39. See J. G. A. Pocock, "Civic Humanism and its Role in Anglo-American Thought," in *Politics, Language and Time*, p. 85, and, more generally, pp. 80–103.

40. Ralph Waldo Emerson, "Nature," *The Works of Ralph Waldo Emerson*, Fireside Edition, 12 vols. (Boston: Houghton Mifflin, 1909), I, 44. "Nature" first appeared in September 1836.

41. Emerson, "The American Scholar: An Oration Delivered Before the Phi Beta Kappa Society, at Cambridge, August 31, 1837," *Works*, I, 112–113.

42. Morton J. Horwitz, *The Transformation of American Law, 1780–1860* (Cambridge, Mass.: Harvard University Press, 1977), p. 30, and more generally, pp. 1–30. See also Robert M. Cover, *Justice Accused: Antislavery and the Judicial Process* (New Haven: Yale University Press, 1975), pp. 25–30.

43. Lucid, ed., *Journal*, II, 661.

44. Lucid, ed., *Journal*, 1, 26–27.

45. R. H. Dana, Jr., *Two Years Before the Mast and Twenty-Fours Years After*, Harvard Classics (New York: P. F. Collier and Son, 1937), pp. 7–11. All later references in the text are to this edition. Dana's book was first published by Harper Brothers in 1840 under the title *Two Years Before the Mast: A Personal Narrative of Life at Sea*.

46. Richard Henry Dana, Sr., to Richard Henry Dana, Jr., November 25, 1834, and November 27, 1835, and Richard Henry Dana, Jr., to Richard Henry Dana, Sr., March 13, 1835, in *MHS Papers*.

47. Lucid, ed., *Journal*, 1, 28, 35.

48. Dana Sr., "The Son," *Writings*, 1, 375–386. For Dana's obsessive interest in the memory of his mother, his strong emotional reaction to "The Son," and his pleasure in the resemblance between his mother and Sarah Watson, the woman he married, see Lucid, ed., *Journal*, 1, xxxvii, 6, 11. See also Robert F. Metzdorf, ed., *Richard Henry Dana, Jr.: An Autobiographical Sketch (1815–1842)* (Hamden, Conn.: Shoe String Press, 1953), p. 100.

49. For the origins of this standard reading, see Bliss Perry, "Dana's Magical Chance," *The Praise of Folly*, pp. 53–57.

50. Lucid., ed., *Journal*, 1, 44.

51. For a good analysis of *Two Years Before the Mast* as a novel of initiation, see Robert L. Gale, *Richard Henry Dana, Jr.* (New York: Twayne, 1969), pp. 108–111, 130–134.

52. Richard Henry Dana, Jr., to Richard Henry Dana, Sr., March 13, 1835, in *MHS Papers*.

53. D. H. Lawrence, "Dana's 'Two Years Before the Mast'," *Studies in Classic American Literature* (New York: Thomas Seltzer, 1923), pp. 163–192.

54. Dana adopts a conscious strategy in sticking to superficial circumstance. "There is no exposure or development of my own mind & feelings," he writes later of *Two Years Before the Mast*. "Nothing more than mere external circumstances." Quoted in Shapiro, *Richard Henry Dana, Jr.*, p. 8.

55. Dana fears that a longer stay in California will make him a permanent sailor by initiating bad habits and eliminating the gentleman's opportunities back in Boston. *Two Years Before the Mast*, pp. 91, 265.

56. Lucid, ed., *Journal*, 1, xxxviii, 77, 119–120, 232–233.

57. Herman Melville, *White Jacket or The World in a Man-of-War*, ed. Harrison Hayford et al. (Evanston: Northwestern University Press, and Chicago: Newberry Library, 1970), pp. 145, 279–281, 17. Melville read *Two Years Before the Mast* before going to sea in 1841. He admired Dana's work and refers to it directly in *White Jacket*. For an analysis of the influences involved, see Robert F. Lucid, "The Influence of *Two Years Before the*

Mast on Herman Melville," *American Literature*, 31 (November 1959), 243–256.

58. The "conflict pattern" of natural law theory and legal positivism in antebellum America is extremely complicated. When and how one replaces the other is a matter of lively conjecture. Legal positivism can be traced as early as the writing and acceptance of the Declaration of Independence and the Constitution. These documents are an expression of the people's will beyond natural law. The distinction between the two Danas in the text has to do with the extent to which father and son use natural law to justify positive law. For interesting analyses of the relationship between natural law and positive law in the period, see Cover, *Justice Accused*, pp. 22–30, and Redmond J. Barnett, "Professionalism and the Chains of Slavery," *Michigan Law Review*, 77 (January–March 1979), 669–677.

59. See, in particular, Perry Miller, *The Life of the Mind in America from the Revolution to the Civil War* (New York: Harcourt, Brace and World, 1965), pp. 239–265, and Lawrence M. Friedman, *A History of American Law* (New York: Simon and Schuster, 1973), pp. 351–358.

60. Lucid, ed., *Journal*, 1, 50.

61. Emerson, "The Over-Soul" and "Spiritual Laws," *Works*, II, 254, 151. See as well Henry David Thoreau, "Higher Laws," *Walden*, in *The Writings of Henry David Thoreau*, 20 vols. (Boston: Houghton Mifflin, 1906), II, 232–246.

62. See Nathaniel Hawthorne, *The Scarlet Letter*, in *The Centenary Edition of the Works of Nathaniel Hawthorne*, ed. William Charvat, Roy Harvey Pearce, and Claude M. Simpson, 14 vols. (Columbus: Ohio State University Press, 1962), I, 252–259; *The House of The Seven Gables*, in *Works*, II, 237, 268–283; Herman Melville, *Billy Budd, Sailor (An Inside Narrative)*, ed. Harrison Hayford and Merton M. Sealts, Jr. (Chicago: University of Chicago Press, 1962), pp. 124–125. Subsequent references will be to these editions.

63. Melville, *White Jacket*, pp. 320–321, 393.

64. Melville, *White Jacket*, p. 390.

65. Hawthorne, *The Scarlet Letter*, in *Works*, I, 258–259. See as well F. O. Matthiessen, *American Renaissance: Art and Expression in the Age of Emerson and Whitman* (New York: Oxford University Press, 1941), pp. 276–277, and James E. Miller, Jr., "Uncharted Interiors: The American Romantics Revisited," in Cameron, ed., *Romanticism*, pp. 34–39.

66. Herman Melville, *Moby-Dick or, the Whale*, ed. Charles Feidelson, Jr. (Indianapolis: Bobbs-Merrill, 1964), pp. 26, 406, 249.

67. For an analysis of these forces at work in antebellum America, see David Donald, "An Excess of Democracy: The American Civil War

and the Social Process," *Lincoln Reconsidered: Essays on the Civil War Era* (New York: Random House, 1956), pp. 209–235, and Oscar Handlin, *Boston's Immigrants: A Study in Acculturation* (New York: Atheneum, 1968).

68. Hawthorne, *The House of The Seven Gables*, in *Works*, II, 178.

69. Thoreau, "Civil Disobedience," *Writings*, IV, 356–358, 368, 376, 385–386. The relationship between individual right and natural law is only loosely drawn in "Civil Disobedience," though Thoreau clearly relies here upon natural images to justify individual human behavior. The much greater, implicit reliance is upon the thought of Emerson, who repeatedly placed nature *in* man. Emerson, "Nature," "The Poet," "The Over-Soul," "The American Scholar," *Works*, I, 31, 38; II, 19, 253; I, 88.

70. William H. Gilman et al., eds., *The Journals and Miscellaneous Notebooks of Ralph Waldo Emerson*, 16 vols. (Cambridge, Mass.: Harvard University Press, 1960–1982), II, 3; Thoreau, *Walden*, in *Writings*, II, 94; Hawthorne, *Life of Franklin Pierce* (Boston: Ticknor, Reed and Fields, 1852), p. 137; Melville, *White Jacket*, p. 151. For relevant analyses of concepts of country in these writers, see Larzer Ziff, *Literary Democracy: The Declaration of Cultural Independence* (New York: Viking Press, 1981), pp. 299–301, and Sacvan Bercovitch, *The American Jeremiad* (Madison: University of Wisconsin Press, 1978), pp. 176–190.

71. Dana Sr., *Writings*, II, 423, and Emerson, "Fate," *Works*, VI, 49–50.

72. Herman Melville to Richard Henry Dana, Jr., May 1, 1850, in Merrell R. Davis and William H. Gilman, eds., *The Letters of Herman Melville* (New Haven: Yale University Press, 1960), p. 106; Dana, *Two Years Before the Mast*, p. 6; Melville, "The Encantadas or Enchanted Isles," *Piazza Tales*, ed. Egbert S. Oliver (New York: Farrar Straus, 1948), p. 154 ["The Encantadas" first appeared in *Putnam's Monthly Magazine* in 1854]; Melville, *Moby-Dick*, p. 27.

73. Herman Melville to Richard Henry Dana, Jr., May 1, 1850, *The Letters of Herman Melville*, p. 108.

74. Compare Dana Sr., "Paul Felton," *Writings*, I, 305–374, and Melville, *Moby-Dick*, pp. 659–660, 667, 672. All quotations in the rest of the paragraph are from these pages.

75. Philip Rahv, "Introduction," *Literature in America* (Cleveland: World Publishing, 1957), p. 21. Rahv refers here to the thought and language of William Butler Yeats.

76. Thoreau, *Walden*, in *Writings*, II, 356.

77. Hawthorne, *The Scarlet Letter*, in *Works*, I, 35–36.

78. Herman Melville to Nathaniel Hawthorne, November 17(?), 1851, *The Letters of Herman Melville*, p. 143.

10. End of the Configuration

1. For an analysis of democratic fears of change using the writings of Andrew Jackson, Theodore Sedgwick, and Robert Rantoul, Jr., lawyers all, see Marvin Meyers, *The Jacksonian Persuasion: Politics and Belief* (Stanford: Stanford University Press, 1957), pp. 1–23, 124–140, 157–178.

2. Seth Ames, ed., *Works of Fisher Ames with a Selection from his Speeches and Correspondence*, 2 vols. (Boston: Little, Brown, 1854), II, 250–255; William Kent, ed., *Memoirs and Letters of James Kent, LL.D.* (Boston: Little, Brown, 1898), p. 209; Samuel Gilman Brown, ed., *The Works of Rufus Choate with a Memoir of His Life*, 2 vols. (Boston: Little, Brown, 1862), II, 315.

3. Andrew Jackson, "Farewell Address (March 4, 1837)," in Francis Newton Thorpe, ed., *The Statesmanship of Andrew Jackson as told in his Writings and Speeches* (New York: Tandy-Thomas, 1909), p. 514.

4. *Works of Fisher Ames*, II, 345.

5. John Adams to Thomas Jefferson, July 15, 1813, in *The Adams-Jefferson Letters: The Complete Correspondence Between Thomas Jefferson and Abigail and John Adams*, ed. Lester J. Cappon, 2 vols. (Chapel Hill: University of North Carolina Press, 1959), II, 358, and Gouverneur Morris to Timothy Pickering, October 17, 1814, in Jared Sparks, *The Life of Gouverneur Morris with Selections From His Correspondence and Miscellaneous Papers*, 3 vols. (Boston: Gray and Bowen, 1832), III, 312.

6. Quoted in Harry R. Warfel, *Noah Webster, Schoolmaster to America* (New York: Macmillan, 1936), p. 424, and quoted in John P. Kennedy, *Memoirs of The Life of William Wirt, Attorney General of the United States*, 2 vols. (Philadelphia: Lea and Blanchard, 1850), II, 324.

7. Perry Miller, *The Life of the Mind in America from the Revolution to the Civil War* (New York: Harcourt, Brace and World, 1965), pp. 207–209, 215.

8. See Grant Gilmore, "The Age of Faith," *The Ages of American Law* (New Haven: Yale University Press, 1977), pp. 41–67.

9. My language and thought on the jeremiad here and in the next paragraph come from Sacvan Bercovitch, *The American Jeremiad* (Madison: University of Wisconsin Press, 1978), pp. 4–11, 23. Bercovitch both clarifies the meaning of the term and demonstrates the essential underlying optimism that other scholars have missed. See also Perry Miller, *The New England Mind from Colony to Province* (Boston: Beacon Press, 1961), pp. 27–39 [originally published in 1953].

10. "Speech delivered in the Odeon, at Boston . . . on the 12th of October, 1835," and Daniel Webster to Caroline Le Roy Webster, January

10, 1836, in J. W. McIntyre, ed., *The Writings and Speeches of Daniel Webster*, 18 vols. (Boston: Little, Brown, 1903), II, 186, and XVI, 264.

11. "Literary Tendencies of the Times: A Discourse Pronounced Before the Society of the Alumni of Harvard University, At Their First Anniversary, August 23, 1842," in William W. Story, ed., *The Miscellaneous Writings of Joseph Story* (Boston: Little, Brown, 1852), pp. 746–747, and Joseph Story to James Kent, August 31, 1844, in *Joseph Story Papers, 1808–1845*, 3 vols., in the Massachusetts Historical Society.

12. Rufus Choate, "The Position and Functions of the American Bar, as an Element of Conservatism in the State," *Works*, I, 429.

13. John Marshall to Joseph Story, September 22, 1832, and James Kent to Joseph Story, October 5, 1842, in *Joseph Story Papers*.

14. For my description of the conservative view of republican government, I am indebted to three sources. R. A. Humphreys, "The Rule of Law and the American Revolution," in John R. Howe, ed., *The Role of Ideology in the American Revolution* (New York: Holt, Rinehart and Winston, 1970), p. 27; John William Ward, "Jacksonian Democratic Thought: 'A Natural Charter of Privilege'," in Stanley Coben and Lorman Ratner, eds., *The Development of an American Culture* (Englewood Cliffs, N.H.: Prentice-Hall, 1970), p. 51; and Arthur O. Lovejoy, "The Theory of Human Nature in the American Constitution and the Method of Counterpoise," *Reflections on Human Nature* (Baltimore: Johns Hopkins University Press, 1961), pp. 40–45.

15. *Swift v. Tyson*, 41 United States (16 Peters' Reports), 11 (1842). See also Gilmore, *The Ages of American Law*, p. 33, and Lawrence M. Friedman, *A History of American Law* (New York: Simon and Schuster, 1973), pp. 388–389.

16. Ward, "Jacksonian Democratic Thought," p. 51.

17. See Richard Hofstader, *The Paranoid Style in American Politics and Other Essays* (New York: Alfred A. Knopf, 1965), pp. 11–40; John R. Howe, Jr., "Republican Thought and the Political Violence of the 1790s," *American Quarterly*, 19 (Summer 1967), 147–165; and Marcus Cunliffe, "Conservatism and Democracy," *The Nation Takes Shape 1789–1837* (Chicago: University of Chicago Press, 1959), pp. 150–180.

18. See Thomas L. Haskell, *The Emergence of Professional Social Science: The American Social Science Association and the Nineteenth-Century Crisis of Authority* (Urbana: University of Illinois Press, 1977), pp. 27, 80, and Burton J. Bledstein, *The Culture of Professionalism: The Middle Class and the Development of Higher Education in America* (New York: W. W. Norton, 1976), pp. 185–186.

19. Joseph Story to James Kent, August 31, 1844, *Joseph Story Papers*.

20. Plato's *Republic* describes the disintegration of the ideal republic

through timocracy, oligarchy, democracy, and anarchy to despotism or tyranny. For the place of the classics mentioned in early American culture, see Meyer Reinhold, *The Classick Pages: Classical Reading of Eighteenth-Century Americans* (University Park, Pa.: American Philological Association, 1975).

21. See in particular Edwin A. Miles, "The Whig Party and the Menace of Caesar," *Tennessee Historical Quarterly*, 27 (Winter 1968), 361–379. The quotation is from Miller, *The Life of the Mind*, pp. 215–216.

22. William Campbell Preston, *Eulogy on Hugh Swinton Legaré; Delivered at the Request of the City of Charleston on November 7, 1843* (Charleston: Published by order of the Mayor and Alderman of Charleston, 1843), p. 14.

23. Joseph Story to Samuel P. P. Fay, February 18, 1834, in William W. Story, ed., *Life and Letters of Joseph Story*, 2 vols. (Boston: Little, Brown, 1851), II, 154. See also Stephen Botein, "Cicero as Role Model for Early American Lawyers: A Case Study in Classical 'Influence'," *Classical Journal*, 73 (Spring 1978), 313–321. For specific examples of the American lawyer's obsessive interest in the downfall of Demosthenes and Cicero, see Rufus Choate, "The Eloquence of Revolutionary Periods: A Lecture Delivered Before the Mechanic Apprentices' Library Association, February 19, 1857," *Works*, I, 439–463, and Hugh Swinton Legaré, "Demosthenes, the Man, the Statesman, and the Orator," and "Cicero de Republica," in Mary Swinton Legaré Bullen, ed., *Writings of Hugh Swinton Legaré . . . Prefaced by a Memoir of His Life*, 2 vols. (Charleston: Burges and James, 1846), I, 443–502, and II, 216–254.

24. Daniel Webster, "Remarks in the Senate, on the 1st of April, 1850, on the occasion of the decease of Hon. John Caldwell Calhoun, Senator from South Carolina," *Writings and Speeches*, X, 101–102.

25. Edward Shils, "The Intellectuals and the Powers: Some Perspectives for Comparative Analysis," *Comparative Studies in Society and History*, 1 (October 1958), 7.

26. Charles Grandison Finney, *Memoirs of Rev. Charles G. Finney Written By Himself* (New York: A. S. Barnes, 1876), pp. 12–24. For the importance of Finney's career, see William G. McLoughlin, "Introduction," in Charles Grandison Finney, *Lectures on Revivals of Religion*, ed. William G. McLoughlin (Cambridge, Mass.: Harvard University Press, 1960), vii–lv.

27. For the essential facts of Field's career, see Helen K. Hoy, "David Dudley Field, 1805–1894," in William Draper Lewis, ed., *Great American Lawyers*, 8 vols. (Philadelphia: John C. Winston, 1907–1909), V, 125–174, and Henry M. Field, *The Life of David Dudley Field* (New York: Charles Scribner's Sons, 1898).

28. Finney, *Memoirs*, p. 256, and David Dudley Field, *Speeches, Ar-*

guments, and Miscellaneous Papers of David Dudley Field, ed. A. P. Sprague and Titus Munson Coan, 3 vols. (New York: D. Appleton, 1884–1890), I, 364.

29. Finney, *Memoirs*, pp. 7–8, 42–43, 52–53, 89, 155.

30. Finney, *Memoirs*, pp. 83–89.

31. Finney, *Memoirs*, pp. 56, 91, 5, 302, 326.

32. Finney, *Memoirs*, pp. 25, 36, 166, 205, 263, 287, 359–366, 436.

33. Finney, *Memoirs*, p. 24.

34. Miller, *The Life of the Mind*, pp. 100, 133. For Miller's interpretation of Finney, see pp. 30–35.

35. Finney, *Memoirs*, pp. 36, 25.

36. For Finney's relationship to Jacksonianism in general and to the Second Great Awakening in particular, see McLoughlin, "Introduction," *Lectures*, vii–xix, xl. See also Donald G. Mathews, "The Second Great Awakening as an Organizing Process, 1780–1830: An Hypothesis," *American Quarterly*, 21 (Spring 1969), 23–43, and Alan Heimert, *Religion and the American Mind from the Great Awakening to the Revolution* (Cambridge, Mass.: Harvard University Press, 1966), pp. 534 ff.

37. Finney, *Memoirs*, pp. 161–164, 221, 263, 83–86.

38. Finney, "Hindrances to Revivals," in McLoughlin, ed., *Lectures*, p. 306.

39. Finney, *Memoirs*, pp. 81–84.

40. Field, *Speeches*, III, 408–409; I, 350; III, 240.

41. Field, *Speeches*, I, 363, 337, 377.

42. Field, *Speeches*, I, 310, 326, 514; II, 508–509; I, 349, 360–361.

43. For a history of the codification movement, see Friedman, *A History of American Law*, pp. 340–353. See also, Field, *Speeches*, III, 408. Field identified the five states in 1889, five years before his death. They were California, North and South Dakota, Georgia, and Louisiana.

44. Field, *Speeches*, II, 508, 498–499.

45. Field, *Speeches*, I, 485–493, 499–501.

46. Field, *Speeches*, III, 245; I, 376–377, 333.

47. Field, *Speeches*, I, 379, 321; III, 407; I, 510, 515.

48. See Finney, *Memoirs*, pp. 170, 293, 298, and Finney, *Lectures*, xxxvi, xli–xlv, 307–308.

49. Field, *Speeches*, I, 347, 342, 383, 522–523; III, 407–408.

50. Haskell, *The Emergence of Professional Social Science*, p. 237.

51. See James E. Miller, Jr., "Uncharted Interiors: The American Romantics Revisited," Arthur Schwartz, "The American Romantics: An Analysis," and Luther S. Mansfield, "The Emersonian Idiom and the Romantic Period in American Literature," in Kenneth Walter Cameron, ed., *Romanticism and the American Renaissance: Essays on Ethos and Perception*

in the Age of Emerson, Thoreau, Hawthorne, Melville, Whitman, and Poe (Hartford: Transcendental Books, 1977), pp. 34–44, 23–29.

52. Haskell, *The Emergence of Professional Social Science*, pp. 236–237.

53. Richard Henry Dana, Jr., "Rufus Choate: Remarks At The Meeting Of The Suffolk Bar In His Honor," *Speeches In Stirring Times and Letters to A Son*, ed. Richard Henry Dana, 3d. (Boston: Houghton Mifflin, 1910), p. 289.

54. Allan Nevins and Milton Halsey Thomas, eds., *The Diary of George Templeton Strong*, 4 vols. (New York: Macmillan, 1952), II, 397.

55. Theodore Sedgwick, *A Treatise On The Rules Which Govern The Interpretation And Application of Statutory And Constitutional Law* (New York: John S. Voorhies, 1857), pp. 1–3, 20–21. See also Perry Miller, ed., *The Legal Mind in America from Independence to the Civil War* (Garden City, N.Y.: Anchor Books, 1962), pp. 296–297.

56. For a contrast between "the Grand Style" before the Civil War and "the Formal Style" after, see Karl N. Llewellyn, *The Common Law Tradition: Deciding Appeals* (Boston: Little, Brown, 1960), pp. 36–39.

57. Friedman, *A History of American Law*, pp. 530–537.

58. Oliver Wendell Holmes, *The Common Law*, ed. Mark De Wolfe Howe (Cambridge, Mass.: Harvard University Press, 1967), p. 32 [originally published in 1881]. See also Oliver Wendell Holmes, "Natural Law," *Harvard Law Review*, 32 (November 1918), 41, and "The Path of the Law," *Harvard Law Review*, 10 (March 1897), 459–464.

59. Oliver Wendell Holmes, "The Use of Law Schools: Oration Before the Harvard Law School Association at Cambridge, November 5, 1886, on the 250th Anniversary of Harvard University," in Mark De Wolfe Howe, ed., *The Occasional Speeches of Justice Oliver Wendell Holmes* (Cambridge, Mass.: Harvard University Press, 1962), pp. 40–41, 46. See also Leon Edel, *Henry James: The Master*, in *The Life of Henry James*, 5 vols. (New York: J. P. Lippincott, 1953–1972), V, 165, 571.

60. For the references in this paragraph to the story, see Herman Melville, *Billy Budd, Sailor (An Inside Narrative)*, ed. Harrison Hayford and Merton M. Sealts, Jr. (Chicago: University of Chicago Press, 1962), pp. 98–99, 96, 112, 110.

61. Robert M. Cover, *Justice Accused: Antislavery and the Judicial Process* (New Haven: Yale University Press, 1975), p. 2. Cover's excellent analysis influences my own, though in his association of *Billy Budd* with Lemuel Shaw, Melville's father-in-law, and the fugitive slave cases of the 1850s, he misses what I take to be the later character of Melville's thinking in the 1880s. For another study that documents Melville's strong interest in legal reasoning, see Brook Thomas, "The Legal Fictions of Herman Melville and Lemuel Shaw," *Critical Inquiry*, 11 (September 1984).

62. This difference between *White Jacket* and *Billy Budd* is raised in Warner Berthoff, *The Example of Melville* (1962; rpt. New York: W. W. Norton, 1972), p. 190. For explicit references to Billy Budd as the angel of God, see *Billy Budd*, pp. 101, 120.

63. In the "Custom-House" section of *The Scarlet Letter*, Hawthorne defines the romance as "a neutral territory, somewhere between the real world and fairyland, where the Actual and the Imaginary may meet, and each imbue itself with the nature of the other." In *Billy Budd*, Melville raises these diverse elements but deliberately keeps them apart. See Nathaniel Hawthorne, *The Scarlet Letter*, in *The Centenary Edition of the Works of Nathaniel Hawthorne*, 13 vols. (Columbus: Ohio State University Press, 1962), I, 36. For the passages referred to here and in the remainder of the paragraph, see *Billy Budd*, pp. 53, 49, 100–101, 108–111.

64. Holmes, "The Path of the Law," p. 464. For a good parallel analysis of Holmes's possible influence on Melville in *Billy Budd*, see John P. McWilliams, Jr., "Innocent Criminal or Criminal Innocence: The Trial in American Fiction," in Carl S. Smith, John P. McWilliams, Jr., and Maxwell Bloomfield, *Law and American Literature* (New York: Alfred A. Knopf, 1983), pp. 74–76.

65. Holmes, "The Path of the Law," p. 464.

66. Holmes, "The Use of Law Schools," p. 36.

67. Jack Nortrup, "The Education of a Western Lawyer," *American Journal of Legal History*, 12 (October 1968), 294–305.

68. Thomas Nelson Page, "Authorship In The South Before The War," *The Novels, Stories, Sketches and Poems of Thomas Nelson Page*, Plantation Edition, 18 vols. (New York: Charles Scribner's Sons, 1908–1912), XII, 76–81. See, more generally, Richmond Croom Beatty, Floyd C. Watkins, Thomas Daniel Young, and Randall Steward, eds., *The Literature of the South* (Chicago: Scott, Foresman, 1952), and Drew Gilpin Faust, ed., *The Ideology of Slavery: Proslavery Thought in the Antebellum South, 1830–1860* (Baton Rouge: Louisiana State University Press, 1981). Other leading lawyer-writers included: Richard Henry Wilde (1789–1846), Edward Coote Pinkney (1802–1828), Philip Pendleton Cooke (1816–1850), and Paul Hamilton Hayne (1830–1886). More important after the war and providing an ongoing tradition were John Esten Cooke (1820–1886), Henry W. Grady (1850–1889), Thomas Nelson Page (1853–1922), and Irwin Russell (1853–1879).

69. Allen Tate, "A Southern Mode of the Imagination," *Collected Essays* (Denver: Alan Swallow, 1959), pp. 557–558.

70. For the combination of traits mentioned here, see Thomas Nelson Page, "The Old South," *Novels, Stories, Sketches*, XII, 4–5, 28–29, 51–55; Edwin A. Miles, "Classicism in Early American Thought," *Journal of the*

History of Ideas, 35 (April–June 1974), 273; Allen Tate, "The Profession of Letters in the South," *Collected Essays*, pp. 271–277; Richard Beale Daivs, "Law and Oratory," *Intellectual Life in Jefferson's Virginia 1790–1830* (Knoxville: University of Tennessee Press, 1972), pp. 351–386; Lewis P. Simpson, *The Dispossessed Garden: Pastoral and History in Southern Literature* (Athens, Ga.: University of Georgia Press, 1975), pp. 13, 25, 55, and *The Brazen Face of History: Studies in the Literary Consciousness in America* (Baton Rouge: Louisiana State University Press, 1980), p. 86; Waldo W. Braden, "Repining over an Irrevocable Past: The Ceremonial Orator in a Defeated Society, 1865–1900," in Braden, ed., *Oratory in the New South* (Baton Rouge: Louisiana State University Press, 1979), pp. 8–37; Clement Eaton, "The Dynamics of the Southern Mind," *The Civilization of the Old South: Writings of Clement Eaton*, ed. Albert D. Kerwan (Lexington: University of Kentucky Press, 1968), pp. 288–296; and Willard Thorp, "The Writer as Pariah in the Old South," in R. C. Simonini, Jr., ed., *Southern Writers: Appraisals in Our Time* (Charlottesville: University Press of Virginia, 1964), pp. 2–18.

71. Tate, "A Southern Mode of the Imagination," pp. 555–556, 560–562, and Lewis P. Simpson, "Discussions: Thematic Problems in Southern Literature," in Louis D. Rubin, Jr., and C. Hugh Holman, eds., *Southern Literary Study: Problems and Possibilities* (Chapel Hill: University of North Carolina Press, 1975), p. 207.

72. For an excellent treatment of the movement from sectionalism to nationalism in the South in the 1850s, see John McCardell, "A Southern Republic of Letters," *The Idea of a Southern Nation: Southern Nationalists and Southern Nationalism, 1830–1860* (New York: W. W. Norton, 1979), pp. 141–176.

73. William Gilmore Simms to William Porcher Miles, December 28, 1857, in *The Letters of William Gilmore Simms*, ed. Mary C. Simms Oliphant, Alfred Taylor Odell, and T. C. Duncan Eaves, 5 vols. (Columbia: University of South Carolina Press, 1952–1956), III, 518. See also Jon L. Wakelyn, "A Political Theorist of Southern Nationalism," *The Politics of a Literary Man: William Gilmore Simms* (Westport, Conn.: Greenwood Press, 1973), pp. 158–187, and Simpson, *The Brazen Face of History*, p. 78. More generally, see William R. Taylor, *Cavalier and Yankee: The Old South and American National Character* (New York: George Braziller, 1961).

74. Page, "The Old South," *Novels, Stories, and Sketches*, XII, 62.

75. For the importance of political involvement for the antebellum intellectual, see Drew Gilpin Faust, "Uniting Our Minds and Energies: The Practice of Stewardship," *A Sacred Circle: The Dilemma of the Intellectual in the Old South* (Baltimore: Johns Hopkins University Press, 1977), pp. 87–111. For the greater importance of ceremonial oratory in the postwar South, see Braden, "Repining over an Irrevocable Past," pp. 11–12, 36.

For the centrality of patriotism in the southern sense of duty, see W. J. Cash, *The Mind of the South* (New York: Alfred A. Knopf, 1941), pp. 98–99.

76. For treatments of the postwar debates over the New South and the Old, see Jay B. Hubbell, "Authorship in the New South," *The South in American Literature 1607–1900* (Durham, N.C.: Duke University Press, 1954), pp. 709–716; Wayne Mixon, *Southern Writers and the New South Movement, 1865–1913* (Chapel Hill: University of North Carolina Press, 1980); and J. V. Ridgely, "The New South: The Past Recaptured," *Nineteenth-Century Southern Literature* (Lexington: University Press of Kentucky, 1980), pp. 89–111.

77. Page, "The Old South," *Novels, Stories, and Sketches*, XII, 54, 60.

78. Simpson, *The Brazen Face of History*, p. 236.

79. These competing frameworks are described in full by Charles S. Sydnor, "The Southerner and the Laws," *Journal of Southern History*, 6 (February 1940), 3–23. The succeeding analysis relies upon Sydnor's findings, but see also Daniel J. Boorstin, "The Unwritten Law: How It Grew in Slavery," and "How Southern Gentlemen Became Honor-bound," *The Americans: The National Experience* (New York: Random House, 1965), pp. 199–212.

80. F. D. Srygley, *Seventy Years in Dixie: Recollections, Sermons and Sayings of T. W. Caskey and Others* (Nashville: Gospel Advocate Publishing, 1891), p. 310.

81. See Faust, "A Sacred Duty: The Proslavery Argument," *A Sacred Circle*, pp. 112–131. Four of the five intellectuals that Faust treats in depth read law: William Gilmore Simms, James Henry Hammond (1807–1864), Nathaniel Beverly Tucker (1784–1851), and George Frederick Holmes (1820–1877).

82. Faust, *A Sacred Circle*, pp. 116–120.

83. Jack K. Williams, *Dueling in the Old South: Vignettes of Social History* (College Station: Texas A & M University Press, 1980), pp. 16–19, 40–41.

84. John Lyde Wilson, *The Code of Honor; or Rules For The Government of Principals and Seconds in Duelling* (Charleston: James Phinney, 1858), pp. 4–7, 32 [first printed in 1838]. See also Robert Sobel and John Raimo, eds., "John Lyde Wilson," *Biographical Directory of the Governors of the United States, 1789–1978*, 4 vols. (Westport, Conn.: Meckler Books, 1978), IV, 1396–87.

85. The contradictions in southern culture have been summarized in many different ways: philosophically and politically in Louis Hartz, "The Reactionary Enlightenment," *The Liberal Tradition in America: An Interpretation of American Political Thought Since the Revolution* (New York: Harcourt, Brace and World, 1955), pp. 149–172; socially in Clement Eaton, "Plan-

tation Life as a Moulder of Opinion," *Freedom of Thought in the Old South* (Durham, N.C.: Duke University Press, 1940), pp. 32–63; psychologically in W. J. Cash, "Of the Man at the Center," and "Of an Ideal and Conflict," *The Mind of the South*, pp. 29–99; and ideologically and mythologically in Simpson, *The Dispossessed Garden*, and Taylor, *Cavalier and Yankee*.

86. "The Archer, No. II," *Monthly Register, Magazine and Review of the United States*, 1 (June 1, 1806), 308.

87. For a full account of all of the characteristics listed above, see Thomas Nelson Page, "The Old Virginia Lawyer," *Novels, Stories, Sketches*, XII, 281–294.

88. Tate, "A Southern Mode of the Imagination," *Collected Essays*, pp. 563–564.

89. A. B. Longstreet, *Georgia Scenes: Characters, Incidents, Etc., in the First Half Century of the Republic* (New York: Sagamore Press, 1957), pp. 10, 182–198. See also Ridgely, *Nineteenth-Century Southern Literature*, pp. 56–58.

90. William Gilmore Simms, "How Sharp Snaffles Got His Capital And Wife," *Stories and Tales*, in *The Writing of Willian Gilmore Simms*, ed. John Caldwell Guilds et al., Centennial Edition, 24 vols. (Columbia: University of South Carolina Press, 1969–), V, 421–465.

91. For descriptions of Simms's and Kennedy's attempts to bridge the contradictions in southern culture through their fiction, see Ridgely, *Nineteenth-Century Southern Literature*, pp. 40–42, 50–56, and Richard Gray, *The Literature of Memory: Modern Writers of the American South* (Baltimore: Johns Hopkins University Press, 1977), pp. 19–27.

92. Joseph G. Baldwin, *The Flush Times of Alabama and Mississippi: A Series of Sketches* (New York: Hill and Wang, 1957), pp. 52–76, 82–103, 15–33.

93. Thomas Wolfe, *You Can't Go Home Again* (New York: Harper and Brothers, 1940), pp. 70–84, and William Styron, *The Confessions of Nat Turner* (New York: Random House, 1966), pp. 58–68.

94. William Faulkner, *Requiem for a Nun* (New York: Random House, 1951), p. 49, *Go Down, Moses and Other Stories* (New York: Random House, 1942), p. 382, and *Knight's Gambit* (New York: Random House, 1949), p. 60.

95. Faulkner, *Requiem for a Nun*, pp. 40, 88. See also Faulkner, *Intruder in The Dust* (New York: Random House, 1948), pp. 243–244.

96. For Cooper's many law suits, see James Grossman, *James Fenimore Cooper* (New York: William Sloane Associates, 1949), pp. 110–111, 134–135, 141, 152–157, 168–170, 186–188. See also Susan Fenimore Cooper, *The Cooper Gallery; or, Pages and Pictures from the Writings of James Fenimore Cooper* (New York: James Miller, 1865), p. 367.

97. Edwin Harrison Cady, *The Gentleman in America: A Literary Study*

in American Culture (Syracuse: Syracuse University Press, 1949), pp. 4, 19, 104–125, and J. Fenimore Cooper, *A Letter to His Countrymen* (New York: John Wiley, 1834), p. 98.

98. Both the importance and the nature of the law in Cooper's writings has been traced in detail in John P. McWilliams, Jr., *Political Justice in a Republic: James Fenimore Cooper's America* (Berkeley: University of California Press, 1972). My own analysis, like any other on this subject, begins and ends with McWilliams' definitive findings.

99. Subsequent references in the text to these novels will be from the following editions: James Fenimore Cooper, *The Pioneers* (New York: Holt, Rinehart and Winston, 1964), *Home As Found* (New York: Capricorn Books, 1961), and *The Ways Of The Hour; A Tale* (Upper Saddle River, N.J.: Gregg Press, 1968).

100. For two other analyses that insist upon the centrality of these novels to an understanding of Cooper's social vision, see Joy S. Kasson, "Templeton Revisited: Social Criticism in *The Pioneers* and *Home as Found*," *Studies in the Novel*, 9 (Spring 1977), 54–64, and Eric J. Sundquist, *Home as Found: Authority and Genealogy in Nineteenth-Century American Literature* (Baltimore: Johns Hopkins University Press, 1979), pp. 1–40.

101. The standard analysis of this conflict remains Perry Miller, *The Life of the Mind*, pp. 99–102.

102. The slaughter of the pigeons by the citizens of Templeton, the destruction of the fish in Lake Otsego, and the forest fire at the end of the novel are all examples of the way in which man destroys the natural world if left to his own devices. *The Pioneers*, pp. 243–264, 420–431.

103. For the need of external standards of conduct in Cooper, see Frank M. Collins, "Cooper and the American Dream," *PMLA*, 81 (March 1966), 81–84, and McWilliams, *Political Justice*, pp. 18–20.

104. My characterization of Bragg as the "Representative American" comes from Donald Kay, "Major Character Types in *Home as Found*: Cooper's Search for American Principles and Dignity," *College Language Association Journal [CLA]*, 14 (June 1971), 432–435.

105. Donald A. Ringe, *James Fenimore Cooper* (New York: Twayne, 1962), p. 142, and Barbara Ann Bardes and Suzanne Gossett, "Cooper and the 'Cup and Saucer' Law: A New Reading of *The Ways of the Hour*," *American Quarterly*, 32 (Winter 1980), 499–518.

106. Kasson, "Templeton Revisited," p. 59, and Howard Mumford Jones, *History and the Contemporary: Essays in Nineteenth-Century Literature* (Madison: University of Wisconsin Press, 1964), p. 79.

107. Paul Stein, "Cooper's Later Fiction: The Theme of 'Becoming'," *South Atlantic Quarterly*, 70 (Winter 1971), 80.

108. James Fenimore Cooper, *The Crater or Vulcan's Peak*, ed. Thomas Philbrick (Cambridge, Mass.: Harvard University Press, 1962), p. 459.

Lincoln: An Epilogue

1. Edmund Wilson, "Abraham Lincoln," *Patriotic Gore: Studies in the Literature of the American Civil War* (New York: Oxford University Press, 1962); David Donald, *Lincoln Reconsidered: Essays on the Civil War Era* (New York: Random House, 1956); Don E. Fehrenbacher, *Prelude to Greatness: Lincoln in the 1850's* (Stanford: Stanford University Press, 1962).

2. George B. Forgie, *Patricide in the House Divided: A Psychological Interpretation of Lincoln and His Age* (New York: W. W. Norton, 1979); Dwight G. Anderson, *Abraham Lincoln: The Quest for Immortality* (New York: Alfred A. Knopf, 1982); Charles B. Strozier, *Lincoln's Quest for Union: Public and Private Meanings* (New York: Basic Books, 1982).

3. Roy P. Basler, *A Touchstone for Greatness: Essays, Addresses, and Occasional Pieces About Abraham Lincoln* (Westport, Conn.: Greenwood Press, 1973), p. 225.

4. Roy P. Basler, ed., *The Collected Works of Abraham Lincoln*, 8 vols. (New Brunswick, N.J.: Rutgers University Press, 1953), II, 249, 122–123; III, 29; II, 282, 367, 383. All further references to Lincoln's langauge in the text are to this edition. See also Richard Nelson Current, "Lincoln and Daniel Webster," *Speaking of Abraham Lincoln: The Man and His Meaning for Our Times* (Urbana: University of Illinois Press, 1983), pp. 6–13.

5. For a quick summary of the Ciceronian ideal in America and of Lincoln's place within it, see William K. Wimsatt, Jr., and Cleanth Brooks, *Literary Criticism: A Short History* (New York: Alfred A. Knopf, 1967), p. 74.

6. See John P. Frank, *Lincoln as a Lawyer* (Urbana: University of Illinois Press, 1961), p. 144, and Richard M. Weaver, "Abraham Lincoln and the Argument from Definition," *The Ethics of Rhetoric* (Chicago: Henry Regnery, 1953), pp. 85–86.

7. For still the best account of Lincoln's language, including his mastery of rhetoric, and his use of literary cadences, see Roy P. Basler, "Abraham Lincoln's Rhetoric," *American Literature*, 11 (May 1939), 167–182, and Basler, *A Touchstone for Greatness*, pp. 53–100, 206–227.

8. For a general account of the weakening of American faith in the Constitution and the debasement of nationalistic oratory in the 1850s, see David Herbert Donald, *Liberty and Union* (Boston: Little, Brown, 1978), pp. 63–81.

9. Alexis de Tocqueville, *Democracy in America*, 2 vols. (New York: Alfred A. Knopf, 1945), I, 166–167. [First printed in 1835.]

10. For the great impact of the Cooper Institute Address, see Benjamin P. Thomas, "The Making of a President," *Abraham Lincoln* (New York: Alfred A. Knopf, 1952), pp. 201–213.

11. See, for example, Basler, *A Touchstone for Greatness*, p. 93, and Strozier, *Lincoln's Quest for Union*, pp. 63–65.

12. Gideon Welles, *Diary of Gideon Welles, Secretary of the Navy Under Lincoln and Johnson*, 3 vols. (Boston: Houghton Mifflin, 1909–1911), II, 190. For a complete treatment of Lincoln's use of religious language and imagery, see Anderson, *Abraham Lincoln: The Quest for Immortality*.

13. See, for example, Fehrenbacher, *Prelude to Greatness*, pp. 11–14, and Albert J. Beveridge, *Abraham Lincoln 1809–1858*, 2 vols. (Boston: Houghton Mifflin, 1928), II, 221–223.

14. Edward Shils, *The Intellectuals and the Powers and Other Essays* (Chicago: University of Chicago Press, 1972), p. 17.

15. Noah Brooks, "Personal Recollections of Abraham Lincoln," *Harper's New Magazine*, 31 (July 1865), 226.

16. For the precipitous decline in oratory in the quarter-century following the Civil War, see Barnet Baskerville, *The People's Voice: The Orator in American Society* (Lexington: University Press of Kentucky, 1979), pp. 88–114.

17. Lincoln frequently questions both the notion of the speech and his role as speaker in his last years. See, for example, Basler, ed., *The Collected Works*, V, 358–359; VII, 17; VIII, 360, 393. For a more detailed account of Lincoln's impersonality of tone and self-effacement in the Gettysburg Address and the Second Inaugural Address, see Weaver, *The Ethics of Rhetoric*, pp. 109–111.

18. As early as 1838, Lincoln speaks of the Founders as engaged in a "practical demonstration of the truth of a proposition," and his close study of Euclid leads him to rely upon the technical meaning of the word. A proposition is a statement of a truth to be demonstrated. That Lincoln thought of liberty and equality *as a sequence* is clear from his statement that " 'all men are created equal' was of no practical use in effecting our separation from Great Britain; and it was placed in the Declaration, not for that, but for future use." See Basler, ed., *The Collected Works*, I, 113; IV, 62; II, 406; and Noah Webster, *An American Dictionary of the English Language* (Springfield, Mass.: George and Charles Merriam, 1856), p. 879.

19. Basler, *A Touchstone for Greatness*, p. 94.

20. Lincoln almost certainly takes his incantation concerning the government of the people from Webster's Reply to Hayne, the speech that William Herndon, Lincoln's friend, law partner, and later biographer, claims that "Lincoln thought . . . was the very best speech that was ever delivered." See "Second Speech on Foot's Resolution delivered in the Sen-

ate of the United States on January 26, 1830," in James W. McIntyre, ed., *The Writings and Speeches of Daniel Webster*, 18 vols. (Boston: Little, Brown, 1903), VI, 54; and Emanuel Hertz, *The Hidden Lincoln: From the Letters and Papers of William H. Herndon* (New York: Viking Press, 1938), p. 118.

21. In his fragmentary notes for a law lecture from 1850, Lincoln argues for this function of peacemaker: "As a peacemaker the lawyer has a superior opportunity of being a good man." Basler, ed., *The Collected Works*, II, 81.

INDEX

p seven: Lead by example

od manager is also a role model, so it almost goes
out saying that you must set an example for how you
your team members to behave. Lead by involving
ple in establishing group objectives, setting standards,
achieving deadlines, and demonstrate your own strong
onal commitment to achieving the team's goals. Set an

TOP TIP

In most workplaces, there's nearly always
someone who is a nightmare to work with.
Before you were a manager, if you had a
troublesome colleague you may have let off
steam about him or her to a friend in the
ffice. Being a boss doesn't mean you have to
be a saint, clearly, but it does mean that you
have to be extremely careful about what you
say about colleagues and to whom. Even if
you feel like screaming, don't commit any
derogatory comments about a colleague to
e-mail: it's all too easy to inadvertently send
them to the wrong person. Also be careful
about conversations you have in the office—
you could be overheard. Use your common
ense and, if you can, wait until you get home
and unburden yourself to someone
completely outside of your work life: your
partner, friends, family members, or pet!

---

about them as individuals. Most importantly, ask each
person the question: what should I do or not do to help you
perform your job effectively?

TOP TIP

Listening—and tuning in properly—to
your team's concerns is a key part of
your early days in a new job. That doesn't
mean for a moment that you should promise
them the moon, but simply that you'll be in
a much better position to represent those
concerns to your own managers.
You need to be able to fight your
team's corner.

Step four: Plan some 'quick wins'

Next, plan a few targets that you can hit quickly and easily,
all of which will help you to feel more at home and on top of
things. Achieving these also eases the pressure you feel to
perform and create a positive first impression and begins
the relationship-building process. Quick wins might include
things like familiarising yourself with systems or ways of
working if you're new to the company (for example, the
internal e-mail system); setting up an early discussion with
your line manager, arranging introductory meetings with
suppliers or customers (external and internal), or even taking
your team to the pub one lunchtime.

Step five: Clarify what expectations others have of you

You may be lucky enough to have been given a detailed job description, but the chances are there are still large gaps in your understanding of the task and priorities, what is or isn't acceptable in the new environment, and on what criteria you will be judged by your boss, peers, customers, and others. Don't be afraid to ask a lot of questions to clarify these issues, and then be very honest with yourself. Can you meet these standards? If not, what might you need to do? Who could help, and what might the price be?

The perils of the 'new broom' syndrome

While you'll be keen to get going in your new role and make your mark, do tread carefully—at least to start with. Don't assume that your new team will welcome your style or your ideas with open arms, even if your predecessor was unpopular. Before you can count on their support and co-operation, they need to feel that they can trust you and that you respect what they've been doing previously.

Above all, don't depart too dramatically and quickly from established practice: even if you're desperate to change 'the way things are done around here', people are much less likely to throw their hands up in horror if you tackle

things gradually. That doesn't mean that you simply that you filter in new ideas and ways o by bit.

Step six: Show your commitm individual development

From your initial meetings with your team, you what their individual aspirations and hopes are going forward. Follow up by setting a code of practice that you tell all team members about follow it rigorously. This code might include c assess training needs, to hold regular team m one-to-one sessions, to set specific goals, an performance against these goals.

Support this code by the way you yourself be team members. Make a point of appreciating effort that people put in, listen properly to wha be generous in your praise of their good qual achievements. The point is, that by demonst team that you as their manager are on their s everything in your power to support them, yo trust and acceptance, and the performance team will be greatly enhanced.

example too by maintaining high standards in your appearance and general behaviour and by establishing warm, friendly relationships.

Step eight: Take stock regularly

At the end of your first week, identify issues that need attention and make a plan for the following week. Get into the habit each week of setting aside some time for review and planning. Don't let your mistakes lead to self doubt: everyone makes them. The key thing to remember is that good managers learn from their mistakes, while bad ones repeat them.

Common mistakes

✗ **You make promises that may be difficult or impossible to keep**

It is very tempting, during the phase of settling in and relationship building, to make all kinds of promises to your team, boss, or customers in the interests of creating a good impression. Do remember, though, that you'll be judged on whether or not those promises are fulfilled, so be cautious about what you say you'll deliver. It's much better to under-promise and over-deliver.

✗ **You make alliances based on first impressions**

Common myth has it that first impressions usually turn out to be accurate, but this is often not true. Your understanding of people and circumstances may change substantially as you learn more about them—especially if you've moved company and are grateful for a friendly face in your few weeks—so don't cement yourself into new relationships that later turn out to be inappropriate or that might alienate other, potentially more useful, allies.

✗ You miss being friends with your team

This is probably the hardest part of promotion for many people: you're thrilled at the great opportunity you've earned, but know that your relationships with many people will change irrevocably. Whether you're new to just the job or the company, you need to build good relationships with your team members but also distance yourself a little from those who report to you so that you can be objective and unbiased in the way you work with them. This can be difficult when you have previously been a member of the team yourself, but, if you don't, you run the danger of being seen as a manager who has 'favourites' and of allowing your personal feelings to affect your judgment. This won't be good for your team's morale and you'll also lose much of your authority. It's probably best to be honest about how you feel with particular friends so that you are seen to maintain a professional relationship at work, and you can then keep purely social activities for outside the office.

✗ You're trapped into accepting the status quo

Whatever anyone says about 'the way things are done round here', the old ways are not always the best. Reserve your right to postpone judgment until you are thoroughly familiar with your team and your role and then, if things need changing, change them – remembering, of course, to be tactful in the way you do it.

STEPS TO SUCCESS

✔ Don't let worries about your new job get the better of you. Your skills and experience have got you this far, so keep positive and enjoy this challenge as much as you can.

✔ If you're a 'details' person, you might find it hard to let go of some tasks so that you can concentrate on the bigger picture—the goals your team, department, and company need to meet. That's exactly what you must do, though, so be ready to adjust.

✔ Research and planning will help you to make a smooth transition into your new role. Find out exactly what's expected of you and come up with a basic plan of how to make it happen.

✔ Spend time getting to know your team and listen carefully to what they have to say—they could prove to be your greatest allies.

✔ Don't overpromise. It's tempting to get people on-side by telling them exactly what they want to hear, but you'll end up backing yourself into a corner.

✔ Plan some quick wins to help you feel more in control.

✔ Tread carefully at first if you're introducing change. People's knee-jerk reaction to change tends to be negative, but, if you bring it in gradually, you'll get a less panicky response.

✔ Lead by example. You can't expect others to behave professionally if you don't.

✔ Be very careful about what you say—and to whom— about your colleagues at work, even if they're driving you mad. Use your common sense and be discreet, however angry or upset you are.

✔ Don't beat yourself up if you make mistakes. Experience is the best teacher you'll ever have.

Useful links

HR Guide:
www.hr-guide.com
HR Village:
www.hrvillage.com

Building great teams

As we saw in chapter 1, one of the challenges of being a new manager is getting to grips with the fact that you're now running a team, rather than just being part of one.

A good manager possesses authority along with strong communication skills and a lightness of touch that draws the various personalities present in the team together so that they work well towards achieving their joint goals. This may seem like a tall order in the early days but it *is* something that can be developed through experience.

Every leader has his or her own style, and when developing a high performing team this needs to be combined with an understanding of:

- the benefits of team-building—what it can achieve and what the leader should be striving for
- team roles and dynamics—how teams work and achieve their greatest success
- the key stages of team development— what they are and how to support the team in each stage

- **the features of a successful team and team leader**
- **how to avoid potential problems and pitfalls.**

Step one: Understand what makes a good team leader

Leadership, in broad strokes, is the capacity to establish direction and motivate others towards working for a common aim. Successful teamwork depends on the team leader's ability to make sure all team members know what that aim is and what they each need to do to achieve it.

Naturally, all teams are different and have their own dynamic, and all leaders develop their own style for forming, developing, and leading them, but there are some general characteristics of a good team leader. For a team to work, it's essential that all members are committed, so leaders must be supportive, enthusiastic, and motivating people to work with. They must organise and communicate well in order to co-ordinate team efforts both *within* the team and with others *outside* the team. During difficult or stressful times, team leaders need to be approachable, good listeners who can offer feedback and advice. Turn to chapter 3 for more advice on ways to boost your leadership skills.

What are the features of a good team?

It goes without saying that successful teams are ones in which people don't waste time trying to achieve success at the expense of others. Instead, they work at understanding each other, and communicate honestly and openly. They're committed to the team's success and are respectful and supportive of each other, sharing information and experience.

Conflict is unavoidable in most work situations, but a good team will work through it and reach an understanding by generating new ideas. A good team also acknowledges the role of the leader and understands when he or she needs to act and make a decision (in an emergency, for example, or if there is a major problem or disagreement). See Step six for more advice on this issue.

Step two: Focus on the work

For anyone interested in productive teamwork, it's often better to start with the work rather than the team. First of all, think about whether the job in hand really does need a team to tackle it. Some types of work, such as repetitive or unskilled tasks and, at the other extreme, specialist activities, are best performed by loners. Rounding up such people and forcing them to work as part of a team risks producing a double disadvantage: their personal productivity falls and they feel that their privacy has been invaded.

While it's currently popular to strive for such an 'all inclusive' approach in the workplace—and some people argue that isolated workers need a social dimension to their work—there are often few benefits from forcing this set-up on someone. Introverts need work suitable for introverts, while extroverts need work appropriate to extroverts.

Step three: Help the team succeed

The team approach for organising work depends on empowerment–that is, making sure that each person is allowed to perform to the best of his or her abilities. This relies on trust, the confidence that a manager places on the qualities and calibre of the employees. It also depends on how well members of a group have developed an understanding of each other's strengths and weaknesses. That's why, if your budget allows, training in teamwork is so important and why it helps to understand the language of team roles.

TOP TIP

As a team leader, remember that you have to allow team members the freedom to do what their role entails—empower them. Give them all the information they need and set boundaries to make sure that things happen.

Communicating clearly

One essential part of working well with your team is communicating clearly with them. It is also useful to know that different people absorb information in different ways. So, when you're communicating, it's important to do so in a manner that gets through to as many people as possible.

Research into learning styles during the 1970s established that people fall into four main categories:

1 **'Why?' people:** who want all the reasons for doing something
2 **'What?' people:** who want all the facts about it
3 **'How?' people:** who want only the information they need to get on and do it
4 **'What if?' people:** who are more interested in the consequences of doing it.

It was also found that if any of these kinds of people don't get the type of information they naturally prefer they tend to switch off. So every presentation, information booklet, team talk, or other communication device you use has a much better chance of being heard and absorbed by everyone in your team if it contains all four elements.

TOP TIP

It's also worth remembering a very useful concept known as the 'three times convincer'. This is based on the fact that 80 per cent of people need to hear a message three times before they buy into it; 15 per cent need to hear it five times, and five per cent up to 25 times! Bearing this in mind, then, messages should be restated at least three times, preferably in different forms, with a few days between each time. It's also a good plan to vary the message so that it's saying the same thing in three different ways.

Step four: Reward teams at the right time

All teams need to be assessed, but how should it be done so that it's positive and constructive? One way is to set objectives for teams and judge how well these have been met. This view is popular in the 'top-down' school of management, where, as the name would suggest, senior managers make all the decisions and these are then passed down through the ranks to employees. In larger organisations, this approach is given added impetus by performance-related bonuses.

The argument is that teams need fixed incentives to perform

well, an assumption linked with the opposite view that without such an incentive a team won't perform well. This approach can, however, backfire. Success in meeting given criteria depends partly on circumstances and contingencies, and may not be a completely honest reflection of effort or skill. Also, objectives may be too easy to reach, or too difficult. In the end, people may focus more on the shortcomings of the incentive than on the work they're doing. Retrospective awards for good team performance (that is, given once the project is complete) are better received than prospective rewards for teams given set targets.

Step five: Stick to the essentials of effective teamworking

Again, start with the work and think about whether it really calls for a team at all. If you do decide that a team is the best way to tackle a task, work out who will be doing what; also, decide which remaining tasks can be assigned to others and make sure those involved know the responsibility for completing those tasks rests with them.

TOP TIP

If possible, train your team so that it plays to the best strengths of its individual players. Make sure each person is allowed to develop ownership, pride, and maximum commitment to the team's responsibilities. One way you

---

can do this as team leader is by delegating effectively (see chapter 5). Finally, understand what motivates the team—what gives it its momentum?

Step six: Resolve conflict

Whatever your line of work, conflict is bound to arise from time to time. Complex projects in particular are breeding grounds for conflict because they are temporary situations and tend to change continually. Unresolved conflict can be very destructive, so it needs to be tackled immediately. Here's how:

1 Recognise conflict

Conflict can be either overt (clearly visible and stemming from an easily identifiable cause) or covert (bubbling under the surface, from a less obvious or apparently unrelated cause).

2 Monitor the climate

Look out for early warning signals so that you can deal with the conflict quickly, before it gets out of hand. Early action saves time and stress later.

3 Research the situation

Spend time finding out the root cause of the conflict, who is involved, and what the potential effects are. Putting yourself in other people's shoes will enable you to understand and empathise better.

4 Plan your approach

Encourage everyone involved to be open and understanding in the way they interact with others. It might be a good idea to ask people to write down their thoughts and feelings, so that they can express themselves logically and constructively.

5 Tackle the issue

✓ Give everyone a chance to express their point of view.

✓ Avoid fight or flight: fighting back will only make the situation worse, while running away from the situation will show that you don't feel up to resolving the situation, and it may lead to a loss of respect.

✓ Remember to be assertive. Becoming aggressive will get you nowhere, but being passive won't achieve anything either.

✓ Acknowledge the views and rights of all parties.

✓ Encourage those involved to come up with their own solution—if they've created the solution, they are more likely to buy into it.

✓ Suggest a constructive way forward.

Common mistakes

✗ You misunderstand people

While it's obviously crucial that you understand the nature of the work being undertaken, you also need to be aware of the skills, experience, and approach of those doing the work. Taking account of people's strengths, motivations, and working patterns can certainly help to build or break teams.

✗ You don't understand teams and what they need to succeed

Don't become too glib about the terminology—'team' and 'teamwork' too easily become meaningless words, so make sure you're not bandying about terms that you don't really understand. Remember to spend time evaluating whether you really need a team to complete a given task before you begin the project, and, if you do go ahead, bear in mind that not everyone flourishes in a team—some people will need more support than others.

STEPS TO SUCCESS

✔ Understand what makes a good team leader. You need to establish direction, communicate your team's goals clearly to them, and then motivate everyone towards achieving them.

✔ Focus on the work at first, rather than the team.

✔ Help the team succeed by communicating effectively and understanding that you'll need to amend your approach depending on who you're talking to.

✔ Reward teams at the right time.

✔ Stick to the essentials: think about whether the whole team needs to be involved in a project at once, if at all; work out who will be doing what and when; monitor progress and offer support as necessary.

✔ If conflict arises, as it is bound to from time to time, act quickly to resolve it rather than let it fester unchecked.

Useful link

Belbin Associates:
www.belbin.com

Developing your leadership skills

Part of being a good team leader is, of course, knowing how to lead. There are rafts of heavyweight management tomes about this very topic, but a lot of it boils down to common sense. In this chapter we'll discuss practical ways to help boost your confidence about this part of your new job.

There are many myths about leaders—'leaders are born and not made' being a prime example. It *is* true that some people are naturally better suited to leadership roles than others, but the good news is that the necessary skills *can* be learned. Read on to find out how.

Step one: Understand that there are different types of leader

As you'd imagine, there are as many different types of leadership styles as there are personalities. For example, think of three shepherds.

- The first opens the gate and walks through, allowing the flock to follow—this shepherd **leads from the front**.

- Another stands behind the sheep and pushes or guides them through, demonstrating a **supportive leadership style**.
- The third moves from front to back and sometimes to the middle of the flock, demonstrating an **interactive leadership style**.

TOP TIP

Flexibility is key to good management. For leaders to exist, there must be followers, and the needs of followers change depending on the context. Knowing how to apply different leadership styles can help you to respond equally effectively in many different kinds of situations.

Another school of thought recognises four leadership styles:

- directive
- process-based
- creative
- facilitative

Each one is related to a personality trait. Being more relaxed doesn't necessarily mean you can't be a leader—in fact, it's a positive boon in some circumstances—it just means that you have a natural tendency towards a certain type of leadership. As you become more confident and practised in leadership, you may be able to learn other styles—more dominant, intuitive, or structured, for example. Try to work *with* your preferred style until you are comfortable enough to branch out.

Clearly, certain styles are suited to particular situations. For example, a structured leader is likely to succeed in a situation where process is important, such as running a complex project. The relaxed or facilitative leader may be one who manages a professional group of people, while dominant leaders may be needed in businesses where there is a real drive or need for change.

Transferring your skills between different arenas

Don't worry if you feel more comfortable in some situations than you do in others—as you gain more experience and practice, you'll see that your skills really transfer across the different strands of your working life.

For example, let's say you can command an audience easily when you make presentations, but don't know if you'll be able to do the same with the team you've just started managing.

Commanding an audience is a great skill, and many leaders have it, but it's not the sole requirement. Leaders also need to be problem-solvers and have originality and flair, confidence and self-knowledge, strong interpersonal skills, the ability to listen, vision, good organisational skills, and so on. Your ability as a speaker suggests that you're articulate and self-confident. If you possess the other qualities too, you are well on the way to being the leader your business needs.

Step two: Get some training

If the training budget in your business or organisation permits, a leadership course will help you to gain a fuller understanding of what leadership is, and, by extension, how it will work for your business. Courses usually range from business theory to developing strategy, to understanding business risk.

TOP TIP

Even if the benefits of some training are crystal-clear to you, it's no bad thing to spell them out clearly to your own boss when you ask to go on a course. A short e-mail explaining what you and the organisation gain from it will show that you are taking your new role seriously and that you're keen to take positive steps towards boosting your essential management skills. Also appeal to your boss's pocket if you can; for example, find out if you could get a discount for a group booking if other colleagues might benefit from this type of training.

Having well-developed commercial awareness and a good business education will not only give you confidence, but will also help you command respect from others in the organisation.

Step three: Build self-awareness

Your leadership style is the means by which you communicate. The more self-aware you are, the more effectively it will work for you. This means knowing:

- what you are like
- what your preferences are
- what your goals are
- how you are motivated to achieve them
- how other people perceive you and your goals

Numerous tests and questionnaires can be used to help you explore your personality and preferences; they are widely available online as well as from books, consultancies, and other sources. Surveys are also useful, and business schools have valuable data on expected leadership behaviours. You can combine information from all these sources to establish a benchmark for yourself.

Step four: Use it or lose it

Some leadership positions require you to set the objectives for others to follow. In these situations, scheduling, consultation, and the team building discussed in chapter 2 are essential to success.

Leaders often need to work as intermediaries between two groups—those wanting the results (boards, investors, and so on), and those who will deliver them. Establish good communication channels with both parties that allow everyone to have the information they need at the right time.

The nature of the team you work with depends very much on your organisation and the type of work you do. You could, for example, work with one small 'core' team all the time, or you could need to build different teams for each different project you work on, selecting from across the business key people with the right skills to tackle the task at hand.

If you need to put a team together from scratch, try to select a group of people that contains a good balance of competent managers and energetic, loyal team members. Teams need consistent, positive energy levels to sustain momentum, so it's critical that you choose a team based on the mix of talent required, rather than on friendships or office politics.

If you are trying out new systems or approaches, do surround yourself with the right people, create a framework for support, and document the process so you can later evaluate what you have done.

Common mistakes

✗ You mirror other leaders too closely

People new to leadership roles may try to copy a leader they respect, because the person provides an easy model. This is understandable if you're feeling a little unsure of yourself in a new role, but you do run the risk of creating a false impression of what you are *really* like, or, worse, of making yourself look foolish for trying to mimic a style that's incompatible with your own personality. Good—and genuine—leadership comes from within. Rather than follow someone else's style slavishly, understand what it is you respect in the other leader and think about how you can best display that attribute. If it doesn't work, don't be afraid to try a new approach.

✗ You don't work at it

Many people hope that they have natural leadership skills, and accept leadership positions without proper training or mental adjustment. This sink-or-swim approach works sometimes, but not always! You're much more likely to be successful if you build up leadership skills, increase your self-awareness, and evaluate what you do.

STEPS TO SUCCESS

✔ Try to be your own person. By all means observe good leaders in action and learn what you can from them, but don't mimic them. Be yourself, but get the training you need to take your skills to the next level.

✔ Remember the importance of context. There are many different management styles to suit a variety of occasions. Be flexible and be prepared to change your style depending on what you need to do and who you're working with at the time.

✓ Don't be afraid to ask for advice. We don't wake up in the morning instinctively knowing how to deal with every tricky situation we might come across at work, so do ask for help if you need it. The advice of your manager, mentor, or a trusted colleague, coupled with your own thoughts about how best to approach a situation, will help you as you build your own 'brand' of leadership.

✓ Give yourself a chance. Your first few months in a new job, especially one with management responsibilities, can be challenging. Don't get too downhearted if things don't go to plan: reflect on them, draw out the lessons to be learned and act on them as appropriate, and then move on.

Useful links

Management First (Emerald):
http://first.emeraldinsight.com/management_styles/ index.htm
The Leadership Trust:
www.leadership.co.uk
University of Exeter, Centre for Leadership Studies:
www.ex.ac.uk/leadership

Communicating assertively in the workplace

Part of the challenge of any new job—and of a new managerial position in particular—is that you start having to deal with a wider range of people, some of whom may be easier to work with than others.

If you're naturally a shy person or someone who feels unsettled by people who adopt a confrontational approach to work, you might find that you need some help when it comes to making your voice heard or dealing with difficult people. Learning how to communicate with others more assertively could be just what you need.

Assertiveness is an approach to communication that honours your choices as well as those of the person you are communicating with. It's not about being aggressive and steamrollering your colleague into submission—in fact, it's about seeking and exchanging opinions, developing a full understanding of the issues, and negotiating a win-win situation, one that everyone can benefit from.

Step one: Choose the right approach

Becoming assertive is all about making choices that meet your needs and the needs of the situation. Sometimes it is appropriate to be passive: if you're facing a snarling dog, for example, you might not want to provoke an attack by looking for a win-win situation! There may be other occasions when a more bracing approach is the answer. It may feel as though you're being aggressive, but you're actually displaying assertive behaviour, as *you*, rather than other people or situations, are in control of how you react.

After a lifetime of being the way they are, some people are daunted by the prospect of change. But, if you don't change what you do, you'll never change what you get. All it takes to change is a decision. Once you've made that decision, you'll naturally observe yourself in situations, notice what you do and don't do well, and then you can try out new kinds of behaviour to see what works for you .

TOP TIP

If you feel you need some formal training, look into some specially tailored courses so that you can try out some approaches before taking on a colleague or manager in a 'live' situation. This sort of thing takes practice, so don't pressurise yourself even more by thinking you'll 'just know' what to do—get some help if you need it .

Step two: Project a positive image

✔ Use 'winning' language. Rather than saying 'I always come off worst!', say 'I've learned a great deal from doing lots of different things in my career. I'm now ready to move on and give my new job all I've got'. This is the beginning of taking control in your life.

✔ Visualise what you wish to become, make the image as real as possible, and feel the sensation of being in control. Perhaps there have been moments in your life when you naturally felt like this, a time when you have excelled. Recapture that moment and 'live' it again. Imagine how it would be if you felt like that in other areas of your life. Determine to make this your goal and recall this powerful image or feeling when you are getting disheartened. It will re-energise you and keep you on track.

TOP TIP

If you're not very tall, it's easy to think you can't have presence because people will overlook you. Many successful people in all areas of life are physically quite small, though. Adopting an assertive communication style and body language has the effect of making you look more imposing. Assume you have impact, visualise it, feel it, breathe it .

Step three: Encourage others to take you seriously

As well as doing all you can to help yourself in terms of what you say and how you say it, you need to get other people to 'buy into' your new approach to communicating at work. You can do this through non-verbal as well as verbal communication.

✔ If someone is talking over you and you are finding it difficult to get a word in edgeways, you can hold up your hand to signal 'stop' as you begin to speak. 'I hear what you are saying but I would like to put forward an alternative viewpoint . . . '

✔ Always take responsibility for your communication. Use the 'I' word. 'I would like . . . ', 'I don't agree . . . ', 'I am uncomfortable with this . . . '

✔ Being aware of non-verbal communication signals can also help you build rapport. If you mirror what others are doing when they are communicating with you, it will help you to get a sense of where they are coming from and how to respond in the most helpful way.

TOP TIP
Until you get used to being assertive, you may find it hard to say 'no' to people. One useful technique is to say, 'I'd like to think about this first. I'll get back to you shortly.' Giving yourself time and space to rehearse your response can be really helpful.

Step four: Use positive body language

✓ Stand tall, breathe deeply, and look people in the eye when you speak to them.

✓ Instead of anticipating the negative outcome, expect something positive.

✓ Listen actively to the other party and try putting yourself in their shoes so that you have a better chance of seeking the solution that works for you both.

✓ Inquire about their thoughts and feelings by using 'open' questions, that allow them to give you a full response rather than just 'yes' or 'no'. Examples include: 'Tell me more about why . . . ', 'How do you see this working out?', and so on.

✓ Don't let people talk down to you when you're sitting down. If they're standing, stand up too!

Step five: Recognise different communication styles

There are four types of communication style:

- **aggressive**—where you win and everyone else loses
- **passive**—where you lose and everyone else wins
- **passive/aggressive**—where you lose and do everything you can (without being too obvious) to make others lose too
- **assertive**—where everyone wins

Remember that people communicate in a variety of ways. Your assertiveness, then, needs to be sensitive to a range of possible responses. Here are some tips on how to deal with the different communication styles outlined above:

✔ **Passive/aggressive people**. If you are dealing with someone behaving in a passive/aggressive manner, you can handle it by exposing what he or she is doing. 'I get the feeling you are not happy about this decision' or 'It appears you have something to say on this; would you like to share your views now?' In this way, they either have to deny their passive/aggressive stance or they have to disclose their motivations. Either way, you are left in the driving seat.

✔ **Passive people**. If you are dealing with a passive person, rather than let them be silent, encourage them to contribute so that they can't put the blame for their disquiet on someone else.

✔ **Aggressive people**. The aggressive communicator may need confronting, but do it carefully; you don't want things to escalate out of control. Using the 'I'd like to think about it first' technique is often useful in this instance. The main thing to remember is that you have equal rights to everyone else that need to be taken into account, including the right to say 'no'. Remember this when you are feeling badgered or defeated by someone.

Conflict is notorious for bringing out aggression in people. However, it is still possible to be assertive in this context. You may need to show that you are taking them seriously by reflecting their energy. To do this, you could raise your voice to match the volume of theirs, then bring the volume down as you start to explore what would lead to a win-win solution. 'I CAN SEE THAT YOU ARE UPSET and I would feel exactly the same if I were you . . . however . . . ' Then you can establish the desired outcome for both of you.

If you become more assertive, people won't necessarily think that you have become more aggressive. Be responsive to their communication styles, and their needs will be met too. All that will happen is that your communication style becomes more effective.

Common mistakes

✗ You go too far at first

Many people find that they go too far when they start to practise being assertive and end up acting aggressively by accident. Remember that you are looking for a win-win, not a you-win-and-they-lose, situation. Take your time. Observe yourself in action, practise, and ask for feedback from trusted friends or colleagues as and when you need it.

✗ Others react negatively to your assertiveness

Your friends and family will be used to you the way you were, not the way you want to become and some of them may try to make things difficult for you. With your new assertive behaviour, however, this won't be possible unless you actively allow it to happen. If you find yourself in a situation like this, try explaining what you are trying to do and ask for their support. If they are not prepared to help you, think long and hard about whether they're really the right friends for you.

STEPS TO SUCCESS

✔ Try to avoid feeling resentful—if you are feeling 'put upon', act on it!

✔ Remember that sometimes passivity is the best approach. Don't mistake aggressiveness for assertiveness!

✔ Speaking positively and using positive body language will encourage others to take you seriously.

✔ It is important to listen carefully to other people's opinions so that you are clear about which points you differ on and which points you agree upon.

✔ Try your techniques out in a safe environment until you feel comfortable with them.

✔ Build up a toolkit of assertive techniques and responses that have worked for you in the past and reuse them.

Useful links

Assertiveness tip sheet, Tufts University:
www.tufts.edu/hr/tips/assert.html
The Oak Tree Counseling Self-Help Assertiveness Quiz:
www.oaktreecounseling.com

Delegating without guilt

Now that you have a team working for you, you need to get to grips with delegation. It's a key skill to develop. Delegation isn't about giving tasks to others because you can't be bothered to do them yourself—it *is* about getting a particular job done, clearly, but it's also about encouraging people to learn new skills and reach their potential, all of which helps a business to grow.

For many of us, it seems to be a natural tendency to want to be in control of everything. We find it difficult to let go of things we know we can do well ourselves. If you want to be a successful manager, though—and preserve your own sanity—that's exactly what you must do.

Step one: Don't fight it!

Some people do genuinely find it difficult to delegate, for a variety of reasons. Often, it seems quicker to perform the task yourself rather than to bother to explain it to somebody else and then correct his or her mistakes. You might worry that the person will make a bit of a hash of it and it'll take a long time to put right the mistakes they make. On the other hand, you may feel threatened by the competence of a person who is quick on the uptake and does well. You might worry that the employee may take over the role of being the person the rest of the staff goes to with their problems. They may even find something wrong with the way *you* do things.

If you lack confidence, you may find it hard to give instructions and you'll put off delegating. If you do delegate and problems arise because the employee fails to do what you've asked him or her to do, you may doubt your own ability to confront the person about his or her actions. If staff have been given increased responsibilities and have done well, you may not be confident of being able to reward them sufficiently. You might even be reluctant to delegate tasks that you think are too dull.

Finally, you may realise that delegation is necessary, but you don't know where to start or how to go about it. You need some kind of method to follow. The following paragraphs will help put you on the right track.

Step two: Understand how delegation can help you

Delegation offers many benefits:

✔ it allows you to concentrate on the things you do best

✔ it gives you the time and space to tackle more interesting and challenging tasks

✔ you'll be less likely to put off making key decisions

✔ you'll be much more effective overall.

Your team will benefit too; everyone needs new challenges, and, by delegating to them, you'll be able to test their ability in a range of areas and increase their contribution to the business. They'll be able to take quick decisions themselves and develop a better understanding of the details involved in the process. In short, good delegation can make everyone more productive.

It's all too tempting to withdraw into 'essential' tasks and not develop relations with your team. The bottom line, though, is that it's wasteful for senior staff to be paid a lot of money for doing low-value work, and passing tasks down the line is essential if other people are to develop.

TOP TIP
Delegation doesn't make things easier—there will always be other challenges—but it does make things more efficient and effective. Essentially, it represents a more interactive way of working with a team of people, and it involves instruction, training, and development. The results will be well worth the time and effort you invest in doing it properly.

Step three: Know when to delegate—and what

Delegation is such an important part of successful management that you should actively look for opportunities to do it. If you have too much work to do, or if you don't have enough time to devote to important tasks, delegate. When it's clear that certain staff need to develop, particularly new employees, or when an employee clearly has the skills needed to perform a specific task, delegate.

Start with any routine administrative tasks that take up too much of your time. There are likely to be many small everyday jobs which you've always done. You may even enjoy doing them, but they're not a good use of your time. Review these small jobs and delegate as many of them as you can. Being your company's point of contact for a particular person or organisation may well be important, but can also be time-consuming—this is an excellent task to delegate.

On a larger scale, delegate projects that it makes sense for one person to handle; this will be a good test of how the person manages and co-ordinates the project. Give the person something he or she has every chance of completing successfully, rather than an impossible task at which others have failed and which may well prove a negative experience for the person concerned.

TOP TIP
Make an effort to delegate tasks for which a
particular team member has a special
aptitude. For example, if you have a partner
company overseas, make someone with good
language skills the new point of contact. He or
she will enjoy the chance to use their
languages, and colleagues overseas will
appreciate the fact that someone is taking
the trouble to speak to them in their
own language.

Who should I delegate to?

Make sure you understand the people you're delegating
to. They must have the skills and ability—or at least the
potential—to develop into the roles you have in mind, and
must be people you can trust. Test them out first with a
few small jobs so that you can gauge their strengths and
weaknesses. Also make sure that the employee is
available for the assignment—the last thing you want to
do is put too much pressure on your most effective team
members. Aim to share the delegation among as many
employees as possible, so think about the possibility of
assigning a task to two or more people.

Step four: Be positive

Think positively: you have the right to delegate and, frankly, you must delegate. You won't get it 100% right the first time, but you will improve with experience. Be as decisive as you can, and, if you need to improve your assertiveness skills, consider attending a course or reading one of the many books on the subject. A positive approach will also give your team members confidence in themselves, and they need to feel that you believe in them.

If you expect efficiency from the person you delegate to, you need to organise yourself first. If there's no overall plan of what's going on, it'll be hard to identify, schedule, and evaluate the work being delegated. Prepare before seeing

---

TOP TIP

Use your common sense about how much detail or how many instructions you give about the task to be done. Depending on the type of job that needs to be done, you may not be able to be very detailed at all—if the task is a creative one, for example, you'll need to give the person you're delegating to some leeway so that they can test out a few different approaches. If the task to be done is urgent and critical, though, it's essential that you're as specific as possible.

---

the person (but don't use this as a ploy to delay!). Assess the task, decide how much responsibility the person will have, and keep an eye on progress.

Step five: Discuss the task to be delegated

When you meet the person or people you're delegating to, discuss the tasks and the problems in plenty of detail, and explain fully what's expected of them. It's crucial to give people precise objectives, but encourage them to seek these out themselves by letting them ask you questions and participate in setting the parameters. They need to understand why they're doing the task and where it fits into the scheme of things. Ask them how they'll go about it, and discuss their plan and the support they might need.

Step six: Set targets and offer support if necessary

Once you've discussed the details of the job to be done, agree some targets with your colleague and schedule some deadlines into your diaries. Summarise what has been agreed and take notes about what the person is required to do so that everyone is clear—sending a brief summary e-mail so that you both have a record of what's decided is a good idea.

How much support you offer and give will very much depend on the person and your relationship with them. In the early stages you might want to work with him or her and to share certain tasks, but you'll be able to back off more as your understanding of the person's abilities increases. Encourage people to come back to you if they have any problems— while it's important to let them get on with things, you should be accessible if anyone has a problem or the situation changes. If someone needs to check something with you, try to get it back to him or her quickly. Don't interfere or criticise if things are going according to plan, though, as you'll sap their confidence.

Monitoring progress is vital. It's all too easy to forget all about the task until the completion date, but in the meantime all sorts of things could have gone wrong. When you're planning the task, build in as much time as you can to review progress. If more problems were expected to arise and nothing has been heard, check with the team member that all is well. Schedule some regular update meetings with the person and be flexible enough to revise deadlines and objectives as the situation changes.

Step seven: Look at how it went

When a task is complete, give praise, and review how things went. If an employee's responsibilities are increased as the result of a job well done, make sure as far as you can that he or she receives fair rewards for it. Make a note of what the person has achieved when it comes round to appraisals or general feedback sessions: when it comes to making a case for your team member to have a salary increase, all of this will help you to build a stronger argument in his or her favour.

On the other hand, if your team member has found the task delegated particularly challenging, or hasn't been able to deliver in the way you'd expected, discuss it with them, find out what went wrong, and aim to resolve problems in the future. Listen carefully to what they have to say and try to see the bigger picture: did he or she need more time or support, or an extra budget? What would help him or her to handle that task differently next time?

Common mistakes

✗ You think you 'haven't got time' to delegate

This is very common reaction among people who are new to delegating, but try not to fall into this trap. It's particularly tempting to think like this if you're new to a job, as you may feel that others will think you can't cope if you don't do everything yourself. In fact, delegating less important or very time-consuming tasks to your new team is one of the best things you can do. It will free you up to concentrate on the big jobs to be done, and make your team feel that you trust them and want to involve them in what you're doing.

✗ You expect people to do things like you do

Managers often criticise the way things are done because it isn't the way they would have done it themselves. This is unreasonable and unfair. We all work in different ways, so try to concentrate on the results rather than the methods used to obtain them.

✗ You don't give people a chance

If you're giving someone something new to do, you must be patient. It'll take time for employees to develop new skills, but it's time that will pay off in the end. Have faith in the people around you.

✗ You delegate responsibility without authority

It's unfair to expect results from someone who has one hand tied behind his or her back. If you're going to delegate responsibilities, make sure that everyone else involved with this task knows this too. Make clear that the person you've delegated to is the contact person for all matters related to that task and that you've given them the authority to get on with doing the job well.

STEPS TO SUCCESS

✔ Take every opportunity you can to delegate tasks to your team. You will all benefit from it.

✔ When you're delegating a task, take some time to pick

the right person for it, rather than hand out work randomly to the next person who passes your desk. If at all possible, tailor the tasks you delegate to people with the right skills, or those who have the potential to develop them.

✓ When you're discussing a task with the person who will be taking charge of it, give as much information as you can about what you are expecting, the deadline, and any other relevant information. Encourage your team member to ask as many questions as they need in order to feel confident about it.

✓ Be ready to answer any extra queries as and when they come up. It's important to offer support while at the same time letting the other person get on with the job.

✓ Don't interfere if things are going well!

✓ When the task is over, review it with the team member, offering praise, feedback, and learning points as appropriate. Make a note of successes and let your own managers know of other people's successes.

Useful link

Mind Tools:
www.mindtools.com

Giving and receiving feedback positively

As part of your new job, you'll need to get to grips with the idea of *giving* feedback to others on their performance—normally as part of a performance appraisal—as well as receiving it about your own. Most people dread even the idea of it and assume that the experience will be a negative and uncomfortable one.

It doesn't have to be like that, though—feedback is, in fact, a gift. If you're giving feedback, your main motivation is usually to see people change their behaviour for the better or to help them to make the most of their potential. Feedback is rarely given maliciously and it can genuinely help others to understand how they're perceived and how they can make positive changes to influence those perceptions. Perceptions are, of course, not always reality, but they're very real in their consequences, so being aware of them will help people choose whether or not to perpetuate them.

This is something to bear in mind when you're receiving feedback yourself. In the early days of a new job you can feel a bit beleaguered and not as confident as usual, so you may be more likely to take well-meaning advice as criticism. Keep your

perspective, though, and listen carefully to what is being said, rather having a knee-jerk reaction and imagining you'll never get it right: it's likely that there is lots of constructive advice you can take.

Step one: Understand the benefits

Giving and receiving feedback is one of many forms of communication that goes on every day at work. One of the reasons that it's so unappealing is that, unlike a lot of the abstract, theoretical, or downright useless information we may encounter at work, feedback is essentially extremely personal and, as a result, highly relevant to the recipient.

Unfortunately, many people feel that the most common type of feedback they receive is critical. Sadly we rarely receive as much praise as we do criticism, even though we know that someone receiving lots of positive encouragement performs much more effectively than someone who is constantly put down.

As part of your own objectives in your new role, you'll be doing yourself and your team a big favour if you can encourage in everyone a positive attitude towards the sharing of feedback. It is, without doubt, a challenge to do this, but remember that:

■ feedback is a useful way of letting people know how they're perceived by others

■ it gives recipients an opportunity to take decisions about whether or not they wish to change their behaviour and the consequences of doing that

Step two: Give feedback constructively

There's no way round it: giving feedback just isn't easy. If you've been on the receiving end of badly thought-out or tactless feedback yourself, the very thought of it may conjure up bad memories, and, if it's an area with which you're unfamiliar or uncomfortable, a feedback session can easily spiral into a critical and defensive exchange rather than be a positive and illuminating experience.

There are plenty of ways to make sure that the feedback session you're in charge of does remain positive and constructive, though. For example:

✔ **Find an appropriate venue**. Make sure that the feedback session is held in a private place and that you can speak to the recipient without being distracted or interrupted. If you have an office, turn your phone on to voicemail or ask someone to field your calls, and remember to turn off your mobile phone.

✔ **Make sure you're prepared**. Don't go 'cold' into feedback sessions of any type; it's not fair on the recipient and is likely to increase any tensions that may be there. Check that you've collected all the information you need and that you've thought through what you'd like to discuss during the meeting.

✔ **Make sure the reviewee is prepared**. If you're conducting a performance review, brief the reviewee so he or she has clear expectations on what will be taking place. Even if the reviewee has had an appraisal within the business before, it never hurts to run over timings and boundaries—some organisations prefer to hold performance appraisals and salary review meetings separately, for example.

TOP TIP

Some organisations have a standard form that all employees use to help themselves and their managers prepare for a performance review. These can include questions such as 'what do you see as your main achievements in the past year?', 'what are your personal objectives for the next twelve months?', and 'how could your manager help you more?'. Not all of these questions are pertinent to every organisation, clearly, but they may be a good starting point for your discussion.

✔ **Be positive**. Start off the session with some praise that shows you've noticed and valued particular behaviour. Remember not to use a one-size-fits-all approach in feedback sessions; you may have quite a range of personalities in the team you manage, so naturally you'll need a range of approaches to suit each person's personality. That doesn't mean that you can't address an issue directly, just that you need to make sure you broach it in the right way for the person you're talking to at that moment.

✔ **Focus on behaviour, not personality**. Make sure that any feedback you give focuses on the person's behaviour (that is, something that can be changed) rather than on their character. For example, it's much more useful to ask someone if they're happy in their current position than to tell them abruptly that they're not pulling their weight! Always acknowledge a positive achievement first, so that the person you're talking to doesn't feel attacked. You can then have a discussion about what's going on, what you'd like to see happen to resolve it, and how you might help to make that happen.

TOP TIP

It's a good idea to find out whether the reviewee is willing to receive your feedback before you attempt to give it. If you think you feel defensiveness at the outset, address it directly. 'I sense that you're uncomfortable with this process. Is there anything I can do to make it easier for you?' You might want to add some reassurances also, such as 'Any comments we make today will stay within the confines of this room.'

✓ **Take responsibility**. As part of your new role, remember to speak for yourself only. Use 'I' statements rather than hiding behind the views of a colleague or group.

✓ **Ask for feedback on the way you handled the feedback session**. Even if the session was difficult, it's an opportunity to build bridges and show your willingness to learn.

✓ **Honour any agreements made during the meeting**. If you've promised some additional resources, greater involvement in a project, or some training, confirm this afterwards in writing and follow it through.

TOP TIP

Always make a point of demonstrating yourself the behaviour you wish to see from others. It's no good asking for something from others that you're not prepared to do yourself. You can't expect people to speak to you openly about issues that concern them if you are impatient, defensive, or obstructive at every turn .

Listen!

Sometimes when you are nervous about something, you become so focused on what you want to say that

---

you don't pay enough attention to what is being said to you. This can cause all manner of problems, including knee-jerk reactions to problems that aren't really there but that you *think* you've heard. If you're nervous about giving feedback to others as part of your new job, you'll benefit greatly from practising 'active listening'. This is a technique which will improve your general communication skills but which is particularly useful when you need to absorb and react to what others are saying to you in potentially tense situations.

Active listening involves:

- concentrating on what is being said, rather than using the time to think of a retort of your own.
- acknowledging what is being said by your body language. This can include keeping good eye contact and nodding.
- emphasising that you are listening by summarising your understanding of what has been said and checking that this is what the communicator intended to convey.
- empathising with the communicator's situation. Empathy is about being able to put yourself in the other person's shoes and to imagine what things are like from their perspective.
- offering interpretations and perceptions to help move the communication forward, then listening for agreement or disagreement. This enables both

parties to start exploring the territory more openly. It is important to listen *for* at this point, which enables you to remain open to new ideas and to think positively about the other's input. Listening *against* results in your closing down to new information and automatically seeking arguments as to why something won't work.

■ questioning and probing brings forth more information and will clear up any misunderstandings about what is being said.

■ not being afraid of silence. We often feel compelled to fill silences, even when we don't really have anything to say—yet silence can be helpful in creating the space to gather thoughts and prepare for our next intervention.

Step three: Receive feedback positively

However much experience you have of working life, the prospect of getting feedback about the way you do your job can be nerve-wracking. The way we act reflects who we are to the world, and when this is criticised or questioned it can feel like an assault on our personalities. If you receive feedback that you find challenging or hard to deal with, try to put it into perspective—work is just one part of your life—and see it as information that allows you to make informed choices about how you're perceived by others.

In some circumstances, of course, the feedback (or the manner of it) may say more about the person communicating it to you than it does about you, but, whether this is the case or not, the best thing to do is to thank the person for their feedback and assure them that you'll think about it further.

TOP TIP

Do remember that you're not compelled to accept the feedback you get from others; it is, at the end of the day, their view of things. You can, of course, choose to carry on as you've been acting before, but do try to be pragmatic and see if it might be useful to bear in mind *some* elements of the feedback, even if other parts of it just don't chime with you at all.

Remember the following when you're receiving feedback:

✔ **Listen carefully**. Even if you feel under attack, try not to leap to your own defence until you've had a chance to think about and understand the feedback thoroughly. Be genuinely open to hearing what the other person is saying and try not to interrupt or jump to conclusions. The active listening techniques discussed above may be helpful to you here.

✔ **Ask questions to clarify what's being said and why**. You are completely entitled to ask for specific examples and instances of the types of behaviour that are at the root of the feedback. Let's say that the person you're speaking to thinks that you should be more vocal in meetings. So that you can adjust your approach best, ask him or her to tell you when they felt you needed to put yourself forward more. If the atmosphere is becoming tense, introduce a more positive approach by asking for examples of the behaviour they'd like to see more of.

✔ **Keep calm**. Even if you feel upset, try not to enter into an argument there and then; just accept what's being said and deal with your emotions at another time and in another place. Stay calm and focus on the rest of the feedback.

TOP TIP
As outlined above, giving feedback can be an uncomfortable experience too, and people generally don't do it unless they feel that you can benefit from their observations. Try to remain engaged throughout and don't start a 'tit for tat' exchange .

Receiving feedback doesn't mean that you can't talk to the other person about your behaviour. For example, you may want to ask if the giver has any suggestions about what you could do differently or to explain why you did things in a certain way at a certain time—the person you're speaking to may not be aware of all the pressures you were under at the time, or of the background to the issue at hand. You don't have to accept what the other person says, but asking for suggestions from them demonstrates a willingness on your part to take the feedback seriously. Round off the session by thanking the person giving you feedback for taking the time and trouble to share their perceptions with you.

Step four: Think about ways to improve the process

Honest and well-presented feedback allows people to enjoy good, open relationships. If feedback is a common feature of the way people communicate, issues aren't left to fester and grow out of all proportion—as they often can in a pressurized work environment.

Some organisations have benefited from encouraging a culture of 'instant constructive feedback', which encourages employees to address issues as they crop up, rather than to leave them to fester or develop into full-blown crises. This approach not only takes the heat out of more destructive or passive—aggressive styles of relating to others, but it can have a genuine impact on profitability, as ideas may be freely exchanged and innovative approaches discussed. If you think this would be appropriate for your workplace, why not suggest it to your own manager or raise it with your team?

Common mistakes

✗ Both parties get defensive

As people can often feel under attack in a feedback session, they can become defensive. This often happens when either or both parties believe they are right and identify strongly with their 'cause'. As a result, people are unreceptive to suggestions about ways to work differently, however useful they might be. Tense situations of this type are difficult for most people to cope with, never mind someone new to a management position, but the best thing you can do is to keep calm and to try to maintain good rapport throughout. This involves the free expression of views and a genuine desire to understand each other's perspectives.

If you hit a rough patch, take a step back for a moment and quickly summarise what you've covered and agreed on so far: this will highlight the positives and hopefully lead to more constructive discussion.

✗ You make assumptions

Jumping to conclusions about other people's values, motivations, or intentions can quickly cause relationships to deteriorate. Rather than wading in armed with only your assumptions, give the other person the chance to explain how they've been acting or feeling early in the feedback session. Ask open questions and be patient: some people take a while to 'warm up' and feel comfortable in this type of setting.

STEPS TO SUCCESS

✔ Giving and receiving feedback doesn't have to be an uncomfortable or tense experience. See feedback for what it is: a useful way of showing people how they're perceived by others.

✔ If you're giving feedback to others, give yourself plenty of time to prepare. Remember to:

- find an appropriate venue
- make sure the reviewee is prepared and knows the scope of your discussion
- be positive, and start the session off with some praise
- focus on behaviour (which can be changed) rather than personality (which is unlikely to!)
- take responsibility for what you're saying
- be sure to follow up on any agreements made in the meeting

✔ Make use of 'active listening' techniques. These will make sure that you concentrate on what is being said, rather than just wait for an opportunity to speak again yourself.

✔ When you're receiving feedback yourself, try not to take it personally. Work is just one part of your life and feedback is very rarely given maliciously. Remember to:

- listen carefully
- ask questions to clarify what is being said if you're not sure about it
- ask for specific examples so that you can see how you can do things differently next time
- keep calm, even if you feel upset; you're under no obligation to accept the feedback given to you, although it's wise to be pragmatic and to see if any (even if not all) of the points raised are useful.

Useful links

Giving and Receiving Feedback, mapnp.org:
**www.mapnp.org/library/commskls/feedback/
feedback.htm**
PersonnelToday.com:
www.personneltoday.com

Fighting back against information overload

There are many exciting aspects to a promotion—a better salary and benefits, or getting your 'dream job', for example—but one of the downsides is having to deal with a lot more information. Being copied in on more e-mails, writing extra reports, and keeping relevant notes on your staff's progress can take up a huge amount of time, and that's on top of doing your 'day job' too!

So where has all this extra information come from?

- There are many more means of instant communication and data access. Mobile phones, the Internet, voice-mail, e-mail, instant messaging, and tele- or video-conferencing have all contributed to the vast and fast flow of information.
- Despite this increased access to information, fewer people are employed to manage it. Secretaries and personal assistants have been replaced by laptops, PDAs, and BlackBerries.
- Everybody expects information much more quickly. For example, customers are getting used to completing transactions at the click

of a button, within just a few minutes. They no longer have to wait for endless copies of paperwork to pass through several pairs of hands before they can place an order.

■ Business structures have changed so that many projects are now outsourced, demanding clear and rapid communication between many groups of people at once. If your role dictates that you're involved with several projects at once, you could be deluged with information from all sides!

The problem is that we've all had to deal with this influx without any preparation, training, or time! Often, we find it difficult to process the flood of information—we feel as though we're drowning, struggling to find time for more important tasks. The good news is that there are steps you can take to keep your head above water and to concentrate on succeeding in your new role.

Step one: Understand the scale of the problem

Although information overload is a fairly recent phenomenon, it's already claimed casualties. Many of us feel that we have to keep up with the information flow in order to perform well, yet increasing amounts of time are required to help us wade through the massive amounts of data available. This time pressure is resulting in stress and, in some cases, burnout. A worldwide survey conducted by Reuters found that two thirds of managers suffer from increased tension and one third from ill health because of information overload.

What's the result?

Information overload contributes significantly to workplace stress. This is turn affects all areas of your life as it manifests itself in many ways, including increased levels of anxiety, short-term memory problems, poor concentration, and a reduction in your decision-making skills—the last thing you need when you're getting to grips with a new job. You can, though, take control of the problem and regain control of your desk

Step two: Take control of the problem

Information management, like time management, is a matter of discipline. To get on top of things, you need to set boundaries around how much time you're prepared to spend processing information.

First of all, decide what your limits are and create a personal information management system that works for you. This may be setting boundaries around the time you spend responding to e-mails, filtering them through your assistant (if you're lucky enough to have one), or responding only to those e-mails that hold high importance for you. Draw up some criteria to work out what you allow through your filter and what you want to screen out. This may mean putting priorities on your e-mails and deleting those that are low priority, returning calls only to those people you need to speak to, and only looking at a piece of data once before deciding what to do with it. If you miss something important, don't worry; if it's really that important, it'll come back to you in one way or another.

TOP TIP

Identify time-wasting information and cut it out of your day. For example, you could ask to be removed from your company's list of often unnecessary 'everyone' e-mails; request a good spam filter from the IT department; or ask for a summary of overly long minutes or reports.

Step three: Look for information efficiently

Whenever you're looking for information—when you're writing a report, for example, or researching a new market—keep the 'Pareto principle' in mind. This holds that 20% of what has been accessed probably holds 80% of the information you need. So much information is now at our disposal that anxiety about missing something prompts us to spend far too much time wading through every piece of data available.

TOP TIP

Remember that before the Internet, people used to make decisions in ambiguous situations; it was considered to be a management skill. Aim to develop your instincts along with your knowledge—both will stand you in very good stead as you progress through your career.

As part of your new, efficient approach to knowledge-seeking, find your own preferred places for accessing information and discipline yourself to go there *only*. You already know the high-quality sites for your particular field of work, so why waste time elsewhere? Failing this, you could make use of the information officers in the library of your professional body, if you have one. They're experienced at finding relevant information and can often save you a great deal of time.

Finally, look only at data that is relevant to your job, the project you're working on, or the decision you're making. Bear in mind the principles of time management, as they're just as effective for dealing with information overload. For example, surfing the Web is incredibly seductive, with each link taking you further and further into fascinating, but unnecessary, detail. Decide how much time you'll spend in each session, print the information that is relevant, and leave the rest in the ether. You often pick up all the information you need in a few hits, the remainder being less fruitful.

TOP TIP

The more specific you make your searches, the
more efficient they will be—you'll probably
pick up most of the information you need in
the first ten minutes or so.

Step four: Learn to say 'no'

Try not to be the dumping ground for information that others
don't want to wade through. This will involve being polite but
assertive and also being sensible; if you're snowed under as
it is, don't even hint at being receptive to this type of task.
Take control of what passes over your desk and decide not
to be held to ransom by a piece of information.

To give yourself some much-needed space, limit your
availability. Leave your mobile phone switched off for periods
during the day when you can be quiet and restful, or let your
voicemail field calls for you. This way you can decide who to
speak to and when to schedule the conversations. Anyone
who needs to speak to you urgently will find a way of getting
through to you.

Step five: Learn to throw things away!

Don't be a hoarder. Have the courage to throw data away or
delete files when you've exhausted their usefulness. You can

always access the same data again and when you do, it will probably have been updated.

Step six: Use some tools to help

It may seem rather self-defeating to resort to technology to solve a problem that technology produced in the first place, but there are useful electronic devices that can help alleviate information overload. BlackBerries and other similar devices are one example. They have many functions that can be accessed while travelling, making use of otherwise 'dead' time: you can read your e-mails, edit documents, plan meetings, write reports, and even read the newspaper. Any changes can be automatically transferred to your PC when you get back to the office.

Managing your inbox

What do you do with incoming messages once you've read them? If the information is important, you may want to keep it for future reference. However, hoarding all your messages in no particular order will not only slow you down when you are looking for information, but may also make your computer system unwieldy and likely to crash.

✔ Check whether your company has a policy for retaining and storing e-mails. Archiving may be essential for legal reasons, and, if there is a policy in place, you must comply with it. Your company may have a central facility for storing or accessing archived e-mails; so investigate with your computer officer or helpdesk, if you have one. You'll be making their lives easier as well!

✔ If you have a lot of important information you need to hang on to (deals done by e-mail for example, or sign-offs from partners), create your own filing system. For example, you could sort messages into folders arranged by:

- customer or supplier name
- project name
- date of receipt
- research topic

✔ Use subfolders: for example, for each project it may be useful to subdivide everything into monthly or yearly folders. This will also make it easier to see what should be archived and when.

TOP TIP

To save space in your inbox, you might want to copy important e-mails relating to a specific project or programme into other applications. For example, you could create a Word document called 'project communications', in which all relevant e-mails or messages are

> held centrally. **Everyone will then be able to access the information if you are away for any reason, and you will all be able to find what you need quickly.**

Common mistakes

✗ You get bogged down in detail

Getting drawn into the detail of all the information that's available wastes a lot of time. People often fear they'll miss an essential piece of information if they don't comb through every available source, but in fact this rarely happens. Resist the temptation to scutinise every piece of information that appears on your screen or arrives on your desk.

✗ You don't prioritise

Being able to prioritise information will save you hours, and you may even find that you can delegate some of the processing to a member of your team, outlining what they should focus on and report back to you. Remember to give your colleague clear instructions and a deadline and try not to contribute to their information overload problem!

✗ You never switch off

Not being able to switch off from the need to absorb or generate information can be tiring and stressful. Blood pressure can rise, your memory suffers, and any

patience you may have had can disappear altogether.
Just as the body needs time to relax, so does the mind—
and not just when you're asleep. Quieting the mind
through techniques such as meditation or yoga has been
proven to increase health, improve memory, and
stimulate creativity. It has also been linked to increased
productivity and a sense of wellbeing. If these techniques
don't appeal, try other recuperative pursuits such as
listening to music, reading, or taking gentle exercise.
Anything that allows the mind to 'freewheel' will help a
great deal.

STEPS TO SUCCESS

✔ Take charge of the problem by being disciplined.
The longer you put it off, the worse the overload
will get.

✔ Set boundaries around the amount of time you spend
each day dealing with new information. For example, you
could decide to check your e-mails twice a day rather
than every hour—if you have an assistant, you could ask
him or her to filter them for you first.

✔ Similarly, if you have an important task to complete and
you're not getting enough peace and quiet in which
to concentrate, put your phone on to voicemail for a
few hours. If people need to speak to you about a
genuinely urgent matter, they'll find a way of reaching
you.

✔ Cut time-wasting information right out of your day. If you're spending an hour a day wading through junk e-mail, ask the IT department to do something about it. If you work for yourself, take some professional advice about how to combat spam.

✔ Don't end up being 'held to ransom' by pieces of paper. Clearly, you need to keep copies of important paperwork, but file them away properly as soon as they appear—the longer you leave them lurking on your desk, the less likely it is that you'll ever put them away safely. Throw away anything you genuinely don't need it.

✔ Learn to say 'no'. Don't agree to hold on to unimportant documents that no-one else will take responsibility for.

✔ Be efficient in the way you look for information as well as in the way you store it. If you know exactly what you're looking for, go to the best sources of information for it rather than search randomly. If you are researching online, remember that the first hits you get via a search engine will probably be the most useful. Once you have the information you need, stop looking and don't be tempted to click onto less-relevant (but still interesting!) sites.

Useful link

Chartered Management Institute:
www.managers.org.uk

Building your network of contacts

Everyone at work can benefit from building an excellent network of useful contacts. Business today is driven by relationships. Starting or growing a network—and marketing yourself along the way—requires you to build strong and meaningful relationships; many will be long-term and some may be extremely helpful as you settle into your new role as a manager.

Before you plunge in, ask yourself the following questions:

- Why am I networking? What's my personal or professional goal?
- What are my strengths that will help me to market myself?
- What organisations or events will be valuable places for networking?
- How much time do I want to spend on networking, and when will I do it?
- How will I know when I've been successful?

Step one: Find out more about the ideas behind networking

The more self-effacing amongst us may feel uncomfortable about the idea of networking and worry that it will appear to others that you're blatantly 'after something'. If you're one of those people, try to see the positive benefits of putting yourself 'out there'.

For example, research has shown that people who have a good network of contacts, who are involved in professional and community activities outside the normal job, and who look for opportunities to be visible are more successful in their careers and contribute more effectively to the company they work for.

TOP TIP

Once you start to build your network, you'll find that it becomes a way of life, and is something that you do all the time and instinctively. As you build professional relationships, be constantly thinking: 'What can I offer this person?', 'How can I be of help?' The more you try to be of service to others, the more people will want to do things for you.

Step two: Be clear about the purpose of your networking

There are many reasons why you might want to network and market yourself. Our main focus here is on building on your recent promotion and getting your name more widely known, but, if you're looking for a new job or even hoping to gain support for a major project, networking can help you too. Your efforts will be much more effective if you know exactly why you're building these relationships and what you hope to accomplish. Everyone has limited time, and this will help you to decide how to prioritise your networking activities.

Step three: Make a list of your strong points

When you're networking and marketing yourself, it's important to have a sense of who you are and what your strengths are. Think about:

- your special skills and abilities
- any unique knowledge you have
- experiences that other people may find valuable
- characteristics and beliefs that define who you are

Knowing your strengths will give you a confidence boost and

also help you to remember that other people will value what you have to offer.

TOP TIP

Never network from a position of weakness. Networking from a position of strength—and always having something of value to offer others—means that people won't see you as an annoyance. Also, try as far as you can to begin networking *before* you need anything from other people. People will be much more inclined to help you if you join or create a network to build relationships, and do what you can to help others or the organisation before you ask for help for yourself.

Step four: Make a list of helpful organisations and events

Once you know your own overall goals and what you have to offer others, you can make a start on getting to know people who can help you.

First of all, find out about professional organisations and events that may be helpful to you in your career or with your project. Look for special interest groups, like those for 'entrepreneurial women', for example. Take the plunge and get involved! When you're at professional events, like conferences, make sure that you attend social functions, that you join people for dinner, and that you seek out volunteer opportunities. Don't hide in your room and hope that people will come and seek you out.

If you're aiming to network within your current workplace, find out whether there are any special interest groups or social groups to join. If not, start some! Do a bit of 'market research' beforehand among your colleagues, and, if they're willing to come along, ask each of them to bring someone else that the other attendees won't know—that will widen your pool of contacts. You could also look for committees to be involved in. Don't be shy about asking questions and making suggestions.

TOP TIP

If you aren't sure where to begin on this step, ask for advice from a mentor, from your boss, and from trusted colleagues. If you are naturally a shy person, try not to get paralysed by nerves, but see it as a real step in the right direction—networking could mean the difference between getting a dream job and feeling unfulfilled for ages in your current position.

Step five: Create a contact list

Keeping in mind your reasons for networking, come up with a list of all the people you know who might be of help to you. Next, prioritise the list according to who is most likely to be helpful. Think about people you've done favours for in the past who might not be of direct help but who may know someone who can be. After you've spoken to each person, ask him or her if they know of anyone else who might be able to help you. That way, your network grows larger at a stroke, and you have a personal recommendation to boot.

Step six: Create an action plan with a schedule

Take your list of organisations and events and your contact list, and put together an action plan for making connections. Schedule networking events in your diary, along with organisational meetings, conferences, and so on. If you're really determined, you could set up a timetable for making a certain number of calls per day or per week to the people on your contacts list.

Step seven: Meet up with people and attend events

It's now time to step out from behind the telephone or e-mail inbox! Meeting people and attending useful events is probably the best way of making the most of your network. Beforehand, review your list of strengths and focus again on why you're networking and marketing yourself in the first place. All of this will help you to visualise a successful outcome and thus banish any last-minute nerves or self-doubt. Be friendly and professional—but most of all, be yourself.

TOP TIP

Always spend time connecting with people on a personal level *before* you ask for their help or share your reason for networking. If you're meeting in person with someone on your contact list, always bring a gift—something they can remember you by.

Networking on the Internet

While there's no substitute for meeting people face-to-face, it's not always possible. The Internet is a valuable place to make connections and to learn fruitful information from contacts all over the world. If you

have a special interest or a special field, there is sure
to be a newsgroup or threaded bulletin board on
your topic.

Step eight: Market yourself

Marketing yourself goes hand-in-hand with building a
network, and the two can complement each other
powerfully. The strategy you use to market yourself will
depend very much on your own personal goals, but,
as a general rule, think of yourself as a brand: 'Brand
You'.

For example, when marketers are marketing a product,
they look for the 'Unique Selling Proposition' (USP),
something relevant and original that can be claimed for a
particular product or service. The USP should be able to
communicate: 'Buy our brand and get this unique
benefit'.

If you're marketing yourself, you need to use the same
principles and define who your 'customers' are and what
your USP is. Your list of strengths above should give you
some clues, but the best USPs are short and snappy,
such as 'I solve problems quickly and simply' or 'My
leadership brings out the best in others'. The people
closest to you can often give good suggestions if you
get stuck.

TOP TIP
Once you know your USP, think about ways
that you can market yourself and your unique
qualities. The key is to let people know what
you have to offer. For example, you could
design a project that uses your talents and
propose it to the right people; volunteer to
give a talk; or write an article for an in-house
or external publication that shows your skills
off to best advantage. Don't be afraid to be
visible!

Step nine: Keep an eye on your progress

It's always a good idea to keep track of your progress and of
where you are in your action plan: a notebook or simple
planner is all you need. It also helps to have someone as a
sounding board, such as a friend, a family member, your
boss, a mentor, or a professional adviser. When we feel
accountable for our actions to someone we trust, we're
much more likely to follow through. Plus it's always a great
boost to be able to celebrate your successes with someone
else.

Step ten: Always say 'thank you'

As you build your network, many people will offer you information, opportunities, and valuable contacts. In your notebook, keep track of the favours that people have done for you and make sure that you write each one a short and simple thank-you letter or e-mail. People are always more willing to help someone who has been appreciative in the past.

Common mistakes

✗ You come on too strong

Networking isn't about selling someone something they don't want. You're looking for opportunities to create a relationship where there is give and take. For networking to be successful, you absolutely have to be interested in developing a long-term connection rather than grabbing a quick answer to a problem you're facing. Remind yourself that your focus is on relationship building, not on immediate results, and not exclusively on **you**.

STEPS TO SUCCESS

✔ Understand that networking is an excellent way of building strong, long-term professional relationships that benefit everyone concerned, not just you.

✔ When you first think about networking, make sure you're absolutely clear about what you're hoping to achieve. Knowing your own goals is just as important as finding people to help you to reach them.

✔ Make a list of your strengths to remind yourself of the skills, experience, and knowledge you have to offer others.

✔ Try to build your networks before you need to ask others for help. This will show that you're interested in building helpful alliances rather than just looking out for your own interests.

✔ Put together an action plan of who you intend to contact when, and which events might be useful to attend. Keep track of your plan and your progress so that you can change tack if you need to.

✔ Think about how you can market yourself as well as network. Take a step back and see yourself as a 'brand' for a few minutes. All successful brands have USPs, which set them apart from others. What is your USP?

Useful links

City Women's Network:
www.citywomen.org
Vault:
www.vault.com

Where to find more help

The Leadership Challenge 4th ed
James M. Kouzes, Barry Z. Posner
San Francisco, California: Jossey-Bass, 2008
416pp ISBN: 978–0787984922
This key title aims to help people to further their abilities to lead others so that they can get 'extraordinary' things done, presenting principles and practices that are based in solid research. It describes the five practices of exemplary leadership, discussing the characteristics that people most admire in leaders, the motives of leaders, how leaders foster collaboration and create a climate for high performance, and how leadership practices can be learnt by anyone.

Network with Confidence
Daphne Clifton
London: A & C Black, 2007
96pp ISBN: 9780713681468
Networking is something that can really improve our career prospects, but it is something that many people actively dread. With advice on how to conquer your nerves, ask the right questions, find out about the right events (and work out which ones to avoid), this book offers a straightforward approach to networking that will build confidence in basic skills, as well as tips to hone the skills of the most seasoned networkers.